WEB WAREHOUSING AND KNOWLEDGE MANAGEMENT

Other titles in the McGraw-Hill Enterprise Computing Series

Berson/Smith *Data Warehousing, Data Mining and OLAP*
  0-07-006272-2
Inman *Data Stores, Data Warehousing, and the Zachman Framework*
  0-07-031429-2
Narayanan/Liu *Enterprise Java Developer's Guide* 0-07-134673-2
Sanders *ODBC 3.5 Developer's Guide* 0-07-058087-1

Other titles by Rob Mattison

Data Warehousing Strategies, Technologies, and Techniques
  0-07-081034-8
Object-Oriented Enterprise (with Michael J. Sipolt) 0-07-041031-3
Understanding Database Managing Systems, 2/e 0-07-049999-3

To order or receive additional information on these or any other McGraw-Hill titles, in the United States please call 1-800-722-4726, or visit us at www.computing.mcgraw-hill.com. In other countries, contact your McGraw-Hill representative.

Web Warehousing and Knowledge Management

Rob Mattison

Edited and illustrated by
Brigitte Kilger-Mattison

McGraw-Hill
New York   San Francisco   Washington, D.C.
Auckland   Bogotá   Caracas   Lisbon   London
Madrid   Mexico City   Milan   Montreal   New Delhi
San Juan   Singapore   Sydney   Tokyo   Toronto

Library of Congress Cataloging-in-Publication Data

Mattison, Rob.
   Web warehousing and knowledge management / Robert Mattison.
     p.   cm.
   ISBN 0-07-041103-4
   1. Data warehousing. 2. Information resources management.
I. Title.
QA76.9.D37M38745 1999
658.4'038'0285574—dc21   99-18755
                                                                                                                         CIP

McGraw-Hill
A Division of The McGraw-Hill Companies

Copyright © 1999 by The McGraw-Hill Companies, Inc. All rights reserved. Printed in the United States of America. Except as permitted under the United States Copyright Act of 1976, no part of this publication may be reproduced or distributed in any form or by any means, or stored in a data base or retrieval system, without the prior written permission of the publisher.

2 3 4 5 6 7 8 9 0   AGM/AGM   9 0 4 3 2 1 0 9

ISBN 0-07-041103-4

Printed and bound by Quebecor/Martinsburg.

The sponsoring editor for this book was Simon Yates, the editing supervisor was Ruth W. Mannino, and the production supervisor was Claire Stanley. It was set in Century Schoolbook by Don Feldman of McGraw-Hill's Desktop Composition Unit in cooperation with Spring Point Publishing Services.

Throughout this book, trademarked names are used. Rather than put a trademark symbol after every occurrence of a trademarked name, we use names in an editorial fashion only, and to the benefit of the trademark owner, with no intention of infringement of the trademark. Where such designations appear in this book, they have been printed with initial caps.

 This book is printed on recycled, acid-free paper containing a minimum of 50% recycled de-inked fiber.

Information contained in this work has been obtained by The McGraw-Hill Companies, Inc. ("McGraw-Hill") from sources believed to be reliable. However, neither McGraw-Hill nor its authors guarantee the accuracy or completeness of any information published herein and neither McGraw-Hill nor its authors shall be responsible for any errors, omissions, or damages arising out of use of this information. This work is published with the understanding that McGraw-Hill and its authors are supplying information but are not attempting to render engineering or other professional services. If such services are required, the assistance of an appropriate professional should be sought.

To Pam Levin, the best mom a guy could ever hope for.

CONTENTS

Preface xiii
Acknowledgments xv
Introduction xvii

PART 1 APPLIED KNOWLEDGE MANAGEMENT 1

CHAPTER 1
Web Warehousing and Knowledge Management 3
Introducing Web Warehousing 4
Web Warehousing: A Formal Definition 8
Future Systems Profiles 10
Web Warehousing Business Applications 12
Web Warehousing for Consumers 15
Web Warehousing: A Compelling Technology Story 16
An Introduction to Knowledge Management 17
What Is Knowledge Management? 21
What Is Knowledge Management Theory? 23
What Are the Knowledge Management Principles? 23
Application of Knowledge Management Principles to the Consumer World 26
In Pursuit of a Definition of Knowledge 26
Knowledge Management and Computers 27
What Are Knowledge Management Systems? 31
Databases, Data Warehouses, and Knowledge Bases 36

CHAPTER 2
From Edison to Berners-Lee 37
A Revolution with a Cost 38
Your First Web Warehousing Project Will Be a Failure! 38
The New Technology Assimilation Process 40
The Role of Knowledge Management in the Future 54
Knowledge Management for Corporate I/T Departments 54
Major Planning Implications 57
The Future of Knowledge Management 59

CHAPTER 3   Value Chains and Killer Applications   61

Corporate Strategic Perspectives	62
Understanding Business in Its Most Basic Form	67
Introducing the Value Chain	72
Telecommunications Example	75
Value Chain Implementation—Key to Corporate Differentiation	77
A High-Volume, Low-Cost Retailer	78
The Value Chain and Killer Applications	79
Value Chains and Knowledge Management	80
Value Chain Alignment Issues	82

CHAPTER 4   Modeling, Visioning, and Value Propositions   85

Too Much Technology, Too Little Time	86
Principal Challenges to Web Warehouse Solution Selection	87
Value Propositions	91
The Nature of the Value That Systems Deliver	95
Turning Potential into Realization: The Role of Models and Visioning	96
What Is a Model?	99
Visioning	102
Conclusions	105

CHAPTER 5   Knowledge Networks, Neighborhoods, and Economics   107

Definition of Terms	108
Cultural Shift and New Technology Assimilation	113
Knowledge Exchange, New Technologies, and Their Role in History	117
Knowledge Exchange, New Technologies, and Their Role in Business	120
The Right to Knowledge—Special Consequences for Business	121
Your Right to Knowledge Defines Your Economic Worth	122
The Hard Economics of Knowledge Exchange	122
Secondary Cultural Conflicts	127
Knowledge Management Consequences for the Systems Development Life Cycle	127

Contents

PART 2   WEB WAREHOUSING IN ACTION   **131**

CHAPTER 6   Traditional Warehousing   133

- Introduction   134
- The Theory of Data Warehousing   134
- What Is a Data Warehouse?   138
- Barriers to Successful Data Warehousing   140
- Really Bad Data Warehousing Approaches   146
- Data Warehousing Approaches That Work   148
- The Data Warehouse (Mart) Functional Model   153
- The Layers of a Warehouse Environment   162
- Conclusion   165

CHAPTER 7   Web-Based Query and Reporting   167

- Delivering Information over the Web   168
- Example: Global Sports   174
- Conclusion   196

CHAPTER 8   Web OLAP   197

- The World of OLAP Reporting   198
- OLAP Architecture and Performance Problems   205
- Aperio from Influence Software   212
- Conclusion   219

CHAPTER 9   Web-Based Statistical Analysis and Data Mining   221

- The Analytical Tools   222
- Business Value from Analytical Tools   223
- Statistical Products Overview   228
- Data Discovery Tools Overview   229
- Comparison of the Products   232
- Architectural Approaches for Statistical and Data Discovery Tools   234
- The Intelligent Miner for Relationship Marketing Product (IBM)   235
- Organization and Use of the IM for RM Product   236
- Architecture of the IM for RM Product   244
- Conclusion   245

CHAPTER 10   Web-Based Graphical and Geographic Information Systems   247

Contents

	Graphical Information Systems	248
	Types of Graphical Information Systems	249
	The Autodesk Geographic Information System	258
	Starting the Autodesk MapGuide Displays	262
	Conclusion	265
CHAPTER 11	An Introduction to Text Information Management Systems	267
	The Potentials and the Pitfalls of Textual Management	268
	Getting Business Benefit from Text Information Management Systems	272
	Areas Where Text Management Systems Have Already Delivered Big Business	274
	The History of Textual Information Management	279
	Conclusion	288
CHAPTER 12	Architecture of Text Information Management Systems	289
	Text Management Systems Review	290
	Major Categories of TIMSs	291
	Functional Components of a TIMS	302
	Conclusion	306
CHAPTER 13	Search Engines and Facilities	307
	Search Engines and the Web	308
	Search Engine Architecture	309
	Variations in the Way That Search Facilities Work	311
	Variations in Indexing Schemes	316
	The Excalibur RetrievalWare Product	323
	Excalibur RetrievalWare—Product Organization	324
	Excalibur Screen Examples	332
	The Excalibur RetrievalWare Report Card	334
	Conclusion	335
CHAPTER 14	Text Mining Systems	337
	Text Mining—An Introduction	338
	IBM Text Mining Product Offerings	341
	Business Applications Making Use of Text Mining Products	342

Contents

		IBM Customer Relationship Intelligence Product—	
		Text Mining in Action	343
		Using the IBM Intelligent Miner for Text	347
		Conclusion	354
	CHAPTER 15	Multimedia Information Management Systems	355
		Defining Multimedia Information Management Systems	356
		The Excalibur Visual RetrievalWare Product	363
		Components of the Visual RetrievalWare SDK	364
		Practical Applications of the Visual RetrievalWare SDK	366
		Conclusion	368
	PART 3	**TECHNOLOGY FOUNDATIONS**	**371**
	CHAPTER 16	The Internet and Internet Services	373
		Introduction	374
		The History and Taxonomy of the Internet	374
		URL: Uniform Resource Locator	383
		Hooking Up to the Internet	384
		Internet Services	389
		Conclusion	406
	CHAPTER 17	Web Components and Communications	407
		Web Architecture Review	408
		Understanding HTML	411
		The Stateless Web	427
		Browser-Server Communication in Depth	429
	CHAPTER 18	PPP and CGI: Database Access to the Web	433
		Delivering Traditional Data over the Web	434
		The PPP Approach	435
		The CGI Approach	438
		The Basic CGI-Based Architecture	439
		INPUT with CGI	440
		Communication within the CGI Environment	446
		Processing under CGI	451
		Conclusion	457

CHAPTER 19 Java: The Alternative Approach to Web Programming — 459

An Introduction to Java — 460
The Java Runtime Environment — 465
Components of the Java Language — 474
A Closer Look at Some Critical Extension APIs — 480
Conclusion — 483

CHAPTER 20 JDBC: Accessing Databases with Java — 485

JDBC — 486
Programming with JDBC — 491
JDBC Working with Specific Databases — 498
The Next Generation of Web Technology — 505
Conclusion — 511

CHAPTER 21 Architecture, Performance, and Management — 513

Web Warehousing Topology — 514
Capacity Planning, Performance Tuning, and Troubleshooting — 518
Step-by-Step Guide to Capacity Planning — 521
A Step-by-Step Guide to Performance Troubleshooting — 531
Conclusion — 539

APPENDIX — 541

GLOSSARY — 545

Index   563

PREFACE

You might ask, "Why read a book about knowledge management and Web warehousing?" "What makes these two subjects so interesting and important?" "Why put both of these subjects in the same book?"

On a simplistic level, the answer is obvious, a little frightening, and also a little embarrassing. You will want to read this book for the same reason you buy most of the other new technology books, namely, *buzzword phobia!* Readers in the computer systems development world know that the industry is constantly inundated with new buzzwords—and that professional survival depends on understanding what those buzzwords mean.

So now that we have established that your professional success may be helped by reading this book, let us consider why Web warehousing and knowledge management are so important and how are they related.

Knowledge management and Web warehousing are the dominant direction-setting paradigms of today. Further, these two disciplines will be instrumental in the development of many computer-based applications well into the twenty-first century. They contain the substance needed to address the many issues that confound us as we struggle to keep up with the ever-increasing rate of change in the computer systems development community. Although fundamentally different in content and scope, they are undeniably intertwined.

My objective is to provide you with a resource and reference book that will give you a set of information and a complete perspective to help you understand:

- What Web warehousing and knowledge management are
- How they work
- How they can be effectively deployed in a typical business environment

I hope, more than anything else, that this book will serve as a source of clarification, demystification, and simplification of a subject area that may seem overwhelming and complicated, but is, in fact, simple and straightforward.

Further, I hope that this book will provide you with the background information, technological foundation, and business common sense to see for yourself the potential value of the many offerings, as well as the most likely pitfalls.

It is my hope that you find reading this book as exciting, interesting and enlightening as my experience in writing it. I also hope that you will find yourself referring to it again and again, as you continue to explore the exhilarating new worlds of Web warehousing and knowledge management.

Rob Mattison

ACKNOWLEDGMENTS

I would like to thank the many people who helped make this book a success. First, and foremost, I want to give credit to the book's technical editor and graphics artist, Brigitte Kilger-Mattison. Brigitte's tireless work is an important contribution to the quality of this book, and creating it would not have been possible without her considerable effort.

I would also like to thank the individuals from the different software products companies who helped provide the detailed information that is included here:

Chapter 7, Mike Durnwald, Vice President of Product Planning for IQ Software.

Chapter 8, Marvin Mouchawar, President of Influence Software.

Chapter 9, Rick Jensen, Information Miner for Relationship Marketing Product Manager for IBM Corporation's Global Business Intelligence Solutions, North America.

Chapter 10, Dan Ahern, Sr. Marketing Manager for the MapGuide Product from Autodesk, Inc.

Chapters 13 and 15, Mark Demers, Director of Corporate Marketing for Excalibur Technologies Corporation.

Chapter 14, Dr. Michael Hehenberger, Manager of Text Mining for IBM Corporation's Global Business Intelligence Solutions, North America.

INTRODUCTION

Before I decided to take on this project, I made several assumptions about the subject matter and about the people who will pick up this book. Web warehousing and knowledge management systems are a new technology area, ungrounded in any specific field of expertise. Therefore, I take a very tolerant, broad-based, and open-minded approach to the disciplines. My experience has been that the majority of attempts to strictly define these new technologies are both hopeless undertakings and fruitless ones. I remember, for example, the years spent debating what relational databases are and are not. Vendors fought to come up with a definition that made their products look better than the competition's offerings. In the long run, however, nobody cares. All most of us really want is to solve business problems with technology, and that is what I will try to focus on.

Since the area is new, ungrounded, and untested, literally hundreds of product vendors, consultants, and conference tours will offer you a large, expensive dose of what is "good for you," trying to convince you that this technology is *hot,* that you need to be part of it, but that you are incapable of understanding it or making good decisions about it, and need them to make it work for you.

These would-be-saviors might be well intentioned, but their primary motivation is *not* to simplify and clarify issues for you, but to filter, befuddle, and distort your view so that they show up as the "solution" to the "problem" that, in many cases, they themselves have invented. (This may sound a bit pessimistic, but for me it is the only explanation for the unbelievable amount of waste, misdirection, confusion, and utter chaos that seems to follow new technology introductions around like a plague.) The typical professional in the computer industry today has gone through enough of these bleeding-edge technology bloodbaths to be extremely wary about new technologies as they come along.

This same professional is fully capable of understanding what these technologies do, and how they can be best deployed with a minimum of fuss. All that is needed is good, objective factual data that is organized in a nonproprietary way without the prejudice of underlying agendas of product vendors and consulting companies, and that is presented in a form that allows the readers to apply what they know to the situations they face.

It is my objective to provide that information.

Who Should Read This Book?

You should read this book if you want to understand

- *What Web warehousing is:* the technical details about how a Web warehousing system can be deployed; the different methods used by companies and software vendors to bundle, package, and deliver Web warehousing solutions to the business community; the ways in which a Web warehousing solution can be of value to your organization; and the methods for dealing with Web warehousing issues on all levels.
- *What knowledge management is:* the fundamental principles behind the knowledge management approach; the different ways that the knowledge management approach can be used to help build computer systems of all types.
- *What knowledge management systems are:* value chains, value propositions, visioning, and killer applications; using the discipline of knowledge management in the deployment of Web warehousing systems.

Among those who will find this book useful are

1. Web technology professionals interested in applying their valuable Web technology skills to the practical solution of business problems
2. Data warehousing professionals interested in understanding how the deployment of Web warehousing solutions is different from and similar to the work they do with existing technologies
3. Business professionals interested in using Web warehousing technology to help them address the many challenges they are facing today
4. Software developers looking for help in turning their client/server-based systems into Web warehousing solutions
5. Software developers deciding how to design and package specific Web warehousing solutions
6. Database administrators who need to understand how Web applications are connected to database software
7. System administrators who need to understand how to architect, configure, and manage complex Web warehouse type applications
8. Computer systems consultants wishing to move into the lucrative Web warehousing development business

Introduction

9. Computer systems executives wanting to understand what Web warehousing is and how it can be worked into existing corporate computer environments
10. Students and teachers interested in understanding these technologies from both a theoretical and practical level
11. And anyone else with the need to have intimate information about this fast-changing technology area

How This book Is Organized

First and most important, you will need a set of tools that can help you to best deploy these technological solutions in your own business situation. Part 1, "Applied Knowledge Management," provides some basic definitions of Web warehousing and knowledge management, and explains how some of the key underlying concepts behind knowledge management can help guide the Web warehousing developer.

Second, you will need to see examples of different kinds of Web warehousing business applications, how they work, and how they are used to make better business decisions. Part 2, "Web Warehousing in Action," is dedicated to the exploration of the different categories of Web warehousing applications that are in use today. You will get a high-level view of the breadth and depth of the Web warehousing world as it is shaping up today, and as it will continue to advance in the future. This part covers data-based, text-based, and multimedia-based applications.

Third, you will need to understand how the technology physically works, and how the "plumbing" provided by the Web/Internet/intranet environment can most effectively be hooked up and assembled into business relevant applications. Part 3, "Technology Foundations," deals with the underlying technology that makes the Web warehousing world work. This part is written for the serious technician who wants to know exactly how Java, JDBC, HTML, and CGI help to create a Web warehousing physical environment.

Applied Knowledge Management

Here we discuss the many challenges that the developers and designers of Web warehousing and knowledge management solutions face in today's ever-changing business environment.

Chapter 1, "Web Warehousing and Knowledge Management," supplies the reader with basic definitions of the terms *Web warehousing* and *knowledge management* and provides some perspectives about where they came from, where they are going, and why they are so important.

Chapter 2, "From Edison to Berners-Lee: New Technology Assimilation," examines the special challenges the implementers of Web warehousing systems face as they move into this brave new world of systems development. To help us understand exactly what some of the challenges to new technology are, we begin with the history of the assimilation of many of the recent paradigm-shaking technologies. We consider the challenges that the developers of products such as electricity, the radio, and the automobile had to face, and see how the assimilation of these technologies into our society was managed.

When we examine the way other products were assimilated, we discover that there is a consistent pattern to this process. We then propose that the knowledge management principles can be used to help us understand it, and to be proactive in our management of this same assimilation process for Web warehousing technologies.

Chapter 3, "Value Chains and Killer Applications," addresses the specific and detailed world of management theory's applicability to business computer systems development. We begin by developing an appreciation for the most valuable tool at the corporate knowledge engineer or disposal, the value chain. We discover what a value chain is, how it is developed, and how it can be used to develop an approach to Web warehousing design, and see how the concepts of the value proposition and the killer app come into play.

Chapter 4, "Visioning, Modeling, and Value Propositions," continues with the development of an understanding of the knowledge management principles by taking a closer look at the concepts of the application value proposition (the statement that defines what value the Web warehousing solution is supposed to deliver to the organization and describes how this value will be delivered) and the process of modeling and visioning. By using the value proposition statement, we can see how the developer can incorporate the knowledge management concepts into the very definition of the systems under development. Thus, both the developer and the systems user will better understand exactly how a new system will help with the running of the business.

I then introduce visioning and modeling, the processes one goes through to figure out what the value propositions for a given application actually are and how they "fit" into the business world into which they are being injected.

Introduction

In Chapter 5, "Knowledge Networks, Knowledge Neighborhoods, and Knowledge Economics," I review the last and perhaps most interesting of the knowledge management perspectives, the role of *knowledge networks*, and the rules of *knowledge economics*. We consider some of the significant ways in which people and organizations are forced to redefine themselves and their roles, and their relationships to one another, based on the way that new technologies wreak havoc with the status quo, and some techniques for managing that process in the future.

Part 2, "Web Warehousing in Action"

Part 2 has been provided for those individuals who are interested in the real world, practical application of Web warehousing technology. While I spend a little bit of time on some of the theoretical aspects and positioning of the different solution areas, for the most part I deal with the cold hard facts of real applications. I show you how they work and where they work well.

This part is dedicated to the investigation and exploration of Web warehousing in action. Each of the major areas where Web warehousing applications are having a positive impact on the businessperson's world today is organized and highlighted.

Each chapter is dedicated to a different application and includes:

1. A description of the application area
2. A description of the kind of business problems that these types of applications solve
3. A description of how the applications work
4. An investigation of how the applications are typically put together
5. An example of a "typical" product from that application area in action, so that you can see how it works in the real world

The chapters in are divided into three major groupings. The first group is concerned with the data-based information delivery applications, the second group addresses the delivery of text-based information, and the last group focuses on the delivery of multimedia-type information.

Data-Based Web Warehouse Applications   Included here is information about the fundamental data-based information that can be delivered from within a Web warehouse type of environment. These application areas are all extensions of the already existing data warehousing environment, and function in the same way as far as the businessperson is concerned. The only difference between these applications and their data warehousing-based counterparts lies in the delivery technology they use.

Chapter 6, "Traditional Warehousing: Architecture and Technology," reviews the technological, organizational, and business organization of the data warehousing environment. Included are the definition of a warehouse environment, a description of the three principal functional components of a warehouse (acquisition, storage, and access), and the history of data warehouses and the business premise for their existence.

Chapter 7, "Web Query and Reporting," looks at the continued role that query and reporting tools play in the business world, and how a Web-based query and reporting tool can work.

Chapter 8, "Web OLAP," discusses one of the latest and greatest types of query applications. It reviews what OLAP is, how it works, and how it is deployed in a Web environment.

Chapter 9, "Web-Based Statistical Analysis and Data Mining," focuses on the transition of both traditional statistical analysis products and the new generation of data mining products to the Web.

Chapter 10, "Web-Based Graphical and Geographic Information Systems," discusses how these systems are helping business people solve problems and how they are being deployed to the Web.

Text-Based Web Warehousing Applications The next several chapters of the book turn our attention from the traditional *data*-based world of business information systems to the newer exciting *text*-based systems. Text-based information management is clearly opening up many new and exciting application areas for business, but as a whole it remains a relatively little understood discipline.

In these chapters we look at the concept and practical application consideration of text applications and examine how they can be integrated into the businessperson's workaday world.

Chapter 11, "An Introduction to Text Information Management Systems," explores exactly what text information management systems are, and examines the broad range of capabilities that such systems offer. We look at the potentials and the many pitfalls, and review a survey of the different business benefits that companies are accruing. In addition, we discuss the history of their development, and the many special challenges that the builders of these types of systems face.

Chapter 12, "Architecture for Text Information Management Systems," considers the many specific technical challenges and the various kinds of architecture alternatives that vendors and companies have developed to create and deliver effective text information management systems. Included in this chapter are:

1. The different major categories of text information management systems (search engines, search enablers, text analysis, text mining, collaborative work environments, subscription and conscription services)
2. The different architectural structures they employ
3. The principal approaches that these products manifest (push versus pull, agent versus user-based)

Chapter 13, "Search Engines and Facilities," concentrates on the specific delivery of search engine capabilities. We review the various types of search engines, their major architectural components, and the principal differentiators between search engine products. We then take an intimate look at a highly specialized, high-end search engine product.

Chapter 14, "Text Mining Systems," looks at the last of the text information management systems, the text analysis and text mining systems. We examine how they work, how they are used to solve business problems, and then see what products one vendor offers in this space.

Multimedia Applications The last chapter of this part focuses on applications and products in the area of multimedia offerings.

Chapter 15, "Multimedia Information Management Systems," is the newest and least mature of the Web warehousing technologies. This chapter is dedicated to the exploration of the multifaceted world of the delivery of multimedia information. Included are issues revolving around the delivery of image, video, audio, 3-d, 4-d, and other nontraditional media via a Web/Internet/intranet technological framework. Included here is a look at a product that does image search based on image-based input and comparisons.

Part 3, "Technology Foundations," is aimed at those individuals who are interested in understanding exactly what Web technology is all about, and how it can be harnessed to do Web warehousing types of work.

Throughout Part 3, I spend a significant amount of time on the development of raw technical information. I do so for some very specific reasons.

Although it is certainly true that there are a lot of books available that talk about Web technology, I was unable to find one that did a good job of focusing on those issues that the developer of a Web warehouse would care about. Each of the dozens of books I reviewed has the same basic shortcomings, namely:

1. They are typically focused on the technology from the programmer's, not the warehouse developer's, perspective, meaning that they spend too much time burying the core information about the Web technology with details that are simply not important to us.
2. They typically are trying to push one form of programming or another. You can get a book about Java and one about CGI, but you cannot get a book that shows you how they relate to each other.
3. They typically are either too detailed, or too generalized.

This part will help you to understand the details of how the Web functions, and how Web-based database and text based access works. This section is for programmers, database administrators, and system architects. Here we cover all of the basics of Web technology, from the lowest technical level and the earliest days of Internet development to today's world of HTML, JAVA, and Coffee Beans.

Chapter 16, "The Internet and Internet Services," considers the history of the technological and organizational foundations of the Web. We discuss where the Internet came from, and the core technological foundations that define an Internet and, subsequently, a Web application.

Chapter 17, "Web Components and Communications," looks at the higher level of operability within the Internet, the level of Web activity. Here I define each of the critical components of Web-based processing and show how they are assembled into Web applications.

Chapter 18, "CGI and PPP: Providing Database Access to the Web," departs from the generalized discussions to consider the specific issues involved in the storage and delivery of information via the Web. We consider the first two methods of data retrieval available to the programmer/designer, the PPP and CGI approaches.

Chapter 19, "JAVA: The Alternative Approach to Web Programming," introduces the reader to the Java technology paradigm. We see how the Java programming approach radically changes the practicality of corporate production Web development by addressing many of the native Web technologies' shortfalls.

Chapter 20, "JDBC: Accessing Databases with Java," concentrates on developing an understanding of how JDBC, the Java-based connectivity standard, improves the developer's ability to deliver data and text to the user.

Introduction

Chapter 21, "Web Warehousing: Architecture, Performance, and Management," considers many of the issues that the designer of a system, or architect of a Web warehousing environment, needs to take into account to make the systems efficient, effective, and manageable.

WEB WAREHOUSING AND KNOWLEDGE MANAGEMENT

PART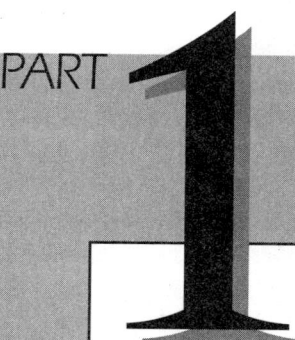

Applied Knowledge Management

Knowledge management and Web warehousing are shaping up to be the preeminent paradigms to drive the development of the next generation of computer systems in the business world.

—Rob Mattison, 1998

CHAPTER 1

Web Warehousing and Knowledge Management

- *What is Web warehousing?*
- *How are data warehousing and World Wide Web technology related to Web warehousing?*
- *What are some of the different types of Web warehousing applications?*
- *What is knowledge management?*
- *What are the principles of knowledge management?*
- *What are some of the alternative definitions for knowledge management systems?*

Introducing Web Warehousing

With all of the technological change that is going on today, the last thing anyone needs is yet another technological revolution to tackle. Computer systems development professionals are forced to deal with a staggering amount of change, generated at an unbelievable speed, and increasing in complexity with every passing day. Many of us would rather avoid taking part in any more of these "revolutions." Many of us would like to "Just say no" to new technologies altogether.

Like it or not, though, we are in the midst of yet another technological and organizational revolution, and we have about as much choice about it as we had about the earlier ones. We can embrace it, learn about it, and master it, or we can get left behind as it sweeps into the business world and the previous technologies are once again replaced.

The revolution, Web warehousing, is one of the most interesting and dynamic of the new technological transitions. Its history is short, but its genealogy is lengthy and complex, and its potential for the delivery of new, powerful, useful, and profit-producing systems is substantial.

Web warehousing, as we describe it here, is really much more than just another new technology. It is actually an entirely new approach that represents the culmination of several trends that have been going on in the business computer systems industry for some time. Web warehousing is the technological world you are left with when you merge data warehousing/business intelligence systems with the new Web technology.

The Data Warehousing Genealogy of Web Warehousing

One half of the parentage of the Web warehousing movement can clearly be traced back to the development of data warehousing systems in the corporate world. These systems have a history that goes back almost as far as computer systems themselves, and have emerged as one of the principle technological approaches to the development of newer, leaner, meaner, more profitable corporate organizations.

Stated in simplistic terms, data warehousing is the computer systems development discipline dedicated to systems that allow business users to analyze how well their systems are running, and figure out how to make them run better. Data warehousing systems are the diagnostic systems of the business world.

In the earliest days of computer systems, developers quickly found out that they really needed to create two kinds of systems to meet the needs of the business.

The first systems, the "bread and butter" systems of the business world, are called the on-line transaction processing (OLTP) systems. These are the systems that actually manage the business itself and allow corporations to coordinate the activities of hundreds of employees and meet the needs of millions of customers, all at the same time.

All businesses need OLTP systems to compete in today's corporate environment. However, people also discovered very quickly that OLTP systems cannot really help a businessperson analyze how well the business is running and how to improve performance. So, some different kinds of systems were invented, the *management information systems* (MIS) and the *decision support systems* (DSS). These systems were concerned not with the day-to-day running of the business, but with the analysis of how the business is doing. Of course, as technologies have improved, the sophistication of both OLTP systems and MIS/DSS systems has improved right along with them.

Ultimately, the MIS/DSS family systems gradually evolved into what we now know as data warehousing systems. These systems are typically put together by using client/server technology [that is, they consist of PCs hooked up to a local-area network (LAN), which connects those PCs with database server machines, which in turn deliver information to the business user]. They typically deliver information to users in one of six formats: query and reporting, on-line analytical processing (OLAP), agent, statistical analysis, data mining, and graphical/geographic. (For more detailed information about data warehousing and the different kinds of applications see Chapter 6, "Traditional Warehousing.")

Data Warehouse Contributions to the Web Warehouse Data warehousing is actually responsible for two major contributions to the new Web warehousing world. First, it provides a large number of the applications that run within the Web warehousing environment. All of the data-based applications that run in the data warehousing world also run in the Web warehousing arena, including query, OLAP, agent, statistical analysis, data mining, and graphical/geographic systems.

Second, data warehousing contributes its organizational principles and objectives. The data warehouse attempts to ease the job of business analysts by organizing and managing the sources of information they need, and making it easy for them to get what they want when they want it. In the same way and for the same reasons, the Web warehouse attempts to organize all of the different sources of information it manages.

One of the most important aspects of Web warehousing, therefore, is that it delivers all of the same kinds of applications that the data warehousing solutions deliver. The only difference is that the applications are delivered via Web technology, as opposed to the traditional client/server technology.

Web Technology Genealogy of Web Warehousing

Migration of the existing population of client/server-based data warehousing applications into the world of Web warehousing is only half of the true Web warehousing story. There is another whole set of applications that the Web warehouse will inherit from its other parental line, from the Web technology genealogy, and those applications will provide some of the most interesting new wrinkles for business.

Web technology will not only bring to this environment a new way to deliver information to users, but it will also allow business people to access, search for, analyze, and make use of *non-data*-based information in much the same ways as *data*-based information.

While the people in the client/server-based business area have been concentrating on mastering data (numbers and letters) to bring information to business users, the developers of Web technology have focused on the delivery of things other than data.

Web Technology's Contribution to the Warehouse Web technology allows business users to manipulate different kinds of information and objects—one of the two great contributions it makes to the Web warehousing world, as noted above. For many years now, people have been able to search for, retrieve, and store things in the World Wide Web environment that are *not* data. The Web's major claim to fame, of course, is the way it allows people to manage text, documents, and other versions of the written word. Users can search for documents and descriptions from around the world, from any number of different entry points. In addition to the development of ways to efficiently manage text, however, the Web has also figured out how to deliver the same kinds of capabilities for the users of graphics, images, pictures, sound, audio, video, and three-dimensional and four-dimensional (3-D and 4-D) displays. See Table 1-1.

Chapter 1: Web Warehousing and Knowledge Management

TABLE 1-1 Contributions to the Web Warehousing Environment

Data Warehousing Contribution	Word Processing and Image Contributions	Multimedia Contributions	Unifying Technology
Data management capabilities	Text management capabilities	Multimedia management capabilities	Web
Data analysis capabilities	Text analysis capabilities	Multimedia analysis capabilities	Web
Legacy data sources	Corporate text sources	Corporate multimedia resources	Web
External data sources	External text sources	External multimedia sources	Web

This then defines the other half of the mission and the capability of a Web warehouse, and presents the user and developer with the truly awesome new capabilities of the Web warehousing environment. A Web warehouse, therefore, can deliver to the user all the things a data warehouse can, but the Web technology adds the capability to perform the same kinds of operations (search, statistical analysis, mining, etc.) with business-related objects made up of pictures, sound, graphics, video, and more (Figure 1-1).

Figure 1-1 The hybrid genealogy of Web warehousing.

Data Warehousing
contributes
    data management
    warehousing approach

The Web
contributes
    Web technology
    text and multimedia management

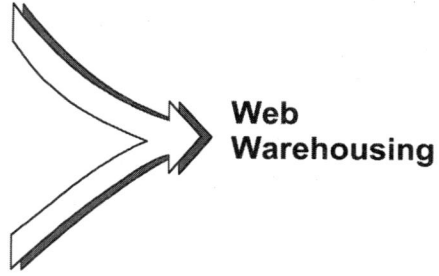

Web Warehousing: A Formal Definition

Let me propose a definition for the term *Web warehousing*. It is clear, at least to me, that a Web warehouse can best be defined as some combination of data warehouse technology and World Wide Web technology that leverages the strengths that each discipline has to offer. Therefore, we can define Web warehousing as below.

WEB WAREHOUSING An approach to the building of computer systems which have as their primary functions the identification, cataloging, retrieval, (possibly) storage, and analysis of information (in the form of data, text, graphics, images, sounds, videos, and other multimedia objects) through the use of Web technology, in order to help individuals find the information they are looking for and analyze it effectively.

It is appropriate to consider some of the more important aspects of this definition.

1. Web warehousing is an approach to the building of computer systems. Web warehousing in and of itself, therefore, is no help in defining the business problems that it is used to address. Web warehousing defines a set of tools for building useful business systems, but we need something else, a different kind of discipline to help us figure out what to have that system do and how to make it work effectively.

2. The purpose of the Web warehouse is to organize and manage the storage, cataloging, retrieval, and analysis of information that users want access to. This aspect of Web Warehousing is significant for two reasons:

    a. It tells us that the job of a Web warehouse is to deal *passively* with information, not actively. Web warehouses are not used to create information, or to run the day-to-day operations of the business. In other words, Web warehouses are *not* on-line trans-

Chapter 1: Web Warehousing and Knowledge Management

action processing systems. They are not e-commerce, net-business, or any of the other forms of e-business that constitute the other half of the business utilization of the Web. Not included in this definition of the Web warehousing universe are applications developed using Web technology, which are concerned with the delivery of transaction-based activities. Also not included are any of the other types of information delivery technologies (data warehousing, image and text processing, multimedia delivery via cable, etc.) which are not based on TCP/IP/Web technology as their delivery vehicle.

b. It also tells us that the world of Web warehouses deals with the organization and management of these items, but not especially with the collection of them. This is another place where Web warehousing differs slightly from its data warehousing predecessor. Whereas the primary function of a data warehouse is to identify, collect, and re-store information, the Web warehouse may or may not involve these tasks. That depends on how easily it can be made available for the user's access. (Text that is stored on the World Wide Web can often be identified, cataloged, and accessed by end users without their needing to copy it first to a new database.)

3. The media delivered by a Web warehouse include not only data, but text, graphics, image, sound, video, and other forms as well. This expansion of the types of things that the Web warehouse can manage means that the level of sophistication and the range of functionalities that can be delivered is greatly expanded, especially for applications that combine some or all of them.

It is also important to note that Web warehousing technology is not limited to the delivery of information to business people (though most of this book will be concerned with the business applications of the technology). A vast majority of search engine applications at work on the World Wide Web today are perfect examples of Web warehousing in action.

The Consequences of This Powerful Combination At first glance, you may think that this will not have much impact at all. "So what," the skeptic might say, "Now you can show fancy pictures and make sounds. That's only cosmetic. There is no real business value to be gained from this kind of capability."

Let's consider just a few of the ways that the force of these combined technologies might express itself. First, and most obvious, the transition of business intelligence and data warehousing applications from the extremely expensive client/server platform to the inexpensive and far-reaching Web platform will provide an incredible boost to productivity and expand the delivery capabilities as well.

Second, as time goes on, the hybrid applications that combine data with text, graphics, video, audio, etc., will surely provide us with yet another quantum leap in corporate productivity. It is always true that the initial introduction of new technologies leaves the first generation of users and developers a little bit short on creativity and insight (see Chapter 2, "From Edison to Berners-Lee: New Technology Assimilation," for more information on that particular aspect). But it is also true that, after the initial learning phase, people have figured out how to use these new capabilities in exciting new ways for great business value.

So, what kinds of systems are these Web warehousing applications? What is so different and special about them? And why should anyone believe that these systems will become a prerequisite part of any successful corporation's technology portfolio in the next century?

We will spend a significant amount of time talking about the specific, immediate ways that these applications make a positive impact on the business world today. But first, let's consider what the computer systems–based business world might look like in the future, say, 10 years from now.

Future Systems' Profiles

To get an idea of where systems are heading, all we need to do is look at the systems of today and of the past, see how they have evolved over time, determine where the current systems are still short of what we would like them to be, and then extrapolate from there. From that perspective, a relatively clear picture comes into focus.

The Media One of the most consistent themes in the evolution of computer systems is the continued demystification and humanization of the computer/human interface. As computer systems have evolved, so too has the "face" the computer shows to the user. There is no reason to assume that this trend will not continue.

Without a doubt, 10 years from now the corporate computer system will include:

- Voice response systems and microkeypads that reduce or eliminate the need for human typing on a keyboard.
- Proliferation of visual displays as bulky computer screens are replaced by wafer-thin, easily moved video display units.
- Full incorporation of multimedia (video, audio, 3-D/4-D, graphics, etc.) into the corporate computer systems world as "primitive" tools like PowerPoint and CorelDRAW are replaced by multimedia presentation makers.
- Continued consolidation and spread of World Wide Web technology (and/or its successors).
- Instantaneous, worldwide communication between corporate users.
- Greatly increased computer power with greatly enhanced storage capacity.

This Web warehousing picture only scratches the surface of the immense enhancements that we will eventually see, and I believe that it is the Web warehousing technology and the Web warehouse platform on which these new types of applications will be based. Web warehousing represents the unifying medium that will pull it all together and deliver it to users.

The Structure of Business and Consumer Behavior Are Changing
If the current pattern continues, then there is no doubt that the corporation of tomorrow will have fewer people doing more work, assisted by incredibly powerful computer systems that have replaced hundreds of people.

The organization of the future will be even less structured and less formal than it is today, as more and more people become subcontractors to the corporate organizations, and as corporations continue to try to create optimum, short-term teams of people to meet short-term project needs. This kind of an organization will depend more heavily than ever on the computer systems to keep track of, organize, and manage the corporate work force and asset base.

At the same time, the relationship of the consumer to business is also undergoing a revolution. As on-line banking, Internet-based sales, and the preference of consumers for electronic forms of commerce increase, the way people prefer to shop will more and more be Web-based.

Web Warehousing Business Applications

With these conditions in place, there is no doubt that the computer systems of the future will be smarter, faster, and more comprehensive, and will exhibit more human-like "intelligence" than ever before. The historical event which best indicates this pattern occurred when the IBM "Deep Blue" computer was able to beat the world's best chess player in a much-heralded media event. Although the "intelligence" of these computers will still be limited, it will certainly be much greater than ever before imagined.

Data Warehousing on the Web

Without a doubt, the first, biggest, and most obvious display of Web warehousing technology in the business world will be the rapid deployment of hundreds and thousands of traditional "data warehousing" applications, which will make use of Web technology to help drive down deployment costs and greatly increase the scope of the systems being delivered. These systems will provide business users with the ability to check inventories, sales volumes, stock locations, and myriad other pools of corporate data, from remote locations as well as from within corporate offices.

Everything that data warehouses can do today, Web warehouses will be able to do tomorrow, only they will do it better and less expensively.

Delivery of Document-Based Knowledge to the Businessperson

Although still in its infancy, the delivery of document-based information to the desktops of corporate users will soon become the norm, as businesses discover all of the many ways that the cataloging, distribution, and sharing of documents within the corporation can help them to reduce costs and improve efficiencies even better than they have so far.

Business Utilization of Multimedia

Not far behind the implementation of corporate-wide document retrieval systems will be the new generation of business-based multimedia management systems. While many people find it difficult to understand how the management of sound, images, pictures, video clips, and 3-D/4-D capabilities will provide any real value to the business world, it is equally difficult to find anyone who doesn't believe that eventually it is going to happen. Web warehousing is how these media will be delivered to the business.

Collaborative Work Groups

The continued breakdown of the corporate hierarchy, and the continued ability of the computer to structure people and situations effectively and to track details better than any person could, will undoubtedly lead to replacing the transaction processing systems with collaborative work environments.

These environments will allow a number of people, spread across the world, to collaboratively participate in complex tasks that currently require the application of millions of lines of computer code and dozens or even hundreds of people's time. These systems will make it possible, for example, for an insurance company to reduce the number of agents, underwriters, and adjusters that it supports.

Imagine this:

A customer drives into a registered auto body repair shop, which is integrated with the insurance company's claim system, the police department's traffic management computer, the auto manufacturer's parts allocations system, and the customer's own home computer system. While waiting for the car to be repaired, this customer can process the insurance claim, file the police report, receive the traffic ticket, automatically deduct the traffic fine and the insurance deductible from the bank account, and then drive away with a car that is good as new.

Or consider this possibility:

The manager of a manufacturing facility watches a fully digitized simulation of the plant in operation hundreds of miles away. Real-time monitoring of each step of the process allows the manager to anticipate problem areas, streamline supply chain issues, and make spur-of-the-moment changes to the manufacturing process and bill of materials by simply making a few requests of the system. Just a few highly trained individuals, whose job is to monitor the systems that run the systems, will manage quality assurance, warehousing, procurement, assembly, and all the other major processes that support the operation of the plant.

The Paperless Bureaucracy

Finally, business will be able to run without all of the paper that it now requires. An abundance of lightweight video screens, combined with incredibly flexible and responsive reporting systems, will make the need for printed reports obsolete.

As text, computer, and image continue to merge, the very need for the printed word will subside as voice messages, visual displays, and graphical representations replace detailed printed reports.

Corporate Learning

During the last decade of downsizing, corporations learned that their assets included much more than just capital, computers, and cash. They learned that their people and their people's maturity, experience, and knowledge all contributed greatly to their ultimate success.

In response to this, more and more corporations are instituting practices and systems that attempt to capture this knowledge, experience, and know-how and make it available to future generations. These systems will involve the combination of written reports, audio- and videotaped interviews with the employees, and the application of new system development techniques that capture this kind of information and make it available to users.

Analysis of Massive Amounts of Input

One of the things computer systems do best is analyze huge masses of raw information and look for patterns and insights that the businessperson can use. These systems, already being used in the data warehousing arena, will continue to grow and mature, allowing business people to analyze not only data-based information, but text, audio, and video as well.

Closed-Feedback-Loop Business Systems

We will see the most dramatic and pronounced impact when we get to the point where this new generation of systems can provide the business with instantaneous in-depth analysis and reaction to any given situation, sometimes even before the businessperson realizes that a problem has arisen. This vision is by far the most aggressive, frightening, and interesting of all. Under this scenario, intelligent Web warehousing systems, driven by intelligent query, analysis, and decision-making software such as data mining applications, are hooked up directly to transaction processing systems. These systems could then monitor the progress of the business and effect changes in the way the business is running. In this way, the business computer systems could become a self-regulating source of constantly renewing business change.

For example, consider a Web warehousing application that keeps track of product inventory levels, sales figures, the weather, and the ever-changing cost of doing business. This system could "learn" the relationship between the weather and people's buying behavior, and automatically raise or reduce the price of products depending on the elements and current inventory levels.

Web Warehousing for Consumers

Consumer applications are by far the most interesting and potentially most profitable aspects of the Web warehousing revolution.

Information Warehouses for the World

The World Wide Web and the current generation of text search services on the Web have demonstrated that there is a world of people who are hungry for as much low-cost, instantaneously accessible information as they can get their hands on. Some may think that the area of search engines is a well-established market with well-defined limits of what people want and how to deliver it. Quite to the contrary, however, I believe that delivering information to consumers through this medium has hardly even gotten started yet.

Looking to Buy Something? Surveys about Web use have shown, again and again, that the number one reason why people use the Web is to get information on something they want to buy. Whether they use the Web as an on-line catalog, as an avenue for direct communication with the manufacturer, or as a virtual showroom, it is clear that the Web is becoming an increasingly important channel of commerce.

Most notable is the fact that, while many organizations use on-line Web commerce systems to take orders and receive payment, a vast majority of people use the Web as a reference source. Current estimates indicate that over 90 percent of all Web activity is simple search and retrieval activity and less than 10 percent is actual commerce.

In other words, the majority of activity on the Web today involves Web warehousing.

Hobbies, Travel, and Leisure Pursuits Not only will Web warehousing continue to play the preeminent role in the support of "traditional" e-commerce, but it will also demonstrate its value in the support of leisure activities. Web information helps people decide where to go on vacation, find out which flights are available, learn how to do a better job of gardening, and pursue stamp collecting and whatever other hobby strikes their fancy.

Delivery of this kind of information will undoubtedly continue to increase in sophistication.

Keeping Track of Your Service Providers Web warehousing systems that allow customers to track services will also see a huge increase. Some people can already check their bank account balances or stock portfolios through on-line Web warehouse information delivery. There is every reason to expect that, in the future, your bank, telephone company, utility, government offices, school, and providers of any other kind of consumer service will be required to provide their constituency with the ability to check status through some Web media.

Hard-Core Research Without a doubt, some consumers and businesses will develop a taste for hard-core research of many different kinds. For these people, specialized services will be able to provide in-depth information about subjects as diverse as the status of a Mars space probe or the full collection of Mozart's symphonies.

Web Warehousing: A Compelling Technology Story

All of this tells us that there is a very compelling technological story and an even more compelling commercial story driving the avalanche of interest in Web warehousing. There is no doubt in anyone's mind that the sudden ability to integrate data, text, information, and multimedia objects from around the world and make them available to business people for analysis and strategic review will result in yet another quantum leap in "progress" on many different business fronts.

This, then, explains and justifies the first part of the title for this book, *Web Warehousing*. It also explains the reason why most of this book is dedicated to communicating what Web warehousing is, how it is executed, and how it can be applied to the solution of business problems. The implementation and integration of high-powered Web warehousing solutions is not a simple, straightforward technical operation, hence the second part of the title, *Knowledge Management*.

Looking backward through the history of OLTP and business intelligence (data warehousing) systems, we can easily say, "Aha, this is what the developers did and that is how it worked." In reality, however, people did not simply walk up to problems and intuitively and automatically know what approach to take and how the technology could best be implemented. No, there was significant investment in trial and error, failure and superfailure. For every successful data warehousing project on the corporate landscape, there are literally hundreds that failed.

The fact that we are presented with a remarkable potential and a great opportunity does not necessarily mean that we will succeed. No doubt, someone will succeed eventually. No doubt, some businesses will figure out just the right combination of technologies, business problems, and operational insights to make those quantum leaps into the next generation of "superapplications" and marvelous success stories that everyone points to. At the same time, there will be hundreds of "bodies" lying along the road, organizations and professionals who "bet the bank" on something that didn't quite work.

It is for this reason that we need to combine our technological understanding of Web warehousing with another perspective. If we are going to be more than just followers in the game of Web warehouse implementation, if we are going to be the leaders and the winners, then we will need some help in understanding these other aspects of system implementation strategy. This is where the knowledge management discipline comes in.

An Introduction to Knowledge Management

We introduce knowledge management against the backdrop of Web warehousing technology and the new age of business advancement. As stated earlier, the discipline of knowledge management is extremely new to the business world at large, and is certainly new to the area of computer systems applications. That is not to say that the foundational concepts for it have not been developing for some time now.

Peter Drucker and the Knowledge Worker

Perhaps the earliest, and certainly the most famous, references to the concept of knowledge management were created by Peter Drucker, the management science guru.

For decades now, Drucker has talked about the concept of the "knowledge worker." As early as the 1970s, Drucker observed that the composition of the gross national product of the United States and most other economic leaders was undergoing a significant shift and that the contribution of "knowledge workers" was growing while the contribution of the traditional "direct labor force" was shrinking.

In the business world that we have known up until now, the value of a business's products was considered to be the direct result of the efforts of the work force that actually did the lifting, welding, moving, and stacking of goods and materials. However, as businesses become increasingly efficient, the intelligent and strategic use of those resources and the clever application of principles of finance, logistics, and management can be combined to accelerate and multiply the initial value of the items, sometimes manyfold.

What Drucker recognized was that the added value of economic activities was not being created by the "real workers," but by the middlemen, the strategists, and the planners who helped the overall engine of business run more efficiently.

Drucker referred to this new breed of employees as *knowledge workers* because it was through the application of their knowledge to the challenges at hand that a business was able to succeed.

Viewing a Business as a Knowledge Factory

Advocates of knowledge management theory argue that our old concepts of what a business is are in the process of being abandoned. The traditional views of business and the traditional organizational structure have certainly been undergoing a radical series of changes. No one could disagree with the observation that the old ways of looking at corporate structure, planning, and development are quickly becoming irrelevant.

As the pressures of business continue to accelerate, we find ourselves working in a corporate environment where none of the old values or old ways seem to make sense anymore.

What is sorely needed, and what the knowledge management perspective provides us with, is a fresh, consistent and functional model for the business, one that can help us explain why things worked in the past, how they can work better in the future, and how we can get there.

The Traditional Corporate Model In the good old days of corporate management science, the corporation was understood in terms of the technology that shaped it. The factory was the epitome of corporate organizational structure, and the factory organizational concepts—the assembly line, the specialist, the compartmentalization of tasks, and the creation and maintenance of an organizational hierarchy—defined how corporations were developed and run.

For whatever reasons, we can still see the signs of these roots in the way corporations are run today. Corporations still spend thousands of worker-hours on building, rebuilding, and remodeling corporate organizational charts. Unfortunately, these corporate structures hardly last longer than the time it takes to get them published and distributed. Corporations still spend thousands of hours on the development of organizational strategies and approaches that do little more than temporarily upset everyone's work schedule, but ultimately leave people less organized than ever before.

The Breakdown of the Traditional Model Unfortunately for most employees in a corporate environment, a loosely organized and annually recurring chaos has replaced planning and order. The corporate structure still exists, at least on paper, but an almost meaningless shell has replaced the intent of corporate structure.

Many things led to the demise of the corporate structure. The breakdown was inspired and created by innovations such as:

- Operational computer systems that eliminate the need for middle management
- The concept of matrix management, which allows multiple people to "belong" to multiple organizations with a minimum amount of accountability or structure
- The continued pressure from competing management consultants to trim the fat and create a lean and mean corporation without the entire overhead of human beings

The traditional corporate organizational model continues to erode and the parade of new organizational theories continues to fall short of providing businesses with the structure, focus, and direction that they really need to move forward.

What is missing is a discipline which:

- Creates a framework for understanding the relationships between capital, people, computer systems, culture, and knowledge, and how to manipulate and manage those relationships effectively
- Is robust enough to explain why successes and major innovations occurred in the past
- Is flexible enough to apply equally well to a wide variety of businesses of all sizes, shapes, and degrees of sophistication
- Is detailed enough to provide a systematic process for diagnosing existing situations, developing new directions, and anticipating future directions

There are many individuals, including this author, who believe that the discipline of knowledge management may provide that structure and framework.

The Knowledge Management View of the Corporation

The advocates of the knowledge management approach say that a business is more than a simple collection of people, assets, and computer systems. They believe that what defines a company and its success is how well it functions in disseminating and managing knowledge. In other words, companies are nothing more than groups of people who collectively apply their knowledge to the solution of customer problems. The more knowledge those people have, and the better they share it, work with it, and propagate it, the better the company runs, the happier the customers are, and the more efficient the entire operation is.

Now, at first glance, this concept may seem a bit simple or obtuse depending on how you look at it. But, doesn't this really explain how companies work in a very fundamental way? Doesn't it explain why some companies succeed and others fail? More important, doesn't this perspective explain the powerful role that computers have played in the success of many businesses? For, when you think about it, what is a good computer system other than a well-designed, automated way to collect, store, and disseminate knowledge to large groups of people?

This perspective also provides us with some fresh insight into the kinds of systems we should be building, and with a new set of criteria for defining how good a computer system is.

What Is Knowledge Management?

There are actually many ways in which we can use the principles defined by knowledge management to help us with the development of Web warehousing systems. Knowledge management provides us with a road map for understanding what the true underlying core processes of the business are. The road map identifies the individuals who execute those processes, and indicates how they relate. We can, therefore, gain extremely valuable insight into how systems can be built to maximize their impact.

The knowledge management principles can be used as follows:

1. To determine how to get Web warehousing applications to function smoothly as part of the overall business processes (the operational aspects of the system).

2. To figure out and deal with the issues of cultural impact and the roles and responsibilities of individuals as they relate to the applications that are being developed (the organizational aspects of the system).

3. To develop techniques for managing the changes in the way people view themselves and their work groups, and the ways in which they deal with each other as a result of the new system (the cultural aspects of the system).

4. To learn how to make sure that the Web warehousing applications will make money for the firm, once deployed (the financial aspects of the system).

5. To resolve how to motivate the organization and the individuals within it to undergo the work and pain necessary to change themselves, and come to accept and embrace the new technological solutions (the promotional aspects of the system).

6. As a guide to describing, designing, and building a special kind of system (a knowledge management system).

Unfortunately, when you mention knowledge management to a group of people, you generally get some glassy-eyed looks or some long-winded, complicated explanation. Some will ramble on and on about knowledge networks, cultural impacts, and other such concepts without ever really saying anything.

This happens, I think, for two reasons:

- The people don't really understand what they are talking about, and they are "faking it."
- The knowledge management subject area is so broad and so weakly defined that you can talk about almost anything and relate it to the knowledge management theme.

To bring some order to this chaos, I have tried to separate the parts of the ocean of knowledge management rhetoric that is flooding the marketplace, and divide them into three major categories.

1. *Knowledge management theory.* We have the philosophical, theoretical concepts of knowledge management that have been proposed by several authors. These concepts (some of which we have considered here) are interesting and insightful, and offer the *potential* for driving some revolutionary changes in the world of business and computer systems over the next couple of years. These concepts, however, though certainly valid, are also for the most part being expounded at a very high level, and serve more as general directions and vague indicators, rather than as specific, tangible instructions or next steps.

2. *Knowledge management principles.* Most important from the perspective of this book, we have the quickly expanding body of tangible, specific instructions, techniques, and guidelines which I refer to as the core *knowledge management principles.* I will identify, explain, and describe the ways in which these core concepts—concepts inspired and directed by the knowledge management view of the world and business—can provide immediately useful guidelines for the developer of Web warehousing systems to follow.

3. *Knowledge management systems.* I undertake to provide several alternative definitions for the latest buzzword phrase to hit the computer systems software sideshow, *knowledge management systems.* This phrase, in theory at least, describes an exciting new type of information system that heralds a whole new generation of business/computer innovation.

In addition, I propose a formal, computer systems–based definition of knowledge itself.

In the next chapter, we will consider these issues in greater depth, but let's pause here for some formal definitions of each.

What Is Knowledge Management Theory?

We start with a formal definition of knowledge management theory itself:

KNOWLEDGE MANAGEMENT THEORY *An approach to the study of business that attempts to describe the effectiveness of organizations as a function of the efficiency with which they create, store, and apply knowledge to the creation of goods and services.*

Knowledge management theory proposes that knowledge constitutes a heretofore unrecognized form of currency which helps define how a business operates, how people relate to each other, and how businesses create real value to the consumer.

According to knowledge management advocates, no value can be created by a corporation unless it figures out what it can offer that a purchaser will perceive as valuable (value propositions), and the most efficient way to deliver it (the value chain).

What Are the Knowledge Management Principles?

Most people will agree that the definition of knowledge management theory that I have provided here is relatively accurate and consistent with most of the writing and speaking going on today about the subject. However, this definition, and knowledge management theory itself, is simply too broad and too general in scope to allow us to do anything very specific with it.

Because of this, I have attempted to identify some specific principles that seem to underlie what people mean when they talk about knowledge management as it is being applied in the business world today. This collection of principles is by no means exhaustive or definitive in any way, but it does provide us with some specific concepts for making useful observations. In my opinion, these principles provide the substance that knowledge management can offer, and can be used to help us manage, design, and build Web warehousing applications in the future. These principles are the core, underlying, defining concepts and organizational insights which allow us to understand how the business itself, the people working in it, and the computer systems that tie them all together work.

The body of knowledge about knowledge management is growing larger daily, and the knowledge management "toolkit" for developing systems is, therefore, growing as well. At this time, there are several concepts that we can use effectively today. These include:

1. *Value chain.* Without a doubt, the notion of the corporate and industry-based value chain is the most often quoted and best understood of the knowledge management principles. The concept of the value chain describes the way a business is organized in terms of its functional components (rather than organizational, political, economic, etc). This organization of functional components, therefore, defines the process by which the business delivers value to customers. Chapter 3 is dedicated to exploring the application of value chains to the Web warehousing world.

2. *Value propositions.* Related to the value chain is the concept of the value proposition. It is the proposition that a business makes to the customer, basically stating that the company agrees to deliver a predefined set of benefits in exchange for money or some other form of consideration. The creation and delivery of value propositions is the purpose of a value chain. [Value propositions can also be used to define the internal exchanges that occur within the business as well. For example, the vendor (or developer) of a software product must describe a value proposition to the clients if they are to understand the benefits the application will deliver.] A large part of Chapter 4 is devoted to the role of value propositions in the Web warehousing world.

3. *Modeling and Visioning.* The functional components of the business and its value propositions describe what the business will do. However, until the employees understand how they will accomplish the objectives in cooperation with the other people in the business and with the new technologies, the business cannot actually do anything. The method of figuring out how people will organize themselves around the use of these new technologies is referred to as the *modeling process*. The method of turning those models

into actionable templates for behavior is referred to as the *visioning process*. We introduce these concepts in the next chapter, and the second half of Chapter 4 is dedicated to an exploration of these theories.

4. *Knowledge networks (and knowledge neighborhoods).* The term *knowledge network* has been coined to describe the network of individuals within an organization who share a common interest in the same set of knowledge. For example, all the people concerned about human resources policy (the legal and human resources departments, and the managers of various other departments) define a knowledge network. Identification of knowledge networks is key to the development of systems which leverage knowledge within the organization. A portion of Chapter 5 considers this concept.

5. *Knowledge economics.* This concept is one of the newest, most powerful, and least understood of the knowledge management principles. Knowledge economics describes how individuals and organizations value, give away, buy, sell, and trade knowledge as a form of currency. Knowledge economics defines how people working along the value chain contribute to the delivery of the corporation's value proposition through their contribution and use of knowledge. As we will see, the ideas of knowledge economics are some of the most difficult to deal with, impacting corporate cultures and values and the very nature of business itself. Chapter 5 considers these issues as well.

In the next few chapters we will explore these terms in greater depth and provide some context for understanding how they are all related. In later chapters we will look at how they can help us in the Web warehousing development and design process.

Knowledge Management Principles— Definition and Listing

In keeping with our structure, therefore, we offer a formal definition of the knowledge management principles.

KNOWLEDGE MANAGEMENT PRINCIPLES *Key concepts that provide insight into the ways businesses and people relate to each other through the creation, manipulation, and application of knowledge. These principles include:*

Value chain analysis
Value propositions
Modeling and visioning
Knowledge networks and knowledge neighborhoods
Knowledge economics

Application of Knowledge Management Principles to the Consumer World

The original focus of the developers of the knowledge management theory was on the behavior of businesses. As we begin to look at the underlying principles, it is obvious that many of them are equally applicable to consumer behavior. All consumers have their own day-to-day value chain. Consumers maintain their own functional "chain of activities" (shopping, lodging, commuting, working, for example). They also have their own value propositions (what they value in the products and services they purchase), problems with operational and functional visioning, knowledge neighborhoods in which they participate, and a set of knowledge economics that they work with. There clearly are parallels in the consumer products market that will bear future investigation, but any great detail is beyond the scope of this book.

In Pursuit of a Definition of Knowledge

Another way to approach the whole process of defining knowledge management is to start with a definition of knowledge itself. This is actually much more difficult than it might seem. Philosophers and semanticists have argued and debated the definition for centuries, and as soon as we change cultural or language contexts, we immediately find that it no longer applies. The definition of knowledge is not easy to develop and, frankly, I don't believe it is very important to our purpose. Throughout this book, we are using the term *knowledge management* in a particular context. What we are concerned with here is the definition of knowledge as it applies to the management of businesses and computers. Taken within this much more limited context, I think that we can develop a definition that makes sense.

Knowledge Management and Computers

If we are to apply the theories of knowledge management to the development of computer systems, then some basic concepts and vocabulary need to be established. Computer systems have played a pivotal role in the evolution of corporate environments into their current state and will continue to do so in their further development.

We need to understand, however, the nature of that relationship in a way that is functional for us and which looks at the computer in a new light, not as a transaction processing engine or a computing machine, but as a highly sophisticated, incredibly efficient, tireless manager of corporate knowledge.

The Evolution of the View of the Computer's Role

People's perceptions of the role that the computer plays in the business world has evolved over time. From the simple computer of the 1950s to the multimedia Web-based thinking machine of the twenty-first century, the role continues to redefine itself as the technology and the business mature.

If we are to succeed at understanding how the computer can be so instrumental to the management of the corporation's knowledge, then we will need to know what the raw material is that computers actually manage, and see if we can make any sense out of this set of assumptions.

Data, Information, and Knowledge

One useful way to look at the evolution of computers and their relationship to business is through people's perceptions of the raw materials that computers create and work with.

The Age of Data Processing In the earliest days, computers dealt with data, pure and simple. Data was defined as those discrete bits of information that were important to the execution of some analysis. The data, in and of itself, was nothing more than a meaningless string of numbers and/or characters. The data became meaningful only when:

- Its storage was structured in a certain way (cataloged, indexed, and made available for retrieval)
- The programs that accessed it knew what to do with it
- The people interpreting the output could make sense out of it

So businesses discovered that, if they combined raw data with smart programmers and good programs, they could get the information they needed from the computer systems. During those early days, the computer industry was known as the *data processing* area, and that is basically how it worked. The business created data that was stored and processed by the computers. Programs then turned that data into information, which users could apply to the solution of business problems (thereby creating knowledge).

Under this model, therefore, we have the three building blocks necessary to understand the relationship between business people and computers. These blocks are *data, information,* and *knowledge.* In this case, the computer manages the data, the programs turn it into information, and the users interpret the information and use it to create and manipulate knowledge.

Of course, in the old days of data processing systems, the computers were incredibly crude by today's standards. It took many people and a lot of programming work to get the computer to help support the business. At that time, the knowledge that the corporations managed was still under the control of the people running the business.

Even at that stage, however, we started to see a shift. The computer started to keep track of many of the details for the business. It also allowed business people to manage and manipulate those details in ways they never could before. Even in those early times, the burden for the management of corporate knowledge started to shift to the computer.

The Age of Information Management As computer systems got bigger and faster, and as business people got more sophisticated, more was asked of the computer systems than simple processing of data. It seems that working with data all the time is an incredibly painstaking and resource-intensive process, and since the computers had more power than ever before, it was worth it to "up the ante" a little bit and have the computers do even more of the work.

Business people soon discovered that they really wanted to work with information, not data. [We define information as the combination of data (which has no inherent meaning) with contextual information (which allows us to assign meaning).] And so, the computer systems took on additional functionalities. Instead of just keeping track of the details for the businessperson, the newly available computer power was harnessed to actually manage information, not only process data (ergo the new name *management information systems*).

As these systems got better at the management of information, the need for programs became less. Eventually, special information management databases (called *relational databases*) were created. These databases allowed business users to store real information, not just data (because the database's structure forces all data to be stored within a meaningful context).

The relational database spawned a new generation of systems. Now that the computers could manage the information itself, a whole new generation of end-user tools (query, OLAP, analysis tools, etc.) were invented. In a very real sense, the maturity of relational databases and the user enablement tools are what spawned the current data warehousing revolution, as business people have started to realize the full potential of power that working directly with information can provide them. Of course, under this information management model, it is still the business users and their business acumen that turn that information into truly useful business knowledge.

However, as we look for the next quantum leap in computer processing power, through the Web warehousing tools combined with the interconnectivity of the Web and the soon-to-be-enjoyed exponential power increases in personal computers, we are preparing for yet another shift along the knowledge management continuum.

Systems That Create and Act upon Knowledge without Human Intervention

Clearly, we are standing at the brink of an even more sophisticated world of computer-enhanced business functionality. If the progression of systems continues as it has (and there is no reason to believe that it will not), then we can count on seeing the role of the computer refined even further as these new technologies are applied.

In this new world, the computer systems will manage not only data (the raw material) or information (that data combined with a meaningful context). What we will most likely see is a new generation of systems that actually store, manage, retrieve, and apply knowledge itself.

How can this be? How can we get mindless computers to actually apply, create, and evoke changes on the basis of knowledge? That will depend on how we establish these systems. It is certainly true that computers are a long way from being as creative, innovative, and intelligent as humans, but it is also true that there are software programs today that can observe patterns, learn to anticipate those patterns, and provide recommendations for how to proceed that are amazingly accurate and useful.

These new systems, in their many different forms, will simply combine data, information, and the application of that information to specific situations and objectives to create the first generation of systems that will actually create, manage, and apply knowledge to the solution of business problems without any kind of human intervention.

Business Knowledge The philosophical discussion about what knowledge is, in all of its many manifestations, is certainly an interesting one. The objective for this book, however, is to limit the use of the term to a particular type of knowledge, namely, knowledge that is useful to business people in the execution of their duties. Our definition of business knowledge, therefore, will be based on this foundation.

Business knowledge, from our perspective, is a collection of information, which has been specifically assembled to support a businessperson's development of specific solutions to specific business problems. In other words,

> Data + context + application to specific business objectives = business knowledge

Throughout the rest of this book, when we use the term *knowledge*, we mean this business-specific, problem-solving type of knowledge.

For decades now, we have talked about getting data and information into the hands of users, knowing all along, intuitively, that this is what they were really interested in. At this point, the astute reader may have a question. "If knowledge is what people were really after all along, and if that is exactly what these previous generations of systems created, then what is so different about defining knowledge and knowledge management now? Aren't we just renaming the same old things?"

Yes and no. In one sense, the relabeling and redefinition of the output of these kinds of systems as knowledge is a meaningless exercise. On the other hand, however, by relabeling we hopefully change our perspective of what we are doing and how we are doing it. For that reason, making the shift to knowledge management–based terminology is critical.

The development of a very specific computer system– and business-related definition of the terms *data, information,* and *knowledge* is key to our understanding of the knowledge management discipline and its relationship to the business computer systems industry.

While these definitions might at first seem somewhat arbitrary, or less than complete, it is my belief that the definition is precisely what is needed to develop a foundation upon which we can build a truly functional knowledge management discipline that can serve our industry.

Granted, this falls far short of capturing the essence of what knowledge truly is in an all-encompassing and theoretical sense. It still, in my opinion, provides all the definition that the designers of business computer systems need. The collection and application of knowledge (data + context + application) to the attainment of business objectives is the only thing business people care about. The definition of these terms, their hierarchy of complexity, and applicability to the stated purpose of a business computer system, specifically to help the businessperson solve business problems, is both eloquent and functional.

What Are Knowledge Management Systems?

Now that we have some definitions for the theory of knowledge management, a collection of principles, and a proposal for a formal definition for knowledge itself, we are finally ready to attack the trickiest definition of all, the definition of knowledge management systems.

Why is it important that we come up with a definition of knowledge management systems? Why is this actually more important than the other definitions? The answer depends on your perspective, but from the computer systems industry point of view, the definition of what is or isn't a knowledge management system also defines what is or isn't a part of the latest, greatest fad in computer systems development. This is important for only one reason. The people who are able to associate themselves, their products, and their services with the term *knowledge management system* are those who are going to be recognized as part of the new wave, the bringers of the hot new technology, and the winners in the next round of new technology sales. Companies not associated with the phrase will be called the dinosaurs and the laggers.

When it comes to defining a term such as *knowledge management system*, one has to be particularly careful. The computer industry can get to be confusing enough when the technology is simple and straightforward. For something as complex as a knowledge management system, it can become just about impossible to propose a formal definition that everyone can agree to. There are in fact, several schools of thought about what the term should mean. I will not pretend to be an authority who can dictate which definition is "correct." All I will do is propose the four most likely categorization schemes, and leave it to the marketplace to actually "slug it out" over the next few years.

On the basis of everything we have considered, there are four different criteria that can be applied to define knowledge management systems. We can say that a knowledge management systems is:

1. Any computer system
2. A computer system that operates according to knowledge management principles
3. A computer system that creates, manipulates, and applies computer-generated knowledge itself
4. Any arbitrary grouping of products that various special-interest groups advocate. (Some groups, for instance, define text management, multimedia, and data warehousing systems as knowledge management systems.)

Let's consider each of these proposed definitions in greater detail.

All Computer Systems Are Knowledge Management Systems

The case can be made that any computer system that helps run a business or provides information to a user is a knowledge management system. In fact, there are systems called *knowledge bases,* there is even a database product called *KnowledgeBase,* and there are hundreds if not thousands of customized corporate information systems that either have the word knowledge in their name or are referred to as *knowledge systems*. It therefore becomes extremely difficult to nail down a meaningful definition for the term. After all, the word knowledge itself has broad meanings.

This means, of course, that you are just about guaranteed to have an argument on your hands when you try to debate with someone what is or isn't a knowledge management system. Since any computer system that delivers any kind of value, can, in this broadest sense, be said to be a knowledge management system, then on what grounds can any one product or application be excluded or included?

This semantic and logical reality, however, has not stopped anyone from starting up yet another new technological approach bandwagon for knowledge management systems. Here are just a few of the other classification schemes to consider.

Knowledge Management Principle–Based Systems

An equally compelling case can be made for the definition of systems which attempt to capitalize on one or more of the knowledge management principles as the true bearers of the knowledge management systems label. Taking this categorization, we would classify systems according to:

- *Value chain efficiency.* In this category we can include the knowledge management systems as well as the efficient customer response (ECR) systems, which attempt to automate and streamline supply chains; the customer relationship marketing (CRM) systems, which try to streamline and manage the relationship of the business with the customer; and any other form of efficiency-generating system that is based on the underlying value chain to help the business run better.

- *Knowledge neighborhoods.* In this category, we can include all systems concerned with the collection and sharing of knowledge within the business. The corporate digital libraries, the corporate knowledge repositories, the systems that gather and disseminate research information, those that create on-line virtual work teams, and even generic applications such as Lotus Notes, all support knowledge neighborhood development and, therefore, are knowledge management systems.

- *Others.* Applications have been developed to help with visioning, modeling, development of value propositions, and management of cultural issues.

While there is certainly a case to be made for allowing these kinds of products to claim the knowledge management systems title, it would probably be most helpful for everyone if they would preface their self-definitions with the additional characterization of value chain, knowledge neighborhoods, or whatever other principle they are associated with, thereby helping everyone understand what they really do.

The Buzzword-Based Method of Categorizing Systems

Another currently popular trend is to apply the term *knowledge management systems* to all of the latest, greatest technologies that are showing up in the business world. This school tends to come up with lists of totally unrelated applictions that supposedly fit under the knowledge management system umbrella. One popular grouping of applications, for example, will list text management, text mining, collaborative software, and customer relationship management as an inventory of knowledge management systems.

The problem with this approach, of course, is that the particular grouping of applications is unrelated to any formal definition or criteria and is most likely based on the list author's desire to be associated with a certain "leading edge" banner.

This method of categorization is in fact the most common way in which we are introduced to collections of products. A new buzzword becomes popular (such as data warehousing, relational database, or knowledge management) and before you know it everyone is placing ads in magazines, writing books, publishing white papers, and giving speeches, associating themselves with that new buzzword. You hear them tell that their random list of products and applications is the one and only defining list that will tell you what is or is not a knowledge management system, for instance.

Systems That Create and Act on Knowledge Automatically

Earlier in this chapter, we considered the possibility of creating computer systems that are able to identify problems, and develop solutions to those problems, all without the benefit of human interaction.

There are already computer systems that independently check inventory levels and reorder products, and systems that monitor stock price activity and make buy/sell decisions. We will most certainly see more and more of the analytical capabilities of these systems being integrated together. They are clearly candidates for the title knowledge management system.

Formal Criteria for the Definition of Knowledge Management Systems

The fact is that companies are already advertising everything from query tools to enterprise resource planning (ERP) systems as knowledge management systems, and there is every reason to believe that the hoards of wannabes will soon overwhelm the market with an even greater variety of products to squeeze in under the same banner.

For all practical purposes, then, the attachment of the label *knowledge management system* provides us with absolutely no net informational value. It does not tell us what the product does or doesn't do, nor what philosophical precepts it is based on. All it really does is allow the product vendors to label their offerings with the latest buzzword and try to impose their interpretation of knowledge management on unwary product shoppers.

There are so many different ways to look at the knowledge management system label, and these conflicting uses of the term pretty much nullify its usefulness as a name. My own opinion is that we should concentrate on developing better, more accurate, and more meaningful labels for the products and services we deal with, and stop wasting our time in fruitless debates.

However, for the sake of completeness, I will provide a formal definition for knowledge management systems.

KNOWLEDGE MANAGEMENT SYSTEMS *Computer information systems that can be defined according to one of four criteria. We can say that a knowledge management system is:*

1. *Any computer system that works for a business or individual, managing data or information in the support of decision making.*

2. *Any computer system developed in support of the efficient exercise of one of the knowledge management principles, including value chain, value proposition, modeling, visioning, knowledge neighborhoods, and knowledge economics.*

3. *Any computer system which integrates the collection and application of business knowledge (data + context + application) to the solution of specific business problems.*
4. *A system identified by the right buzzword. One can define a select list of unrelated software applications and claim that this particular grouping defines the set of knowledge management systems.*

For all practical purposes, using the knowledge management system label has almost no practical value because of the many different ways that it can be interpreted.

Databases, Data Warehouses, and Knowledge Bases

In a related flurry of activity, we can expect to see the emergence of a new generation of products known as *knowledge bases,* and we can also expect a great amount of confusion and misdirection. In fact, there is already a patented database called *KnowledgeBase,* and even one called *Knowledge Man.* These products were created long before the concept of knowledge management existed and simply functioned like any other database. So we can expect to see a group of database vendors claiming to have made the magical shift to becoming knowledge bases.

At the same time, we can probably also expect to see a new generation of database-like products that will actually be knowledge bases, software products which, in the business sense, store and manipulate knowledge as well as data and information.

CHAPTER 2

From Edison to Berners-Lee

New Technology Assimilation

- *What are the major impediments to the deployment of new technology solutions?*
- *How can we best categorize each of the impediments, and how can they be effectively addressed?*
- *What are the mechanical, architectural, operational, organizational, cultural, financial, and promotional aspects of new technology deployment life cycles?*
- *How can we use Web warehousing and the knowledge management principles to help us address each of these aspects of the cycle?*

A Revolution with a Cost

In the previous chapter, I draw a picture of a world full of opportunity and revolution, one where new information systems, new ways of dealing with computers, businesses, and each other will be the hallmarks of a wondrous new society. I describe some of the technology that would get us there, namely Web-based technology, both in the form of e-commerce/Web-based transaction processing systems and Web warehousing technologies. I also propose that knowledge management theory, and more importantly, the knowledge management principles (value chain analysis, value propositions, modeling/visioning, knowledge neighborhoods, and knowledge economics) will provide us with some of the more important structural concepts and insights to make this new world a reality.

What we didn't talk about, specifically, is how that new world will be created and what we can do to help it along. We tend to forget the hidden costs that accomplishment of these objectives involves.

We forget that for each new "miracle" that arises out of new technological development, there is a concomitant armful of adjustments that we have to make. Each time we go through one of these technological revolutions we tend to experience a lot of painful trial and error as we learn how best to make it work. We immediately forget about the dozens of *failed projects* we witnessed over the years and cling to the memory of the one successful project we were a part of. We all focus on the stories about the million dollar home-run paradigm-busting applications that turned the industry on its ear, and we pretend to look somewhere else when we hear about the many hundreds of projects that attempted to do the same thing and failed.

Yes, there are some very significant costs associated with the deployment of new technologies that we tend to overlook when we start planning these projects and, unfortunately, these costs have continued to get higher and higher as the complexity and speed of technological progress continues to increase.

Your First Web Warehousing Project Will Be a Failure!

Statistically speaking, I would be on very safe ground if I were to say that your first Web warehousing project will be an abysmal failure. In fact, we can be pretty sure that the first *several* projects you are associated with will not be raving successes. That is not because I think we are all incompetent, but it is what historically has happened each time we have had to struggle with a new technology as complex and untested as this.

Understanding What It Takes to Master a New Technology

As we rush to jump onto the next new technology bandwagon, we tend to forget that each of these technological revolutions has associated with it a technology assimilation process similar to the consumer marketplace life cycle. We also need to remember that we have to first figure out how the technology itself works and how we will work with it before we can learn how to best make use of it.

Technologies that do not require us to change the way we do things are typically not the revolutionary kind. Look at every technological innovation that has come along—the automobile, the airplane, the telephone, electricity. In each case, the technology itself was around for some time, but it was only after people changed the way they did things that it became popular and accepted.

For example, automobiles were not really revolutionary until people started building roads. The concepts of travel, distance, and road making had to change before the automobile could become a miracle of transportation. The telephone forced people to change the way they thought about conversation and the accessibility of other people, and the airplane caused our whole concept of the size of the world to shrink dramatically.

Before the promised potential can be fully realized, each generation of technological advancement, therefore, requires that we reinvent ourselves, and reorganize the way we approach and look at things on many levels.

Web Warehousing Is No Exception

So, to get the full benefit of what Web warehousing has to offer, we will have to do more than simply learn how the mechanics of the technology work. To make full use of it, we have to rethink our assumptions of what computer technologies can be used for, and we have to figure out how to adjust our attitudes and our organizations.

There is clearly a common learning curve that one must go through each time new capabilities are worked into our day-to-day world.

Why So Many Projects Fail

Failure to address all aspects of the technological assimilation process is part of the reason so many projects fail. As a matter of fact, when we look at the history of technological innovations, both in the consumer world at large (electricity, telecommunications, etc.) and of the computer-specific "revolutions" (mainframe, client/server, data warehousing, etc.) we can identify a common pattern that reveals how the winners in the new technology deployment game were able to score, and how the losers managed to miss the boat.

In general, we find that the people who got the most benefit out of the technologies and were the most successful were those who managed to understand and address all of the different aspects of this complicated technological assimilation process.

The New Technology Assimilation Process

In general, when you look at any kind of technological innovation, its integration into our day-to-day lives follows the same basic pattern. Study of the assimilation of other new technologies shows a very consistent pattern that we can use to determine what will make a new technology work as well.

This process describes the way a technological innovation moves from the drawing board to the office or home, and it describes the changes that people, society, and business have to go through to integrate the new capability that the technology offers into their lives.

This process involves the following steps:

1. *Invention.* The actual creation of the new technology.
2. *Development of operating principles.* The period of time when developers create a new set of principles and create a new "physics," which explains to people how the new technology works and how it can be managed effectively and safely.

3. *Modeling and visioning.* Creation of clear ideas about when, where, and how the new technology will be made useful.
4. *Promotion.* Development of new understandings and expectations on the part of the users and consumers of the new technology.
5. *Acceptance.* The point at which the new technology becomes an accepted part of the consumer's view of the world.
6. *Dependence.* The point where the technology is no longer viewed as an option, but as a necessity.

In the following sections we look at each of these steps in detail and see how the historical development of previous generations of new technologies (electricity, radio, automobiles, etc.) can be shown to reflect these different phases in their development.

Invention

First, of course, something has to be invented that didn't exist before. This invention can be unexpected, as in the case of electricity, or it can be a creative new combination of things that have existed for some time, like the World Wide Web. With new technology it is important to realize that the inventor often has little or no clear idea of exactly what the invention will do for people—ironic, but often true. The originators, first and foremost, invented a new set of principles and a new capability, which simply showed a lot of potential.

Lee De Forest and the Audion One of the best proofs of my contention that the inventors often have no idea what they have created is the case of Lee De Forest and the audion or triode.

The audion, invented by De Forest in 1907, is the component that made modern broadcast radio possible. Before the audion tube, radios had only crystal-based receivers that were so weak that only faint sounds could be produced from broadcasting stations. The audion tube made it possible for radio broadcasters to greatly amplify the radio and sound waves so that voice and music could be broadcast over a much larger area, with more clarity and volume than ever before possible.

What is ironic about De Forest and the audion tube is that, many years later, when testifying in a patent suit to defend his invention, De Forest was unable to explain specifically how his audion tube worked. The person who actually figured out how it worked and built on those principles was Edwin Armstrong, an engineer at Columbia University, who figured out how to modify the base audion tube so that it could be used to selectively amplify radio signals. Armstrong's device, invented in 1918, called the superheterodyne, was the little gizmo that actually made commercial consumer radio broadcasting possible. So, while De Forest really invented the tube, it was Armstrong who figured out how it worked and how it could be manipulated.

The Invention of Electricity The development of electricity as a useful consumer product has a similar set of progressive steps. Electricity itself was first discovered by the ancient Greeks. They found that, if they rubbed a piece of amber against some cloth, things would stick to it (the first case of creation and use of static electricity). Over the centuries people continued to experiment with electricity, but things really started to happen when Michael Faraday, an uneducated chemical lab assistant, began playing with magnets and motors. Faraday invented the first electric motor and he developed the first electric generators using magnets and wire.

As in the case of De Forest and the radio, Faraday may have invented two of the most critical building blocks for the viable use of electricity (the ability to generate the electricity and to use it to power a motor), but he did nothing to move it any further along the developmental trail.

The Invention of the Web and Web Warehousing In the case of the World Wide Web, we also know who the original inventor is. Tim Berners-Lee, a graduate of Oxford University, England, is credited with developing the concept in 1989 while working at CERN, the European Particle Physics Laboratory.

Since its invention, the Web has gotten much bigger and a lot faster than even Berners-Lee could have imagined. In this case, at least, Berners-Lee has been involved in more than just the invention of the Web. He has been and continues to participate in the next phase, the development of operating principles.[1]

Development of Operating Principles

Given that the originators may or may not be the ones to make the inventions truly usable, we arrive at the next step in the process of assimilat-

---

[1] In the case of Web warehousing, there is yet to be a truly credited inventor (possibly the author of this book?).

ing a new technology into the real world. This next step is to put together a solid set of operating principles so that people can understand what this new technology is and how they can work with it. There are actually two sets of principles that we need to be able to work with: mechanical principles, which define the detailed workings of the technology itself, and architectural principles, which describe the way the detailed workings can be organized into larger, more complex configurations.

Mechanical Principles   It is actually easy to see the way the mechanical principles were first developed for electricity and radio. In radio, a long line of inventors and engineers, including Marconi and his wireless telegraph in 1895 and Edwin Armstrong and his FM radio in 1925, developed a body of knowledge about how radio worked and published the information in papers and journals. In the same way, a long line of contributors from Faraday up to Alexander Graham Bell and Thomas Edison all worked toward a basic mechanical science of electricity for people to use.

Two key observations about the development of these mechanical principles can help us understand what we are dealing with in today's world of technological innovation:

The mechanical principles are developed over a long period of time and by a wide assortment of contributors. No one person or institution has ever been able to completely define any set of new technological principles like the ones we are talking about here.

These new mechanical principles need to have new concepts and new vocabularies so that the characteristics of the technology can be described to people.

While the full collection of Web warehousing's mechanical principles may not yet be assembled, it is certainly true that quite a bit of it is already in place. The combination of the mechanical principles underlying data warehousing with those developed in the Web environment, including the latest developments in the areas of Java, Java Beans, and possibly XML, has contributed to a full set of robust mechanical principles to work from.

In fact, you can read through Chapters 16 through 20 of this book for a well-organized introduction to precisely what the mechanical principles are.

Architectural Principles   The area of architectural principles is another one where the development of core principles is important. While mechanical principles describe how the new technology works at a detail level, development of architectural principles describes it at the higher macro level.

The Development of Architectural Principles in the Electrical Field The fact that Edison worked with electricity in his laboratory provided him with very little information of value when it came time to make the electric light a common household appliance. It seems that the generation and management of electricity to light a few bulbs in his laboratory was a very different exercise from trying to create and distribute enough power to light up the entire city of New York.

The basic mechanical principles that Edison worked with in his lab helped him to get electricity into the commercial world, but an additional set of principles would be required before his inventions could be truly viable. Circuit breakers, switches, transformers, rheostats, and all those other things necessary to produce and distribute large amounts of electricity over a wide geographical area had to be developed on the fly. We tend to overlook the fact that, when Edison installed his first commercial electrical plant, he and his workers had no idea what might happen and what kinds of challenges might arise.

We take for granted the volumes of books and classes available today for anyone wishing to work with electricity. We tend to forget the fact that many people died while learning to work with the first few generations of electrical energy.

Ultimately, though, the result was a clear set of guidelines that tells people how to deploy the technology at an incredibly high level.

Architectural Principles and Web Warehousing While we certainly have a large body of knowledge concerning the mechanical realities of Web warehousing, we are still very unfamiliar with the architectural principles that will govern its deployment on a large commercial scale. Web warehousing is still, for the most part, a young, untested technology and it will take a lot of work over the next few years before a good, solid architectural framework has been developed.

In this book, I have devoted all of Chapter 21 and sections of each of the chapters about specific technology deployment areas (Chapters 7 to 15) to the consideration of Web warehousing architecture issues.

Modeling and Visioning

After our technological innovation has been created and the underlying principles developed, there is usually a long period of time when people look at it, scratch their heads, and try to figure out what to do with it. Throughout history, this process of making that invention practical has involved the work of many people in a lot of situations. Sometimes it is the inventor who makes the innovation practical. Other times, someone else, days, months, or years later, figures out how it can be practically applied.

The process of making a new invention practical involves the development of a series of related *visions, perspectives,* or *models* which explain how you can take the basic functionality that the invention delivers and harness it effectively for practical applications. Unfortunately, people usually fail to realize just how important the development of these practically based models is to the overall success and eventual deployment of technologies.

In retrospect, our observations about some of the things that people tried to do with new technologies in the past can seem comical. In reality, we continue to experiment and recreate similarly comedic situations on almost a daily basis.

There are actually many different aspects of the modeling process that need to be in place before we can see clearly how a new technology will fit into our work-a-day world. Some of the models that need to be developed are:

- *Functional model.* Describes the work that the new technology will do for us.
- *Operational model.* Tells us how the new technology will fit into the way we do things and how we will use it.
- *Organizational model.* Describes the roles and responsibilities people will play in the world that this new technology creates.
- *Financial model.* Describes the monetary value that the technology will deliver.

In the following sections, we will consider each of these in more detail, and discuss some of the ways these visions have manifested themselves in the past, and how we need to address the same issues in the development of our new Web warehousing environment.

Functional Model The functional model of a new technology provides us with a description of what the innovation will do for us. The development of a functional vision, which describes what the practical application of the new technology will be and what it will do, is key to the measurement of its ultimate level of assimilation into our day-to-day lives.

For example, the invention and mastery of electricity itself was meaningless. It was the development of the functional vision of the light bulb (to provide light for homes without fire) or the electric motor (to turn the wheels that make a washing machine work) which turned the basic invention into something that people could understand, relate to, and work with.

Functional Vision in the World of Radio   Marconi, De Forest, and Armstrong are credited with the development of the mechanical technology that would one day become the world of radio as we know it. However, it was a different person, a gentleman by the name of David Sarnoff, who was responsible for turning the technology of radio into the *business* of radio.

Sarnoff, originally an employee of the Marconi Wireless Company, saw the potential that radio represented, and went off to become the president of RCA, the Radio Corporation of America. Sarnoff first submitted the idea for a "radio box," an appliance which could be placed into everyone's home, and could receive broadcasts of music, sporting events, and news from around the world. He came up with this idea in 1916 and by 1926 he helped to form NBC, the National Broadcasting Company, which set up the first coast-to-coast network of radio stations.

While De Forest and Armstrong could make the technology of radio work, they never envisioned a world where every home would have one, and every person could listen to entertainment broadcasts from hundreds or thousands of miles away. Before Sarnoff, everyone's functional vision for the radio was some advanced form of telephone. In fact, the original inventions were referred to as *radio-telephones*. With Sarnoff's vision of the radio as a broadcast medium, instead of a point-to-point communications medium, came the real radio revolution that we experience even today.

Functional Vision in the World of Electricity   The original developers of the commercial applications of electricity had to undergo a paradigm shift very similar to that undergone by the developers of radio before the full potential of electricity in the home could be realized as well. While the use of the electric light bulb and its functional vision were pretty straightforward, there was actually a serious lag time before the electric motor found its way into the home.

It seems that a majority of the engineering minds of the day could not conceptualize of any way that an electric motor could be functional in a typical home environment. These engineers, whose only experience with motors was with the large steam engines and waterwheel generators of the day, envisioned large electric motors in people's basements. These motors could be hooked up to a series of pulleys and wheels which would then make the rotating energy of the motor available to washing machines, water pumps, and other mechanical devices. This functional model was, of course, very clumsy and cumbersome and not at all practical. It was only when some bright young inventors figured out that you could build very small, portable motors, place them into each individual appliance and simply run wires full of electricity to each of the devices that the full exploitation of electricity in the home became possible.

The Functional Model for a Web Warehouse The development of a functional model that explains to people exactly what a Web warehouse is and how it can be used can actually be an extremely challenging exercise. Unfortunately, as new technologies become more sophisticated, the paradigm shifts that must occur in order to make them useful become equally more sophisticated.

The development of good functional models for the different capabilities that a new technology can deliver is one of the many things that the knowledge management principles can provide us with.

Operational Model Associated with the functional model that describes what the new technology will do is an operational model that tells us how it will be integrated and made usable in people's lives.

Operational models for new technologies usually start out as variations on some other aspect of peoples lives with which they are familiar. For example, when the developers of the light bulb first reflected on electric light in homes and streets, they immediately envisioned a device that looked and acted very much like the gaslights and oil lamps they would replace. So, the original operational paradigm for electric lights was devices that looked very much like chandeliers and gas lamps. They were found in the home in the same places, and were used for the same basic reasons.

Over time, of course, the operational model for electric lights changed as people became more comfortable with the technology and as the devices got smaller and more portable. Today, you can find lights inside vacuum cleaners, hanging from chains, mounted under windowsills, and in all kinds of places that never would have occurred to the original developers.

Similarly, the original developers of commercial air transportation based their idea for the airport on the paradigm of the train station. The developers' conception, their operational model for how airplanes could be used commercially, centered on the concept of the "airplane station," a building that looked just like a train station, where people would buy tickets and board a regularly scheduled plane to their destination.

The operational vision is what provides people with an understanding of how the invention's functions will be integrated into their daily routines.

We have found, again and again, that our operational model for the use of a new technology, especially in the business world, is an extremely important aspect of how well it is utilized. Unfortunately, as new technologies are deployed in the workplace, they are often so complex and intimidating that people are not exactly sure how they are supposed to be used. When you combine the complexity of the technologies themselves with the complexities of the working environments they are placed into, it should come as no surprise that developing a clear operational blueprint for how the technology will fit into a person's work world will be difficult.

Our historical analysis has shown repeatedly that people fail to truly capitalize on a new technology until they abandon their preconceived notions about how things should be done, and develop new, nonconventional perspectives that make better use of the new technologies at hand.

This can have disastrous consequences if the new technology does not fit into the old model very well. Consider, for example, the use of OLAP technology in the data warehousing world. Only a few years ago, business users were introduced to OLAP on a broad scale. Users fell in love with it, and technicians tried desperately to make use of the technology in all sorts of situations.

Unfortunately, what people failed to realize was that the operational model for OLAP technology was not the same model that the previous generation of reporting tools and query tools supported. As a consequence, you saw hundreds of OLAP applications developed with the wrong operational assumptions; the end result being that you had a lot of OLAP systems that failed miserably.

We can expect to face similar kinds of challenges as we forge into the world of text-based information. While text information can now be delivered to the desktop, there are things about text that are very different from data, and without doubt, we will see our fair share of failed text warehousing projects that try to implement applications using text-based technology and data-based operational models.

Organizational Model Not only do we need to develop functional and operational models to help us understand how the new technology will be made useful, but we also need to have an organizational model. The organizational model describes for us the different jobs that people will do and roles that they will play in relation to the technology, and provides people with a context for understanding how it will be used.

For example, trains require engineers and conductors. Airplanes, on the other hand, need pilots, navigators, and cabin attendants. (What would you do with a navigator on a train?) Similarly, the development of electricity required all sorts of new roles for people and new places for them to work: electricians, electrical engineers, electrical trade schools, electrical research laboratories, professors who specialize in the study of electricity, government agencies that create laws about the use of electricity, building inspectors who enforce electrical codes, and so forth. The invention of electricity itself was only the tip of an iceberg of millions and millions of ripple-down jobs, roles, and responsibilities.

New technologies create new roles, but they also require that we define how those jobs will be carried out, the qualifications of the different participants, and their subsequent responsibilities. This is why the study of people and their relationships through the vehicles of knowledge networks, knowledge neighborhoods, and knowledge economics is so critical to the development of this part of the system.

Financial Models Not only does the presence of a new technology wreak havoc with our understanding of how to do things and who to use to get them done, it also creates a need to rethink the entire economics of running a business or accomplishing something.

For example, did the invention of electricity change economic considerations? Most certainly! What business would try to function without electricity? What business would build a factory without an assurance that there is enough low-cost electricity available to support it? How could any business's financial plan be put together without the inclusion of the costs, benefits, and risks associated with the use of electricity?

Of course, when electricity was first presented to the business world, no one was really sure how to manage the finances associated with its use. Is it an expense? Is the investment in electrical equipment deductible? Will the investment in electrical equipment pay off?

For every new technology that comes along, there is a concomitant set of financial models that needs to be developed in order to make it fit into the business world.

Financial Modeling Challenges in the Web Warehousing World The job of figuring out the functional, operational, and organizational aspects of a new system is a big challenge in and of itself. Those challenges can be minimal, however, compared to the problems of trying to figure out just how much the new technology will contribute to the financial well-being of the company.

While it is relatively easy to associate a cost/benefit ratio when it comes to on-line transaction processing systems and e-commerce applications, it is often difficult or impossible to come up with similar estimates for new technologies. Web warehousing applications help to make business people smarter and to make better decisions, but do not directly contribute to the financial workings of the business. For this reason, special efforts must be made to help develop financial models that make it possible for the businessperson to develop these kinds of estimates.

Knowledge Management Principles and the Development of Models in the Web Warehousing World

We face some substantial challenges in the Web warehousing world when we set out to look for the functional, operational, organizational, and financial models for exactly when, where, and how this capability will be useful. Unfortunately, people have become so involved in the process of trying to integrate new technologies quickly that they often rush to bring the technology in before they have figured out exactly what it will do for them.

The best example of this is the area of text- and multimedia-based Web warehousing applications. While it is certainly possible for us to build such systems (there are plenty of examples of applications like this in this book), it is not clear how useful these systems will be.

Developing clear functional, operational, organizational, and financial visions for new technologies is the key to their eventual success. (Just think about where radio or electricity would be if these models had not been developed!)

Because developing these models is often difficult, and always important, we have dedicated several sections of this book to addressing the issues. In Chapter 4, we discuss the process of figuring out exactly what the value of the new technology will be to the business, and how the different models for its use can be developed. In Chapter 5, we take a closer look at the ways people organize themselves around new technologies. In Chapters 7 to 15, we look at each of the different types of Web warehousing applications, and examine the value propositions and modeling assumptions involved in the deployment of each.

Promotion

After the basic technology has been defined and the details of how it will be applied via its functional, operational, organizational, and financial models have been developed, we face the next challenge. Someone has to seriously promote it and encourage people to try it. People generally don't like to do something that is new to them, and they don't want to be involved in the utilization of something that will make them look bad. Therefore, the developers need to figure out how to make the new technology look socially, morally, and personally appealing to people. This is where the process of *promotion* comes in.

While we are all well aware of exactly how pervasive promotional activities are in today's hustle-bustle world of new computer technologies, we tend to overlook the fact that every new technology developed since the beginning of time has had to undergo some form of promotion to get people to accept it.

One of my favorite stories is the one about the grand parades that Thomas Edison put on through the streets of New York and at fairs and conventions. You see, although Edison had proved that the electric light was viable, he still needed to prove to people that it was *safe, easy to use,* and *modern,* and that their image would suffer if they were not associated with it. To do this, Edison would hire hundreds of people to wear costumes made up of electric light bulbs. These people would have light bulbs on their heads and shoulders, along their arms, and up and down their legs. Wires connected them all to each other and to wagons that held the batteries or generators. Then the whole cavalcade would march through the streets late at night accompanied by marching bands and hawkers. Ultimately, Edison was able to convince enough people that using electricity would be safe and socially acceptable, and the electricity revolution finally began in earnest.

Web Warehousing and Promotional Considerations We are all familiar with the high-powered promotion that the manufacturers of computer products sponsor; the introduction of Microsoft Windows 95, for example, was said to be the single largest new-product launching in history. Clearly, the promotion of new computer technologies is just as important today as it was to the inventors and promoters of products like electricity and the automobile.

Surprisingly enough, the message you need to give people to promote new technologies today is not that different from what it used to be. Basically, people want to know that using the new technology will be *safe, easy, inexpensive,* and *beneficial,* and will enhance their *image.*

Equally surprising is how many developers of new technology solutions have not recognized this fact. People need to be convinced that positive things can be had if the new technology is used. Nobody wants to undergo the degree of change that new technologies bring with them, and only incentives and convincing will get people to make those changes.

In an interesting twist of fate, the role of the promoter of new technologies has been undergoing a shift over the past few years. In the past, the developers of software and hardware products were the principal promoters of new technologies in the business world. Today, however, because there are so many hardware and software vendors, promoting so many easy solutions, the systems developers have had to step in and play that role just to maintain their relative positions of credibility and authority with the business users.

Evangelizing The first and most obvious form that promotion takes is evangelizing. Evangelizers are individuals and companies that go out of their way to bring the word about how this great new technology will solve your problems and make things better in many different ways. Evangelizing involves the normal forms of communication such as advertising, as well as the funding of extraordinary means such as live demonstrations, free samples, and myriad other attention-getting schemes.

The key to the evangelizing process is the way in which the person bringing the message is able to convince people to take the risk and invest the time, energy, and effort to make the changes that accepting the new technology implies.

Enculturation The second form of promotion necessary to make assimilation of the technology complete is to change the culture so that the use of the technology, in the ways prescribed, enhances the self-image and perceived status of the person using it.

For years, a large percentage of business people refused to use computers for two reasons:

Computers were what clerical people used to do trivial tasks.

Computers and keyboards were only for secretaries.

Only within the last few years, since the explosion in the popularity of personal computers and the Internet, have business people come to change their perceptions of whom a computer user is.

Knowledge Networks, Knowledge Neighborhoods, and the Assimilation Process

To understand how the process of promotion of business products takes place within a corporate environment, however, we need to go a little deeper in our investigation than simply looking at the advertising and promotion of software products that the makers of those products go through. Today's software solutions (like Web warehousing solutions) are not simple products that one buys off the shelf. The Web warehousing solution of today's corporate world is a sophisticated combination of hardware, software, and a whole lot of customization and consulting work, which makes it the unique and powerful application that it is. So, the promotion of these solutions and the development of their cultural profile and eventual acceptance by users requires the developer to understand a lot more about those users, their jobs, the ways they interact, and the cultural rules they work under.

It is within the context of these issues that we take a closer look at the knowledge management principles associated with knowledge networks, knowledge neighborhoods, and the entire promotion and business solution development process in most business environments. Chapter 5 has been put together for this reason.

Acceptance and Dependence

After all of the development and maturation of the new technology is complete, and after all of the promotional activity is through, we enter the next phase of the assimilation process, full consumer or user acceptance. During the *acceptance* phase, we see a shift in people's perceptions. Use of the new technology is no longer considered to be a novelty or a "leading edge" kind of activity, but just another thing that people do.

One might think that moving into the acceptance phase would be the goal that every inventor and developer of new technology solutions is looking for. After all, with acceptance comes the reduction in the objections that people have to the product, as more and more of them want it.

Unfortunately, there is another side to this phase. As the technology moves from promotion to acceptance, what typically happens is that the demand for the product rises, which encourages standardization as well as competition, and then reduces the price of the product.

This standardization and price reduction, while good for the consumer, is not the best imaginable world for the seller. Suddenly, the profit margin is gone from the product and it is time to get into some other business. In some cases, the product becomes so popular and so standard, that it becomes a commodity that people have become *dependent* on.

Of course, this book is not too concerned with the acceptance and dependence stages of Web warehousing development. They are a long way off, if they ever happen at all. What we are most concerned with now are the second, third, and fourth stages—development of operating principles, establishment of models, promotion of the Web warehousing solutions—and the knowledge management principles associated with them. These stages are detailed in the next several chapters.

The Role of Knowledge Management in the Future

In this book, I will introduce a core set of principles, all associated with the discipline of knowledge management, and all directly related to the challenges and success factors of the implementation of Web warehousing solutions. In the future, however, as these principles become better understood and more thoroughly developed, obviously there will be many other ways that they can be used to help manage and control the software development process even further.

The area of computer systems software design would seem to be one important place for implementation of this knowledge management–based perspective of computer systems. These concepts provide computer software developers—people not usually involved in running the corporate enterprise—with a framework that can help them better understand what is to be accomplished.

Not explored within the context of this book, but certainly worth further investigation, is continued application of these principles to all sorts of other areas, including the following.

Knowledge Management–Based Design

A software developer should come away with a clear perspective of how the software being designed will need to fit into the business world. By understanding the specific value chain that the application is supposed to address, and by developing functional visions, the developer will move a long way toward building a product that does a better job for the customer than any competitor's products.

Knowledge Management–Based Marketing

Even more important than making use of knowledge management in developing the software itself are the implications this perspective can have on the marketing of products. The customers are happier, more likely to buy, and more pleased with the results when the marketers of software products do a good job of defining the value chain positioning, the value propositions, and the functional and fit visioning.

Knowledge Management/Web Warehousing–Based Development

When software developers make use of Web warehousing and knowledge management approaches to automate and drive their own manufacturing processes, they gain another bonus. In my capacity as manager of software development projects, I found that the creation of a Web warehouse, which holds all of the code, documentation, marketing materials, and everything else concerned with the development of the product, provides immeasurable assistance in running the project.

Knowledge Management for Corporate I/T Departments

While the software development company can certainly gain from the application of the knowledge management perspective, the benefits for a large corporate computer system are far greater still. These concepts, if applied with vigor, have the potential of changing everything we understand about how to build systems, how to plan and budget them, how to staff our departments, and so forth.

Knowledge Management–Based Systems Development Life Cycle

If the systems development life cycle were modified so that it is driven from everyone's understanding of the corporation's value chain (rather than organizational structure, technology, outmoded models, etc.), then the most profound changes could be made to corporate computer systems groups.

A knowledge management–based systems development life cycle would propose that every implementation start with identifying the value chain links to be addressed, proceed through functional and fit visioning, continue with developing precise value propositions, and then drive all development efforts off that document.

A value proposition–based methodology would create far less pain and suffering than today's obsolete life cycles, and with far better, more tangible results.

Knowledge Management–Based Budgeting and Planning Processes

It is mind-boggling to think what systems development would be like if the budgeting and planning processes were value proposition–based. With tangible, measurable deliverables associated with every project, and with the built-in accountability of both users and developers, a very different world of computer systems development financing would undoubtedly emerge.

Knowledge Management for Software Procurement

As we note in the previous chapter, making use of the value proposition statement as the principal criterion for the acceptance of a software product can be a powerful and expedient way to make sure that the corporation is getting the best software deal for the dollar.

Requiring software vendors to think through the functional visions can make the process of developing a fit vision as painless as possible and can go a long way in minimizing the energy organizations spend on nonproductive, noncritical, non-revenue-producing tasks.

Major Planning Implications

Application of knowledge management approaches can also assist the corporate computer systems department in the development of longer-range plans as well, specifically in the way the computer systems infrastructure is organized and in the way the organizational structure is arranged.

Knowledge Management and System Architecture and Infrastructure Design

A major concern for the developers of corporate computer system infrastructures is the organization of the information systems themselves. Currently, corporate information systems represent a hodgepodge of conflicting and overriding organization schemes that have come and gone as the corporation and the current state of computer systems theory have varied. As we enter the next generation of systems deployment, however, we will become hard-pressed to continue to manage these systems in such a haphazard manner.

As more and more databases come on line, and as the new generation of text bases and knowledge bases becomes commonplace, we will undoubtedly see an incredible increase in the amount of stored disk space managed by the corporation, not to mention the computer systems that will manipulate it all. What is needed is an organizational framework that allows people to understand where things are, how those things interconnect with everything else, and how to best navigate throughout the system.

Using the Value Chain as the Guide As more and more corporations move forward into Web warehousing and knowledge management, we will see a gradual shift of the underlying structures along value chain lines. Clearly, systems organized according to the structure of the value chains they serve will be much more easily managed.

Value Chain–Dependent Applications The other trend that is already underway in the business and software world is the development of more and more solutions that are specific to the industry value chain link. The development of the "generalized" software product that can be used by one corporation to do one job and another corporation in a completely different way, is quickly being replaced by the special-purpose software package.

As more and more products and solutions become value chain–specific, there will be more and more need for a logical grouping of that knowledge neighborhood's resources in one place.

Using Web Warehousing Technology to Help As was true in the area of the software developer, we are beginning to see organizations who have figured out that they can use Web warehousing technology to help with their own development efforts. The development and management of computer systems is a documentation- and context-intensive process that Web warehouse environments and knowledge management frameworks can help with.

A Web site, dedicated to the storage, retrieval, and updating of project requirements, specifications, progress, and development efforts, as well as to holding the code itself, and allowing people to run all of it interactively, creates a highly productive, collaborative work space for all of the participants in the development process.

Knowledge Management–Based Organizational Structures

In our listing of all of the different ways that knowledge management concepts are apt to permeate the corporate computer systems support departments, last but not least is the very way that these departments are organized.

Designation of people's roles according to technological specialty and/or functional skills will likely be superseded by the placement of individuals on the basis of their understanding of the different value chain links themselves, how they relate to other links, and how the operational and informational knowledge management systems within their space interact and relate to the users.

Knowledge of the value chain will become a criterion as important, or more important, than any of the other skill sets, and the organization of computer systems teams is likely to be framed in terms of that value chain as well.

The Future of Knowledge Management

Although knowledge management is still in its infancy, the potential benefits that computer systems developers and corporations can enjoy from fully embracing it are clear.

Undoubtedly, over the next few years an avalanche of conflicting stories will follow about what it is, how it works, why it is important, and why some products are knowledge management–based and others are not. Eventually, a core set of principals and concepts will emerge that will define what the market thinks it is and what it is good for, accompanied by a quantum leap forward in the functionality and complexity of Web warehousing solutions themselves.

CHAPTER 3

Value Chains and Killer Applications

- *What is the relationship between BPR, ECR, and customer-centric corporate strategies and value chain analysis?*
- *What is a value chain, and what is value chain analysis?*
- *What is a killer application, and what does it have to do with computer systems and knowledge management?*
- *How can we combine value chain analysis with knowledge management to create a new universal systems development methodology?*

As I establish in the previous chapters, my goal in taking a closer look at knowledge management as it relates to Web warehousing is very specific in its application. What is clearly lacking in the computer systems development industry overall, and in the Web warehousing area specifically, is a clear-cut set of guidelines and approaches that can help the developer to:

1. Integrate the business and technological objectives that an organization faces
2. Provide a consistent, focused direction that both business and technology strategists can follow
3. Provide insight into what the best directions of pursuit for a given organization might be
4. Provide a methodology that unites the strategic and tactical planning processes of both the business and technology communities under the same consistent set of operating principles.

It is my belief that the following set of assumptions, principles, and approaches can provide that coordination and synergy between these two dynamic environments, and that the basic tenets of knowledge management will provide us with the key to making it happen.

Corporate Strategic Perspectives

If the objective of this study is to create an approach to systems development that successfully unifies the development of strategic initiatives on both the business and technology front, then it is important to understand the basic directions that each of these disciplines has followed up until now.

While the strategic initiatives of both business and computer systems are related (that is, most business strategies include technology in their solution and most technology strategies refer to the need to include business perspectives in their analysis), they are still fundamentally different in their approaches and give only secondary attention to the other side of the equation. What we really need is a strategic perspective that integrates business and computer systems equally, dynamically, and completely.

We have already discussed many of the insights and directions that the technology world is pursuing as we enter this new and exciting age of Web-based knowledge management systems development. What we have not even begun to consider, however, is the nature of the equally fascinating and important efforts that are under way in the area of management theory. On the business front, we need to pay attention to some very different kinds of initiatives.

Business Process Reengineering

One of the major disciplines to come upon the corporate scene over the past decade has been the business process reengineering (BPR) movement.

The BPR Approach The basic premise behind this approach is that business processes, over time, get moved further and further away from the most efficient possible arrangement of people, processes, and deliverables. While business processes might be well set up to begin with, they quickly get out of sync with reality as market conditions, technology, financing, and the world in general changes around them.

Stagnant, out of date, inefficient processes can quickly become the bane of the large corporation, and business process reengineering provides the executive with a fresh, objective look at what the processes are today and how they can be fixed to make for a better, more efficiently run business.

BPR Strengths Business process reengineering has had many advocates over the past few years, and many corporations have spent millions of dollars in reengineering their organizations. Clearly, there are many inefficient and sometimes even ridiculous processes in a business, and BPR has been instrumental in helping to eliminate many of them.

BPR Weaknesses Unfortunately, the application of BPR has turned out to be not quite the panacea people had hoped it would be. The weaknesses that it propagates often fall under several different categories, most of them having to do with the consequences of budget cuts and staff layoffs based on short-term, limited-scope analysis of what are actually extremely large and complex organizational networks of people, processes, and computers.

Some of the negative side effects of BPR have included:

1. *Weakening of customer service and customer focus.* Often, the apparently "redundant" or "trivial" processes and roles within an organization turn out to be the very roles that maintained a high-quality, meaningful relationship between the customer and the organization. The net result of the "efficiency," therefore, might

yield limited revenue increases in the short run, because of reduced salary and overhead, but disastrous shortfalls in the long run as a result of lost market share.

2. *Erosion of the quality of work life.* The working environments of those few people lucky enough to survive a BPR exercise are often reduced to a shadow of what they used to be. Highly splintered, defocused, and widely spread responsibilities tend to leave people with little room for creativity, a sense of accomplishment, or any sense of loyalty to the organization.

3. *Destruction of corporate culture.* Even more disturbing and less obvious is the way in which corporate cultures are undermined by these kinds of efforts. Many corporations have been forced to abandon long-standing, people-supporting sets of assumptions about what the jobs of employees are and how people are supposed to work together.

4. *Destruction of corporate memory.* Even more devastating in the long run is the net effect that this kind of efficiency has on the corporation's future. As fewer and fewer people spread themselves thinner and thinner, with less and less structure to help hold them together, the more common it is for valuable experience and expertise to disappear as time goes on. With the experience and expertise gone, the corporation is left in the unenviable position of having to constantly reinvent the same things at an incredible cost.

Efficient Customer Response

The next big movement in management circles is an initiative known as efficient customer response (ECR). ECR has gone under several different names over the past several decades, but has made a big resurgence in recent years.

The ECR Approach *Efficient customer response* is the business strategic approach that attempts to help companies reduce cost and speeds the time it takes to get products into the customers' hands by examining, tuning, modifying, and perfecting the supply lines that feed into the manufacturing or delivery process.

A manufacturer, for example, might find that it takes 4 weeks from when an order is received until it can deliver the product to the customer's door. Its goal will be to reduce that time to, say, 2 weeks, cutting the "to market" time in half.

Speeding up the manufacturing cycle in this way can create many financial benefits for the company:

- It can be more responsive to customer demand, thereby winning more business.
- It can reduce the costs of inventory, shipping, and materials management by eliminating those functions from the manufacturing process and getting suppliers to carry more of the load.
- It can trim product shipping and delivery costs by eliminating the need to inventory and warehouse the product, shipping it directly to the customer from the manufacturing line.

ECR Strengths ECR systems have certainly helped companies to reduce costs and increase productivity in many different areas. New computer systems and vendors that are more responsive (being also powered by new, more responsive computer systems) are making many corporations run at levels of efficiency never before imagined.

ECR Weaknesses The bad news, as far as ECR is concerned, is that, as more and more corporations get efficient, fewer jobs and even fewer companies (and sometimes industries) are required. ECR has had a devastating effect on industries like trucking, international trade and transportation, warehousing, wholesaling, and a myriad of other intermedidary functions that are being squeezed out of business by this efficiency-creating process.

Customer-Centric Corporations

The other big initiative at work in the corporate world today is the "customer-centric" and the customer relationship management (CRM) approach to systems development.

The Customer-Centric Approach It should actually come as no surprise that, as corporations continue to get more efficient, with fewer and fewer people around to worry about customers, a countermovement has arisen. The customer-centric approach to corporate strategy says that corporations need to be much more focused on customer service and customer satisfaction if they are to be competitive in the future.

As "overhead" customer service departments and sales staffs are replaced by Web-based and telephone ordering systems, corporations are beginning to see that if they are to maintain their market share, they will have to figure out how to identify, attract, and retain their most valuable customers.

This approach, best symbolized by the customer marketing database and the customer-based data warehouse, attempts to get the entire corporation, at all levels, to focus specifically on the customer's needs and wants. The epitome of this approach is summarized in the works on integrated marketing by Donald Schultz of the Northwestern University Marketing Department. His approach advocates the reengineering of the organization with marketing at its core.

Advantages of the Customer-Centric Approach The good news is that the customer-centric approach is helping organizations to become reacquainted and more intimate with their customers. These systems allow savvy business people to identify who their customers are and what they want more quickly than their non-customer-centric counterparts, with corresponding differences in profits.

Weaknesses of the Customer-Centric Approach Even the customer-centric approach falls short of providing the organization with the answers to many of the questions they have about what to do, what the best strategy is, and what information systems to build next.

The Convergence of Corporate Strategic Initiatives

In general, each of the initiatives we have just discussed have much value and contribute to the corporate planner's frame of reference for how to proceed, but none of them, in and of themselves, really provide the businessperson with a universal and unprejudiced view of the problem. What is really needed is a higher-level, nonproprietary view that provides direction for all businesses in all situations, not just in the limited kinds of cases that have been described here.

We will see in this next section that each of these initiatives is really nothing more than a different expression, a different way of attacking common underlying parameters. I will show that the business itself can be defined as a set of processes known as the *value chain,* and that performing BPR, ECR, or customer-centric management is just another way of looking at the value chains for different industries and making them more efficient.

Understanding Business in Its Most Basic Form

It is actually amazing that underneath these apparently diverse strategic initiatives is a common, knowledge management–based thread. That underlying thread is what is referred to as the *value chain*. It is examined by value chain analysis.

What Is a Business?

The key, of course, to understanding knowledge management and the value chain view of business is to start with the basic definition of what a business is. In the simplest terms, the corporate world is made up of only two participants: businesses and customers. A customer is anybody who buys what the business has to offer and businesses are groups of people who make or provide what people want or need.

So, if a business is a collection of people who work to meet the needs of customers, then what is competition all about? Competition occurs when more than one company tries to become the customer's preferred agent for getting its wants and needs. The key to the survival of the business, therefore, lies in its ability to:

- Identify the needs of a group of people
- Figure out how to meet those needs
- Meet those needs better than anyone else.

Our basic model of the business world, therefore, would look like the diagram in Figure 3-1.

Figure 3-1
The business universe simplified.

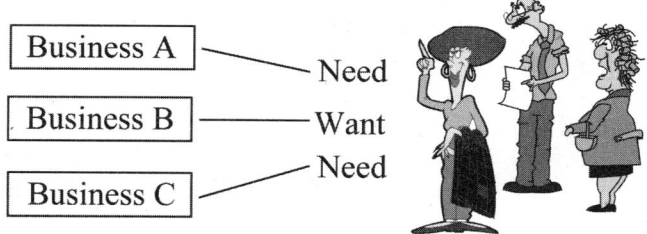

Part 1: Applied Knowledge Management

How Do Businesses Meet Consumer Needs?

The process of running a business is actually a lot more difficult than this initial depiction of a universe appears. There are several problems that big companies face:

People's needs and wants are complex. Meeting the needs of people, especially in today's complex world, is not always an easy thing to do. People's desires and definitions of what they want and need are constantly changing over time, as they gain more money, prestige, or experience. All styles, fashions, and tastes change over time.

People's needs and wants are not easy to determine. Not only are these needs hard to define, but it is extremely difficult to figure out who will want what, and when. In fact, people may say they want one thing, and then buy something else, often for unknown reasons, even to themselves.

It takes a lot of work to build, find, or arrange for the things that people want or need.

So, in today's world of business, people have organized themselves into logical groups that work together to meet a particular set of needs. Basically, a company is a group of people who have gotten together and agreed to share the responsibility of meeting those needs. See Figure 3-2.

Ultimately, as companies become bigger and people become more specialized, we end up with insurance companies, banks, stores, manufacturers, brokers, television stations, restaurants, and farms, all of them

Figure 3-2
Specialization of roles and the value chain.

existing to do only one thing, meet the needs of some group of consumers somewhere in the open marketplace.

How Are Businesses Organized?

Of course, as soon as two or more people try to work together to accomplish something, they end up needing to get themselves organized so as to make their efforts more efficient. And so businesses develop organizational structures. These structures let people know who reports to whom, and defines for all exactly what role they will be playing in meeting these needs.

And so the different business specializations are created. Marketing people concentrate on figuring out what people want and how to best convince them that their company has it. Manufacturing people figure out how to most efficiently make what people are interested in. Finance people figure out how to make the best use of the money the company has. Computer people figure out how to get computers to make the business run more efficiently. The list goes on and on. The business is formed; the people within it get organized around the execution of different tasks.

The Competitive Perspective If this were a perfect society, and if businesses were organized perfectly, then there would be no need for more than any one company to do any one job. As we know, this is not what really happens. In reality, many different groups of people get together and compete for the customer's interest and money.

In fact, the particular organization of people, functions, money, computer systems, and facilities that is the most efficient in the marketplace will usually end up becoming the biggest supplier of those particular goods and services. Our entire economic system is designed to encourage groups of people to meet consumer needs better and more efficiently. The competitive struggle continues.

The Challenges of Infrastructure and Organizational Structure

So far, hopefully, everything we have been talking about is perfectly logical, if somewhat simplistic. Businesses compete for supremacy through their ability to better organize a group of people around the task of meeting a particular consumer need. As times, needs, and businesses change, there is a constant state of flux as some things become important and others fall by the wayside.

Given this understanding, it is easy to see where many of the problems faced by large organizations come from, and why small upstart specialty firms are a constant threat. In fact, a company that is very large and very successful on one day can become an unprofitable dinosaur the next.

There are a number of things that can hold back organizations and make it difficult for them to adjust. All of them have to do with the same dichotomy. Large organizations gain competitive advantage by building large infrastructures (factories, sales organizations, distribution centers, store locations, etc.), that allow them to capitalize on the economies of scale that high-volume activities make possible. Unfortunately, these same size and scale advantages can become their downfall when business or technology conditions change. Many organizations suddenly find that their investment in infrastructure has been made in the wrong place and that newer, better, less expensive ways have subsequently been invented. In these cases, the business is stuck with an investment in something that it would rather do without, but which it cannot get rid of without an excessive amount of expense.

Included in this category of "mixed blessing" infrastructure investments are:

1. *Physical facilities (factories, offices, stores, etc.).* The business's facilities infrastructure is by far the single most limiting factor when it comes to the ability to change quickly. As a company invests in buildings and real estate, it becomes linked to those investments in many ways. A company that spends millions of dollars on a factory assumes that this factory will support the production of goods for many years.

2. *Computer systems (online transaction processing systems).* A company that invests in a large corporate on-line transaction processing system is betting that the transactions will continue to be managed in the same way for a long time to come. As long as that is true, the investment pays off. When the nature of the business changes, however, the company faces the prospect of having to rewrite or replace the system, an extremely expensive and painful process.

3. *Organizational structures.* The same can be said for the company's investment in an organizational scheme. People need to have a structure that helps them understand what is expected of them. Changing this structure takes a severe toll on morale, productivity, and efficiency.

4. *Processes, policies, and procedures.* The very foundation of any business is its processes, policies, and procedures. It takes a lot of time, trouble, and investment to get these in place, and it can cost even more to change them.

In the short run, the investment in infrastructure (whether in machinery, buildings, people, or processes) will usually prove to be quite successful as the required capacity meets its target.

However, in the long run, as conditions continue to change, that investment can become less and less economically feasible. Suddenly, the great benefit that the infrastructure investment was providing becomes a liability. As new companies enter the market with a newer and more focused understanding of what today's infrastructure should look like, the large corporation moves from an advantageous to a disadvantageous position. Now, suddenly, the firm is saddled with an infrastructure that is out-of-date, inefficient (according to modern standards), and far from optimal.

The Alignment Problem

As the corporation continuously tries to adjust to the demands of the marketplace, competition, technology, and employees, its biggest challenge becomes one of alignment.

The optimum corporate structure is one that can constantly realign the organization of people, infrastructure, processes, and objectives with the realities of today's demands, and then realign them again tomorrow on the basis of a new set of conditions, with a minimum penalty cost associated with the write-off of obsolete skills, plant, equipment, and facilities.

Of course, while this analysis may very well describe the nature of the business world as it should be, it does little to tell us what, if anything, we can do to achieve it. If the nature of business is to constantly change everything, how can we possibly hope to tie things down? How can we inject some sanity into the constant reinventing of the universe?

This is precisely the challenge that advocates of business process reengineering, efficient customer response, and a customer-centric approach face when they try to practice what they preach. What causes each of these initiatives to bog down are the problems of costly infrastructure investment, inflexible organizational structure, and the inability of the business to change quickly.

The builders of large corporate information systems, whether they be OLTP, client/server, Web-based, or any other kind of technology, are confronted with the challenge of computer systems' functional alignment. Systems are designed to meet today's structural needs, but are difficult and expensive to change when those needs change.

Trying to get a large corporation to change direction quickly is like trying to turn an ocean liner at a 90-degree angle. There is just no way to do it. The structure is too big, and the momentum will carry it a long, long time in the present direction no matter how hard you try to turn it.

Introducing the Value Chain

To figure out how to create this flexible, easy-to-change, large corporate organization, we need to understand what the underlying principal building blocks of the business organization are. We need to understand what the foundational, immutable core structures are that do not have to be revised each time conditions change.

Every approach that has been tried up until now has shared a common shortcoming: Each approach has tried to build a model for the business that was dependent on the very things that needed to be constantly changed in order for the business to survive. Is it any wonder that business people and computer systems developers are confused?

Historically, people have tried to manage the change of the business environment by changing the:

1. Organizational structure
2. Computer systems infrastructure
3. Processes (business process reengineering)
4. Focus (customer-centric corporations)
5. Supply chains (efficient customer response)

These efforts are constantly making adjustments to an underlying structure that is already there and is relatively stable, and that structure is known as the *corporate value chain*.

What Is the Corporate Value Chain?

Value chain is the term used to define the logical organization of fundamental, functional building blocks that businesses use to

1. Identify the needs of customers
2. Define solutions to those needs
3. Create those solutions
4. Finally, deliver them to those customers

In other words, a value chain is a description of the chain of events, or the linkage of functions, which describe how a business or an industry meets the needs and wants of consumers effectively.

Every industry has a common value chain and every company has a specific treatment of the value chain that it adheres to as the principle underlying definition of itself as an organization. While the specific nature and organization of a value chain will undoubtedly vary from one company to the next, the basic structure of these chains is surprisingly similar across industries.

The value chain perspective, originally proposed by Harvard professor Michael Porter, defines the value chain as "The set of activities an organization performs to create and distribute its goods and services, including direct activities (such as procurement and production) and indirect activities (such as human resources, finance, and I/T)." Competitive advantage, according to Porter, is achieved when an organization links the activities in its value chain more cheaply or more expertly than do its competitors.

A Retail Industry Value Chain Example

To help illustrate what a value chain is, and how it can be used, let's take a look at a specific industry and see how its value chain is put together. Let's start with the retail industry.

To define a value chain, the first thing we must do is determine exactly what needs or wants the industry is setting out to satisfy. This definition is known as the *industry value proposition*. The industry value proposition defines the need or want that the industry has chosen to target, and the things that it believes are important to the customer about meeting that need or want.

For example, the objective of the retail industry is to satisfy the needs and wants of consumers by providing them with the products they want, in places where they can find them quickly, at the price they are willing to pay. Value propositions that a retail firm can offer to consumers will therefore include availability, convenience, and price. By providing better value propositions for the consumer than the competition, that company obtains a competitive advantage in the marketplace.

Once we understand what the objective for an industry or company is, we can then begin to assemble the logical organization of functional components that make up their approach to delivering those value propositions.

Figure 3-3

The retail value chain.

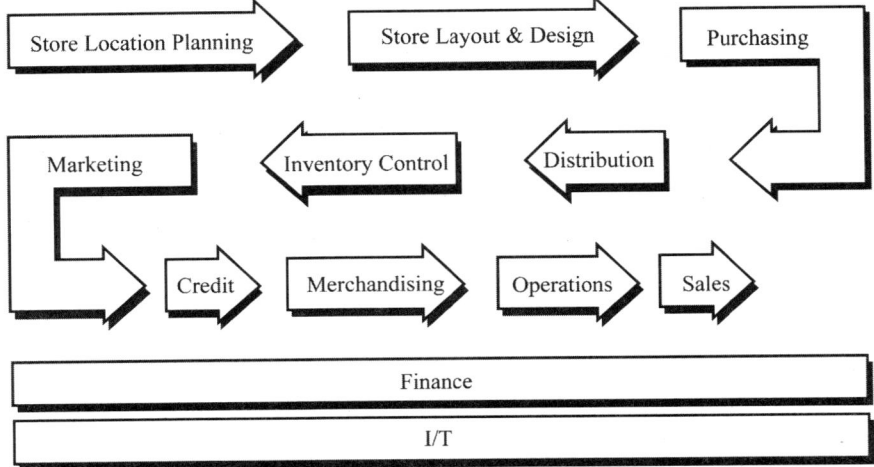

Principal Value Chain Components In the retail industry, the value chain is made up of the following principal components:

Marketing. The process of figuring out which customers to go after, which value propositions are the most important to them, and how to attract and keep them as customers.

Store location planning. The process of determining where stores should be located, how large they should be, and how they should be designed.

Store layout design. The process of determining how the merchandise should be organized and displayed to make it easy for the consumer to find and purchase.

Merchandising. The process of determining what, where, and when merchandise should be carried and how much it should be sold for.

Purchasing. The process of finding the items that customers are interested in and acquiring them at the best price possible.

Distribution and inventory control. The process of acquiring, transporting, and maintaining reserves of those items the customers are most likely to buy, to increase availability and convenience while simultaneously minimizing the distribution and inventory costs.

Operations and sales. The process of staffing, stocking, and running stores, and performing all the other functions necessary to do business.

Look at any retail firm in business today and you will see that each of them performs these functions in one way or another. In fact, not only does every firm take part in these functions, but no firm could exist if it did not have a specific strategic and tactical approach to addressing the specific functions defined in the chain. See Figure 3-3.

Telecommunications Example

While the telecommunications industry is certainly different from the retail industry, there are many common functions when you look at their value chains. As you can see in Figure 3-4, there are several functions that both chains share: marketing, purchasing (or acquisition), operations, and sales; and several that they do not: activation, provisioning, network planning, and network management. It is important to understand, at this level, that all firms have a similar type of value chain to deal with, and that those value chains can be used as guides to the development of Web warehousing and knowledge management applications.

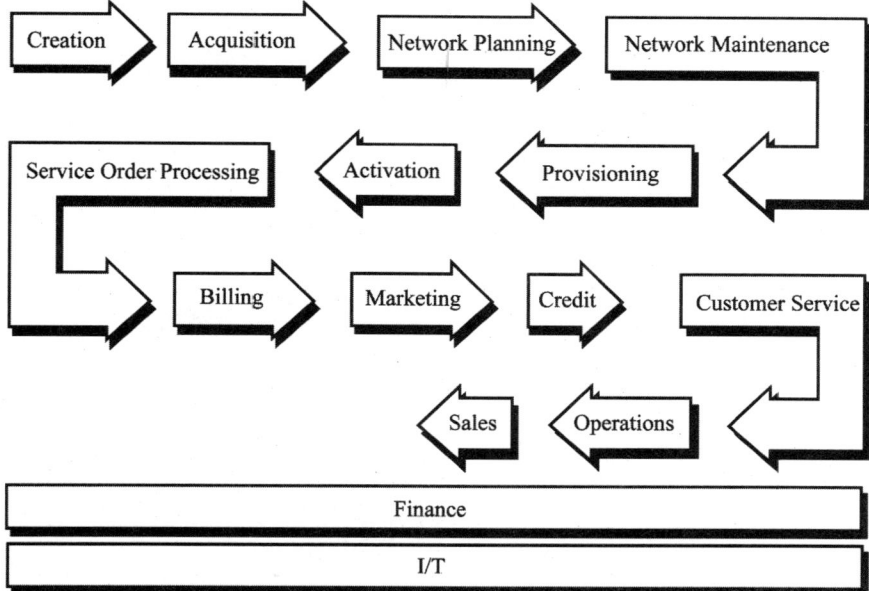

Figure 3-4
The telecommunications value chain.

Value Chains and the Role of OLTP Systems

To help us understand exactly how value chains and legacy/OLTP systems get out of alignment, let's look at a typical situation. In the telecommunications industry, the system that is the heart and soul of any company is the billing system. Because of this, the billing system will tend to keep information, not only about bills, but also about a lot of other things. See Figure 3-5.

When the billing system was first created, it was put together to support one part of the value chain, the billing function. As long as the computer system is focused on the management of one, and only one, aspect of the business, that system will be efficient, easy to understand, and easy to change in response to the demands of the business.

However, because of the way that most telecommunications firms have evolved over time, the billing system ends up supporting all sorts of value chain links that are not part of its primary function. What happens, then, when the functionality of the computer system is expanded to support more than one part of the value chain? What happens when we expand its functionality to include customer service, sales, and a dozen other functions? The system gets incredibly slow, complicated, difficult to manage, and impossible to replace. In other words, what happens is that the billing system becomes inflexible.

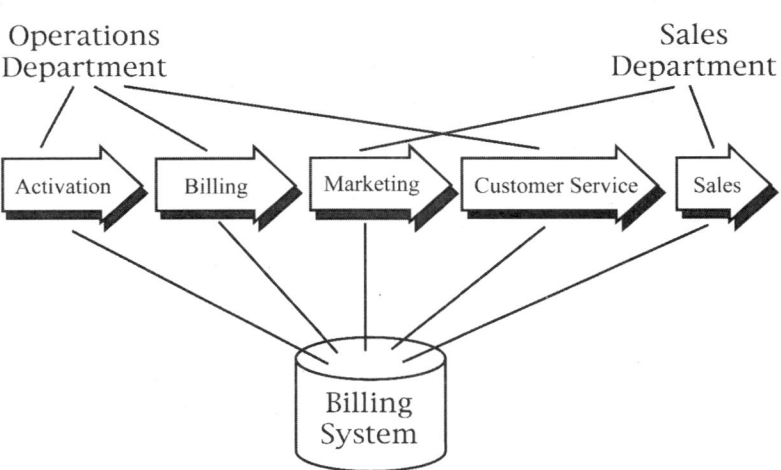

Figure 3-5

The telco value chain and the billing system.

Now, as the business changes, and as the company tries to change its emphasis on certain parts of the value chain, it finds that it cannot adjust. That one billing system that does so many other useful things is now one large albatross, which prevents the company from generating many of the changes that it would like to make.

The short-term solution to this problem is to develop yet another computer system, one that takes the information out of the billing system and makes it available for restructuring. (This is the primary role of the data warehouse and Web warehouse.)

The long-term solution to the problem is for businesses to develop their computer systems on the basis of their value chains. That way, they can make adjustments to their operational flow without having to rewrite their core systems.

Value Chains and the Creation of Web Warehouses

Once we have used value chain analysis to understand where alignment problems exist with legacy systems, we can quickly turn around and use those value chains to help us unravel the problems and create extremely useful value chain linkage-based systems.

In fact, if you look at most of the successful data warehouse and Web warehouse applications today, I would be willing to bet that most of their success can be explained in light of the company's value chain alignment problems and the resolution of those problems through the use of the warehouses. See Figures 3-6 and 3-7.

Value Chain Implementation—Key to Corporate Differentiation

The companies that participate in the same industry share a common set of goals, objectives, and perspectives. For each and every industry there is a basic, fundamental value chain that defines the process it participates in and allows us to see how it relates to the ultimate objective of meeting customer needs. In fact, once you put together a basic plan of the value chain for a particular industry, you begin to see how companies are able to differentiate themselves from each other. In general, a company

Figure 3-6
A value chain/legacy system view of a corporate Web warehouse.

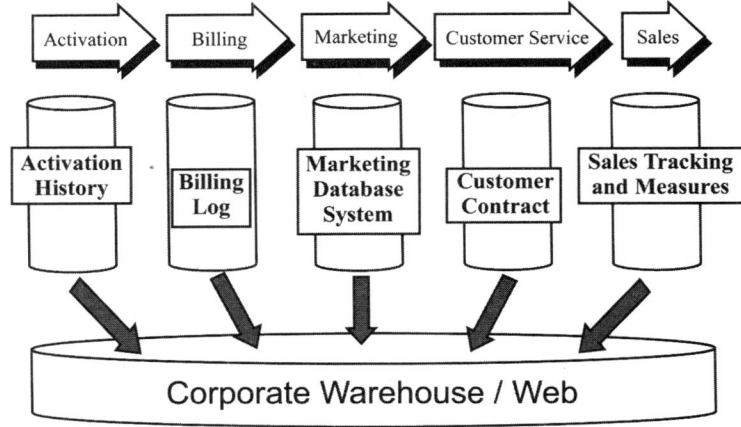

Figure 3-7
A value chain/legacy system view of a knowledge mart.

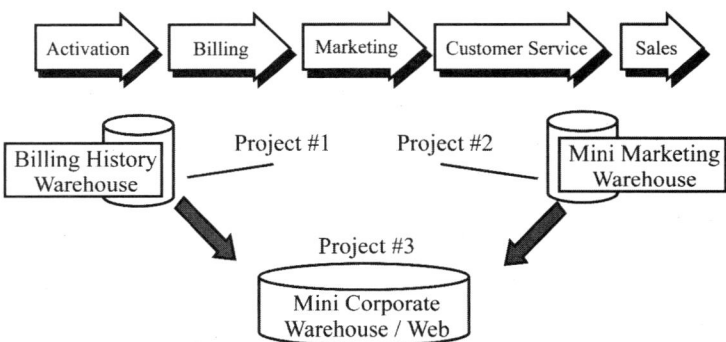

differentiates itself from its competitors in the way it chooses to customize its value chain approach.

Let's look at a couple of examples.

A High-Volume, Low-Cost Retailer

One retailer may decide that the value proposition most important to the customers it has chosen to target is that they be able to buy decent clothes at a low price. These consumers do not care about how conveniently or attractively the clothes are displayed, and are not nearly as interested in the latest fashions as in low cost and easy access.

This retailer, therefore, will construct a value chain that deemphasizes store layout and advertising (which add to the cost of the goods). It is much more likely that this organization will instead build a value chain where purchasing and distribution are emphasized (concentrating on finding the best bargains and getting them delivered to stores quickly). It will probably own its own trucks and schedule infrequent deliveries to many locations.

A Low-Volume, High-Profile Retailer

Another retailer may decide to focus on the high-end consumers who need to be fashion-forward and leading-edge, with little regard for price. A value chain based on these assumptions will dedicate much more effort to running effective marketing and merchandising efforts and will spend a lot of time enhancing store locations and store layout capabilities. In the meantime, the emphasis on low-cost acquisition of product and high-volume delivery of items will be minimized as the company attempts to make each store look unique and stylish.

The Value Chain and Killer Applications

As business people have become more aware of the value chain concept, they have gained several interesting and powerful insights. One of the most powerful "proofs" for the value chain can be seen in the phenomenon known as the *killer application*.

Killer applications are those computer systems applications that uproot people's understanding of what their value chain is. These applications are so radically different that they basically kill the existing status quo between competitors in that industry. They put many of the participants out of business, giving one company (the one that created the application) a devastating competitive advantage, and create a whole new level of participation for those competitors that survive.

Examples of Killer Apps

The computer industry is full of stories about the killer apps that changed various industries:

- The Sabre reservation system revolutionized the airline industry and gave American Airlines a competitive advantage that it enjoys to this day.
- The American Hospital Supply on-line purchasing system, which allows hospitals to order supplies directly from the supplier's inventory, eliminates the need to deal with hundreds of vendors and jobbers.
- The WalMart data warehouse revolutionized the integration of distribution, inventory, and merchandising and helped WalMart to soar to the number one retailer position in its marketplace.

Analysis of Killer Apps

These applications are especially interesting not for their differences, but for what they have in common. Each and every one of them made use of the latest available technology to destroy preconceived notions about what the industry value chain was and how it could be most efficiently executed.

These killer app systems radically changed and shortened the value chain for a given industry through the use of the latest technology. In other words, the companies who sponsored these projects were the first to effectively recognize the technology-based opportunity and capitalize on it.[1]

In general then, what knowledge management and value chain analysis advocate, and what the killer application phenomenon proves, is that the company that understands its value chain and uses technology effectively to manage it will come out on top in the competitive arena.

Value Chains and Knowledge Management

So, what is the relationship between value chains and knowledge management? What does the one have to do with the other? The answer to these questions can be found by looking back at our objectives for exam-

---

[1] For a more detailed examination of this issue, see the explanations offered by Larry Downes, Chunka Mui, and Nicholas Negroponte in their book *Unleashing the Killer App: Digital Strategies for Market Dominance*, Harvard Business School Press.

ining knowledge management in the first place. If the knowledge management perspective is correct, and I believe that it is, then the key to improving a business's performance is in understanding how you can better apply computer systems to improve the collective application of knowledge to the customers' problems. To do that, however, you need to understand what the customers' problems are and how the corporation is organized to address them. This is precisely the information that the value chain provides.

A Knowledge Management–Based View of Computer Systems

In knowledge management terms, we could say that:
"The role of every business computer system is to help organizations create, manage, and control their value chains through the collection, storage, and dissemination of knowledge. Therefore, every computer system can be defined as either working to help maximize the efficiency of one of the links of the value chain, or working to help maximize the cooperative activities of two or more links in the value chain."

This means that the first step in understanding what you are trying to accomplish with a given computer system is to understand it in terms of the value chain links it is associated with.

My conclusion, therefore, and my recommendation, is that any attempt to make decisions about what technologies to use where, can only be made effectively with a clear understanding of the industry and corporate value chains. This value chain–based view of the business will guarantee that everyone involved in the development of new computer solutions will understand exactly how the technology they are deploying fits into the grand scheme of things.

The Value Chain–Based View of New Technology

This first conclusion then points to a second one, that every computer systems effort, every system upgrade, every set of requirements, and every proposal to build a new system should also be based on the same business-oriented value chain.

The consequences of this approach are both profound and difficult to deal with, at least at first glance. I am proposing that we abandon our subject area–based, object-oriented, and, in general, abstract theory-based foundation for systems development approaches, and replace it with a value chain–based approach.

If computer systems design is to continue to contribute to the forward progress of business, then it will have to become significantly more business-focused than it has up until now. The value chain/knowledge management–based view actually provides the universal perspective that can do that.

Value Chain Alignment Issues

Once we are armed with a value chain for a given industry, we are provided with the yardstick, the barometer, if you will, by which we can identify, measure, and assess our strategy. Unfortunately, we discover that the corporation still has problems with alignment as it attempts to change in response to market demands, the demands of competition, and the demands created by the availability of newer and better technology.

Organizational Misalignment

While everyone can pretty much agree to the nature of the value chain for a given industry, it is rare to find a corporate organizational chart (the definition of departments, roles, and functions) that aligns itself exactly with the value chain approach that the corporation is pursuing. The corporate organizational chart and corporate value chain were probably in alignment at one point in the business's history. However, as companies get bigger, more political, more unclear in their mission, and more mature in their history and culture, the organizational structure and the value chain get more and more out of alignment.

Computer Systems Misalignment

Not only do the corporation's organization and value chain get out of sync, but so do the computer systems that support it. If 100 percent alignment of value chain linkage and computer systems existed, you would expect the retailer, for example, to have systems called Store Layout, Store Location, Merchandising, Purchasing, etc. What you end up with instead are dozens of systems, many of which have the value chain component names in their identifiers, but none of which really performs the specific jobs mentioned.

Using Value Chain Analysis and Knowledge Management to Help with Alignment Challenges

The fact that the goals and directions of the corporation are constantly getting out of sync with its organizational structure and computer systems infrastructure should come as no surprise to anyone. Solving this problem—that of getting large corporations to leverage the advantages that large budgets, large departments, and large computer systems can offer, while at the same time making it possible for that same corporation to "turn on a dime" in response to myriad changes in market conditions—is the art and science of modern corporate management. Value chain analysis, knowledge management, and knowledge management systems offer a framework for understanding the nature and degree of misalignment, and painlessly restoring alignment as quickly as possible.

So far we have established that there is something called a value chain and that it can be incredibly helpful in understanding how the business is functioning and how we can make it run more effectively. We have not yet shown how the concept of the value chain can be tied to the concepts of knowledge management to provide us with an understanding of how to manage the development of new technology solutions.

To make this connection, we have to go back to our definition of what knowledge management is and how we want to make use of it. At the end of the previous chapter, we proposed a definition of knowledge management, from a computer systems development view, as a unifying discipline and perspective that will tie the business view and technology view together into one universal position.

We also proposed that knowledge itself is the combination of data and context applied to the solution of specific problems (data + context + a business objective = business knowledge), and that knowledge management, therefore, is the process of identifying and managing that data, its context, and the associated business objectives in an efficient, meaningful, and repeatable way.

The value chain provides us with a piece of the knowledge management formula that we have had no access to before, a discipline that allows us to define, model, and plan the business objectives piece of the knowledge management equation. In other words, we will use the concept of the value chain as our unifying element, our central icon, that will allow us to build a knowledge management discipline that accomplishes all of the objectives we have set forward, and that will ultimately guide us in the development of effective Web warehousing systems.

Our objective in Chapters 4 and 5 is to explore this perspective of the development of computer systems as nothing more than the expression of the company's value chain. We also explore the use of this powerful concept in tandem with the concepts of knowledge management itself to help direct the development of specific Web warehousing applications and the overall Web warehousing infrastructure and environment.

CHAPTER 4

Modeling, Visioning, and Value Propositions

- *What is a value proposition?*
- *How is it related to knowledge management and the value chain?*
- *How is it used to help drive Web warehousing systems development?*
- *What are modeling and visioning?*
- *How are modeling and visioning used to help identify value propositions?*

Too Much Technology, Too Little Time

With all of the wonderful new technology available to choose from, and all of the great opportunities that business presents us with to make improvements through the use of that technology, you would think that the computer systems development world as we know it today would be in its heyday. Just as with everything else, though, there can be too much of a good thing, and that adage certainly holds true for the developers of computer systems.

One of the biggest problems faced by the computer systems developer in the world of business today is clearly a shortage of time. Both technology and business are changing at such a hectic pace that it is impossible to do everything we all know we should do, before moving ahead with different projects.

Business Pressure

Everyone knows that, before you deploy a new business computer system, you need to study the business, study the problem, look at alternative solutions, and then write an extensive requirements document that can be used by the technician to build the system. Unfortunately, despite years of experience in the development of business computer systems, the reality is that no company can afford to invest the time and money that this extensive process would require.

Web Warehousing Deployment Reality

The reality is, again, that there is no time for any kind of due process or set of standards we would like to see enforced. In the final analysis we will be forced to deploy much new technology a lot faster and much more haphazardly than we would like to. Despite our best efforts, there are just too many forces at work in the business and technology world which make it necessary for the Web warehousing practitioner to become a "fast-draw" artist, and simply learn newer, more effective, more efficient, and faster ways to make good decisions.

We are faced with a world where there are hundreds of problems that need to be addressed and hundreds of potential solutions that the Web warehousing practitioner can choose from. Unfortunately, there is simply not enough time in the day to review them all, consider the strengths and weaknesses of each, and develop a well-meaning, overall consensus from large groups of people. Instead, we have to go for the best-we-can-get approach. By making use of our understanding of business, computers, knowledge management, and value chains, we should be able to come up with a "quickie" approach that actually brings us pretty close to the mark in the majority of cases.

Principal Challenges to Web Warehouse Solution Selection

For the would-be Web warehousing practitioner, the challenge of trying to determine which solutions to deploy—and when and where—is particularly challenging. Many things conspire against us, making this decision particularly difficult. In general, we can summarize these problems into three major areas:

1. How to apply the technology to the solution of a particular problem.
2. How to change the ways people work together in order to make use of it.
3. How to cost-justify the deployment of the technology solution.

But Is It Useful?

When we consider a new technological capability, our first problem is deciding whether the technology will actually be of any use to anyone in the business. Now, at first glance, this might seem like a silly problem. Isn't it *obvious* whether something has value or not?

Lack of Clarity about the Functions That New Types of Systems Perform In many cases, it is not clear at all whether something has value. There are many reasons for this. Some of them occur when overzealous practitioners try to jump into the use of systems before they fully understand them, some happen when well-meaning marketing professionals and industry analysts attempt to explain these approaches without applying a sufficient amount of rigor, setting the context, and making the necessary assumptions. These practices often make the process of choosing a technology extremely difficult:

- *Telling only half the story.* When it comes to evaluating new technologies, one of the greatest difficulties is the fact that vendors will often tell you less than everything about what you are getting into until after you are committed to the purchase. A potential user will be told, for example, that "users of these kinds of system are often able to reduce inventory expenses by 25 percent or better." The unwary purchaser is not told that, in addition to installing the software, the company also needs to close down warehouses, lay off staff, and change their way of doing business before any of those benefits will occur. The problem with incomplete definitions is that there is an unstated list of other things you have to buy or do to get the system to deliver, and you are not told about it until too late.

- *Generalization.* Another problem occurs when advocates of a solution list potential benefits in only the most generalized terms. For example, a vendor might suggest that you could reduce inventory, improve efficiency, and increase customer satisfaction with their product. While those are certainly things any business person would want, they are stated at such a high, general level, that there is no way for you to know whether it can actually deliver those benefits. Many times people purchase products based on such high-level claims, expecting these business values to be delivered somehow.

- *Obfuscation.* Sometimes vendors or developers simply make the descriptions of their product so complex, confusing, and contradictory that there is no way anyone can figure out what the product does or doesn't do. (This is *not* an exaggeration. After working for several software development firms, I can guarantee you that there are companies that develop products that are so complex that no one can figure out exactly what they do or how they work, and that includes the manufacturers themselves.)

The easiest way to deal with these situations, you might think, would be to simply avoid any and all products whose marketing materials are not clear, or whose marketing personnel don't seem to be able to explain precisely how the product works. Regrettably, you cannot really afford to deal with it in this way. First, almost *all products* come across as overwhelming, contradictory, and difficult to understand when you first meet them (or at least, when you first meet any particular category of product). Second, the fact that some or all of these factors may be present in the marketing materials and the way the system has been presented

Chapter 4: Modeling, Visioning, and Value Propositions

does not especially mean that it is not a good, viable solution once you cut through the smokescreen.

How You Use It Is More Important Than What It Does What we need is a way to look at the different solutions that are offered to see whether we really understand what they will do. Then we need a way to compare system alternatives according to equivalent evaluation scales. This is not as simple as it might sound. The capabilities and the value that a product or system delivers are defined within the specific context of a given business problem and a given approach to solving that problem.

In the old days of OLTP systems, the problem was much easier to deal with. For example, the business function that an airline reservations system performs is to efficiently keep track of all ticket sales. The economic value of this functionality can be measured in terms of the additional customers you can attract with the capability and the additional revenues you can gain by more efficiently loading the planes. This is clear, simple, and straightforward, and it is obvious to us what this system does.

It gets trickier to figure out the business function and value, however, when you have a data mining system that evaluates the information collected by that reservation system. A data mining product might be able to analyze the behaviors of different types of customers and help determine who the most profitable ones are. It might also be used to help the operations department figure out which flights are going out at capacity and which are taking off with so few passengers that they are running at a loss. The important question is not whether the system can, theoretically, produce that kind of information, but whether somebody needs to know those things and could use them to make changes that will benefit the corporation.

Actionability, the Key Ingredient The key term used to describe this aspect of a system's deliverability content is *actionability*. The question we need to ask ourselves about any system is, "Can the users, as a result of what the system tells them, take a meaningful action which cost-justifies the installation of the system?" If the answer is yes, then you have a system of value. If the answer is no, then you can provide interesting and amusing information, but not anything that the business is concerned about.

To answer the question, we need to understand not only what the system can produce, but also under what conditions and assumptions this value can actually be delivered. Unfortunately, the vendors who sell and promote systems of this type tend to use generalization, incompleteness, and even obfuscation in their descriptions. They too often leave on us the burden of figuring out the details of how these products are supposed to work.

Special Challenges for New Technologies Each generation of new technologies and new approaches to solving business problems tends to become more sophisticated and complicated and, therefore, more difficult to explain in simple business terms. It is ironic that some of the hardest-to-explain technologies are often some of the most useful and most powerful. What we need is a method for defining just what a system is supposed to deliver—the nature and substance of the value it will bring if employed—expressed in terms that make it immediately obvious exactly what it will do and how.

Just because we have established that the application or tool in question exhibits some kind of tangible value to the business, however, does not guarantee that it is a solution that we should actually consider. Just because something is useful does not mean that it is economically viable. Many times users want something that is appealing to them, but delivers no value at all. Other times they may want a system that delivers some value, but not enough to justify the cost of acquiring it.

So, another challenge we face in deciding whether to deploy alternative solutions is to determine whether the deployment will be economically justified. While it is certainly true that many implementations of new technologies have resulted in astounding returns on investment, it is also true that for every success story there are hundreds of disaster stories. We need a way to select solutions that help us to weed out the bad choices.

There are actually many reasons, other than good economic business sense, that people deploy new technologies. A Web warehousing practitioner must determine whether these other forces are at work and ameliorate them as much as possible. Computer systems that are implemented for reasons other than those of sound economic value and contribution to the efficiency of the corporate value chain are a dismal waste of money and will generally fail to meet the needs of the business.

Reasons other than Economic for Systems Deployment People are attracted to new technologies for a variety of reasons other than sound economic ones including:

The gee whiz factor. Many times, users become enamored with new, flashy systems that attract them for esthetic reasons.

Convenience. It makes my life easier. Users will often ask for systems that deliver no real additional value to the business, but will be more convenient for them. There is certainly nothing wrong with making a user's life more convenient, but doing so needs to be evaluated in terms of how much more it will cost. Many times, the multimillion-dollar cost of correcting a little inconvenience is deemed unwarranted.

Neatness. Sometimes users or developers are attracted to solutions that "tie things together" or get rid of "loose ends." These consolidating systems, again, may be attractive or convenient, but still offer no additional value to the firm.

Curiosity. Many information systems' requests are based on a user's curiosity about information that is unrelated to the solution or does not address specific problems or concerns.

Power. Knowledge is power, and sometimes users ask for information because they know that access to it will give them power over others—again, of little value to the overall business itself.

Technology du jour. Unfortunately, many organizations purchase new technology because it is "hot" and the latest thing to have. Web warehousing and knowledge management are two good examples of that.

Status. Sometimes users are trying to keep up with the Joneses. They simply want what other users have.

Value Propositions

So, given all of these reasons and problems, how do we go about figuring out which Web warehousing systems to deploy and where? More important, how do we evaluate each new technology as it is presented to us for consideration as part of the corporate computer systems arsenal? The answer is a concept known as the *value proposition*.

Different Types of Value Propositions

There are actually several definitions for a value proposition that we need to deal with to make sense out of this situation. We will start with the business-level, generalized definition, and then work our way down to the more detailed, application-specific ones.

Value Chains and Customer Value Propositions In the previous chapter, we talk about the value chain and the highest-level form of a value proposition, the customer value proposition. As we say there, the whole objective of a company is to identify, create, and deliver the solutions for problems to customers. The description of what that solution is—what a company offers to the user—is known as the customer (or corporate) value proposition.

Customer value propositions come in many forms. These offers can be physical (an automobile manufacturer proposes to provide customers with high-speed, low-cost transportation), emotional (an insurance company offers peace of mind to its customers), or conceptual (a fashion designer offers to make a person feel young and cool). It can be an offer of something tangible or intangible, anything that anyone could possibly want.

Application Value Propositions The corporation survives by offering and delivering value propositions to customers. It delivers them through its exercise of the value chain that it subscribes to. Each computer system at work in that organization, therefore, contributes to the delivery of that value proposition, either directly or indirectly, through management of the knowledge it deals with. (Billing systems contribute by helping customers pay for the products, data mining systems help marketing analysts figure out what people want and need, etc.)

We can now carry this thinking one step further by realizing that each computer system, in fact, has its own value proposition (or propositions). If computer systems did not offer value to the corporation and ultimately contribute to the execution of the value chain, they would not be purchased. We specifically define this kind of value proposition as an application value proposition or a system value proposition.

(Throughout the rest of this book, unless otherwise specifically noted, the phrase *value proposition,* refers to the specific application value propositions described here and specifically to those value propositions made by the developers of Web warehousing systems to the owners of corporate computer systems.)

Objectives for Using Value Propositions We introduce the concept of the application (Web warehousing) -based value propositions here for several reasons. Up until this point, in the process of defining the development of the Web warehousing environment, we have talked about the framework for organizing our efforts (knowledge management and value chains), but we have delivered nothing in terms of a specific plan of attack for using that framework. The concept of the value proposition provides us with that capability.

Chapter 4: Modeling, Visioning, and Value Propositions

Value propositions are the nuts and bolts, the foundation, the rubber-meets-the-road portion of the entire knowledge management/value chain–based approach to systems development. It is through the value proposition that we get out of the area of generalized descriptions and non-reality-based suppositions about what will and will not work in a given situation, and into the area of practical, discrete reality.

We will use the value proposition as the mechanism through which we:

1. Compare and equate the value that a system can deliver to the business
2. Define and declare the system's place within the business
3. Guarantee that the solution will meet the content, context, fit, organizational impact, and cultural content that the business demands of it
4. Assure ourselves that the deployment of the solution is economically valuable to the firm

Formal Definition of Web Warehousing Value Propositions To complete our description of the knowledge management–based view of the business world, we need to include value propositions. Every system, feature, and software product brought into the firm has associated with it a value proposition. The job of the Web warehousing developer and designer is to make sure that the value proposition for the system under consideration is well understood, qualified, and communicated to everyone involved in the process.

WEB WAREHOUSING VALUE PROPOSITION *A statement made by a businessperson that states that if the described information (in the form of data, text, video, audio, or any other medium) were to be delivered to the business, and made available through the use of the proscribed access tools or technologies, then the following value could be delivered to the business.*

For example, the marketing department's value proposition for a data mining application, as stated by the head of marketing, might read as follows:

"The marketing department will be able to increase the company's market share by 5 percent if information about customer buying behavior were made available to the market research department and they could make use of data mining tools to analyze that behavior and make appropriate changes to our strategy."

The practice of requiring that all new systems be sponsored by a businessperson who can state the value the system will deliver in business terms, and is willing to back up that sponsorship with a statement about who will provide the benefit and where it will come from, can make all the difference in the world when it comes to deciding which technologies to work with and when.[1]

Using Value Propositions My recommendation, then, is that every solution under consideration must provide a value proposition as part of its description to the users and implementers.

We can create an environment where many different kinds of applications, from many different areas (data, text, image, video, audio, etc.), can be evaluated and compared with some clarity, focus, and efficiency by making the proposer communicate the following information in the value proposition:

- The value chain of the affected business
- The specific business areas being affected
- The nature of the tasks that the business users are expected to perform
- The population and nature of the knowledge being managed
- The business value expected to be delivered

A properly stated value proposition provides the person responsible for selecting a Web warehouse application with all of the information needed to determine:

What the system will do

How much it will contribute to the business (its economic contribution)

By establishing a policy of requiring that value propositions be associated with all Web warehousing activities, management can quickly and effectively make decisions about which applications to accept and which to avoid.

---

[1]For a more detailed exploration of the concept of value propositions and their use in data warehousing, see *Data Warehousing: Strategies, Technologies, and Techniques* by Rob Mattison, McGraw-Hill, New York, 1996.

Chapter 4: Modeling, Visioning, and Value Propositions

Discovering Value Propositions Now that we know what a value proposition is, what it is made up of, and how we are supposed to use it, we are left with only two more small problems:

1. Determining what the value propositions are for a given tool or solution
2. Determining which value propositions apply to which areas of the business

At first glance, the process of assigning a value proposition to a solution would seem to be an obvious, straightforward, and relatively simple thing to do. This is not always the case. In fact, we often find that the solutions that ultimately deliver the *most* value to the corporation, and the most competitive advantage, are the value propositions that are the most difficult to identify and verbalize in the early stages of systems development.

Several factors contribute to this condition, but two of the more formidable are:

Value propositions that deliver significant competitive advantage are usually neither obvious nor easy to figure out. When you think about it, this makes perfect sense. If it was easy or obvious, then everyone would do it, and there would be no advantage in it. It would simply be the way everyone does business.

As technologies become more mature, they also become a lot more complicated. For sophisticated leading-edge technologies to work well, they require users that are both business-savvy and technically proficient.

Identifying what value propositions are associated with a given tool and figuring out where they are most appropriately applied in a given business situation are two very important tasks we need to tackle. To make the value proposition approach work, we need to understand a little more about how to handle these tasks.

The Nature of the Value That Systems Deliver

Figuring out exactly what value a particular system or capability will deliver to the user is actually a lot more complicated than it first appears. This is because there are so many ways that value can be delivered, some simple, obvious, and tangible, and some complicated, obscure, and intangible. We will be successful when we have figured out some way to recognize and categorize all of them.

How Does Value Get Delivered?

Figuring out the value that a data warehousing or Web warehousing solution will deliver to the business is made difficult by the fact that the tools that people purchase in this area (the query products, the search engines, etc.) are tools, *not* applications. When you purchase a Web warehousing solution, you are not actually buying the capability itself. It can be delivered only if:

- The Web warehousing solution has been put together the right way.
- The right equipment has been assembled (hardware, software, databases, knowledge bases, etc.).
- The correct raw materials have been brought together (data, text, and other media).
- The users know what they are supposed to do and are qualified to do it.

In other words, a Web warehousing solution may physically have everything that is needed, but actually accomplishing the objective depends on the user. (This is very different from OLTP systems, where the system basically tells *you* what to do. The user simply follows instructions and the job gets done.) So, part of the challenge we face is that, when we put these systems together, we must make sure that the people will use them correctly and effectively.

Turning Potential into Realization: The Role of Models and Visioning

In assigning value to the implementation of a particular solution, we need to determine two things:

The potential benefits if the capability were deployed. In other words, we need some kind of functional and financial model that tells us what benefits will be provided.

The who, what, where, when, how, and why of that deployment within the context of the business. In other words, we need to develop an organizational and an operational model of how the solution is going to work.

Let's consider each of these problems in more detail.

Developing the Functional and Financial Models

Imagine that you have just been introduced to a new Web warehousing software product. It has a functionality that is very familiar to you. It reads files and databases, creates reports, and sends output to any place you want it to go. Even though this is a new product, and it may be a little difficult to use at first, you will probably have no problem determining what it does and how it can be used within your organization. In this situation, the functional model for the product is clear, because you are familiar with it. Since the type of product is well known and its benefits are generally understood by all, it is easy to imagine how it is going to be used.

But what do you do when the technological approach is new and no one has any experience with it? What do you do with OLAP, data mining, and the host of other leading-edge applications?

In such cases, you need to think through some typical situations, and try to imagine what role the technology will play and how well it will work. When the product is not known, you need to apply imagination and mental discipline to understand whether and how the solution can provide value, and then make some estimates about the outcome. That is critical! If you do not understand how a product can potentially solve problems, then it certainly never will in reality.

Let's consider an example. One of the new functions that Web warehousing will make available to the businessperson is the ability to search for text documents. The mechanics of how text document search systems work is clear. We know that with a search engine you type in key words, which tell the system what kinds of documents you are looking for. So, the mechanics of the application are understood.

But what kind of business functionality will this capability provide to business people? How will text search improve their ability to do their jobs? What business value will it deliver?

These questions are actually a lot more difficult. You could cite situations where a businessperson had to look for a lost document for a few hours, and propose that a text search system might have saved valuable time. Or, you could say the person should have kept track of the document better. At first glance, there is no apparent business reason (other than possibly convenience) for us to consider deploying this search technology. (For some examples of how some companies are using text search capabilities to improve business performance, see Chapters 11 to 14.)

Clearly, we face a problem when we know what the product or application does mechanically, but cannot see how it can be harnessed to improve the running of the business. And, as we have already stated, even though we may understand what the system will do, that is no guarantee that the effort will make good economic sense. The functional model we develop must be accompanied by a financial model to explain that aspect as well.

Identifying Who, What, Where, When, How, and Why: The Operational and Organizational Models

Even if we have calculated, theoretically, how the new value can be attained when this technology is deployed, we still need to figure out the who, what, where, when, how, and why of its use. You see, if the technology is new, and the application of it to the business is untested, then there is a very good chance that:

- Nobody has ever done it before.
- There is no "department" responsible for the execution of those functions.
- There are no policies, procedures, or standards for making it work.
- And, one of the most devastating consequences of all: There is no way for anyone to do anything about it when the system provides new insights and information. (In other words, there is no one to take action, when actionable information is produced.)

To make use of the new technology, we must put all of these pieces together as well. For example, many organizations today are excitedly developing a new kind of data warehouse system called *marketing databases*. (A marketing database system is a data warehouse that keeps track of a company's customers. The system records information about everything those customers have bought, every contact they have had with the company, and a lot of other information about their preferences and behavior.) Once a company has a marketing database, they usually analyze it to determine the different types of customers they have (segmentation), their likes and dislikes (behavioral modeling), and the likelihood of their buying again (predictive modeling). All is useful information.

Most companies that are new to marketing databases fail to realize that having access to this kind of information does not guarantee that anything will be done about it. In business, just having the facts is not enough to make changes happen. The company has to change itself so that it is able to act on the information that is discovered.

The fact is that it takes a specialized person to interpret the information that a marketing database holds. Once all of this information in the database is gathered and interpreted, it takes a specialized group of people, working within all areas of the company (advertising, customer service, etc.), to take this information and make good use of it. Many times, companies build systems like this without even realizing what the organizational and operational consequences will be until after the fact.

What Is a Model?

Up until now, we have spent a considerable amount of time talking about what the different types of operational models are and how they apply to the business world in a conceptual sense. What we have not discussed, however, is what they really look like and how they can be made useful in the world of systems development. We now turn to understanding models from that perspective.

Webster's dictionary defines a model as "a representation to show the construction or appearance of something," or "a simplified representation of a system."

As we have already established, the operational models we are talking about here are descriptions of how new technology products and applications can be made a useful part of the business's activities. But what do these models look like, where do they come from, who invents them, and how are they propagated within the business? Actually, the toughest question about these models is "What do they look like?"

Implied Models

Up until very recently, we have not had to get explicit about the form of modeling that we are talking about here. In the past, when it came to making use of new computer technologies, we all just kind of figured it out as we went along. We allowed the process of modeling to happen automatically, implicitly, and, in many cases, subconsciously. Indeed, for many of the technologies that we have implemented so far, the operational models can be derived intuitively.

Unfortunately, as the level of technology and complexity increases, the number of people who are able to intuitively understand the model is dwindling rapidly. More and more, people try to use technologies without any clue as to how they are supposed to fit into their workplace environment. A new type of model, however, is quickly replacing the implicit models of the past, one that spells out the functionalities of new systems in ways that can easily be understood.

Approaches to Model Development

If the organization is to successfully deploy knowledge management/Web warehousing solutions, then some form of modeling process will have to take place. The nature of this process varies by organization, industry, culture, and history, but somehow it must be done. If we do not figure out specifically how a new technology will fit into the business, then we will be left with new systems implementations that are disastrous exercises in futility and waste. (How many of these have we had recently?) The development of a solid model for the business is the first step, the leading edge in implementing new technologies with consequent changes to the business itself.

There are several ways in which organizations have developed their models for integration of a given solution or product into their workplace. Some approaches have worked well, and others have failed to prevent the implementation of a system where no one understood what was being delivered. What is critical is not so much that you choose the right technique, but that you use it (or several of them) effectively.

Internal Research and Development Departments Perhaps the oldest and most formal of the methods to bring the operational modeling process to the business is the research and development approach. In this approach, a special department is set aside whose job it is to identify, test, verify, and assign value propositions and "official" corporate models to all technologies under consideration. This approach, when applied correctly, can be quite effective. Unfortunately, politics (both technical and financial) have conspired to eliminate these positions from most firms.

Chapter 4: Modeling, Visioning, and Value Propositions

Special Study Teams Sometimes organizations will assign to teams of individuals temporary part-time duties as the "studiers" of some type of solution. These special study teams can acquire whatever background or education they feel is important and then report back to the organization at large with their findings.

Study teams can, in fact, be one of the more effective responses to the problem of evaluating alternative solutions, as long as the participants:

- Take the responsibility seriously
- Are qualified to do the evaluation
- Are thorough in their study
- Provide well-documented feedback to the organization

Consultants Sometimes organizations will hire consultants specifically experienced in the technology area in question to provide some real-time, on-the-spot education to the organization. In fact, the use of consultants, paid experts in the use of new technologies, is without doubt the number one technique that people use to get information about how other companies have successfully integrated the new technologies into their workplaces.

Help from Outside Parties The organization can get the functional visioning help they need from several sources:

1. *Formal education.* Classes at educational institutions on the subject matter (often light, academic, and theoretical in nature).
2. *Intensive tutorials.* These are provided by consulting or training organizations. They can be effective, but they can also be light and generalized in nature. They often turn into "how to use the software" classes, offering little or no help in the identification of value propositions.
3. *Vendor briefings or training.* Educational experiences sponsored by the vendors of hardware or software with an expected bias toward their own solutions (often forcing users to stop thinking about what they need and instead focusing on how to make this product work for them).
4. *Magazines, advertisements, and trade shows.* Articles, specials, advertisements, and advertorials tend to be light and heavily biased toward the vendors who run the ads or sponsor the booths.
5. *Borrowing from competitors and related industries.* Actually seeing others make it work (extremely effective when possible).

6. *Books (such as this one).* In the second section of the book I provide you with one chapter for each category of product, with an in-depth analysis of what it does, how it works, what its value propositions are, and how people use it in reality.

Any or all of these approaches can help the organization gather initial intelligence about the effectiveness of these technologies. Unfortunately, in far too many cases, the organizations putting on the training or writing the articles are professional trainers and writers, not professionals in the use of the technology. These offerings can be overgeneralized, and can gloss over or avoid completely the issues regarding the application of the technology to specific value propositions, value chains, and solutions.

How Do You Know When the Modeling Is Done?

Of course, since so much of the modeling process is a cultural, subconscious process, it is very difficult to know when or if the modeling job has been completed. In general, if the use of a new technology seems to be understood and accepted by the majority, then the organization can be said to have a functional model for that technology.

For example, most organizations are very clear about what personal computers are and are not good for. There is very little argument about their applicability, and it is clear to everyone how they can be used. However, there is probably no large business organization today with the same understanding of Web technology. People have confused and conflicting goals, experiences, and expectations for what the technology can and cannot do, and what it will cost to gain the benefits. At this point, the world of Web technology suffers from a severe lack of meaningful models in the functional, financial, organizational, and operational perspectives.

Visioning

After we have developed a good understanding of what a system is going to deliver, we are left with only one small problem. We have to figure out how to get a very large group of very busy, very focused, very reluctant business people to come to understand what these new models are and how they should be used. More important than that, we then need to convince and motivate these people to:

- Change the way they look at things (such as their jobs, their roles, and their sense of order)
- Change the way they do things (abandon processes, stability, and a sense of status quo that they have worked years to attain)
- Possibly change the way they are viewed by others in the business and the way they view themselves

Helping people to integrate these new models into the way they interact with each other, computers, customers, and the business itself is what is known as the visioning process.

Objectives for the Visioning Process

The visioning process, then, is what we go through to help people examine the new capabilities we are delivering and figure out how to integrate them into their routines. It allows people to examine what the system can do and how it can be utilized, and gives them the opportunity to fine-tune those models into a truly workable scenario.

Reasons Why Good Technologies Do Not Get Applied This problem of figuring out when and where to deploy new technologies is a very tricky one. While no organization wants to be the one that experiments and fails, every organization wants to be the first one to successfully implement approaches that benefit its stockholders, customers, and employees.

There are several reasons why good solutions go untried in large organizations. They include:

- *No experience.* The number one reason that companies do not use a lot of the newer technologies is because no one inside the company has ever used them before, and so nobody understands how they work or how they can help.
- *No vision.* The second biggest problem occurs when organizations are unable to figure out how to get "outside the box" in their thinking, and try to see how the new approaches might work.
- *Conservatism.* The implementation of new technologies is painful. It is hard on the organization and the individual. Many simply cannot handle that kind of pressure.

Developing a Vision

After the organization has determined what a technology can deliver and how it can be applied, the second half of the process requires that they figure out how it will be implemented. Remember, just because you know how a particular technological solution *might* help the business is no guarantee that it actually will be able to. There are innumerable issues, challenges, and exceptions that can turn a seemingly obvious fit for an organization into an implementation nightmare.

To get an idea of how the product will actually work, it is important that we somehow learn:

- How users currently do things
- How this new product/approach will make that process easier or better
- How the processes will have to change to realize that value
- What kinds of reconstruction the organization will have to go through to make those changes happen
- Whether the users are capable of learning how to use the new product and process, and are motivated to do so

The problem of trying to figure out what the "fit" issues will be, and how to resolve them, is *not* a trivial one. Many times, systems fail, not because the technology didn't work, but because the organizational consequences of its implementation were not understood until long after the commitment to use the new product was made.

Remember, the installation of these kinds of systems is supposed to have a major impact on the business, and to be focused on making sure that the management of knowledge within the organization is improved. Therefore, the fit issues are often the most critical.

Some of the approaches utilized to make this happen include:

1. *Surveys.* A team of individuals determines what the most important questions are regarding the implementation of the solution, and develops questionnaires that are then distributed to the end users for their input.
2. *Consultants.* Expert consultants, experienced in the implementation of these types of systems, can be called in to assist with the determination of fit issues.
3. *Visioning sessions.* Many times special, collaborative, educational/work sessions are put together. During these sessions users are presented with the *functional vision* of the potential solutions

and asked to participate in the development of the *operational vision* for their particular application areas.
4. *Interviews.* Often one-on-one interviews with the people who will be using the system are scheduled to make the operational determinations.
5. *Role playing.* One of the more popular approaches is to get all of the individuals targeted for the new technology involved in role playing. These exercises make it possible for individuals and groups to see themselves in the new situations, and allow them to work out any kinks that the proposed technology may impose in a safe, nonthreatening environment.
6. *Interactive games.* Some of the most sophisticated experts in the area of vision development have actually developed board games and other types of play tools that allow people to learn while they have fun with the onerous task of reinventing themselves and their organizations.

Conclusions

In this chapter, we take a closer look at three of the most important aspects of new technology implementation in the business world today. We find that with new technologies often come new paradigms for understanding how those technologies could fit into the business world. We also see that, through the use of value propositions, models, and the visioning process, we can help the organization ameliorate those challenges.

Value propositions, as we have described them here, are one of the best means available to establish technology-independent valuation criteria for the implementation of any new technologies.

The modeling process is something we go through every time a new technology comes along; it forces us to rethink how to get things done.

The visioning process is the method many organizations advocate to help people more quickly and efficiently transition into the use of new technologies through role playing, games, and other imagination-provoking techniques.

CHAPTER 5

Knowledge Networks, Neighborhoods, and Economics

- *What is a knowledge network?*
- *What is a knowledge neighborhood?*
- *How does one define knowledge economics?*
- *What is a knowledge exchange?*
- *What cultural and organizational impacts do new technologies have on the organization?*
- *How can implementers of Web warehousing solutions take these factors into account?*

Definition of Terms

To effectively address these last areas of knowledge management—knowledge networks, knowledge neighborhoods, and knowledge economics—as they relate to computer systems development in general, and Web warehousing specifically, we once again need to come up with a set of definitions. In this case, each of the terms is related to the same area of the knowledge management discipline. Each has to do with the roles individuals play, how they perceive their roles, and how they deal with the changes in those roles (and the related changes in their self-perception and personal reality) as new technology solutions are forced upon them.

The Knowledge Network

The first and perhaps easiest term to describe is *knowledge network*. This term has come into popular use over the last couple of years and has become a standard part of the knowledge management vocabulary. We use the term to describe that group of individuals within the organization who share a common pool of knowledge, and who, through the sharing of that knowledge, help make the business operate more effectively.

For example, take a specific collection of information in a particular industry, say, insurance policies and fraudulent claims in a large insurance company. The knowledge about these claims will include information about the insurance policies themselves, information about the people who made claims, investigators' reports, court proceedings, pictures, interviews, legal briefs, and any number of other types of text, video, audio, or audit information. This pool of knowledge, then, will be of interest to a diverse group of people within the organization, including:

- Underwriters, who, with access to the information, will be able to make better underwriting decisions in the future
- Attorneys, who will want to review how other cases were handled and dispatched
- Fraud investigators, who need access to the information to help with future cases
- Management, administrative, and other personnel for a variety of reasons

We would include all these people in our definition of the knowledge network for fraud and claims knowledge in the firm.

Why Define Knowledge Networks at All?

An amazing thing about the concept of the knowledge network is that it is relatively new and that the term has only recently come into wide use. The concept is absolutely logical and incredibly useful in helping us understand and define who needs to gain access to what kind of information within the business.

The developers of computer systems have dealt with a similar concept for many years, but never as formally. In the past, every time a new computer system was being installed, the developers had to interview all users and figure out which of them did or did not need access, starting from scratch each time. Often, people who did need access were skipped. Other times, people who didn't need access were included. Just about every time, the issues uncovered or created conflicts about security and access rights (topics we will consider later in this chapter).

Perhaps the biggest reason for the failure of the computer systems community to recognize the term and its usefulness was a combination of factors, including:

- Most new computer systems are managed and budgeted through a process which requires that particular departments and other types of economic and political units within the corporation sponsor their development. Under this kind of financing scenario, it logically follows that the organization paying for the system would be interested in the delivery of information to only the people within its own economic sphere of influence.

- The history of the development of computer systems has been incredibly short-term-focused. The fact that the grouping together of these types of individuals could have long-term, strategic benefit is therefore missed in the pursuit of quick returns and short-term objectives.

These previous conditions notwithstanding, it is clear that knowledge networks will begin to play a critical role in the development of systems in the future as we shift our emphasis from the OLTP mode and toward the business intelligence mode or systems development and definition.

Knowledge Network Definition In keeping with our practice of providing formal definitions, we come up with the following for knowledge network.

 **KNOWLEDGE NETWORK** *A group of individuals who share a common interest in the same collection of information and knowledge about a particular subject area and use it effectively.*

Knowledge Neighborhoods

Whereas the term *knowledge network* has been around for a few years and has common acceptance in the industry, this second term, *knowledge neighborhood,* is much newer and has a much more specific application. The term *knowledge network* is useful in helping us understand who the people are that participate in the collection, processing, and utilization of a given set of knowledge. The term, unfortunately, does little to help us understand the nature of those people's relationships or their intentions for the utilization of it.

What we need, in addition to this general term, is one that defines for us that group of people who share not only the knowledge, but also a fundamental relationship to each other based on that same knowledge. We refer to those individuals as a *knowledge neighborhood* (or *knowledge community*).

A knowledge neighborhood is that group of people within the organization who share a common vocabulary, a common set of goals and objectives, a common view of the world, and, consequently, a common pool of knowledge as well. A knowledge neighborhood, in other words, is that group of people who work with, and participate in, the management of one of the links in the corporation's value chain, regardless of where they happen to reside organizationally, politically, or professionally.

An example can help us illustrate this explanation. Take, for instance, a telecommunications company. If this is a typical company, it will be undergoing a significant amount of change due to competitive pressures in the world today. It will probably manage three to five different product lines (local, long distance, cellular, pager, Internet), have several different operational units based on geographic regions, and support residential and corporate sales forces. Now, with an organizational structure like that, how many people do you suppose are involved in the processing of marketing? How many people put together ads, develop marketing strategies, work on customer satisfaction issues, and do the myriad of other things concerned with marketing to the telco customers?

One might assume that there is one large marketing department that takes care of all these things for all product lines, all geographies, and all customer types. For most organizations, however, there will be anywhere from 1 to 30 official departmental designations, all of which identify their personnel as having marketing responsibility for some aspect of the business. At the same time, any number of individuals or subcontracted organizations will have additional unofficial or implicit responsibility for marketing aspects as well.

We refer to the overall community of marketing people within the organization as the *marketing knowledge neighborhood* (or *marketing knowledge community*).

While the concept of the knowledge network is useful, the concept of the knowledge neighborhood is crucial, if we are to successfully build the next generation of computer systems, based not on organizational and budgetary alignments, but on the efficient operation of the different value chains that drive the business.

Knowledge Neighborhood (Community) Definition This leaves us then with the need to develop our formal definition for the term *knowledge neighborhood.*

KNOWLEDGE NEIGHBORHOOD *A group of individuals who share a common vocabulary, a common set of perspectives and objectives, and a common responsibility for the efficient management of one of the links of the corporation's value chain. This is also referred to as a knowledge community.*

Knowledge Economics

Now that we know who the participants are in the knowledge-based world, our next job is to come up with some definitions for the rules by which they relate to each other. You will recall that the whole point of the knowledge management perspective is to look at the corporation as a collection of individuals who manage knowledge more or less effectively. Of course, if you recognize that management of knowledge is the key to corporate success, then the next logical step is to figure out how that value is assigned and paid for within the context of the overall business.

In other words, you cannot have a meaningful theory of knowledge management in business without assumptions about the economics of how business works and, most important, how people are paid. This is what we call the discipline of *knowledge economics.*

Definition of Knowledge Economics Within the field of knowledge economics we include all of those issues pertaining to how the business places value on knowledge itself, on the systems that manage and maintain knowledge, and on the people who process it and make decisions based on it. Webster's dictionary defines economics as follows: "Of or pertaining to the production, distribution, and use of wealth." It therefore follows that the definition of knowledge economics would be:

KNOWLEDGE ECONOMICS The study of those issues pertaining to the production, distribution, and use of knowledge within the organization.

The Rules of Knowledge Exchange

This then brings us to the final definition in our knowledge naming spree, to the term *knowledge exchange*. Knowledge exchange is, of course, directly related to our study of knowledge economics and defines for us the rules by which people participate in the knowledge economy.

The rules of knowledge exchange have actually been in effect within our business and personal lives for as far back as anyone can determine. Just as with the other aspects of the knowledge management revolution, the only real surprise to be found in this area is that it has taken us so long to recognize and label the phenomenon for what it really is. As we explore that subject further we will discover that organizations have been forced to continually deal with problems in the development of equitable and acceptable rules for the management of knowledge exchange within the firm, and between the firm and the public in general. We will also see how the foundational concepts provided by knowledge exchange help us to understand a lot of the technology assimilation resistance and cultural revolution issues that we have experienced in the past. In fact, it is not unfair to say that in the majority of situations, especially in the areas of communications technologies (printing, radio, television, telephone, music, etc.), the sundering of the preexisting status quo regarding the rights and prerogatives revolving around knowledge and its control has been responsible for a great many of the advances and declines in business and our civilization as we know it today.

Definition of Knowledge Exchange This leaves us, finally, with a definition of knowledge exchange.

Chapter 5: Knowledge Networks, Neighborhoods, and Economics

KNOWLEDGE EXCHANGE The economic system through which people place value on the creation, storage, manipulation, distribution, and application of knowledge and define the terms under which they will participate in the knowledge economy.

Cultural Shift and New Technology Assimilation

Given this understanding of knowledge management, defined by knowledge neighborhoods and the rules of knowledge economics, we are ready to consider the many issues that these topics engender.

One of the most obvious, and yet overlooked, aspects of technological assimilation is the incredible impact it will have on the culture into which it is introduced. It is ironic that governments and corporations will spend millions of dollars studying and recognizing the impact that technologies have on "primitive" people, but almost everyone takes for granted the impact that the newer technologies have on "advanced" societies. (As a matter of fact, one of the most pronounced characteristics of our society is our ability to handle the massive amounts of cultural change that the constant assimilation of new technologies causes.)

The key to rapid deployment and economic capitalization of new technologies is mastering the cultural shifts they demand. This is especially important to the people who manage corporations since it applies as much to the survival and economic enrichment of a business as it does to the survival of a society. (In other words, the corporation that survives and thrives is the one with a culture and a group of people who can manage cultural adjustment quickly and effectively.) Unfortunately, what the introduction of new technologies usually creates first and foremost in the business is an awful lot of chaos.

Technological Impact on Cultural Memberships

While it is relatively easy to observe the effect that technology has on the culture of "primitive" people, trying to figure out how the latest technologies will impact our culture is much more difficult.

For example, the introduction of the gun and snowmobile to the Inuit peoples of Canada and Alaska caused them to make notable shifts in their life styles. When you can kill a polar bear from 500 yards away, you change the way you hunt significantly.

These cultural changes, however, are not so drastic that people abandon all of their values. Some values are changed, but, for the most part, the culture simply adjusts to the new reality. In the same way, the introduction of new Web warehousing technologies will force us to undergo some changes in our business and personal culture. These impacts can take many forms.

1. *New ways of getting things done.* New technologies provide people with new ways to get things done, which are usually easier, faster, more efficient, and more intuitively natural than previous generations of the technology.

2. *Elimination of people roles.* New technology often brings with it a reduction in the number of people needed to get things done. In other words, new technologies make people obsolete. This has been true throughout the history of technology and continues to be true with the latest generation of systems. It also continues to be true that, eventually, the economies manage to create new jobs in other places which more than make up for the temporary shortfall they create. (Consider the industrial revolution and its impact on jobs. Initially, it appeared that the factories would wipe out the "cottage industries" that dominated manufacturing before that time. In reality, the industrial revolution created more jobs than anyone could have imagined possible.)

3. *New roles and responsibilities.* New technologies create new jobs. Just think of any technology—electricity, the airplane, the computer—each brought with it new jobs, new careers, and new cultural identities. Clear your mind for a moment and then conjure up a picture for each of these words: *engineer, astronaut, pilot,* and *programmer.* Each "picture" associates with it a role and a status for the person who does the job. As the new Web warehousing technologies unfold, new roles will be invented for them too, and each of those roles will engender a status and a fit within the new culture that it creates.

4. *New relationships between parties.* Since the new technologies are creating new ways of doing things, eliminating some roles, changing others, and creating new ones, it should come as no surprise that the introduction of a new technology requires that people

renegotiate their relationships to each other. As the roles change, so does the status associated with them.

New Identities for People and a New Cultural Reality New technologies force us to redefine who we are and how we relate to each other. The same thing applies to the society or culture we belong to.

The process of this redefinition can be quite traumatic and painful for some people (especially to those who are at the heart of the change). Not only does the technology force us to make these adjustments, but it also puts in jeopardy many of the old standards and ways of doing things. This is where some serious conflicts can occur.

Cultural Membership and the Cultural Hierarchy

As soon as we probe the shifting cultural issues in the corporation, we open a virtual Pandora's box of related issues. The reason is that the people who work within a corporation actually subscribe to many different cultural identities simultaneously. If we try to measure, understand, and work with the cultural impacts that new technologies create, then we need to understand how they relate to each other in the face of the disruption of the status quo that they create.

This problem of redefinition and cultural chaos is exacerbated by the fact that people identify with more than one cultural group at any given time. Therefore, we need to also consider the consequences if the new technology creates a conflict for the individuals themselves when their own personal allegiances become conflicted.

Let's consider some of the different cultural memberships that employees of a company will subscribe to.

- *Personal image and personal values.* The first and often most difficult cultural characteristics to deal with are those associated with the individual and his or her own personal image and personal value issues. People have a complex network of beliefs and values that help them decide what to do and what not to do. Any plan to deploy new technologies requires people to assume new roles and responsibilities. It is critical that we understand the effect of new technology on the way people feel about themselves, in particular on their perception as to whether association with the technology will enhance or downgrade their status in the eyes of others.

- *Professional image and affiliations.* Strong cultural identification and participation also occur in the area of professional identity. Groups of people in the same profession often form strong organizational alignments that serve to reinforce and promote their identities both personally and economically. These groups can be especially resistant to the changes new technologies impose.
- *Corporate organizational memberships.* Within the corporate environment, one does not have to look far to find smaller groups which have their own identity and sense of loyalty. These organizational alignments can be based on geographic location, department, division, or even profession. In all cases, these groups will have something to say about how, when, and where new technologies will be deployed.
- *Corporate identity.* Despite the lower orders of cultural membership, people also feel that they belong to the overall culture of the corporation for which they work. This corporate identity brings with it certain attitudes of belonging, entitlement, and access to people, places, and things.
- *Citizenship and societal identity.* Beyond these other memberships is the people's sense of belonging to the city, state, country, and continent where they reside, and the different subcultures in which they participate.
- *Global and human affiliation.* Finally, people feel an affiliation with all other persons on the planet and a sense of the global community that we are all becoming part of.

The Cultural Hierarchy and Cultural Conflicts When we consider the many different groups a person may feel an affinity for, it should come as no surprise that the challenges of new technology assimilation are compounded by the fact that the individual may experience a personal conflict with the technology on any number of levels at the same time. For example, a person might personally feel that making more aggressive use of computers would be a fun thing to do, but membership in a professional group that frowns upon such things might discourage him or her.

An interesting study of precisely this kind of conflict can be seen in the ranks of corporate upper management today. For a very long time, the highest levels of management of big corporations refused to have anything to do with a computer. The use of computers was associated with clerks, secretaries, accountants, and nerds, not big-time executives. The recent explosion in the popularity of the use of the Internet has changed that for almost everyone. Use of the computer might be menial, but use of the Internet is absolutely acceptable and, suddenly, a new cultural norm is set.

Knowledge Exchange, New Technologies, and Their Role in History

Communications technologies have had an especially profound effect on cultures. When we look at the impact these special kinds of technologies have created, we gain an insight into what we can expect from this next generation of systems.

Knowledge Economics in Primitive Societies

Even the most primitive societies practice their own forms of knowledge economics. In these societies, different groups of people within the tribe hold the knowledge about different aspects of the real world. There are the "men's practices" and the "women's practices," there are the ways of the shamans, and the knowledge of the chiefs. In each of these cases, ritual, ceremony, and membership in a certain part of the culture determines who is allowed to know what skills and insights.

Men's and women's ways are taught to boys and girls through sophisticated rites of passage. The shaman takes an apprentice to be sure that knowledge is passed on to the next generation. The "council of elders" serves as the forum where special knowledge, special either because it is sacred or because it has to do with military intelligence, is shared, remembered, and manipulated.

Even in these societies, knowledge and its management serves as the underpinning for the entire social and economic order.

The Printing Press and the Industrial Revolution

One tends to forget, for example, that there was a time when the printing press represented a new technology. With the invention of this device came a cultural revolution so profound that there is almost nothing left of the way things were before. With the invention of the printing press came the ability to capture knowledge on paper and distribute it in ways never before possible. In the wake of the printing press came the Protestant Reformation, and the Renaissance with its associated recommitment to the pursuit of science. With its invention came the ability to build upon the knowledge of others, and greatly accelerate the rate at which things could be discovered, mastered, deployed, and assimilated.

Without a doubt, the invention of the printing press changed the rules of knowledge exchange for the society of the Middle Ages. Before that, only a small group of professional scholars and a select group of theologians even knew how to read or write. Consequently, the only way to transfer knowledge was through personal meetings and word of mouth.

The church and the kings of the day jealously protected access to knowledge, and this stranglehold on knowledge helped to keep them in power. It is no surprise that throughout history, some societies made it illegal for certain types of people to learn how to read. With the invention of the printing press, however, came the ability to teach the masses to read and to involve many people in the process of learning, growing, and changing.

Radio, Movies, and Nationalism

The next quantum leap in the area of communications technologies occurred with the invention of broadcast radio and movies. These media, again, greatly increased the amount of knowledge that could be distributed, and even more important, drastically changed the economic rules by which that distribution occurred. With radio and movies, people suddenly had the ability to communicate single, powerful, and motivating messages to extremely large groups at a very low cost. Before radio and movies, communication occurred in person or through the written word. So, a new level of knowledge distribution was created, and a new generation of people struggled with how it was to be managed and used to drive the economic machine of society.

Propaganda and Knowledge Control One of the first experiments in knowledge management on a massive scale occurred during the middle of the twentieth century. During that time, some governments began to understand the immense power that the media of radio and movies represent, and set out to consciously manipulate the way people feel, think, and act. These governments used the media to explicitly engineer their societies and change their cultures to fall into alignment with their plans.

The socialist and nationalist movements that overran Germany, Italy, and Japan were based upon the conscious cultural engineering envisioned by their leaders. Before the World War II was over, even the United States was involved in social engineering through movies and radio to the tune of several hundred pro-U.S. movies and radio programs.

Luckily, these attempts at social change through knowledge control have been permanently abandoned, but as each new generation of technology arises, we are faced with similar possibilities if we are not careful.

Television and the Global Community

Today, the entire world is engulfed by the next generation of experiments in knowledge management as people everywhere gain access to globally circulated movies, music, and television programs. The society and cultural standards of our world are homogenizing as more and more people fall under the spell of the latest generation of communications technologies.

Even this technology finds itself in the throes of battle over the distribution of knowledge as governments fight for the right to decide who gets to see what, where, when, and how. To this day, the citizens of Iraq, for example, are subjected to a completely different view of the world than those of the United States.

The Role of the Internet and Web Warehousing

Now, we find ourselves once again at the beginning of a revolution. The consequences of global communication (as in the broadcast media of the last generation) combined with the ability to communicate individually (as in email and Web sites) guarantee yet another round of issues about the control of the knowledge being distributed—and the economic benefits to be gained from it.

Knowledge Exchange, New Technologies, and Their Role in Business

Of course, there is no way that we could consider the economic consequences of knowledge management at the macro level of society at large without seeing a parallel and even more pronounced consequence in the world of business.

Throughout the history of business and technology, each generation of technological innovation has forced renegotiation of the relationship between customer, company, and employee. Each new technology, especially in communications, creates a new set of issues to be dealt with. Just imagine what this will mean over the next few years as the Web warehousing technologies start to take hold.

In the past, corporations needed to worry about only two kinds of knowledge management: management of data and of printed documents. In the case of data, business took control over the medium by building large, elaborate, complicated database systems to manage the security issues that the mass distribution of data can create. In the case of printed materials, knowledge was managed by controlling the physical distribution of the medium.

Let's now consider the world that the wholesale distribution of Web warehousing technology will create. Look at just a few of the Web-related court cases that are already being heard. Imagine a world where a memo sent by one corporate executive to another is intercepted by a corporate spy and immediately distributed, via email, to all of that company's competitors. Think about an inventor who cannot patent a new invention because the plans and details of it are immediately made available to everyone in the world. Picture a disgruntled employee who can send an email to everyone in the company, airing personal grievances, and calling for the other employees to rally around the cause. This world is not science fiction. It is the world that Web technology has already created, and it is only the beginning.

Chapter 5: Knowledge Networks, Neighborhoods, and Economics

> Every new medium that becomes available for manipulation by an organization or machine creates the need for another round of negotiation about what the rights to that knowledge are.

The Right to Knowledge—Special Consequences for Business

Let's consider, for a moment, some of the consequences this process will have on the workings of the business itself.

Cultural Conflicts across the Cultural Hierarchy of the Individual

We will see conflicts when individuals are allowed access to knowledge because of their membership and identification with a cultural group whose goals and objectives conflict with those of another group.

Right now, so much that happens within corporations occurs in little pockets. There is such a lack of communication in most corporations that it is a miracle anything gets done at all. The left hand often does not know what the right hand is doing. But what will happen when that changes and all of the little corners of the corporate world are brought into the light? What happens when people know exactly what other employees are doing? How will the individual handle the conflict?

For example, what happens when the employee of a computer software company, a person who believes in the process of free enterprise and the whole open systems movement, gains access to emails that describe how the company is planning to circumvent that process and unfairly monopolize the industry? A cultural conflict occurs. This person needs to choose between membership in the corporate culture and professional association with the larger industry to which he or she belongs.

Consider a company involved in doing experiments with dangerous chemicals. This firm may be building products that help protect farmland from infestation. But what happens when those experiments go awry? Suddenly, a lot of people in the company know something that they might feel the public should know about, while, of course, the management and stockholders of the firm would prefer that the public remain decidedly ignorant of the event.

In these cases, and in millions more just like them to come, corporations and individuals will have to learn how to deal with the new level of knowledge accessibility that Web warehousing provides.

Your Right to Knowledge Defines Your Economic Worth

These cultural conflict issues, however, are small change compared to the much bigger and more ominous consequences of new technology deployment in the business. Culture and value issues aside, the reality is that the deployment of any new technology of this kind could very well threaten your livelihood. It most certainly requires that you renegotiate your basic contract for employment. Let's consider why.

In a very literal sense, the very structure of the business and the subsequent definition of people's roles and relationships with one another within that business are defined by the rules that govern people's rights to different kinds of knowledge.

For example, in most situations, the boss has the right to know anything and everything that the employees know. That is part of what being the boss is all about. However, employees almost never have the right to know anything that the boss knows, unless the boss chooses to give them that information. The right to knowledge defines the very relationship.

Of course, the employees have some subtle ways of reattaining some of their knowledge power. Employees can simply choose not to pass on certain information to their bosses, or they can choose to allow the level of detail at which they work to obfuscate issues so that they maintain a level of control that they wouldn't otherwise have. In fact, one of the oldest and soundest strategies in business is to *make yourself indispensable* by knowing what your boss or others don't know. Of course, this personal survival strategy will no longer be effective once the corporation decides to capture all of the knowledge that is out there.

The Hard Economics of Knowledge Exchange

Let's take a much closer look at this aspect of knowledge economics and see how far-reaching the consequences could be for a few careers that we are all familiar with.

Sales People

Let's start with the role of the salesperson in the automotive industry, for example. In this industry, the salesperson is the primary agent through which cars are sold to individuals. The entire economics of the automotive business is based upon a model that dictates that manufacturers work with dealers who employ sales people who work with customers.

Now what is the role of that salesperson? There are several.

- The salesperson is an educator, telling the customers everything about the car they want to know. The salesperson provides customers with technical, emotional, historical, and experiential information about the car they are looking at, and this information helps them make a decision.
- The salesperson is an agent, simplifying the process of working with the dealer. The salesperson helps the customer choose financing, order special options, and put together a complete sales package.
- Finally, the salesperson is a negotiator, driving the best deal possible between the customer and the dealer.

But what happens when all the information about the cars and the mechanics of putting together financing and special car options can all be managed by a Web application? The answer is obvious: You no longer need the car salesperson. The role of the salesperson is being weakened as the strength of the knowledge management capabilities of computers continues to grow.

Doctors

While it is unlikely that the role of the doctor will be reduced to quite the degree of the salesperson's, the effects will be felt here too. Even in the medical field, knowledge management is forcing a renegotiation of doctors' roles and the economic worth of the job they perform.

Where is this happening? On several fronts simultaneously.

First and foremost is the area of medical knowledge itself. In the past, and until quite recently, the sum total of current medical knowledge that doctors could apply to problems had to be stored inside their heads. There were many medical books available to consult, but medical problems can be so multidimensional, and the sources of information so diverse, that only a human brain was capable of cataloging and using knowledge in a time frame useful for diagnosis purposes.

Fortunately, that has begun to change. Large medical databases, full of compilations of medical histories, diagnoses, and applications, are now available. These medical knowledge bases make it possible for doctors to input symptoms and conditions and be rewarded with immediate possible diagnoses in less time than it takes to formulate the question. One result is that doctors no longer need to try to memorize and remember everything. The other is that they are beginning to loose their grip on the status, prestige, and financial security they once enjoyed.

But this is only one aspect of the ways in which the medical profession is loosing its foundation to technology. On the business side, doctors are succumbing to the mind-numbing level of detail that they have to administer in dealing with hospitals, insurance companies, government agencies, and individuals, by outsourcing the management of the marketing and business knowledge to the specialty medical centers and HMOs. Consequently, doctors are losing the business relationships and knowledge about their customers (patients), suppliers (insurance companies), and industry groups and thereby undermining their financial power even further.

In both cases, loss of control of the knowledge is causing a loss in economic power.

Consultants

One of the most obvious and difficult professions to wrestle with issues of knowledge economics is that of consultants. Consultants, after all, are paid for only one thing: the knowledge they bring to the business they consult with.

How then do consultants feel about the idea of transferring their knowledge into a computer for others to use? They are not too excited about it. Nevertheless, the consulting profession, along with every other profession, will have to undergo major retrofitting and renegotiation of employment relationships before Web warehousing technologies find their way into the mainstream of corporate business.

Without a doubt, as these new Web warehousing technologies are deployed, we will see some pretty dramatic shifts in the status, compensation, and personal prestige that different participants in society will be able to command.

Special Web Warehousing Considerations

Until now, we have limited our discussion on the issues of knowledge economics to data and the written word. But stop and consider for a moment how much greater the conflicts will be as companies and individuals collect knowledge bases full of video clips, audio recordings, fingerprints, and all of the other media that the Web now makes accessible to us. The consequences could very well be staggering, and are most probably beyond our ability to anticipate at this time.

The History of Knowledge Exchange Conflict Resolution in Business

Although we are currently placing a lot of emphasis on the issues of knowledge exchange and conflict over the ownership of knowledge at a very explicit level, that is not to say that the business and computer industries have no experience in dealing with such issues. On the contrary, the history of computer systems' deployment is one of conflict resolution in precisely these areas. In general, the developers of business computer systems have, over the decades, come to develop two paradigms for understanding and dealing with these security and ownership issues.

Security Issues The most obvious battlefield on which issues of right of access to computers get resolved is in software security systems. These systems "secure" information and limit access. In their heyday, corporate security packages were incredibly large, complex, and sophisticated, and attempted to ease the many headaches that security issues always create. Unfortunately, the recent popularity of open systems and personal computers has left most corporate software security systems in a shambles. The new generation of Web technology provides even less security.

One of the biggest consequences, therefore, of the full-scale deployment of Web warehousing and e-business solutions will be a massive reinvestment in the development of corporate security systems. There is a need for security systems that will be able to handle data, text, and multimedia and allow the soon-to-be-developed rules of knowledge access to be enforced.

Ownership Issues Another way to address issues of access rights to knowledge is to declare them ownership issues and to pass them to the people financing the system for a ruling. Since business systems, after all, are created to make money, the people holding the purse strings make the major decisions.

How Business Resolves Conflicts Regarding the Right to Knowledge

When a simple yes/no answer, or the application of security software, or the invocation of a management ruling fails to resolve knowledge exchange issues, then the computer systems department has to come up with a more "ergonomic" approach to the problem. In general, the developer of a new system will attempt to resolve these issues through the following means:

- *Overt negotiation.* Trying to get the conflicting participants to agree to a compromise.
- *Promotion.* Trying to convince people that changing their status and power has positive effects.
- *Attrition.* Removing the people who went by the old rules and replacing them with those who learn the new rules as the only rules.
- *Structural reorganization.* Changing people's official status to reflect the new, desired order.
- *Structural disintegration.* Eliminating certain organization areas with the intent of allowing other people to figure out how to get the job done.
- *Systemic.* Letting the group gradually migrate to the new set of rules.

Consequences of Knowledge Exchange Conflict on System Developers Developers of Web warehousing systems are just about guaranteed to face issues about the right to knowledge and knowledge exchange in the near future. It is critically important that they be well informed as to the nature of the problems and the options for their resolution.

System developers have dealt with these issues for years and never realized their underlying import. For the developers of Web warehousing systems, then, it is critical that they:

1. Be aware that the issues are there, and be ready to address them squarely and overtly whenever possible. (It is easier to resolve conflicts when everyone understands what the real problems are.)

2. Recognize the issues and build capabilities into the system to address and minimize conflicts. (For example, the presence of good security mechanisms can do a lot to resolve these issues.)
3. Be prepared for the worst. This means that: (*a*) You will see good systems fail to be built simply because these issues could not be resolved to everyone's satisfaction. (*b*) You will need to make your systems a lot more complicated than you would like in order to build in all of this security.

Secondary Cultural Conflicts

While the resolution of the primary economic concerns of individuals will be your first concern, cultural conflicts will make themselves felt in the secondary areas as well. Unfortunately, most individuals are unfamiliar with the concepts of knowledge economics, and most will fail to realize what the consequences of the deployment of these new technologies will be. People's self-images, the convenience that systems provide them, and the restructuring of their roles and the workplace at large will all serve to make the end user of the future a tough customer to deal with.

Fortunately, with the shift that the overall society is making in this direction, and the globalization of technologies and functions, the job of getting users to integrate new technology into their work lives is getting easier. We do, however, have to recognize the critical role that promotion has in the overall process, and the importance of continued development of useful, engaging visioning processes that can make integration easier.

Knowledge Management Consequences for the Systems Development Life Cycle

Our main purpose in this exploration is to obtain a much better understanding of the systems development life cycle as it used to be practiced, and as it will have to be practiced in the future.

Up to this point, we have considered different aspects and disciplines of the knowledge management approach to business. They provide the developers of Web warehousing systems with insights and guidelines that can help them anticipate many of the challenges they are most likely to face, and provide them with specific remedies for many of them. Among the disciplines we have considered have been:

1. *The value chain.* The value chain describes the major functional components of the business which work together to allow people to coordinate their knowledge creation, collection, and application activities in order to deliver value to customers. By understanding what the corporation's value chain is and how it works, the developers of Web technology can quickly identify those areas of the business that can best be aided by the application of the new technology. Web warehousing solutions can be used to help organizations:

    a. Make individual links in the value chain work more effectively by using technology to more efficiently share knowledge within the link (systems like text sharing applications, for example, which allow members of the knowledge neighborhood to share access to a common set of documents in their area of expertise).

    b. Make the overall business run more effectively by better bridging knowledge gaps between the different links (with value chain software, such as efficient customer response systems, which streamline the corporate value chain, thereby making the delivery of goods and services to customers faster and more efficient).

2. *The value proposition.* The value proposition, or specifically the application value proposition, describes the criteria we use to define which applications we want to apply to the business, and a method for assigning a valuation to them. The value proposition is a statement, made by a businessperson, that says that if the Web warehousing capability were to be delivered, then that business area would see an easily recognized benefit to the company, in terms of increased revenue, decreased cost, increased market share, or any other valuation scheme. Making the development of application value propositions a key ingredient of Web warehousing deployment strategies is a technique that can help guarantee that every application that is deployed will:

    a. Have an immediate, tangible, recognizable value to the business.

    b. Have a predefined, proactive knowledge neighborhood interested in making use of it.

3. *The new technology assimilation cycle.* We described the series of steps that every new technology goes through as it moves from its creation to the point where it is considered a necessity by the people who use it. We found that understanding this cycle can allow us to look at a new Web warehousing technology and quickly assess exactly where

it is in the life cycle, and therefore, what we have to do to make it useful. This cycle includes:

  a. Creation of the basic new functionality.

  b. Development of operational principles (mechanical and architectural). During this stage, people determine exactly how to build the new creation. This includes establishing the detailed mechanical principles that make the system work, and the architectural principles by which a large functional system is assembled from the discrete technological parts.

  c. Modeling and Visioning. During these stages, people figure out how to make the new technology useful and fit it into their day-to-day lives. Modeling and Visioning occur on the operational, organizational, functional, and financial levels.

  d. Promotion. During this phase, aggressive developers and investors take the story to the people. Consumers are encouraged to accept the new technology and give up their old ways of doing things. Promotion is really the process of overcoming the natural inertia and resistance to change that most people have when presented with new ways of doing things. In the Web warehousing world, the job of promotion is a burden shared by product sales people and the computer systems department.

  e. Acceptance. At this point, the product has been accepted by most people. The new technology acceptance cycle is at an end, and the technology follows a normal product life cycle.

  f. Dependence. Now, the new technology is no longer new. In some situations, it can be considered something that everybody must have in order to function.

4. *Modeling.* This is the process whereby the organization figures out exactly how the new technology will fit into the day-to-day running of the business. Modeling is purely a conceptual process, many times occurring automatically, and involving the development of models that describe how the technology will fit functionally, operationally, financially, and organizationally.

5. *Visioning.* In visioning, people use the new models to work with a technology and turn it into a set of viable, personal, acceptable practices which they can employ in the future. While modeling is a conceptual process, visioning is an experiential one. People use techniques such as seminars, discussions, training, role playing, and game playing to accomplish visioning objectives.

6. *Knowledge neighborhoods.* Knowledge neighborhoods are groups of people who share a common interest in the execution of a particular link of the value chain, a common vocabulary, a common view of the world, and common objectives. The knowledge neighborhood is the primary building block of a knowledge management–based systems development scheme.

7. *Knowledge exchange.* Knowledge exchange is the set of rules that the members of a community use to establish the value placed on different parts of the knowledge creation, storage, manipulation, and application process. The rules of knowledge exchange change whenever a new technology is introduced to the organization, and the Web warehousing developer needs to be aware of these issues and be ready to address them as part of the system development process.

We conclude on the basis of these insights that the currently understood systems development life cycle falls far short of providing developers with everything they need to do an effective job of Web warehousing development. (The "classical" definition of the systems development life cycle includes such approaches as business case development, collecting user requirements, and establishing return on investment, but they are much too generalized to be useful.) Therefore, a newer, more robust systems development life cycle is needed that:

- Is based on the formal definition and understanding of the corporation's value chain strengths, weaknesses, and strategic directions, and the composition of existing and future knowledge neighborhoods.
- Involves the identification and classification of Web warehousing applications in light of the specific application's position within the new technology assimilation life cycle.
- Includes the specific requirement that developers provide value chain analysis, value propositions, explicit modeling definitions, plans to enable the visioning process, and an analysis of the security, cultural, and economic impact of the technology on the knowledge networks on which it will be imposed.

In other words, the successful deployment of Web warehousing solutions and other new technologies will depend more and more on the effective understanding and application of knowledge management principles to the overall systems development process.

PART 2

Web Warehousing in Action

"Products, tools, and specific business applications turn the high-level business vision promised by knowledge management, and the detailed, technical foundation provided by Web warehousing into something of true business value. The organization of people, data, multimedia, and computational capabilities into living systems that actually accomplish their goals is what Web warehousing is all about."

—Rob Mattison

CHAPTER 6

Traditional Warehousing

Architecture and Technology

- *What is a data warehouse?*
- *What is a data mart?*
- *What is the theory behind data warehousing?*
- *What are the major components of a data warehouse?*
- *Where do data warehouses come from?*
- *What is the underlying physical architecture of a traditional data warehouse?*
- *What are the rules for data warehouse architecture design?*
- *What is an operational infrastructure?*
- *How are data warehousing environments managed?*

Introduction

In the first chapter of this book, we consider some of the history, background, and business value that data warehousing has to offer. In several subsequent chapters, we take a closer look at the physical workings of the Web environment. Now, however, we talk about exactly what a data warehouse is, and, more important, how it is physically put together.

To be able to describe how a Web warehousing environment should be constructed, we have to first understand how the traditional data warehouse environment is put together. That will be the objective for this chapter. In the next several chapters, we will take a fresh look at the Web and see how that physical environment is set up. Armed with this background, we will then be able to combine what we know about the Web environment with our understanding of the data warehousing environment and assemble a pretty good picture of how the Web warehousing environment can be architected effectively.

To appreciate how the data warehousing environment is built, however, it will be helpful to answer such questions as: What is behind data warehousing? What is the history of legacy systems development?

The Theory of Data Warehousing

While we have also looked at some of the history of data warehousing, we never really set out to describe the theory behind it. It should come as no surprise that, like most things in business, the theory behind data warehousing is an economic (money-based) one.

The Nature of Information Systems Architecture BDW (Before Data Warehouses)

Anyone familiar with the history of data processing in the business world knows that databases and reporting systems have been around almost as long as computers have. These same amateur historians will also quickly be able to tell you that the business user's need for newer, better, faster, and more accurate information has always been insatiable.

What then is the big fuss about data warehousing? How is data warehousing different from anything before? And how did we end up doing it this way today? These are good questions.

Chapter 6: Traditional Warehousing

The First Generation of Computer Systems Back in the "Stone Age" of computer information systems, the world was a much simpler place. The early computer technology consisted of very, very large mainframe computers, which were fed instructions and data with punched cards and large reels of magnetic tape. In those days, information systems were very simple, very focused, and very operational in nature.

For example, you might have had a payroll system that kept track of payroll records and wrote checks, or an accounting system that kept track of the general ledger.

In these kinds of situations, the user's need for information was simple and straightforward—summary reports and tabular reports that proved that the books balanced, for instance. In these cases, there was no sharing of information between systems, and there was no need to analyze data too deeply. See Figure 6-1.

Second-Generation Systems Environment As computers became more powerful and businesses became more sophisticated, however, information management needs changed. During this time period, tapes and punched cards were replaced with direct-access storage devices (DASD), also known as *disk drives*. With the creation of disk drives and on-line terminals came all sorts of new applications. Eventually, the first generation of databases was developed, together with products such as IMS (Information Management System) and IDMS (Information Data Management System).

Suddenly, we found that the businessperson's need for information changed. Computer systems were not just doing special-purpose, isolated tasks anymore. It became possible for computers to actually start running these businesses. With real-time databases and terminals, it was

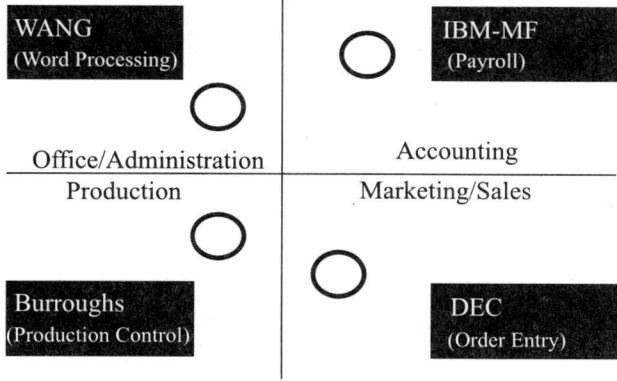

Figure 6-1
First-generation information systems.

suddenly possible to create organizations that could function on a scale never before imagined, because companies could use the computer's ability to keep track of details to coordinate everybody's activities across time and distance.

With this expanded role of importance on the business scene came a huge increase in the demand for information. Now that everything done in the business was being captured on the computer, all kinds of additional reports were required.

At this time, the need for reporting, however, was not too different than it was earlier. It was just that people wanted more and more of it. In response to this demand, some crude report writing packages were developed, but with limited usefulness. The vast majority of reports were still written in COBOL by the information technology (I/T) department.

While the demand for the number and types of reports increased, another phenomenon occurred. As more and more operational systems were created (systems such as payroll, accounts payable, and production control), a new kind of information requirement was born. It was a demand for information that combined the data from two or more of these other systems. In most cases, the need for this kind of reporting was met by the creation of a special reporting program. Occasionally, however, it was decided that there were so many combined data reports required that a more formal "bridge system" was needed. Bridge systems extracted data from the two sources in question and placed them into a separate, special reporting database, which could then be used to generate these hybrid reports.

Hybrid reporting database systems represent the first generation of true data warehousing applications. They were given cute names such as "the PHOENIX system" or clever acronyms such as CRAS (Combined Reporting and Accounting System) or CORE (Consolidated Operational Reporting Environment), and allowed to function as free-standing systems. See Figure 6-2. Notice the degree of data sharing and interdependency in the second-generation environment.

The Relational Database Era Is Born As time went on, systems got bigger and bigger. Organizations got larger, more diversified, and more complex. Eventually, there were so many individual operational systems and hybrid systems that the existing technology could not handle them all. In an early attempt to address the pending data management problems that were looming on the corporate horizon, the relational database was invented.

Unfortunately, while the relational database did make it easier to get reports out of the databases (using the SQL language), it did nothing to

Chapter 6: Traditional Warehousing

Figure 6-2
Second-generation systems.

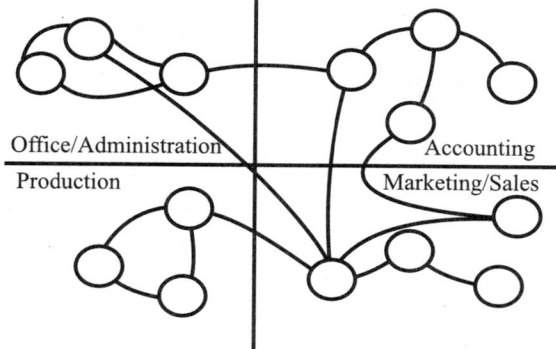

slow the upward surge in computer systems growth—more legacy systems, more needs for reporting, more specialized, hybrid reporting systems, and no end in sight to the growth of the environment.

In addition to the continuing problems associated with the management of data that must be combined from multiple systems, there is the business's needs for new, different, and more expansive free-standing systems, and more in-depth analysis of them. These needs often made it necessary for the I/T departments to create new reporting systems with these new capabilities even when no additional data source was required.

The Client/Server Revolution About the time when everyone thought that corporate computer systems were going to fall apart because they were getting too big, complex, and unmanageable, along came the client/server revolution. The makers of personal computers, UNIX servers, and a host of personal and departmental support software told people that the solution to their problems was to downsize their I/T and to expand into the client/server world instead.

With this advice, people jumped onto the PC/open systems client/server bandwagon with both feet. However, the effect was the opposite of the one desired. Instead of simplifying the environment and reducing data management complexity, this new revolution made it all worse.

More data was stored, in more kinds of databases, serving more business areas, than ever before. What was needed was a way to finally get ahead of this data quicksand, a way to efficiently and effectively provide consolidated reporting, without building customized, hybrid reporting systems each time. See Figure 6-3. Notice, when the client/server revolution occurs, how much more complex everything becomes. Hundreds and thousands of personal computers appear, hooking up to hundreds of

Figure 6-3
Client/server revolution.

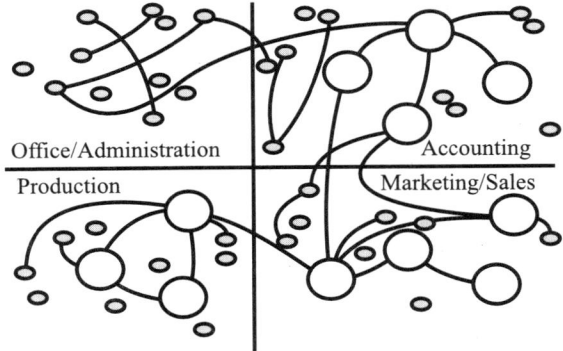

servers, which must all in turn somehow synchronize with all of the legacy system activity that was already present.

The Data Warehousing World Somewhere along the line several people had a clever idea. Why don't we stop pretending and recognize that these interim, intermediary reporting databases and systems are an afterthought? Why don't we stop fighting this overwhelming deluge of computer systems, and start figuring out how to harness their power instead? What if we start developing sophisticated tools, methodologies, and approaches that will enable us to manage this "after the fact" non-operational data with the same professionalism and discipline with which we manage the operational information? Couldn't we, in fact, find some cost savings if we started to attack this informational glut with centralized approaches and discipline? Wouldn't you think that we could experience some economies of scale if we stopped developing hundreds of free-standing information repositories and built one central repository instead?

In short, that is the business justification and the theory behind data warehousing.

What Is a Data Warehouse?

From this background, the data warehousing movement was born. Throughout the rest of this chapter, we will be spending a lot of time considering why data warehouses are built and how.

At this point, however, let us stop for a moment to propose a definition.

Chapter 6: Traditional Warehousing

DATA WAREHOUSE *Any of a large variety of computer systems initiatives, whose primary purpose is to extract information out of legacy systems, and make it usable to business people, in the support of their efforts to reduce costs and improve revenues.*

Later in this chapter, we will spend quite a bit of time talking about some of the different approaches to building warehouses and managing them, but ultimately this simple objective is what all of them are about.

The Economic Justification for Data Warehousing

To appreciate the underlying justification for a data warehouse, let's look at some simple economics. Assume that an organization has several different areas, each with its own information systems, and each with the need for a new kind of reporting environment. See Figure 6-4.

In this example, we have a situation where four different areas of the business all decide that they need to enhance their information reporting capabilities. Each new system will make use of information coming from the plethora of operational and reporting systems that support the area, and all four will require the creation of yet another reporting environment with its own hardware, software, and support staff. See Figure 6-5.

In a situation like this, it is easy to imagine an environment where these four systems could be delivered at a much lower cost, if they could share the underlying infrastructure costs. See Figure 6-6. Of course, while this explanation certainly describes what can be considered to be

Figure 6-4
Business needs for new kinds of information.

Operationally Focused Systems

Overall Trends Analysis	*Customer Tracking*
Management	Marketing
Production Control	Finance
Manufacturing Tracking	*Integrated Portfolios*

Figure 6-5
Autonomous information delivery solutions.

The need for decentralization and tactical solutions.

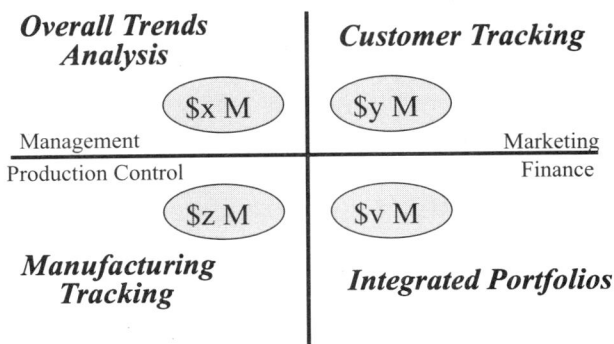

Figure 6-6
Economies of scale through centralization.

Leveraging efficiencies between applications

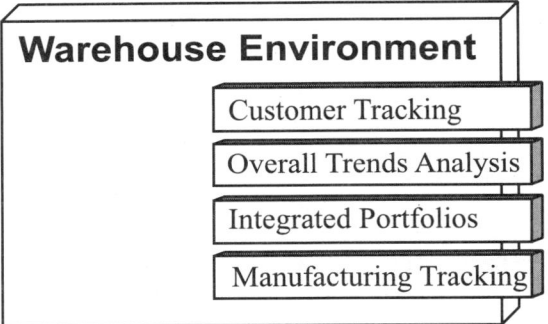

the "common understanding" of what data warehousing is all about, it actually is not quite that simple. Several factors make accomplishing this objective extremely difficult.

Barriers to Successful Data Warehousing

The perfectly obvious and apparently simple approach of creating a centralized information and reporting environment that can be shared by many different parts of the business often turns out to be an incredibly difficult process. Several factors seem to conspire to make this the case.

There are three areas in particular where major problems occur again and again:

1. *Problems with data sourcing.* Converting legacy system data into a usable form for some other system is a very difficult process.
2. *Problems with systems specification.* With new technologies and new approaches, users can face serious struggles in figuring out just exactly what they would like the system to do.
3. *Problems with business prioritization and organizational struggle.* These are also known as "political problems."

Let's look at these three problem areas in some greater detail, and see if we cannot gain some useful understanding of the challenges that we will face when we try to build a data warehouse (whether it is a traditional or Web-based one).

Data Sourcing Challenges

The biggest single problem that people run into when they try to do data warehousing is that of trying to find the data that they want to put into the warehouse in the first place. The problems of data sourcing have turned out to be so common that many organizations have started to refer to their data warehouses as *data horror houses.*

It seems that, without fail, every organization needs to make the same basic mistake when it comes to their legacy systems data. What is this problem, and how does it occur? A typical scenario goes something like this:

A business area decides that it needs new kinds of informational reports. The existing reports are slow, outdated, and full of ambiguous and meaningless information.

The business manager calls the I/T department and a new set of reports—data warehousing reports—is designed. The users are encouraged to be creative and really think about all of the different kinds of information that they would like to have. They will be using a data warehouse this time, so it would be best to get all of the important information identified and stored in the warehouse right away.

So the requirements are collected, the reports are designed, the budget for new hardware and software is approved, and the system developers start building the warehouse.

The Typical Systems Development Life Cycle Usually, developers use the following system development approach.

1. Design the reports that the user is looking for.
2. Design the database that will hold the required information.
3. Locate the data necessary to load these databases.
4. Load the databases and produce the reports.

Our project will go along smoothly—until step 3. At this point, things usually grind to a screeching halt. The problem is that when I/T people go to the legacy systems to get the data needed for the reports, they encounter all kinds of problems they never anticipated. They discover that the information they need is not so easily found. In fact, sometimes they learn that the information does not exist anywhere. And so, in a great many cases, the developers of the data warehouse project find that they must either cancel the project or greatly increase the allotted budget. It usually turns out that it will be a lot more expensive and complicated to load the data warehouse than originally imagined.

Common Data Sourcing Problem Areas How can this be? How could the developers possibly go through the process of conceiving, designing, and building a warehouse and not realize that the data is not available? How could the users who made up the specifications for the system not know that the information they want is unavailable? It just does not seem to make any sense.

Sadly, this happens all the time. In fact, I am not aware of *any* data warehousing project where this is not the case at least once. But how does it happen? Well, there are several reasons, some obvious and some not so obvious. Some of the bigger reasons include:

1. The complexity of the underlying legacy systems. By far, the number one reason that people find themselves caught short in the data sourcing game is the simple fact that they greatly underestimate exactly how complex the underlying legacy systems really are. Users tend to base their impressions of information systems on the parts that they see, not on what is happening under the covers. Layer upon layer of legacy system, each with a serious amount of overlap with other legacy systems in the same environment, conspire to create an environment where it is almost impossible to sort out the underlying detail on which decisions are based.

2. Conflicting interpretations of the meaning and sources of the data. Even in those situations where the information required is easy to find, you can still run into problems when two groups of users insist on interpreting the same numbers differently. In these situations, many hours of the developers' time can be spent in trying to help business people resolve their philosophical and numerical differences.

3. False confidence based on legacy system reports. When users look at the reports that come out of legacy systems, they tend to accept them at face value without questioning how the numbers were derived. Unfortunately, those legacy report numbers have often been "adjusted" for any number of reasons, and those "adjustments" can be misleading.

4. Blind faith and assumptions. People just assume that the information they want must be located someplace.

As we have already stated, the problems associated with legacy system data sourcing is no small part of the challenge of data warehousing. In fact, it is by far the number one expense of almost every project. Numbers quoted by experienced data warehousing professionals indicate that anywhere from 50 to 80 percent of the data warehousing budget should be allocated to this part of the process. As we proceed with the development of a physical model for the warehousing environment, our design will be affected a lot by this factor.

System Specifications Challenges

The second area of data warehousing challenges is no less painful and surprising than the first. It concerns the process of figuring out exactly what it is you would like the data warehouse to do. In many situations, determining what kind of output the warehouse should produce can be an extremely challenging exercise in and of itself. Why is the question of what kinds of reports to create such a big challenge?

There are many reasons for this phenomenon as well. Some of the contributing factors are discussed below.

The Paradigm Shift Problem Without a doubt, much of the confusion in figuring out what to do with a data warehouse application occurs because people do not understand how the new technologies can be leveraged.

New technologies such as data warehousing and data mining represent a much bigger change to the businessperson than just the simple replacement of one kind of reporting tool with another. Data warehouses make more information available to business people than ever before imagined, and they make that information more accessible, more manipulatable, and more analyzable than ever before.

Unfortunately, a group of users who have never been exposed to this kind of power and capability are often left at a loss. Several interesting kinds of aborted data warehousing attempts can occur in these cases.

Sometimes, some very smart, business-savvy, proficient designers will build a data warehouse application with all of the latest, greatest, and most sophisticated capabilities. After the system is deployed, however, management often finds that none of the real end users will have anything to do with it.

In other situations, users will get involved in the purchase of a new, high-powered end-user reporting tool (such as OLAP), and then a system gets designed with it that would be better delivered by using older report writer types of technology.

In many situations, the computer systems and data warehousing professionals are more excited about the technology than the end users. This is, of course, understandable, but it also can be fatal to the project's success. What is required, in these cases, is a process whereby end users can become familiar with what these technologies have to offer, and develop an understanding of how they can be leveraged to their advantage.

We spend some time considering the issues of business value and paradigm shift management in the Web warehousing environment in the chapters about knowledge management.

Unfamiliarity with Tools and Techniques Another big reason that organizations have trouble getting data warehousing requirements done well is that many of the end-user reporting tools are so new and unconventional in their approach that many people have trouble figuring out what to do with them.

A good example is OLAP tools. One OLAP tool vendor we worked with traveled around the world, giving demonstrations that showed off how well the tool managed the inventory of a hypothetical store. Unfortunately, the vendor gave the same demonstrations to telecommunications, retailers, banking, insurance, and manufacturing companies without any attempt to gear the presentation to the specific industry. The net result was a lot of confusion; the customers got angry and asked, "What does *this* have to do with *my business*?"

Indistinct Business Case Development Even when the users and the systems development team know how to use the tools in question, there is still usually a challenge associated with figuring out what specific business problem the warehouse is being targeted to solve. Again and again, we face user groups that say they need a database to support marketing, and insist that that is all the detail needed to put a business case together. Typically, the end users get excited about general concepts and broad, far-reaching ideas, but get a lot less enthusiastic when pressed for the details. A fuzzy requirement for a data warehouse can do a lot more damage than no requirement at all. Successful warehousing requires that users and developers jointly develop good, solid business cases for the systems they are building.

User Reluctance to Change Not to be missed on our list of reasons for trouble in figuring out what to do with a warehouse is the situation where end users do not want to get involved in the design because they are resistant to change. Forcing users to go through the process of learning new tools, new approaches, and new technologies is an uphill battle any way you look at it. The smart developer figures out ways to minimize this impact on the users and maximize the benefits they receive.

Political Issues

In some cases, data warehouse developers will find that they have mastered or avoided the problems of data sourcing and requirements development, but still run into grief. This time the problem comes from political struggles in the organization.

Data warehouses are typically large, expensive, powerful additions to the corporate armory. They require large capital outlays and the dedication of a large number of resources, and usually produce systems that deliver potent, useful, and actionable information. Because data warehouses involve all of that, they usually loom large on the political playing field of most organizations for several reasons, including:

1. The budget levels are typically high. A lot of money requires much political concurrence from many areas of the business.

2. The information that data warehouses carry often crosses organizational boundary lines, combining information sources from two or more distinct organizations. When this happens, the organizational units in question often become concerned about any shift in power that the new system may represent.

3. Even when a new system does not cross organizational lines, the issue of "who will own the system" often arises.

Political issues, such as paradigm adjustment issues, are a subtle but critical piece of the data warehouse development puzzle. Our chapters about knowledge management consider these political aspects of systems development as well.

Really Bad Data Warehousing Approaches

Given all of this information, then, we can see that there are many challenges for the data warehouse builder to face. In fact, many, many books have been written about the best way to build a data warehouse. Unfortunately, not all of these approaches work equally well. In fact, some are actually disastrous. Let's look at a couple of the worst.

The "Build It and They Will Come" or "Dump and Run" Model

According to this model for data warehouse design, the best way to build a data warehouse is to simply gather up all of the data that the organization has and dump it into a large, well-organized data warehouse environment. Then, after all the data has been cataloged and loaded, we can turn to the users and say, "Okay, all of the data is here. Come and get it!" See Figure 6-7 (the PM in the figure stands for "pure magic," which is what supposedly happens to make this data useful).

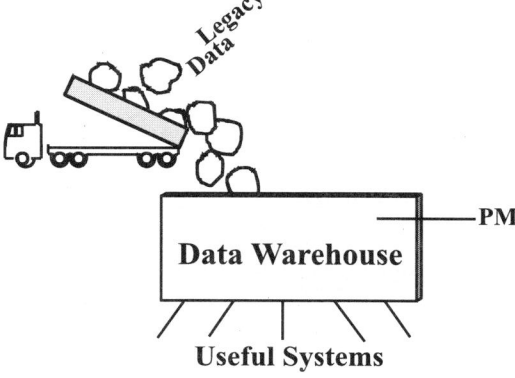

Figure 6-7
The "dump and run" model of data warehousing.

Unfortunately, this approach never works very well. There are several causes for this, but the biggest reasons are:

1. There is a very good chance that you will never get to the point of telling the users that you are done and that they can now come and get it. It is very easy for projects like this to go on forever, with no business value delivered anywhere along the way.
2. If you do actually "finish" building the warehouse, the chance of users actually caring about using it is slight. (See the issues about specifications gathering in "System Specifications Challenges," earlier in this chapter.)
3. Finally, even if you finish and actually get specifications, the chances are very good that you will have gathered the *wrong data,* and that you will have to go back and get different data from the legacy systems anyway. User requirements are very broad, and the stores of legacy data almost infinite. No one has figured out a better way to get data requirements from users than to ask them what they need to know.

These aborted projects are among the most abysmal and expensive in the history of data processing, and there are dozens of multi-million-dollar "bombs" of this nature to point to within the industry.

The Data Mart Mania Approach

An alternative approach that some organizations take is to stay away from building any kind of large, centralized warehouse. These organizations prefer to build many little "data marts" instead. Each business problem, each user, each tool gets its own mart (or marts).

This approach is by far preferable to the first approach. In the data mart mania mode, the business people at least get short-term, recognizable value for the data warehousing efforts.

The downside of this approach is that:

1. You get no leverage or economies of scale.
2. You create many schisms within the data architecture, and it gets more and more difficult for people to get an accurate, consolidated view of the business.
3. You can also create a technological morass of momentous proportion. Hundreds of little marts, on hundreds of platforms distrib-

uted around the world, can tend to create a maintenance headache that is difficult to imagine.

Data Warehousing Approaches That Work

While the approaches mentioned above exemplify two extreme ends of the warehousing approach spectrum, there is clearly a lot of middle ground that can be considered. Some of the less extreme solutions which seem to have done well include approaches that use centralized data warehouses to support all of the business's needs, and others that use a limited number of well-managed mega-data marts.

In general, however, most organizations find that a hybrid approach, one that sees the realistic deployment of warehouses and marts where each makes the most sense economically and technically, has been the most successful.

Data Warehouse versus Data Mart

This is probably a good time to clear up a couple of terminology issues. One of the many inane controversies in data warehousing centers around the definition of the terms *data warehouse* and *data mart*. While almost everybody feels that the two are somehow related, no one seems to agree on exactly what the terms mean and what the differences between them are.

There are three general schools of thought, each believing that size, user population, and content, respectively, define the difference between marts and warehouses.

1. Some practitioners hold to the belief that data warehouses are large, enterprise-wide repositories of data which are designed to meet *all* of the informational needs of the organization. These same practitioners will then state that data marts are smaller, departmentally based "mini" data warehouses that meet the specific needs of a smaller group of users.

2. Others believe that the difference between a mart and a warehouse is determined organizationally, by how many people use it. They believe that any data environment, no matter what size, is a warehouse if it meets the needs of two or more groups of users, and is a mart if only one group utilizes it (regardless of what it contains).

3. Still others believe that the differentiation is based on content, stating that a warehouse is any data environment that manages information from two or more subject areas, while data marts are data environments that manage information about only one subject area (regardless of size).

As far as we are concerned, the differentiation of these two terms has become so muddled, controversial, and meaningless that we just use the two terms interchangeably. At best we use the terms *data mart* and *data warehouse* to differentiate the size of the warehousing efforts, with marts being smaller and warehouses larger.

Typical Architectural Deployment Models

Typical data warehouse and data mart deployment models include the following:

1. *Departmentally based marts.* Organizations deploy marts based on organizational structure. Warehousing efforts are centralized and leveraged up to the departmental level, but no effort to consolidate at higher levels is attempted.
2. *Enterprise-wide shared master warehouse.* Organizations create a centralized enterprise-wide warehouse environment. All departments come to this central location to get their information processing needs met.
3. *The two-tiered "waterfall" model.* This is an interesting model that attempts to split the difference between the two above.
    a. Under this scenario, a large, enterprise-level data warehouse is developed to serve as the centralized clearinghouse for all data acquisition and preliminary storage efforts. The mission of this warehouse is to make all data at a very granular and nonspecific level available for the use of the entire organization.
    b. When individual departmental groups need information, their first option is to go directly to the "big" warehouse to get it. If, however, they need to have a more specialized subset of information, which is better defined, consolidated, and formatted in a manner specific to their needs, then a data mart is developed and deployed instead. This mart, however, will still use the data warehouse as its primary source of data.
    c. By using this model, the organization is able to leverage the strengths that centralized data acquisition and storage offer,

while at the same time gaining the flexibility and convenience of the smaller departmental-type solutions.

The Need for Balance

In general, any of a variety of architectural approaches can serve the organization well. There is clearly never any one right or wrong approach to architecting these environments, because every organization has its own needs and infrastructure.

What is critical for the success of these efforts, however, is a balanced approach, that is, an approach that takes into account:

- Existing hardware and software environment
- Current business needs and objectives
- The existing user comfort level and familiarity with the technology
- The existing I/T support staff's comfort level and familiarity with the environment
- The available hardware, software, and technology
- The presence of clear business problems that the technology can most appropriately address

The "Real" Warehouse as a Guide

One analogy that we like to draw for people, to help them to understand how best to set up these kinds of environments, is the world of real warehouses.

When you build a warehouse for a manufacturing, wholesale, distribution, or retail organization, you do it for a specific business reason. You build a warehouse because you need to make something more accessible to more people in a shorter amount of time. No businessperson would build a real-world warehouse because everybody else is building them. No, business people would build one only if they were having trouble getting products delivered on time. In the same manner, we need to approach the building of a data warehouse on the basis of our need to move data from one place to another. See Figure 6-8.

Another good measure of how well your ideas about data warehousing are grounded in reality is the answer to this question: How do business people measure the effectiveness of a real-world warehouse?

Chapter 6: Traditional Warehousing   151

Figure 6-8
The real-world warehouse.

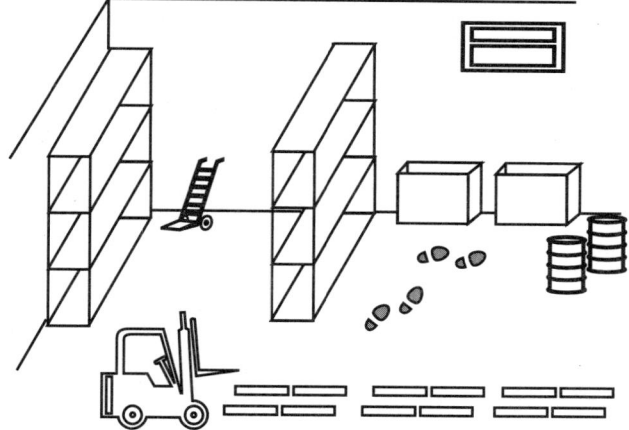

Measuring Warehouse Effectiveness Do business people want to know how big a warehouse is? No. Do they want to know how many blue shoes are stored in it? No.

What business people measure when they evaluate a warehouse is how many *turns* of inventory the warehouse experiences. (Turns are a measure of how many times the complete contents of the warehouse are moved out and replaced.)

A warehouse with a lot of turns is one that is doing well. A warehouse with no turns or only a few turns is a failure. (In other words, items go into the warehouse, but no one ever takes anything out.) When designing your warehouse, you need to keep that in mind. If people are not frequently using the data in the warehouse, then that data probably doesn't belong there.

Prioritizing the Design and Build Process Our real-world warehouse analogy can also help us with determining how to design the warehouse in the first place. All too often, individuals attempt to start the warehouse development process by trying to get people involved in the exercise of figuring out all of the data models necessary to support its development. These modelers want to get everyone to agree on what will be in the warehouse before they even know what the warehouse will actually be used for. This is, of course, a disastrous approach.

No businessperson would get involved in the development of a list of products to put into a warehouse (7 red shoes, 12 blue shoes, etc.), before determining:

- Where it should be located
- What kind of sales and supply problems it needs to address
- How big it needs to be
- How it will be managed and run
- When it will be needed

All of these things are much more important than the specific details about what will go into it. We need to establish the same kind of criteria before undertaking a detailed warehouse design effort.

Business Value Is the Key

The single key to any warehousing effort, whether it is data warehousing or Web warehousing, is business value, pure and simple. If the warehouse (or mart) is built with a clear business objective in mind, then the chances of success are high. Without this, there is no chance of success. (Again, we cover these issues in detail in the chapters on knowledge management and business value development.)

Viewing the Warehouse as an Environment

To develop an appreciation for the fact that a data warehouse (or Web warehouse) is not a system or an application in the traditional sense is probably the most difficult thing for systems developers to do. A warehouse is an environment whose job is to extract information from legacy systems, format it, and make it available for new applications and user analysis needs.

A truly effective warehouse environment is one where the data content is constantly being reviewed, changed, upgraded, and eliminated according to the ever-changing needs of the business users. A warehouse set up this way, as an environment, is a truly dynamic, powerful, and organization-supporting behemoth that helps the business change its direction and focus quickly and efficiently with a minimum of pain and a maximum of benefit.

When we start to view the warehouse or mart as an environment, instead of as a stagnant application, we begin to make sense of the confusing architectural and design problems that exercises of this type involve.

When architecting a warehouse environment, our primary objective should be to figure out how to most effectively transition legacy data into usable information. The following functional model provides an initial framework for understanding this process and building the infrastructure to support it.

The Data Warehouse (Mart) Functional Model

No matter what the size, shape, purpose, or flavor of a data warehouse, or data mart, there are three fundamental functions which it must always support: acquisition, storage, and access. While various vendors and designers may put a different emphasis on each, or attempt to hide the functionalities behind software components, underneath it all, these are the functions that must be provided. Figure 6-9 shows a diagrammatic representation of these three functions in action.

In the following sections, we will consider the functionality of each of these components in detail.

Acquisition

The first and most critical link in the warehouse environment development chain is the acquisition component. Acquisition is the process of:

1. Identifying the necessary data from legacy systems (and other data sources)
2. Validating that the data is accurate, appropriate, and usable
3. Extracting the data from the original source
4. Preparing the data for inclusion into the new environment. This includes the processes of:
   a. Cleansing—making the data usable (eliminating meaningless values, etc.)

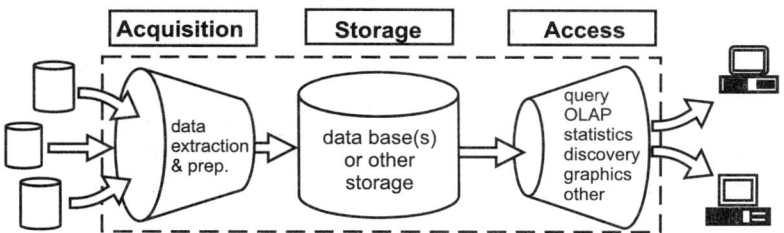

Figure 6-9
The three components of a data warehouse system.

      b. Formatting—establishing the correct format for the data (EBCIDIC conversions, etc.)

      c. Standardizing—getting all data into a consistent form

      d. Matching and reconciling—matching up data from two or more disparate sources so that the one "true" value is represented

      e. Merging—taking information from two or more sources and consolidating it into one place

      f. Purging—eliminating duplicate and erroneous information

      g. Establishing referential integrity—making sure that all referential values are accurate (i.e., state codes match the corporate list of state codes and the like)

5. Staging the information—making the data ready for loading into the warehouse itself.

The acquisition process is usually a long, painful one. There are many reasons for this, but it is important to remember that, for the most part, acquisition is what makes the warehouse valuable to begin with. If all of the information that people needed were already accessible, usable, and available, then there would be no need for a warehouse to begin with.

In trying to understand the physical architecture that supports acquisition, there are actually several things to consider:

Acquisition—Hardware Architecture First, it is important to realize that a vast majority of corporate legacy system environments are disparate in nature. Organizations tend to have a myriad of different hardware, software, and networkings holding the corporations together. See Figure 6-10.

This can create some interesting architectural challenges. One of the biggest revolves around the issue of where and how the actual acquisition process (extract, cleanse, format, merge, purge, etc.) needs to occur. The thought of dedicating one hardware platform to the acquisition process is an attractive one (allowing you to consolidate skills, locations, and functions in one place). In most cases, however, acquisition chores are distributed throughout the organization, according to the available resources, skills, and existing utilities. See Figure 6-11.

Notice how different functions are done on different platforms. Notice too how complicated this makes the issues of architecture and system management. One of the critical components of the acquisition architecture that many designers miss is the intermediary or "staging" area. This is an area of disk storage that is used to hold data that has been

Chapter 6: Traditional Warehousing

Figure 6-10
Disparate legacy systems environment.

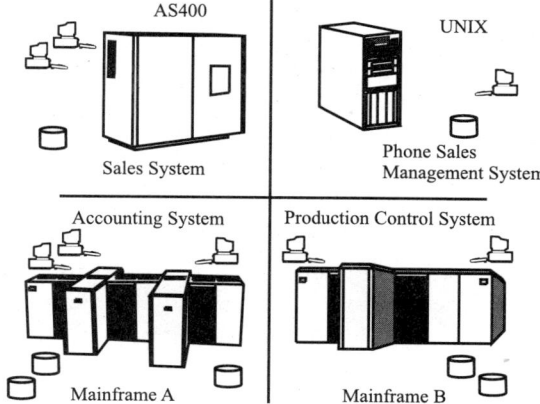

prepared by the acquisition process and is ready to be loaded into the storage area.

Acquisition Management Software One of the biggest markets for data warehousing support software is in the area of acquisition management and support. The job of extracting and preparing the large amounts of data required to populate a data warehouse can be extensive, and it is logical to assume that large, powerful data warehouse loader, preparation, management, and control packages would be great to have.

While there are a number of good products available to support many of these functions, in general, the area leaves a lot to be desired. Data warehouse acquisition is *so* complex, *so* specific to an organization, and *so* complicated that the current benefit from using these types of tools is very difficult to substantiate in most cases. When preparing to under-

Figure 6-11
Multiplatform acquisition processing.

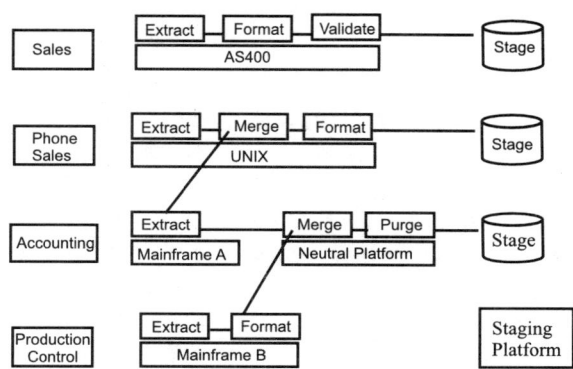

take your first data acquisition efforts, be prepared to do much of it *the hard way*.

Acquisition and Web Warehousing There are some isolated cases of people using the Web to help with the acquisition process in data warehousing. Unfortunately, because of the extremely complex, and legacy architecture–based nature of the acquisition process, the applications are limited.

Some enterprising companies and organizations have developed interesting tools, however. These vendors have created a suite of data acquisition and transportation products that allow the manager of a warehouse to schedule the running of data extraction and preparation jobs from a Web browser–based control panel. This application then uses the Web infrastructure to "order" the execution of extraction programs on the legacy systems. Upon completion of the extraction and preparation process, the same systems then make use of the Web to facilitate the population of remote warehouses and marts via HTTP or FTP services.

In other cases, the vendors of data transportation and replication software have created products that support the automated synchronization of remote data marts using Web-based applications. For the most part, however, acquisition is *not* the main reason to leverage the strength of the Web environment.

Storage

Storage management is the component that most people associate with data warehousing. Storage, or the creation and management of an environment where the prepared information can be stored while waiting for users to access it, is the heart of any warehousing or mart environment.

It is important for us to remember, especially when discussing Web warehousing architectures, that a database (whether it is a relational, star schema, or Lotus Notes database) is only one form of informational storage. There have been very large, very successful warehouses which made use of simple flat files, Excel spreadsheets, Web server home directories, and object-oriented databases as their storage mediums.

What is important about the storage component is not that it be made up of a certain kind of technology, but rather that it consist of whatever technology best addresses the needs of the warehouse environment.

Storage—Hardware Architecture Another issue to be resolved is where the database itself should reside. If you think about our "real" warehouse analogy, you will realize that figuring out *where* the warehouse should be located is a very important part of the decision-making process. There are several ways in which people approach this decision:

1. *Legacy system hosting.* Despite the many great inroads that client/server and UNIX technology have made in recent years, a majority of data warehouses are still built with the corporate mainframe platforms as the host. In these situations, organizations simply include the warehouse as another one of the many applications that the mainframe supports. In other cases, organizations with UNIX-based production environments will end up doing the same thing. There are many advantages to this approach including:

    a. The production/legacy system environment (whether it be a mainframe or UNIX system) represents the lowest cost per transaction of any hardware environment.

    b. Organizations with mature legacy environments in place can expect good administrative support.

    c. These environments tend to be very stable.

    d. Large data volumes are easily managed at low cost.

    e. The staging and loading of data from other legacy systems is simplified when the target warehouse is also on the same type of platform.

2. *Dedicated platform hosting.* The next most popular alternative, and running a very close second to the legacy system hosting solution, is for the organization to purchase a special, separate, dedicated platform for the purpose. The majority of data marts are hosted in this manner, and several data warehouses have been handled successfully this way as well. (Several organizations have actually dedicated complete mainframe systems to function solely as warehouse platforms.) This approach offers a number of advantages, including:

    a. A separate platform guarantees that the warehouse/mart will have good performance (since the hardware is not shared with a separate application).

    b. It often helps the organization get around internal staffing, budgeting, and support issues that the larger, shared legacy environment entails.

c. Specialized hardware, tuned specifically to the needs of warehouses and marts, can do a better job of delivering warehouse information than a general-purpose legacy platform.
3. *Multihosting.* As stated earlier, most organizations end up supporting a warehousing environment that includes many different storage areas, depending on the specific demands of the user organizations, and the available skills and capacities in the existing environment. This approach will obviously lead to the development of an extremely complex and unwieldy environment, but usually ends up being the most common because of the economic and organizational realities we need to deal with.

The hardware architecture of the storage component of the warehouse environment is based on the decisions made by the warehouse's developers. In all cases, the machine will have to be big enough to handle large volumes of disk space and run the data management software in one form or another.

Storage—Network Architecture Although the hardware that houses the warehouse data is the most critical component of the architecture, it is also important to understand the role of the network infrastructure.

The data storage area must be able to:

- Manage a large volume of data, which must be reloaded and/or refreshed on a regular and timely basis
- Provide access to a large number of users, allowing them to have simultaneous access to those large information stores

Because of that, the nature and bandwidth of network connections both into and out of the warehouse are critical. In the case of inbound network capacity, the crucial requirement is that there be enough network bandwidth to support the loading and refreshing of the data warehouse on a timely basis. Some data warehouse's tables have been known to take days, or sometimes even weeks to load. When it takes that long to load the warehouse, it is critical that the developer think through beforehand how the system will handle problems with failed disk spaces, loading of corrupted data, and other typical database backup and recovery issues. Many organizations discover too late that their data warehousing inbound network configuration is not robust enough to support their processing requirements.

In the case of outbound network capability, we have a different kind of challenge. The data warehouse is a centralized location, which leverages economies of scale and allows the organization to put all of the relevant data into one location for management. When you do this, however, you must stay aware of just exactly how many users the system will have, and how many concurrent users it will need to support. If you do not, then you can end up with a warehouse that is network traffic–bound.

The network capacity coming into the warehouse must be able to support a steady stream of short, intense query and reporting traffic (as opposed to the inbound capacity, which is more concerned with moving very large volumes of data in a very short time).

Storage—Support Software (Databases and Others) Of course, no discussion of data warehouse storage would be complete without addressing the databases and other forms of storage management software that we use to make the warehouse work.

There are three major categories of data that need to be managed and two approaches to managing it. In general, "traditional" warehouses are called upon to manage:

1. Extremely high volumes of low-level reference type data. This is the data that is typically used to support statistical analysis and data discovery types of applications. While a relational or some other form of database can support it, it is often best managed by simple flat file structures.
2. High volumes of traditional query and reporting support data that are typically supported by relational database structures.
3. Less extreme volumes of OLAP cube supported "star schema" type data, which can be housed in modified relational databases or special OLAP structured databases.

Of course, in the Web warehousing environment we also have to worry about images, sound, video, and many other things that we expect the storage component to handle as well, but we will investigate this in Chapter 21, "Web Warehousing: Architecture, Performance, and Management."

Access

After preparing and storing the warehouse data, the final step in the process is to consider the access component. This warehouse component is the process of providing end users with access to the stored warehouse information through the use of specialized end-user tools. While there are literally hundreds of end-user data warehouse and data mart access tools available in the marketplace today, most of them fall into a limited number of categories. These categories include query and reporting, OLAP, statistics, data discovery, and graphical and geographic information systems. The following sections provide some basic information about each. We will actually dedicate a separate chapter to each of these tool categories, showing you how they work, where they are most effectively used, and walking through an example of how one of them can be specifically integrated into the Web warehousing environment.

Access Using Query and Reporting Tools The first and most common category of warehouse/mart access is the query and reporting tool category. Within this group, you can find hundreds of products of every size and description.

At the very low end of the spectrum are simple "query manager" products that allow users to input SQL commands and see the results in tabular form. Products such as ISQL (Interactive SQL) fall under this description.

At the highest end of the spectrum are full-service query management environments such as Business Objects and Cognos. These products provide users with an incredibly user-friendly, business-level view of the data, tables, and information that they want, while at the same time providing administrators with a suite of tools to manage the environment.

In between are the vast majority of the products, including the number one and number two query access tools in the marketplace today, Microsoft Excel and Lotus 1-2-3. That's right! These two spreadsheet products, with their backend database attachment capabilities, are used more often to support data warehouse access than any other products.

Access Using OLAP Tools A wide assortment of products known generically as OLAP tools are available. OLAP tools are a relatively recent invention and are little more than a specialized form of reporting tool.

Query and reporting tools concentrate on making it easy for users to dynamically request and view information. OLAP tools, in contrast, give those same users the ability to interactively and dynamically navigate throughout a large database and explore different aspects of their data warehouse information without having to write queries or format reports.

Access for Statistical Analysis Statistical analysis is actually the oldest form of data mining. By applying statistical analysis techniques to large stores of data warehouse data, organizations have been able to

Chapter 6: Traditional Warehousing

optimize performance, improve profitability, reduce waste, and make all sorts of operational improvements.

Data warehouses and marts support statistical analysis through end-user spreadsheets such as Lotus 1-2-3 and Excel at the low end, and through powerful statistical analysis packages such as SPSS and SAS at the high end.

Access and Data Discovery Data discovery tools represent one of the newest introductions to the user access scene. They are used to solve the same kinds of problems as the statistical analysis products, but use the newer sciences of chaos theory and approaches such as neural networks and chi-square analysis.

Access Using Graphical and Geographic Information Systems Not to be underestimated, the graphical display products and geographic information systems (GISs) continue to make inroads into the corporate information access and delivery space, providing some unconventional ways to examine problems. With these products, users can envision very large, very complex multidimensional problems in ways that allow them to intuitively interpret the results.

Especially popular are the geographic information systems, which allow for the dynamic assignment of numeric data to different sections of a map. These systems present organizations with a bird's-eye view of territories, trouble reports, demographic densities, and many other aspects of a population that would be almost impossible to envision with normal tabular-type reports.

Access—Hardware Architecture The access component has one of the simplest parts in warehouse hardware architecture. Access hardware in the traditional environment can be identified as:

1. *Standard Windows 95.* Intel-based personal computers running Windows 95 or later are by far the most typical of end-user platforms, an almost solid standard that can be counted on.

2. *Pre-Windows 95 Microsoft.* Many organizations have a backlog of older personal computer hardware and software. This pre-Windows 95 type of environment will present the architect with many challenges, especially in the areas of network connectivity, disk capacity, and CPU availability.

3. *OS/2.* There are still organizations running a pretty solid OS/2 platform environment. These environments are very similar to the Windows 95 environment.

4. *Macintosh.* The Apple is present in many locations as well.
5. *UNIX workstation.* In some rare cases, or in firms especially involved in engineering or graphical design, or in other industries where the use of high-powered UNIX workstations is common, we will find that we have to use these workstations as user front ends.
6. *Dumb terminals.* While hardly sought after as data warehouse front ends, there are occasions when the old-fashioned "dumb" terminals will be called into service.

Included in our definition of the access hardware environment, regardless of the platform type, is an area of disk storage known as a *work area*. A work area is a special allocation of disk space, made available to the end user, that allows the user to extract data from the warehouse environment and store it somewhere temporarily for future processing. The inclusion of work areas in the warehouse architectural model creates an environment that is extremely flexible and powerful.

Access—Network Architecture Given the wide variety of end-user platforms and database platforms to choose from, it should be obvious that the network infrastructure in a client/server-based warehousing environment will be extremely complicated. Networks tend to be based on MS-Net Beui, Novell-Netware, TCP-IP, or IBM-SNA. While more and more organizations are cutting over to a standard TCP/IP mode, there are enough of the other kinds of network around to warrant attention.

In fact, it is here, in the network infrastructure area, that Web warehousing solutions can provide considerable short-term economic benefit, since Web-based solutions can bypass much of this network infrastructure detail.

The Layers of a Warehouse Environment

After this basic explanation of the parts of the data warehouse from a functional perspective, we look at the different "layers" of the environment. While the components of the warehouse help us to understand the horizontal flow of data through the environment, they do nothing to help us grasp the many layers of complexity that make up that entire system. Figure 6-12 shows the different components of the warehouse and how they can be assembled via different layers.

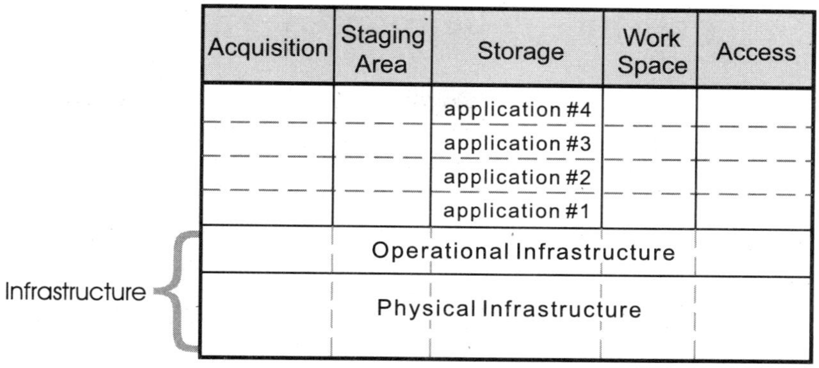

Figure 6-12
Layers of a data warehouse environment.

Acquisition	Staging Area	Storage	Work Space	Access
		application #4		
		application #3		
		application #2		
		application #1		
		Operational Infrastructure		
		Physical Infrastructure		

Infrastructure {

The Physical Infrastructure

The lowest and most basic layer of the warehouse environment is that area known as the *physical infrastructure*. It defines all the hardware, software, and networking components, which, when connected together, form the core of the warehouse environment. The physical infrastructure is used to define the physical architecture and is key to the establishment of an efficient, responsive, flexible environment.

The Operational Infrastructure

The next higher level of the warehouse environment is the *operational infrastructure,* which includes:

1. The definition of roles and responsibilities within the warehousing environment
2. The definition of policies and procedures for warehouse use
3. The metadata management and other warehouse management software in use (if any)

Organizations often build a data warehouse on the physical and application level and completely ignore the operational infrastructure issues. This ultimately turns out to be a mistake, as, sooner or later, the lack of operational guidelines leads to system problems, and sometimes even failure.

The Application Layer

Of course, the physical and operational infrastructures of the warehouse are meaningless in and of themselves. The real "guts"—the value delivery component—is what we call the *applications layer*. It consists of all of those activities and data stores within the acquisition, storage, and access areas which, when combined, produce an "application" of value to the business. We call this view of a data warehouse an *application-based* or *value proposition–based* view.

With this perspective, we define the following two terms:

1. *Data warehouse application.* A data warehouse application is a contiguous assembly of acquisition, storage, and access components, which, when assembled and executed, deliver a specific value proposition to a specific area of the business.

2. *Value proposition.* A value proposition is a statement, made by a businessperson in authority, which states that:

    a. If the following data or other form of information
    b. Were delivered to our organization
    c. Within the specified timeframe
    d. And delivered through the use of the specified end-user "tool set"
    e. Then the following business value (impact to the business's top or bottom line) will be experienced.

This layered view of the warehouse presents a radical departure from the traditional "dump and run" model in several ways.

First, when approached in this manner, we basically say that nothing should be put into the warehouse—no acquisition job stream, no data element, and no reporting tool—unless an already identified business value requires it. By incorporating this discipline into our view of the warehousing process, we establish a very rigorous and valuable prerequisite for warehouse activity. There is absolutely no risk of building a warehouse that no one will use if we require that everything be useful before we start.

Second, this approach takes the "religion" out of data warehousing tool selection, database selection, and other decisions, and makes everything a nice simple case of economic analysis. We put only those things into the warehouse that contribute directly to the solution of a business problem. This will greatly reduce the "blue sky" design, modeling, and tool selection efforts.

Third, the approach helps keep everyone working on the project focused on the business problem at hand.

This approach, though a little difficult to establish at first, has proven to be extremely helpful in establishing very successful warehouse environments.

Conclusion

In this chapter, we review the background and foundational information which establish the history, the business justification, and the architectural organization of a typical data warehousing environment. We explore the jargon surrounding data warehousing, including the difference between data warehouses and data marts, and look at a componentized and layered framework for understanding those parts that make up a data warehouse, how they fit together, and how they work.

This foundational vocabulary and the corresponding concepts will help us in future chapters to understand better how traditional warehousing architecture, justification, and business value is being modified and blended with the business values and architecture of the Web environment.

CHAPTER 7

Web-Based Query and Reporting

- *What are the six main reasons for choosing a Web warehousing solution?*
- *What kinds of business value can be delivered with a query or reporting tool?*
- *What value propositions help justify the investment in query/reporting solutions?*
- *What are some of the typical architectural approaches to delivering query capabilities?*
- *What is IQ (from IQ Software)?*
- *How does IQ deliver query and OLAP information over the Web?*
- *How does a user access reports and OLAP cubes in this environment?*
- *How does a developer create reports and cubes in this environment?*
- *How are things scheduled and managed?*

Delivering Information over the Web

While having a good understanding of the business situations, the organizational issues, the physical infrastructure, and the Web architecture is important in crafting a Web warehousing solution, there comes the time when you must actually *do something*. At that point, you usually resort to some kind of end-user reporting tool. In this chapter, we look at some of the more popular Web warehousing end-user access tools, in order to develop an appreciation for how Web warehousing looks when it is actually being delivered.

There are basically three ways that the developers of Web warehousing tools can arrange for the delivery of data to a Web browser via the Web: They can use PPP (Pre-Process and Publish), CGI (Common Gateway Interface), or Java, and JDBC (Java DataBase Connectivity). As we look at these products in this chapter, we see how each of them combines the power of the Web and their individual characteristics to create an extremely viable and practical Web warehousing delivery capability.

Query and Reporting Tools and Business Value

In Chapter 6, we consider the many different categories of data warehousing tools in the "traditional" data warehousing environment. In subsequent chapters, we discuss the categories of Web warehousing tools that can also be used to deliver value to the business. The list includes query, OLAP, statistical analysis, data discovery, graphical, geographic, image, document, video, audio, and many other types of tools. In the final analysis, however, the one tool that gets more use than any other and delivers more value to the business is the first one, the humble query and reporting tool.

There are a number of reasons, the bigger ones being that query and reporting tools are:

1. *Easy to use.* Query and reporting tools provide end users with an environment that is relatively easy to figure out. You can usually learn how to build a query or format a report in a matter of minutes. After decades of building query tools, the developers of the latest generation of offerings seem to have finally figured out how to make the process of getting information out of the computer a relatively painless one.

2. *Extremely flexible.* All you have to do is point query and reporting tools to a different database, and hundreds of different kinds of reports become instantly available.
3. *Extremely powerful.* The products can browse through billions of records, searching for the exact piece of information that a user is looking for, and deliver it, in the form desired, in a few seconds. That is power!
4. *Well suited to many different demands.* Query and reporting tools are classics. They never get out of date. You can always get more use out of them.

Query and Reporting Tool Value Propositions In general, people estimate the economic value that a query or reporting tool can deliver in any number of ways. One of the easiest ways is to calculate how much it would cost to deliver the same kinds of reports if they had to be written by I/T professionals in a language like COBOL. The cost savings measured in these terms will be astronomical. Of course, this is usually not a very fair cost comparison, and the savings don't really represent new value brought to the company.

In the vast majority of the cases, however, the value that a query or reporting tool delivers to the business is directly related to the savings in operational costs that the delivery of the information to the user makes possible. This category of business valuation, known as *operational enhancement,* is used to justify a great number of data warehousing projects, and the vast majority of these is made possible through the use of the humble query and reporting tool set.

Characteristics of a Good Fit for Query Tools Not *all* situations are ideal for the use of these kinds of tools, however. Here are some of the strongest indicators that bringing in a query or reporting tool will be a good idea:

- The user needs to know that condition *right now.*
- The mode of operation is *proactive.*
- The information required is volatile in nature.
- Users require different information at different times.
- Timeliness and immediacy of the information is important.
- The information gathered is actionable.
- The users are analytical in their mind-set.
- The users are motivated to find things out.

Characteristics of a Good Fit for Reporting Tools Whereas the benchmark for a successful query tool implementation is that the users' need for information be immediate, volatile, and ever changing, the requirements for successful report writing are different. For reporting tools to be successful, we need conditions where:

- The format and nature of the information is stable for a given period (daily, weekly, monthly, etc.). In these situations, the user needs to know what the conditions were like.
- Users need to see the information in the same format each and every time.
- The users need not be proactive. Reports best support *reactive* modes of operation.

Query, Reporting, or Both? While the business situations and user profiles of report users versus query users are very different, the fact is that most organizations have both kinds of tools in operation, and, in general, users make use of both when the situation warrants it. It is critical for us to understand, however, the differences in operational and user profiles, so that when we are architecting an environment for the first time, we have the best chance of choosing the right mix of products.

Architectural Approaches to Delivering Query Capabilities over the Web

The challenges of deciding how to deliver reporting and query capabilities over the Web can be tricky.

Supporting Query Capability Delivery Our options for the delivery of real-time query capabilities over the Web are in fact a bit constrained. [For a more detailed description of each of these approaches (PPP, CGI, Java) see Chapters 16 to 21.]

1. *PPP.* Since, by the very nature of most query processing, users need to see absolutely current and accurate information, we find that the PPP (Pre-Process and Publish) approach is hardly ever used. Unfortunately, the ad hoc nature of query activity, the volatile nature of report layouts, and the timeliness requirements preclude this approach as an option.

2. *CGI.* In contrast, the CGI approach to delivering query capabilities over the Web is in fact pretty simple and straightforward. HTML forms were made to support this kind of activity, and back-end CGI programs can easily handle most database query needs. Under this kind of approach, HTML forms are used to call CGI programs that perform native database calls. The data returned from these calls is formatted and returned to the browser.

3. *Java and JDBC.* While CGI can meet the processing requirements of any of the simple, basic query processes, any sophistication in the creation of reports will require that we build the query tool front end with Java (or ActiveX). As soon as a user wants to have the convenience of interactive drop-down boxes, "pick lists," and radio buttons, the reasons to go with a Java (or ActiveX) solution get stronger. The Java/JDBC combination certainly offers the user the most sophisticated of the native Web environment options.

4. *PC-based front ends.* It is also possible for a vendor to take some existing query management applications (applications written in C, C++, Powerbuilder, or any of the hundreds of PC programming languages) and modify those to leverage the TCP/IP network connections of the Web. By doing this, a vendor can deliver the same rich end-user desktop functionality, and use it to gain access to remote Web-based databases, without the use of Web browsers or Web servers. (This is certainly possible, but involves some disadvantages including high cost, lack of leverage of Web technology investments, and lack of standardization.)

Support Report Delivery Capabilities While the PPP approach is anathema to the demands of the query user, the exact opposite is true for the report viewer. For people who need to see reports on a regular basis, the use of the Web and the periodic publication of standard reports represents an easy, fast, low-cost way to disseminate a lot of information in a hurry. While the CGI and Java approaches can be utilized, the PPP approach is the hands-down winner for report distribution.

The Case Study Approach

To develop an appreciation for exactly how different Web warehousing tools can help us deliver traditional information via the new medium, we will start by reviewing several examples of real-world situations to see how the products are used to address them. We do this for several reasons:

The variety of products, features, and functions available are so broad and diverse that it is almost impossible to keep track of them all when viewed from a "contextless" perspective.

It is much easier to understand what the different product features and functions are, and what impact they have on people's job assignments, when you view them from within the context of a real business situation.

By understanding how these products are actually used to solve real-world business problems, you can get a much better appreciation for the needs that they address.

In each example, we will create a fictitious company, describe the different business challenges that they face, and see how the Web warehousing solutions can help. After learning about these different applications and how they work, we will then take a look at how different vendors deliver these capabilities. We will examine both the mechanics of building the applications and the architecture that makes the delivery of the applications possible.

Due Diligence in the Development of Solutions

In all the situations we describe, we assume that the company has gone through an exhaustive "due diligence" before deciding to move forward with these kinds of applications. As we discuss earlier in this book, the prerequisites for the development of any Web warehousing solution include the identification of the value propositions that the application will support. Every successful Web warehousing application has, at its core, a value proposition, a statement that describes clearly and simply:

- The business opportunity that the application will address (financial savings or benefits)
- The business organization that will be using it (that will actually make the financial benefits a reality)
- The value that the application will deliver (an approximation of the size of the financial benefit in absolute or relative terms)

In its simplest terms, a value proposition is a statement that says "If a certain collection of information were delivered to a specified group of users, within a specified time frame, and the specified application functionality were provided, then the following business benefits could be received by the organization:

1. Advocacy and support of the business area that will ultimately make use of the application (sponsorship and a commitment to take action).
2. Identification of the type of business opportunity being addressed and selection of an appropriate information delivery mechanism. The business opportunities and value propositions that Web warehousing solutions can address include:
    a. Operational enhancement (supported by query, reporting, and OLAP mechanisms). Operational enhancement value propositions are concerned with delivering operational information to end users in a way that makes it possible for them to make decisions that improve the operational efficiency of the organization. These value propositions calibrate their value in terms of the reduction or avoidance of expenses that would be incurred if the information were not otherwise available.
    b. Forecasting—explanatory, exploratory, and predictive (supported by statistical analysis, data discovery, graphical, geographic, and data mining mechanisms). Forecasting value propositions are concerned with the development of models that help the businessperson understand why things happened the way they did in the past and how things will happen in the future.
    c. Knowledge management and collaboration enhancement (supported by intranets, text search engines, nontraditional search engines, push technology, email, and other forms of nontraditional information delivery). These value propositions are concerned with the enhancement of the ability of large groups of people to work together in more unstructured ways.
3. Analysis of the existing operational and technological infrastructure and determination of the best architecture to deliver the capability. (Just because this book is about Web warehousing does not mean that we assume that a Web technology solution is the best for every situation.)
4. Selection of a particular product to deliver the capability—a tool that can deliver the type of information required (query, OLAP, text, etc.) and can run on the physical infrastructure described.
5. Selection of the right data storage medium to store and manage the information or data being delivered. The selection may be a relational database or a Web server's file structure.

The Case for Web Warehousing

While there are situations where the selection of a Web warehousing solution might not be the best alternative, there are many situations where it is. Delivering an application via the Web will accomplish several things:

- Savings on the cost of network infrastructure. By having information delivered via a Web interface, the organization can get around the need to network all of their different people and locations together (a project that could easily run into the millions of dollars for large organizations).
- Savings on the cost of end-user workstations. Since the application is delivered via a Web browser, the organization does not need to upgrade anyone's existing workstations.
- Savings on the cost of end-user software. End users need invest in a Web browser and nothing more. No special software is purchased at the end-user location.
- The ability to work remotely. By deploying via the Web, the company makes it possible for users to dial in from home, from the airport, or anywhere else they want.
- Worldwide consistency in application approach. By deploying one Web application that everyone uses, the company creates a consistent management structure that the entire organization can share.
- Savings on software maintenance and end-user support. Since hundreds of software packages are not being migrated to hundreds of workstations, the cost and trouble of maintaining that software is reduced tremendously.

It is no wonder that so many organizations are turning so quickly to Web warehousing as an alternative worth consideration.

Example: Global Sports

In this first example, we will be working with a fictitious company called Global Sports, and consider how this company might go about making decisions. Global Sports is a retail distributor of sporting goods, with store locations all over the world. As you might imagine, any company of this size, with this kind of geographic distribution, will face many chal-

Chapter 7: Web-Based Query and Reporting

lenges in keeping everyone around the world provided with all the information that is critical to their success.

Management at Global Sports realized that they were facing a serious problem. Recent acquisitions and mergers had turned them into the largest distributor of sporting goods around the world. Unfortunately, that same rapid growth has left them with some serious challenges.

Among the biggest problems are those associated with inventory management and sales forecasting. With so many stores, in so many places, it has become extremely difficult for Global Sports management to keep track of how well the business is actually running. Stock shortages and overages have started to cost the company millions of dollars in lost revenue and underutilized inventory. In a very short time, inventory problems (no product where it was needed and too much where it wasn't) and an inability to know how well individual stores were performing overall have placed the company in serious jeopardy.

Management determined that Global Sports was in need of serious help in the operational enhancement area. It was therefore decided that if the information about current sales and inventory levels for all of the stores were made available to the management teams of each store location, then inventory and sales problems could be addressed and corrected in short order.

Global Sports is dealing with a business environment that is geographically dispersed all over the world, and the existing information systems infrastructure is nothing more than a hodge-podge of several different I/T infrastructures which have been inherited as a result of their recent mergers and acquisitions. Because of these factors, it was decided that the deployment of a Web-based query, reporting, and OLAP environment would be the best solution.

Ultimately, management would like to see an inventory and sales reporting system made available on the Web to everyone in the organization. Ideally, managers, anywhere in the world, could show up for work in the morning, bring up their Web browsers, and be presented with a menu allowing them to choose from many different kinds of reports. (See Figure 7-1.) From the menu, managers would be able to pick and choose different reports, all of which could help them make better decisions. (See Figure 7-2.)

Global Sports chose some of the product offerings from IQ Software to help them make this vision into a reality. There is no reason, however, that they could not have chosen another product vendor. We use the IQ Software products here as an example to help the reader conceptualize

Part 2: Web Warehousing in Action

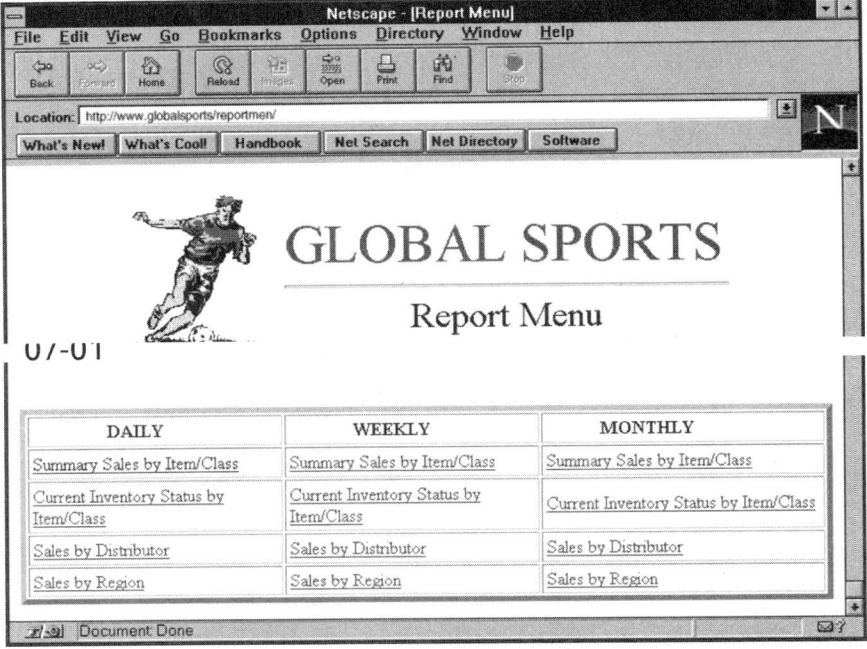

Figure 7-1
Global Sports main Web menu screen.

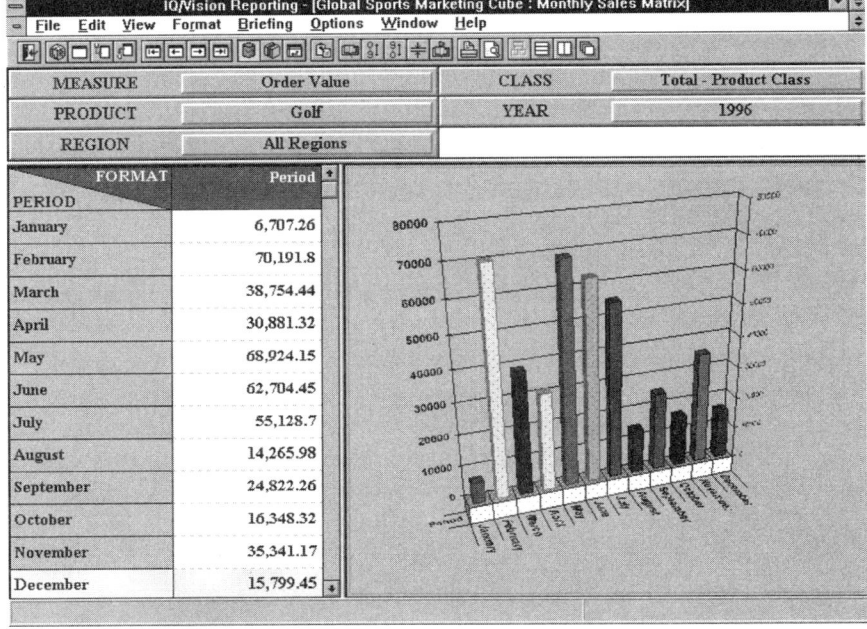

Figure 7-2
Global Sports monthly sales report.

exactly how all the pieces of this application fit together. (For example, since every product vendor's screen development approach is different, we need to provide you with one particular vendor's perspective in order to leave you with a concrete example. We will use this same approach throughout our review of each of the product types.)

IQ Software Background

IQ Software is one of the largest providers of these types of solutions, with an enviable customer base of over 1.5 million users. The company was founded in 1984 and has its corporate headquarters in Norcross, Georgia. They have been profitable for each quarter of their existence. Their current employment ranks boast over 165 employees, including approximately 17 in Marketing, 35 in Research and Development, and 45 in Consulting. This company has survived and thrived through the pursuit of their main vision, which is "To empower end users with data access, analysis, and reporting tools for transforming corporate data into useful information."

IQ has become the leading supplier of business intelligence tools in many marketplaces as the result of an unending dedication to the principles of product innovations and a consistent emphasis on service. Their current product offerings include tools which offer end-user report writing via the Web in addition to the more traditional forms of data delivery. They pride themselves on the ability to provide an interface for users that allows them to get at data without requiring them to have a high-tech background.

The IQ Product Family (Overview)

Global Sports I/T and management first had to decide which of the six IQ products to include in their solution. Three of them can be delivered in either a Web or client server mode (Objects, SmartServer, Vision), two are platform-specific (Intelligent Query for UNIX and DOS and Intelligent Query for Windows), and one is a Web-delivery-only hybrid. The IQ product family includes:

1. *IQ/Objects:query and reporting.* IQ/Objects is an enterprise reporting solution that gives end users with widely differing skill sets a

full range of decision support capabilities. With IQ/Objects, users can view preexisting reports, perform ad hoc queries, analyze data, and create simple to sophisticated reports. It can be used in a stand-alone mode to make direct access to corporate data sources, or in tandem with the IQ/SmartServer product.

2. *IQ/SmartServer:query and OLAP scheduling and management.* IQ/SmartServer is a three-tier reporting server that lets query processing and report execution be offloaded to powerful server environments and provides the capability and manageability required for deploying enterprise-wide decision support solutions.

3. *IQ/Vision:OLAP.* IQ/Vision takes advantage of three-tier architecture to provide powerful multidimensional analysis capabilities. It is ideal for business analysts, managers, and executives to use in performing "what if" analysis to review performance of business operations and help forecast future results. IQ/Vision applications can go directly against Applix TM1, Arbor Essbase, or a star schema in a relational database.

4. *IQ/LiveWeb:query and reporting via the Web.* A complete Web-enabled database reporting solution that includes everything a company needs to disseminate database information on an intranet. It provides server-based processing, comprehensive management facilities, and capabilities for automatic and on-demand report publishing to an intranet.

5. *Intelligent Query:query and reporting for UNIX, DOS, XBMS, Alpha-OSF (native UNIX).*

6. *Intelligent Query for Windows:query and reporting for Windows (client/server) (ODBC/native database drivers).*

Because of the nature of its infrastructure and business problems, Global Sports has decided to deploy its inventory and sales tracking application using the IQ/Objects, IQ/Vision, and IQ/SmartServer products.

The company's strategy calls for allowing the corporate information systems group to begin by developing queries and OLAP reports at the corporate offices using the IQ/Objects and IQ/Vision tools. This will allow the developers and corporate users to get comfortable with the quality of the information being distributed and with the utilization of the products. After upper management approval of these reports, a worldwide deployment strategy will be developed to make use of the IQ/SmartServers Web publishing capabilities.

Chapter 7: Web-Based Query and Reporting

Using the IQ Products

To make this possible, the systems developers will follow several steps, and make use of several of the IQ products. The following procedure will be followed:

1. Identify the data sources that hold the information of interest to end users.
2. Create an inventory of database objects that will make it easy for developers and users to gather the specific information they require (using the IQ/Objects administration capabilities).
3. Develop a specific set of queries that will report on the things most critical to the users. The queries developed will make use of the database objects created in step 2 (using the IQ/Objects query capabilities).
4. Validate that the information being reported is accurate and useful.
5. Format the approved information into a highly readable format (using the IQ/Object report writing capabilities).
6. Publish the reports to the Web (using IQ/Objects and SmartServer).

We will now review each of these steps in more detail and see how the IQ/Objects environment makes it easier.

The IQ/Objects Editions and Their Functions When you decide to make use of IQ/Objects, you have a choice of four different versions of the product. They are called *editions* and include:

Personal Edition supports the basic light user. With the Personal Edition a user can view predefined queries or reports and perform basic manipulation of the information. This edition basically allows the user to look at the reports that others have prepared.

Query Edition allows end users to actually create and submit queries that can run against any ODBC data source, in addition to the fundamental Personal Edition functionality. With this edition you can "roll your own" queries and interact with the database in any way you choose.

Report Edition includes the capabilities of both the Personal and Query Editions, but also allows the user to take those simple queries and turn them into full-fledged, sophisticated reports (with report formatting, control breaks, etc.).

Administration Edition allows users to do everything that the other editions can, but also provides for the ability to create metadata and objects that can be stored and used later. (Metadata consists of table names, column names, join columns, calculated columns, and formalized abstractions, format settings and overrides, etc.). With this edition you can create queries and reports and store them as objects that can be executed by users having only one of the lower-level editions.

In addition to offering these four standard editions of the IQ/Objects product, IQ makes it possible for developers to integrate their product into other applications. For example, you can build a front-end application using Visual Basic, Powerbuilder, or even Java, and have them call IQ/Objects queries and reports in the background. In other situations you may decide to run existing IQ/Objects reports and queries and have their output routed to other desktop products such as Excel, Lotus, Word, WordPerfect, or email.

Identifying Data Sources   The first step in any development effort of this nature is to identify where the data of interest will be coming from. As we have noted in earlier chapters, these areas, the data acquisition and "data storage" areas of the warehouse, are fraught with perils and pitfalls. Since we have already spent a considerable amount of time on these issues in the chapter on data warehouse architectures and procedures (Chapter 6), we will assume that all that work has been done in advance, and that a collection of data tables has been identified that already holds all the information needed.

Creating Database Objects   After we determine where the data of interest will come from, our next challenge is to make that information available to developers and users with a minimum of hassle. In the early days of data processing, figuring out how to get your hands on the data and pulling it into your reports was the toughest part of the job. These days, the administrative and technological tedium is greatly reduced by using metadata and database objects.

Generically speaking, database objects are high-level descriptions of data sources (tables, fields, etc.) that can be manipulated easily by the user and make the process of building queries and reports a whole lot easier and more intuitively obvious.

To create database objects, you develop a collection of the names and descriptions of the different data sources that the users will choose from.

Chapter 7: Web-Based Query and Reporting

Instead of asking users to memorize table names, column names, and data types, and having them write that information into queries, you simply provide them with a list of choices. They pick and choose the data elements they are interested in, and let the system worry about building queries, inputting appropriate column names, and all that other technical and administrative detail. By organizing the environment in this way, the user can concentrate on the business aspects of the reports being developed, while the system itself keeps track of the administrative detail. In the specific case of IQ/Objects, the Knowledge Base Manager, a feature of the IQ/Objects Administration Edition, provides this database object management capability.

So, to create the database objects for our reports, we will go through the following steps.

1. Invoke the knowledge base manager from within the IQ/Objects environment. There are several ways in which this can be done.
2. Identify the ODBC data source on which this object is to be based. A typical ODBC data source selection screen will be displayed. This will show all data sources registered with the ODBC manager.
3. Select the specific tables to import. From the provided ODBC list, choose whichever data sources you want to make available for end users and developers.
4. Define standard join conditions between those tables (including intermediary join tables). In those cases where joins between tables are required, it is a good idea to create "virtual tables" which represent these combinations of tables in a prejoined manner. Setting up these prejoins ahead of time takes a huge burden off the users, and goes a long way to protect the performance of the system by guaranteeing that any join activity will be done according to the database administrator (DBA)-defined criteria.
5. Select the specific columns and give them business user names, default fonts, formats, hide columns, derive columns, etc. [the system checks for previously defined metadata that will be imported and overlaid (special menu option)]. This will allow the development team to create a "business level" view of the data, insulating the user from cumbersome detail.
6. Click on close and save. As soon as this information is saved, it will be made available for use by the query and report creation components of the system.

See Figure 7-3.

Figure 7-3
A list of database objects.

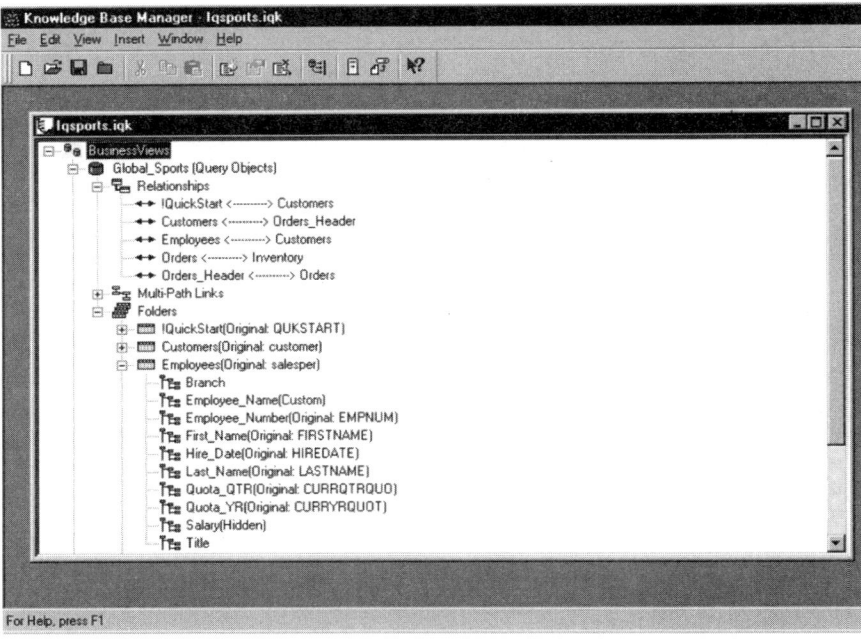

Developing Queries Once the database objects have been created, developers or end users will be able to build queries. The query building process is made easy through the use of a "Quick Query Wizard" that guides users through the query building process with questions and list selections.

After invoking the wizard, users are carried through the following options.

1. Choose the type of report you want to create. There are four types: *Detail,* a simple listing of rows; *Summary,* a row for each group, usually with subtotals; *Grouped Detail,* all rows and subtotals; and *Overall Summary,* a single row with just grand totals. See Figure 7-4.

2. Choose the tables and columns of data you want to include in the query. Simply select from the list of database objects in the Object Directory. The Object Directory shows the information in your database as defined with the Knowledge Base Manager. It provides convenient names and groupings of your database information to make it easy to define your query. See Figure 7-5.

3. Set filters that allow the user to specify which information to include or exclude from the output.

Chapter 7: Web-Based Query and Reporting

Figure 7-4
Choosing the query type.

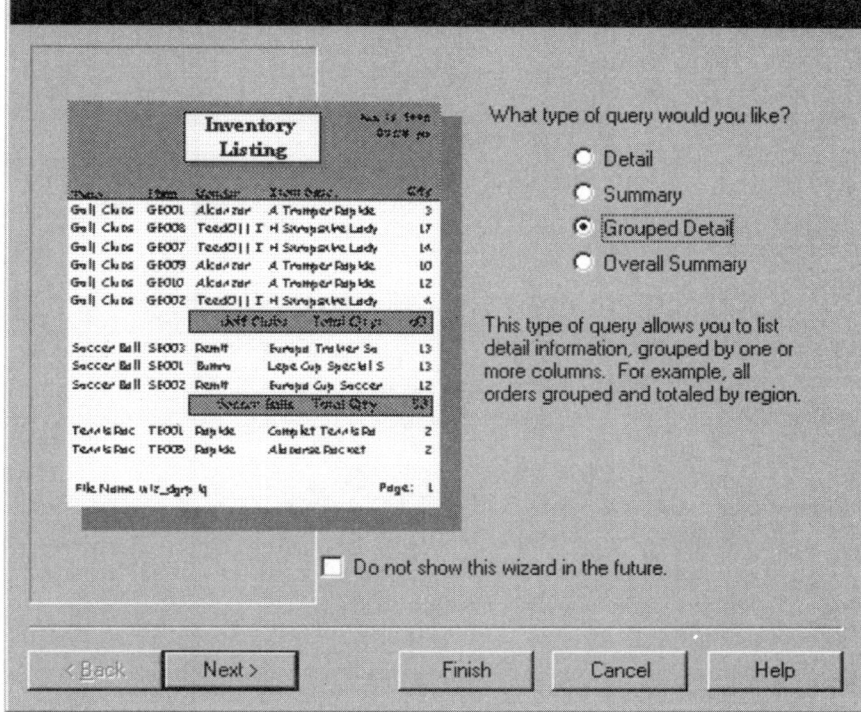

4. Define sorting and summarization criteria that determine how output is to be displayed.
5. Save and make use of predefined "styles" that establish how the output should look.
6. Finally, save the query, run it, and view it online or export it to several different file types, printed, or sent by email to another user.

Validating the Reports After creating the queries that we suspect will deliver the information that is needed, it is very important that the developers of the reports get feedback from the real users of the system before formalizing and distributing the data on a worldwide basis. Many times, a report developer's ideas about what is or is not important are different from those of the users.

Even more important, until end users actually look at the information being distributed there is no way to be sure that the content of the reports is accurate or useful.

Figure 7-5
Choosing columns.

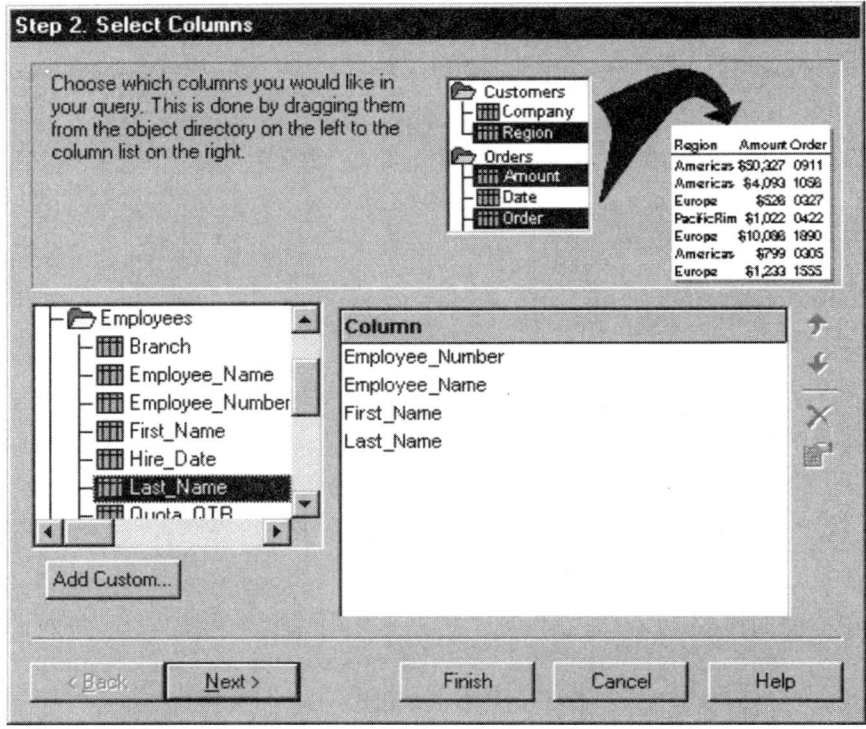

Formatting Report Output After validating content, the report developer can then proceed to clean up and pretty up the output. Under IQ, this is done with the Reporting Edition. To invoke it, you choose Free Form from the Window menu or click on the Update\New Free Form toolbar button.

From within the Reporting Environment you can then refine an existing query or begin from scratch. This is done by working on different kinds of object descriptions. The types of objects that you can operate on include:

- *Text objects.* Simple strings of text
- *Column objects.* Objects from your database
- *System objects.* These provide for the creation of easily formatted date and time stamp displays
- *Prompt objects.* These allow a report designer to build an interface so that the user can input information (parameters and query data) at run time

Chapter 7: Web-Based Query and Reporting

- *Component objects.* Predefined output such as charts and crosstabs that can be reused across several reports
- *Area objects.* These provide a mechanism for implementing common sets of behaviors or interfaces
- *Hot objects.* These make it possible to create special "parent-child" type links between reports. In the hot objects mode of reporting, you are able to define a higher-level report, from which users can choose to "drill down" to the lower-level reports. (When defining a hot object, you have a choice of whether the child reports should be dynamic or passive. "Normal" reports are always dynamic.)
- *Composite objects.* These allow for the combination and hybridization of report objects
- *OLE objects.* These provide for the inclusion of standard object linking and editing capabilities

See Figure 7-6.

For any object type, you can build conditional output or exception reporting (setting parameters for the display of output). For example, you can create an object that will trigger the running of an additional report if certain conditions are met.

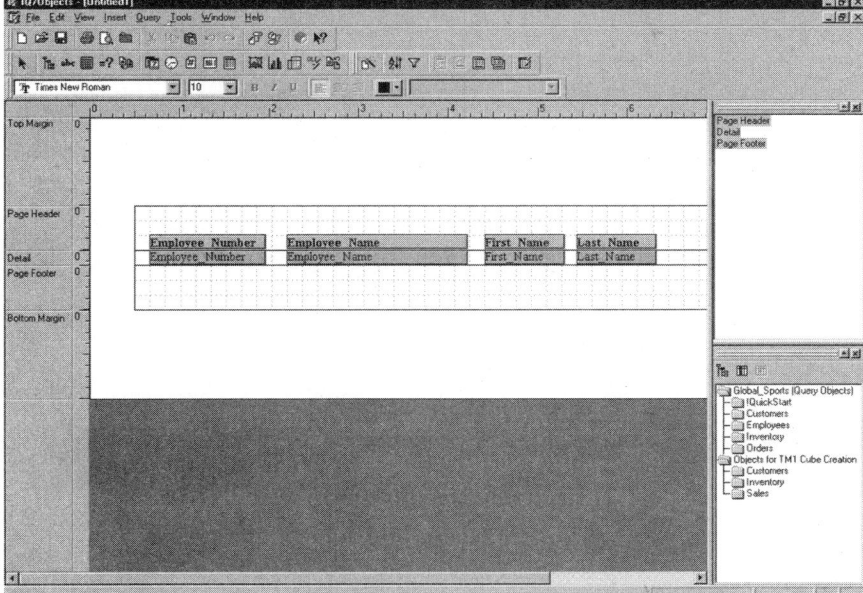

Figure 7-6
Formatting report output.

After you complete this formatting effort, the report should be ready for distribution.

Distributing a Report for Viewing Once the report is ready for display, we can turn again to the administrative capabilities of IQ, specifically the IQ/SmartServer product. With IQ/SmartServer developers can manage many different functionalities, including support for:

- *Standard query processing.* Making standard queries and reports available to all users.
- *Batch processing.* Allowing users to schedule reports to be run (and distributed) at a specified time, or on a preset schedule.
- *Repository storage.* Both knowledge bases and reports can be stored in a centrally located and managed repository.
- *Web publishing.* The ability to make reports available via the Web.

At the same time provision is made for:

1. *Standard three-tiered, application server functionality.* The IQ/SmartServer can function as a report server (sitting between the workstation and the database), making it possible for developers to offload processing from the workstations and databases, placing the burden on the IQ/SmartServer itself.
2. *Job monitoring and tracking.* Allowing users to schedule jobs and monitor their performance
3. *Notification of task completion.* Sending electronic notification of job completion to the appropriate parties via email
4. *Job submission and system access authorization management.* Creating an environment where the access to things, including the authority to submit jobs for execution, is centrally managed and administered.
5. *Extensive error handling.* The ability to keep track of, report on, and manage errors as they occur.

In terms of specific report publishing functionality, the IQ/SmartServer can be used to:

- Schedule a report to run periodically
- Schedule a report to run at off-peak times
- Publish a report to the Web
- Execute a report real-time from the Web

Chapter 7: Web-Based Query and Reporting 187

In the following sections, we review a few of the different ways in which these things can be accomplished by using the SmartServer functionality.

Distributing a Report for Viewing via the Web Let's assume that management has approved the inventory and sales reports that we have been working on, and we are ready to place them on the Web and make them available for the entire organization to see. To do this, we will go through the following steps.

1. After finishing the report, choose the submit icon from the IQ tool bar.
2. Select a specific SmartServer to work with from the server info tab (many organizations have more than one SmartServer active simultaneously; they can be set up to serve different functions, i.e., one for test, one for production, etc.).
3. After choosing a specific SmartServer, you will be given access to its functionality via three folders, one for the submission of jobs (submit job), one to define information about the job (job settings), and one with information about the SmartServer itself (server info). See Figure 7-7.

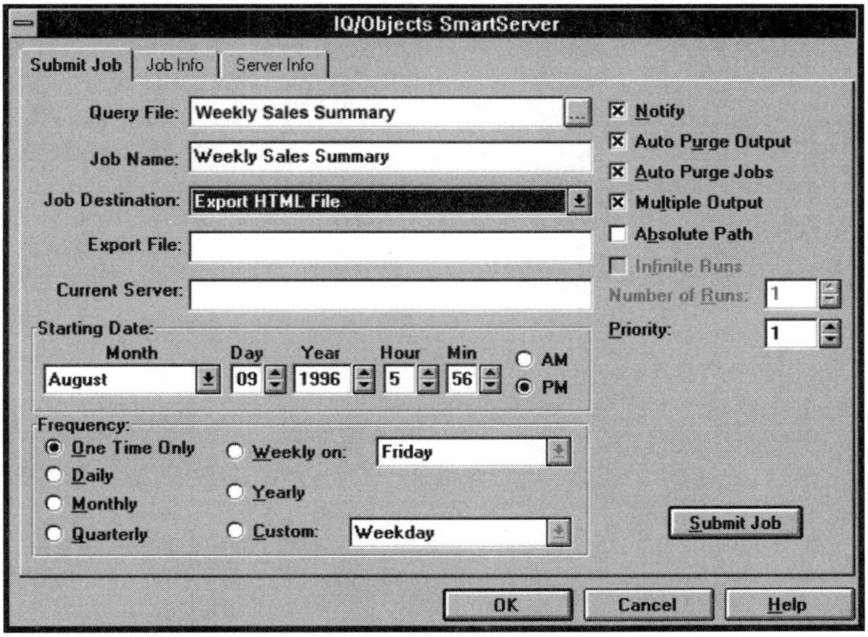

Figure 7-7
The IQ/SmartServer submit job.

4. To submit a job, move to the submit job tab.
5. Input the name of the report that you want to submit for publication (query file:).
6. Give the report a Web name (the name by which it will be known by Web users) (job name).
7. Select the type of output—in this case, choose HTML file).
8. Move to the job settings tab and set the starting date and scheduling frequency (daily, weekly, etc.).
9. Click on the submit job button. See Figure 7-8.
10. The report will now be automatically posted to the Web and as specified.

It's as easy as that! Of course, while the process of publishing this report to the Web has been made easy for the report developer, that does not mean that what is really going on under cover is anywhere near that simple.

Figure 7-8
The IQ/SmartServer job info.

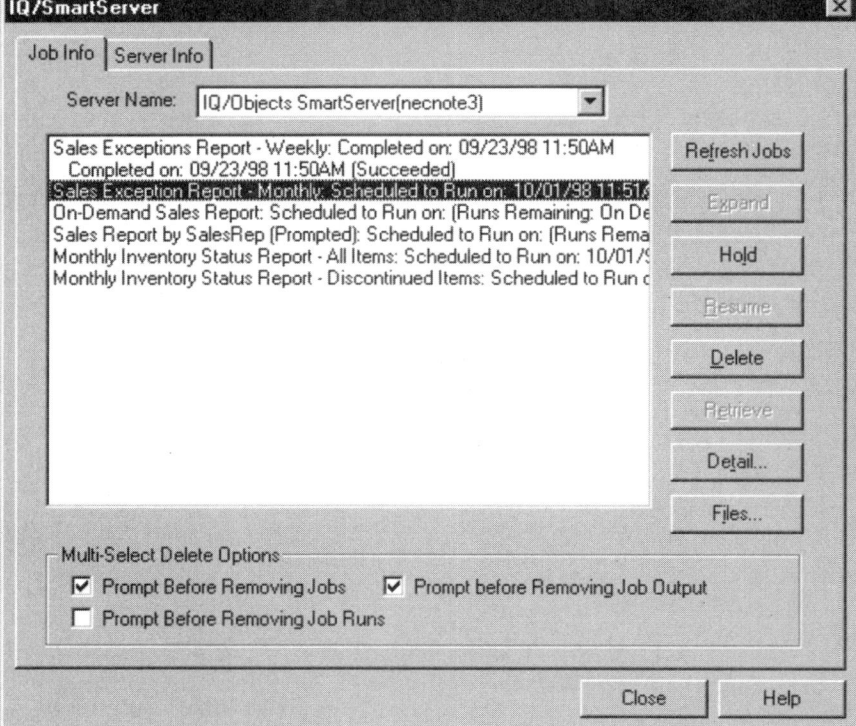

Chapter 7: Web-Based Query and Reporting

We will now take some time to review the physical architectures which make this kind of functionality possible and then look at the actual Web support architecture in greater detail.

IQ Product Architectures

To better appreciate how the different pieces of the process are put together, it is helpful to review the architecture and design of the overall IQ products environment.

IQ/Object Architecture To make use of the IQ/Objects product you need several components:

- The IQ/Objects software itself (which runs on the developer's workstations)
- Network access to the databases from which queries and reports will be built (via ODBC)
- Network access to the IQ/SmartServer which will schedule, run, and publish the reports

The specific hardware/software configuration requirements for each of these includes:

Platform: The IQ/Objects product (the software that we used to create the reports) runs on 16-bit Windows 3.1, 32 bit on Windows 95 and Windows NT.

Database: The product is able to work only with databases registered with a locally accessible ODBC manager.

Network: TCP/IP connection to the SmartServer is required, but access to databases can be through whatever is supported by ODBC.

In Figure 7-9, you can see this arrangement of components. Note that the ODBC server and the IQ/SmartServer do not have to reside on separate platforms; they can be and often are resident on the same machine. Notice also that the ODBC server is then connected to whatever data sources you want to pull from, and the IQ/SmartServer is subsequently connected to whatever Web Servers you will want to publish to.

IQ/SmartServer Architecture Of course, the architecture for the IQ/SmartServer product is a little more complicated. The IQ/SmartServer itself consists of several components, including *jobs database,* a database

Part 2: Web Warehousing in Action

Figure 7-9
Architecture for IQ/Object and IQ/SmartServer.

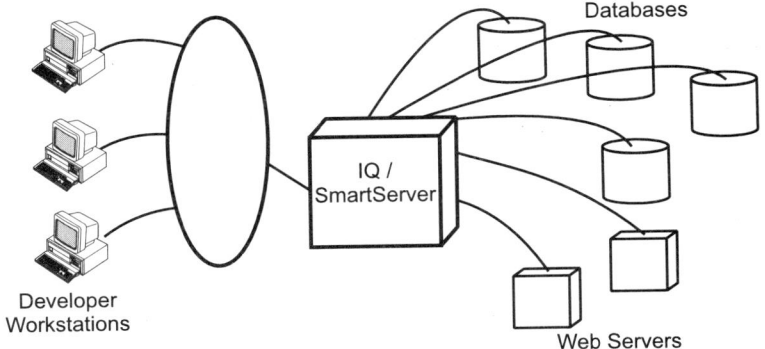

that holds all the information about jobs that need to be run (their name, type, frequency, etc.) and several daemons, such as:

- *Job server.* A process that manages the jobs database.
- *Job monitor.* Polls the jobs database at a preset frequency looking for jobs to execute. If there is something to execute it tells the multi-threaded server process to run the job.
- *IQ server.* Multithreaded server task that is actually the execution engine of the product.
- *Web publisher.* Takes care of interaction between the Web server and SmartServer and publishing of HTML and ActiveX output. It also creates the default report menu.

See Figure 7-10.

The specific hardware/software configuration requirements for these components include:

Platform: The IQ/SmartServer product (the software that we used to manage the environment and run the reports) runs on NT servers, AIX, Sun Solaris, and HP-UX.

Database: The product can work with any database that has an ODBC driver.

Network: TCP/IP connection to the IQ/Objects environment is required, but access to databases can be through whatever is supported by ODBC. Access to Web Servers is usually via TCP/IP.

Web servers: Netscape, MS-IIS, Lotus Domino, and others.

Chapter 7: Web-Based Query and Reporting

Figure 7-10
IQ/SmartServer internal architecture.

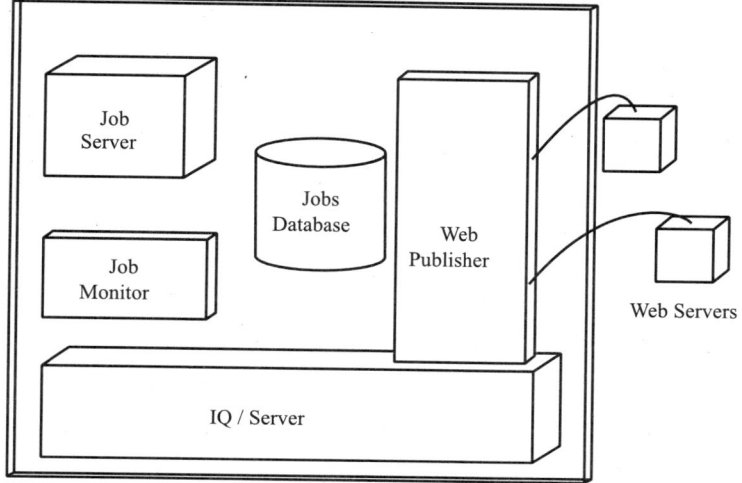

The IQ Web Architecture

Given this basic understanding of the way that the IQ products work, we can now take a much closer look at how the products work with the Web. As we have already seen, you can tell the IQ/SmartServer product that you would like to publish a report for viewing on the Web. What we have not seen, however, is exactly how that is accomplished.

The IQ product line is unique in that it supports both a PPP (Pre-Process and Publish) and a modified CGI "real-time" implementation for Web publishing. This means that you can use the product to publish pre-defined HTML pages, formatted to look like your reports, or you can make it possible for users to dynamically execute reports on the fly and view the results from their Web browser in real time. Let's see how these things are accomplished.

For the user of the IQ/SmartServer, deciding on how to publish reports to the Web is easy. As you may recall, we tell the IQ/SmartServer where to publish the reports via the definition of the report type from within the submit job process. (See Figure 7-7). You should also remember that there are two ways that IQ can perform that publication.

Creating HTML-Based Output We have already reviewed the process a developer needs to go through to get the IQ/Server to create a "passive" HTML report. The user will:

1. Finish working on a report.

2. Choose the submit icon from the IQ tool bar.
3. Move to the server info tab.
4. Select the specific SmartServer to work with.
5. Move to the submit job tab.
6. Input the name of the report to be submitted for publication (query file).
7. Give the report a Web name (the name by which it will be known by Web users) (job name).
8. Select the type of output. In this case, choose HTML file.
9. Move to the job settings tab.
10. Specify the execution schedule parameters.
11. Click on the submit button.

When the user clicks on the submit button, the following occurs:

1. The SmartServer product generates the report just as it would for any user.
2. The report is then read and passed through an HTML converter, which inserts the various HTML tags and values necessary to create an HTML version of the report.
3. The newly created HTML version of the report is then copied to the Web site location specified within the IQ/SmartServer.
4. After it copies the HTML page to the Web server, the SmartServer creates an HTML hyperlink statement that points to where the page is stored.
5. This hyperlink statement is then inserted into a master menu page which holds the hyperlinks pointing to all the Web pages the SmartServer has posted.

Figure 7-11 provides a diagrammatic view of this process, showing the five steps and the relationship between them.

In this case, the implementation of Web publishing is very simple and straightforward. The IQ/SmartServer converts the report to HTML and posts it. No fancy machinations are required. Of course, while posting passive reports to the Web can provide for some value, it would be even more useful if the user at the browser could get reports generated on the fly. For this, the makers of IQ had to get a little more creative.

Supporting Real-Time Report Generation over the Web For the user to generate a report on demand via the Web, several enhancements

Chapter 7: Web-Based Query and Reporting   193

Figure 7-11
The HTML export generation process.

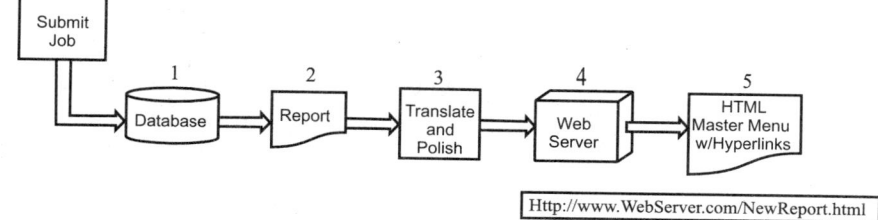

to the standard architecture need to be made. To make this kind of functionality possible, the makers of IQ have implemented support for the industry-standard CGI approach.

The steps we will follow to generate a report on demand are similar to those required to make a report of the passive HTML type. The user finishes the report, chooses the submit icon, selects an IQ/SmartServer to publish to, provides a Web report name, and then specifies the report type. In this case, the report type is still HTML, but it is specified with an on-demand schedule on the job settings tab. In this case, when the submit button is pressed, the IQ/SmartServer will do something very different:

- Instead of generating a report and storing it on the Web server, the IQ/SmartServer will start by creating an entry in the jobs database that defines the report and stores the instructions for executing it.

- Instead of creating an HTML hyperlink that points to the page itself, the IQ/SmartServer creates one that points to the IQ/SmartServer, including the name of the report as a parameter which it can then read and execute. (You can also code your own hyperlink statements in exactly the same manner.)

When the user then clicks on the hyperlink for that report, the following sequence occurs:

1. The Web browser interprets the hyperlink as a CGI call. This CGI call specifies the IQ/SmartServer as the program being called and passes the name of the report as the parameter the SmartServer is supposed to read.

2. The Web Server invokes the SmartServer and passes it the report name.

3. The SmartServer reads the report name and schedules the running of the report.

4. After the report has completed its execution, the output is translated into HTML and copied to the Web server location.

5. The Web server is then instructed to send a copy of the HTML page to the browser.
6. The Web server sends the page.
7. The browser receives the page and displays the result.

All of this happens very quickly and it may appear to the user that there is little or no difference in response time between this method of report distribution and the passive method we covered earlier. There are, of course, big differences when it comes to the amount of burden that gets put on the system.

Handling User Input Parameters The scenario we just described is not the most complicated situation we can imagine. What do we do, for example, when we want to create reports that allow users to input some search parameters before the report is actually run? How would we handle an application that would provide users with detailed information about the sales results from an individual store for a given date? In this case we would have to create some kind of parameter input screen into which users could specify the details about the specific store they wanted to see.

To make this kind of report possible we have to get even more sophisticated. The user prepares the submit job screen just as in the other cases. When the submit button is hit, the IQ/SmartServer stores the specifications for the report in the jobs database and creates a hyperlink that points to the SmartServer. When the report is then invoked, the SmartServer goes through the following steps:

1. The user chooses the hyperlink that invokes the report.
2. Selecting that option causes the browser to issue a GET command to the Web server instructing it to invoke the SmartServer program. The name of the report is sent as a parameter.
3. The SmartServer runs the program.
4. The program determines that input is needed and dynamically generates an HTML form, which collects the required information and returns it to the browser.
5. The user fills in the form and hits the submit button.
6. The browser issues a post command to the server with the instruction to send it to the SmartServer program.
7. The SmartServer receives the parameters and runs the report.
8. The report is published to the Web site.

9. The Web server is instructed to forward the document to the browser.
10. The user sees the report.

As you can see, by adding this functionality to the IQ product capabilities, there is almost no limit to the types of reports that you can generate.

ActiveX and Java Reporting

In some situations, end users have discovered that normal Web-type functionality is not good enough to meet their reporting needs. For those situations, IQ software has created reporting capabilities that make use of either an ActiveX (Microsoft) or Java (Sun) -based method of delivery as well.

ActiveX Reporting and the Web Viewer IQ Software has named the invocation of their ActiveX-based reporting capability the *Web Viewer*. Under this model, the request for an ActiveX-based report results in the following steps:

1. The user asks that an ActiveX-based report be run from the menu.
2. The browser issues a GET command asking the server to invoke the SmartServer program, passing the name of the report as a parameter.
3. The SmartServer program looks up the name of the report and sees that it is an ActiveX report.
4. The SmartServer then sends a message to the browser, asking if ActiveX is present.
5. If yes, the system asks to see the version number. For MS Windows it simply checks for installation and version; for Netscape or other browsers, it checks for the presence of an ActiveX plug-in and its version.
6. If the version is old or if the ActiveX plug-in does not exist, the SmartServer program sends a copy of the plug-in or updated module to the browser. [The ActiveX control (plug-in) is only 360 Kbytes in size.]
7. Once the viewer is present on the browser, it is invoked.
8. A copy of the ActiveX report is sent to the browser.
9. The user can view the results.

Java-Based Reporting with IQ Included in the IQ product offerings is the *Java Report Requestor*. This product allows users to simultaneously view and run multiple production and on-demand reports in much the same way the CGI-based reporting is done, only in this case, it is made possible through the use of Java applets in lieu of the HTML menu for the Web. In this situation, the user can invoke the report from the browser window and then execute more than one job at a time.

Conclusion

In this chapter, we introduce some of the major criteria that one must consider when choosing a reporting tool in a Web-based environment. We also take a detailed look at one of the products that provide Web-based reporting and OLAP capabilities. We see how the product is used and how its architecture supports many different kinds of Web implementations. In the next few chapters we examine some other types of products and see how they also accomplish Web functionality.

CHAPTER 8

Web OLAP

- *What is OLAP?*
- *What is Web OLAP? ROLAP?*
- *In what ways can Web OLAP be delivered?*
- *What are the Big Cube and Little Cube approaches?*
- *What is the business value of an OLAP application, and what kinds of value propositions are associated with it?*
- *What is the Aperio product offering from Influence Software, and how does it work?*
- *How do you use it to define OLAP cubes?*
- *What is the Aperio's architecture?*

The World of OLAP Reporting

In Chapter 7, we got our first look at a specific Web reporting product and the way it might be utilized by a company. We will now continue to expand our understanding of these types of products by looking at another one with some different kinds of characteristics.

Where previously we limited our discussion to the development of the most basic kind of information delivery through the execution of queries and report writing, here we will take a closer look at a more advanced form of report delivery known generically as *OLAP reporting*. (The product demonstrated in the preceding chapter can also deliver OLAP functionality, but using another product for this chapter's example will give the reader an appreciation for the different ways in which these products work.)

The acronym OLAP stands for on-line analytical processing. In recent years, this type of reporting has become the hottest and most popular form of reporting to hit the industry. OLAP systems can go by many different names, including such high-sounding technical labels as MD-DBMS, ROLAP, MOLAP, hypercube, and MDD. Despite the variety of names and types of OLAP systems, they all do pretty much the same thing.

What Exactly Is an OLAP System?

As with so many technological innovations, describing in simple terms exactly what OLAP systems are like is a little difficult. OLAP is very easy to understand once you have used it a few times, but is difficult to describe to a person who has never seen one before. Actually, OLAP systems are nothing more than a special category of query and reporting tools and as such can be used to pull data out of a database (or a collection of databases) and display it in a way that makes it easy to find information. OLAP products allow you to build and submit queries to ask for specific kinds of information, and they provide you with a way to format the output and organize it in a way that makes it easy to use.

The uniqueness of the OLAP systems lies in the way the data is queried, accessed, and displayed. OLAP systems provide users with a unique format for the execution of queries and reports. This format presents the system user with some very powerful features that a typical query or reporting product does not have, but it also forces some limitations on that user which a query and/or reporting tool would not. Some examples of how an OLAP system looks and acts follow.

Chapter 8: Web OLAP

The Characteristics of OLAP Reports

You really need to understand only two things to get a good idea of how OLAP reporting works, the concepts of *base report* and *report navigation*.

Base Reports The base report is a predefined report layout that forms the basis of all subsequent OLAP reporting activity. Probably the best way to think of a base report is to view it as a template or a reporting guide that all the different reports will use during the OLAP session. Typically, an OLAP base report looks much like a spreadsheet section, a collection of rows and columns of information important to the user.

OLAP base reports have different layout styles. Some of them include the straight display style, the "sparse/nested" style, and the "stacked/nested" style. In all cases, the base report page will show the information of interest for a given section of the business.

In Figure 8-1 we see the straight display style. This style makes the report look very much like a simple spreadsheet. In Figure 8-2 we see the

Figure 8-1
The straight display style.

Country	Region	City	Zone	Sales
United States	East	New York	30293	362930
United States	East	New York	30299	9800
United States	East	Boston	31293	88382
United States	South	Atlanta	98392	70000
United States	South	Memphis	89392	22039
United States	Central	Chicago	60016	98002
United States	Central	Detroit	32093	2400
Mexico	Central	Mexico City	1	100300
Mexico	West	Acapulco	4	98383
Mexico	South	Cancun	9	37372
Mexico	East	Veracruz	2	100

Figure 8-2
The sparse/nested style.

Country	Region	City		
United States	East	New York	30293	362930
			30299	9800
		Boston	31293	88382
	South	Atlanta	98392	70000
		Memphis	89392	22039
	Central	Chicago	60016	98002
		Detroit	32093	2400
Mexico	Central	Mexico City	1	100300
	West	Acapulco	4	98383
	South	Cancun	9	37372
	East	Veracruz	2	100

Figure 8-3

The stacked/nested style.

United States	Sales	Revenue	Costs
East			
New York			
30293	36,230	15,000	3,500
30299	9,800	5,000	4,000
Boston			
31293	88,382	22,000	52,000
South			
Atlanta			
98292	70,000	15,000	55,000
Memphis			
89392	22,039	7,000	12,000

sparse/nested style. In this case, the repeating report labels (i.e., country name, region name, and city name) are displayed only once. This style tends to free up the report, making it easier to read. In Figure 8-3 we see the stacked/nested style. In this approach, the region name and city name columns have been removed from the top of the report, and indented titles have instead been stacked along the left-hand side. This style of report allows for even more compaction of information and allows for more hard data columns on the right-hand side of the report.

Navigational Capabilities Your first step in making an OLAP report is to create a base report format that shows the kind of information you want. Of course, this formatting approach is no different from that for a spreadsheet or report writer. But this is where the much more powerful feature of the OLAP product comes into play. If you look at the base reports, you will notice that while they provide the format for a lot of specific information, it would be very easy to use that same format for all different kinds of reporting. For example, look at the report in Figure 8-2. It should be possible, using the same basic report format, to show the sales results for *any* combination of country, region, city, and zone in the world, not just the United States and Mexico. All we would need to do is to display the information from a different part of the sales database and use the same base format. See Figure 8-4. By simply changing the data that we feed into the OLAP system's base report, we are able to create an entirely different report, one that is just as valuable but which focuses on a different area of the business.

Trying to get a normal reporting or query system to create this second kind of report would require that the user build it from scratch. With an OLAP system, however, this is not necessary. With an OLAP system, we

Chapter 8: Web OLAP

Figure 8-4
Germany and France sales data.

Country	Region	City	Zone	Sales
Germany	North	Berlin	5746	32833
			5987	1039
		Hamburg	5122	103982
	South	Munich	3008	9829
		Stuttgart	55	392
	West	Dortmund	5111	928
		Bonn	3737	111
France	North	Paris	3928	4342
	West	Nantes	3482	3383
	South	Toulouse	9382	4092
	East	Dijon	2928	300

simply instruct it to navigate to the new set of data, and it will immediately display it. This ability to dynamically navigate through a huge database and to tell the database exactly what to show next and at what level of detail is what makes OLAP systems so popular.

Types of Navigation To describe the many different kinds of navigation that are possible with an OLAP system, we need to become familiar with a few of the terms that OLAP uses to describe reports. If you look at any predefined OLAP base report, you will notice that there are two very different kinds of report elements.

Most of the information that shows up along the left edge and top edge of the report, the labels and column headings, is known as *dimensional* data. Dimensional data provides report viewers with contextual information about what they are looking at. For example, the country, region, city, and zone labels in Figures 8-2 and 8-3 identify the context of the sales numbers.

The other kind of information carried on an OLAP report is *factual* data. In the case of the report in Figure 8-2, the sales column displays the only facts. In the report in Figure 8-3, however, facts include sales, revenue, and costs.

The real power of an OLAP system comes into play when the designer of a report provides the viewer with many different facts and lots of different dimensions, all of which can be navigated by the user. In fact, you can ask an OLAP system to navigate through a set of data in many different ways. You can navigate:

- *Across facts,* asking the system to display different *facts* for the same set of dimensions. For example, you might want to start by looking at sales and revenue data as displayed on the report in Figure 8-3, and then ask the system to show returns and margins numbers for those same cities and zones.

- *Horizontally* within the same dimension, asking the system to display the same information for a different set of locations (as we did in our example in Figure 8-4).
- *Vertically upward* within the same dimension (known as a *rollup*). When we navigate upward in a report, we summarize lower levels of detail into higher-level reports. The report in Figure 8-5 uses the same base report as the ones in Figures 8-3 and 8-4, but shows a summarization by country.
- *Vertically downward* within the same dimension (known as *rolldown*). These reports are the opposite of rollup reports. They allow the user to break down a summary level report into its lower-level components.
- *Horizontally across different dimensions.* Not only can we navigate up and down a dimension, but usually we can have the system traverse other available dimensions as well. (For example, while looking at a report that defines sales for the United States, you might decide to traverse the time dimension and ask the system to show sales for last year as well as this year.)

By allowing users to interact with the system in this way, OLAP systems provide business persons with the ability to analyze and investigate the state of the business in a way that has never before been possible.

Figure 8-5
A rollup report by country.

Country	Sales (m)	Revenue (m)
Albania	500	1,345
Canada	1,500	9,345
Costa Rica	265	985
England	3,276	9,374
France	1,922	5,678
Germany	5,211	18,983
Greece	683	98
Japan	7,490	−908
Mexico	3,433	159
United States	12,911	1,764
Venezuela	2,909	22

The Business Value of OLAP

While OLAP systems have certainly generated a lot of interest from many different business users, it is often very difficult to figure out exactly what extra value the application may bring. OLAP systems clearly are exciting and fun to use, but what real value does an expensive solution like this offer when compared to the much less expensive options of query and reporting tools? (Remember, anything that you can create with an OLAP tool can also be created with a report writing package.)

The sad truth is that, in many situations, users and I/T departments, swept up in the excitement of harnessing this new technology, find, after they have built their systems, that the true additional business value has been minimal. Determining the value that a specific kind of application can deliver to your business depends on many factors. Some dos and don'ts about OLAP implementations follow.

OLAP Implementations That Deliver Little or No Business Value
There are several mistakes people often make when implementing OLAP types of systems for the first time. While the technology itself is very exciting and appears to be extremely user-friendly, there is, in fact, a very high price associated with its power. Some of the biggest mistakes are:

- *Using an OLAP tool as a report writer.* Because the format and flexibility of OLAP reports is so appealing, many system designers mistakenly assume that OLAP systems provide a good way to create large numbers of printed or on-line reports, but they are much more easily and economically developed with a report writer. OLAP is first and foremost an *on-line* activity, and use of the tool to do noninteractive kinds of analysis is a waste of the resources (and will create serious performance problems besides).

- *Using an OLAP tool as an ad hoc query manager.* Almost as bad as trying to get an OLAP tool to meet all of your reporting needs is trying to get it to meet all of your needs for query processing. As we have seen, the core functionality of an OLAP report is the base report structure. Any attempt to use an OLAP tool to support information that is reported in a different format will be extremely cumbersome, time-consuming, and less than satisfactory.

- *Creating systems with no specific business purpose.* By far the biggest trap that the developers of OLAP systems fall into is to build systems with only very general ideas about the business value that they hope to deliver. An OLAP system whose requirements are defined through generalized statements is one that is sure to be overengineered and underutilized. Specific value propositions and specific anticipated benefits are the key to successful OLAP system implementation.

OLAP Implementations That Deliver High Business Value Of course, OLAP has not become as popular as it is by delivering no business value. Hundreds of companies have discovered the value of delivering multidimensional information to the executives' desktops.

OLAP implementations that have traditionally delivered the most value can be found in almost every industry. Reporting in the areas of financial analysis and budgeting, where the ability to roll up and roll down financial reports assists accountants in the analysis of the firm's financial position, has proved to be very useful. Inventory management (as in the retail, manufacturing, and distribution industries) and sales and marketing analysis (for all industries) have been big winners in the race to get value out of an OLAP system. The ability to uncover trends in availability, profitability, and consumption can provide big benefits to those organizations that are able to figure out how to manage them.

Characteristics of Successful OLAP Implementations The key indicators for a successful OLAP implementation can be identified through the acronym VAINS, which stands for:

Volatile content. The area of information being navigated must be one that is constantly changing. OLAP is most effective when utilized to help business people continuously monitor conditions that are constantly changing. The type of information being viewed is meaningful when displayed in a set format (base report).

Actionable. OLAP systems provide little value if the information displayed to people reveals conditions that they can do nothing about.

Important. Not only should the information be actionable, it should also be important. Every fact and dimension included in an OLAP system is expensive, and great care should be taken to make the system so that only that information critical to the success of the business is included.

Navigable. The ability to navigate up, down, and across hierarchies will provide business users with insights into their environment that would be either impossible or extremely difficult to glean from reports.

Stable Format and Dimensions. The information that people want to get out of a report should be easily displayed on one or two well-defined base reports (each taking up one screen). The number and types of dimensions should be simple, consistent, and nonvolatile. (OLAP systems are great at reporting things along standard time, geography, and organizational lines. That is because the relationships between the different levels of these dimensions are consistent and predictable. This fits well within the OLAP architectural model. If you try to create reports that require the designers of the system to continually add, delete, and modify dimensions or facts, then you will quickly find out just how difficult, expensive, and impractical an OLAP system can be.

OLAP Architecture and Performance Problems

Assuming that you have identified an appropriate kind of application, and have designed it in a manner appropriate to the tool you have selected, you will find that OLAP applications can provide an organization with an extremely powerful addition to their information management arsenal. Of course, very few people can build a large production OLAP application without running into some serious performance problems eventually. It is simply the nature of the beast for this to happen. In fact, the data processing industry is full of stories about companies who built large, complex OLAP systems, and found that they had created a monster whose performance was so bad that they had to scrap the whole project. While OLAP may look deceptively simple and straightforward to the user, from the developer's perspective it is extremely complicated and cumbersome to build.

Design Challenges

What exactly is the problem with OLAP systems? Why are they so difficult to design and build? Why are there so many different approaches to them? Before we can understand how the makers of different kinds of OLAP products deliver those capabilities via the Web, it will be extremely helpful if we can first understand how those capabilities are delivered in a non-Web kind of world.

Data Volume Challenges The basic challenge behind the development of an OLAP solution has to do with the sheer volume of data that a typical OLAP application has to manage. When you look at an OLAP report at first glance, you really get no idea of how immense the required data stores have to be to support it. To understand this problem, let's look at some typical OLAP applications.

Let's assume that the developers of an OLAP report would like to provide sales information. We will assume that this is a simple system, one that will only report on one fact for the company, sales volume. One fact— easy enough. Now let's look at the dimensions we will want to use to manage this fact.

- *Time.* We will certainly want to have a time dimension. This dimension should allow us to view daily, weekly, monthly, quarterly, and yearly sales data for the past 5 years.
- *Geography.* We will also want to see sales volume data from our different store locations. This dimension will carry sales data at the store, region, city, state, and country levels.
- *Product line.* We would also like to see sales data by product line, including major category, minor category, product type, and SKU/UPC (stock keeping unit / universal product code).

So, for these hierarchies, how many different sales volume values do we need to store to have our system be functional? Let's figure it out. Table 8-1 shows the calculations for the number of different sales volume facts we will have if we store one fact per time-reporting dimension: a grand total of 2170. Table 8-2 shows the calculations for the number of different sales volume facts necessary to cover one time period: a total of 732. Table 8-3 shows the calculations for the total number of product dimensions for one time period and for one location: a total of 12,162.

TABLE 8-1

Calculating the Number of Time Dimensions

365 days/year	×	5 years	=	1825
52 weeks/year	×	5 years	=	260
12 months/year	×	5 years	=	60
4 quarters/year	×	5 years	=	20
1 year/year	×	5 years	=	5
				2170

Chapter 8: Web OLAP

TABLE 8-2

Calculating the Number of Geography Dimensions

stores	325
regions	200
cities	120
states	75
countries	12
Total	732

Table 8-4 shows the final calculation: how many fact values we need to store to provide full OLAP navigational capabilities. The number, obtained by multiplying the three other numbers, comes out to a whooping 19,318,607,280. That's over 19 billion! This is how much we need to store for only *one fact*. To get the number of values to be stored for 10 facts, just multiply this number by 10 (that will be over 190 billion). Compare this to the number of records that you typically store in an extremely large database. Really big "traditional" databases are usually measured in the hundreds of millions of records, not billions. When you look at it this way, it becomes pretty obvious why OLAP systems can get into performance problems so easily.

TABLE 8-3

Calculating the Number of Product Dimensions

Major categories	12
Minor categories	30
Product type	120
SKU/UPC	12,000
Total	12,162

Table 8-4

Calculating the Total Number of Facts

Time	×	Geography	×	Product	=	Total
2170	×	732	×	12,162	=	19,318,607,280

Basic Approaches

With so many different values to manage, OLAP systems have had to come up with many different approaches to minimize the performance problems and maximize response time. In general, products use three approaches.

1. *Precalculate and store.* The builder of the OLAP system figures out all of the different values that anyone might ask for (all 19+ billion of them) and stores each in a database. With this approach, people have built very large, very fast OLAP systems, but it has two shortcomings:
   a. It requires the dedication of large amounts of disk space, driving the cost of the system up.
   b. When you precalculate everything, you make it very difficult to apply updated values to the database. You would have to recalculate *all* the values the database contains.
2. *Calculate on the fly.* In this approach, the database stores all the lowest-level data values, and allows the system to dynamically calculate and roll up the values only when requested. This uses a lot less disk space and is much easier to update. Unfortunately, it can also tend to get very slow when the database is especially large or complex.
3. *A hybrid approach.* In many cases, the creators of these products have developed hybrid products which attempt to split the difference between the two approaches, allowing the designer to dynamically generate some numbers, and precalculate others.

Data Management Approaches Not only do OLAP products have to figure out *how* they will manage the data logically, they also need a physical data management mechanism to deal with. This is handled in three ways :

- *Relational OLAP.* One of the most common mechanisms is the ROLAP system, which is nothing more than an OLAP system that uses relational databases as the underlying data engine.
- *Multidimensional Database Management Systems (MDBS).* These special breeds of databases have been developed to deliver only multidimensional kinds of information.
- *Proprietary/internal.* Sometimes vendors build a special database right into their product.

Big Cube, Little Cube A more fundamental difference between OLAP products can be found in the way they approach the storage, retrieval, and management of their multidimensional data. A collection of multidimensional data is referred to in the industry as a *cube*. There are two schools of thought on how big a cube you should try to build. Some vendors, the makers of the big, high-end OLAP products (such as Essbase and Information Advantage) advocate the creation of very, very large cubes. These cubes, holding billions of facts and hundreds of dimensions, tend to be very expensive, but provide organizations with a very high degree of cohesiveness and consistency in their reporting and, consequently, in their decision making.

The other school of thought is to deploy smaller, more specific cubes that contain less information, but which focus on the area of most interest to the user. Smaller, more meaningful cubes are built on the fly and only when the user requests them.

Both approaches present Web warehousing practitioners with their own sets of challenges.

Web Approaches

Given what we have already learned about OLAP systems, their engineering challenges, and their basic approaches, it should be obvious why deciding how to deploy an OLAP system over the Web is a complicated process. There are several approaches that seem to be the most popular with vendors.

Precalculate and Publish as Web Pages Actually, there is a very easy, quick way for makers of OLAP products to convert their products to Web functionality. Simply stated, all they need to do is arrange that all the values that people want to see on a report page are precalculated, preformatted, and stored in an HTML format. What this amounts to is figuring out ahead of time each and every possible screen a user might want to see, and then storing that screen image as an HTML document.

Providing users with the impression that they are "drilling up" and "drilling down" is easily done through the clever use of HTML hyperlinks. By embedding these hyperlinks in their OLAP report pages, the product designers are able to create an environment that appears to be completely interactive and dynamic to the user, but is actually prestaged.

It should come as no surprise that the advocates of a "little cube" kind of approach find this method of deployment to be quite satisfactory (as long as the users do not need a real-time view of the information). This approach requires that no changes be made to the user's environment (they can do everything with generic browser functionality), and that no real-time OLAP engine be provided. Of course, it does take a lot of disk space and the creation of many Web pages.

As the number of screens that a user might want to look at increases, or as the need for information becomes more time-dependent, or as the number of dimensions and navigational options get greater, the viability of the prepublish option becomes weakened. At that point, alternative approaches are needed.

The Client/Server-Based Front End (Using the Internet as a Network Path) At the other extreme end of the spectrum are those products that attempt to create an application delivery environment exactly like a typical client/server implementation. The vendor creates a completely functional, workstation-based OLAP navigational management application, which runs on the user's PC. This application is then hooked up to an OLAP engine located somewhere on the Internet. In this environment, the only role that the Internet plays is to provide the network infrastructure to allow the user's PC-based client to talk to an OLAP server.

Applications built this way certainly provide end users with a high degree of functionality and can be attractive to many organizations. However, they have several drawbacks. With this approach, the two principal components of any Web application, the Web browser and the Web server, are bypassed and we lose many of the benefits that choosing the Web warehousing solution offer us in the first place.

The Web browser is bypassed because the application that is running on the user's PC has no need for it. The application can run on *any* PC, whether a browser is present or not. Because we are not taking advantage of the browser's capabilities, we are not getting any of the benefits that browser-based applications offer. We lose the platform independence that browsers give us. In this kind of an environment, you will need a different version of the software for every different kind of workstation a user wants to run. We also lose the consistency of an operational environment that the Web browser provides.

The Web server is bypassed because communication between the application and the OLAP engine occurs at the lowest (TCP/IP address) level and there is no reason to leverage. By bypassing the Web server we lose the rest of the big benefits that a Web-based environment can deliver: We lose the network management and centralization of control that Web servers provide, and we lose any Web server-based security or administration functionality that the server environment offers (meaning that we have to write our own).

Hybrid Approaches Most product vendors choose to split the difference and combine the strengths that these approaches can offer. There are two tricks that product developers can use to maximize the benefits of the Web environment, while at the same time infusing as much control and flexibility as they can into the architecture.

First, however, a vendor must figure out how to get a standard Web browser front end to provide the additional functionality that a typical OLAP application requires: buttons that allow users to tell the system which way to navigate and how to display the information. Vendors have approached this problem in two ways:

- *The modified HTML approach.* Developers put together template HTML screens which include buttons to provide navigational direction. These buttons are tied to Java applets or CGI scripts which convert instructions from the user into commands that are fed to the OLAP server engine. The engine can then put together the next set of data and send the next screen to the user.
- *The Java approach.* Developers write full-blown applications as Java or ActiveX modules, which run as a session under the control of the browser. This approach gives the developer more control over the user environment, but is quite a bit more complicated. (The problems of code maintenance can be handled by dynamically downloading applets or modules.)

By using either of these approaches, the product developers are able to create highly versatile OLAP front ends that are as functional and user-friendly as any client/server application.

After surmounting the front-end challenge, an OLAP vendor faces a second problem: how to deliver this kind of functionality in a Web environment, while managing the incredible processing and I/O workloads that typical OLAP applications generate.

In a typical client/server environment, the product developers have complete control of the architecture that they sell to customers. They can, therefore, architect a solution that meets the processing needs of their customers.

In the Web warehousing environment, however, you have some additional considerations. Here, you still need to manage the workload that your OLAP application creates. You have to architect an environment that provides users with the responsiveness and accuracy they require. However, in this environment, you need to figure out how to make this happen while passing the functionality through a Web server and a Web browser over which you have no control.

In general, most vendors use an application server (that is, they create a four-tiered architecture to enable their products to fit into a Web-based environment, leverage the strengths that the environment has to offer, and maintain the performance control that they need). In this kind of environment, the vendor places an additional server application into the architecture. This additional server ameliorates the load balancing and traffic control problems that neither a Web server nor a traditional database could handle on its own. See Figure 8-6.

Provided with the generalized background, let's consider an example of a Web-based OLAP product to see how the implementation looks in a specific case.

Aperio from Influence Software

A good example of a Web-based OLAP tool is the Aperio product from Influence Software. Influence is a relatively new start-up company that has recently begun to get some attention. The company was founded in October 1996 and consists of about 25 people (at the time of this writing).

For example, Aperio applications help a large manufacturer manage and coordinate inventory for 12 plants located around the world. In this case, the value propositions accomplished are doubly potent. By making it possible for management to stay aware of excess and obsolete inven-

Figure 8-6
The four-tiered application server architecture.

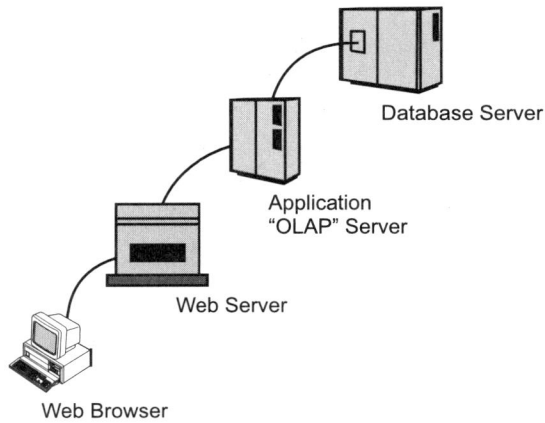

tory items, the organization saves money by reducing the amount of scrap they have to write off while at the same time reducing the number of orders for material that can be satisfied by reallocation of inventory from one location to another.

Product Offerings

Influence Software actually offers several products to help organizations manage their information over the Web:

Aperio OLAP.   Provides for Web-based OLAP reporting over the Internet or an intranet. Aperio OLAP allows users to perform on-line, real-time rollup and rolldown reporting with a standard Web browser.

Aperio Knowledge Gallery.   Functions as a Web-based data and information broker, making it easy to disseminate preconstructed reports of any form. The Knowledge Gallery provides users with an easy-to-access central location from which they can gain access to all the different types of information that they may need. You can set up the Knowledge Gallery to manage not only Aperio OLAP reports, but also many other types of information that people need to share, including the most popular desktop data sources such as Excel, PowerPoint, Web pages, and Notes databases.

Aperio Knowledge Agent.   Helps users manage their data acquisition needs.

Aperio Administrator.   Allows the system developer to create Aperio OLAP cubes and to manage their distribution via the Knowledge Gallery.

Product Architecture

The Aperio products are integrated into a complete architecture that provides for a lot of power and flexibility. See Figure 8-7 for a diagrammatic view of the architecture.

Front Ends   The user front end for all four of the Aperio products is Web browser-based, and absolutely no other end-user software is required. Currently, the product runs under Netscape, Internet Explorer, or any Java-compliant browser and can be run from UNIX, Apple, Microsoft, and Network Computing types of workstations.

Part 2: Web Warehousing in Action

Figure 8-7
Architecture for the Aperio products.

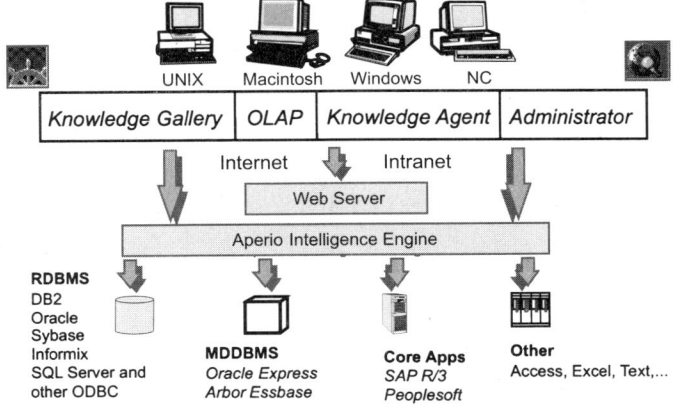

Web Servers All traffic is managed through the Web browser to the Web server first and is then passed to the Intelligence Engine. In a Netscape server environment, NSAPI (the Netscape Server's native language) is used to manage communication. With a Microsoft server, the Microsoft (ISAPI-MS) native language is used. In all other cases, the product defaults to a native CGI mode. The Intelligence Engine's queuing application keeps track of which application server is doing which job, and of who requested which work. Basic communications between the browser and the Intelligence Engine consist of the return of either standard HTML or Java applets.

Applications Server The workhorse of the Aperio environment is the Intelligence Engine. It is responsible for management of all work functions and can be run on Windows NT or on any of the major UNIX platforms (IBM, HP, SGI, etc.). It is scalable at the application level, and built-in load balancing will distribute work evenly over any number of platforms. (The Intelligence Engine includes a built-in queuing mechanism that manages those processes.)

Back-end Data Sources Aperio can work with DB2, Oracle, Sybase, Informix, and SQL-Server with native connectivity, and with just about every other database using ODBC. (There is no JDBC, OSF, ORB, or OLE support). The product itself is built on the Net Dynamics product, and provides for an enterprise-class Web development environment that is both Java- and HTML-based.

Categorization of Aperio Architecturally, we would refer to the Aperio OLAP product as a modified HTML, calculate-on-the-fly, ROLAP, four-tiered, little-cube product. That means:

- *Modified HTML.* The product provides most of its functionality through the delivery of custom-generated HTML to the browser. (The only exception is when special graphics are displayed, in which case Java applets are used.)
- *Calculate on the fly.* Aperio OLAP builds the cube requested at the time the user asks for it (although precalculation is possible).
- *ROLAP.* The product makes use of an underlying relational database to provide its data management structure.
- *Four-tier.* The product inserts a fourth tier, the Intelligence Engine, into the Web architecture to provide processing support.
- *Little cube.* The Aperio OLAP product works best when small, specific-purpose cubes are dynamically created on the fly and immediately loaded directly from the underlying relational databases. (Although precalculation and aggregation are also possible with the product.)

Developing an OLAP Application with Aperio OLAP

If we wanted to put together an application for a hypothetical organization, how exactly would we do it with Aperio? We would follow these steps:

Step 1. To create an Aperio OLAP cube, you first log on to the Aperio Administrator. See Figure 8-8. This screen can be invoked by keying in the appropriate URL on your Web browser.

Step 2. After logging in, you execute the workflow tool. This tool is called the *Subject Wizard*. It takes you step by step through the process of defining the subject area for the report.

Step 3. The Subject Wizard then does the following:
- It prompts you to name the subject you want to create a report about. (For example, we might want to create a cube that assists with revenue analysis.)
- It asks you to define the data source that will be used. This could be a view, a database (star schema), one large denormalized table, or some other kind of data source.

Figure 8-8
The Aperio Administrator login screen.

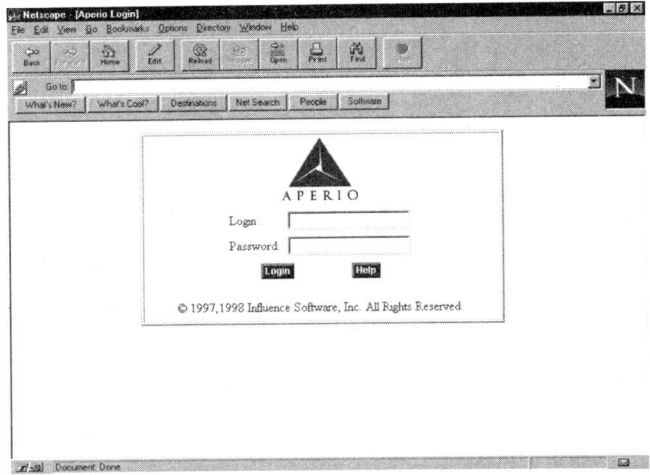

- It asks you to identify the fact table (star schema) that will serve as the basis for the report. (You can also provide the name of a large denormalized table as a default fact table.)

Step 4. You identify the measurements in the fact table. (Choose the columns to report and navigate on.) Figure 8-9 shows an example of the fact table specification screen.

Step 5. Within the fact table, you identify the low-level (starting) dimension keys (typically time, customer, geographic, etc.) which point you to the hierarchies of keys.

Figure 8-9
Specifying a fact table.

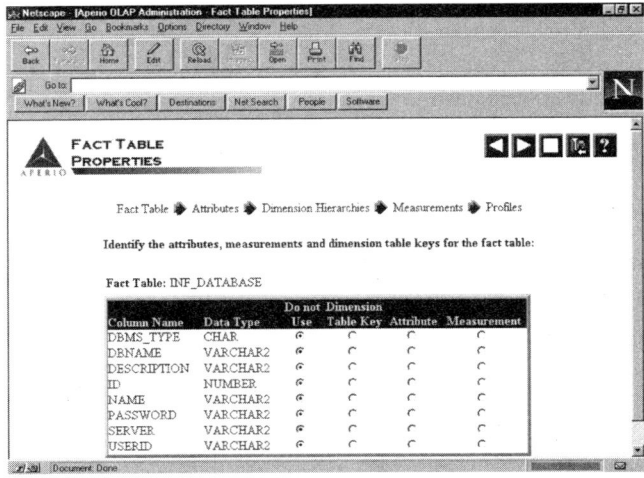

Chapter 8: Web OLAP

Step 6. After defining the basic facts for the report, you have to instruct the system where to find the dimension tables. These tables tell the system what the different kinds of navigation will be.

Step 7. You identify which columns of the dimension table are to be used (e.g., parent corporation, market, size).

Step 8. Finally, you define output and format for output, define any calculated measurements, and authorize access to the newly created subject. (You can authorize different levels of access to different groups for different pieces.)

After you create the subject, it is ready to use. Anyone authorized will now see the cube on its subject dropdown.

Looking at the Report Output After successful development of the cube, you can provide users with direct access via an HTML-based menu system, but most organizations prefer to use the Knowledge Gallery, which allows users to gain access to all kinds of information from the same set of menu selections. See Figure 8-10.

Of course, with any OLAP system, navigating around within the cube can get to be a challenge. Navigation around the Aperio OLAP reports is

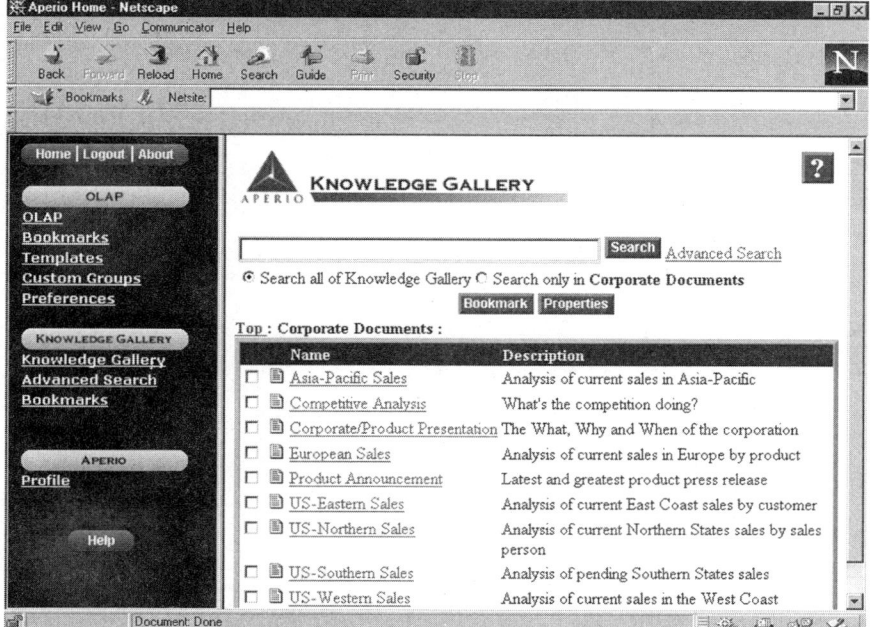

Figure 8-10
The Knowledge Gallery menu of available information.

Figure 8-11
Aperio query submission screen.

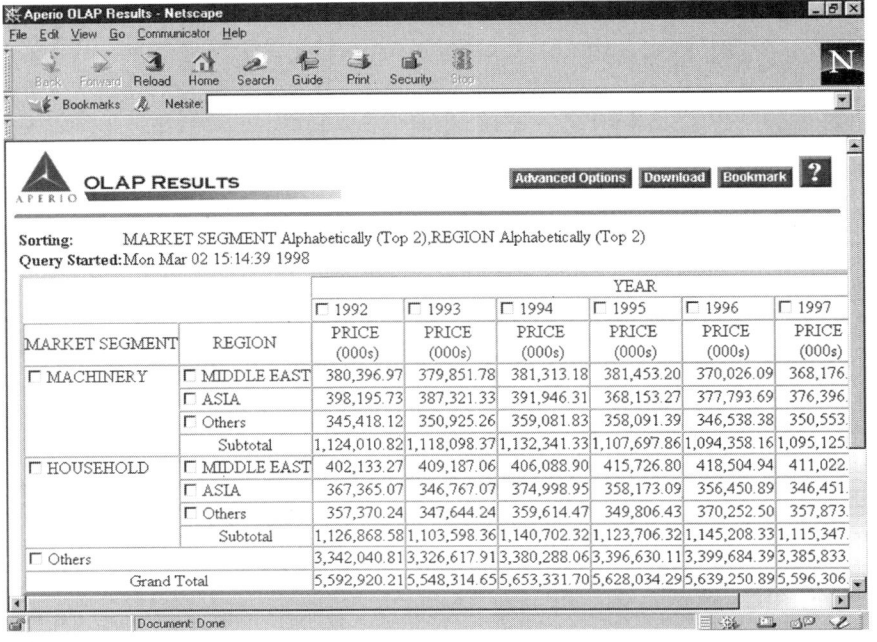

Figure 8-12
Market segmentation OLAP report.

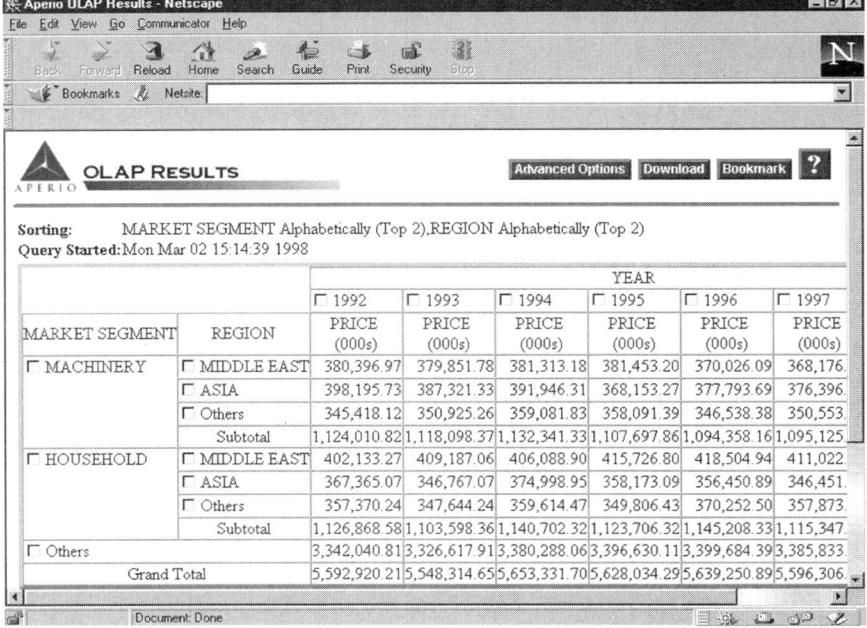

Chapter 8: Web OLAP

Figure 8-13
Graphical display of market segmentation data.

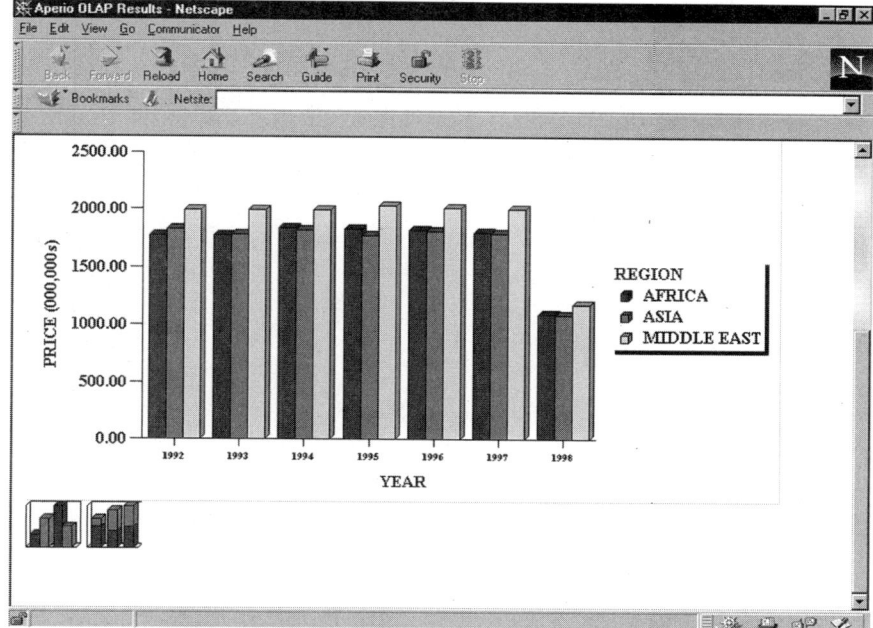

made simple with a predefined query submission panel. This panel allows users to specify the rows, columns, and other reporting characteristics required. See Figure 8-11.

Finally, the user is able to look at the requested report. See Figure 8-12. This report shows sales totals for the last 6 years across a number of different geographies. In addition to standard reporting, Aperio also allows the user to view the same data in a graphical form. See Figure 8-13.

Conclusion

In this chapter, we continue our exploration of the world of warehousing functionality delivery over the Web with a look at the way OLAP tools work and a review of several of the ways this functionality is converted to the world of the Web. Finally, we take a closer look at one of the many Web-based products available today, Aperio. In the next several chapters, we will continue our investigation of some of the other traditional Web warehousing tools, in addition to some of the newer, more exciting multimedia, video, audio, image, and text warehousing that is becoming popular.

CHAPTER 9

Web-Based Statistical Analysis and Data Mining

- *What is statistical analysis, and what is its business value?*
- *What is data discovery, and what is its business value?*
- *What is data mining?*
- *What are the similarities and differences between data discovery and data mining and some typical value propositions associated with each?*
- *How are these capabilities delivered via a Web warehousing configuration?*
- *What is the IM for RM product? How does it work? How does it leverage Web technology?*

The Analytical Tools

While the query, reporting, and OLAP products we have been discussing in the last few chapters define a large segment of the Web warehousing–based information delivery space, there is another whole category of tools which we have yet to consider. Whereas the query, reporting, and OLAP categories of product all help business people address their day-to-day operational concerns, this second group addresses a completely different set of needs. We call this general area of Web warehousing tools the *analytical toolkits* area.

Included in the analytical toolkits category are those products that help the businessperson figure out how or why things are the way they are and also predict how things will be in the future. Products of this type include two major categories:

- *Statistical analysis.* Products that execute the traditional statistical analysis functions, such as standard spreadsheets (e.g., Excel and Lotus 1-2-3), SPSS, SAS, and StatLab.
- *Data discovery.* Products that execute the new generation of nontraditional statistical analysis approaches with such concepts as neural networks, CHAID (chi-square automatic interaction detection), and decision trees.

What Is Data Mining?

Anyone familiar with the world of analytical processing and data warehousing has more likely than not heard of the term *data mining*. Although data mining is often associated with statistical analysis and data discovery types of applications, it is not exactly the same thing. In its most common application, the term data mining is used to describe those applications of either statistical analysis or data discovery products which analyze large populations of unknown data, to identify hidden patterns or characteristics that might be useful. Many of these technologies deliver their greatest business value from these types of applications. The examples "Predicting Buying Behavior" and "Discovering the Cause of Production Problems" presented later in the chapter are representative data mining applications.

Business Value from Analytical Tools

Trying to figure out how to economically and efficiently make use of these tools can be very challenging, however. These technologies tend to be so entertaining, exciting, interesting, and novel in their approach that organizations and individual users often fall in love with them before establishing a business case for their use. Just because a product is able to do "neat" things that amuse an end user does not mean that it will actually deliver good business value. Truly successful implementations must be based on the solution of business problems, not the amusement of users.

Categories of Business Value There are actually four major categories of information delivery that can be readily associated with real business value:

1. *Descriptive information.* Information that helps people to get a better understanding of the composition of a population. Descriptive techniques include the calculation of averages, maximums, minimums, modes, distribution curves, and a host of other descriptive statistics. Descriptive information helps marketers understand their customers. It helps production control people understand the products they make. It helps the logistics experts understand the behavior of their distribution channels. And there are dozens of other situations. Descriptive information can be obtained from statistical, data discovery, and graphical tools.

2. *Predictive information.* This is information that actually helps people predict future behaviors on the basis of historical information. The predictive tools include regression analysis, forecasting techniques, CHAID, neural networks, decision trees, and a long list of other pattern-studying tools. The predictive tools have had some especially useful applications in the areas of marketing, fraud detection, and production quality control, where they have been successfully utilized to anticipate buying trends, fraudulent acts, and product control problems by studying the conditions that seemed to contribute to those happenings in the past. In general, predictive information is obtainable only by statistical or data discovery methods.

3. *Exploratory/explanatory discovery.* Information of this type is generated by techniques such as correlation analysis, factor analysis, and neural networks. These help people to identify the conditions that may have contributed to a particular situation, so that proactive steps can be taken to prevent or encourage the occurrence of those same conditions or behaviors in the future. Explanatory and exploratory types of information are nothing more than extremely sophisticated in-depth types of descriptions. In general, the difference between descriptions and explanations is that descriptions offer no information to help the person understand *why* a condition is the way it is, while exploratory/explanatory efforts usually do. These values are also typical of the statistical and data discovery set.

4. *Specialized insights.* This category includes specialized forms of analysis such as graphical analysis, geographic analysis, and ANOVA (analysis of variance), which fulfill the specialized needs of individuals. These highly specialized tools help analyze extremely complex sets of variables by simplifying and codifying them into forms that make it easier to identify patterns and anomalies. A good example of this type of information display is the graphical information systems that turn the 20 different characteristics of the performance of a stock into a graphical representation, using colors, height, thickness, and position on the chart to display its long-term price movement behavior. This kind of system makes it possible for a stock analyst to spot a glitch in a stock's behavior at a glance (while analysis of the same information in a raw data form could take hours).

Examples of Analytical Tools in Action

Let's look at some of the ways that these tools provide value to their users.

The Humble Spreadsheet By far the most popular and most frequently used tool in the statistical analysis arsenal is the humble spreadsheet. Spreadsheets like Lotus 1-2-3 and Excel have become standard desktop fare on personal computers around the world. One of the functions of these spreadsheets is to allow users to quickly and easily apply statistical analysis functions to tables of data. See Figure 9-1. To invoke these statistical functions, all the user has to do is input the for-

Chapter 9: Web-Based Statistical Analysis and Data Mining 225

Figure 9-1
A standard spreadsheet report.

XYZ Company Sales Analysis Report	
Region	**Sales Total**
North	$256.00
South	325.00
East	765.00
West	125.00
Total	$1471.00
Average	367.75
Minimum	765.00
Maximum	125.00
Standard deviation	277.52

mula into the cell. See Figure 9-2. Of course, while this statistical functionality provides a lot of flexibility to the typical user, more advanced tools can be used to deliver results that are even more powerful.

Predicting Buying Behavior One of the most fundamental challenges to any organization is to accurately predict how their customers

Figure 9-2
Standard spreadsheet with formulas displayed.

XYZ Company Sales Analysis Report	
Region	**Sales Total**
North	256
South	325
East	765
West	125
Total	= SUM(C8:C12)
Average	= AVERAGE(C8:C11)
Minimum	= MIN(C8:C11)
Maximum	= MAX(C9:C12)
Standard deviation	= STDEV(C8:C11)

will behave in the future. No matter how successful you have been in the past, you are always interested in doing better. More important, it is critical for most organizations to try to understand what effects different actions or events will have on buying behavior. For example, if I raise prices by 5 cents, how many customers will I lose? If I lower prices by 10 cents, how many will I gain? How can I predict what will happen if I change my advertising campaign? Should I be spending more money or less?

Obviously, the ability to answer questions like these accurately will have a huge impact on the organization's ability to function in a profitable manner. Luckily, statistical analysis and data discovery tools can help answer those questions. In any situation where we want to predict what large populations of individuals will do, we can make use of statistics and data discovery to look for the underlying patterns and causal relationships. No matter which technique you use (we will address the specific techniques in the next section of this chapter), the basic approach is as follows:

1. Identify the population you want to analyze.

2. Collect a large amount of information about that population. (This collection should include descriptive information that tells you how the individuals in this population are different from one another and behavioral information which tells you what the people did in the past.) For example, I might have a file with information about all my customers—their names, ages, addresses, and how many times they bought my products last year.

3. I can then take this file of information (descriptive and behavioral) and analyze its content, using any of a large number of statistical or data discovery tools. These tools will then tell me about any hidden dependencies within that population. For example, I might take my file of customer information and analyze it by factor analysis, correlation analysis, CART (classification and regression tree), CHAID, or even a neural network. Each of these tools reports different kinds of associations. I might discover, for instance, that mostly x-generation females buy a certain type of product, while mostly y-generation urban males buy other types. This insight would allow me to reexamine my marketing efforts, to see if I was targeting the right kinds of people with the right kinds of ads.

Discovering the Cause of Production Problems Another very popular application of analytical tools is helping people to discover less-than-obvious reasons for production problems. If a factory is producing thousands of units a day, and 3 percent are flawed somehow, it is very important that the engineers figure out what combination of conditions might lead to the production of a bad unit.

In this situation, the engineers will pull together a file of all the information they can gather about the entire population of units. They will attempt to gather as many details as they can about each unit's assembly history (what lot the unit is from, or what time the various operations were performed on it, etc.) and its ultimate quality. This file is then turned over to an analytical tool (statistical or data discovery), which looks for hidden patterns behind the failures.

For example, one organization discovered that 50 percent of all failed units were being assembled during the late morning (11 a.m. to 12 noon) and the late afternoon (4 to 5 p.m.). This led them to investigate the shop floor conditions around those times. They found that people were not concentrating as well near the end of their shifts, causing them to be sloppy in their performance. A system of staggered shifts with more breaks was instituted, and the failed unit rate dropped by 50 percent.

Determining the Business Value That an Analytical Tool Will Deliver

It can be a difficult process to get business people to face up to the hard job of assessing the real business value that can be delivered by these tools. While there is frequently an undeniable value that can be associated with each of them, the nature of the value is often discovered only after the tool has been used for a while.

In general, the effective use of analytical tools requires some faith on the part of the people using them—faith that by using the tool, they will discover something of value. Think about it. If I could tell you what the analytical tool was going to discover, and how you could use that insight, why would you bother using the tool? I would have already told you what you wanted to know.

The use of analytical tools requires that we understand what it is that we want to analyze, and think we have a good chance of accomplishing that analysis and then building the system, taking it on faith that those values will be delivered. Luckily, in most cases, the organization's investment has been easily justified.

Let's look at each of these types of tools in a little more detail, and then see how they can be deployed in a specifically Web warehousing environment. The statistical and data discovery tools work pretty much the same way (reading large, complex input files, analyzing the results, and providing the answers to the users). Therefore, we will consider these products' architecture and deployment as being the same.

Statistical Products Overview

One of the oldest and most common applications of mathematics to the solution of business problems is statistics. Unlike most of the products we have talked about, statistics is an approach that you can apply with absolutely no computer assistance of any kind. Statistics is statistics. However, in recent years, the extreme power, flexibility, and user-friendliness of PC applications have made it possible for statisticians to get a lot more of their work done in a much easier manner through the use of high-powered statistical management tools. The two biggest vendors of statistical analysis tools are SPSS and SAS. But you can do a lot of statistical analysis with LOTUS 1-2-3 or Excel spreadsheet.

As we have already stated, the basic operational model for a statistical analysis tool is simple. A large file of information about the population that you want to study is collected, and then the file is read into the statistical analysis tool and analyzed, according to the instructions given to the tool by the statistician.

Statistical Analysis Applications

While you could write an entire book just listing the different types of statistical applications to business problems (and many people have), some of the more popular and useful applications include the following:

Correlation Analysis This type of analysis allows the users to examine a population and detect if there is any correlation between its members. In other words, are the members of this population somehow related to each other? Correlation analysis will help us to discover the natural groupings of individuals within a population. (For example, correlation analysis might show us that there is a large group of single, female professionals who shop at our stores.) Correlation analysis, however, does nothing to determine the reasons for the correlations, or if they are significant groupings. This type of analysis is often used to help a user zero in on areas that warrant more attention by another technique.

Factor Analysis As opposed to correlation analysis, which only tells you about groupings of individuals within a population, factor analysis provides the user with insight into what different factors tend to be associated together. For example, factor analysis might tell us that in those cases customers state that the main reason they shop at a certain store is its location, and that they tend to buy fewer items during each trip, but shop more often each week. Factor analysis actually does begin to provide some causal information in its results, but still focuses on simply reporting on patterns that it finds.

Regression Analysis By far the most popular of the statistical analysis toolkit for business people (especially marketing and quality assurance people) is regression analysis. This application allows the user to analyze a population and identify the nature of the relationship between two or more variables. Regression analysis will actually provide us with the mathematical relationships two or more variables may share. This is obviously an extremely powerful capability where business is concerned. For example, I might use regression analysis to tell me the relationship between sales and dollars spent on advertising. This formula could then be used to predict customer behavior on the basis of my advertising budget. (By the way, while this specific kind of formula is theoretically possible to develop, the number of factors involved makes it extremely difficult.)

Data Discovery Tools Overview

Data discovery tools, in contrast, represent one of the newest applications of mathematics to the real world. And whereas traditional statistics has been around for hundreds of years, data discovery math is based on many of the latest theories in applied mathematics. While the truly sophisticated statistical analysis capabilities can be found only in a small, exclusive group of vendor products, the market for data discovery products is crowded with dozens—even hundreds—of vendors.

Data discovery tools, also referred to as *data mining, information discovery,* and *knowledge discovery* products, can be found all over the place. In fact, a quick search of the Internet under these topics will provide you with the names of a whole lot of products with a dizzying array of names, functions, and explanations. It is interesting to note that, although there are dozens of products, the vast majority of them are small, "skunk works"-type products created by students and universities.

Data discovery tools work in a way very similar to that of statistical tools. Large files are assembled, which are then read and interpreted by the data discovery product to provide the analyst with new insights. The big difference between the data discovery tools and the statistical analysis tools is in the nature of the participation of the user. For data discovery applications, the user is much less active in the analysis process. These tools are much more user-friendly and self-managing than the statistical tools. While the user of a statistical tool must be a statistician to make use of them effectively, the user of a data discovery tool really just needs to know how to run it to get good answers from it.

Data Discovery Applications

There are many dozens of different kinds of data discovery applications in the market today. Some of the more popular include neural networks and CHAID, but many more, with names such as CART, decision tree, and binomial analysis, are also in use. All of these tools use different logical and mathematical foundations as their underlying premise but do the same kind of thing and work the same way. In all cases, these tools are used to help business people identify patterns within large populations of data. They can be used for either explanatory/exploratory or predictive objectives.

Neural Networks The glamor applications of the data discovery and data mining product category, neural networks represent one of the latest in a long line of artificial intelligence approaches to the solution of complex business problems. Over the past several decades, scientists have tried to learn how the brain, especially the human brain, actually works on a mechanical and electronic level. It has long been known that the brain consists of networks of neurons, which are small electrochemically charged circuits. The brain and central nervous system are nothing more than large, complex networks of these very simple circuits.

Until now, no one has been able to figure out exactly how neurons, working together, could actually contribute to the processes of thinking and the application of logic. Recently, however, a large body of knowledge has been accumulated which suggests that a complex organization of

Chapter 9: Web-Based Statistical Analysis and Data Mining

relatively simple "circuit programs"—called *neural networks*—have actually been able to simulate this kind of activity electronically.

Neural networks are programs designed to mirror the structure of a biological central nervous system. The networks consist of a collection of hundreds or thousands of miniprograms, called nodes, that are organized into a structure known as a *network*. To use these networks, all you need to do is feed information to them. The system reads in the information, sends it cascading through its network of nodes, and learns things about that information. (What actually happens is that each node is assigned to learn about one aspect of the tons of information being fed into it. Eventually, the overall system learns. The individual nodes each remember their detailed portion, and the system is said to be *trained*.)

Once you feed enough historical information into a neural network—that is, once it is properly trained—you can then use it to do analysis on other populations of files. When you feed it the new information, it compares the new file against what it has already learned and tells you what differences and similarities it has noted.

Neural networks have proved to be extremely successful in the accomplishment of predictive tasks. There are many neural network-based applications that have been used to successfully predict future customer buying behavior, to accurately predict or detect fraudulent behavior, and to effectively evaluate the potential credit risk that an individual represents.

CHAID   CHAID, or chi-square automatic interaction detection, is one of the newest applications of nontraditional statistical methods to the solution of business problems. The CHAID approach uses an already established form of statistical analysis, the chi-square test and, with the help of software, applies it to the solution of larger, more generalized problems.

The chi-square testing method, when applied in its original, statistical mode, allows the analyst to look at the relationship between two variables in a population and determine their dependency on each other. Under CHAID, a chi-square test is applied to all possible combinations of variables within a population and the results of the analysis are used to tell which combinations of variables are the strongest and which are the weakest. A CHAID analysis will show the analyst what the most likely and least likely combinations of traits will contribute to a desired outcome.

CHAID is therefore very useful in situations where organizations are totally unaware of what kinds of possible combinations of variables are important. CHAID analysis provides individuals with valuable input. The findings of a CHAID analysis are usually of limited value, in and of themselves, but the application of a CHAID tool can save analysts days and days of work, allowing them to zero in on those areas where more in-depth study will be of the most benefit.

Comparison of the Products

So, if the statistical analysis and data discovery products generally try to accomplish the same things, and if they work pretty much the same way from an operational and mechanical perspective, what is fundamentally different about the two approaches? In general, the differences can be found in the following areas:

- The level of sophistication of the person running the tool
- The level of sophistication associated with the preparation of the data to be analyzed
- The level of confidence that one can place in the answers received
- The mathematical principles on which the analysis is based

What Kind of User Is Required?

Both the statistical and data discovery tools require the user to have some level of familiarity with and understanding of the application of sophisticated analytical concepts. In general, however, the statistical tools require much deeper understanding of advanced mathematics to make their outputs useful.

Running the Tools To run applications effectively in the world of the traditional statistical analysis system, you need to be a relatively sophisticated and experienced statistician. There are several reasons for this. First, running a statistical model usually involves setting dozens of variables to make the test run effectively. To use the tool, therefore, you need to understand what all these variables are and how they affect the outcome.

However, the data discovery tools, in general, have few, if any variables to set before they can be run. A data discovery tool has been built in such a way that it can practically run itself. This is not because the data discovery tools are in any way less sophisticated, but because these products are usually developed with a very narrowly defined, well-focused, specific business application in mind. Therefore a lot of the "variables" can be preconfigured into the system.

In contrast, statistical analysis packages are usually nothing more than statisticians' general-purpose workbenches. They are useless if you do not know what problem you are trying to solve, and how to convert that problem into statistical terms.

Interpreting the Results   Besides the differences in execution between these types of products, there are big differences in their outputs. The output of a statistical model is very difficult to interpret without a sophisticated statistical analysis background. Without statistical sophistication, the results of a statistical analysis can be easily misinterpreted.

Data discovery tools, because they are narrowly focused on the solution of well-defined, specific problems, usually have outputs that are easy to understand and difficult to misinterpret.

Data Preparation Discipline

Because of the nature of formal statistical analysis, extremely high standards have been established regarding the amount of data, its cleanliness, and its completeness in order to make reliable predictions or draw meaningful conclusions. This is because the traditional statistical approaches are deemed valid only when the strictest standards are adhered to.

Data discovery tools, on the other hand, can accomplish more insight with significantly less data, and data of lower quality. This means that using data discovery tools can often cost a lot less money (because of the data preparation costs) than using statistical tools.

Mathematical Foundations

Statistical analysis is based on the formal, well-defined body of knowledge associated with traditional statistics. It is highly dependable and well respected because it is based on extremely high standards for conducting tests and making measurements.

Because of this, statistical analysis is a respected but very expensive form of business discovery. Building statistical models usually involves the employment of several high-level, experienced statisticians, many hours of preparation time, and running dozens of tests and proofs.

Data discovery disciplines, in contrast, involve the application of advanced, new-age, less traditionally defined or proven forms of mathematical theory. Because of this, the models tend to be much easier to build, with a lot less rigidity associated with their execution—but also with a lot less "provable" dependability behind them. For example, there is no way to prove or explain the conclusions drawn by a neural network. The network is too complicated to disassemble in that way. The only proof we have of the neural network accuracy comes when we apply the results and see if the desired positive impact will occur.

Confidence in the Results Received

Because they are based on different mathematical foundations, these approaches yield results with different levels of confidence. In general, the statistical models are much more dependable and accurate than the data discovery solutions. However, because of the huge differences in costs between the two methods, data discovery tools are often chosen as the preferred method of investigation. This is especially true in those situations where a slight inaccuracy in an analysis will have little or no impact on the business risks or costs.

Architectural Approaches for Statistical and Data Discovery Tools

Because the natures of statistical tools and data discovery tools are similar, they are integrated into the world of Web warehousing in very similar ways. You may recall that the basic architecture of data discovery and statistical analysis systems is relatively straightforward. The tools function by reading large volumes of data into the product, which are then analyzed.

A typical arrangement of components in this environment is:

- *100 percent host-based.* Under this model, the end user simply triggers off programs that run on the host which do the analysis. The user workstation serves as the launching point for programs and as the place where output reports are read.

Chapter 9: Web-Based Statistical Analysis and Data Mining

- *100 percent client-based.* In this case, all of the data to be worked on is copied to the workstation. The locally housed analysis application then reads the data and reports on its findings.
- *Hybrid approach.* In some situations, the allocation of functions is split between these two ends or is managed through a distinct application server.

Since the major job of these particular analytical tools is to read in large volumes of data and interpret it, the typical Web warehousing configuration offers little in the form of architectural enhancement. The typical configuration in this environment, therefore, involves either PPP, a very passive implementation via the PPP model (Figure 9-3), or CGI/Java, or a remote execution model, using CGI or Java, which turns the user's workstation into a control panel, where remote execution of the programs is controlled from, and which allows for downloading of the output reports to that workstation.

The Intelligent Miner for Relationship Marketing Product (IBM)

Perhaps one of the best examples of a leading-edge analysis product using Web technology, statistical analysis, and data discovery techniques is the Intelligent Miner for Relationship Marketing (IM for RM) product from IBM. The IM for RM product is the latest addition to IBM's

Figure 9-3
A typical PPP implementation.

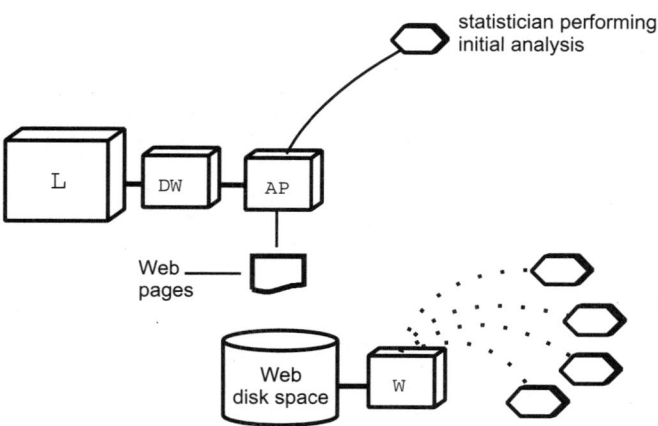

Intelligent Miner family of statistical and data discovery products, which provides users with a wide range of data and text analysis capabilities that can be used to address a variety of business problems.

IM for RM Background Information

IBM's Intelligent Miner for Relationship Marketing is a suite of applications designed to help users gain valuable insight into the behavior of their customers. It uses the powerful data mining technology of the underlying Intelligent Miner for Data product to drive its functionality. These applications provide the marketing executive, manager, or analyst with the ability to perform sophisticated analysis with data mining tools, all from the convenient interface of a Web browser and without having to possess any specialized analytical skills.

Using Intelligent Miner for Relationship Marketing, individuals with marketing expertise can tap their company's data resources to better understand their customers' behavior. They can then use this knowledge to more precisely target their market segments and optimize the spending of their marketing dollars. Specific business problems that IM for RM can address include:

- *Customer attrition prevention.* Allowing the analyst to identify which customers are most likely to defect to a competitor so that preventative marketing actions can be taken.
- *New customer acquisition.* Making it possible for the analyst to determine the most likely profile of prospective customers and to further identify ways to locate and approach them with offers.
- *Customer win-back.* Figure out how to reattract customers that have drifted away to competitors' ranks.
- *Cross-selling.* Showing companies how they can sell more to existing customers by figuring out what other products they have bought in the past and are likely to buy in the future.

Organization and Use of the IM for RM Product

The Intelligent Miner for Relationship Marketing product is organized into four major functional components. The components are designed to allow analysts to concentrate on different parts of the relationship marketing process, and organized so that they can be executed in the logical progression that an analyst would follow in developing a predictive model. These components are:

Data Preparation. A series of screens that allow the analyst to define the data to be input into the system for modeling.

Model Build. Screens allow the user to actually define and analyze alternative models.

Customer Focus. Allows the analyst to look at reports that help decide which subset of customers will be the best one to target (e.g., which will be the most responsive).

Business Insights. Allow the analyst to actually decompose the targeted population into its most meaningful characteristics, making it possible to gain truly useful insights into the nature of these "best-targeted" profiles.

So, in general the analyst will:

1. Select a population of data to model.
2. Build a model (to select those characteristics that will make up the best target population).
3. Analyze the model (to see exactly how good a predictor the selected model actually is).
4. Decompose the model (examine the different aspects of the model in greater detail to learn what the most important characteristics of the population are).

Each Intelligent Miner for Relationship Marketing application provides a flexible data template that is industry-specific, and a four-phase methodology for analysis. The data templates and methodology follow this progression:

Data Preparation

This area is concerned with identification, extraction, cleansing, standardizing, and incorporation of data into the model. Anyone who has tried to execute models in the past knows that the quality of the incoming data is critical to success—and is usually of questionable value.

The Data Preparation functions include the ability to:

- Identify different input files.
- Analyze the quality and content of each field using statistical analysis and graphical display techniques (see Figure 9-4).
- Fix aberrant data by eliminating it, eliminating the records it is in, or changing the values to more appropriate ones.
- Run a correlation analysis of the data included in the input file.

Correlation analysis is the statistical analysis technique that examines a population and tells the user how strongly the different values are correlated across the population. A strong correlation means that, when value A shows up, there is a very high likelihood that value B will show up as well. For example, suppose the customer file you are reading into IM for RM has a column called State_Name, where the name of the state is spelled out, and another column called State_Code, which has a two-digit code number for each state (e.g., 01 = Alabama, 02 = Arkansas, etc.). Then the correlation analysis will show that these two columns have very high correlation. (When I see a State_Code of 1, I always see a State_Name of Alabama.) Very high correlation is very bad for a predic-

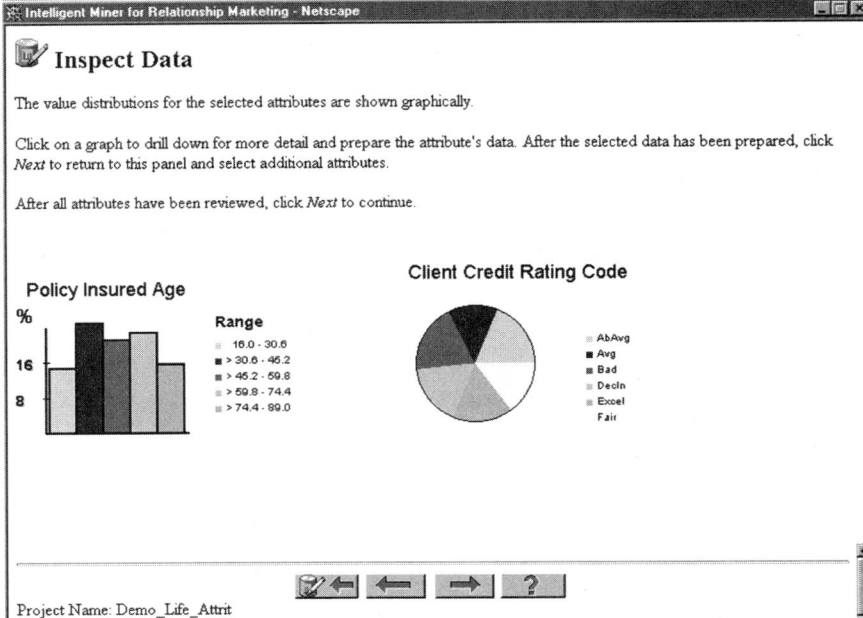

Figure 9-4
IM for RM inspect data screen.

tive model because it tells the analyst that the correlation is the most predictive of relationships. (It is 100 percent predictive.) However, anything this highly predictive is usually not very useful.

Strongly correlated variables can ruin the viability of the model because they indicate a relationship that is not meaningful. IM for RM, therefore, allows the analyst to identify this aberrant correlation and to eliminate it before the actual analysis of the model takes place.

Figure 9-4 shows the IM for RM Inspect Data screen. This screen appears when the user selects a field to analyze. You can see that the Policy Insured Age field shows five different age ranges, and that the Client Credit Rating Code field has six potential values (from fair to above average). By examining the contents of each field, the analyst can determine the best way to clean up the data and prepare it for use.

Model Build

After preparing the data for analysis, the analyst moves into the Model Build area of the product. During model building, the user can develop a number of different predictive models to determine which variables from the input file provide the most predictive capability. Model building involves the following steps:

1. *Choose the predictor.* This means that you identify the kind of behavior or result you are trying to predict (e.g., buying behavior, machine component failure, credit card fraud, etc.).

2. *Create a sample file.* Sample files are used to quickly assemble and run many alternative models. Typically, the input files for this kind of analysis are so large that statistical model building will take too long if the entire file is used. The analyst, therefore, picks a subset of the data, using either random or enriched selection techniques. In some situations, using a sample of the file instead of the file itself can actually increase the accuracy of the model developed.

3. *Choose a modeling technique.* After choosing a subset of the data to "play with," you decide whether to run an RBF (Radial Basis Function), a cluster tree, or both kinds of model. Both of these techniques apply data discovery disciplines to the sample file to draw conclusions about the population's behavior.

4. *Run the analysis.* The product applies the chosen modeling technique against the sample file and creates a report that shows

which variables will be useful in predicting behavior and which ones are the more predictive.

5. *Analyze the results.* The product outputs a special graphical display known as a *gains chart*. The gains chart shows how effective the specified model will be. See Figure 9-5.

6. *Save.* The user saves the best model and then applies it to the entire file.

Understanding the Gains Chart A gains chart is an industry standard report that shows the user how effective the proposed model will be. Understanding how to read and interpret gains charts is the key to building and understanding effective models. Let's break one down into its component parts. Figure 9-6 shows a simplified, generic gains chart that we can use to explain its functionality. This default gains chart shows us the response rate we could expect if a promotional campaign were to be run without any analysis—in other words, if we were to simply send our marketing material at random to anybody at all.

Viewing the Random Response Rate The x axis (horizontal axis) in Figure 9-6 charts the percentage of the total population of potential cus-

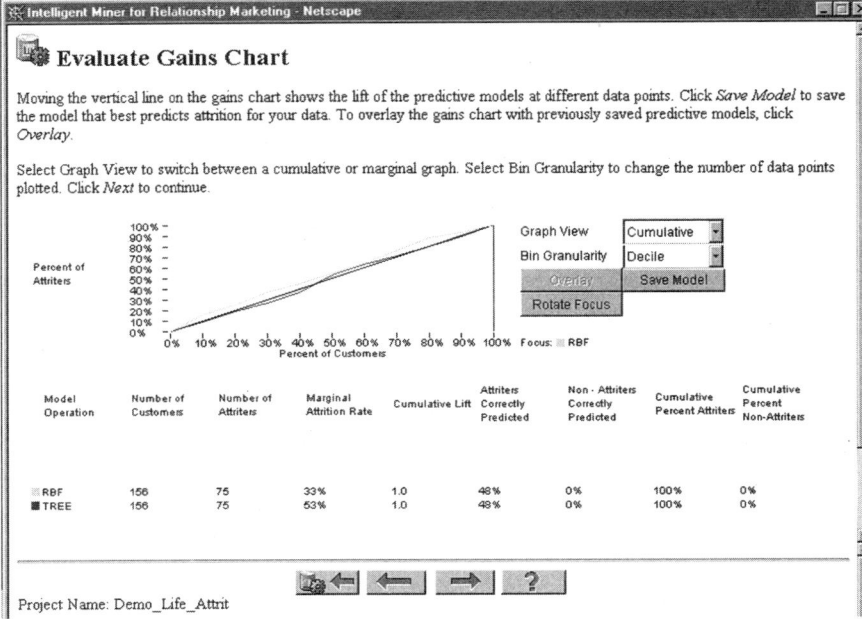

Figure 9-5
IM for RM gains chart.

Chapter 9: Web-Based Statistical Analysis and Data Mining

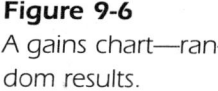

Figure 9-6

A gains chart—random results.

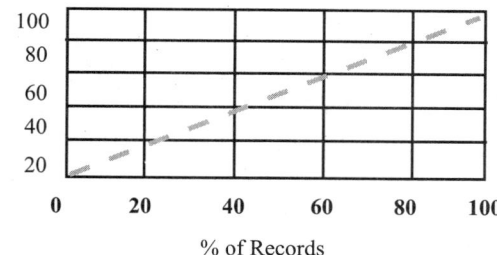

tomers (percent of records) that we would mail our advertisement to. From left to right, we go from 0 percent to 100 percent of the population. The *y* axis (vertical axis) charts the percentage of the full population of positive (or "good") responses we will get back after a certain number of advertisements have been sent out.

The diagonal line through the middle of the chart graphs what our random response rate will be. Our default gains chart tells us that, when 20 percent of the advertisements are sent out, 20 percent of the positive responses will come back. When 40 percent are sent out, 40 percent of the positive responses will come back, etc. (Please note, this does not say that 20 percent of the people will respond, but only that 20 percent of the positive responses will come back. In other words, assuming a population of 1000 potential customers, only 5 people will buy something: 1 person = 20 percent of the total responding population.)

The random response rate chart now says that:

- When I mail out 200 advertisements (20 percent of the 1000 total),
- I will get 1 response back (20 percent of the responding population).
- When I mail the second 200 (I have now mailed 400 total, or 40 percent of the entire population),
- Then 2 responses, or 40 percent of the responding population, will be accounted for, etc.

Seeing Your Lift Of course, the objective of doing a modeling exercise is to improve this response rate. If we know that only five people will respond out of 1000, then we would ideally like to mail our ad to only those five people. This would be called a 100 percent response rate.

Unfortunately, 100 percent response rates are difficult (but not impossible) to accomplish. Most people, however, will settle for any kind of improvement they can get. For instance, for this same example, it may be unreasonable to hope to reach those five buyers by sending out only five mailings, but it might be possible to catch all five by sending out 500 or maybe even only 100 mailings. Even that would be a great improvement.

The measured rate at which a proposed model improves the response rate over the random response rate is known as the *lift*. The better the lift, the more profitably the model can be used. Figure 9-7 shows a typical gains chart with the diagonal random response rate line and the lift line. The lift line shows the analyst how much improvement the new model will produce over the random response rate. As we can see on this gains chart, the model creates a lift line where better than 80 percent of the positive responses occur after only 40 percent of the advertisements are sent out. This represents an incredible improvement in response and will allow the company to save 60 percent of its mailing expense, while still gaining 80 percent of the potential revenue.

Too Good to Be True?   Care must be taken, however, when you look at gains charts. Sometimes statistical anomalies (such as high correlation variables that were not removed) can cause the gains chart to show improvements that are too good to be true. See Figure 9-8. This chart shows such a good response rate that the analyst should be suspicious.

Using Gains Charts to Polish the Model   After building the model and examining the gains chart created, the analyst can:

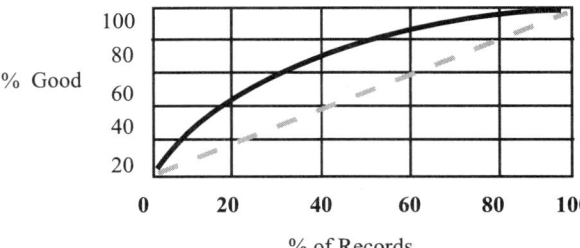

Figure 9-7
Gains chart with lift.

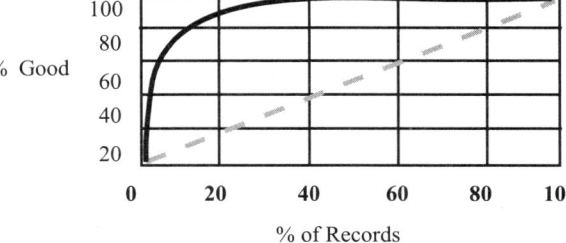

Figure 9-8
Gains chart: too good to be true.

- Go back and build a different model.
- Decide that the lift accomplished is good enough and proceed to the next step of the process.

Customer Focus

Once you have picked the model you like, you can move on to the Customer Focus section and identify all of those specific customers who will actually receive an advertisement. You go through the following steps in the Customer Focus part of the IM for RM.

1. Select a subset of the entire file to mail to (optional). If you want to apply the model to only a subset of records (only mail to a certain state, for example), then specify that here.
2. Score the list. This is the process of going through the file and assigning a likelihood to respond to each of the records. This ranking of the customer record is known as its *score*.
3. View the gains chart. Another gains chart, this one based on the complete file, is generated so that you can verify that the lift is sufficient.
4. Choose the cutoff point. Decide how many of the people should actually be advertised to. Look at the gains chart and the lift and decide to mail to the top 20, 40, 60 percent, or more, of the list that will yield the most economical campaign.
5. Export the scored list for execution. Finally, the best-candidates list is exported and used for mailing.

Business Insights

At this point, you will have completed the actual modeling, scoring, and execution process. The mailing or other type of campaign can be run and the results tracked. However, many analysts will want to go even further with their analysis. For them, it is not enough to know that the people being approached will be the best responders. What they really want to know is what these responders have in common. Who are they? How do they find them again? To gain this kind of insight, the analyst can make use of the Business Insights functionality of IM for RM. Business Insights allows the analyst to examine a list for its characteristics in greater detail. Figure 9-9 shows the Profile Customers screen of the

Figure 9-9
Profile customers screen.

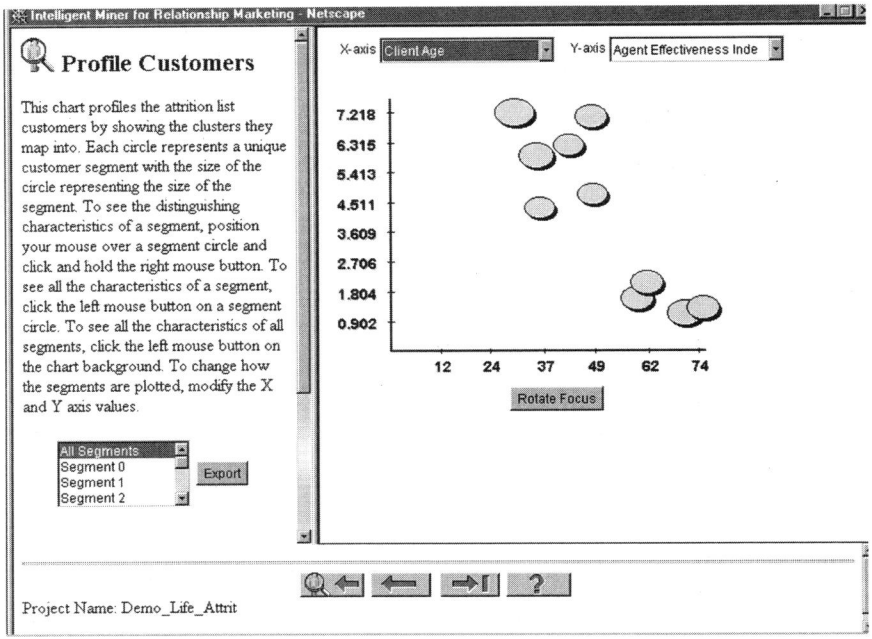

Business Insights area. This chart is a collection of circles; each circle represents a different group of customers who share a common set of characteristics. Each circle, therefore, represents a unique market segment, and the size of the circle reflects the relative size of the population.

Starting from this display, the user can select any one of these segments and "drill down" into a better understanding of the characteristics that make that segment unique. For example, the large segment represents a group of people with high income between the ages of 25 and 35. The size of the circle indicates that this is an important group of people to cater to.

Architecture of the IM for RM Product

The IM for RM product not only provides highly functional, user-friendly, advanced statistical analysis capability, but also runs completely under a Web technology umbrella. The product itself is written in Java and uses a three-tiered architecture (Web browser, Web server, and Intelligent Miner server) to deliver this capability. In this particular case, the majority of the product's functionality is delivered via a direct linkage between the Java code executing on the Web browser and the Intelligent Miner server, with the Web server being invoked only for initialization and screen management.

Conclusion

In this chapter, we look closely at the second major category of data and Web warehouse application delivery tool sets, the analytical tools. We discover that there are several different kinds of analytical tools, with some very different sets of operational and architectural assumptions.

We discuss the statistical tools and see how they help businesses uncover patterns in behaviors with traditional, mathematically based statistical techniques. We also look at the newer, nontraditional data mining/data discovery tools and see how they deliver the same kind of information, though using different techniques. We see too that the nature of these products and their architectures makes them less-than ideal candidates for conversion to a Web, Internet, or intranet type of architecture. They are run better in traditional single-platform or client/server configurations. Several products of this category are currently being converted over to Web warehousing frameworks, however, and we should see a lot more of them in the near future.

CHAPTER 10

Web-Based Graphical and Geographic Information Systems

- *What is a graphical information system?*
- *What are the different types of graphical information systems?*
- *What is a geographic information system?*
- *What business value do graphical information systems deliver?*
- *What are some examples of successful GIS implementations?*
- *How does the Autodesk GIS product work?*
- *What is the GIS Web architecture?*

Graphical Information Systems

So far in our investigation of the different types of information and knowledge delivery that we can expect from a Web warehousing system, we have tended to concentrate on the more traditional forms of data delivery. Starting in this chapter, however, we investigate some of the newer, more exciting, and profoundly less traditional ways that Web warehousing is helping to change the way business works.

The first nontraditional area that we look at is graphical and geographic information systems. Despite their differences, all the business applications that we have considered so far have one important thing in common: They are all concerned with the management and display of data—hard, cold numbers. This latest area of information delivery, however, though it still makes use of hard numbers, provides users with insights into their business operations by displaying that cold, hard data in colorful and interesting forms.

A Definition: Graphical Information System

As with all aspects of this technology, it is important that we clearly define what we mean by graphical information systems. For our purposes, a graphical information system is any application that accepts traditional numeric and descriptive data as input, and formats and displays that data in some graphical or visual form. In other words, included in the category of graphical information systems are any of those products that can graphically display raw information in any form. What are not included in this category are those systems that gather and store images, audio or video, and redisplay them.

The Business Value That Graphical Systems Deliver

All the reporting systems that we have been talking about until now not only concentrate on the storage and retrieval of basically raw data, but also center on presenting that data in a fundamentally tabular, mathematical, and accounting mode. While this kind of information is important to running a business, it is far from the only kind of information that is of value.

It is a well-known scientific fact that different parts of our brains participate in different cognitive processes, and that different forms of input

Chapter 10: Graphical and Geographic Information Systems

are of more value to these different areas. It is also known that different people favor different degrees of exposure to these diverse areas.

Until now, the world of corporate data processing has largely favored the number- and fact-based forms of communication and analysis. The latest generation of information systems, however, including the graphical information systems, open up new doors for business productivity by applying the power of computer systems to the management and manipulation of nontabular items as well.

When it comes to determining the business value that the graphical information systems deliver to the business, we need to use some different kinds of metrics and perspectives to make any business sense of them. Each of the major categories of graphical information systems addresses a different set conditions. However, they do have the same underlying core values in common. In general, the graphical information systems allow the user to be aware of, review, and analyze information that is so complicated, so multidimensional, and so overwhelming in detail that the simple numeric, tabular forms of reporting and communication are inadequate. In the following section, we will investigate how some of these tools actually work.

Types of Graphical Information Systems

The area of graphical information systems is large and growing quickly. Organizations have found many ways to display data graphically to their advantage. The major categories of these products include:

- Traditional charting and graphing software
- Virtual-reality mapping (2-D/3-D) software
- Abstraction (multidimensional) mapping software
- Geographic information systems

In this section, we provide some background information about each of these categories.

Traditional Charting and Graphing Software

Included in the ranks of the traditional charting software packages are an extremely wide array of products that turn plain, boring data into pie charts, bar graphs, and other forms of visual reporting. There are very few, if any, traditional charting software packages in existence anymore. Nowadays, traditional charting and graphing capabilities are built into almost every Web warehousing product.

You find these capabilities built into many products:

Spreadsheets such as Lotus 1-2-3 and Excel

Query tools such as Brio or Impromptu

OLAP tools such as Influence or Essbase

Statistical analysis tools such as SPSS or SAS

Data discovery tools such as the IBM Intelligent Miner

Word processing tools such as MS-Word or Lotus Word-Pro

Just about every other kind of end-user tool on the market today.

Delivering Business Value with Charting and Graphing Software
It might seem strange that this very non-businesslike functionality is being built into all these end-user business tools. Who says that showing your spreadsheet data in the form of a pie chart delivers a real value to the business? Nevertheless, it is clear that these capabilities contribute significant value to many of the operations they are associated with; otherwise they would not be so popular and critical to the success of these tool sets.

I believe that the reason for this confusion is the fact that people do not always use the tools for the right reason. Let's see if this scene is familiar: You are sitting in a meeting room. The presenter is an incredibly boring person, talking about something that only he or she is interested in. This person then proceeds to flash full-color slides on the screen. For a moment, your interest is piqued. The slide has added some color to an otherwise dreary presentation. The colors attract you, entice you. But then you look closer; and you realize that the slide has so many colors, is so complicated, and has such small type that there is no way you can make any sense out of it. Slide after boring, unreadable, full-color slide is displayed, as you slowly nod off to sleep.

The problem with this presentation has nothing to do with the usefulness of the graphical reporting tool, but a lot to do with the presenter. When graphics (or any other materials) are used haphazardly without any notion of their value or strengths, then they are in fact quite useless. See Figure 10-1.

Consider another situation. Here, the speaker has been focused and interesting and is trying to present a strong case. Suddenly, a pie chart appears. The bright, primary colors and the conspicuous discrepancies in

Chapter 10: Graphical and Geographic Information Systems   **251**

Figure 10-1
A less-than-informative graphical report.

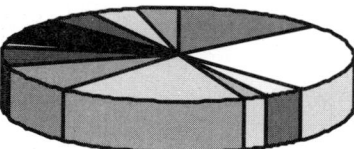

29 May 99
Sales Report

- Boston Crab Market
- Carnavaron Tigers
- Escargot de Bourgogne
- Gravad lax
- Ikura
- Inlagad Sill
- Jack's New England Clam Chowder
- Konbu
- Nord-Ost Matjeshering
- Röd Kavair
- Røgede slid
- Spegesild

the size difference of the slices clearly reinforce the point this person is trying to make. In this case, the saying "A picture is worth a thousand words" is certainly true. See Figure 10-2.

These well-known graphical capabilities do, in fact, provide real value to the organization, as long as they are used correctly. Charting and graphing software can enhance the abilities of the businessperson by:

- Summarizing large amounts of detail into clear patterns of anomaly conditions
- Focusing in on problems or growth areas
- Showing clear trends and directions
- Simplifying the communications process

With intelligent use of these capabilities, people can review more information, more quickly, and more accurately and respond more appropriately to conditions that may arise.

Figure 10-2
A meaningful, informative bar chart.

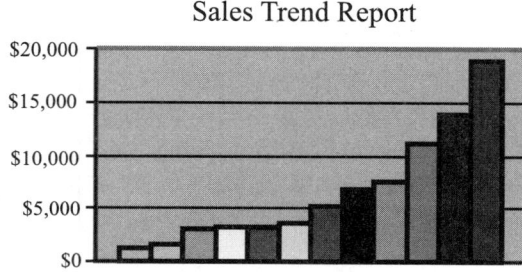

A good example of this can be found where charting and graphing capabilities are added to existing OLAP or query and reporting tools. In those situations, graphical capabilities can be utilized to create high-level summary reports that allow the user to scan millions of records by simply observing the colors and patterns that the graphs display. Many executives have found this capability to be well worth the small additional expense.

Virtual Reality (2-D/3-D/4-D)—Reality Representations

A second category of graphical information systems is virtual-reality (2-D/3-D/4-D) products. When we talk about virtual-reality products, we do *not* mean video games, virtual-reality game rooms, or the vast assortment of virtual-reality toys that are so popular these days, although these entertainment products have spearheaded the development of the technology that makes useful business products a reality.

When we discuss Web warehouse–based business virtual reality products, we mean those applications that provide *reality representation* services. A few examples will help explain what this exciting branch of graphical information systems is all about.

The fundamental purpose of a reality representation application is to collect a large amount of specific tabular data about a situation or condition, and then use that data to create a graphical representation of what is happening. A person looking at it can then get a more accurate and complete picture of what is going on.

A Power Plant Application An excellent example of this is the use of reality representation inside nuclear power plants. There are two extremely large challenges that the manager of such a plant (or any large power-generating facility) must face.

First is the fact that there are many areas of the plant that are inaccessible, either because they are too dangerous, too hot, too cold, or too cramped to get into. This means that there are miles and miles of pipes, conduits, and wires, running in every direction, that cannot be easily monitored.

Second is the problem of interdependency. This problem occurs whenever you have a large number of components, all of which work together and are dependent on each other to do their job. The problem is that, in order to really understand what is going on with those different parts, you need to see what all of them are doing at the same time.

Chapter 10: Graphical and Geographic Information Systems 253

Unfortunately, simple gauges and reports will not give you a good and accurate picture of all of these unknowns and interdependencies. This is where reality representation comes in.

In a reality representation application, the user is provided with a graphical 3-D view of the specific area that is to be examined. The physical layout of the pipes and wires is already known to the system, and the 3-D software allows the user to "walk around" in the facility.

Instead of simply showing the physical pipes and wires in their real colors, the virtual-reality software can read all the different meters and gauges planted throughout the system and use that data to color-code the objects. For example, a blue pipe would be cold and a red pipe hot; the hotter or colder the pipe, the deeper and darker would be the color of the display. By showing the user the physical plant layout, color-coded to show temperature, voltage, radioactivity level or any other characteristic that is important, the user can monitor all activities and situations, and see the interdependencies in a way that no report could ever show. Such systems can give people a level of control and a troubleshooting capability whose value cannot be underestimated.

Layering Applications Another variation of reality representation is the layering application approach. These types of products have had a long and fruitful history of applicability in many areas:

- *Computational and experimental physics.* Fluid dynamics, electromagnetics, heat conduction, neutron flux, groundwater flow
- *Engineering.* Mechanical, civil, automotive, aeronautical, electrical, petroleum
- *Sciences.* Oceanography, medical imaging, biology, earth sciences, geography, geophysics

In all cases, the product's main strength is that it allows the user to take a multilayered object, separate each of the layers from each other, and explore details and interdependencies between them.

A good example of this kind of product is Tecplot, the data visualization and plotting software from Amtec. Tecplot allows engineers to decompose geologic and engineering spaces into their component parts for analysis and design purposes.

Other Reality Representation Applications While the power plant case is certainly an interesting and glamorous one, it is only one small example of how this technology is being used to support business applications. Some other interesting examples follow.

- *Medical systems.* They allow doctors in remote locations to monitor the progress of patients long distances away. The vital signs, temperatures, and other critical data points are collected and fed into a virtual-reality representation of the patient's body.
- *Oil well drilling services.* One leading-edge organization has figured out how to feed specific data about the progress of drilling operations at sites around the world. This real-time data is fed into reporting systems that allow customers to log onto the Web, view the progress of each drilling operation, and make up-to-the-minute decisions about all their operations from one centralized location.
- *Traffic and transportation management.* Almost everyone is aware of the awesome capabilities represented by scanning technology, where data on packages and/or freight loads is scanned into the system at every step in the transportation process. Global positioning systems (GPS) and centralized reality representation software allow people to actually track their packages and loads from one location to the next. This capability enables people to make up-to-the-minute, accurate decisions about how to best move goods at the lowest cost and with the most impact.

There are dozens of other applications of this technology that we could talk about, but suffice it to say that these capabilities will continue to develop and will continue to be added to the successful corporate arsenal of business intelligence capabilities.

Multidimensional Abstract Representations

Another form of advanced graphical representation software that is becoming extremely popular is a class of product that displays extremely complex, multidimensional conditions in greatly simplified graphical formats. These types of applications reveal underlying patterns that are not obvious in tabular representation or other forms of straightforward graphing and modeling. These products are often referred to as *visual data mining* applications, since they allow users to take multidimensional relationships, display them with customized layout schemes, and then explore more deeply in the areas of interest.

Visual Data Mining When there are so many variables that colors and shapes fail to communicate the complete situation, then multidimensional abstraction tools can prove extremely valuable. The user customizes the reporting environment so that more dimensions and relationships are exhibited.

One of the earliest and most powerful collections of products in this category was developed by Silicon Graphics Inc. Silicon Graphics, the pioneer hardware vendor in the area of graphics display and manipulation, created a series of visual data mining applications to address some very specific business needs.

1. *Splat and Scatter Visualizer.* For situations more complex than two or three dimensions can handle. Data is displayed in many dimensions (3-D coordinates, two independent slide bars, size, color, and orientation). This approach is ideal for simultaneously analyzing the behavior of data in many dimensions. This visualizer can be used to analyze complex interrelationships, such as market basket applications, where the analyst is interested in determining the interdependencies between the shoppers' selections. For example, when consumers buy milk, do they often also purchase cereal or baby food?

2. *Map Visualizer.* Displays geographical maps, using the same dimensional configurations (3-D, size, color, etc.). The application can help users understand the complex interrelationships among different areas of the country, for instance.

3. *Tree Visualizer.* Displays hierarchical data structures in a 3-D landscape, revealing quantitative and multidimensional characteristics of data. Utilizing a fly-through technique, users view data as visual representations of hierarchical nodes and associations. Users explore data with any level of detail or summary, from a bird's-eye perspective down to detailed displays of source data. This is used to analyze market segments, allowing users to organize their understanding about groups of buyers of different products.

4. *Stat Visualizer.* Provides in-depth analysis of standard statistical relationships in a graphical format.

Drug Development Cost Savings A company called Spotfire Inc. has developed another very powerful product in this category. The Spotfire product allows users to graphically display the relationships between their data in the same way as the other products. In this case, however, the vendor has tailored the application to the needs of specific industries.

Although it is a well-focused product, Spotfire has been utilized in several different industries with excellent results. In one application, drug companies use it to assist their research and development teams in the reduction of research costs. Drug companies spend billions of dollars on the development of new drugs, and millions of files full of valuable information about other research efforts are available to them for review. Unfortunately, it is very difficult to weed through all of this data and discover any useful new insights. The Spotfire application brings out patterns in research that others have already discovered. It can save the users years of wasted research. See Figure 10-3.

Other applications include the analysis of marketing databases and the review of complex financial portfolios.

Geographic Information Systems

The last type of graphical system we will consider is geographic information systems (GIS). These systems represent a highly specialized niche in the overall graphical display market, but the GIS functionalities too have begun to find their way into the mainstream of desktop software. For example, MS-Excel now comes with a GIS component included.

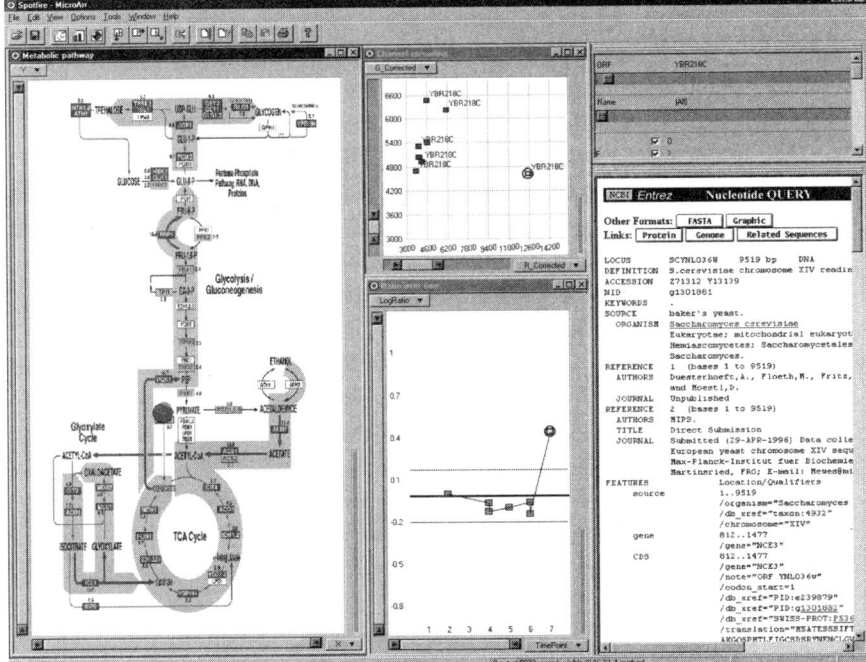

Figure 10-3
Spotfire application.

Chapter 10: Graphical and Geographic Information Systems

Basic GIS Functionality The fundamental operation of a GIS is simple and straightforward. A user is provided with a series of semitransparent maps, often referred to as *layers* or *overlays*. An overlay is like a clear piece of plastic with certain objects "painted" onto it (except, of course, that it is built into the software).

Each overlay contains a different collection of map objects, such as:

The political boundary lines between countries, states, cities, or counties

The interstate highways

All available properties zoned for business

A color-coded demographic map, indicating the income level of residents in their postal code

Figure 10-4 shows an example of two layers for a map of the world: an *oceans* layer and a *continents* layer. When these two are laid over each other, a complete map of the world results. Once the collection of overlays is selected, the user can begin analyzing the relationship between the various layers and develop a better understanding of the nature of a particular geographical area.

There are several application areas where GIS technology has proven profitable to employees. A couple of examples follow.

Picking the Best Store Location A major problem for managers of large store chains is deciding where to establish new shops. Since store location can literally make or break the entire undertaking, it is one of the biggest decisions these managers will make.

Before a new store is built, many factors need to be taken into account. A few of the many questions that need to be answered are:

- How close are we to our competitors' stores?
- How far away are our own stores?

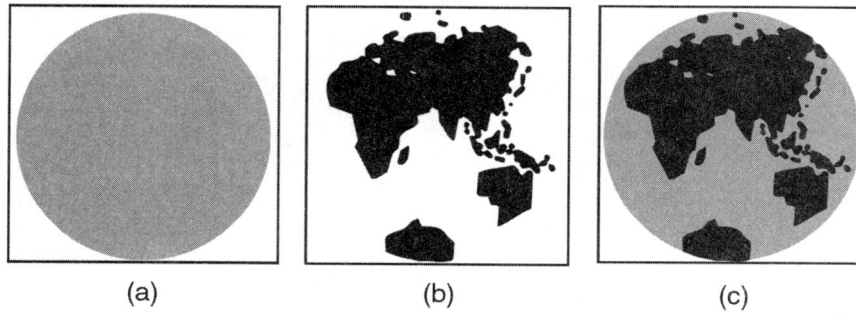

Figure 10-4
Layers and overlay. (a) Oceans, (b) continents, and (c) combined layers.

- How good is the highway access?
- What is the demographic information—income, age, and other facts—about people in the area around the potential location?

By limiting their search to available properties within 1 mile of a freeway, at least 10 miles from a competitive store, and within a prosperous and attractive community, GIS analysts can quickly generate a list of prospective properties.

Analyzing Cell Phone Locations Another place where GIS products have found wide acceptance is in the telecommunications and, specifically, the cellular telephone area. In this industry, determining the locations of cellular antennas and the geographical areas they cover can be a tricky engineering problem. Complicated terrain, the presence of hills, valleys, buildings, structures, other cell sites, and many other factors can make cell location and maintenance an interesting problem, especially when real estate costs and establishing right of way can be incredibly variable from one location to the next. Evaluating locations is often referred to as *line-of-sight analysis,* and telephone companies have found GIS technology to be extremely helpful in such analyses.

The Autodesk Geographic Information System

A good example of a geographic information system that leverages the power of the Internet and corporate intranets is the Autodesk MapGuide product.

Company Background

Autodesk Inc. was founded in 1982. The first product offered to consumers was called AutoCAD, which was a revolutionary new approach to the development and deployment of CAD/CAM (computer-aided design/computer-aided manufacturing). This software automates and standardizes engineering and architectural design and manufacturing processes with graphically based programs that allow designers to electronically create and manipulate drawings and specifications.

Chapter 10: Graphical and Geographic Information Systems

By 1987, Autodesk had sold 100,000 copies of its flagship product and had begun to diversify into many other areas of graphical support software. The company is headquartered in San Rafael, California, and currently supports 2540 employees worldwide. Autodesk claims to be:

- The largest personal computer software company in the world
- The number one personal computer design software company
- The number one personal computer 3-D animation company
- The eighth largest developer of multimedia tools

Product Overview

The Autodesk GIS product family allows users to create, manage, view, and analyze complex geographical images (maps and map overlays). One of these products, Autodesk MapGuide, allows organizations to inexpensively distribute their maps and GIS data by using a standard Web browser interface.

The Autodesk GIS has been used by hundreds of customers, and has helped to solve even more business problems. Two examples of these implementations follow.

- **Telia.** A large Swedish telecommunications company, Telia has invested millions of dollars to record geographic information, including digital maps of streets and paper maps of telephone wires and facilities. Paper maps can be easily scanned electronically for inclusion in the system. Once collected, the data is distributed by Autodesk MapGuide to thousands of employees throughout the company. Gone are the days when staff had to request originals or copies of existing maps now that they can access this information from their personal computers.

- **City of Oakland.** The staff at the City of Oakland, California, administrative offices opened up their map vaults and GIS data to the public by building an Autodesk MapGuide system. From the comfort of home, users can browse the city's geographic database, viewing and querying home ownership, aerial photos, and more. The lengthy process of traveling to city headquarters to obtain this information is now streamlined. Built alongside the city's live "Map Room" is a permitting application that enables the public to avoid long lines and hassle to obtain building permits. Moreover, with the GIS distributed in this way to the public, developers and investors can perform research efficiently and thereby speed the city's revitalization efforts.

Product Architecture

The Autodesk MapGuide GIS software consists of several key components and supports a number of different GIS file types.

Autodesk MapGuide Key Software Components A typical Autodesk MapGuide implementation involves the installation of the following Autodesk MapGuide specific components:

1. *Autodesk MapGuide Viewer.* Web browser–based software that allows the user to communicate directly with the Autodesk MapGuide server. The Autodesk MapGuide Viewer is what a user actually employs to view, analyze, and print maps.
2. *Autodesk MapGuide Author.* The component used to create and manage the maps provided to the user.
3. *Autodesk MapGuide Server.* The system component that manages the distribution and display of maps and overlays to users via the Autodesk MapGuide Viewer.

To know how these components work together, we need to understand the different types of files that Autodesk MapGuide uses as its raw material, and the way it manipulates these files to provide the functionality described.

Principal File Types Autodesk MapGuide makes use of three types of files:

- *Autodesk MapGuide (SDF) Storage Files.* The physical files that support the Autodesk MapGuide system.
- *.html files.* The industry standard Web documents that provide text, formatting, and contextual information.
- *.mwf files.* The primary intelligent mapping document. This is a self-contained file that holds general map properties, security information, map layer properties, raw map data, and user interface specifications.

The Construction of an Autodesk MapGuide Display To construct an Autodesk MapGuide display, the system follows the following progression.

1. The system invokes an .html document that provides the initial user display.
2. The user selects an Autodesk MapGuide application from the screen.

Chapter 10: Graphical and Geographic Information Systems

3. The Autodesk MapGuide Viewer is invoked.
4. The viewer invokes the appropriate .mwf file (the master control file for an Autodesk MapGuide display).
5. The viewer interprets the .mwf file and displays each of the different layers of the display.
6. The user can then manipulate the display, adding and subtracting layers (overlays), zooming in and out, etc., all through the viewer software.

The Overall Operation of the Autodesk MapGuide Environment

From an overall operational perspective, the Autodesk MapGuide environment is built to integrate with existing Web-based architecture. For an illustrated view of this organization, see Figure 10-5.

Creating Autodesk MapGuide Systems   The users or administrators of the Autodesk MapGuide system are able to create and manage the maps and overlays they distribute with the Author product. This product works in a standard client/server mode, either through the Internet or via a direct connection to the Autodesk MapGuide Server. The server collects the user's instructions, creates the maps, and delivers a meaningful report.

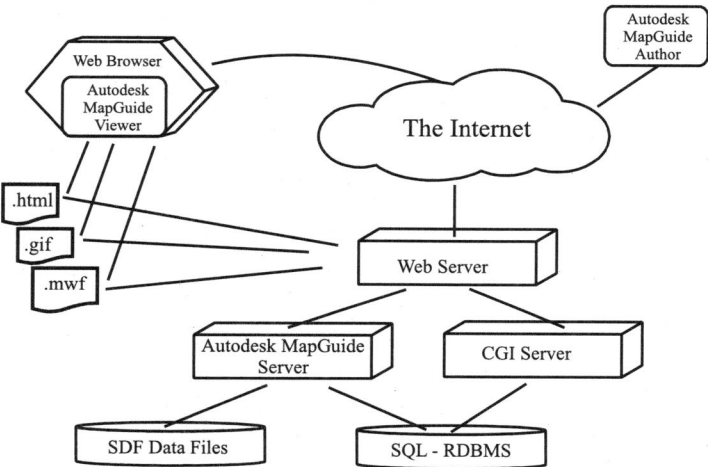

Figure 10-5 Autodesk MapGuide GIS product architecture.

Starting the Autodesk MapGuide Displays

The user starts up the Web browser and invokes Autodesk MapGuide. The viewer then manages the sending and receiving of instructions, data, and images from the Web server, and through the Web server to both the Autodesk MapGuide server and any database servers. In the example in Figure 10-6, we can see a map of the United States, which includes three layers: the U.S. State Capitals, Major Cities, and States, as indicated in the upper left-hand corner of the display.

Manipulating a Map View

After becoming familiar with the initial display screen, the user will have the option of navigating within the display or manipulating the map. One way to manipulate the map is by using the Autodesk MapGuide toolbar. See Figure 10-7. The toolbar, which can be displayed in various locations on the screen, allows users to

1. Make a copy (first icon)
2. Zoom in or out (using the magnifying glass with + or −)

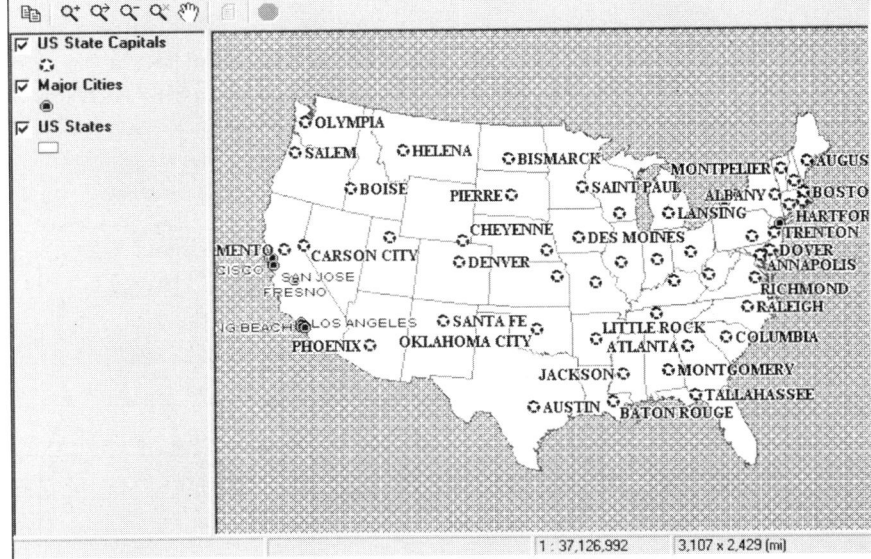

Figure 10-6
Initial display of a map view.

Chapter 10: Graphical and Geographic Information Systems 263

Figure 10-7
The Autodesk MapGuide toolbar.

3. Slide to the left or right (using the magnifying glass with arrow)
4. Stop sliding (using the magnifying glass with X)
5. Grab the map and change its physical location—a process known as *panning* (using the small hand)
6. View help or comments

The other option for mapview manipulation is to use the menu bar at the top of the screen or a pop-up menu. See Figure 10-8. The menu offers many of the same options as the toolbar plus a few more, including the option to:

Create .html bookmarks so that the user can return to these views at a later time

Reload the image to get a fresh view of the map

Select certain areas of the map for more specific investigation

We will now look at a few of these capabilities in more detail.

Zooming in on a Map If the user looking at the map of the United States in Figure 10-6 were interested in getting more detailed information about specific parts of the country, all that user would have to do is click on the zoom-in facility and point to the specific area of the country.

The system would then automatically redraw the map, presenting a close-up of that particular part of the country and eliminating the rest of the map from the display. Figure 10-9 shows a zoomed-in view of the state of California.

Figure 10-8
Autodesk MapGuide pop-up menu.

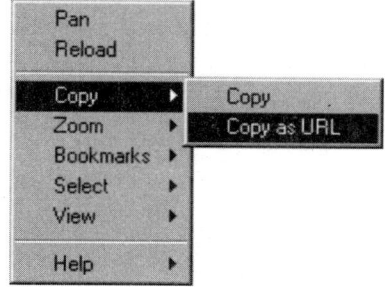

Figure 10-9
Zooming in on the state of California.

Finding a Specific Item on the Map If, however, the user did not know where a particular object was (say a certain city), the MapTip capability would help find it. Figure 10-10 shows the resultant display when a user searches for the city of San Francisco using the MapTip capability.

Selecting a Particular Object Besides simply allowing users to identify specific areas of a geographic display, Autodesk MapGuide also provides all sorts of underlying analytical and reporting capabilities. To see population, sales, pollution, or any other tabular information about a particular area, all the user has to do is select the object, and then ask to

Figure 10-10
MapTip identifying a major city.

Chapter 10: Graphical and Geographic Information Systems

Figure 10-11
Selecting the state of California.

see the corresponding data. Objects can be selected via the select option of the pop-up menu, or through a point-and-click approach. Either way, the result is the highlighted display of the item. See Figure 10-11. Once the particular object is displayed, any specific tabular and referential data for that object can be revealed on the screen.

Conclusion

In this chapter, we discuss the category of Web warehousing products known as graphical and geographic information systems. The main functions of these applications are to display data graphically and to allow that data to be manipulated by users. In Chapter 15, we talk about a closely related category, the multimedia applications. These applications also display graphical information, but their job is to display graphics and images for their own sake, with no data transformation and display included.

In addition to reviewing the general category of graphical information systems in this chapter, we choose one of the GIS products, Autodesk MapGuide, for a closer look.

CHAPTER 11

An Introduction to Text Information Management Systems

- *What is a textual information management system (TIMS)?*
- *Where do these systems come from?*
- *Why does anyone need a text information management system?*
- *What business opportunities does a TIMS present?*
- *What are the challenges to TIMS implementation?*
- *What are some of the approaches to putting a TIMS together?*

The card catalog at your local library, the bibliography at the back of this book, a Web-based search engine, an on-line news service, Internet-based usenets, text mining systems—what do all of these products and services have in common? Although the items in this list share no common technology, professional discipline, or population of users, they are still very similar in one very important way. All of them have been created and organized to help people find the textually based information they need.

The human need for textual information management is as old as the art and science of writing things down. Since the first person put chisel to clay tablet and created the first cuneiform "novel," there has been a need to store information in a place and in a way where it could be retrieved quickly. During the Dark Ages, entire orders of monks were dedicated to the task of copying documents, cataloging them, and saving them, so that the information they contained would not be lost. After the invention of the printing press, and with the dawn of the age of scientific discovery and exploration, our need for documenting, storing and retrieving just about everything has become almost obsessive. It should come as no surprise, therefore, that there is really only one reason that society and businesses are in the place they are in today. It is that we humans have learned to store, retrieve, and take advantage of what has been mastered by those who came before us.

The process of capturing information in a textual form is an incredibly powerful one. In fact, the procedure of organizing one's thinking and writing it down is the most powerful form of communication ever known. With this medium we can actually *store knowledge* and make it available for other people to tap. With the written word, men and women are able to stand on the shoulders of the people who came before them, making it possible to communicate across space and time and to contribute to the ever-increasing body of knowledge to which all human beings have access.

The very nature of this capability, and the power that it includes, makes the job of managing this medium extremely difficult. In many ways, the storage, retrieval, and cataloging of knowledge defies our puny attempts at cataloging and disseminating. In contrast to the storage, retrieval, and management of data, which is relatively straightforward, the problems of managing textual information seem infinitely complex.

The Potentials and the Pitfalls of Textual Management

Once you accept our basic premise about the nature and the importance of the written word in the history of mankind, you begin to see the immense opportunities that the current generation of Web-based information systems represent. Today's crude first generation of HTML-based text search engines have introduced the world to a small sample of what a globally based textual information management system can do. Clearly, we have only begun to scratch the surface of the potential of such systems. With a little work and organization, we all, collectively, can be in a position to propel business and the human race forward into an entirely new plane of human communication and coordination through the intelligent, focused harnessing of the Web's capabilities. Imagine a world where people, anywhere on this planet, can ask for information about any subject and instantaneously be rewarded with a condensed, focused response of exactly what they want to know.

Current Web-Based Text Search Shortcomings

Let's be honest; there are several barriers to the exploitation of the written word, all mechanically based. For all its power, global scope, and gee-whiz appeal, the Web delivers several shortcomings with its convenience. When you do a search on the Web today, you will find a lot of information that you do not want; a lot more information that is related to what you are searching for, but not precisely what you need; and, if you are lucky, a little bit of what you really want to know. Of course, the only way to claim your search results is to read through dozens and dozens of pages to get down to the item you really want.

Suppose we had a globally based system, like today's Web, that would not only find the documents of interest, but would read them, weed through them, and extract only the information that we are really looking for in the first place. Suppose we could have a system that could do all that looking, searching, and prioritizing for you, leaving you free to fret over the actual information you were worried about in the first place.

This is exactly the kind of system being built in the newly emerging world of text management in the Web warehousing arena. It may be a while before that kind of capability is made available to the general public through the local Internet service providers, but we are already seeing many firms spending large sums of money to put systems like this in place for corporate users. These systems are being viewed as the latest generation of mission-critical, survival-based weapons in the corporation's arsenal of technologies, and it will not be too long before every corporation has a powerful, sophisticated tool delivered to every decision maker's desktop.

The Availability of Information to the Businessperson

Without a doubt, today's businessperson has access to more information than anyone has ever had before. Hundreds of corporate computer systems, thousands of personal computers, and millions of knowledge workers are daily creating, storing, accessing, and analyzing information in all sorts of different forms in order to help them make good decisions.

A contemporary businessperson reads newspapers, magazines, and reports at corporate, local, and other levels every single day. The businessperson also gains access to the Web, new services, usenets, and a myriad of other Web-based information sources. In addition to business people, there are the hundreds of thousands of people who work in the intelligence, research and development, industry consultant, and think tank industries, creating millions of pages a week of new information on top of everything that is already there. It is clear that a businessperson has access to—and a need to work with—a lot of information.

The Businessperson's Need for Masses of Information

Just because business people *can* and *do* have access to so much information does not necessarily mean that they need it to do their jobs. Everyone knows instances of the many ways business people can abuse their corporate Internet access:

They do research for their children's homework assignments.

They shop for personal items.

They review vacationing options.

They participate in chat rooms and/or personal special-interest usenets.

Providing people with full access to information is not always a good thing in and of itself. However, for every one of those abusive situations, there are examples of productive use of information access.

Competitiveness in Today's Business World Without a doubt, the business world is becoming increasingly competitive. This competition, however, is not the same kind that business people have had to face in the past. Every day businesses are merging, diverging, divesting, and investing in each other. Every day the very economic, technological, organizational, and financial foundations upon which businesses are based are changing.

As conditions change, it becomes increasingly important for business people to understand how that change is happening, and how their company can best take advantage of it. Every day businesspeople become more dependent on more and more information (from both the traditional data sources and the nontraditional text-based informational sources) in order to keep their companies in the business "game."

The Knowledge-Is-Power Paradigm For many years, the saying "knowledge is power" has been accepted as a fundamental truth. We live in a world where knowledge is available in more forms, from more places, and deliverable in more ways than ever before. It is obvious, therefore, that the business that stays on top of the new forms of knowledge is one that will survive and thrive. This paradigm has proven itself true over and over again, as industry after industry succumbs to the relentless onslaught of information technology in all of its many forms.

The latest generation of "killer apps" (technology solutions that reinvent an industry, unseat the former main players in the industry, and create a whole new generation of winners), has been based on data warehousing and data mining. These technologies have been wreaking havoc in the areas of marketing and sales, forcing companies to reexamine exactly who their customers are, what they want, and how they can best be served.

There is absolutely no reason to believe that this latest generation of information technology will not lead to yet another such revolution. The fact that this newest technology will be text-based and not data-based is inconsequential. More important, this latest revolution will most likely combine the first-ever opportunity to manage huge volumes of textual information electronically with the first real opportunity to share access universally and globally via the Internet and the World Wide Web.

This would seem to indicate that this next escalation in the corporate war for knowledge will be for much bigger stakes than ever before imagined. After all, more tightly coupled governments, multinational businesses, and the Internet are creating an ever-shrinking global marketplace. The next battles for technological and information supremacy will be defining not just who will be the biggest corporate players on a regional or national scale, but will in fact define which organizations will be the survivors in the newly emerging single worldwide business marketplace.

Getting Business Benefit from Text Information Management Systems

So let's say that a lot of different kinds of text management, data management, and combined text/data management systems (TIMS) are available to the typical business user. Just precisely what are businesses going to do with these kinds of systems? It is one thing to talk about the "big picture" and "vision" that a text-managed world might represent, and another thing entirely to translate those "visions" into short-term, tangible, measurable benefits to the businessperson and the corporate top or bottom line. There are in fact many ways that this kind of capability is being harnessed today in businesses around the world, and ways in which they will most certainly be harnessed in the future.

New Technologies Force Business People to Redefine Themselves and Their Roles

At first glance, the power of text management might seem deceptively simplistic and irrelevant to the running of most businesses. After all, businesses have been functioning for years without these capabilities, and people understood how to do their jobs without needing to lean on TMSs.

Unfortunately, in the case of text management systems, we will probably find that we have to face the same kinds of challenges that we experienced with every new generation of business-based technological innovation. Business people will not understand exactly how these technologies can help them because they will want to continue doing their jobs the same old way.

The quantum leap in business efficiency and capabilities that a new technology provides is recognizable only when the users redefine themselves, their jobs, and their work structure to capitalize on that technology.

Early Computers Redefined the Business Itself Imagine the skepticism and chagrin that accountants felt when the first computers were introduced into business back in the 1960s. "Computers! Hah! Those big, expensive things are nothing but glorified calculators. You're never going to get a machine to replace the work that *we* do!" Well, what happened? It turned out that the computers could do what the accountants did; and they did it better, faster, and cheaper.

Chapter 11: Text Information Management Systems

There was, of course, an incredibly painful period of adjustment that businesses and accountants had to go through to make the change and to experience the benefits of those computers. When it was all said and done, the job of the accountant had to be shifted significantly and the structure of the business had to change. But ultimately, the computer provided a benefit that far outweighed the cost of its implementation (the cost in both *hard dollars* and the *soft dollars* of human reorganization).

Client/Server Technology Is Still Redefining the Business
Maybe you think that the accountant story is a really obvious example, that computers needed a little redefinition of business roles to make them pay off, but that the change they had to make was pretty logical anyway. What about in more modern times, though?

Let's consider the personal computer and client/server revolution. Did these technologies deliver value, and did they lead to the redefinition of business roles? On the surface, you might think not. The presence of the personal computer certainly did not lead to as sweeping of a change or as measurable an improvement to business operations as the first computer revolution did—or did it?

Consider for a moment what the business world is like today compared to 10 years ago. Every businessperson has a personal computer on the desk. Every personal computer is hooked up to a corporate local area network (LAN). People are totally dependent on such things as email, personal calendars, the exchange of word processing documents, and presentations to do their day-to-day jobs.

But has this yielded any economic value? Let's see what else has happened in that decade. Where are the armies of secretaries, administrators, and typists? What happened to the leagues of middle managers whose jobs it was to keep everybody organized and to provide organizational cohesion and structure? All of those jobs have been deemed unnecessary to the modern business. Today's businesses run leaner and meaner and more efficiently than ever before, and the personal computer has played an instrumental role in that process. However, to capitalize on it, businesses had to undergo some growing pains.

Redefining the Business under Text Management We will probably see over the next few years yet another major shift in the way business people think about their jobs and pursue their tasks. If this happens, then the new generation of text management systems will yield the same kinds of significant improvements in business performance that the earlier generations of systems did.

If this implementation pattern is consistent with earlier patterns, then we will be functioning in a business world with:

- Fewer people to do more of the work
- A less formal structure for people to function in
- More responsibility for those people involved in the process
- More pressure to continue to learn, grow, and expand horizons

I am not so sure that this is the kind of world we would want to work in, but the following facts remain: Nobody wanted to go through the changes imposed by each previous generation of technology. Everybody thought that we had gone as far as we could go with the last set of changes. But eventually, we adjusted, got used to it, and moved forward again.

Areas Where Text Management Systems Have Already Delivered Big Business Benefits

We will assume that the business people who want to cash in on the benefits of text management systems are willing to pay the price, measured in terms of their understanding of themselves, their jobs, and the way their businesses are organized and run. Then let's look at some of the different places where implementation can, and will, occur over the next few years.

There are really two major areas where text management systems will most likely have a major impact on the ways businesses are run; not too coincidentally, these are precisely the two areas where data information management systems have an impact as well. These are the operational enhancement area (helping business people make better short-term tactical decisions) and analytical enhancement (turning business decision makers into better strategists).

The world of the business today is full of data-based tools that help keep track of how well things are running. It seems that for every process, for every machine, for every person there are dozens of different computers that are monitoring, measuring, and controlling everything that happens, all to better manage the way the business performs. Despite all of this automation, there are still many, many areas where the data-based information system simply cannot perform well. Consider a few situations from different industries.

Manufacturing—Complex Machinery Maintenance and Repair

There are, in fact, hundreds of situations in the manufacturing world today where very large, very complex machinery needs to be maintained by a small, specialized staff of individuals who do not have the time to learn all the details about each of their charges. In these situations, the presence of user manuals and access to manufacturers' representatives are never enough. The failure of a large complex machine can cost an organization millions of dollars in lost production time. Many times, there is someone, somewhere in the organization, who has had to fix that same problem once before.

These organizations are creating on-line troubleshooting logs, which allow individuals to record the problems they encountered and the way they resolved them. These logs are then available to other technicians who work in other locations or on other shifts. When similar problems arise, the technician on the spot can do a text-based search for similar symptoms or conditions and receive a listing of all log entries with similar conditions.

In other situations, the sheer volume of text documents that a service and repair organization needs to keep available to technicians has led to the elimination of printed service manuals in favor of on-line manuals, which are not only available immediately, but also can be:

Shared among as many technicians as required

Immediately updated as changes occur

Footnoted with comments from field personnel, relating their own experiences and challenges in working with these items.

Systems like this save organizations millions of dollars a year in manual maintenance and distribution costs and untold millions in savings for the repair processes themselves.

Research and Development—Don't Reinvent the Wheel

Text management systems are yielding huge cost savings in the area of research and development. Almost every major industry has a research and development aspect to it, and the implementation of newer, better ways at a lower cost is the key to their success. Companies such as drug firms, food manufacturers, and auto manufacturers thrive on their R&D efforts.

For the people who run these R&D units, the key to efficiency is to try to never invest in the development of something that has already been developed by somebody else. If these groups can find ways to leverage the work that other organizations have done in the past, then they can cut years off their own research and development budgets. Nowadays, these organizations can gain access to millions of pages of research material, created by their own research and development departments or in other divisions, published within government or university semi-public repositories, or available for purchase.

The problem, of course, is that, even when you can gain access to other people's research notes, there is no way to know whether the work being discussed is relevant to what you are trying to do. Research and researchers are notoriously nebulous in their categorizations and cataloging. The only way, then, to figure out what is pertinent is to find all work that might be related and read everything.

Modern text management systems can spare organizations all that work. Text mining and text analysis systems can read these documents and summarize their content, saving researchers weeks of work.

Travel and Transportation—People's Preferences in Hotel Rooms
A big problem for developers and maintainers of travel agency and reservation systems is keeping track of all of the customer preferences in their travel arrangements. At first glance, the capture of this kind of information might seem to be just another trivial task for a normal data capture and management system. Just figure out everything that people might want or prefer, make a database to hold the information, call up the customers and ask them which of these preferences apply to them, and voilà, you have your information.

Unfortunately, people and their wants, needs, and interests are much too volatile for that. In fact, different kinds of things are important to different kinds of people under different kinds of conditions, and any attempt to capture all of that information in a database form is an exercise in futility.

For example, one person wants to vacation only where the days are warm and sunny, unless it is an area where there are a lot of trees and water, then cooler weather will be okay. Some people want a view of the water, others want to see the sunset. Some want rooms with blue curtains, others want a hotel with a masseuse on duty. Some want a vegetarian menu, others want English-speaking waiters. The list is infinite.

Some travel and transportation firms are discovering that it is much easier and more economical to go ahead and capture any and all preferences that a person might have in textual form, and allow intelligent text mining and analysis systems help agents match up people and preferences.

What is the benefit to the company? The company that gets the best match of customer preferences and travel conditions is the one the customer will come back to. Systems like this provide significant competitive advantage in the marketplace.

Real Estate—People's Preferences in Homes The customer preference story for the travel and transportation industry is equally true for the real estate salesperson. A system that can keep track of a person's likes and dislikes in a nonstructured, *subjective* way, and applies those preferences to an analysis of equally unstructured information about available homes, is a system that can make the real estate agent's job a lot easier.

Customer Service—Analysis of Consumer Letters and Email
Another clever and relatively new application of text mining is in the area of customer service, where more and more customers are sending requests, complaints, and comments to corporations via email and Web page forms. It is now possible for those organizations to enlist the aid of text analysis software and actually "read" the mail and report to the customer service department information such as how many people are pleased or angry and which products they like or don't like.

Assigning a human being to actually read this much mail would cost the organization many worker-weeks of effort. More likely, though, the mail will not be read at all. The discipline and accuracy of the software-based analysis can help the company make quantitatively based decisions about which products are liked/disliked and how to improve them.

It is even more interesting to think about what will be possible as more and more written communication becomes email-based. What about software that reads homework assignments and essays and grades them? What about software that manages politicians' mail and sends appropriate responses? The possibilities are endless and perhaps a bit frightening.

The Knowledge/Text-Based Organizational Structure It is becoming clear in most businesses today that organizational structure is on a serious downturn. Companies are daily removing more and more of the guidelines, policies, and organizational hierarchies that hold people together, let them know how they fit into the organization, and inform them what they are supposed to do and how to do it.

In place of this structure is a dizzying array of contradictory policy, procedure, and guideline setting, supported by an even more confusing arrangement of "matrixed" management structures. These pseudo-structures actually do very little to help people understand their place in the scheme of things, and as the rate of change in the business continues, this lack of structure is beginning to take its toll.

In the meantime, knowledge management storehouses have been created in which systemically defined resources provide people with a text-based structure to support and shore up the nebulous real-world structure they are forced to deal with. These text repositories provide disenfranchised employees with guidance and instructions, and are a resource that helps them save time and effort in navigating the organizational quagmire that is the business world of today. These systems, referred to as *corporate digital libraries* or *knowledge networks,* allow organizations to enhance their operational efficiency without adding layers of management.

Legal Profession—On-Line Legal Libraries An area that seems to be custom-made for text management systems is the legal profession. The main job of attorneys, other than to appear in court, is to do legal research, pouring through scores of legal documents to identify precedents and previous cases that help shore up the case they are currently working on.

In today's world of textual information management, the traditional law library, ensconced with hundreds of stuffy old law books, has been replaced by a computer terminal. The terminal not only allows a researcher to look up the cases on line, but it also allows that researcher to analyze the targeted cases for some particular nuance of the law that can help fortify a case, thus saving attorneys and researchers thousands of hours of hard reading time.

Insurance—Policies, Compliance, and Correspondence Analysis
Without a doubt, one of the biggest challenges facing the insurance industry is keeping track of myriad and sometimes contradictory governmental and corporate policy guidelines and the way they are stated within policies and reflected in the correspondence that the company sends and receives. Insurance companies have struggled for years with the problem of different rules and regulations that apply to different people, at different times, and under differing conditions. They have created artificial "codified" data-based systems to try to manage and control it all.

With a powerful text management system, however, these companies can do away with much of the cumbersome, constantly changing codification process, and instead store all applicable rules, regulations, policies, and correspondence in an electronic form. By combining this electronic storage medium with powerful text search and manipulation packages, they can greatly reduce their cost of doing business, while significantly improving the quality of their decision making at the same time.

Before getting into a lot of detail about the various text information management systems and how they work, we will review the history of how text management systems got to where they are today.

The History of Textual Information Management

Of course, the process of managing textual information in the business world is not a new one by any means. Businesses have always had a lot of respect for textually stored information and have always found that the manipulation of that information could be profitable.

In the earliest days of business, letters, reports, and correspondence were written by hand, and all of these documents would be stored and filed for future reference. But at the dawn of the Industrial Revolution we found that handwritten letters had drawbacks. First, handwriting is often difficult to make out. Second, it is often useful to have more than one copy of a document so that it can be shared with other people, stored in different places, or for any number of other reasons.

The Dawn of the Textual Information Revolution Luckily, that wonderful invention known as the typewriter came along. (Younger readers who may not be so sure what this ancient device is should think of a typewriter as a mechanical word processing system with a built-in printer but no delete key.) With the typewriter, one could create documents that everyone could read and, with the other miraculous device known as carbon paper, make multiple copies of it. For decades, business thrived on the basis of its ability to create standardized textual information, and to store it in large filing cabinets.

Of course, another "secret" ingredient made all of this possible. That was the secretaries and clerks whose entire careers were based on nothing more than the creation, storage, and retrieval of textual documents. The combination of these people with their typewriters, carbon paper, and filing cabinets defined the first generation of textual information management systems for business.

The First Generation of Computer-Based Textual Information Management In this area, as in so many other areas of the business, microelectronics and the computer would soon make that way of doing business obsolete. When the computer first came onto the corporate scene, no one could have possibly imagined that this technology could ever have an impact on textual information. Early computers required a staff of highly trained technical experts, and the only things the machines could read were punched cards and tapes.

Eventually, however, as the computer became more sophisticated, the possibilities for text management became feasible. Early pioneers such as Wang and the Xerox Corporation created the first generation of computerized word processing systems. These computers, though large and cumbersome, allowed employees to create text documents on a computer screen, print them from that same computer, and then store them electronically for future use.

While difficult to use at first, these systems started a revolution that we are still feeling today. The floppy disks (12- and 18-inch diameter) and printers were large and almost comical looking by today's standards, but they became the forerunners of the automated text processing systems that we see today.

Specialized Text Management Systems   While Wang and Xerox started what we might call the mainstream of corporate word processing, there were also several highly specialized initiatives that were underway at the same time. The hypertext systems became the forerunners to the Web HTML environment. Along with these experiments came a varied assortment of "publishing management" systems.

These systems were developed for and utilized by printers and newspaper, magazine, and book publishers. They allowed these users to capture text, pass it around for editing and review, perform cut and paste operations on it for page layout, and finally, convert it to lithographic or some other kind of plates for final printing. Other systems provided large databases of text, which were accessed by research agencies that provided individuals with the ability to pore through volumes of information and find items of interest in a hurry. Systems of this type had extremely limited business applications, were centered on the execution of very specific business tasks, and were based on a construction using proprietary hardware and software.

The Personal Computer and Its Role   The world of text management stayed fairly stable for a while. Several corporations installed and made use of the large, specialized word processing systems for a certain amount of their correspondence. The lowly typewriter, however, still maintained its position as the principal means of business communica-

Chapter 11: Text Information Management Systems

tion. After all, only the largest, richest companies could afford word processing systems, and it was too difficult to train people to use them. And, if you can't store 100 percent of your documents in electronic form, then you will have to rely on maintaining it *all* manually.

All of this changed, however, with the explosion in popularity of personal computers. Suddenly, almost overnight, all of the reasons not to manage documents electronically seemed to disappear. The typewriter disappeared from the business office, carbon paper became ancient history, and the age of the PC-based word processing package came into being.

What we have seen over the past several years is the proliferation of personal computers into every line of business and almost every home. We have also seen the evolution of computer-based text processing from the crude rudimentary style of the 1960s to the incredibly user-friendly and powerful packaging of the 1990s.

Current State of the Art in Text Creation and Storage Software

If we look at the capabilities of today's modern text processing software package, we will see a combination of several of the different "legacies" of text management.

The Word Processing Legacy One evolutionary path revolves around the "traditional" word processing packages that could format and store letters, memos, and notes rapidly and efficiently. You can consider these packages the software versions of the typewriter.

The earliest generation of these products included WordStar, WordPerfect, and MultiMate on the personal computer and the Script language on the IBM mainframe, to name just a few. These products represented a phenomenal step forward in text management. Users could type in the document in a standardized text form, then place special symbols before and after text to mark sections to be displayed in a different font, spacing, or any other format settings. (Ironically, this is exactly the same text formatting approach that the first generation of HTML documents used to accomplish the same objectives.)

Inserting these control symbols was quite a feat, however. The user needed to memorize complex control key sequences, holding down two or even three keys simultaneously to get the right symbols to show up. Unfortunately, the only way the user could see how the formatted document would look was to actually print it out.

The next generation of word processing packages improved on this paradigm by making the insertion of control characters easier and showing the formatted output on line before actually sending it to the printer.

The (Desktop) Publishing Legacy While companies such as Microsoft and Borland were dominating and reinventing the world of word processing, another group of software developers were doing the same to the publishing business. True, there are many similarities between the needs of a corporate office word processor and the text management capabilities that a typesetter in a printing house may need, but there are also a great many differences. The art and science of typesetting is an extremely complex and demanding discipline. There are many specialized functions that a publishing software package needs to offer, over and above the functions provided by a typical word processing package.

A publishing software package needs to provide the publisher with the ability to take absolute, 100 percent control over every square centimeter of the printed page. Publishers need the ability to:

1. Make hundreds of different kinds of fonts available
2. Control the precise spacing between each letter of a word
3. Set standard headers, footers, and other operational templates
4. Manage the automatic pagination of multifile documents
5. Provide for automated index, table of contents, and other forms of lookup capabilities
6. Allow cut and paste of many different kinds of images and figures
7. Use special control characters, formatting mechanisms, and interfaces so that the output of the software can be fed directly into typesetting and printing machines

In general, the output from a publishing software package is not sent to a printer, but to a typesetting machine in which lithographic or other types of printing plates are cut. These plates are then used to drive the production printing runs.

Just as the word processing business was revolutionized by desktop word processing packages, so was publishing changed forever by such packages.

The Email/Web-Based Legacy In the meantime, another world of text creation and management was being developed in the arena of the UNIX operating system. The universal acceptance of UNIX, TCP/IP, and email created an entirely new branch in the text management family tree. Originally, email was a crude and rudimentary thing, made up of straight text files and circulated around the world with little or no formatting capabilities. Eventually, however, this gave way to the current reality of mail standards such as MAPI and Internet/World Wide Web, which have created universally sharable rich-text documents. Eventually, this branch of text management led to the creation of HTML and what we now know as Web pages.

The Think Tank Legacy Our legacy of text management systems does not end there, however. An entire industry of highly specialized text search and retrieval databases has been springing up over the past 30 years. These databases have been developed to meet the specific research and development needs of different groups of individuals.

Some of the more common "think tank" or "R&D" machines have been developed in the support of the legal profession, specialized scientific areas (chemistry, physics, etc.), and special-interest social and government agency systems. In all cases, these systems were responsible for the development of very sophisticated text storage and retrieval approaches and algorithms that are being employed within today's sophisticated text management systems.

Imaging Systems While most of the world has been busily trying to type their text into a computer, so that it can be stored, manipulated, and printed, there is another group of people using products that take the opposite approach. Several generations of specialized hardware and software have helped to create what is known as the *imaging industry*. Imaging is the name given to the technology that takes handwritten and other forms of hard copy text (text that has already been committed to paper) and captures it in electronic form right off the paper. Imaging is basically a form of document photography.

In a typical imaging system, documents of all shapes and sizes are passed through scanners, which "take pictures" of the text and turn those images into binary data for disk storage. These images can then be cataloged and retrieved later.

Imaging systems have become very popular in governmental and insurance organizations, where many documents need to be captured and stored for long periods of time for legal reasons. They present us with yet another family of text management products that we must include in our analysis of text management as a whole.

Imaging systems, like all of the other systems we have been talking about, are becoming increasingly prevalent in the business world. Almost every business has at least one document scanner attached to a PC. Several photocopy machine companies are creating copy machines that spin off digital image copies of the copied documents as well.

Optical Character Recognition Simply capturing images can be very effective in some situations, but to make images of text especially useful, they should be convertible back into the actual textual characters that made up the original. That way you could edit, analyze, and manipulate them just like you would any other text document. This is precisely the job that *optical character recognition* (OCR) software does: it scans images of text and converts those images back into its basic alphabetic characters.

You can find specialized OCR programs that are tied in with different imaging products, or you can find some versions that work with PC-based fax software. You can get versions that translate only certain sizes or types of fonts, or you can get versions that actually translate people's hand printing or even cursive handwriting. Although the OCR technology itself is far from 100 percent foolproof, it has proved to be useful in a number of situations.

Current Convergence of Approaches, Products, and Capabilities Over the past several years, these different disciplines have begun to converge, as supercharged text management systems become available. At this stage, typical word processing packages include the ability to perform all these functions in a totally interactive mode. Now users can immediately see how formats will look and can incorporate the capabilities of publishing software (such as Ventura Publisher or Quark), email/Web-based compatibility, think tank structures, such as summarization and indexing structures, and non-text-based objects such as graphics, maps, and spreadsheets.

Not only have we seen a convergence in the capabilities of these software packages, but there is also phenomenal progress in the areas of translation between products. In the "old" days, it was almost impossible for anyone to translate text documents from one form to another. Someone writing a document in MultiMate, for example, could not work with it in a WordPerfect software package. Today, virtually any word processing package file can be read by and formatted into any other software package with a minimum of trouble.

The Current State of Chaos At first glance, these conditions would seem to indicate that we are in a very good position to create the paperless society that computer visionaries have been talking about for years. More important, if organizing thought and storing it in written form has been such a powerful means of boosting human abilities for so long, then the current volume of written information available, combined with the current access capabilities, should let us move to whole new levels of knowledge and progress. Just think of it:

- The vast majority of business correspondence is created and stored in computerized form. Paper documents are starting to become "shadow copies" of the real, electronic documents that spawn them.
- The standardization of text management software and the ability to translate between one software product and another makes it relatively easy for nearly anyone, anywhere to send well-formatted, highly readable documents to almost anyone else with very little effort.
- The creation of huge corporate intranets and the use of the Internet mean that it is possible for anyone, anywhere to access the files of anyone else, anywhere in the world, without much trouble (assuming that the security issues are addressed).

However, this incredible increase in connectivity and standardization has not created the visionary world of seamless communication and informational superaccess that one might imagine. There are actually several barriers to accomplishing that goal.

Challenges in Textual Information Management

Language Differences No discussion of the challenges to the development of a text management system would be complete without recognizing the most obvious one, languages. There are hundreds of languages in use in the world today, and many of them are radically different. Therefore, if you are going to tackle the issue of text management, you will have to manage different languages within the same system. This challenge is in no way small or trivial. Some languages use different alphabets, and even different sequencing on the printed page, making the problem of providing text management capabilities in cross-language situations very difficult.

Stylistic Differences After the language problem has been surmounted, the next challenge that makes text management so difficult is the many and varied forms that language can take. Even within the rules of structure of a given language, we have many problems that need to be addressed. These include the infinite variety of sentence constructions, subtle meanings, and other forms of textual communication (bulleted lists, charts, etc.), all of which defy anyone's attempt to catalog the information.

Contextual Differences Besides stylistic and language differences, we run into challenges with the document's informational context. The very same words can have a different meaning, depending on where they occur in the text. As we move from one industry to another, one group of people to another, one area of the country to another, or one subject area to another, we change the meaning of the words we are working with.

This problem is nowhere more prevalent than in the computer industry itself—an industry that invents, reinvents, and recycles words as if they were water. For example, what is a *coffee bean?* A reusable Java code component or an ingredient in cappuccino? What about the words data, information, and knowledge? All these take on a different meaning, depending on the context of the discussion.

The Storage Media Even if all of these underlying problems of meaning, context, and applicability were not enough, there is an issue that can invalidate any attempt to catalog textual information: the fact that textual information gets stored in so many different physical forms.

THE PRINTED WORD By far, the single most common form of textual information storage and retrieval is the written and printed word. It is ironic that 10 years ago people were talking about using computers to create a paperless society. What has happened is exactly the opposite. More printed material is created today than ever before in the history of mankind. Every home has a PC and every PC has a printer. More books are published than ever before, more magazines are printed, and more companies are storing documents than were ever imagined possible.

The huge challenge we face in this arena is to ensure that people who need this particular form of textual information have it in their possession, know that what they need is in it, and know specifically where to find it. A paper copy is eminently useless to someone who doesn't have it handy, doesn't know what's in it, and can't figure out where to find it. Alas, while card catalogs, indexes, and tables of content can help us, there are just too many different kinds of items that we might want to find in a printed document. Ultimately, the only way to discern whether a printed document holds the information we want is to actually read it.

THE DIGITAL WORD While a record-breaking volume of documents is being printed and distributed in the old-fashioned, hard-copy format, that does not mean that these are the only forms of textual storage we need worry about. There is still an unbelievably vast amount of additional textual information that is being captured and managed in a solely digital form every day. Today's generation of PC-based desktop publishing software amasses vast storehouses of textual information and many times leaves them totally inaccessible to anyone but the author. This textual information is stored in a variety of formats, Word processors, spreadsheets, HTML documents, and presentation software and a vast array of other product types, all of which have their own special format and storage requirements.

The challenge then in the desktop publishing area is very different from that in the hard copy, printed materials case. In this particular world, it is actually possible to store and transport the information electronically, eliminating the problems of physical proximity, and develop dynamic indexes and search engines that can analyze the contents of the documents for us, helping us to determine their appropriateness before we have to actually read them and greatly reducing the problem of content validity assessment.

It is for these reasons that digital storage of text has become so popular and is proving so incredibly useful. It is here where the exploitation of Web technology has the greatest impact.

THE HANDWRITTEN WORD Lest we forget, we must include in our discussion this, the oldest and still often invoked form of textual information. Although the writing of documents by hand may someday become an ancient art, today it is still used on a very frequent basis.

Much progress has been made in figuring out how to capture, store, catalog, and make retrievable the many different kinds of handwritten inputs that we deal with in the modern business world. Some of these approaches include OCR and imaging.

With so many different kinds of textual documents, and so many different ways they can be constructed and utilized, one might begin to wonder if any kind of realistic text management strategy is even feasible. We will find that, although not perfect or universal, there is certainly enough standardization and universality to accomplish a lot. We will also discover very quickly, however, that it is not the technological, formatting, and other "mechanical" standardizations that limit our ability to fully exploit the potentials, but rather it is the organizational and business value issues that really hold this progression back.

Conclusion

In this chapter, we review some of the reasons for textual information management. We also discuss the diverse history of many of the different branches of text management that have sprung up over the past several years. We then explore the whole idea of text management in business and consider many of the ways that it can and is being used to help make businesses run better and more efficiently. Finally, we quickly survey some of the many challenges that the developers of today's comprehensive text management systems need to deal with.

In the next chapter, we look at the concept of textual information management systems, what they are, how they work, and the different ways they can be physically organized. In subsequent chapters, we talk about a few of the different implementations of the technology in the Web warehousing space.

CHAPTER 12

Architecture of Text Information Management Systems

- *What are the major functions that a text information management system delivers?*
- *What are the different types of TIMSs?*
- *How are text information management systems put together?*
- *What is a search engine?*
- *What is an on-line clipping service?*
- *What is a conscription service?*
- *What is a spider? How is it used?*
- *What are some of the different delivery models that TIMSs use?*

Text Management Systems Review

To comprehend the vast assortment of text management systems that are in use and under development these days, we need to know what they are, how they work, and for what purposes they have been created. The field of products and services in the text information area is vast, and is being changed and added to almost on a daily basis. Therefore, it is critical to establish what the job of text information management is and how it is handled by different products, before we undertake to understand individual products and what they have to offer. We will begin our investigation of this area with a definition.

Text Information Management Systems Are Systems

Because the area of text information management is so broad, it is important that we clearly identify what we mean by a text information management system. At the outset, let me clarify that when we use the term *system* we mean exactly that. A system, in our terms, is a combination of people, processes, hardware, software, and "raw material" (in this case, textual matter in any form), arranged in a way to deliver some specific capability to a specific group of users.

A text information management system, therefore, is much more than just a search engine, or a word processing package, or a clever little text spider. It is a robust system, with a mission to accomplish. To phrase the preceding definition more precisely: A text information management system is any combination of people, processes, software, hardware, and textual material that has been logically organized to provide a specific set of text management capabilities to a group of users to meet their informational needs. This means that if we really want to understand text management and text management information systems, then we need to know all the different components that make up those systems, especially the processes that they comprise.

Differentiating between Systems

With such a variety of features, functions, and purposes, trying to understand different TIMSs can be a challenge. In this chapter, we see how the different products and applications relate by examining the ways in

Chapter 12: Architecture of TIMSs

which the systems are differentiated. The products and systems can be differentiated by:

1. The major categories of text information management systems
2. Their functional components
3. Their delivery and execution model
4. Their information sources
5. Their text population

Major Categories of TIMSs

The most obvious way to distinguish among different TIMSs is to look at the principal objectives of the system. They include:

Search engines and search enablers. These products make it easy for people to locate the text information they are looking for.

Subscription services. Subscription services allow users to identify the kinds of information that they would like to be kept up-to-date on. The system providing the service then does the appropriate research and/or monitoring of available information sources, and sends the subscribers the information requested.

Conscription services. Conscription services are very similar to subscription services in that they keep the user up-to-date on a certain category of information. The difference is that users do not ask for the service, but instead the conscription service forces it on them. Conscription services are most prevalent in the corporate world, where employees are conscripted into receiving all kinds of information they may or may not want or need, and in the area of marketing, where corporate marketing departments will conscript former customers and prospects into receiving all sorts of updates about products and services.

Collaborative work environments. These are environments where large numbers of people are able to work together on a task, through the shared development and maintenance of documents and presentations.

Text analysis. Much akin to the area of data analysis, text analysis makes it possible for people to feed large volumes of text information into intelligent software programs, which are then able to look for patterns, trends, or insights.

Let's consider each of these areas in a little more detail so that we can get a better understanding of exactly what each of them entails.

Different Types of Search Engines and Search Enablers

The first, most popular, and most prevalent of the text information management systems are the search engines and search enablers. These products are best exemplified by the World Wide Web–based search engines familiar to so many ordinary people, from schoolchildren to grandparents.

Web-Based Public Domain Search Engines A who's who of the ranks of search engines would certainly include products like Yahoo!, Alta Vista, Excite, InfoSeek, Lycos, and HotBot to name just a few. Each of these products has achieved its fame by making it possible for people to weed through the literally hundreds of millions of pages of disorganized information that is currently available on the World Wide Web to find the specific pieces of information that they are interested in.

A student doing research on cellular regeneration can instantaneously gain access not only to an informative tutorial about what the subject area is all about, but also to some of the latest research available at the same time. A gardener interested in finding out how to best grow azaleas in a certain part of the country will find hundreds of references to flower growing strategies. A person shopping for a new car can see pictures of the latest-model cars and get technical information about its construction and performance, then read the opinions of experts on how well the car performed in the field.

There is actually so much information available on the Web, and organized and made accessible by the many different search engines, that it is beyond any single person's ability to catalog and describe. Of course, these search engines are only the most obvious and readily accessible of an entire class of products that provides the same functionality at many levels.

Subscription Search Services In addition to the publicly accessible search engines that everyone is aware of, there is also a surprisingly substantial "private" search engine/search enabler network that individuals or organizations can gain access to for a fee, or with the right security clearances. Many government agencies, universities, and research facilities maintain libraries of text information in the support of specific topical areas. These private or limited-access systems often provide search capabilities similar to—and in many cases better than—those offered by a Web-based search engine. They allow people to scan through millions of files, looking for the specific information they are interested in.

Corporate Digital Libraries A recent and increasingly important type of search system is generically known as a *corporate digital library*. These systems, which are being developed by corporate I/T departments, pull together all the different sources of text information to be found within the corporation (including the collection of correspondence, policy manuals, memos, presentations, reports, etc.), making them available for review by individuals all over the organization. By combining the vast storehouse of text information that the corporation controls with the power of enhanced and specialized search capabilities, corporations are beginning to pull together disparate parts of the organization, and accomplish levels of cohesion never before possible.

Search Engine Functionality

There is actually a progression of capabilities and sophistication that search engine and search enabler products exhibit, depending on who makes them, what purposes they are intended to serve, and how much people are willing to pay for them.

Keyword Search The core minimum functionality of any search engine is the ability to find documents based on *keywords* provided by the user. The search engine software usually starts with a "search parameters" page. From this page, the user is able to input keywords that identify to the search engine what information to look for. See Figure 12-1.

The system then figures out which documents are the most applicable to the keywords entered, and returns a listing of those documents that are the most likely to meet the requirements of the user. See Figure 12-2. The user is then able to select the document or documents that seem pertinent, and view them for confirmation.

Targeting the Search Population Of course, asking the system to review all of the available documents in the universe (or in a particular product's sphere of influence) would mean that it would have to search

Figure 12-1
A typical keyword search screen.

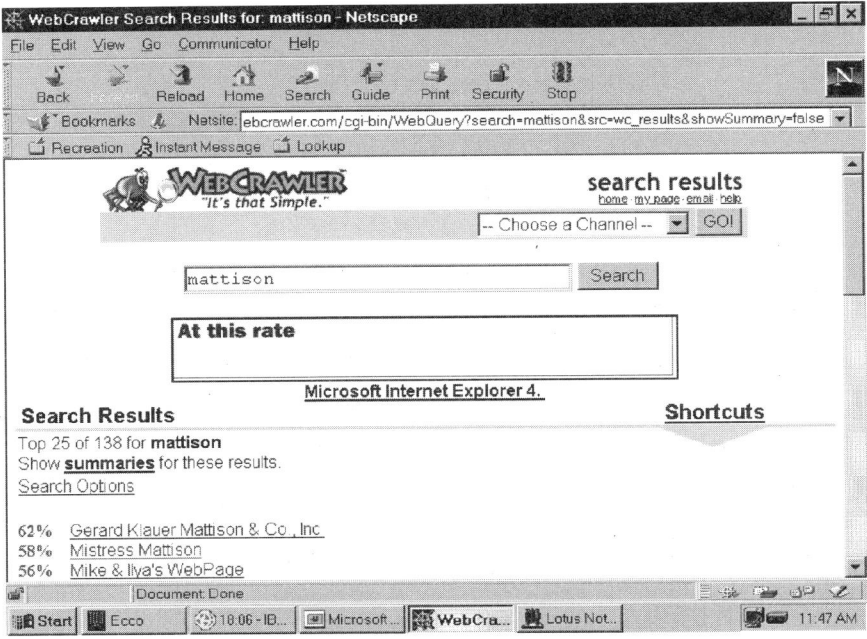

Figure 12-2
A typical keyword search response screen.

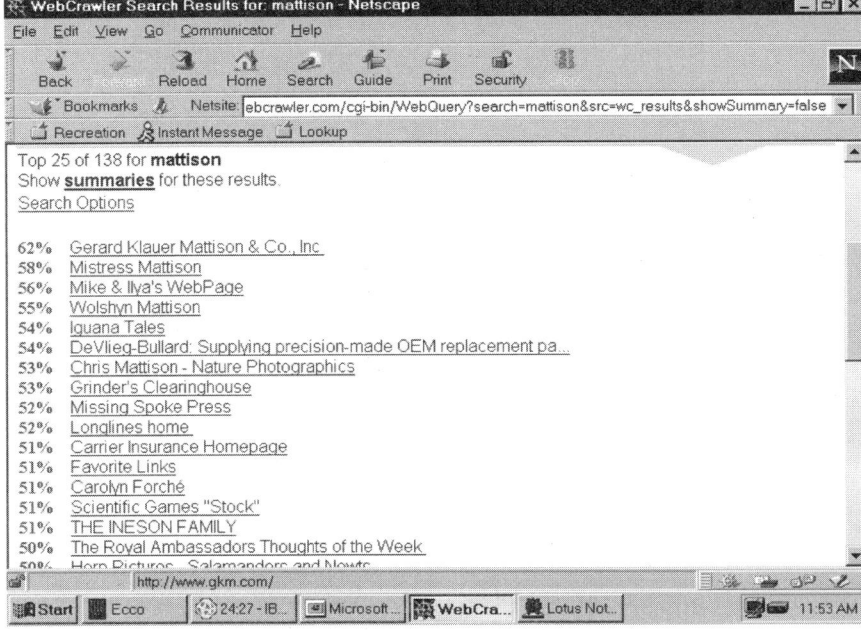

through a lot of documents that could not possibly contain anything of interest. To avoid forcing the system to do unnecessary work, and to speed up the searches, most search engines include search context-limiting parameters. Users specify which populations of files they want the system to search through, allowing it to skip files that are outside of the parameters.

Figure 12-3 shows the HotBot search engine as an example. In this case, the user can ask the system to search:

1. All available locations
2. Documents created during a specific time period (second line)
3. Specific locations (third line)
4. Only documents containing image, audio, video, or Shockwave files, or a combination of these (check boxes)
5. Alternative locations such as Usenet, Yellow Pages, and White Pages (listed on the left)

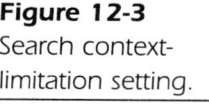

Figure 12-3
Search context-limitation setting.

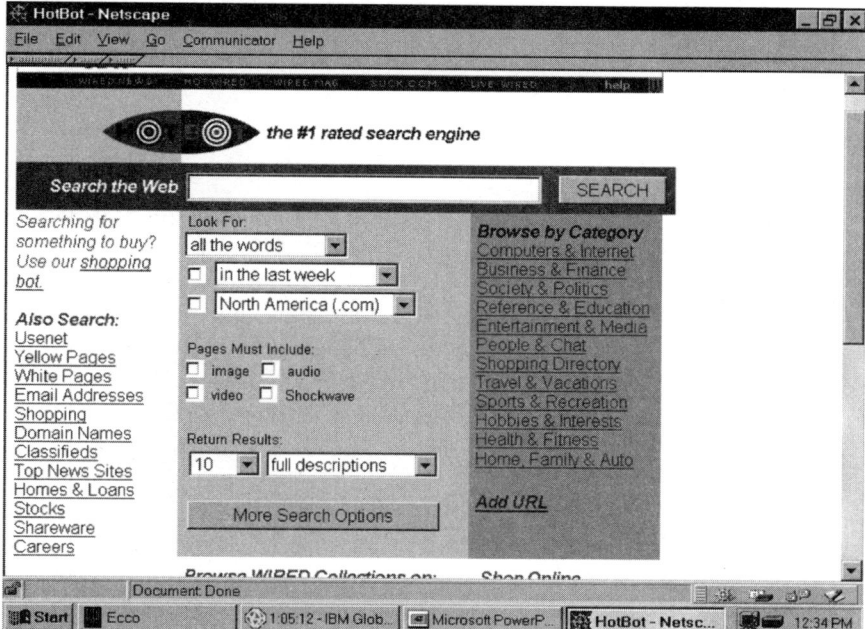

Search Enabler Product Functionality

These keyword searches and context-limiting parameters can certainly help tune the work that a search engine will go through, but these capabilities are, in fact, relatively crude and simplistic. As the population of text information gets greater, and as the sophistication of the documents continues to grow, an even more powerful and precise search engine capability is needed. This is precisely what search enabling technologies provide.

A new generation of "super search engines" is known as *search enablement* products. These search enablers start by providing users with simple keyword search and context-limiting capabilities, but expand to all sorts of sophisticated search, context-limiting, and search parameter-setting capabilities that let users get quite specific about what they want to know. Technologies such as text mining, linguistic analysis, and textual search algorithms provide users with more than a simple "fetch" capability. These systems can make use of full English language (or French, Dutch, Chinese, etc.) questions and descriptions of the information being sought. There are even some products that will read a document or a collection of documents that the user specifies, draw conclusions about the common subject matter that those documents share, and then look for other documents that meet the same criteria. In the next chapter we see how some of the more sophisticated search engine and search enabling technologies work in greater detail.

Text Analysis

While the search engines and search enablers are most certainly of prime interest to most business applications, there are several other areas where text information management is also having a big impact. One of those areas is text analysis.

In a very real sense, the development of search engines in today's text-based environment actually represents little more than the logical extension of the already very well established query and reporting capabilities in the data-based world into the text-based space. We use query tools to find data in a database, and we use search engines to find text information in a text information system space.

It should come as no surprise, therefore, that other disciplines from the data side will apply to this space as well. One of the newest and most interesting of these extensions is the sudden appearance of text analysis software. Just as the data analysis software applies statistical, heuristic, and advanced mathematical analysis to the interpretation of factual data, so do similar products now attempt to apply these algorithmic approaches to the search for new information within text information.

Text Analysis Approaches There is a substantial hierarchy of text analysis approaches that we may choose to diagnose the contents of a particular document. Different products make use of some or all of these approaches. The progression includes:

1. *Keyword or abstract analysis.* This form of analysis assumes that the documents being analyzed have keywords or abstracts associated with them. In these cases, the system simply gathers up the keywords and abstracts and uses them as the basis for index construction.

2. *Word count.* In this case, the analysis software parses through the entire document and makes a list of every single word that it found. These word counts are then used to assign weights to the document. For example, if the word *food* was found 100 times, and the word *apple* was found 3 times, an index for the word *food* with a score of 100 and for the word *apple* with a score of 3 would be built. People looking for these keywords would get a score of 103, which strongly indicates that the document is about food.

3. *Phrase and word combination count.* While word counts can give people clues to the identity of a document, those clues can often be misleading. For example, a search for *apple* might get us red fruit, or it might get us personal computers. Another level of sophistication in the development of text mining systems is the inclusion of the ability to keep track of how may times different phrases or combinations of words appear. For example *apple computer* versus *apple pie* or *navy seal* versus *o-ring seal*, etc. Systems that track combinations and phrases yield matches that are much more accurate than simple word count systems.

4. *Context evaluation.* These systems keep track of the subject area's context, in order to help interpret the meanings of the same words used in different ways.

5. *Advanced analytical techniques.* Even more sophisticated systems use complex statistical analyses, like factor analysis and trend analysis or neural networks, to find even more interesting and insightful patterns.

In the next few chapters, we look at several of the ways that text analysis techniques are applied.

Two Categories of Text Analysis Applications

Text analysis is used in many areas, but the two biggest uses are as adjuncts to the search engine process and as free-standing analytical tools.

Enhancing a Search Engine with Text Analysis As we have already noted, the sudden appearance and rapid growth of search engine technologies have shown that people have a real need for help in figuring out how to best store, catalog, and retrieve documents of interest to them.

In the simplest cases, a search engine can get its job done with basic indexes that associate keywords with different files. Of course, if you are looking for a search approach that does an even better job of finding what you are looking for (and nothing else), then you need to do a better job of analyzing those documents and creating those indexes.

Free-Standing Text Analysis Applications Making use of text analysis is not limited to the enhancement of search engine capabilities. In many situations, organizations have found that they can gain some benefits by using these products to help them understand current text information stores. Among the many areas where this approach is being applied are:

- Analysis of mail and/or email
- Analysis of research papers in hope of uncovering related activity or findings
- Analysis of patents in hope of finding conflicting claims before a violation occurs

Collaborative Work Environments

One of the most interesting and newest of the applications of text management to the solution of business problems is the development of collaborative work environments. These systems, also known as *groupware, collaborative decision-making environments,* and several other buzzwords, all share the common purpose of helping business people function

Chapter 12: Architecture of TIMSs

more effectively. They all attempt to streamline the decision-making and work generation process by providing people with a shared, document-based environment within which they can get their work done.

Some of the several different kinds of collaborative work environments include the following:

Shared Reference Libraries Shared reference libraries are systems that provide a group of people with a common place where they can store, organize, and retrieve text information that is important to them. Included in this category of applications are systems where repair manuals and reference materials are centrally maintained and distributed. These systems are especially important in industries where a lot of very complex machinery needs to be maintained (such as the airlines, mining, and utilities).

The mechanics of these systems are relatively simple and straightforward. Documents are stored and maintained by one group of people in one centralized location, and the users of the system are provided with hard-connected terminals or dial-in capability to gain access to the information. As updates to the manuals are made, the entire user population is immediately updated. Systems like this have saved companies millions of dollars in paper management costs, in addition to the hundreds of thousands of hours of time saved by individual repair and maintenance people.

Work Flow Management Systems Work flow management systems create a document flow–based framework within which people do their jobs. A few of the more interesting and profitable applications of this approach include:

- *Complex sales cycle management.* Sales people and their support teams are carried through the process of putting together complex proposals by the work flow approach.
- *Technically sophisticated sales cycle management.* Sales people are provided with all the required references to technically deep material in support of their efforts.
- *Insurance claims management.* Orchestrates the activities of large numbers of participants in the claims validation process.

Collaborative Problem Solving and Think Tank Applications
While the work flow–based solutions provide a rigidly defined, text-based structure, this type of application supports a much more creative and

unstructured kind of business scenario. Collaborative problem solving software allows large groups of people to maintain a dialogue about the solution of specific problems and save their insights and experiences to benefit others at a later date. These applications have been used for troubleshooting in the field by many different industries including:

- Oil drilling machinery maintenance
- Mining equipment upkeep
- Automotive repair

Organizing these systems is much more difficult than putting the other systems together. Users are usually in the field, meaning that normal computer equipment will not last very long; in addition, the nature of the problems being addressed makes the logical design of the systems and the structuring of solutions extremely difficult. These systems have yielded significant business to those organizations that have figured out how to execute them, however.

Subscription/Conscription Services

While the mainstream interest in text information management is centered on the search engine space, there is a growing level of interest in some of the other text-related management disciplines as well. One area that is growing rapidly is that of subscription and conscription services. These services deliver information to the user as it becomes available and not when the user specifically asks for it. Some of the more popular subscription services are described below.

News Services Provided by organizations like CNN and MSN, these news organizations are getting into the business of sending the specific news that people are interested in, to those who have asked for it.

Stock Quotes/Monitoring An extremely popular form of subscription, stock monitoring systems let people know how well their stocks or others they are interested in are performing, so that they can be much more responsive in the marketplace.

On-line Clipping Services In the old days before computers came on the scene, there were companies, called *clipping services,* in which people who would scan newspapers, magazines, and other publications for the topics that subscribers were interested in. Whenever a pertinent article was found, it would be copied and forwarded to the appropriate subscriber.

Today's on-line clipping services work in very much the same way. People register with the service and tell the contracting organization exactly what kinds of news are of interest. Whenever a new Web site, news release, or any other kind of text information becomes available, it is electronically forwarded to the appropriate user.

In an interesting variation on the clipping service theme, there are a number of Web search–based products that allow the user to put together information requests that go out to the Web and pull down all pages that seem pertinent. The system will then keep track of those Web pages, and rerun the original request on a periodic basis, to see if any newer information is available. When changes to pages, or new pages, show up, the system automatically downloads them to the user's personal computer for review.

Special-Interest Groups   Within both the world of the Web and many corporate environments, there are large groups of people who share a common interest.

In the public domain, there are groups interested in almost anything you can imagine, from antique cars to purebred Shetland ponies to preservation of endangered mushrooms. Many of these organizations provide interested parties with the ability to register for periodic updates on changes that occur in their areas.

In the academic community there are subscription services which keep people posted on the latest research in their respective areas, and most governments at the local, state, and national levels have many kinds of updating capabilities that keep people current on developments in a wide variety of areas.

Marketing Conscription Services   There are a number of text information services that you can enroll in voluntarily. However, there are also literally hundreds of organizations just waiting to get their hands on your name and email address so that they can enroll you in their update service whether you want to belong to it or not.

It is becoming more and more common for the producers of different products and services to enroll their customers in corporate-sponsored update services. These services keep people posted on the status of various product lines, make them aware of upcoming offerings, and, in general, attempt to improve the communication between seller and buyer with a stream of often-unsolicited text information.

Corporate Conscription Services Last but not least is the corporate conscription service. In these environments, corporate management decides which users should be included in special-interest groups, and provides them with any number of unsolicited updates of information.

Functional Components of a TIMS

Given the extremely wide variety of application types included under the text information management systems umbrella, it should be obvious that the problem of developing a good understanding of the systems architectures that support them will be difficult.

The world of text management is a large one, and there are many different products, all of which have a role to play in managing text information. A text information management system is usually a combination of products, each of which contributes to the overall job of managing the information. A typical TIMS will combine products and processes to provide some or all of the following functionalities:

1. *Text creation.* Providing the user with the ability to input text information in a digital, textual form.
2. *Text conversion.* Converting digitally stored information from one physical format to another (for example, converting an MS Word document into HTML page format), or converting nondigital information into a digital form (for example, the conversion of handwritten documents by scanners and optical character recognition), or capturing and converting voice communication into a digital form (by using voice capture and conversion systems).
3. *Text storage.* Semipermanent storage of digital text information on an electronic medium (such as a disk drive, compact disk, or mass storage device).
4. *Directory maintenance.* Creation and maintenance of a directory which defines where documents can be found and what they contain. (Directories typically keep track of only a document's physical location and name, with no special attention given to its contents.)
5. *Text indexing and cataloguing.* Creation and maintenance of specialized lookup lists that allow the system to quickly identify those documents which hold some information of interest to the user and provide the ability to locate those documents.

6. *Text analysis.* Reading a document and drawing conclusions about its contents on the basis of various analytical approaches.
7. *Text search and retrieval.* Locating and retrieving documents on the basis of descriptions provided by users.
8. *Text format and display.* Putting a retrieved document into a form that users can read.

When you organize these different functions in a way that helps business users get their jobs done effectively, then you are creating a text information management system.

Text Information Management System Delivery and Execution Models

Before we take a closer look at each of the different functional areas of a TIMS, it is important for us to realize that these systems can actually function under several different operational models. These include push versus pull, broadcast versus targeted, and agent-based versus user-based models.

Pull Model The most common operational model for a text information management system to work under is a "pull" model. In pull mode, the information that users may want to access is stored in one or several locations. It is passively stored and actively pulled up by a user only when it is required.

Push Model There are a number of text management systems that have begun to embrace a "push" model of access management. Under these systems, users specify the kind of text information they are looking for, but leave it up to the system to decide when the documents should be delivered.

Push models are very popular for those areas where the timeliness of information is important. For example, there are push-based systems that monitor the value of specific stocks as they are traded on the open market. When those stock prices go above or below a certain threshold, the system will automatically push an alert message to the service subscriber. See Figure 12-4.

Another very popular push application has been developed for people who do research on the World Wide Web. These individuals can tell the

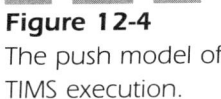

Figure 12-4
The push model of TIMS execution.

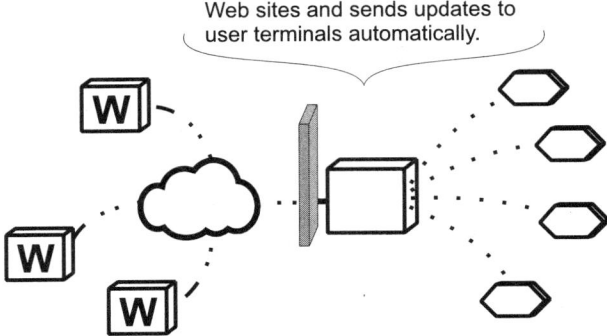

system what topics they are interested in and ask for an immediate display of all pertinent Web pages. The user can then instruct the system to automatically push any new pages or changes to existing pages an extended period into the future. This way, the user is assured of always having the latest information in that subject area, without having to explicitly check for changes.

Targeted Model Under this model of text delivery management, the system keeps track of individual users, and provides the specific information each one asks for. A vast majority of text information management systems are target–based. The targeted model can be used to support both push and pull approaches.

Broadcast Model There are, however, some applications where the broadcast model is more appropriate. In a broadcast scenario, the information that people might need is sent en masse to an entire group of pre-defined users. The broadcast approach is always a push-based application, and is often used to support the needs of special interest groups, subscriber populations, and corporate interests.

The most common form of a broadcast/push model is the corporate-sponsored internal email sent to all employees, or all the employees in a particular department. Other, public sector, broadcast models include news services and special interest group and subscriber services.

User-Based Model The most common form of information delivery is through a user-based model. Under this model the user is required to physically, interactively, and in real time make requests for information. Often, these users also participate in the manipulation of, navigation through, and retrieval of the information being sought.

Agent-Based Model The newest and most popular and powerful trend, however, is to employ special programs called *intelligent software agents*. These agents take responsibility for a lot of the user's work. Agents come in many forms and can do a variety of tasks including:

- Scheduling times for different tasks, making sure that they are performed, and then reporting back on the results
- Reviewing the content of documents (Web pages, text pages, etc.) for relevancy and then reporting back on the ones that are worth further investigation
- Providing automated navigation. There are agent software packages that can actually analyze the contents of a document, look for references which point to other documents, look up these new documents, analyze them for more references which are then subsequently looked up and scanned—ad infinitum

There is in fact a very special category of intelligent agent, known as a *spider*, that has become the core component of many very powerful text information management systems.

TIMS Information Sources

There are an almost infinite variety of places where text information can be found. It therefore follows that there are also an almost infinite variety of places where a TIMS can access it. In general, however, we can categorize the sources of this information as one of the following:

Public domain. Created and published by governmental agencies, charitable organizations, educational institutions, and other groups who compile and distribute information of interest to people.

Marketing materials. Collections of information that are made available to the public through a variety of channels, but which have been produced and distributed by organizations for the purposes of promoting their products and services.

Brokered information. Information that is collected, stored, and made available to the public for sale as part of the main business of an organization. Brokered information is information collected and then resold to people who are interested in it. Many information brokers sell text information through a variety of mechanisms.

Corporate property. One of the biggest and newest sources of information is the vast storehouse of text that can be found on the personal computers and databases in corporations. As LANs and WANs (local area networks and wide-area networks) become standardized, we are finding that it is possible to make use of this rich pool of information as a source for further investigation.

Conclusion

In this chapter, we finish our overview of the area of text information management systems. We look at the different types of systems (search engines and search enablers, text analysis, collaborative work environments, and subscription/conscription services). We then consider some of the major functional components of any TIMS and the different delivery mechanisms they might invoke.

In the next two chapters, we take a much more focused look at two of these four categories of TIMS applications, the search engine and enabler area and the text analysis area. We look at some specific products and see how these products have been put together to address the needs of business people in the text management space.

CHAPTER 13

Search Engines and Facilities

- *What is the basic architecture for any search engine?*
- *What are some of the ways that user requests are gathered?*
- *In what ways can the search population and context be narrowed?*
- *What is Excalibur RetrievalWare?*
- *How does Excalibur approach the challenges of search functionality?*
- *What is the architecture of the Excalibur RetrievalWare product?*
- *What is the future of searching?*

Search Engines and the Web

Without a doubt, when you start talking about text management and the Web, people immediately think about search engines. Search engines, in their many different forms, have revolutionized our understanding of what can be done with computers. Think about it. The widespread use of the World Wide Web, and the vast majority of modern business applications that people are talking about building, would not have been imaginable without the current generation of search engines.

The Differences among Search Engines, Search Enablers, and Search Facilities

Like any other area in the data processing community, the search technology is inundated with conflicting definitions—in this case, for the terms *search engines, search enablers,* and *search facilities.* Suppliers will state that their product is or isn't in one of these categories, depending on how it is put together. It all depends on whether the company believes that it is good or bad for them to have the product categorized that way. For our purposes, we will use the terms interchangeably, making no differentiation between them.

The Critical Role of the Search Engine in the Web Environment

Why is the search engine such a critical component of any Web-based solution? The Internet and an already impressive assortment of textual information sources were available long before the creation of the Web. But just ask people who tried to work in that environment what it was like, and they will tell you the same thing. "The environment was great, but it was just about impossible to find anything."

The fact that textual information is available over a massive global network does not mean that it is usable. The only way information can be tapped is if there is some way to keep track of it all. That is exactly what search engines provide.

These days it is hard to imagine a world without search engines in it. How would we find out anything at all? With a search engine we are able to use our personal computers to type in a couple of keywords and almost immediately gain access to more information than we know what to do with.

The Role of the Search Engine in the Business World of Tomorrow

While some businesses have been slow to jump wholeheartedly into the Internet/intranet conversion effort, it is clear that this will change over the next few years. As businesses tool up for Internet-style connectivity between all of their employees, there is no doubt that search engines will play a pivotal role in their development.

Every developer or manager of corporate information systems knows that the typical corporation's portfolio of applications is far too big for any one person to understand or manage. Situations exist where people know that the information they need is somewhere out there in the vast corporate wasteland, but they are unable to find it.

Search engines will change all of that. Suddenly, people will be able to input a search word string such as "Accounts Payable Reports Taiwan" at their terminals, and have a set of references to output reports, system names, and contact people, all of which can help them solve whatever problems they are facing.

How far are we from making something like this happen? The technological capability is already there. All that is missing is the vision, commitment, and action of a few I/T departments. We will undoubtedly see an avalanche of demand for precisely this kind of system.

Search Engine Architecture

Of course, while the critical current and future role of the search engine is not to be denied by anyone, what is more important to our discussion is that we develop a good understanding of how these search engines are put together. There are many different kinds of search engines, with differing levels of sophistication and functionality. Before we look at some of the more prevalent of these specific cases, however, let's take a few moments to develop a good understanding of the fundamentals of search engine architecture.

Principal Components of a Search Engine

Every search engine and search enabling system must have the following component parts if it is going to be able to function:

1. *User request facility.* This facility allows the user to tell the system what kinds of information to look for.
2. *Search templates.* These define the specific formats and types of values that the system will use to help the user specify:
   a. *What* to look for
   b. *Where* the system should look for it
   c. *How* the results should be reported
3. *A population of documents to search (also known as the search universe).* These are the documents from which the system can select responses.
4. *An index.* A file or database that contains both search parameter information and information about where the documents related to those parameters can be found.
5. *An index builder.* Somehow, the index that the search engine uses must be built. Humans can build it, or it can be built automatically by some specialized software, or a combination of the two approaches can be used.
6. *A query building and execution mechanism.* Also known as the index searching mechanism, this is the mechanism that the product uses to convert the user's input search parameters into an algorithm which allows it to search through the indexes and identify the documents the user is asking for.
7. *A user response facility.* The facility that formats and presents responses to the user.

Figure 13-1 shows all of the components in their respective positions.

The User Request and Response Process The user begins the process by formulating a request. That request is made up of a description of the information that the user wants to look for, translated into the form dictated by the search templates. This request is then submitted to the index searching mechanism, which looks for matching values in the index. The best matches are retrieved from the index and reported to the user via the user response facility.

Chapter 13: Search Engines and Facilities

Figure 13-1
Components of a search facility.

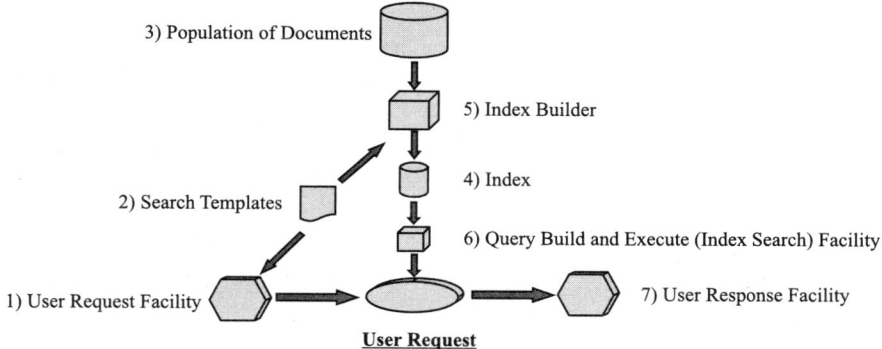

The Index Building Process The index building process begins with the development of the search templates, which are used as input for the index building system. The index building process, using the templates as a guide, goes out to the different information sources and categorizes the information according to the parameters that the templates describe. (For example, if the search template allows room for a keyword search, then the index builder will examine documents and associate keywords with each document.)

The system then builds an index. The index will be nothing more than a list of all possible search template values with an identifier that points to the source document for each value. The complete index is then made available to the index searching mechanism.

Variations in the Way That Search Facilities Work

Of course, the core functionality that we have outlined is a bare-bones description. As the sophistication of search facilities grows, so does the value of the system.

Variations in the User Interfaces (Request and Response Facilities)

One of the ways in which the makers of these products differentiate their wares is to build more sophisticated interfaces for the user to work with.

Part 2: Web Warehousing in Action

By adding more drop-down boxes, check boxes, and other user-friendly characteristics, these vendors provide people with some options that make the system easier to work with.

Variations in the Search Templates

Of course, changing the user interface will not mean very much to a user in and of itself. The first real differences that the maker of a search product can offer is in the assembly of search templates. In general, the more options, and the more different kinds of search parameters the user can set, the more flexible and powerful the system will be.

In the area of search templates, there is as much variation between products as there could possibly be. Each vendor tries to take a different approach, each hoping that their approach will make things easier, faster, and more efficient for their users. The screens in Figures 13-2 to 13-6 show examples of the many different search template approaches taken by some of the most popular Web-based search engine products.

Figure 13-2 shows the Alta Vista search engine's refine search screen. This is the screen that will show up when the user either gets no

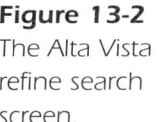

Figure 13-2
The Alta Vista refine search screen.

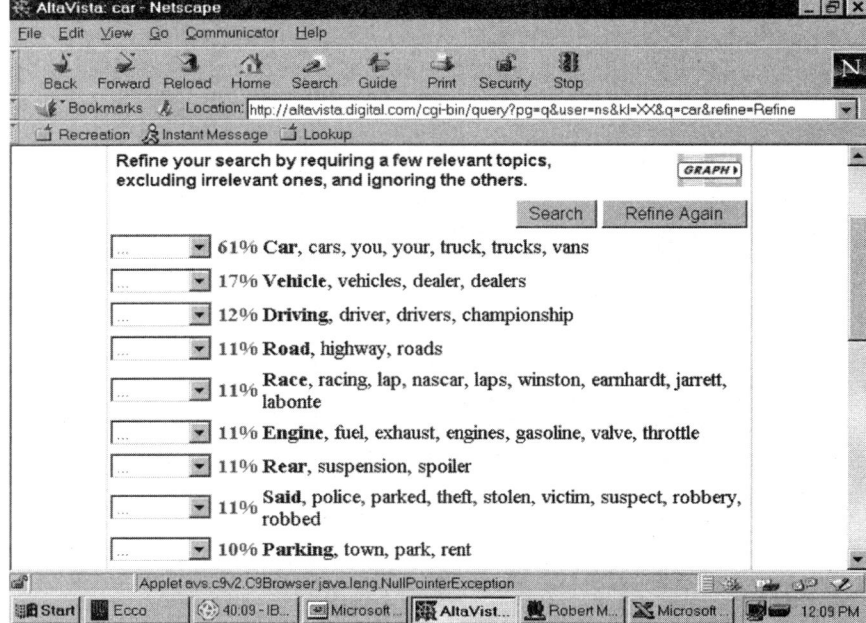

Chapter 13: Search Engines and Facilities 313

responses back from a search or gets so many that it is clear that a more refined search will be desirable.

As you can see, this screen provides the user with an analysis of all the pages found about cars. It reports, for example, that 61 percent of the articles with cars as a main topic include the words cars, you, your, trucks, and vans as part of their text. The next most frequent occurrence is those documents where the word car is associated with the words vehicle, dealer, and dealers. And so forth. After viewing this list of categories, the user can select the subset of documents that seems the most interesting.

This approach is a very good example of both context analysis (showing users the context within which the words are used) and search population limitation. Both cases help define the search template that the Alta Vista product uses to handle user queries.

The HotBot product takes a very different approach to search parameter definition. The HotBot search screen (Figure 13-3) shows that users have a number of different limiting options including:

1. The ability to choose to shop for articles and to choose a specific subset of vendor sites (by using a "shopping bot").

Figure 13-3
The HotBot search screen.

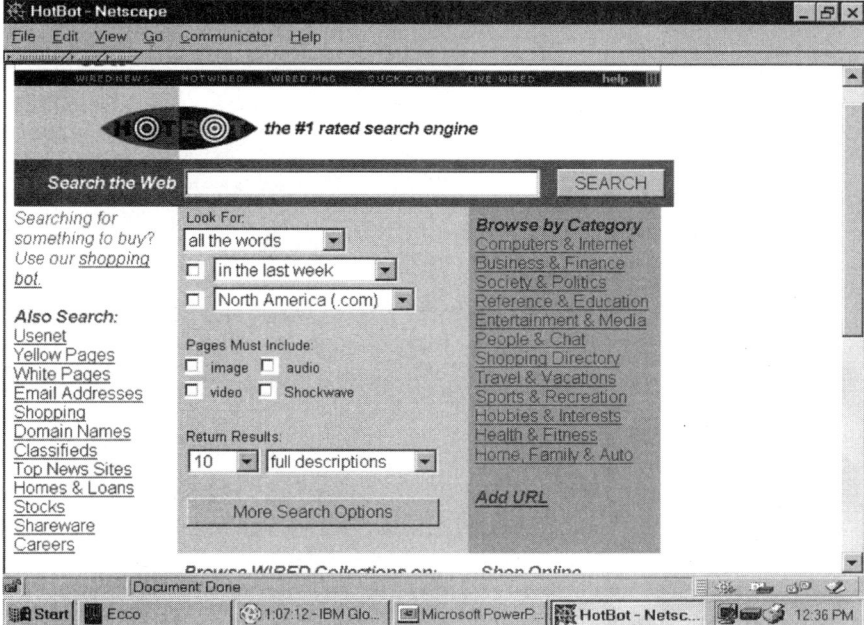

2. The ability to choose different populations of information to limit the search (e.g., usenets, yellow pages, white pages), as seen on the lower left-hand side of the screen.

3. The ability to search only within different categories of documents (e.g., computers and Internet, business and finance), as shown on the right-hand side of the screen.

4. The ability to limit the search by time (e.g., in the last week), geography (e.g., North America), and document content (image, video, audio, Shockwave check boxes), and to define how many "hits" to return and in what form—all shown down the center of the screen.

The Excite search again screen (Figure 13-4) allows users to select from a list of additional words, which when added to the search will help narrow the response. This accomplishes the same as the Alta Vista approach, but in a different format.

With drop-down menu boxes, the Infoseek advanced search screen (Figure 13-5) allows the user to define:

- The item being searched for (i.e., the document)
- The format to be used for the search (the "contain the ____" option)

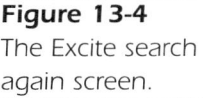

Figure 13-4
The Excite search again screen.

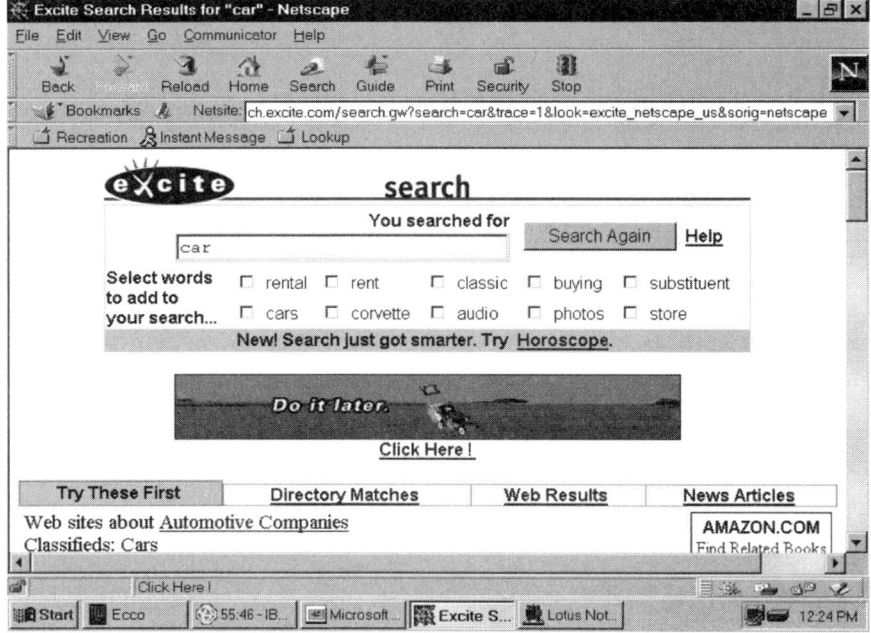

Chapter 13: Search Engines and Facilities

Figure 13-5
The Infoseek advanced search screen.

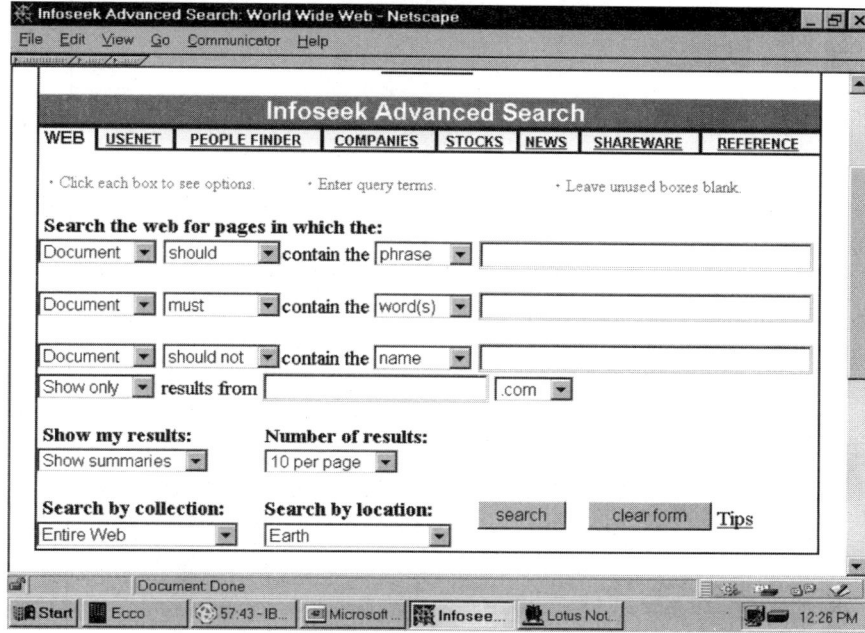

- What should be shown, how many responses, and from what population the choices should come

Finally, we see the Lycos approach (Figure 13-6), which is to offer to the customer all the different categories it maintains that contain information the user is looking for, allowing the user to select the category and resubmit the search.

More Sophisticated Search Templates While these examples of products show a variety of options, there are a number of other ways to define search templates. Ultimately, as more and more information becomes available to users, the quality of the search templates will have to continue to rise.

Some of the most sophisticated products allow users to input documents, conceptual statements, or simple textual descriptions representing the kind of information they are looking for. These systems make use of sophisticated text analysis systems to turn that input text into an internally defined search template, which then does the search for the user.

Figure 13-6
The Lycos matching categories screen.

Variations in Indexing Schemes

Ultimately, the real value of the search engine comes not from the user interfaces or even the search templates, but from the search capability that is built into the product. One key component of that capability is the schemes used to manage the systems' indexes. The index builder they use to scan and categorize all the documents in the targeted population, the technique they use to convert a user's request into an executable search argument, and the mechanism they use to search those indexes all define the quality and capacity of a search engine. There is an incredible variety in the way that different vendors build these indexes and complementary search capabilities. In general, these approaches involve three important characteristics:

How the indexes are organized

The query building and execution technique

How the indexes are loaded

Index Organization

The various ways that indexes can be organized include the following:

A Simple Search Engine Index The way the indexes are designed will ultimately define how good a job the system can do in retrieving what people are interested in. The simplest possible search engine index would consist of only two columns, one to keep track of keywords and another to provide the locations of the files. See Figure 13-7.

Multivalued Index Columns There are several variations on this core indexing scheme. One is to provide the index with many different columns, each column holding a different piece of information about the document and the appropriate search template information.

For example, a more sophisticated index might have columns for:

1. The size of the document
2. The age of the document
3. The type of document (HTML, text, etc.)
4. Several different keywords

One of the more common enhancements to a basic index of this nature is to include the keyword related to a particular file and an associated contextual weighting score. The weighting score is used to indicate just how applicable the keyword is to the document. For example, assume that my keyword search included the words Ford Fairlane. The first document contains a list of all of the cars that Ford has ever manufactured; so the word combination Ford Fairlane shows up only once. In this document Ford Fairlane is mentioned but is not a critical aspect of the document. Therefore, the weighted score for Ford Fairlane would be very low.

Figure 13-7
A simple search engine index.

Keyword	File Name
car	carfile.doc
car	www.car.com/car.html
cat	mycat.doc
cat	cat.txt

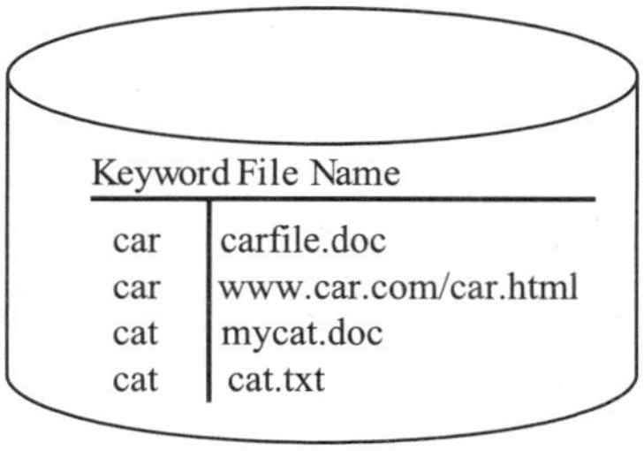

On the other hand, another article might be a reprint of a magazine article reviewing how the car stood up in consumer surveys and exhaustive testing. In this article Ford Fairlane might be mentioned 35 times. The article would therefore be awarded a much higher score.

Using Multiple Indexes At some point in the process, however, a single index will not be able to do the job. In these cases, the builders of the search engine will begin creating multiple indexes, each index capturing and reporting on a different aspect of the document's nature and applicability to a user search.

Ultimately, these multiple indexes become full-fledged, multidimensional, extremely sophisticated databases, holding all sorts of information, all of which is used to help the system better locate the documents being looked for.

Variations in the Query Building and Execution Techniques

Part of the functionality that any search engine delivers is defined by the way that the system converts user search parameters into queries that can check the indexes and identify the documents being searched for. In the simplest cases, a product will take the search parameters input by the user and look for matches to those words within the index itself. More sophisticated query builders will spend a great deal of energy in dissecting (parsing) a user request into more meaningful and manageable components, much as a relational database would do, only in a much more sophisticated and complex way. The most sophisticated systems will actually make use of internal dictionaries and thesauruses to create queries that ask for all possible variations of a word.

Variations in the Way the Indexes Are Loaded with Information

A good indexing scheme, supported by a good index search mechanism, is what makes the difference between a satisfactory search engine and an excellent one. However, the best indexing scheme in the world is worthless until it has been loaded. It is in the area of index loading that some of the most interesting, variable, and pertinent aspects of the search engine come to light. Indexes can be loaded manually, programmatically by job, or programmatically by spider.

Manually Loaded Indexes In an age in which almost everything seems to be computer-automated, it may come as a surprise that one of the most popular and effective ways to build an index to documents is to do so the old-fashioned manual way. Many search engine facilities, including the extremely popular and successful Yahoo! product on the Web do exactly that.

The people who provide the search facility hire a staff whose whole job is to read Web pages, determine their content, subject matter, and quality, and then input information into the indexes to allow people to find the pages when they use the search facility. While this method may seem archaic at first glance, when you think about it a bit, it begins to make more sense. A manually loaded index approach, in fact, has several advantages:

1. Manual loading makes it very easy for the builders of the index to define the scope of what is categorized and indexed. Since you can create any kind of abstract categorization scheme that you like, and then leave it up to the index builder to understand the scheme and use it, you shift a lot of the burden for the quality of the search experience from the system to the human indexer.

2. A human-built index can, in many cases, be counted on to be more accurate than a machine-built index. Machine-built indexes must use tricks, assumptions, and mechanical interpretations to categorize documents. Human indexers can cut through that to the real meaning and context.

3. A human-built index can often accurately and quickly discern many of the tricky contextual and other abstract subtleties of a document.

Unfortunately, these advantages also bring with them some disadvantages. These include:

1. Human indexers are not objective. Their subjective opinions about what something may mean will become integrated into the index.

2. Human indexers are not perfect. They can make mistakes that mechanical systems seldom do.

3. Human indexers must know the subject matter they are reading about if they are to do an accurate job of document scanning and indexing.

4. Manually generated indexes are expensive to build and maintain. The cost of paying people to read all of this material and categorize it is extremely high, especially when the subject matter is highly specialized or technical in nature. Imagine the cost of getting people to build indexes for highly technical and specialized materials that only a Ph.D. in astrophysics could understand. At some point, it would simply make more sense to pay such an expert to classify the documents.

5. Human indexers are far from reliable or consistent in their quality when working on a broad range of topics. Imagine having a person who knows nothing about raising pigs read and appraise the value and meaning of documents on pigsty management techniques. That person's interpretation and judgment will most likely miss many of the subtler points of what is discussed in the documents.

The weaknesses of human-made indexes notwithstanding, many general-purpose human-loaded indexes are in service today, meeting the search needs of millions of users.

Program-Built Indexes (Job-Based) The second option for the building of an index is to use manually controlled programs to do the job. This approach, called the *job-based* approach, makes use of document interpretation programs, in an attempt to automatically categorize documents according to any number of schemes, ranging from highly sophisticated to childishly naïve.

Very simple approaches include copying the name of the document into the index, using the first line of the document as the index entry, and using the title line or abstract from the document as the index entry.

Moderately sophisticated approaches include doing word counts and using the number of times a word appears as a "strength" or relevancy factor, and keeping track of key phrases and using those phrases as the relevancy factor.

Extremely sophisticated approaches include using advanced statistical techniques, using artificial intelligence and data/text mining techniques, and using advanced linguistic interpretation algorithms.

Obviously, as you move from the manually generated index loading scenario to the programmatically defined one, you get a whole new set of pluses and minuses. The advantages of more sophisticated approaches include:

1. *Reduced costs.* Programs can read documents a lot more quickly and less expensively than a human being.

2. *Reduced subjectivity.* Since a program is doing the categorization, there is little chance for personal bias to intrude.

3. *Increased capacity.* It becomes possible for the index builder to take on a lot more documents much more quickly than a human can.

However, some of the disadvantages include:

1. *Lack of subtlety.* Programs do not interpret subtle differences well, and the ability of those same programs to handle anywhere near as great a variety of subject matter and communications forms is certainly lacking.

2. *Adjustment for document types.* While human beings can easily interpret a wide variety of written words with a minimum of effort, setting up programs so that they can review documents created by various word processing packages is a big job. Moreover, any documents stored in image form will have to be either read by humans or fed into an OCR (optical character recognition) system for conversion into an electronically manipulable form.

3. *Need for more rigid criteria and definitional parameters.* Because of these factors, the builders of a system that will use programmatically loaded indexes will have to spend a lot more time in designing those indexes and the programs that search them, since the "facts" that the programs determine about the documents will have to be interpreted by the index search program.

4. *Problems with context, meaning, and accuracy.* Programs can use only "facts" to interpret the meanings of documents. Therefore, the ability of those programs to develop contextually targeted and accurate interpretations is totally dependent on the metrics and algorithms used to categorize them via those facts. Unfortunately, this is not a simple, straightforward process, even in the best of worlds. It creates all kinds of problems with the context, meaning, and accuracy of the indexing efforts.

Until the creation of spider programs, the job-based programmatic approach to building an index was the only option developers had, aside from the manual technique. The original Internet search engine WAIS makes use of this approach, as do a number of other products.

The Spider-Based Approach The undisputed kings in the world of index building are those systems that use spiders—the hottest new programs to hit the computer world for some time. A spider is simply given a set of instructions and is then left to execute those instructions however it best sees fit. It functions autonomously, without any direct intervention on the part of users.

The typical Web-based index building spider works as follows:

1. The spider program is provided with a series of parameters that tell it:
   a. Where to look for documents
   b. What kind of documents to look for
   c. What kinds of categorization to do
2. On the basis of this information, the spider program then begins to run Web search queries that it deems to be the most relevant to the area of interest.
3. The pages that are returned from these initial search queries are then read and interpreted by the spider for relevancy to the requested search. The interpretation might be done by any or all of the programmatic search techniques mentioned in the previous section.
4. In those cases where a hit occurs and the spider determines that the document found is valuable, an index entry is constructed and entered.
5. In many cases, the spider can interpret the returned pages well enough to follow the links provided to yet another set of referenced documents. This second set of returned Web pages is then interpreted and processed in the same way as the first set, and more index entries are made.
6. The spider will then continue to follow the different linkage paths through the Web, until the search has been exhausted.

This approach to index building is certainly the most exciting and interesting of them all, and it offers several major advantages. The spider approach can process a lot more documents much more quickly than the simple programmatic approach. The spider is not restricted in its search, and is able to follow any of the links that it interprets as relevant. It also does not have to interpret many documents that are clearly not relevant. In addition, if the searching and interpretation components of the spider are especially sophisticated, the depth and breadth of the indexes that it builds will be exceptionally valuable and timely. Finally, a spider-based system can automatically keep track of the places it has looked before, and learn not to return there unless a change has occurred.

Products That Use the Spider-Based Approach   Since its creation, the spider-based approach to index building has grown steadily in popularity and utilization. Some of the biggest and most powerful search facilitation systems in the world and on the Web today use spiders as their principal means of index development. For example, the Alta Vista search engine is particularly well known for the use of its spider programs, which read over 1 million Web pages a day, and add them to the Alta Vista indexing system.

So, as we have seen, there is an incredible diversity in the way that search engines are built and managed, providing individuals with a wide variety of choices in the way they can be used. In the next section, we will look at one particular product, the Excalibur system, and see how the vendor has attempted to balance the cost versus value parameters to create a highly effective search facility.

The Excalibur RetrievalWare Product

Excalibur RetrievalWare is provided by the Excalibur Technologies Corporation of Vienna, Virginia. The company, founded in 1980, pioneered the use of innovative technology to help companies transform information into usable knowledge. The company's mission statement says "We empower people and enable organizations to quickly analyze, index, catalog, browse, access, search, retrieve and more easily share all enterprise knowledge assets whether they be paper, text, images or video." The current customer base for Excalibur includes hundreds of the largest and most innovative corporations around the world, and the company's products have been accepted and integrated into the daily business of major publishing houses and Internet search facilities.

The Excalibur Family of Products

Excalibur's lineup of product offerings includes:

Excalibur RetrievalWare.   An enterprise-wide knowledge retrieval system that allows broad flexibility and scalability for implementation across enterprise networks, intranets, and the World Wide Web. This includes the indexing of over 200 document types, as well as Lotus

Notes, Microsoft Exchange, usenet news groups, and all major relational database management systems (RDBMS). This product interfaces with any HTTP server and supports very large scale distributed electronic publishing and enterprise applications on the Internet, translating massive amounts of data into useful information and practical knowledge.

Excalibur RetrievalWare FileRoom. An Excalibur RetrievalWare extension for incorporating scanned paper-based assets into an organization's digital repository. It accurately captures, loads, indexes, and retrieves both image and text documents.

Excalibur Internet Spider. A multimedia, high-performance Web spider/crawler for augmenting the knowledge retrieval capabilities of Excalibur RetrievalWare, for stand-alone use, or for integration with other applications.

Excalibur Visual RetrievalWare. A programming toolkit for the creation of powerful image content-matching applications for digital libraries, document imaging, positive identification, and more. Every aspect of the visual data is "learned" automatically by the system on the basis of patterns in shapes, colors, contrasts, and textures and is then reduced to a searchable index typically 10 percent the size of the original file. (We will take a closer look at this product in Chapter 15, where we discuss multimedia management systems.)

Excalibur Screening Room. Excalibur's newest search and retrieval application and the industry's first comprehensive, integrated solution for fast, easy, and intelligent analog and digital video asset capturing, analyzing, indexing, browsing, accessing, and retrieving.

Excalibur RetrievalWare—Product Organization

Unlike a "traditional" search engine or facility product, which comes as one complete package, Excalibur RetrievalWare is a product that allows developers to create a search facility-type environment based on whatever criteria they want it to contain. In that sense it is more of a toolkit that allows the systems developer to construct a search facility, than it is a search facility product in and of itself.

The product is also licensed as a Software Developer's Kit (SDK), which provides the developer with a comprehensive suite of text servers and optional third-party components.

Chapter 13: Search Engines and Facilities

The product itself provides capabilities in each of the areas typically associated with search engines, but with some very interesting and powerful enhancements.

Excalibur User Interface

Excalibur RetrievalWare provides a native scripting language for creating Web-based HTML interfaces. The scripting language is a way to dynamically create HTML pages based on user session data, search results, relational database questions, and any data or functionality available within the RetrievalWare system. A person purchasing the system is provided with a default set of HTML (actually the HTML from Excalibur's own intranet interface). In addition, Excalibur RetrievalWare 6.6 comes with a sample Internet interface. This can then be easily modified to meet the needs of the users.

Excalibur HTML Interface Architecture

The basic architecture of the HTML interface can be seen in Figure 13-8. As indicated by the diagram, the product architecture includes:

- *Web client.* Provides for the collection of the users' input query parameters and the display of their results. (The RetrievalWare Web client consists of the HTML customized by the system developers and utilizing the RetrievalWare scripting language.)
- *Web server.* This can be any industry-standard Web server (Netscape, MS, or other) that normally manages HTML traffic for the user.
- *RetrievalWare interface.* A common gateway interface (CGI), NSAPI, or ISAPI interface that connects the Web server with the RetrievalWare Web front-end server.

Figure 13-8
Excalibur RetrievalWare HTML interface architecture.

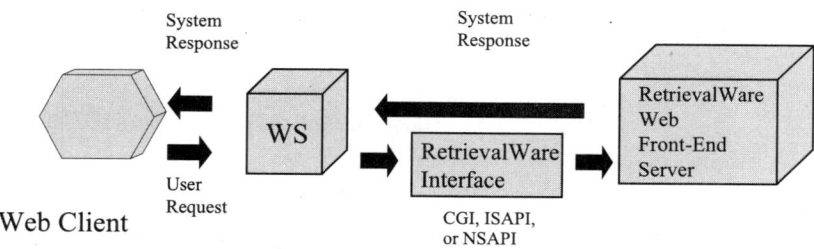

- *RetrievalWare Web front-end server.* The Web-based RetrievalWare "engine" that manages queries and sends responses to the user. This server is manipulated through the issuance of SET and GET commands, forwarded by the RetrievalWare interface.

Java Interface Capabilities In addition to this basic CGI/interface-type capability, the RetrievalWare software development kit (SDK) also supports a Java interface. See Figure 13-9.

RetrievalWare supports a seamless integration with both HTML- and Java-based interfaces. There is no requirement for users to switch from Java to HTML mode to capitalize on the capabilities of both. This is possible because the RetrievalWare CGIs and Java applets talk to the same session server. The RetrievalWare Web front-end server holds the user's session, query status, query results, and other transaction thread-based information, not the Web server or transaction threads themselves, therefore CGI and Java applets are interchangeable.

Excalibur RetrievalWare Search Templates

While other products limit users to only one or two keywords, and/or a small set of other contextual types of options, the Excalibur product actually encourages users to include as many words as possible into the initial search parameter list. The Excalibur RetrievalWare facility allows for the use of keywords, multiple keywords, complete sentences, paragraphs, and even documents as user input. This free-form style of user search parameter input allows Excalibur to be much more comprehensive in its handling of user input, and much more accurate in its determination of user request information.

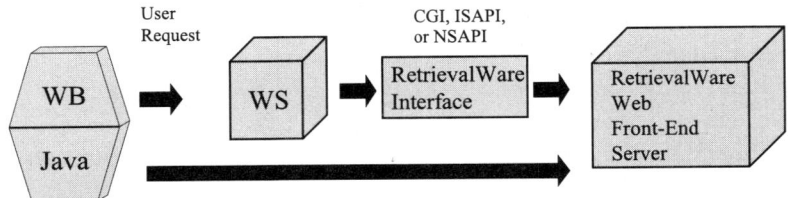

Figure 13-9
Excalibur RetrievalWare Java interface architecture.

Excalibur RetrievalWare Query Building Approach

To understand exactly how different Excalibur RetrievalWare is from the run-of-the-mill search engine, you need to understand just how sophisticated the product is in the analysis of queries and the development of indexes. As you recall from our earlier discussion, the more sophisticated the product, the more sophisticated its approach to query building, and Excalibur is by far one of the most sophisticated of all. Once the Excalibur RetrievalWare product receives the textual input from the user, it carries that input through a series of processing steps. The ultimate objective of these steps is to convert the user's input into a system-savvy, efficient query that can then be run against the system's databases and indexes.

What Excalibur uses to do this is called a *search pipeline* approach. The search pipeline defines the many different checkpoints that a query will go through as it is prepared for submission to the search engine itself. See Figure 13-10.

The pipeline details the following major processing stages that a query will run through:

1. *Preprocessing.* Preprocessing includes several query string preprocessing steps which help to enhance and clarify the characters, tokens, and words in the query. This includes:

    a. *Tokenization.* In this stage, strings are divided into words.

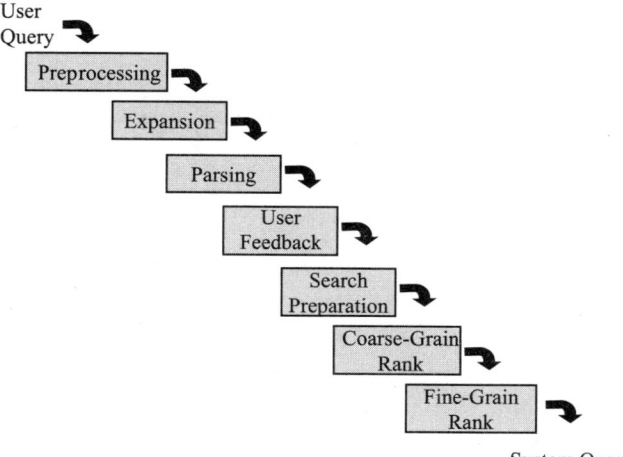

Figure 13-10
Excalibur RetrievalWare search pipeline.

b. *Dictionary lookup.* Words are located in the internal dictionary and user-provided words are augmented with additional dictionary information that might be meaningful (e.g., part of speech, other words with common roots, variant spellings).
   c. *Word reduction.* When a word is not found in the dictionary, rules are applied to reduce the word to its root or simpler form that can be found in the dictionary.
   d. *Token typing.* The types of special tokens in the query (such as numbers, expansion operators, or other query operators) are identified.
2. *Expansion.* During this step various expansion techniques are applied to the words. These include:
   a. *Semantic expansion.* Here the meanings of the word are expanded to include additional words that are semantically related to the meaning.
   b. *Fuzzy spelling.* The word is expanded to include additional words that are similarly spelled.
   c. *Wildcards.* The user can specify word patterns by using wildcards. Words that match the pattern are added to the query.
3. *Parsing.* Query parsing is the technique used to standardize otherwise variable elements. Included are:
   a. *Numeric and date range management.* The user can search for numbers or date ranges contained within a document, including greater-than and less-than criteria.
   b. *Term grouping/query structure.* The user can create statistical groups of terms, which are combined to help establish context and completeness.
   c. *Boolean expressions.* Standard Boolean operators (AND, OR, NOT, WITHIN, parentheses, and ADJ (word proximity with order enforced) are used.
   d. *Fielded queries.* Any query can be applied to any predefined field or zone of a document.
   e. *Exact phrases.* A search is made for a simple sequence of terms in the proper order.
4. *User feedback.* After steps 1 to 3 are complete, the system returns a copy of the query that it has built to the user for review. This review allows the user to be sure that the system has accurately interpreted the request. Upon acceptance by the user the system continues to step 5.

5. *Search preparation.* The system uses its internal setup for the execution of the query (allocation of memory, validating syntax, etc.).
6. *Coarse-grain rank.* This is a first pass at the query to try to reduce the search set from the entire universe of documents to a manageable subset. Once the search set is reduced with these high-level criteria, the lower-level, more detailed criteria can be applied. Coarse-grain ranking includes the following:
    a. *Expansion term distance.* Documents are identified with terms that are more closely related to the original terms.
    b. *Query structure, completeness, and contextual evidence.* Once the set of terms in a document is known, the weights of the individual terms are combined using the structure in the query. This then produces a structure that enhances completeness (documents contain representatives from all main terms in the original) and contextual evidence (terms are weighted to prove that the contexts of the documents are the same).
    c. *Main term weighting.* The term weights, chosen by the user or by automatic statistical techniques, are used to combine term weights.
7. *Fine-grain rank.* More specific tests are made to further differentiate between the documents that are left after the coarse-grain ranking.

RetrievalWare accomplishes these operations by making full use of parallel processing capabilities. It can query across multiple physical machines and databases through a LAN or WAN. Multiplatform query work is load-balanced and managed by the system.

Unique Search Approaches

RetrievalWare incorporates two unique techniques to help find documents in a way that no other product can. They are the semantic network and the pattern search.

Using Semantic Networks Semantic search is used to find words which mean the same thing, or which enhance the meaning of a word. This expansion has two purposes:

- To enforce or enhance the meaning of a word, or the concept the searcher is interested in. For example, finding the word *tank* in proximity to the words *vehicle* and *military* would indicate that the tank in question is a military tank and not a fish tank.

- To paraphrase the user's query so that the author and the user do not need to use the exact same language to find each other. For example, the user might ask for *international commerce,* and this will still find documents that talk about *foreign trade.* The user is freed from the need to anticipate the exact syntax of the writer to get the information of interest.

Using Pattern Search Pattern search, also known by the trademark Adaptive Pattern Recognition Processing (APRP), is used to find words that are misspelled, because of errors made by OCR, by the author, language translation, or by the searcher. (For example, there are 39 ways to spell the name *Muhammad*—the most popular first name on the planet.)

Making Use of Dictionaries In addition to many different kinds of searching techniques, RetrievalWare makes use of internal dictionaries to help verify, expand, and interpret queries. The product comes with a default English language dictionary, which serves most users' needs, but in rare situations, specialized dictionaries such as a legal or medical dictionary can be added.

Index Building with RetrievalWare

Not only does RetrievalWare make use of advanced techniques in the preparation of queries, it also uses a similar approach to the building of indexes.

Indexes Built by Spiders To start with, RetrievalWare makes use of the Excalibur Internet Spider software to build internal indexes. These spiders feed the index building pipeline and profiler.

The Index Building Pipeline Just like the RetrievalWare query building process, the index building process chains together a series of steps which greatly enhance the ability of the system to interpret the meaning and content of the documents reviewed. As Figure 13-11 shows, the main steps of the index building pipeline include:

1. *Tokenization.* Dividing strings into words and identifying the types of special tokens (numbers, dates, etc.).
2. *Morphology.* Dissecting words and finding other words that are like them.
3. *Idioms.* Identifying idiomatic expressions.

Chapter 13: Search Engines and Facilities

Figure 13-11
Excalibur
RetrievalWare
index building
pipeline.

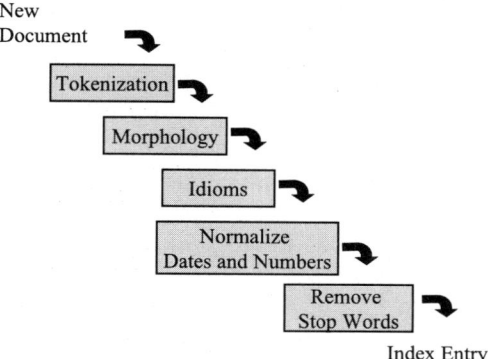

4. *Normalizing dates and numbers.* Standardizing date and number entries.

5. *Remove stop words.* Elimination of all words that add no substance to the content of the document (words such as *but* and *and*).

By using these techniques, RetrievalWare is able to build extremely powerful indexes which, when combined with the already powerful query building process, are unprecedented in the search engine arena.

The RetrievalWare Approach to Synchronization

Unfortunately, no matter how good a job you do at building an index, the system will only be useful as long as the index is up to date. As the population of documents changes, the system needs to stay aware of those changes and keep the system current.

There are basically two ways in which a search engine can keep entries up to the minute: the scheduler (or synchronizer) approach and the search broker approach. RetrievalWare uses the scheduler approach. Under this scenario, the system proactively keeps track of all of its sources of information and periodically checks to see if there have been any changes. If changes have occurred, the system adjusts the index entries to reflect that change.

In the search broker approach, the search engine does not keep its own indexes of the population of documents, but instead forwards all requests to another search engine (such as Alta Vista). These systems have a clear disadvantage compared to the scheduler approach, since their performance depends on systems that are outside of the host system's control.

Searching against Real-Time Data Sources In addition to providing users with the ability to search against passively stored documents, the system also allows those users to query against real-time data sources.

One of the features of the RetrievalWare software package is the facility known as the RetrievalWare Profiler and Disseminator. This facility allows users to build search profiles, collections of queries that define the kinds of information that they would like to be proactively notified about whenever new or different information becomes available. The users define what they want to stay current on, and the profiler proactively works with real-time data sources to guarantee that the user gets the information as quickly as possible.

There are two ways in which the profiler and disseminator can discover new information for the users:

- *Scheduler activity.* To be sure that users are made aware of any changes that may occur within the search universe after they have run an initial query, the profiler takes part in the document integration process. When the scheduler identifies new or changed documents to include in the index, it also has the profiler check to see if any of those same documents include information of interest to the user. If so, the appropriate notification is sent to that user.

- *Real-time data feeds.* In addition to intervening in scheduler activity, the profiler and disseminator can also be used to tap into real-time data feeds. These data feeds (news services, ticker systems, etc.) are scanned for the text of interest, just as any document would be scanned, and when appropriate material is found, the user is notified.

Excalibur Screen Examples

Included in this section are several examples of the Excalibur product in action. The first example shows the main Excalibur RetrievalWare, Version 6.6, Web-based interface (Figure 13-12). This screen has the main menu across the top. Along the left side, it displays a map of an organization's searchable information assets, be they Web-based (from the Internet), text-based (structured or unstructured), or paper-based (scanned documents).

Chapter 13: Search Engines and Facilities

Figure 13-12
RetrievalWare main menu screen.

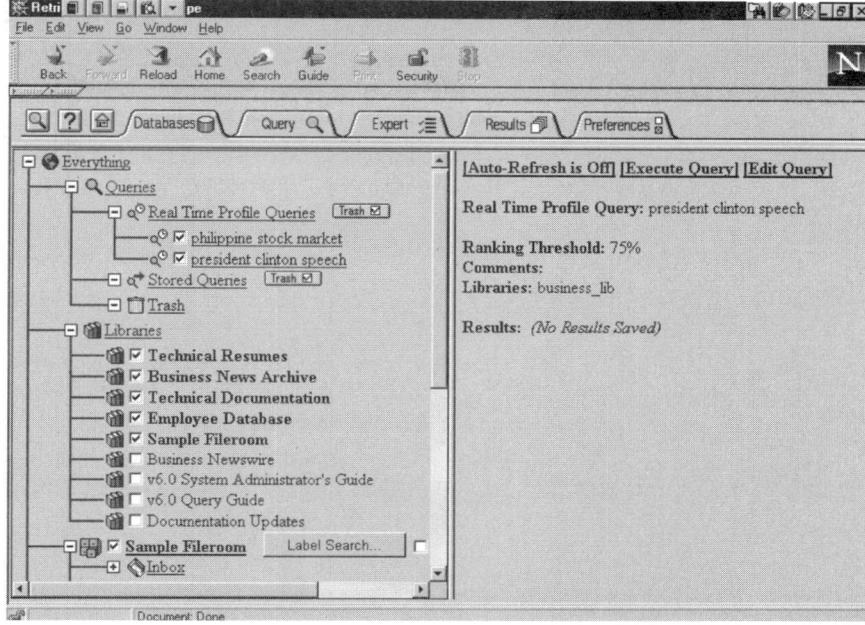

Figure 13-13
Clinton search results.

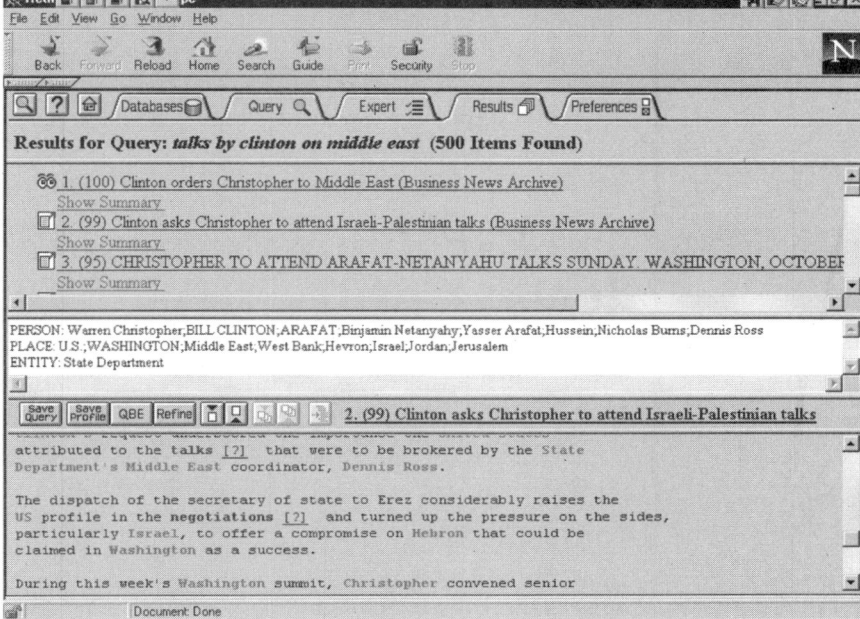

Figure 13-14
Document explorer.

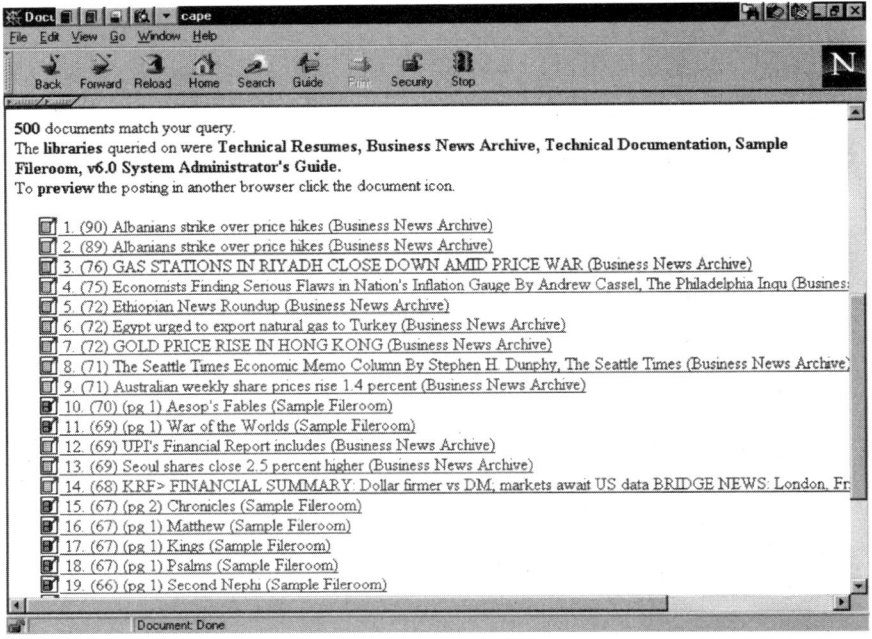

We next show an example of the results of a concepts-based query for "talks by Clinton on the Middle East." Figure 13-13 illustrates the intelligence of the RetrievalWare, which highlights best hits at the bottom of the screen.

Finally, we show the ranked results list after performing a search using the simple document explorer interface. See Figure 13-14.

The Excalibur RetrievalWare Report Card

In general, the Excalibur RetrievalWare product outperforms its competition on almost every front. Two of the most important considerations however, are system accuracy and scalability.

Accuracy

One of the ways to measure how well a search engine does its job is to run benchmark tests [similar to the TPC (Transaction Processing

Council) tests in the database world] to see how quickly and precisely it returns the documents of interest to users. In government studies, a typical text search system was able to achieve an average of about 33 percent for those queries that were run well. In similar tests, RetrievalWare was able to accomplish 71 percent—a significant improvement.

Scalability

RetrievalWare's scalability derives from its architecture, which includes five types of components:

- *Clients.* This is represented by the end user employing HTML on a browser.
- *Executives.* These programs catch user requests and broker communications between the other components.
- *Schedulers.* These make sure that the clients' requests are evenly distributed over multiple search servers (providing an automated load balancing and parallelization capability).
- *Client handlers.* These handle specific client requests for information. (You can have as many client handlers as you need to guarantee good user response time.)
- *Search servers.* These servers actually perform the requested search activity. (You can have as many search servers as you need to guarantee good user response as well!)

This distributed and load-balanced architecture means that there is virtually no limit to the scale to which a RetrievalWare environment can expand.

Conclusion

In this chapter, we discuss search engines, their components, and what differentiates some of the very popular products. We examine various approaches to index generation, including the spider-based scheme. We look at one of the more sophisticated search engines, the Excalibur RetrievalWare product, and see its approach to the many challenges that face the builder of a search engine.

CHAPTER 14

Text Mining Systems

- *What is text mining?*
- *What is the basic architecture of a text mining system?*
- *How are text mining and data mining alike and different?*
- *What kinds of business problems do text mining systems solve?*
- *What are some examples of text mining software, and how do they work?*
- *What is the IBM Customer Relationship Intelligence product, and how does it work?*
- *What is the IBM Intelligent Miner for Text product, and how does it work?*

While the previous chapter provided the reader with information about search engines (by far the most popular form of text information management system), here we will concentrate on the second most common utilization of these types of systems, the text mining systems.

Text Mining—An Introduction

When you consider all the different textual information that is available on the Web and in corporate data stores around the world, it becomes clear that there is much more of it available than any one person could ever actually process. The next plateau, therefore, in the management of corporate information will undoubtedly involve the development of approaches and algorithms that allow business to weed through the masses of textual information and distill out precisely the kind of information that people are looking for.

The discipline and the technologies that focus specifically on the accomplishment of those objectives are known collectively as *text mining solutions*. For the purpose of our book, we will define text mining as the application of computer systems hardware and software to the analysis of textual documents in order to:

1. Extract information and/or knowledge from those documents.
2. Discover trends that those documents might expose.
3. Gain insights into people, places, and things based on what those documents reveal.
4. Classify, organize, and/or categorize the documents or the information/knowledge that they hold.
5. Summarize by condensing a document into a more compact form.

Text Mining as a Separate Discipline

As we discovered in the last chapter, one of the most powerful applications of text mining is accomplished when the text mining tools are integrated with a search engine. However, there is no reason why this same text mining technology cannot also be applied to reviewing textual information for other research, discovery, and pattern matching exercises.

Just as the data information management systems world is typified by both real-time data analysis techniques (via query and OLAP capabilities) and passive, strategic, and analytical investigation (via data mining, neural network, CHAID, and other capabilities), the text information management systems world faces those same options.

Core Text Mining Functions There is, in fact, a considerable variety of text mining tools from which to choose. These tools have been developed to perform a number of different analytical jobs, but all of them tend to make use of the same core analytical approaches, using techniques like:

- *Content summarization.* Using the software to read documents and summarize their contents for the analyst.
- *Content search.* Searching for the specific information you are looking for.
- *Trend analysis.* Attempting to find patterns in the content of documents.
- *Document categorization.* Electronically organizing a large collection of unclassified documents on the basis of their content.
- *Lexical analysis.* Analysis of documents based on the collections of words that they contain.
- *Grammatical analysis.* Analysis of documents based on the way the words are organized.
- *Semantic analysis.* Analysis of a document and conversion of the meanings of words and expressions into codified values.
- *Linguistic analysis.* Analysis of a document to identify which natural language it is written in.
- *Cluster analysis.* Examining a collection of documents and determining the different ways they group together.

The Text Mining Process

The process of text mining is executed in much the same way that data mining is:

1. A businessperson identifies documents that might hold some information worth mining.
2. All potential sources for documents of this type are identified.
3. The documents are collected and standardized in some way. This assumes, of course, that the documents are coming from several different sources. For example, a person might want to combine

documents from the Internet (HTML files), email, Microsoft Word, and Lotus Word Pro sources. In this case, the user will have to get all of the documents converted to some kind of standard format.

4. The user determines the appropriate kind of mining activity that should be applied to that document collection to gain the desired insight (there are several different mining operations including classification, organization, categorization, and the discovery of hidden trends or insights), and selects the appropriate mining tool.

5. The mining tool is allowed to read through the entire population of documents, applying its particular assortment of algorithms and analytical approaches to accomplish the objectives set for it.

6. The tool produces some form of output report, which communicates the results of its process to the user.

7. It is then left to the user to read these output reports and interpret them to gain the objectives desired.

Text versus Data Mining—Similarities and Differences

It is obvious that there are many similarities between text mining and the data mining and statistical analysis approaches that we considered in earlier chapters of this book. What is not clear is exactly how similar and different they are. The similarities between text and data mining are:

- They are executed by the same fundamental process: Identify a collection to mine, prepare it, and analyze it with the software.
- The tools are developed on the foundational concepts of either core statistical analysis functions (such as cluster analysis) or advanced nonstatistical mining techniques (such as neural networks, CHAID, CART).
- Both approaches are most effective when the users have a clear understanding of the kind of information they are mining for and the business value that the information will provide.
- Both approaches must be utilized discerningly; users must be aware of each approach's limitations, or they may draw erroneous conclusions from the data presented.

As similar as these two approaches are, there are also some significant differences we must consider:

Chapter 14: Text Mining Systems

- The most obvious has to do with the nature of what is being mined. Only the rarest of tools can be used to analyze both raw data and textual information at the same time or in the same way.
- While these two disciplines share some of the same analytical approaches, they also have a broad selection of analytical tools unique to their discipline. For example, test analysis includes incorporation of many linguistic, lexical, and contextual techniques to glean a meaning out of the text that data analysis can never accomplish.

IBM Text Mining Product Offerings

One of the companies that is taking the forefront in the field of text mining systems is IBM. IBM has developed a number of product offerings over the past couple of years, each of which attempts to address the solution to specific business problems through application of these different text mining approaches and techniques.

The flagship product of the IBM text mining offerings is the Intelligent Miner for Text. This product is offered as a software development kit (SDK), providing customers with a collection of core, general-purpose text mining software modules that can perform different kinds of text analysis, advanced search engine support, and Web management to allow users to develop customized text mining solutions. Applications built with the Intelligent Miner for Text SDK can search text-based documents, categorize them, create clusters of similar documents, and extract relevant text such as proper names and multiword terms.

The fundamental toolkit of text mining capabilities that the Intelligent Miner for Text product makes available can be utilized by customers in a number of different ways:

It can be purchased as is, and used to assemble specific text mining applications.

It can be incorporated into advanced text mining applications written by specialized third-party software developers.

It can be embedded in specific IBM text mining applications.

Some of IBM's specific text mining applications based on Intelligent Miner for Text are:

- *The Text Knowledge Miner.* A powerful text analysis tool that can be used to analyze tens of thousands of complex, text-based documents in a single iteration, including scientific publications, newswires, and articles. It analyzes and clusters textual data to help companies discover new subject relationships, extract important concepts, and stimulate new ideas.

- *Customer Relationship Intelligence.* A cross-industry text mining solution that extracts information and insight about customer interactions with a company to better understand how customers feel about and are responding to the company's services and marketing efforts.
- *Technology Watch.* A product for analysis of patents, and gathering of competitive intelligence. This product analyzes the keywords of documents found in databases containing patents and references from scientific publications. It classifies the documents according to content in order to aid companies in analyzing vast quantities of technically oriented information.

Business Applications Making Use of Text Mining Products

There is actually quite a respectable array of business applications for text mining products, although the technology itself is quite new. A few examples follow.

Drug Firms—Biomedical Research

In one of the most common applications, several drug development firms have found that text mining of repositories of drug development notes yields significant returns on investment.

For example, a drug firm was looking for ways in which they could reduce their development times and speed their go-to-market time. They used text mining tools to analyze the textual records of researchers doing similar work for other firms, or within their own firm. These tools help researchers speed up their development process by avoiding the pursuit of directions that others have already tried, and by drawing new conclusions based on the combination of their own findings and the findings of others. (In this case, the company made use of both the content search and trend analysis capabilities of the IBM Text Knowledge Miner product to accomplish their objectives.)

Electric Utility—Customer Opinion Survey Analysis

Another strong application of text mining technology can be found in the work done by an electrical utility company. In this case, the company made use of text mining to provide the marketing department with a consolidated view of their customers' opinions about the release of an electric car within their marketplace. The organization downloaded tens of thousands of documents from the Internet, tagged them, parsed them for meaning, grouped them into thematic clusters, and then analyzed them for interrelationships to detect subtle shifts in public perception, all without human intervention.

This company was able to do in hours what would have taken a large group of people weeks or even months. (The tool used in this case was the IBM Customer Relationship Intelligence product with its analyzing, clustering, and interpreting capabilities.)

On-Line Newspaper—Searching for a Job, Car, or House

In an exceptionally clever utilization of a text mining product, a large German newspaper was able to create a powerful and flexible on-line classified ad system where subscribers can search for the precise cars, apartments, jobs, and homes they are interested in. The system allows the users to describe the search parameters for the type of item they are looking for. It then uses a text mining product to analyze the content of each of the thousands of available classified ads, identifying the best match from among them. (The newspaper made use of the IBM Intelligent Miner for Text product to get the job done, using content analysis capabilities to differentiate between the many different types of basically free-form ad layouts.)

IBM Customer Relationship Intelligence Product—Text Mining in Action

One of the most universally applicable of the text mining products is the IBM Customer Relationship Intelligence product. This product was designed to specifically help companies better understand what their customers want and what they think about the company itself.

The information returned from these investigations allows an organization to retain and grow their customer base by developing an earlier and better understanding of:

- Customer needs
- Customer issues
- Industry and market trends
- Product issues, complaints, and acceptance
- Competitive positioning

For many companies, the information analyzed in this way can yield extremely useful, objective, credible, and measurable feedback from the marketplace—feedback that no other technique can deliver.

The CRI Process

The CRI (Customer Relationship Intelligence) product itself operates as part of a four-step process (see Figure 14-1):

1. Input identification and collection
2. Input preparation
3. Analysis
4. Report generation

Figure 14-1
The CRI process.

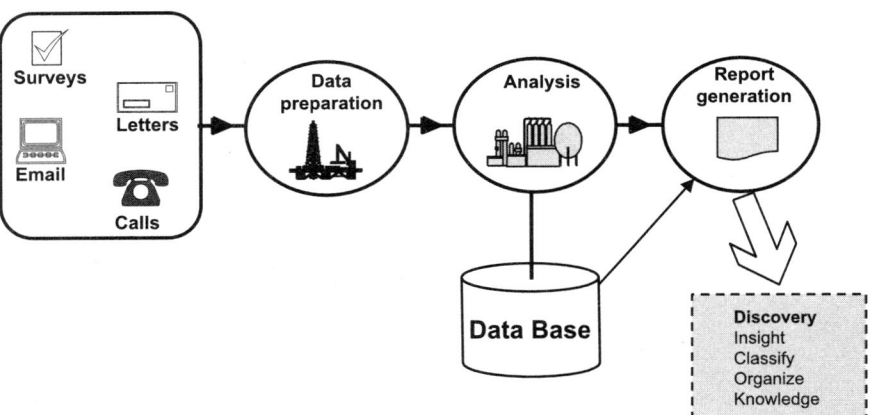

Chapter 14: Text Mining Systems

The following sections will discuss each of these steps in more detail.

Input Identification and Collection The first step in any mining process is identification and collection of all the different inputs that are going to be used. Each company can assemble its own list of textual sources to be used as input. They usually include:

The textual results of customer surveys. (This information can include the surveys themselves as well as the subjective observations made by observers and the people conducting the surveys.)

Focus groups, including the groups' participants and the observations of the people running the groups.

Letters sent in by consumers.

Email received either unsolicited or in response to specific offers or invitations.

Telephone calls in the form of transcripts or notes taken by phone operators.

Input Standardization After the sources of information have been identified, the next step is to make those sources analyzable. The work required to standardize these diverse input sources will vary depending on the method received.

Telephone call responses can be collected by voice recognition systems (systems that listen to voices and create transcripts of what is said) and/or interactive touch-tone systems (users input preferences by pressing different keys). Letters and surveys can be read into the system by optical character recognition systems, or through the translation and transcription of that input into textual form. Email can usually be copied right into the system. In all cases, the different forms of input need to be converted into a standard textual format, which the CRI product will be able to read and interpret.

Analysis After all the input has been collected and standardized, the CRI product itself is ready to run. Analysis is accomplished through the following steps:

1. *Preparation.* The input text is prepared, and core customer data is coded (standardized and converted into the correct codes). During this step, the key data-based identifiers are standardized, such as customer's age, sex, income level, date of input collection).

2. *Conversion of textual information into coded data (linguistic processing).* During this step, the textual information is read into the system. The system is then able to interpret and translate it into one of the predetermined codes set by the system. (In other words, if we are checking for whether the customer likes or dislikes something, we can set the system to look for positive or negative statements, and then have those coded into a 1 for positive and 0 for negative feedback from the customer). This is accomplished by using the following four capabilities:

    a. *Tagger.* Facility that reviews the input and tags recognizable text (looking for things like the company name or product name).

    b. *Expressions.* Facility that looks for known expressions and assigns the related code (for example, the expression "I really like" will be coded as a positive response).

    c. *Terminology.* Facility that looks for known terminology and assigns the related code (looking for special terms or words that are specific to the industry or product).

    d. *Semantics.* Facility that uses semantic analysis of text (referring to the meanings that words and combinations of words are meant to communicate).

3. *Feature selection.* After the initial analysis of the input has been performed, users are allowed to select those features that they wish to have employed through the rest of the processing.

4. *Clustering.* The now codified, but still raw, data is then subjected to several forms of cluster analysis, including:

    a. Simple clustering of 0 and 1 values

    b. Standard statistical frequency clustering

    c. Assignment of cluster values to each entry within the system

5. *Code storage.* The corresponding collections of customer identification information and the codes derived are stored within a customer characteristics database.

Report Generation Finally, the users are able to examine and analyze the feedback by simply running informational reports out of the codified database. (In this case, our text mining exercise has now become a purely data mining exercise, since the user will now be analyzing the data collected about the textual information, not the textual information itself.)

Chapter 14: Text Mining Systems

Figure 14-2
The CRI product architecture.

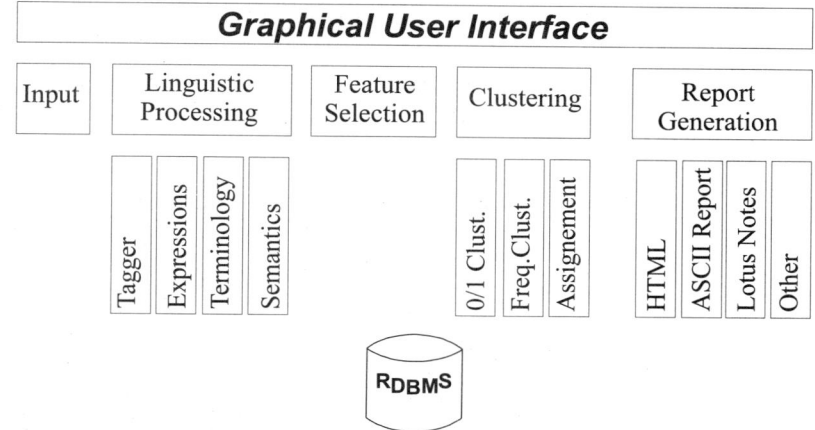

The system can produce output for HTML, ASCII, Lotus Notes, or other reporting formats. The report output depends only on the user's ability to read and analyze relational data, since the codes and customer information have been stored there.

The CRI Product Architecture

We can get some better insights into how the CRI product analyzes and codifies these varied forms of textual input by looking at the architecture of the product itself. As Figure 14-2 shows, each of the parts of the CRI process is supported by a separate set of product components including input, preparation, linguistic processing, clustering, and report generation. All these facilities are managed and made available to the user through the standard graphical user interface.

Using the IBM Intelligent Miner for Text

For those customers with more specific needs for text mining capabilities, the more flexible Intelligent Miner for Text SDK can be the more appropriate solution. While the IBM Customer Relationship Intelligence product is specifically engineered to analyze input from a wide variety of sources and then codify those inputs to provide in-depth data analysis, the Intelligent Miner product allows users to do their analysis without the codification step.

Intelligent Miner for Text comes complete with three text analysis tools, which can be used to address a variety of analysis problems: an extraction tool, a clustering tool, and a categorization tool. We will consider each in more detail.

Feature Extraction Tool

The feature extraction tool of the IBM Intelligent Miner for Text product allows users to analyze documents, finding vocabulary items within the text that are significant to the analyst. The feature extractor recognizes these terms and expressions and reports their presence. Feature extraction occurs in several modules including:

- *Name extraction.* Names provide valuable clues to the meaning of text. Using fast and robust heuristics, the name extraction module locates the occurrences of names in text and determines what type of entity the name refers to (person, place, organization, etc.). The module processes either a single document or a collection of documents, providing a list of names, their locations, and a dictionary or database of all names in the collection.
- *Term extraction.* Another lexical clue to the subject of a document are the domain terms the document contains. The term extraction module uses a set of simple heuristics to identify multiword technical terms in a document.
- *Relations extraction.* This extractor looks for relationships between words.
- *Abbreviations.* The extractor looks for recognized and derived abbreviation forms.
- *Number.* This module looks for both textual and numerically displayed numbers and makes it possible to identify and standardize them.
- *Date.* This module identifies the many different ways that dates can be formatted and communicated.
- *Money.* The money module captures monetary units and displays standards, and textual identification.

Making use of each of these modules, the feature extraction capability of Intelligent Miner for Text allows analysts to learn many different things about the documents being reviewed.

Clustering Tool

Of course, the ability to identify each of the different features of importance within documents will be of only limited value if it is not combined with some other analytical capabilities. One of the most useful of the Intelligent Miner for Text tools is the clustering tool.

Clustering is the process of grouping together objects that are in some way similar to each other. In text mining, clustering is used to segment a document collection into subsets, or clusters, with the members of each cluster being similar with respect to the specified features. When clustering is performed, no predefined criteria for grouping documents are established, and the document population is allowed to organize itself.

The automatic clustering of documents can be used to:

Provide an overview of the contents of a large document collection

Identify hidden structures behind groups of documents

Ease the process of organizing and then browsing large document collections

Find outstanding documents within a collection

Detect duplicate documents within a collection

The clustering tool accomplishes all of this by scanning the contents of the documents and creating the statistically appropriate grouping of those documents according to the criteria that the user sets.

Using the Clustering Tool Figures 14-3 and 14-4 show some typical output from the application of the clustering tool to a population of documents. Figure 14-3 shows a typical entry screen for the clustering tool. From this screen the user can choose the population of documents to be clustered (either the information processing document collection or the opinion survey document collection) and establish the type and degree of clustering to be performed (thresholds, slices, and number of documents).

After filling out this screen, the user can then proceed to view the output of the clustering activity. The screen in Figure 14-4 shows the initial output from the analysis of a population of documents. Note that the documents have been grouped on the basis of several words that they have in common. The first report box, the one that is darkened, shows the first cluster identified. This cluster has two documents, which represent .4 percent of the total document population. These two documents are 28.7 percent similar (the most similar of any documents in the collection) and share the word associations cowboy/dallas, decide/kid, and kid/tho.

Part 2: Web Warehousing in Action

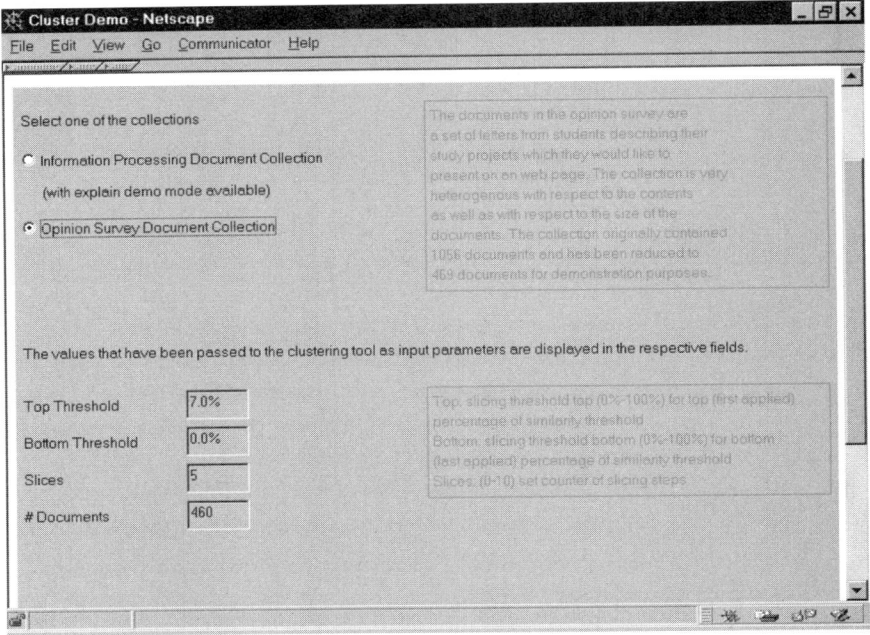

Figure 14-3
Clustering tool entry screen.

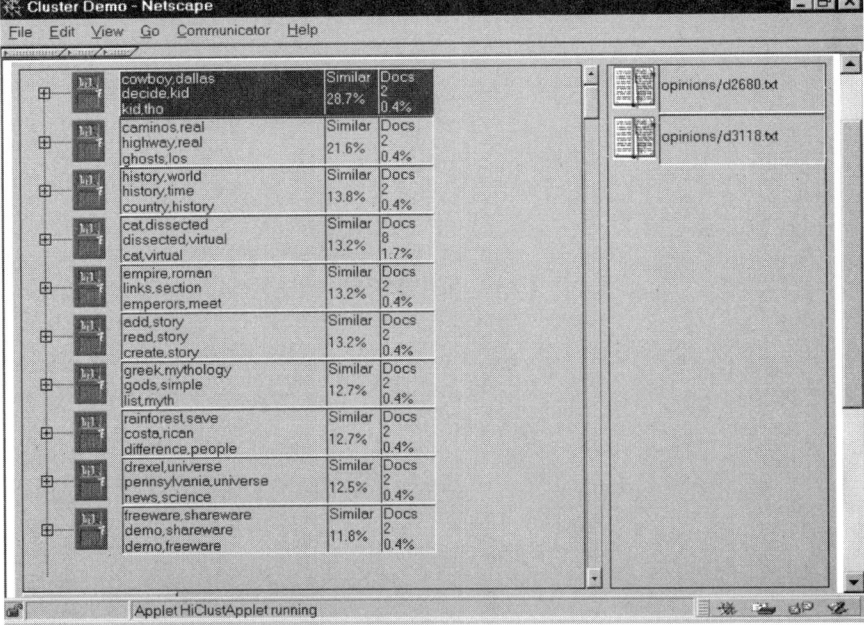

Figure 14-4
Initial clustering output display.

On the far right-hand side of the display, we see the two documents. By selecting and clicking on one of these, we would be able to read the content of that document. Scanning down the screen, we can see each of the different clusters that the system has identified, including eight documents about cats/dissected. By subjecting a document collection to this kind of analysis, the user can learn a lot about the population.

Categorization Tool

The categorization tool of Intelligent Miner for Text allows users to automatically assign documents to predefined categories according to the criteria they have established. This facility helps users to:

Organize Internet documents. The system automatically places user-submitted documents in the appropriate Web site and folder location.

Automatically assign documents to folders. Allows users to automatically file incoming email in the appropriate location, for example.

Dispatch requests. The system accepts incoming email and other types of news or messages and automatically routes them to predefined interested parties. For example, it routes email trouble reports to the appropriate help desk and forwards news to subscribers.

Using the Categorization Tool The categorization tool is able to automatically recognize documents through the execution of the following steps:

1. *Identification phase.* During this phase, the users and designers decide on the scope and breadth of documents they will want included in the schema. Consensus is reached regarding the purpose of the text storage facility and the objectives for the categorization.

2. *Sample (training set) collection phase.* During this phase, samples of each type of document to be included are gathered. This collection needs to hold representative examples of each of the types of input (email, word processing document, etc.) and of the subject matter, date, author, sender, etc.—information critical to the successful creation of categories.

3. *Training phase.* To know where to place different documents, the categorization tool must first be "trained." The training procedure is as follows:

a. Read the training set—To train the product, the user provides it with a training set of documents, which includes sample documents from each category collected during the previous phase.
   b. Analyze each document in the training set. The categorization tool makes use of the Intelligent Miner for Text feature extraction tool (described previously) to evaluate the content of each document in the training set. The feature extraction tool looks for items identified as critical to the categorization approach (authors, dates, etc.) and summarizes them on a document-by-document basis.
   c. Create the category scheme. After reading and analyzing the contents of the training documents, the categorization tool is ready to create the category scheme. It is a dictionary that encodes in a condensed form significant vocabulary statistics for each category.
   d. Create the categorization algorithm. After creating the category scheme, the system can then evaluate the key statistics about the sample population and generate a categorization algorithm. The categorization algorithm is used to evaluate each document as it is submitted for categorization and to determine which category the document should be placed into. It works by scanning the document, returning a ranked list of the categories that apply to that text, and generating a rank value (which summarizes and weights the overall applicability of the document to each of the potential membership categories).
4. *Categorization phase.* During this phase, the previously prepared categorization algorithm is used to scan, evaluate, and classify each document as it is fed into the system.

Special Language Classification Tool

There is an additional specialized module that is used solely to identify the natural language that the document is written in. (In other words, this tool can tell whether a document has been written in English, French, Spanish, or German, for example.) By combining this capability with the other categorization tool features, designers can build powerful, multilingual repositories at a very low cost.

Chapter 14: Text Mining Systems

Figure 14-5
Clustering versus categorization.

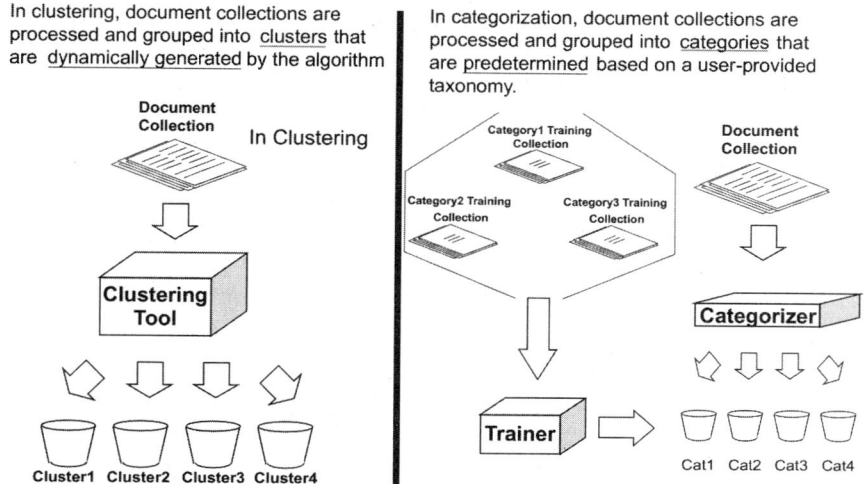

Summarization Tool

Summarization is the process of condensing a source text into a shorter version, while preserving its information content. Version 2.3 includes this new feature. The summarization tool automatically extracts those sentences from a document which are most relevant to its content, and creates a summary of the document from these sentences. The summarizer tool uses a set of ranking strategies on sentence level and on word-level to calculate the relevancy of a sentence to a document. The user can set the length of the summary. An automatically generated summary can be useful to judge the relevancy of a full text, to enrich search results, and to get a fast overview over document collections.

Clustering versus Categorization

Because there is often some confusion over these two terms, we supply a very brief description of the difference. Categorization is supervised classification, with the documents being sorted into *predefined* categories. Clustering, in contrast, is unsupervised classification, with automatic selection of categories by the system, and distribution of documents to be analyzed into these system-generated categories. To teach the system how to do this, it is necessary to use a learning set of documents. Figure 14-5 illustrates the difference.

Conclusion

In this chapter, we finish our examination of the text information management systems by taking a closer look at the specific area of text mining products (that is, products that read and analyze the content of documents to provide business people with additional information or insight about their businesses). We see that text mining, like data mining, is a statistically and mathematically based discipline that involves the reading of massive collections of input files (documents) by smart software—software that knows how to analyze the contents of the files and provide users with useful insights.

We discuss how text and data mining are similar to and different from each other. We also look at some powerful products that have appeared in the text mining space: IBM's Customer Relationship Intelligence, Text Knowledge Miner, and Intelligent Miner for Text.

CHAPTER 15

Multimedia Information Management Systems

- *What is a multimedia information management system?*
- *How do you manage multimedia information?*
- *What are the two major approaches to multimedia management in a Web environment?*
- *What is the architecture of a typical multimedia search engine?*
- *What is the difference between text-based and media-based search systems?*
- *How does the Excalibur visual query product work?*

This is the last of the chapters dedicated to the exploration of knowledge management–based Web warehousing applications. We will look at the newest, the least traditional, and possibly the most exciting of all the application areas, the multimedia information management systems.

Defining Multimedia Information Management Systems

Just as with most of the other categories of information systems products that we have talked about, there is a lot of controversy around exactly what we mean by the term *multimedia management information system*. In this book, we use the term to describe those systems that manage the storage, retrieval, and analysis of nontraditional computer-managed objects (namely, audio, video, graphical, 3-D, 4-D, and other types of objects), in order to help businesses to accomplish their objectives.

What we do *not* include in this category are products that:

Create, manage, store, and display graphical images that are based on and dependent on numeric and textual data. (We have already discussed these types of products in Chapter 10 under "Graphical Information Systems.")

Create, manage, store, and display multimedia-type images (like video, audio, or 3-D) for the purposes of playing games, providing entertainment, or otherwise delivering multimedia as an end unto itself. (This category of products is certainly interesting. It could be considered a "business" pursuit in that the creation and distribution of entertainment is a business, and it could provide us with valuable insights into the ways that such media can be managed. However, to include this category of products would go beyond the scope of what this book has set out to do, and it represents such a highly specialized portion of the business applicability of the technology that I have decided to forgo its coverage here.)

In general, we limit our investigation specifically to those products and applications that address the businessperson's need for information and knowledge in the support of better business decision making and execution.

Categories of Multimedia Information Management Systems

While the field of multimedia information management is certainly new, there is no shortage of applications. Some of the more interesting and popular categories include:

- Hybrid search systems (text and multimedia combined)
- Exclusively multimedia search and retrieval systems
- Multimedia analysis systems
- Security and personal identification management systems

In the following sections, we will review each of these in more detail.

Hybrid Search Systems (Text and Multimedia Combined) By far the most common form of multimedia management system is one that manages the search for both textual and multimedia objects from within the same facility. The evolution of the Internet and the World Wide Web, and their native ability to handle a variety of different types of objects with equal efficiency, has made the appearance of the hybrid text/multimedia search engine a reality.

In general, the only difference between a text information management system and a multimedia information management system from this perspective is the kinds of objects that they retrieve. In fact, almost every search engine on the World Wide Web today, and the vast majority of search engines available for sale in the corporate world, are hybrid systems.

The fact that these systems can do both jobs, however, does not mean that the inclusion of multimedia in a text-based world is a trivial matter. It requires that the builders of the systems consider some additional points.

Exclusively Multimedia-Based Search and Retrieval Engines
There are some systems available on the market today that deal exclusively in the management of multimedia systems. They are obviously not the kind of tools that a typical accountant might use, but are instead created to support highly specialized business needs. Systems in this category are usually provided to support either (1) industries that are heavily multimedia-centric (for example, the recording, movie, or publishing sectors where large libraries of sounds, video clips, or graphics

are needed) or (2) industries in which access to a variety of multimedia objects, unaccompanied by textual information, is needed. While these systems are certainly rare, they do deserve attention, since they show us some of the alternative ways to approach the challenges of Web warehousing in general.

Multimedia Analysis Systems Just as in the data and text area, there are products that allow people to analyze multimedia objects just as they would analyze data or text. For example, several high-tech computer animation and analysis firms have put together software that can analyze a photograph and look for patterns or images that the naked eye cannot detect. Other systems can analyze a series of different sound recordings and identify patterns that otherwise could not be noticed. Still others are used to compare a time series of infrared photographs to look for the patterns in the changes in temperature across a geographical area. While still highly specialized in the government, medical, and scientific areas, multimedia analysis systems can clearly be seen to be paralleling their textual- and data-based cousins and may soon be finding their way into the public eye, helping to address any number of interesting problems.

Security and Personal Identification Management Systems
Perhaps one of the most pervasive and tangible applications of multimedia management systems can be found in the areas of personal identity and security systems. The problem of trying to keep our belongings safe has plagued humanity for as long as people have had possessions. Today, the problems of security and identity are trickier than ever before.

Security problems are pervasive for several reasons. Some of the biggest reasons include:

There are more people than ever before, and therefore more people to keep track of.

Our society is much more impersonal than it used to be. The typical person interacts with dozens of strangers every day, and the local community where everyone knows everyone else on a first-name basis is a thing of the past.

We have more to keep private. We not only have physical property (homes, offices, cars, etc.), to protect, but also money and information about ourselves. All of these things are suddenly vulnerable to the attack of someone who understands computers and security systems and how they work.

Chapter 15: Multimedia Information Management Systems

As our society continues to propel itself ever more deeply into its dependence on computers, so too will its need for sophisticated security mechanisms. There are in fact several types of security systems that have become available recently, which significantly raise the level of security sophistication, and most of them are multimedia-based. They include:

1. *Voice matching systems.* These systems record a person's voice, store it, and use it as an identifier when that person wants access to a system or a building.

2. *Fingerprint identification systems.* These systems store copies of a person's fingerprints, and then use those images to match against a potential violator.

3. *Retinal scan.* Retinal scans take a photograph of a person's eye and use a match of the retinal image as proof of identity.

4. *Hand pattern recognition.* These systems take a system-based impression of a person's hands (the combination of finger size, length, thickness, and arrangement) to provide their security measure.

5. *Photographic identification system.* In addition to the preceding high-technology solutions, there is perhaps one of the simplest methods of identification of all, the photographic recording system. This system takes a picture of the person and then makes it available to security guards, bank tellers, and store clerks, making it very difficult for a person to masquerade as someone else.

With the existence of the Internet and the pervasiveness of corporate information systems, there are all sorts of things we need to protect from intruders.

Why Is Multimedia Search Different from Textual Search?

When looking at textual search and multimedia search systems, someone might ask, "Why do we need to consider them as separate? In fact, don't most of the major search engines retrieve pictures, sound bits, and video clips for us as a part of our textual search anyway?" The answer is yes, these systems do retrieve both text and image, but what they are usually doing is simply retrieving text that happens to have images attached to it. (There are exceptions to this rule—those Web sites that offer image libraries to the user, for example.)

What differences then would there be between a text information system and a multimedia system? The biggest single difference between them is in the way the system identifies, catalogs, and makes the multimedia objects available to the user for search. Think about how textual information management systems are put together, and you see the problem.

Applicability of the Text Search Architecture If we briefly revisit the architecture of a typical text search engine, we can identify where the problem lies. A text search engine architecture consists of:

- *Storage.* A place to store the text.
- *Indexing.* An index to point users to the text.
- *Search criteria.* A facility to allow users to identify which text they want.
- *Index building.* A system to build the index.
- *Query optimization.* A facility to translate user requests into index searches.

Why can we not use this approach to support the user's search for multimedia? Well we could, except for one small thing. How exactly do we go about identifying, indexing, and providing search capabilities for users to allow them to look for something that is not especially definable in terms of text?

Let's try to create the same list for an alternative medium—video, for example:

1. *Storage.* We need a place to store the video. That is certainly easy enough; there are all sorts of different forms of tape, film libraries, and disk to store video information. However, when we want to make that video information available via a Web-type interface, we have to translate the video into a digital form or create some mechanism that allows the nondigital video to be transmitted over the Web and displayed at the terminal.

2. *Indexing.* Now that we have figured out how to store the video, what do we do about indexes? Here is where we begin to see the real problem. What kind of index will we use to identify the videos? For example, if we have a library of classic black-and-white films from the 1940s, we could certainly create an index by the name of the movie. But what if we wanted to look for movies by producer or director or by star? What if we wanted to see all the movies that Jimmy Cagney

ever played in, whether he was the star or not? How could we possibly index all of this information?

3. *Search criteria.* One of the biggest problems with nontextual materials is that there are so many nontextual ways that you might want to create a search. I might want to search video clips by:
   a. How they are made
   b. Where they are made
   c. Who made them
   d. Who is in them
   e. The dialog they contain (I might want to find all movies where the phrase "Frankly, I don't give a damn" is spoken)
   f. The music that plays in the background
   g. The theme songs
   h. The types of camera angles that are used
   i. Any number of a thousand different perspectives.

4. *Index building.* Of course, once you have figured out what to index and how to search it, then you need to come up with a programmable technique for performing the search. In effect, you need to develop a computer program that can "watch" the video and check for what is asked for.

5. *Query optimization.* Finally, you need to figure out how to ask the computer program to perform the right search, and do it efficiently.

As you can see, the job of creating search facilities for multimedia is far from straightforward. It is certainly possible to build rudimentary systems where human beings actually watch the videos and fill out databases and indexes with the information that people might want. Of course, you can translate anything into a textual problem eventually if you try hard enough, but let's consider some of the consequences of what we are saying. In general, we create powerful indexes of information about textual documents with software programs that read the text and categorize it for us in a meaningful way. The better the index building mechanism, the better the search capabilities delivered. It is possible to build indexes based on human input, but these systems are the most expensive and the least objective. If we are to provide the ability to search for nontextual things, then we need to address this problem more directly.

Multimedia Search Requirements The fact is, if you provide the users with a meaningful multimedia search capability, they will have to have the ability to search on the basis of other criteria. For example:

- The user of a video clip search and retrieval system would like to be able to find the scene from an old Jimmy Cagney movie that shows him holding a machine gun and saying, "You dirty rats."
- The user of a graphical image library would like to find a picture with the same color combination as the corporate logo she is working on.
- The user of an audio library keeps hearing the same melody in his head. To find what song it is from, he would like to be able to hum it into his machine and have the system find it.

All these searches are possible, but they obviously cannot be executed by a simple textual search system.

Approaches to the Indexing of Multimedia

There are several ways in which we can index a multimedia collection, many of which are already in use.

1. *Simple name search.* The simple name search approach is the most obvious way to index any multimedia object. The name of the object is made available and if the users happen to know that name, or if it is descriptive (`TeddyBear.gif` as the name for a teddy bear picture), then the system will meet the users' needs.

2. *Keyword search.* A more sophisticated approach is a keyword file associated with each multimedia object. This is more effective than the simple name search, but still leaves much to be desired.

3. *Descriptive document search.* Under this model, someone familiar with the subject area actually reviews (looks at, watches, or listens to) all objects being cataloged and writes up a descriptive text that tells the searcher what it contains. A typical text search engine can then read this document.

4. *Referenceable document search.* This is the approach used most often on the World Wide Web. The multimedia document is attached to a document that references it, or that considers a subject related to it. (For example, a paper written about Mozart might include references to `.wave` clips of his music.)

Chapter 15: Multimedia Information Management Systems

5. *Descriptive database search.* In this case, specialized databases, specific to the media type and subject area, are created to provide the users with a meaningful and in-depth search capability that attempts to identify multimedia objects defined in their own codified terms (as opposed to being defined in textual, descriptive terms).

6. *Multimedia mining tools.* Although they are currently scarce, there are products that can scan multimedia files and create descriptions, which can then be used to populate a search index automatically.

7. *Real-time matching.* Probably the most effective (and most expensive and time-consuming) of the multimedia search techniques is the one that electronically compares multimedia input from the user to the media in its library until a match or similarity is found. For example, a sound file can be reduced to a sound wave image that can be matched against one filed in the library. The computer looks for similarities in the patterns and returns matches.

While the business value of pure-multimedia-based search facilities is viable in only a very limited set of industries, there are clearly many areas where they will begin to make appearances in the future.

The Excalibur Visual RetrievalWare Product

To show how multimedia systems can work outside the text-based arena, we look at the Visual RetrievalWare product from Excalibur. Excalibur is the same company that creates the RetrievalWare product that we introduce in Chapter 13. The product we talk about now has a decidedly *visually* based operational model.

According to the makers of Visual RetrievalWare, one of the greatest challenges facing information systems managers today is to deliver to the businessperson an intuitive, accurate, and rapid method to access information of all types and formats. Excalibur's Visual RetrievalWare is one of the few solutions available today that allow end-user search based on more than just text and numeric input. The Visual RetrievalWare product has extended the RetrievalWare product line to include powerful image content matching ability.

Visual RetrievalWare is not an off-the-shelf application, but is in fact distributed as a software development kit. This SDK provides developers with a set of tools that they can use to build their own custom visually based search and retrieval systems.

While the underlying architecture of the Visual RetrievalWare product is similar to that of the text-based RetrievalWare product, there is one significant difference. In this case, the product actually allows users to create their search on the basis of real images and image definitions, as opposed to textual and contextual reference information.

Components of the Visual RetrievalWare SDK

Visual RetrievalWare SDK consists of programming components that allow developers to build systems that provide a complete visually based search facility. These components include:

1. *Feature extractors.* These are programming modules that take an image as input and identify and describe certain features. (A feature extractor would fit into our category of multimedia indexing approaches as a multimedia mining tool.)
2. *Feature vector indexes.* These index constructs store the information generated by a feature extractor and allow the system to determine how similar two images are by comparing their index entries. (These feature vector indexes fall under our category of multimedia indexing approaches as a descriptive database search.)

The Feature Extractor

The Visual RetrievalWare feature extractor is an image analysis tool that distills the key characteristics of one aspect of an image into a specific string of 1s and 0s that describe that aspect of the image in a standardized format. For example, one feature of an image is its coloring, and the Visual RetrievalWare color-based feature extractor can be used to analyze the colors that make up that image and turn it into a string of 1s and 0s. While the mechanics of how this works is much more sophisticated than we can cover here, a greatly simplified example should help us understand how it works. Let's say, for instance, we decide that the color code for a certain shade of blue is 1001. Let's further assume that

Chapter 15: Multimedia Information Management Systems

the image file in question consists of nothing more than a plain blue screen, all in the same shade. The color feature extractor would then "analyze" this image and create a byte code for it, which might be 10011001100···. The system can then use this codified description of its coloring to compare one image's color coding with that of another and come up with color code matches between them.

Types of Feature Extractors Because there are so many different ways in which an image might be described, there are a lot of different feature extractors that can be used to help the system developer come up with the right feature mix. Some of the predefined feature extractors that the Visual RetrievalWare SDK includes are:

- *Color feature extractor.* Codifies the color scheme of an image.
- *Shape feature extractor.* Codifies the shapes that an image contains.
- *Texture feature extractor.* Codifies the texture of the image.
- *Generalized feature vector extractor.* Creates a codification of a generalized view of an image based on a loose model of a biological retina. This approach allows the system to directly index images "gestalt-style" by scaling the whole image to fit within the retina's fixed dimensions. This extractor is helpful in face recognition support.
- *Kanji feature extractor.* A specialized extractor sensitive to Kanji character sets.
- *Customized feature extractor.* Provides for the customized development of any particular feature that the system developer would like to include.
- *MPEG1 and MPEG2 feature extractors.* Codify video images.

Vector Indexes

The complementary component to the feature extractor is the Visual RetrievalWare vector index. While the feature extractor creates codified descriptions of the image, the vector index captures and stores those descriptions and provides the system with the ability to compare index entries in order to find matches.

Each feature extractor creates an entry to be placed into a specific vector index. These vector indexes allow the system to quickly compare the codification of thousands of entries in subsecond time, making the quick retrieval of close matches possible in a fraction of the time of other techniques.

Practical Applications of the Visual RetrievalWare SDK

There are several ways in which the Visual RetrievalWare product has been used to create unique visual search and retrieval systems.

One such system is the *color, shape,* and *texture* search application. This application allows the users to select the image from the screen that is most like the image they are looking for. The system will check its database of images and look for the other images that come closest. The user can then select an image from the resultant set that more closely matches the target and the system will continue to refine the search. The following screens show this system in action. Figure 15-1 shows the color, shape, and texture initial entry screen. Shown here are the 12 starter images on which further searching can be based. Figure 15-2 shows the resultant set of images that the system retrieved on the basis of the initial selection. Notice how the images all look like pumpkins. (Notice also the available "tuning" slide bars to the right of the image, which allow the users to determine how much of the search they want based on color, shape, and texture criteria.) Figure 15-3 is an example of a screen for video analysis.

Figure 15-1
The color, shape, and texture initial selection screen.

Chapter 15: Multimedia Information Management Systems   **367**

Figure 15-2
The result of selecting the pumpkin.

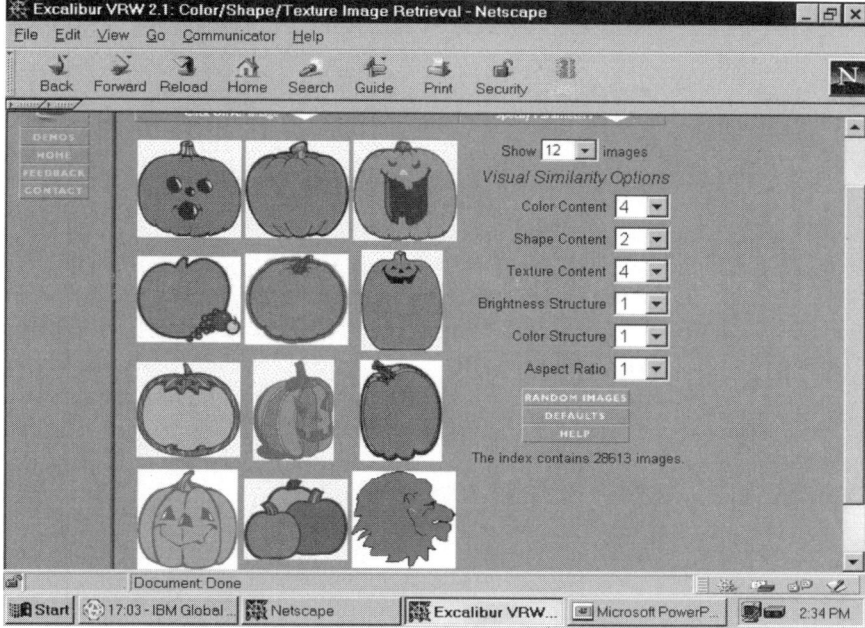

Figure 15-3
A video analysis example.

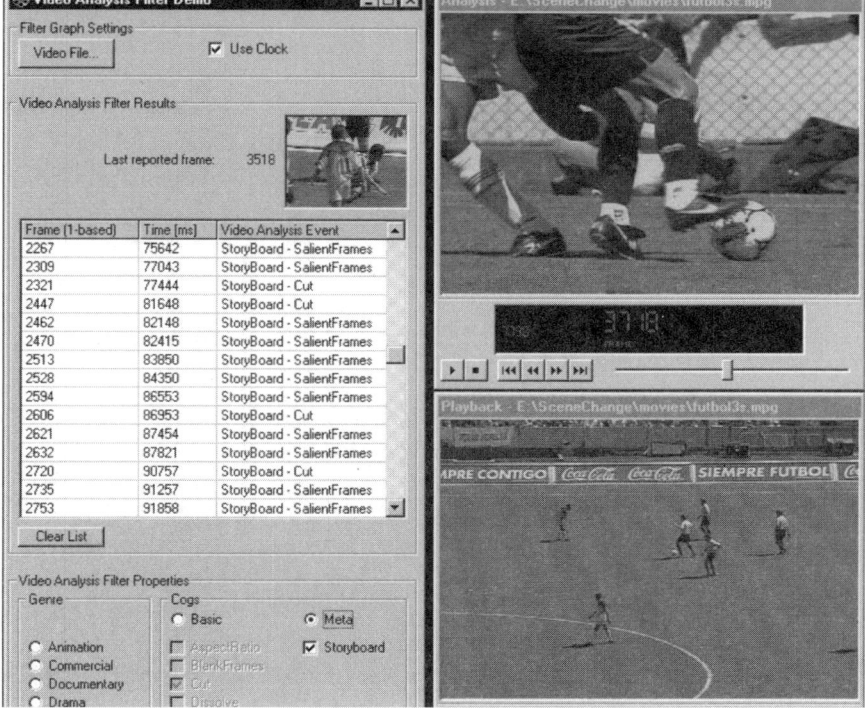

Conclusion

In this chapter, we talk about multimedia-based information systems, and specifically the Excalibur Visual RetrievalWare product, which allows users to look for multimedia objects according to their own, non-textually-based search criteria. While it is clear that this particular aspect of Web warehousing and knowledge management is still in its infancy, it is equally clear that a lot of new innovations will occur in this area in the near future. Already, there are exciting new developments in audio mining, audio search and retrieval, video mining, and search and retrieval and all of the other sections of multimedia management. We can look forward to big changes ahead in this area.

■ ■ ■

At this point we not only finish our discussions of multimedia tools, but we also conclude our look at all of the different types of tools that will make up the knowledge-based, Web-based business environment of the next decade. In review, we see that we could divide the Web-based warehousing tools into several major categories, depending on the kinds of objects they deliver to the users.

We look first at the data-based Web warehousing tools and see that, in general, these products could attribute their history to the data-based, client/server data tools of the previous generation of systems. While there are some products that have been created specifically for the Web environment, each of the categories of data-based Web-warehousing tools consists of products that have been converted from their earlier versions. Included with these products are:

Data query tools. Allow users to ask questions and get answers in an ad hoc fashion.

OLAP tools. Make possible the execution of multidimensional analysis over the Web.

Statistical analysis tools. Employ traditional statistical analysis techniques to analyze data.

Data mining and data discovery tools. Provide analysis based on the execution of specialized nonstatistical algorithms and approaches.

In addition to the data-based applications, we also see that there is a specialized set of applications based on graphical information management. These systems allow users to learn more about their data through graphical manipulation. The most popular of the graphical systems include simple graphing programs and the geographic information systems, which combine map images and numeric data to provide users with geographically based views of the world.

We then spend a significant amount of time considering the area of textual information management systems. We see that these systems allow users to tap into the very heart of human knowledge: textual documents. We identify many of the issues that need to be faced in putting a textually based information system together. We also examine many of the ways people use them to help drive decision making. Specifically, we discover that there are in fact two major categories of textual information management systems that fit well into the Web warehousing space: the search engine systems and the textual analysis systems.

In the area of search engines, we see some of the many different ways that companies have put these search engine systems together, what the critical components of such systems are, and how they are utilized to help solve business problems. We also take a closer look at text mining, and see how organizations can analyze textual documents to gain insight.

Finally, we look at the most glamorous of the Web warehousing tool sets, the multimedia systems. We see that the most common utilization of multimedia is to integrate multimedia and textual search into the same system. We also see how the specialized multimedia systems can function with the benefit of textual information.

In the next chapter, we will continue down to the very lowest, specific technical level of the Web warehousing environment, and see if the Internet, the World Wide Web, and Java-based technical environments can make all of these different kinds of systems work.

PART 3

Technology Foundations

You can't build a house without a foundation, and you can't build Web warehousing and knowledge management systems without technological building blocks. Failure to understand the technological basis will jeopardize even the humblest of projects.

—*Rob Mattison*

CHAPTER 16

The Internet and Internet Services

- *What is the Internet, and what is its relationship to the Web?*
- *What is TCP/IP, and how is it used to make the Web work?*
- *How does the Internet manage to keep track of all the machines within its system?*
- *What is a TCP/IP address, and how are domain names managed?*
- *What is a URL, and how is it used?*
- *What is HTTP?*
- *How do you get an Internet address or a Web site?*
- *What are the different ways of hooking up to the Internet?*
- *What are the following Internet services: Web, FTP, Gopher, WAIS, Telnet, IRC, Mail?*
- *How do they work, and how are they related?*

Introduction

To get to the point where you can wrestle with any of the various aspects of Web warehousing, you first need to be familiar with both the world of data warehousing and the world of the Web itself. Although there are any number of excellent books about the Web environment and architecture, they tend to focus on the programming, Java, and network aspects of that environment and to gloss over the data communications and management issues. I therefore felt it useful to focus several chapters on developing an understanding of the Web architecture environment from a decidedly data warehousing perspective.

In this chapter, we review some of the fundamentals of the Web environment itself, taking the time to consider some issues of vocabulary, topology, and continuity. In subsequent chapters we explore in more detail the specifics of the principal components of a Web architecture and the way they relate from a data movement perspective.

The History and Taxonomy of the Internet

One of the first challenges for a decidedly data-focused person in understanding the Web environment is that the World Wide Web consists of many components, and runs by rules that appear on the surface to be radically different from those followed in the traditional corporate data processing model. The good news is that, once you get past some of the Web jargon and cultural trappings, you will very quickly find an environment that is surprisingly familiar.

The Web itself is a phenomenon that is, frankly, still quite difficult to believe. How could any industry as scattered and competitive as ours (an industry with an incredibly bad reputation for the development of proprietary solutions and infamous for its inability to get anyone to agree on standards of any shape or size) give birth to an environment that allows millions of computers to connect hundreds of millions of people in a way that is fundamentally user-friendly and nonproprietary? The World Wide Web has got to be the single greatest miracle of the twentieth century.

Where Did the Web Come From?

Most people are aware that the Web had its foundation in the development of a government-sponsored network known as the Internet. The Internet was originally established as an environment that would allow government agencies, contractors, universities, and research facilities to share and access one another's information in a relatively noncompetitive and open manner. Funded by the U.S. Department of Defense starting in 1969, the system was originally called Arpanet.

Under Arpanet, all of the parties interested in sharing information agreed to a standard set of protocols and mechanisms for the mutual classification and transportation of electronic data over a "neutral" network infrastructure. Since the Internet was created with the sole purpose of facilitating the mutual sharing of information, it developed from the very beginning as an extremely collaborative type of framework. Anyone, with any kind of computer, could participate, as long as they complied with some basic rules of operation.

Over the years, more and more networks joined up with the core Arpanet group, and adapted the simple standards and procedures that made that network so successful. In 1973 the first international connections were made to Norway and England, and eventually spread all over the world. Today, there is not a country on the globe that is not connected to the Internet in hundreds and thousands of ways.

Of course, as time went on, and the environment got larger, it became more and more difficult to manage. A committee of representatives from each of the participating organizations was set up, and this committee, to this day, "rules" the Internet world.

The Internet of old was a much cruder and more fundamental kind of environment than the explosive world of Web activity we see today. However, the legacy of its birth and progression has had a profound effect on its ability to grow and its continued maintenance of a basically open communications environment.

At this point, you may think, "Wait a minute, I want to learn about Web warehousing, *not* Internet networking. This stuff is too technical and not related to what I am interested in!" Here we must reiterate that, if you want to understand the Web, then you *must understand the Internet,* since the Web runs exclusively on top of the Internet as its technical foundation. Knowledge of the technical details about the Internet is prerequisite to even beginning to discuss Web warehousing issues.

Internet Organization

The architecture of the Internet itself is basically simple and straightforward. The Internet is nothing more than a collection of computers whose owners have agreed to communicate and share network management duties according to an established set of rules. It really does not matter where the computers are, or what kinds of computers they are. They can be personal computers running MS-Windows 95, they can be UNIX-RS6000 workstations running AIX, or they can be big IBM mainframes. All that matters is that they are hooked together, physically, via the Internet network.

Internet Topology One of the most amazing things about the Internet environment is that no one actually owns it. Basically, what you have is thousands of individuals and organizations, each of whom has agreed to share in a piece of the workload that the environment creates, in exchange for their ability to participate in that environment (Figure 16-1).

This means that there is very little structure to the Internet's topology. Each machine on the Internet has one basic job, to check every packet sent to it, and then forward it. The packet will be forwarded to either the next machine down the line (if the packet is addressed to someone on another machine) or to a local user (if that person has a logon on the machine itself).

The TCP/IP Protocol Of course, the fact that these machines are physically connected did not mean that they could actually work together to do this checking of addresses. A network protocol needed to be estab-

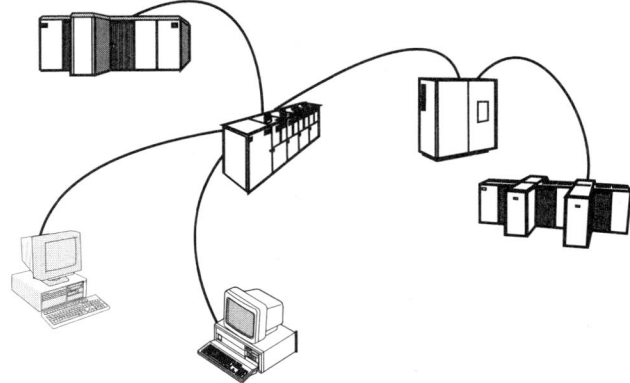

Figure 16-1
Basic Internet topology.

Chapter 16: The Internet and Internet Services

lished to guarantee that they all speak the same language. In the case of the Internet, that protocol is TCP/IP. TCP/IP stands for transmission control protocol/Internet protocol. IP is the foundational protocol that manages the bulk of Internet activity, and TCP manages a small subset of functions.

The role of IP is to manage the transportation of chunks of data, called *packets,* across the network environment. IP determines what the size of each packet of data needs to be and creates the header and other "wrapper" information that packages the block of data. In this way, the different computers on the network can recognize whom the data is being sent to (so that it can be forwarded to the ultimately correct machine) and how to unwrap and use it (when it arrives at its destination).

It is critical that we understand that when data is transported across a network in this manner, it is not possible to send it all at the same time. (Data transmission is not like a telephone call.) Networks cannot usually afford to open up a line between two computers and keep that line open until all of the data is passed. This dedication would cause an interruption of services to all of the other computers on the network, and would *not* be an efficient use of the line. Besides, most lines are of such limited capacity, it would take too long to send it all through at the same time anyway (Figure 16-2).

Instead, network protocols take all of the information being sent (whether it be an instruction, a file, or a program) and break it into tiny pieces. The protocol then sends each piece over the network as individual messages (Figure 16-3). (That way, each packet can find its own, quickest path to the other end.) On the receiving end, the protocol then

Figure 16-2
Trying to move all of the data at once.

Figure 16-3
Breaking data into packets.

reassembles the packet and delivers it to the user. (This process of breaking messages down and sending them in chunks will turn out to be a critical component of our understanding of Web data management issues at a future point in our discussions.)

It is important to reiterate at this point that when the IP breaks the data being sent down into smaller packets, and sends it across the network, there is no reason for it to make sure that all packets take the same path. Remember that the Internet is thousands of computers all hooked up together and cooperating. By managing network traffic in this way, the Internet is able to handle huge volumes of data movement. Unfortunately, the tradeoff is that there is a very serious lack of control over the connection between computers.

Because of this characteristic of the Internet, that is, its ability to break data into autonomous packets and reassemble them at the other end, without requiring that there be any overt control over the specific network path itself, we say that the Internet creates a "stateless" telecommunications environment. In other words, the Internet itself is totally unaware of the status of any particular transmission that is going on. The Internet is aware only of packets that need to be disassembled, moved, and reassembled. Thus, whenever you want to do any kind of "state-based" database activity (such as establishing a logical unit of work, or telling the system on the other end to wait a minute to get a confirmation on the order), the Internet is unable to support it. In situations where we want to establish this kind of control, in an Internet environment we need to do some serious reengineering of our applications and rethinking about how to get the job done.

Internet Addressing Now that we have established the way that the different machines on the Internet are connected, and the way that messages are sent between them, we are ready to talk about the last ingre-

Chapter 16: The Internet and Internet Services

dient that makes the whole thing work, namely, the TCP/IP addressing scheme.

Obviously, if you have hundreds of thousands of computers, all of which are allowed to talk to each other, then you will need some kind of addressing scheme that keeps all of these different participants organized. In the case of the Internet, we have a huge assortment of what are called *IP addresses*.

The IP address is a string of numbers, separated by periods, and each IP address uniquely identifies a different machine on the network. A typical IP address looks like this:

www.xxx.yyy.zzz

So, for example, 127.244.176.222 might be the IP address for Joe's Pizza Parlor and 253.111.276.123 would be the address for the local junior college.

Although these numbers might seem at first to be arbitrary, they are in fact organized in a certain way and for certain reasons. Each set of three numbers is referred to as a triplet, and each triplet—the first, second, third, and fourth—is assigned according to different criteria. In actuality, the IP address is made up of two parts: the first part is a subnet address, which tells the network which part of the network the message is destined for, and the second part is the host-ID, which tells the network the specific machine being identified on that subnet.

Class A addresses are those ranging from 001.xxx.yyy.zzz to 126.xxx.yyy.zzz as part of the first triplet (the www. portion). Class A addresses are assigned to organizations which will have up to 126 networks (subnets) and up to 17 million hosts within the portion of the network that they manage. For class A addresses, the subnet ID is made up of the first three numbers (www.) and the host ID is made up of the last 9 (xxx.yyy.zzz).

Class B addresses are those ranging from 128.000.yyy.zzz to 191.255.yyy.zzz and are given to organizations that have up to 65,000 hosts to manage. In a class B address the subnet ID is made up of the first six numbers (www.xxx) and the host ID is made up of the last 6 (yyy.zzz).

Class C addresses are those ranging from 192.000.000.zzz to 223.255.255.zzz. They are for organizations planning on supporting up to 254 hosts. For a class C address, the subnet address is made up of the first nine numbers (www.xxx.yyy) and the host ID is made up of the last 3 (zzz).

If you look at the IP addresses of some of the machines that you have contact with, you can get a pretty good idea of how big an organization acquired the numbers.

Dynamic IP Addressing Of course, not everyone actually has an IP address assigned all the time. There are simply too many machines and not enough numbers to go around. It is also very difficult to manage today's world of remote dial-in computers, and wireless modems, with any kind of efficiency if you have to keep track of a large number of hard-coded IP addresses all the time. Therefore, what we have instead is a capability known as *dynamic IP address allocation*. Under this scheme, an organization can set up a network environment so that, when a user logs in, an IP address is assigned to the user's computer from a pool of addresses that the organization controls. This way, the same set of numbers can be used repeatedly by a large number of people.

For example, when I dial into my work network from home, the system will assign an IP address to my machine that will remain valid until I hang up. The next day, when I dial up again, a different number will be temporarily assigned. If, later that evening, I decide to dial up my America On Line connection, the AOL network services will assign yet a different address to my machine.

Dynamic addressing is what makes it possible for so many people to access the Internet without requiring complicated registration and configuration exercises (activities that used to be all too common).

Finding the Server You Are Looking for: InterNIC and Domain Name Services

Of course, when we get on the Internet we hardly ever make use of those long cumbersome TCP/IP addresses. Usually we are typing in the names of different server machines, names such as `www.ibm.com`, `www.msn.com`, or `www.usa.org`. Where do these names come from, and how does the Internet know which machines they point to?

Domain Name Services While it is true that every machine on the Internet has a unique TCP/IP address, it is also true that those names are very difficult to remember and use. The makers of the Internet, and of network services in general, are very aware of that fact.

So to make it easier on everyone, they invented a thing called domain name services. A domain name service, or DNS, is an integral part of

Chapter 16: The Internet and Internet Services

most networks. Through a domain name service, network managers make it possible for people to establish user-friendly alias names, for relatively ugly TCP/IP addresses, and then take care of translating those names into addresses whenever they need to.

The mechanics of how domain name servers work can be pretty complex and will be different for each type of machine and network you are dealing with. For example, under UNIX or Windows 95, there is a file, called the HOSTS file, that lists the names that a user has given to a collection of machines, and their related TCP/IP addresses. In the sample HOSTS file in Figure 16-4 you can see entries for:

loopback   A standard network alias used for diagnostics, with an address of 127.0.0.1

lazarus   A server machine on the LAN with an address of 192.192.192.1

gomez   Another machine on the network with address 192.192.192.9

goofy   192.192.192.15

mattison   My own machine, with an address of 192.192.192.11

Figure 16-4

This is a sample HOSTS file.

```
# This file contains the mappings of IP addresses to host names.
# Each
# entry should be kept on an individual line. The IP address
  should
# be placed in the first column followed by the corresponding
  host name.
# The IP address and the host name should be separated by at least
  one
# space.
#
# Additionally, comments (such as these) may be inserted on indi-
  vidual
# lines or following the machine name denoted by a '#' symbol.
#
# For example:
#
#       102.54.94.97     rhino.acme.com          # source server
#        38.25.63.10     x.acme.com              # x client host

127.0.0.1            localhost        loopback
192.192.192.1        lazarus
192.192.192.9        gomez
192.192.192.11       mattison
192.192.192.15       goofy
```

When this HOSTS file is in place, the network management system can substitute the real TCP/IP address for the alias name, whenever someone tries to use it.

If you would like to see for yourself how this works, simply find the HOSTS file in your Windows directory and create an alias name for yourself. Then all you need to do is go to the DOS prompt and type the word PING followed by the alias name you would like to test. (The PING command is a TCP/IP utility that tests the network connection between two TCP/IP machines.)

By typing the command PING LAZARUS at my DOS prompt, I am able to see how the network translates the alias name and returns a message to me that it is trying to communicate with the LAZARUS server machine. Pinging LAZARUS [192.192.192.1] with 32 bytes of data, the network returns a message that will either confirm or deny the connection.

InterNIC and Internet Domain Name Control

Of course, with so many different kinds of domain name services available, maintaining lists of server names and their addresses could very quickly get quite complicated. Because of this, the creators of the Internet established a group, called InterNIC, that is responsible for managing the assignment of addresses and alias names, and making that process and those services available to anyone.

To quote from the InterNIC organization charter: "In January of 1993 the InterNIC was established as a collaborative project between AT&T, General Atomics and Network Solutions, Inc. and supported by three five-year cooperative agreements with the National Science Foundation. AT&T was to manage the InterNIC Directory and Database Services project; NSI was to manage the Registration Services project, and General Atomics was to manage the Information Services project." To this day, these organizations work in a cooperative manner to glue the Internet together into a universally accessible information resource.

These organizations maintain two lists. One is a master directory of all Internet-supported TCP/IP addresses and the other contains the unique Web server names. This list of Web server names is then populated through yet another cooperative network of service providers and domain name services facilities, to make it possible for anyone to find any Web server name at any time, all in a manner transparent to the end user. In fact, the process of managing these resources is so fair that anyone can get an address and a name assigned for a small fee. To find out more about getting your own domain name or TCP/IP Internet address, check out the InterNIC home page at `www.inter_nic.org`.

URL: Uniform Resource Locator

Now that we know how addressing is handled in the Internet environment, we are in a position to understand what a uniform resource locator is. The uniform resource locator, or URL, is the address used to identify specific objects in the Internet/Web world. Anyone who has used the Web has seen a URL. For example, to hook up to the Yahoo! search engine service, you would input

`http://www.yahoo.com/`

The entry `//www.yahoo.com/` is the URL for the Yahoo! home page. In this case, the URL consists of nothing more than the `inter_nic` designated server name. When this address is input by a user, the Web environment is able to check that name against a domain name server, convert it into an IP address, and send the request for a home page.

What happens if we do not want to see a home page? What if there is some other page on that server that we want to see? In this case, we can simply add the name of the page onto the end of the command. For example,

`http://www.yahoo.com/homepage.htm`

is a command equivalent to the earlier one. The only difference is that, in this case, we explicitly ask for the home page. If we have a Web site called `www.animal_server.com`, and we know that there is a page called `animal_crackers.html`, then we can go directly to that page by typing in

`http://www.animal_server.com/crackers.html`

Of course, even though this capability allows us to ask for explicit pages, we will probably find that this can be rather limiting in the long run. To make the URL even more powerful, its developers added one more capability, the ability to specify, within the command, the directory, (and subdirectory, and sub-subdirectory, etc.). For example, assume that the `animal_server` has a directory structure that includes a directory called `cats` and a subdirectory called `lions`. Within this subdirectory is a page called `lazy_lions.htm`, and we can locate it by typing in the command:

`http://www.animal_server/cats/lions/lazy_lions.htm`

URLs are important because they make it possible for anyone, anywhere, to call out any HTML page (or any other type of Web-based object). They are a key component of almost every type of Web activity.

Hooking Up to the Internet

To develop an appreciation for the complexities involved in the running of the Internet environment, we need to take a closer look at some of the different ways that individuals get hooked into the environment.

The Core Internet Environment

The easiest way to understand participation in the Internet is in terms of those machines which are part of the core Internet environment. This core environment, often referred to as the Internet "cloud," is made up of all those machines linked into the Internet network as both a receiver and a router of Internet traffic. These nodes of the network are usually UNIX machines, and typically serve as major doorways into the organizations that have sponsored them.

The base Internet itself, then, for the purposes of our discussion, consists of machines that concentrate on the management of Internet traffic for their sponsoring organizations. In other words, the Internet cloud is really the network traffic management infrastructure that holds the rest of the environment together (Figure 16-5).

Consumer Hookup and Internet Service Providers

Given our understanding of the core Internet, we next want to understand exactly how the typical consumer—someone sitting at home, surfing the net—gains access to this environment.

Chapter 16: The Internet and Internet Services

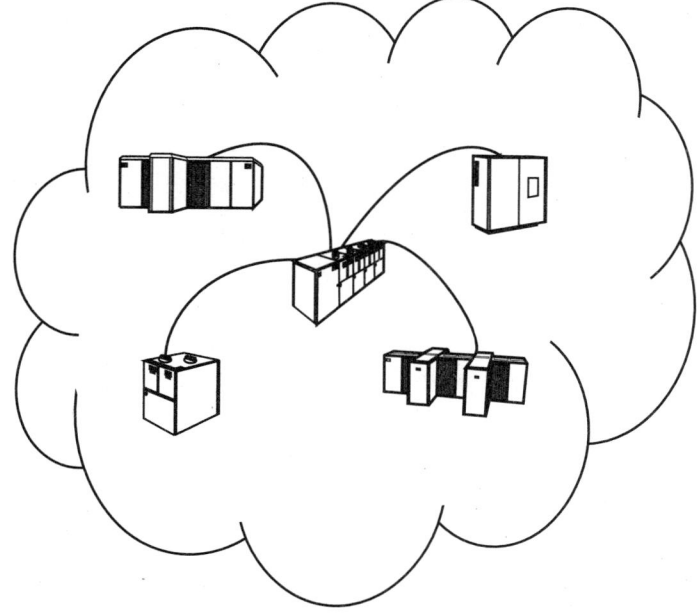

Figure 16-5
The Internet cloud—a network trafficking backbone.

While the typical core Internet machine is a large UNIX processor with a lot of network management capability, the typical home Internet user is hooked up to the environment with a personal computer (with Windows 3.1, Windows 95, Windows NT, or Mac). To get these highly diverse and relatively low-powered machines to participate in the Internet environment, we need a special configuration.

Typically, the home PC user will connect to the Internet through the services of an Internet service provider. These providers, companies such as America On Line, Compuserve, local phone companies, AT&T, and Netcom, all provide an environment that makes these connections possible (Figure 16-6). The Internet service provider (ISP) environment consists of two principal components: a bank of modems and a machine that is part of, or hooked up to, a machine within the core Internet environment itself. In essence, the service that the ISP provides to the consumer is basically a pathway into the Internet cloud.

On an architectural level, the ISP machine establishes a TCP/IP connection between the ISP machine and the user's personal computer. This network connection uses the telephone line as its conduit. Typically, the ISP machine assigns a dynamic IP address (one of the addresses that the Internet service provider has acquired) to the consumer's PC, and then serves as a router, routing PC traffic to the Internet and Internet traffic

Figure 16-6
The Internet service provider environment.

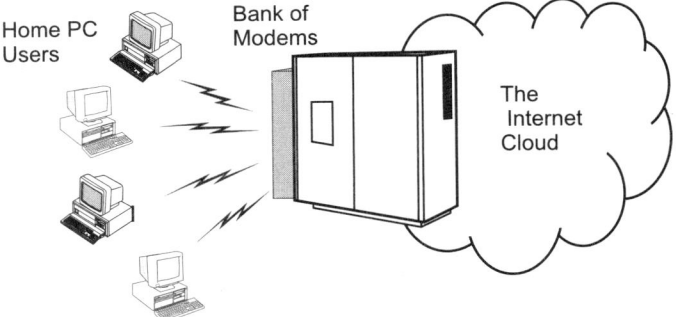

back to the PC. What is critical to understand about this relationship and this mechanism is that:

- The connection between the consumer's PC and the ISP machine is a straightforward TCP/IP network connection, just like any of the UNIX-to-UNIX TCP/IP connections that are typical of the Internet itself. Once this TCP/IP connection is made, the consumer's PC can perform any of the same functions, and make use of the same Internet services as any other participant.

- The connection to the Internet being managed by the service provider is the first hookup to the Internet itself, and could create the first of many bottlenecks into the Internet and contribute to reducing overall response time.

Remember, the speed of delivery via the Internet depends on the bandwidth and capability of each of the nodes along the Internet hookup trail. For example, just because a user hooks up to the Internet service provider with a 28.8-kbps (kilobit per second) modem does not guarantee that the user will get a 28.8-kbps response. How well the Internet responds to the user depends on many other factors, such as the number of other modems the ISP is supporting, the ultimate bandwidth of the ISP machine to the Net, and how much overhead the ISP machine is suffering over all.

Corporate Hookup to the Internet

Of course, individual consumers and their home-based hookups to the Internet represent only a small fraction of the overall traffic on the

Internet today. Besides the millions of home computers that find their way into the Internet via consumer-based Internet service providers, there are many millions more users who gain access to the Internet through their corporations' Internet gateways (Figure 16-7).

In this environment, we find that a corporate-owned and -managed Internet service machine will provide the access to corporate users that the ISP provides to consumers. Of course, the corporate machine may be much larger than the ISP's machine, since corporate traffic on the Internet will typically be much heavier and of a different type than the relatively simple ISP environment.

It is also much more likely that the Internet "bridge" machine will be something other than the typical UNIX servers that typified the Internet world before it became big business. This is because corporations have access to, and are more comfortable with, a wider variety of machines, and different kinds of machines can provide for different strengths, which the corporation may wish to leverage.

In addition to the difference in the nature of the machine that provides this entry into the Internet, the corporate environment will also provide support for many more kinds of access. While the ISP need worry only about consumers who dial in over phone lines, the corporate machine must support not only these kinds of dial-ins through its own external modem mechanisms, but also the traffic generated by users whose personal computers are connected to a LAN or a WAN. (LANs and WANs typically run at much faster speeds, and handle much higher capacities than a simple phone line. Thus, corporate Internet gateway machines must be able to handle much more traffic a lot more responsively than the ISPs.)

Figure 16-7
Corporate Internet connectivity.

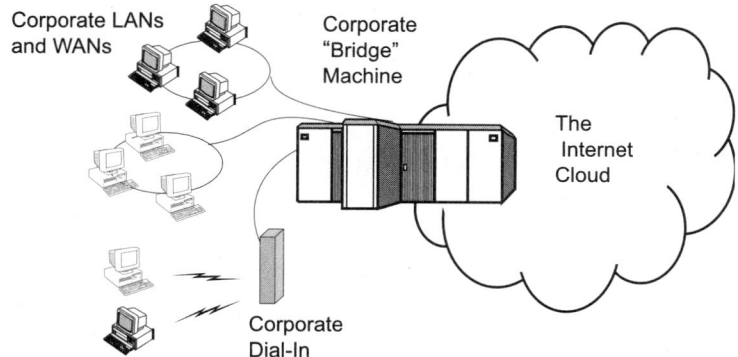

Intranets and Extranets

Of course, the corporate Internet gateway is much more than a simple corporate-sponsored replacement for an independent ISP. This is because corporations do not only gain access to the Internet and pull things from it; they also participate as the sponsors of Internet sites which other businesses or consumers can access.

Physical Corporate Extranets When a corporation establishes a connection to the Internet and then allows consumers or other businesses to gain access to some of their internal computer resources (data, images, programs, etc.), then we say that that corporation is running an extranet environment. In other words, when the corporation allows its internal users to gain access to the external Internet world only, then we call that a simple corporate internet capability, but when the corporation decides to open communications the other way, and allow external users to get into their environment, then we call it an extranet.

Extranets can be extremely large and complicated environments because of the many additional factors that must be taken into account when a business allows outsiders to gain access to its systems. Extranet design requires that the architect be aware of all kinds of capacity, throughput, and security issues that a simple internet service provider could care less about. Besides the security issue, the architect must also be concerned with making it possible for people to execute programs on corporate machines, read corporate files, and send messages to corporate employees. (This can be a logistical, managerial, and capacity planning nightmare, to say the least!)

We will talk more about extranet architecture in future chapters.

Physical Corporate Intranets Some corporations choose to use the Internet to interface better with their customers; others have decided that the Internet architecture is the perfect way to solve their own internal I/T infrastructure problems. Consequently, these organizations create an entire Internet-like world within their own physical environment. They are replacing proprietary LANs, WANs, networks, and applications with the much simpler, more standardized, and much less expensive Internet browsers, servers, and networks. We call these environments where there are no connections to the outside world a *physical intranet*.

Virtual Intranets and Extranets Of course, in this incredibly complex world of technology today, nothing is as simple as it first appears.

While the terms *physical intranet* and *physical extranet* can describe the way that the physical networks have been built, they do not tell us how these networks are intended to be used. There are in fact a few different scenarios to consider.

In the first case, a corporation may decide that it wants to take advantage of the Internet's phenomenal networking and remote accessing capabilities, but utilize it only for its own employees. For example, many companies have built remote order tracking and inventory management systems, which their field sales representatives can access from anywhere by simply connecting to the Internet via a local Internet service provider. When an organization makes it possible for employees to gain access to internal systems through the use of a physical extranet, we call this a *virtual intranet,* running on a physical extranet.

In other situations, a company may allow consumers or business partners to dial directly into the company's own internal systems (or even provide them with direct LAN, WAN, or terminal connections). (For example, a bank might allow consumers to dial in and check their account balances.) In these cases we say that the company has created a *virtual extranet* using a physical intranet environment.

No matter how we decide to put the plumbing together (physical intranet, physical extranet, or simple Internet access) or whom we decide to give access to (virtual intranet versus virtual extranet), ultimately it is always the same core sets of services that people are able to use, leveraging the same basic network/communications standards and capabilities. In the following section, we will review what some of those services are and how they work within the Internet environment.

Internet Services

So what does the history and existence of the Internet have to do with the Web? Are the Web and the Internet the same thing? Can you run a Web without the Internet?

These are all very good questions. Let's start with the distinction between the Internet and the Web. As we have already discussed, the Internet is a worldwide network of computers, all sharing a common set of rules for communicating with each other and sharing information. This network, in and of itself, however, is not robust enough to actually allow people to do anything useful. The network is there, somewhat like a road, ready to be used. What is needed, however, is some kind of application (or better yet, many different applications) that runs on the Internet and allows people to do useful information movement.

Of course, several different applications run on the Internet. Some of them are very simple and crude in their approach, and others are extremely powerful and sophisticated. The fact is that the Web is nothing more than another one of those Internet-based services.

Before we get into a lot of detail about the Web itself, let's take a moment to look at the full range of services that can be utilized on the Internet. Doing this will be important for several reasons:

1. You will quickly find, when you are working within the Web environment, that Web developers often call upon these other Internet services to make their applications more powerful.

2. You may find that certain Internet services (such as WAIS and FTP) are actually more useful than the Web services for some of the things you want to accomplish as a Web warehousing expert.

3. It is important to be aware of what these other services are, and how they work, so that you are not surprised or confused when they come up.

Some of the more important Internet services include:

The World Wide Web

FTP Services

Gopher

WAIS

Telnet

IRC

Mail

Let's consider what each of these does and how it works.

The World Wide Web

The World Wide Web, or the Web, as it is referred to colloquially, is clearly the most prevalent and obvious of the Internet services in the world today. Of course, while the Internet itself is over 30 years old, the Web is a relatively recent phenomenon. The Internet has existed, and provided service to people through its other features (FTP, Gopher, etc.), for many years.

Nevertheless, the Web has become the most popular form of communication between individuals and organizations since the invention of the telephone and the television, and has become the most important of the Internet services available. It is critical to understand, however, that the Web is still at its core just another Internet service, with the same physical, architectural, and organizational limitations as any other Internet service.

Server-Based Architectures The Web is one of several Internet services that are "server-based." Other server-based services include WAIS, FTP, and Gopher. Server-based services function by making use of two principal components: a client and a server. The client is the software than runs at the desktop and provides the end users' interface with the service. The server is a program that runs on a separate machine, somewhere within the Internet environment, and does the work the client asks it to.

So basically, client software gathers input from users and creates network-based commands. These commands are sent over the Internet to server machines, which receive those commands, do the work requested, and send the appropriate response back to the client (via another network-based command). See Figure 16-8.

For example, the following sequence of events occurs when a user on machine 192.25.44.1 decides to ask a name-and-address server machine to find the phone number for Sally in the Engineering department.

1. The user fills in the appropriate information on the client software.

2. The client software creates a message that says "Send this request to machine 107.2.34.17 and ask it to find Sally's phone number and send it back."

Figure 16-8

The generic server-based Internet service architecture.

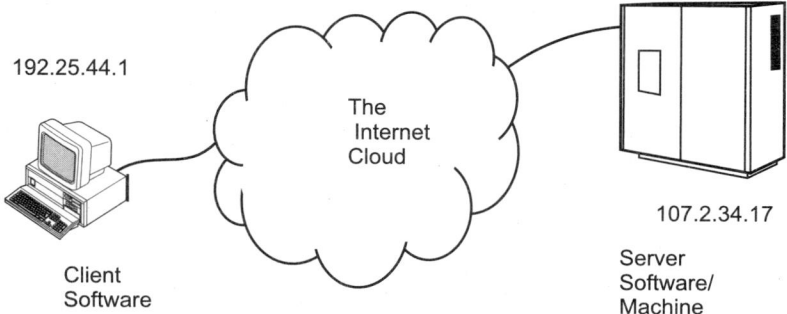

3. The Internet routes the message to the appropriate machine.
4. Machine 107.2.34.17 looks up the phone number.
5. Machine 107.2.34.17 sends the number 875-1004 to machine 192.25.44.1.

The server architecture we have just described is basically the same for all Internet server applications.

Web Architecture Fundamentally, the World Wide Web is a screen management service that runs over the Internet. The two principal components of a Web session are the client, an Internet browser product like Netscape Navigator or MS Internet Explorer, and the server, a Web server product like the Netscape Enterprise server or the Microsoft server.

[An interesting sideline: The "real" name for the service provided by the Web, and the official, definitional name for all Web servers, is actually HT server (or hypertext server), because the documents that are displayed when we use the Web are written in a language called hypertext markup language (HTML). The command to invoke a Web server is therefore not WEB:// (for "Internet please call a Web server for me"), but is instead "http://"; this command stands for hypertext transfer protocol and tells the Internet the protocol to use when connecting with the server. We will, of course refer to these servers by their more familiar and colloquial name, *Web servers,* throughout the book.]

In general, the service consists of the following steps:

1. The client (browser) sends a message to the server asking that a certain screen be displayed.
2. The server receives the message and forwards the requested screen (which has been written in HTML) back to the browser.
3. The browser accepts the HTML instructions and builds a screen for the user based on them.
4. The user then either fills information into blanks on the screen or clicks on some section of the screen, which prompts the browser to build yet another request to be sent to the server.

We can see in Figure 16-9 the command being sent to the server asking that the menu be displayed. The command `http://107.2.34.17/menu` basically says "Please ask machine 107.2.34.17 to send me a copy of the menu."

The second command, which goes from the server to the browser, says "Send the following menu to machine 192.25.44.1." Following the com-

Chapter 16: The Internet and Internet Services

Figure 16-9
Web browser/server communication.

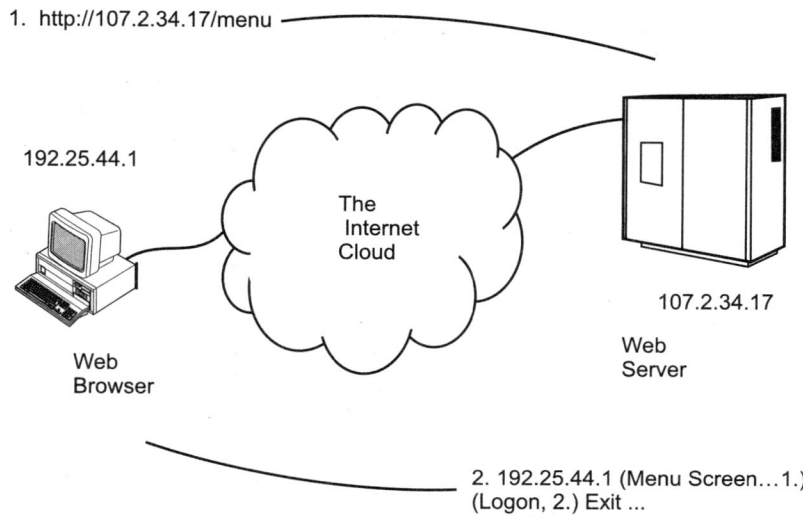

mand and the address are the actual contents of the menu screen. The final menu displayed might look something like Figure 16-10. If the user clicks on item 1, then the browser will send a command back to the server that says "Get me the logon screen" (the command would be http://107.2.34.17/Logon). If the user clicks on item 2, then the browser will send back a command that tells the server that the session is over (http://107.2.34.17/Exit). This process is repeated over and over, as many times as the user wants to investigate further.

In the next chapter, we will go into detail about how the HTML language works and how these clients (browsers) and servers communicate with each other. At this point all we really need to understand is that, ultimately, the Web service boils down to this basic approach.

Figure 16-10
A simple menu screen.

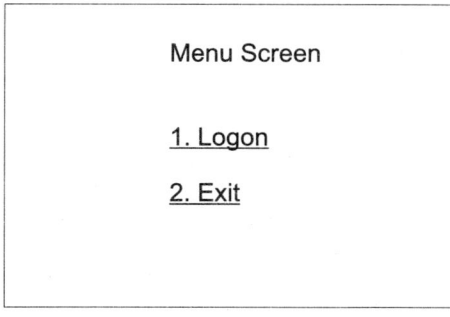

FTP Services

As we stated earlier, the Web is only one of the many services available on the Internet. Another service, which has proved to be extremely useful over the years, is the file transfer protocol (FTP). FTP makes it easy for people to copy things from one machine to another anywhere on the Internet. By using FTP, any person, anywhere in the world, can locate and copy files from any computer anywhere else in the world (as long as they have the right software and security clearance, and as long as both computers are hooked up to the Internet). Imagine how powerful that capability is! FTP service was one of the first and, until very recently, the most heavily used of the Internet capabilities. (Web services have since become the most popular.)

Architecture of the FTP Environment   FTP services, like Web services, are server-based. To make use of FTP, you need two things: an FTP server at the file storage end and an FTP client at the requesting end. The FTP server is a program that performs these functions:

- It allows users to navigate within the file directory structure of the machine it is serving (it functions in much the same way as the Windows Explorer or the UNIX dir and cd commands).
- It allows users to select files from that directory structure and copy them to their own machines over the Internet.

While there are many forms of FTP browser, the most common way to use FTP services these days is with a Web browser. To make use of an FTP server, all the user has to do is insert the command FTP:// plus the IP address or server name of the FTP server plus the user's logonID on the Web browser command line. This will connect the user with the FTP server and display the initial directory of the FTP server.

In Figure 16-11 you can see our initial attachment to the lazarus FTP server. Notice the command line:

```
FTP://mattison@lazarus/lazarus-d
```

This command tells the browser that:

1. We want to attach to an FTP server
2. Our user logon ID is mattison
3. The FTP server we want to connect to is called lazarus
4. The directory we want to access is called lazarus-d

Chapter 16:   The Internet and Internet Services

Figure 16-11
Initial FTP connection (lazarus-d directory).

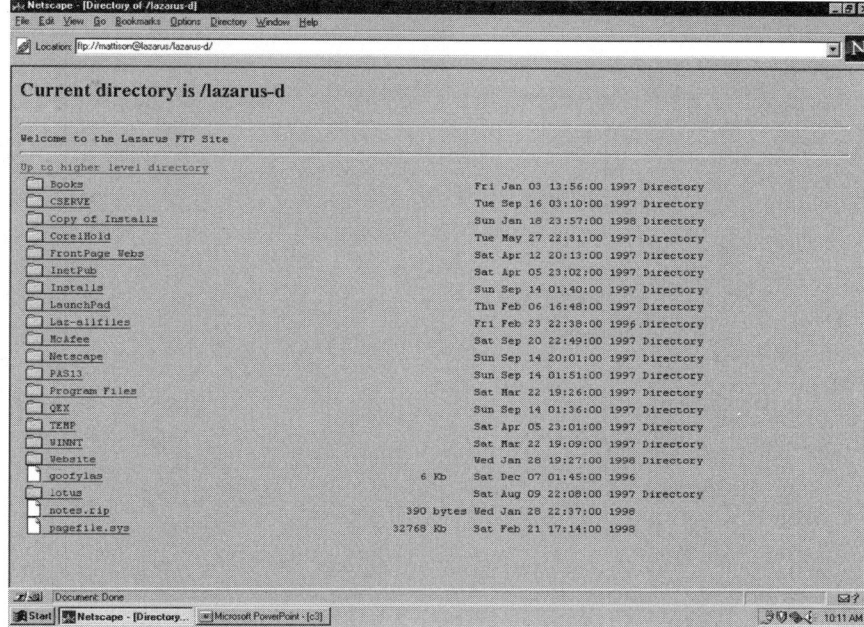

By entering that command line into the browser screen, we access the initial directory structure of the FTP server. As you can see, there are several directories within the lazarus-d directory including Books, CSERVE, Copy of Installs, and many more.

From this initial entry point, we can navigate anywhere within the directory structure by simply clicking on the folder we want to investigate. In this case we will click on the Books folder and see what is in that directory. Figure 16-12 shows the contents of the Books directory. There are additional folders (BOOK-MKT, Database Book, etc.) and some files (Inventory.xls and Text.exe). If we want to copy one of these files to our own computer, all we need to do is click on the file name and fill in the location we want the file copied to on the Save As screen. As we can see in Figure 16-13, the Save As box allows you to choose the directory and the name for the file after it is copied to your own personal computer.

Command Line FTP Of course, FTP was around a long time before Web browsers were. So naturally there are several ways in which you can make use of the power of FTP without fancy screens. The most commonly utilized form is the FTP command line form. With this feature you can log onto any FTP server machine and navigate within its environ-

Part 3: Technology Foundations

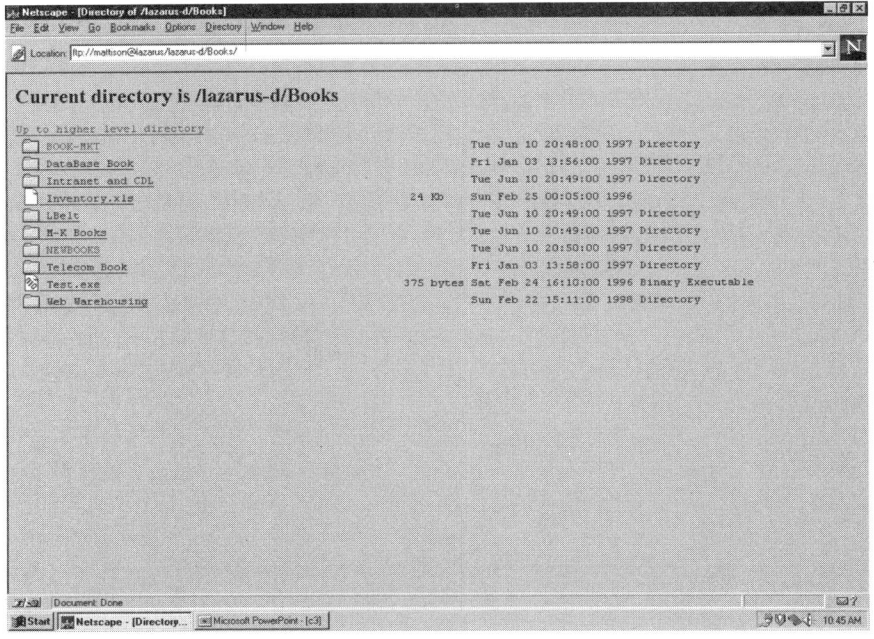

Figure 16-12
The Books directory.

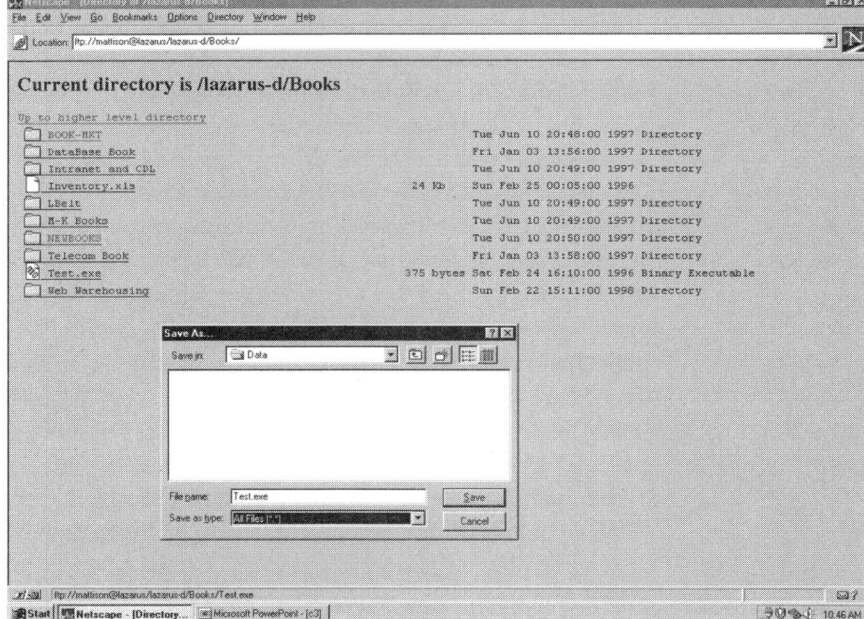

Figure 16-13
Copying the Test.exe file to your PC.

ment, creating and deleting files and directories, and copying files to anywhere you want to. In fact, it is possible to gain access to FTP command line services with any personal computer running Windows 95 that is hooked up via TCP/IP to an FTP server machine. To invoke the FTP server all you need to do is type FTP <servername> at any DOS command line, and the facility will be enabled.

Industrial-Strength Uses for FTP While the ability to browse directories and send and receive files is certainly a nice feature to have, the power and flexibility of FTP goes much further than that simple functionality. In addition to the rather cumbersome directory scanning capabilities of FTP, it is also possible to embed FTP commands into HTML (Web pages), scripts, and programs. These commands allow the Web designer to identify and copy files automatically without ever needing to get the user directly involved.

Another extremely convenient characteristic of FTP is that it places no limits on the sizes, types, or destinations of the files that it manages. FTP, therefore, can become a significantly potent tool to add to the Web warehousing architect's toolkit for moving large files or databases from one location to another. FTP utility jobs can be used to load, update, and resynchronize databases anywhere in the world, without the need to develop any new network connectivity between the sites to be coordinated.

Gopher

Another Internet utility similar to both FTP and the Web is Gopher. Gopher is also a server-based Internet service and was actually a precursor in many ways to the modern Web. The Gopher service was invented by a group of students at the University of Minnesota in 1991 to make it possible for students and faculty to publish interesting information and files that could be shared schoolwide. (The name that was chosen for the utility can be attributed to many origins. Minnesota is known as the Gopher State, and the University of Minnesota's teams are known as the Golden Gophers. Additionally, the Gopher utility can be thought of as an Internet service that burrows into the Internet world looking for information. It is also said that the name was selected because the system will "go for" files.)

The owners of Gopher servers publish menus of pointers to different files of interest. These menus can point to other menus, which point to other menus, which eventually point to the files that the searcher is looking for.

The FTP service is certainly helpful in that it makes it possible to ask for a file and download it, but its biggest weakness is that there is no way to find and retrieve that file if you didn't know where it was located before you started. In the early days, the developers of FTP sites tried to play all kinds of tricks on the system by creating long, drawn-out directory names to guide people to the files they were looking for. In one case, I remember a file structure that a local university put in place to help students find their computer science homework assignments. The directory was named "\This\is\where\the\COMPSCI201\homework\resides."

While clever directory naming helped a little bit, it did not solve the search-and-recover problem. The Gopher service changed all that. With a Gopher server you can publish an extremely detailed and user-friendly collection of menus to allow people to "hunt and peck" their way down to what they are looking for. These early Gopher servers were precursors of the HTML-based Web services that we use today.

The Gopher Architecture Gopher services, like FTP services, are provided by a simple client- (browser-) server architecture. The Gopher server can be located on any machine hooked up to the Internet, and the Gopher client (or browser) can be any machine hooked up in the same way.

Gaining Access to a Gopher Server As with the Web and FTP, the easiest way to gain access to a Gopher server these days is with your Web browser. Simply type the command Gopher://server-name (or IP address) and you will be presented with the Gopher server's initial menu screen.

In the example in Figure 16-14, you can see the command `gopher://192.192.192.1`. This provides the browser with the name of the service we want access to (Gopher), and the IP address of the server machine (192.192.192.1). The first Gopher menu provides us with options for lists of files about types of animals including cats, dogs, lizards, etc.

The Gopher server represented a huge step forward in the area of shared information on computer systems. Shortly after its inception, the Gopher product gained popularity around the world. By combining the networking standards that the Internet provides with the flexible structure of the Gopher service, people were suddenly able to search for and retrieve files from around the world.

Figure 16-14
The Gopher animals menu.

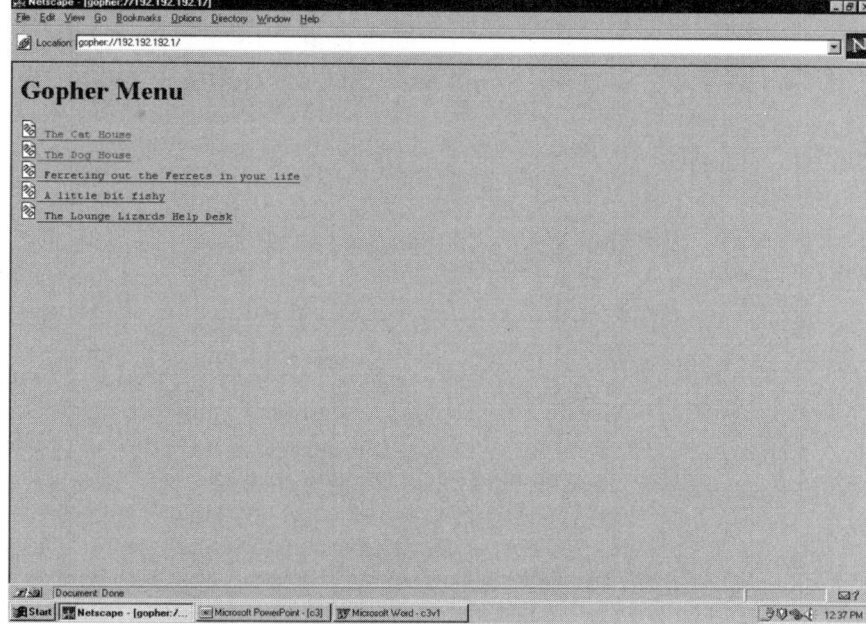

As Gopher gained in popularity, more and more servers were populated around the world. Huge menu directory structures were assembled and transported between Gopher servers. Eventually, of course, the process became unwieldy. It was just too big a job to keep so many menus up-to-date, accurate, and useful.

Several improvements were made to the Gopher services, and thus services with the names of Archie, Jughead, and Veronica were born. Of course, since all of these were file- and menu-based, and since they depended on manually assembled and maintained menus, they too quickly outlived their usefulness. It was only with the invention of HTML and the much more dynamic nature of the Web's navigational style that the Internet became the worldwide communications juggernaut it is today.

WAIS Services

As the popularity of FTP and Gopher services continued to spread, people began to realize that there were still a lot of things that they wished that Internet services could provide. One of the biggest problems that people still suffered from was the continued challenge of finding what they were looking for among this massive population of documents.

While the Gopher approach was far more useful than the simple FTP service, you still had to deal with the fact that you could only find what somebody before you had already found, and took the trouble to register within the Gopher system. As if that was not bad enough, you also had to deal with the fact that the way that one person decided to organize the information might not be the way that somebody else needed it organized. In many cases, the titles and menus used to point to documents didn't really tell you whether they held what you were looking for. Consequently, you had to search through dozens or even hundreds of "potential" sources, before you ever got lucky enough to find exactly what you were looking for.

What was needed was some way to get a software program to read all of the documents that were out there, have that program create an index of all of the different things it found, and make that index available to the searcher. That way, you could look for what you wanted according to what the documents actually contained, not the way that the person who built the menu decided the information should be categorized.

It was in response to this need that the first WAIS (wide-area information service) server was created. The WAIS Internet service is an information location and retrieval system based on the ANSI Standard Z39.50. A WAIS service identifies a population of documents that it will support, and then compiles indexes and dialogs that describe the contents of those documents in a number of different ways. Therefore, whereas a Gopher service simply provides pointers to files based on a navigational menu, a WAIS service allows you to ask it to locate specific kinds of documents for you.

The WAIS Architecture While WAIS is also a server-based service, it is a bit more complicated than the ones we mentioned earlier. A WAIS environment consists of a client (browser) and a server (a machine that manages the documents, descriptions, and indexes), but it also includes special programs called searchers, indexers, and retrievers. We will take a few moments to consider the functionality of each of these components:

The WAIS Indexer The job of a WAIS indexer module is to read through every single word of every single document within the WAIS server's domain and create a collection of indexes that will help people find what they are looking for. The WAIS indexer is able to do this with a specialized program known as a *parser*. (People familiar with databases will be acquainted with this type of program.) A parser is a program that knows how to read through something (a file, a document, or a database) and break it down into its meaningful parts.

In the relational database world, each database has a parser whose job it is to read every SQL command submitted to it and break it down into a series of executable database instructions. In the same way, the WAIS parser is designed to read a document, file, or database, and break the content down into words that it can use to build its reference indexes.

The WAIS parser in fact does several things:

1. It identifies the headline or description of the document it is parsing.
2. It identifies all of the nontrivial words within the document (it skips words like *the, and,* etc.).
3. It creates a relevancy value, which indicates how relevant the word found is to the meaning of the overall document.

This information is then gathered and placed into an inverted list index. Once again database aficionados should be familiar with the term. An inverted list index is an index that stores key values and a series of pointers to their sources. (More about indexes and searching in later chapters.)

WAIS Search and Retrieve Functions Any user of the World Wide Web is familiar with how WAIS search and retrieval functions. A lot of the supposedly Web-based search and retrieval engines, products like Yahoo!, Alta Vista, and others, are actually either based on the way that WAIS services work or are front ends for WAIS servers at the back end.

The WAIS client software provides a box (for example, the one in Figure 16-15), which allows the user to input the keywords on which the search is to be based. When the user hits the execute or run key, the WAIS client (browser) creates a WAIS query that is sent to the WAIS server. The server then executes the query (in much the same way that a database works). The WAIS server searches its indexes, taking into account both the number of times a word shows up in a document and the relevancy of the word to the overall document's integrity, and returns to the user the names, descriptions, and locations of the most relevant documents. In very many ways, the WAIS server works in exactly the same manner as a relational database. The only differences are that the "database" in this case is an organized collection of documents instead of an organized collection of data, and that the query language is HTML, not SQL.

Figure 16-15
The NASA WAIS search and retrieval screen.

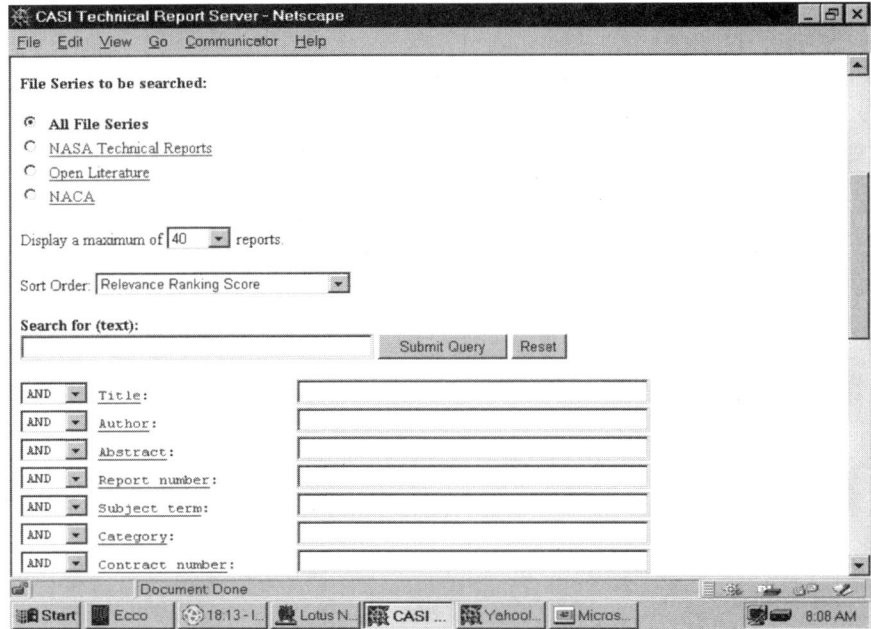

In Figure 16-16 we can see how all of these pieces of the WAIS architecture fit together. In the background, we have the population of documents and other information sources that WAIS will use as its input. (These sources are represented as residing on one disk device in this picture, but the actual population could consist of hundreds or even thousands of disks, holding text, spreadsheet, word processing, data, and other kinds of information.) On a periodic basis, and in a background mode, the WAIS indexer will scan through the information sources and create the indexes that become the intelligence source that the WAIS server will go to.

In the foreground, the users, sitting at a WAIS or Web browser terminal, input the words they wish to be used as search criteria. These words are assembled into a query and forwarded to the WAIS server. The server then checks the index, determines what the best document matches are, and sends that information back to the users.

As we will see in future chapters, the relatively simplistic model under which WAIS operates has been expanded significantly within the World Wide Web and knowledge management space, and we look at some of these more sophisticated solutions in detail later in the book. What is most interesting about the whole process, however, is the fact that the

Chapter 16: The Internet and Internet Services

Figure 16-16
WAIS architecture components.

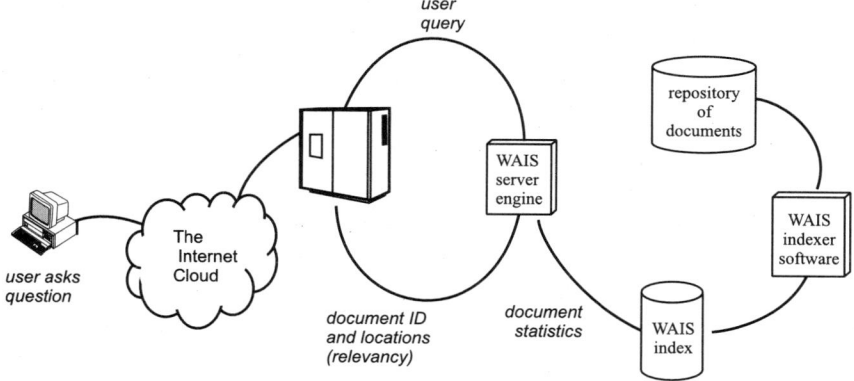

fundamental approach to document management and retrieval that was instigated by the WAIS service really remains unchanged.

Telnet

While the previously mentioned Internet services certainly represent the greatest part of current Internet—and therefore Web—activity, there are a few other Internet services that you should know something about.

One of the most interesting of these additional services is Telnet service. With Telnet capability, a user at one location can connect a personal computer to another computer on the Internet and actually execute commands, run programs, and in general, function as if that remote computer were sitting in the person's own living room. Obviously, the Telnet capability can create all kinds of exciting, and quite frightening, possibilities.

As with the FTP service, it is possible to work with Telnet from a ready-made screen, from a command line, or through background "batch" types of commands.

With Telnet, it is possible for the systems architect to make all kinds of things happen. Since Telnet is just another Internet service, the Web architect can integrate programs that initiate system login and program execution commands from within any Web page or from any Web site.

Like all Internet capabilities that allow outsiders access to the control of your system's hardware and software, it is critically important that you take appropriate security measures to guarantee that hackers (of the benign or malign variety) are not able to damage existing systems, files, or capabilities.

IRC

Another Internet service that has become very popular with the Web consumer is IRC, or Internet relay chat. IRC makes it possible for any two or more users, connected to the Internet, to have a real-time, typewritten "conversation" with each other.

IRC works something like this:

1. First, you need special software to run IRC, an IRC server, and an IRC client.
2. The IRC server software is located on a machine hooked up to the Internet and usually sponsored by an Internet service provider. The server machine provides users with an area where they can log in and look for individuals with whom they would like to have a real-time conversation.
3. The user gains access to the chat room area, and can then check into different chat rooms. Within a chat room, one or more people will be carrying on some kind of conversation.
4. If two individuals decide to go off and have their own conversation, they can create their own "private" chat room.
5. If two people want to schedule a time to meet on the Internet ahead of time, all they have to do is create a private chat room with a name that they both will recognize.

In general, at this phase in its development, the Internet IRC capability has little commercial applicability. More important, the ability to send and receive real-time voice and video over the Internet may make IRC capabilities extinct in a very short time.

Mail

We would be remiss if we did not, at least in passing, mention the phenomenal capabilities Internet mail has created in the business and consumer world today. Suddenly, almost overnight, we find that it is possible for anyone, anywhere in the world, to send a written message to anyone else, anywhere in the world, almost instantaneously, and at virtually no cost whatsoever. This capability is a far cry from the days of slow-moving, handwritten mail that had to travel by pony express, train, or jet airplane.

Not only has the consumer been the beneficiary of this amazing capability, but business has been revolutionized by it as well. Through

Internet mail, it is suddenly possible for people working at the same company, or working on the same project, to share letters, notes, diagrams, plans, drawings, and anything else that might be required to get work done as a group. This capability has enabled some corporations to close down office buildings, abandon their corporate headquarters, and go mobile to an amazing degree.

Ultimately, of course, the mail service that people are using is not actually Internet mail at all. The real mail programs are products like Lotus Notes and Microsoft Mail. However, the Internet has provided the means to standardize people's addresses around the world. (Since every machine hooked up to the Internet has a unique address, it is not very difficult to get a unique address for each person who uses one of those machines.) The Internet also provides a network infrastructure that delivers that mail quickly, efficiently, and very inexpensively.

A typical email address might be something like `mattison@us.ibm.com`. In this case, `mattison` is the unique ID of a person and `us.ibm.com` is the name of a server machine hooked up to the Internet.

As we have seen over the past couple of years, there seems to be almost no limit to the possibilities for the increased communication capabilities that the Internet can provide.

Other Internet Capabilities

Before we wrap up our discussion of the Internet and its many services, it is important to note that we have talked about only a small sampling of the full range of what you can get from the Internet. News, data feeds, and special interest groups are only a few of the many other services that have been available on the Internet for years.

We can be sure that we will see many, many more. Just a few of the ideas that are being cooked up for Internet utilization include:

- *Audio distribution.* Under this scenario people would no longer go to the store to buy records, CDs, and tapes. Instead they would contact a Web site and download the music they want.

- *Video distribution.* What about watching movies over the Internet, or downloading a movie that you want to watch next week?

- *e-commerce.* There is no doubt that in the future we will do more and more of our business over the Internet. It will be possible to order and pay for products, and check on the status of our orders, all through the Internet global infrastructure.

- *Real-time Internet telephone and real-time video conferencing.* Software and engineering are already in place to make it possible for individuals and entire groups to talk to each other face to face, leveraging the Internet infrastructure as a communications media.

And who knows what else?

Conclusion

In this chapter, we took a very cursory look at the Internet, its foundations, basic architecture, and some of the most popular Internet services and how they work. Armed with this general background information, we are now ready to dig deeper into the workings of the thing that we are really interested in, the World Wide Web, and its utilization as a foundation for data and information warehousing capabilities.

CHAPTER 17

Web Components and Communications

- *What are the different types of HTML commands (tags)?*
- *What is the basic HTML syntax?*
- *How do you place pictures and other objects into a Web page?*
- *What are the major Web object types?*
- *What is MIME, and why is it important?*
- *What is hypertext, and how is it related to HTML?*
- *How do you execute programs using HTML?*
- *What are the HTML server/browser communication methods? What are server to browser fields and browser to server fields?*

In the previous chapter, we constructed a generalized, high-level view of the Internet and its services. In the process, we discovered several things of particular importance to the would-be Web warehousing expert.

We saw that what is colloquially known as the Web is one of several Internet services.

We saw that the Web's main job is to manage the distribution of hypertext documents to people asking to see them.

We saw that this hypertext management and display capability is absolutely and totally dependent on the infrastructure provided by the Internet (or intranet or extranet).

We also saw that, no matter how a person is hooked up with the Internet (whether it be via an ISP, a corporate LAN/WAN, or through a direct node of the Internet itself), all participants in the process function as equals, as either clients or servers.

In other words, the Internet is an incredible, large, and heterogeneous equalizer, showing no favor and providing no special treatment to anyone. Ultimately, every node attached to the Internet, and consequently every browser and every Web server, is reduced to communication via the same fundamental TCP/IP based protocols.

Armed with this insight, we are now ready to take a much closer look at the specific workings of the Web itself, and see if we can get a better understanding of how this particular service is being harnessed now and can be harnessed in the future to meet the needs of businesses around the world.

Web Architecture Review

As we saw in the previous chapter, a Web architecture consists of only three basic components (1) a browser, which sits on the user's desk and allows that user to ask that documents be displayed; (2) a server, which is a dedicated program (and sometimes a dedicated machine) whose job is to receive those requests and return the documents; and (3) a connection between the two (either through the Internet itself, or through a network infrastructure that is set up to operate the same way that the Internet does). See Figure 17-1.

We also saw the basic way in which the Web service works: The user asks that a document be displayed (either explicitly through the com-

Figure 17-1
Web components.

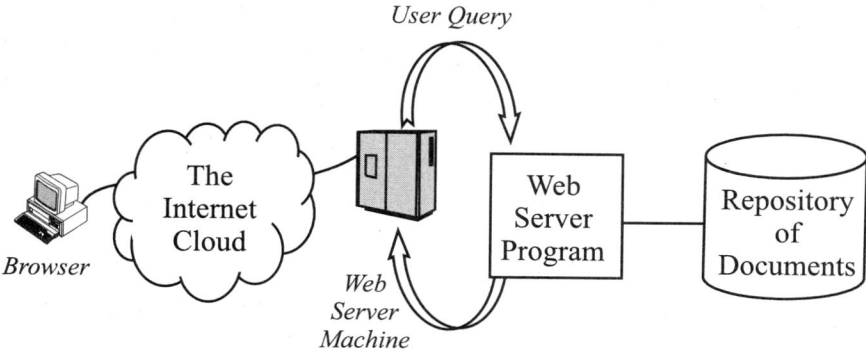

mand line or implicitly through the selection of an item on the screen). The browser translates that request into a command, which is sent via TCP/IP to the server. The server then interprets the command, locates the document, breaks it down into packets that the network can handle, and sends the pieces of the requested document back to the browser. The browser then collects the packets, reassembles the document, and displays it on the user's display area.

Incidentally, this sequence helps explain the dreaded "partial paint" phenomenon. When your Internet service is slow, have you noticed how an especially large or "busy" Web page will be painted on the screen one chunk at a time? You might see the title line and a few icons show up at first, then you wait for a few minutes and half a picture shows up, a few minutes after that some more picture might appear, and so forth. What is happening is that the browser is trying to show you as much of the screen as it can as soon as possible. When the first data packet arrives over the Internet, it is immediately displayed. As soon as the second packet arrives, that is also displayed.

What Makes the Web So Special?

Of course, the basic architecture that we have just described, though logical, is certainly not revolutionary. There is nothing earth-shattering or different about this particular approach versus hundreds of other ways that have been attempted in the past. This then raises some very important questions: What makes the Web so special? Why has the Web taken off the way it has when it is not that much better than systems that came before it? Actually, there are several reasons for the Web's special character and unique success:

Leveraging the Power of the Internet The first and biggest reason that the World Wide Web has become and will continue to be as powerful and visible as it is, is the simple fact that it leverages the universality and global exposure afforded by the Internet.

However, leveraging the power of the Internet, in and of itself, does not fully explain the Web phenomenon. All we have to do is look at the history of the Internet and we will see that there have been many other information storage and retrieval services that had the same global reach as the Web, and provided the same kinds of services as the Web.

FTP has been making it possible for people to copy files from anywhere in the world to anywhere in the world for over a quarter of a century. Gopher, Archie, and Veronica made it possible to search via menus and pointers to files, and WAIS allowed searches for documents on the basis of their contents long before the Web was conceived. Each of the earlier Internet services has contributed to the body of knowledge, expertise, and capabilities that the Web now displays, but the Web has been so successful in so many different ways, that there clearly must be some other factors at work. I think that, to really explain the popularity of the Web, you need to look at the synchronicity of what has been going on for some time now.

Consumer and Business Personal Computer Mania Of course, there is no way that the Web could have gotten as big as it has if it hadn't been for the many millions of personal computers that have invaded the office, the home, and the schoolroom. People have gone PC crazy, and those PCs on their desks paved the way for the Web.

In many ways, it is almost as if the world and the PCs were just waiting for the Web to come along. While stand-alone PCs have their uses, a PC hooked up to a network and other machines is a much more powerful entity, and the abysmal performance and gut-wrenching complexity of client/server technology made it clear that an easier, more straightforward approach to networking was needed.

Web Ease of Use and HTML The combination of the presence of millions of personal computers, the existence of the Internet, and the desire of millions of people to "get connected," for many different reasons, created a world that was ready for the Web.

It is interesting to note that there were dozens of network service providers (NSPs), companies like Compuserve, America OnLine, and the Microsoft Network, all of which provided consumers and businesses with connectivity and access to remote facilities very similar to those of the

Web, long before the Web came into existence. But somehow, these NSPs were unable to really excite people the way the Web did. The Web offers people more than worldwide connectivity, more than the ability to play games on their personal computers, and more than the simple hardcore data processing functions that the earlier generations of Internet services provided.

While many things have contributed to the Web's success, the one that was clearly responsible for a big part of the Web stampede is that humble little language known as HTML.

Understanding HTML

HTML, the hypertext markup language. What is it? Why do we claim that it is the keystone that makes the Web so unbeatable? The following are among the things that make HTML so powerful:

1. It functions as a universal document display language, making it possible for people around the world, with thousands of different kinds of computers, to see the same things in the same way.

2. It provides people with the ability to navigate dynamically from one page to the next via the hypertext capability.

3. It allows people to view and interact with other than simple text, e.g., sound, video, and graphics.

Let's look at each of these functionalities and see how they fit together.

HTML as the Universal Document Display Language

First, foremost, and most obviously, the HTML language describes how a document should be displayed on a computer screen. A vast majority of HTML commands are nothing more than formatting tags that provide instructions like "This line should be printed with a very large font, this one should be colored blue, and this line should be displayed with bold typeface."

Of course, there were hundreds of document formatting languages long before HTML came on the scene, and frankly, almost every one of them does a better job of describing how to format a document than HTML does. HTML is special because it is simple enough, basic enough, and universal enough for almost any computer, no matter how big or small, powerful or weak, modern or ancient, to adequately display the information on the screen, formatted the way HTML wants it to be formatted. HTML documents can be displayed anywhere and will look basically the same!

Let's stop a minute and think about what this means. While companies, individuals, and institutions have fought for years to come up with a way to standardize data processing, and to create "open" systems, when it came to the desktop computer we were on our own. Dozens of standards—the standards created by manufacturers (Macintosh, IBM, and Silicon Graphics), the standards created by software vendors (Microsoft Windows, IBM OS/2, Mosaic, etc.), and the standards dictated by legacy systems—all conspired to keep us from standardizing the desktop. And since we couldn't standardize the desktop, we were unable to standardize much of anything.

But along came this crude, totally unglamorous language called HTML and all of that changed. By combining HTML with the Internet and with powerful Web browsers and Web servers, we suddenly had a world where extremely versatile, globally delivered, standard desktop applications become feasible. This universality of display is made possible through the clever combination of hardware and software.

In the normal world of data processing, the languages that run on a particular piece of computer hardware define how the output from that device will look. User displays are very hardware-dependent. Because of this hardware dependence, it is virtually impossible to get any universal standardization of display, because no two hardware vendors are willing to cooperate. So we end up with a plethora of displays that cannot be merged.

Through the miracle of software, the Internet, and HTML, however, all of that has changed. While we cannot get hardware or software vendors to standardize, it is possible to get Web browsers that can achieve standardization. It is easy to use the same Web browser software on many different kinds of hardware. Basically, what that means is that by combining standard Web browsers, and a standard programming language (HTML) with the standard Internet communications channels, we are suddenly able to mass-distribute identical applications on a scale never before imagined.

For the rest of this chapter, we look at examples of how the standard HTML language works. We see how HTML can be used to format screens, navigate through documents, execute programs, and display other types of objects. In the next chapter we will look at the much more

Chapter 17: Web Components and Communications 413

powerful aspect of HTML, HTML forms, which allow users to input data and manage a much broader range of activities.

In Figure 17-2, we provide a small sampling of some of the HTML document formatting tags. If you take a close look at Figure 17-2, you will get an idea of how HTML actually specifies the formatting rules. The fundamental rules for HTML formatting are simple. A raw HTML document is nothing more than a raw ASCII text file. The words that we want to see on the Web page are simply typed into a file. This ASCII file is then spruced up through the addition of special HTML formatting tags. Some tags apply to the entire document (there are HTML tags to define the background color, dividing lines, etc.). Other tags describe how a particular line should be displayed.

Text modification is accomplished through the use of tag pairs. A tag pair is a pair of tag symbols that are used to surround the section of text that the programmer wants to modify. Ultimately, tag pairs are HTML's way of providing instructions to the browser. There are pairs of tags for each of the different formatting options that HTML provides including:

<CENTER> </CENTER> identifies the text that should be centered on the screen

<P> </P> identifies separate paragraphs (or in this case, lines)

<FONT COLOR = #FF0080> </FONT> tells the browser to paint this text in pink

<FONT SIZE = + n> </FONT> indicates an increase of *n* in the relative size of the font, larger or smaller than the base font (−*n* would indicate a decrease)

In the previous coding example we created a special example screen called Animal World (see Figure 17-2). This screen represents a fairly typical main menu screen for a Web site. The first line, the line that says "Animal World" has been centered (not visible here), and given a font size

Figure 17-2

A sample of HTML text formatting code (the Animal World screen).

```
<BODY>
<CENTER><P><FONT SIZE = +4>Animal World</FONT></P></CENTER>
<P><FONT SIZE = +2>The Place to Learn About Animals</FONT></P>
<P><FONT SIZE = +1>Comforting Cats</FONT></P>
<P><FONT SIZE = +2>Dangerous Dogs</FONT></P>
<P><FONT SIZE = +3>Lazy Lions</FONT></P>
<P><FONT SIZE = +4>Watchful Whales</FONT></P>
</BODY>
```

4 times larger than the base font. The second line, the line that says "The Place to Learn about Animals," has not been centered, has not been given a special color, and is to be 2 fonts larger than the base. The third, fourth, fifth, and sixth lines are all plain, noncentered, and of variable sizes from + 1 to + 4.

Now, let's see how this HTML code will actually look when displayed by a browser. Figure 17-3 shows how that HTML will actually look when displayed from within Netscape Navigator (the Netscape Web browser).

Figure 17-4 shows how the same HTML looks when displayed from within a Microsoft Internet Explorer (the Microsoft Web browser).

As you can see by these two examples, while there may be some minor differences between the displays, in general these two browsers have managed to display the same document in the same way. (Try reading the same document into WordPerfect, MS Word, and WordPro and see how well it works!)

While this powerful capability certainly makes HTML attractive and easy to use, it is far from the only thing that makes HTML so useful.

Figure 17-3
The Animal World HTML screen displayed by Netscape Navigator.

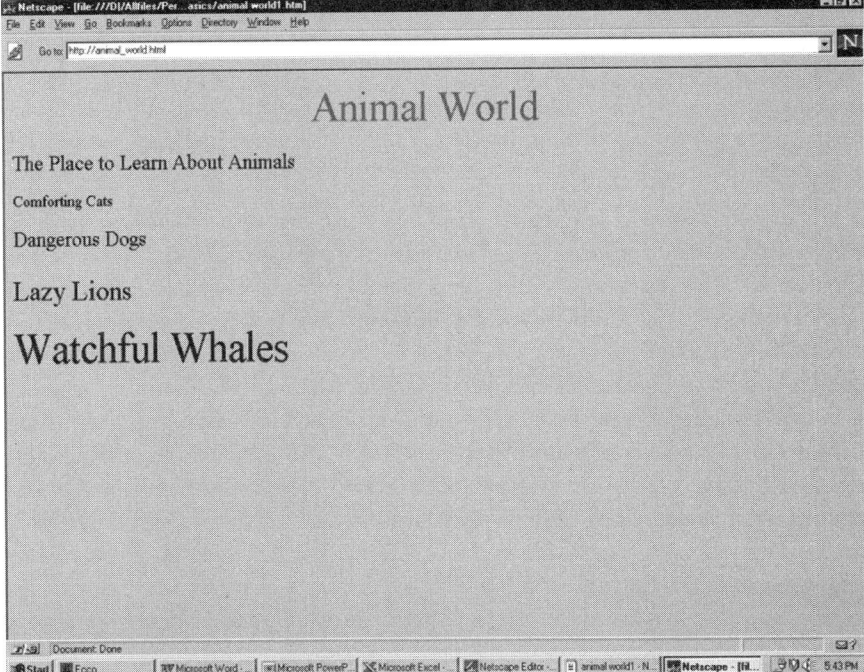

Figure 17-4
The Animal World HTML screen displayed by Microsoft Internet Explorer.

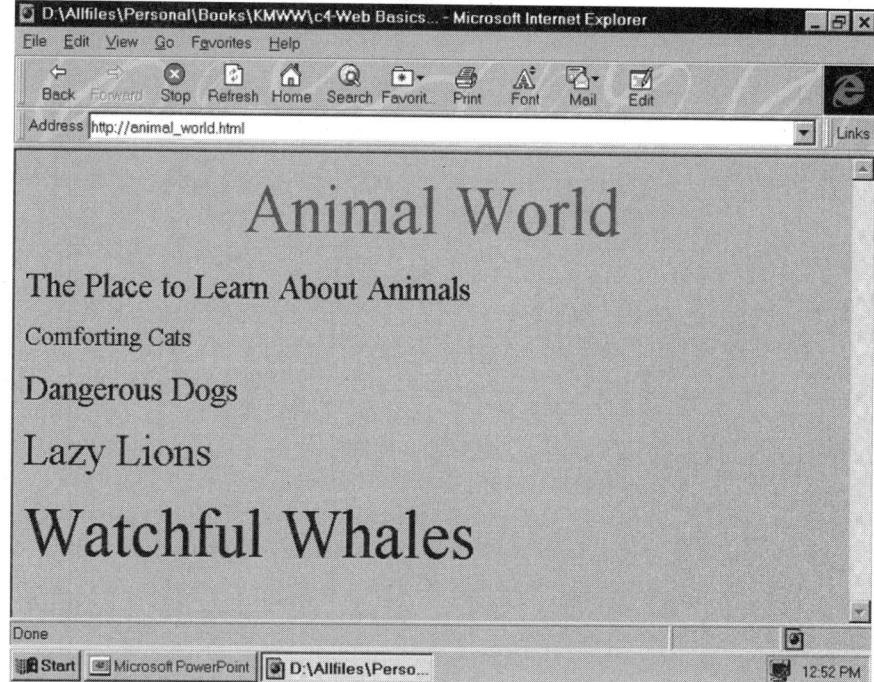

HTML and the Hypertext Paradigm

While the majority of the HTML tags tell a browser how a document is supposed to be displayed, there are also other kinds of commands that are equally important. For example, there are commands that provide the Web with its dynamic navigational capabilities. This navigational capability is known as *hypertext functionality* (thus the name HyperText Markup Language). The HTML formatting tags tell the browser how to display different blocks of text, while the hypertext tags tell the browser which document to retrieve when the user clicks on a particular position on the screen. In other words, it is the hypertext tags, embedded in the HTML document, that make it possible for you as a Web user to read a document, click on an underlined entry which points to another document of interest, and almost immediately have that document displayed for you. Talk about ease of use!

Hypertext and the Web have created a world that not only redefines the role that computers play in our life, but also forces us to reconsider our basic understanding about how to learn, how to find information, and how to place a value on the information we have.

The History of Hypertext In reality, the people who invented the Web did not actually invent hypertext. Hypertext—at least the concept of documents that allow readers to immediately branch off into other documents from anywhere within the current document—was conceptualized as early as the year 1945. At that time, Vannevar Bush proposed that institutions could create vast, interlinked networks of documents, making use of microfilm, documents, pictures, and other media. This creation, dubbed "memex," was supposed to make it possible for someone to read a document, point to a reference, and then automatically pull up the related document, with a minimum amount of effort on the part of the user.

Of course, in 1945 no one had even dreamed of the possibilities that personal computers and the Internet of today could offer. At that time, Bush thought that the linkages between documents could be managed by microdots, which could be scanned by photocells, which would in turn, trigger the retrieval of the documents.

The first legitimate hypertext environment has been attributed to Douglas Engelbart. In 1960, Engelbart created a system that made use of a revolutionary device known as a mouse.

More recently, serious hypertext systems, systems that allow researchers to scan vast libraries of technical materials, in a fraction of the time that traditional methods would take, have flourished in academia and business. The Brown University Intermedia system and the Apple hypercard are a couple of the more prevalent modern hypertext systems.

Of course, as computer technology has continued to expand, hypertext functionality has been replaced by hypermultimedia. In this age of personal computer convenience, any child can plug in a CD-ROM version of an encyclopedia, or a collection of information about movies, authors, poets, artists, or musicians, and point and click through sound and video (and every once in a while, click for more text to read).

With so much ease of use, and with such an intuitively productive way to organize information, is it any wonder that HTML documents have helped make the Web as popular as it is?

HTML Hypertext Examples There is really only one basic HTML tag pair that you need to know about, if you want to be able to set up a document to point to another one, and that is the A HREF = , /A pair. Specifically, the syntax for the A HREF = tag is:

<A HREF = "location of the document you want to point to (usually a URL) "> </A>

Chapter 17: Web Components and Communications 417

Figure 17-5
Animal World document HTML code with pointers.

```
<CENTER><P><FONT COLOR = "#FF0080"><FONT SIZE = +4>Animal World</FONT></FONT></P></CENTER>
<P><FONT SIZE = +2>The Place to Learn About Animals</FONT></P>
<P><FONT SIZE = +1><A HREF = "Main_Cat_Screen">Comforting Cats</A></FONT></P>
<P><FONT SIZE = +2><A HREF = "Main_Dog_Screen">Dangerous Dogs</A></FONT></P>
<P><FONT SIZE = +3><A HREF = "Main_Lion_Screen">Lazy Lions</FONT></A></P>
<P><FONT SIZE = +4><A HREF = "Main_Whale_Screen">Watchful Whales</FONT></A></P>
```

When you surround a line of text with this tag pair, you accomplish several things:

1. You tell the browser to display the text in the special color put aside for "linking" references (usually blue).
2. You tell the browser to underline the text.
3. You tell the browser that, whenever someone clicks on that text, it should retrieve the document specified for the user.

Figure 17-5 shows an example of the code for our Animal World document with the references for each of the menu items included. Figure 17-6 shows how the Animal World document looks when viewed from within a browser. Notice how the menu items are now underlined.

Using HTML to Point to Other Things

In addition to providing for formatting of text displays and navigation between pages HTML can point to

- Pictures and graphics
- Audio (sound) recordings
- Video recordings
- Many different types of documents.

In fact, HTML and an appropriately configured browser can manage and display all of these types of objects and more. More importantly, these objects can be placed anywhere within an HTML document and navigated to in exactly the same manner as any HTML document is managed.

418   Part 3: Technology Foundations

Figure 17-6
Animal World document displayed with pointers.

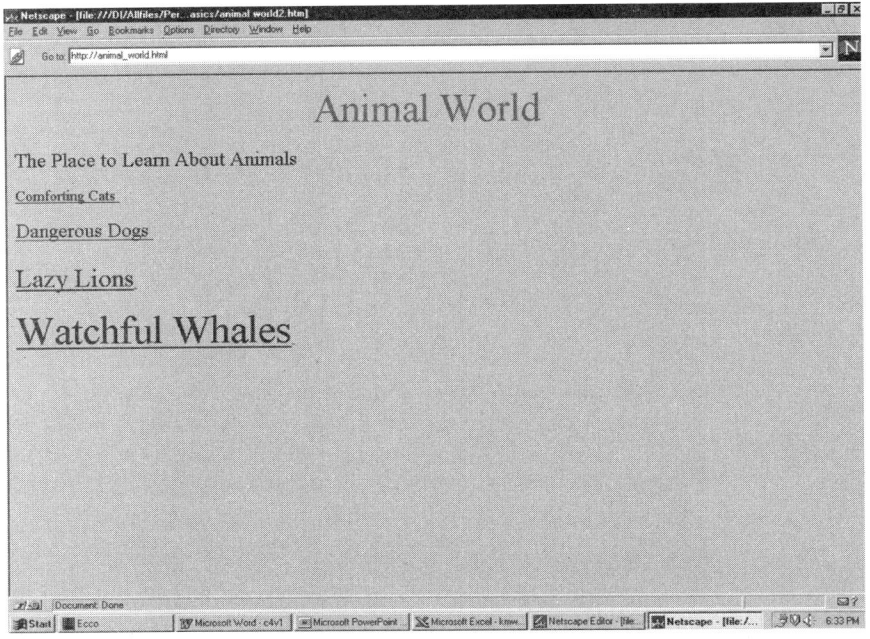

We have seen how the browser and the Web server work together to manage HTML. HTML, which is basically an ASCII text document (with formatting instructions included), is sent to the browser and interpreted by it to create the mutlicolored, multifonted document you see on the browser screen.

Although the browser's main function may be the translation of ASCII HTML instructions into formatted output, it can also manage the formatting and display of the many hundreds of other things we may want to look at.

If we want our browser to display not only ASCII text but also pictures, sound, video, word processing documents, and more, what do we have to change? There are two ways that a Web browser could be modified to support this kind of additional functionality: (1) We can change the functionality of the browser itself, so that it automatically handles these other kinds of objects as well. (For example, we could modify the browser so that it knows how to display graphics files automatically. This is exactly what most browsers do.) (2) Alternatively, we can create a mechanism that forwards those other types of objects on to a different program. (For example, if we want to display a Lotus 1-2-3 spreadsheet, there would be no reason to build a spreadsheet application into the browser. In this case we simply access the Lotus program from within the browser and let it display the Lotus document.)

In the world of Web technology today, we are faced with a situation where different browsers use different combinations of these solutions. When the Web browser handles the automatic display of a non-HTML object, we call this an *in-line display*. The displayed items are referred to as *in-line display objects*. In these cases, the non-HTML objects are sent from the server to the browser just as if they were another block of ASCII text. It is up to the browser to know that the object it is receiving needs to be handled differently.

However, when we want to display, manage, or run an object—a Word document, video clip, or audio track—in a passive mode (in which the object is invoked only when the user clicks on it), then the Web browser will usually display an icon that the user can click on. We call these *static display objects*. In these cases, the action of clicking on the icon causes the browser to invoke some other program (e.g., it will invoke MS-Word to display a Word document) to complete the operation.

To make these techniques work, we need several additions to our Web architecture. We have to arrange it so that the Web browser knows where to place the object, how to execute it, and where to send it for execution. These tasks are accomplished through a variety of approaches.

Placing Nontext Objects on Your Web Page The problem of figuring out where to place a non-HTML object in your display, and of telling the browser how to handle it, is partially taken care of by special nontext HTML display tags. These tags follow a syntax similar to that of the regular display tags, but with special features for the objects they manage. For example, the standard syntax for the simple display of an image is:

<IMG SRC = "image source file name">

So, for example, to show a picture of an elephant on a Web page, we would code:

<IMG SRC = "elephant.gif">

The elephant picture will then show up.

Of course, one of the cool things about the Web is that you can actually call another Web page by clicking on pictures. The syntax to perform this little magic trick is a combination of the A HREF = and IMG SRC = tags.

To get our elephant picture to be the icon that calls up the elephant information page (called elephant_page.html), we would simply code:

```
<A HREF = "elephant_page.html"><IMG SRC = "elephant.gif"></A>
```

Notice how the `</A>` at the end of the line is used to combine the HREF and IMG SRC instructions into one tag.

What if we have the sound of an elephant trumpeting, and we want that to play as soon as a person opens up the page. To do this, all we do is code:

```
<BGSOUND = "elephant_call.wav">
```

The `.wav` file will play immediately upon invocation.

To have the sound clip available via a point-and-click operation, the tag:

```
<embed SRC = "elephant_call.wav">
```

could be used. This tag will set up a small control panel that allows the user to control the `.wav` file's execution.

There are of course a wide variety of tags used to define the different kinds of treatments that a Web page designer would like to see. These few examples are provided to give the reader a general idea of how they work.

Object Types While the command syntax for nontext objects helps the browser know how to treat an object, that alone is not good enough. These tags tell the browser what the general category of the object is, but not specifically what kind it is. For example, you tell the browser to display an image file using the IMG SRC = tag, but what kind of image is it? Is it .pcx, .jpg, .gif? There are hundreds of image file formats to choose from.

To make it easy for the browser to manage multiple object types, we also have to provide it with the means to identify the specific types of objects it is dealing with. There is actually a standardized set of file-naming conventions that are used in support of this Web browser management process. This naming convention helps the different browsers running on different operating systems to coordinate their efforts.

The first line of identification for any file, therefore, is its object type. You can identify the type of object by the file name extension it carries. For example, we know that HTML documents are stored with a name ending in .htm or .html. What this means is that if we want the HTML document to point to another HTML document, all we have to do is be sure that the name of the pointed-to document includes the extension

Chapter 17: Web Components and Communications

TABLE 17-1

Extension Naming Conventions for HTML

Extension	Contents
.htm, .html	HTML documents
.txt	Generic ASCII text
.doc	Microsoft Word document
.tiff, .jpeg, .gif	Graphic display types
.mpeg	MPEG—Video
.wrl, .vrml	VRML 3d
.java	Java applets
.ps	Postscript
.au, .wav	Audio

.htm or .html. To get the browser to pull in an ASCII text file, we simply identify it as a .txt, and so on. Table 17-1 shows some of the more commonly referenced targets of an HTML document and the extensions that identify them.

Browser Settings for Objects Unfortunately, the use of special display tags, and the identification of an object by its object type, is still not enough. To get all of these different kinds of things displayed on our desktop, we have to make sure that our Web browser is capable of handling and displaying all these different types of things. For the individual browser there will be certain defaults built into the system. In addition, many browsers offer a settings or preferences screen that allows the user to specify which programs should be used to run the various object types.

A good example of this can be found in the Netscape browser. Figure 17-7 shows the Netscape browser preferences screen. We can see the preference settings for Lotus 1-2-3 documents. Notice how the extensions for different generations of Lotus 1-2-3 documents (.wk3, .wk4, etc.) are identified. Notice too, the reference to MIME types, the subject of our next section.

MIME and MIME Types

While the establishment of default ways of handling disparate types of objects (HTML, graphics, documents, etc.) works well for the browser,

Figure 17-7
Netscape preferences for Lotus 1-2-3 documents.

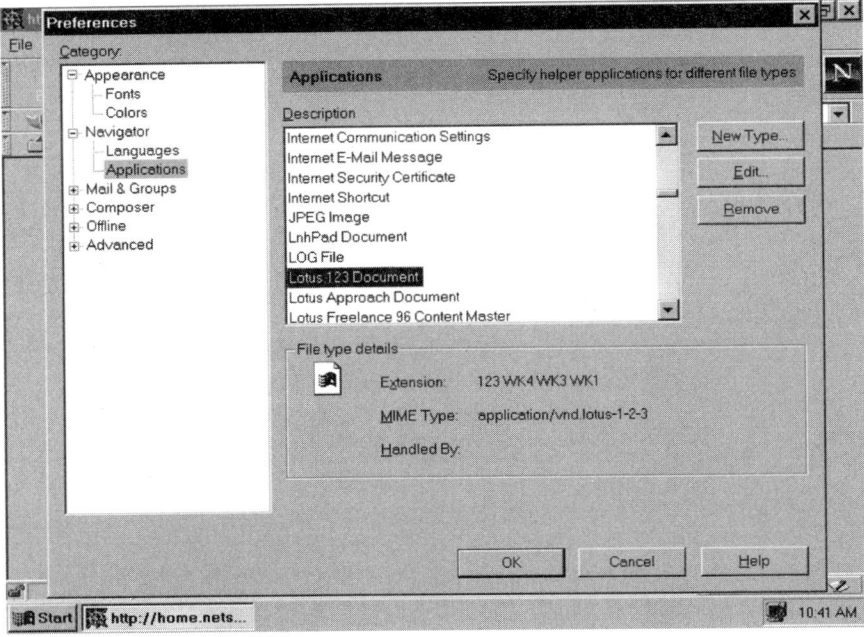

there is no way that the Web environment could function with only that method of object definition. Unfortunately, browser settings for object types can be enforced and referenced only within the browser they are set for. Remember, the Web is an almost universal environment, providing standardized levels of service to hundreds of different kinds of browsers and servers, each with its own, different capabilities. What is needed is a way to standardize document and object types across all environments, without diminishing the flexibility that individual browsers have to offer.

In the case of the Web, this server-side standardization is accomplished through the use of MIME. MIME (multipurpose Internet mail extensions) describes a globally recognized set of data types that is recognized by all servers and all browsers anywhere on the Web. MIME was originally established to make it possible for systems to interchange multimedia mail, and the standard was simply incorporated by the designers of the Web itself.

Table 17-2 shows some examples of MIME types and their meanings. As you can see, the MIME type consists of two parts: the general category of object to be managed (text, video, audio, etc.) and the specific type (lotus, postscript, text, etc.). Between these two settings, the browser and server are able to stay coordinated.

TABLE 17-2
MIME types

MIME Type	Instructions
text/plain	Display plain ASCII text
text/html	Display ASCII text in HTML format
application/vmd-lotus 1-2-3	Invoke the Lotus 1-2-3 program to open
application/postscript	Use a word processing package that can read postscript
Image/gif	Image coded in GIF format
Image/jpeg	Image coded in JPEG format
Audio/basic	Use a sound broadcasting application
Video/mpeg	Use a video projector application
x-vrml	Display using a VRML 3-D scene

How MIME Types Are Utilized To make it possible for browsers and servers to synchronize their efforts, there has to be a way for the browser to tell the server which kinds of objects it is able to handle. An older model browser running on a smaller machine may not be able to display some of the latest and greatest graphics. In another situation, the browser may have no sound capabilities. In all such cases, the browser must be able to tell the server what kinds of things it can handle. Conversely, we would want the server to tell the browser the kind of document or object it is sending, so that the browser knows how to handle it. This communication is handled through the use of MIME types.

Whenever the browser sends a message to the server, it includes within its message a list of those MIME types that it is able to handle. This list of MIME types is called the Accept settings. (It is telling the server, "These are the types of documents I will accept.") Conversely, whenever the server sends a document to the browser, it will include in its message a Content-Type setting, which specifies the MIME type of the object being sent.

Managing MIME Traffic Given the way that servers and browsers are set up, and the way that MIME compatibility information is passed between them, it is easy to see how the Web is able to serve so many different kinds of needs.

In general, when the browser contacts a server, it immediately tells it which MIME types it can handle. The server can then check to see if it wants to send anything that won't run properly. In those cases, the server can send an alternative object (of a MIME type that the browser can use), send only those portions of the response that include valid MIME types (leaving "holes" in the Web page displayed at the browser), or send a message to the browser that it is unable to receive the requested document/object.

Using HTML to Manage Program Execution

While making use of HTML and Web servers to retrieve and display documents and other types of objects is certainly useful, getting the Web server to execute programs for us as well would be even more practical. Then we could actually use the Web for "real" kinds of interactive work, and not just simple display work. Setting up our HTML to do this is actually easier than we might first think.

You will recall that the syntax of our HTTP command requires that we input the name of the server, the directory location, and the file name of the object that we want to display. Our Web server then does nothing more than simply grab the file we identified and send it back to us.

If we want to get the Web server to actually execute programs, then we would have to do two things:

- Modify the server so that it will not only retrieve and send things, but execute them as well. Most of the major Web servers have already been modified.
- Tell the Web server which objects to simply retrieve and which ones to also run as programs.

There are two ways that programs can be identified as such to a Web server:

Identify objects with executable programs by their file extension. For example, we could set up the server to execute any requested object whose object type is a .bat, .exe, .dll, .cgi, etc. (The file extensions that identify the file we are invoking as a program will depend on what kind of system the Web server is running on. If the Web server is running on Windows NT, then the .exe, .bat, and .dll extensions will work. On a UNIX machine, the .cgi extension will identify a CGI script.)

Alternatively, set up a special directory that the Web server recognizes as an executable directory. Any time anyone asks that an object be retrieved from the executable directory, the server will know that that is an object to be run. (The most common name for an executable directory is `/cgi-bin/` which serves as an abbreviation for CGI (common gateway interface)—the standard for Web server/program communication) and binary (or executable).

Either way, all we need now do is simply issue an HTTP command that specifies the server name, directory name, and program name and pass it to the server. The server will then detect that this is an executable request and run the program.

Running a Program with HTML—An Example For example, assume we have a program called `Doggie_count`. `Doggie_count` goes out to a database and figures out how many different breeds of dog are currently tracked. It then returns that count to the user at the browser screen. The command:

```
<A HREF = "http://www.animal.com/animals/dogs/doggie_count.exe">
```

when clicked from within a Web page will call the `www.animal.com` server and tell it to run the `doggie_count` program found in the `/animals/dogs` directory.

Program Output from a Web Server What happens when a browser invokes a program? The name of the program, its directory location, and the name of the server where it resides are sent. The server receives it and checks security. Now what happens? Up until now the Web server has done nothing more than fetch objects and send them back to the requester. Now we are asking it to do more.

The first thing that happens is that the server will execute the program. This program execution, of course, does not occur without some overhead. In fact, this overhead may be significant. Some of the resources of the Web server machines will be taken away from the job of handling requests for objects, and will instead be dedicated to the process of running whatever program was invoked. The user may end up waiting a very, very long time for some kind of response from the server, especially if the program is large, complex, or dependent on outside services (like databases, external documents, or "live feeds") for input.

Let's consider a few of the options that our Web-based program will have regarding sending something back to the requester. The targeted program might:

1. Send nothing back to the browser. This is rarely an acceptable option. However this could happen if the program experiences problems, or if

the program is simply being used to trigger off some other series of events.

2. Send a status report/confirmation back to the browser using simple text. Since the server can send "raw" ASCII to the browser (via the text/ASCII MIME type), it is possible for a program to send back a little text-based message to tell the user one of the following:
   a. There is a problem.
   b. The request was received and is being processed.
   c. The user is being sent the information requested.

3. Send a previously identified and stored HTML document back to the browser. In these situations the program looks at the message sent to it and decides that some other HTML document it knows about should be sent. In this case, the program issues the command to send that document via the server.

4. Create an HTML document dynamically and send it back to the browser. This is an extremely popular option. In this scenario, a program receives input and dynamically decides what the next user screen should look like. The program then builds the screen and sends it to the requesting browser.

In all cases, the intervention of a program into our normal flow of Web processing makes things more versatile but more complicated at the same time.

Security and the Web Having the Web order the execution of programs is certainly a plus, but there are also some serious minuses associated with it. While it is nice to be able to let people all over the world run programs that we want them to run, it can also be very dangerous if those same people figure out how to run programs that we do not want them to run.

Herein lies the single biggest problem with Web services and security today. While it is certainly convenient and powerful for users to trigger commands from their Web pages, the situation is also very dangerous. Because the Internet is so standard, so open, and so stateless, it can be very difficult to keep track of who is doing what and where they are doing it. If you set things up so that a user can run programs on your machine, then you may have inadvertently made it possible for the user to do anything on your machine that you can do. Loose security can create a situation where the user can run *any program*, not just those programs that you code into the HTML. In these situations, experience has shown that clever hackers can figure out ways to delete files, change files, and in general wreak havoc within your system.

If you give global execution permissions to a Web server, you open yourself up to the possibility that a user could wipe out all of your files, execute programs that tie up all of your memory, or even penetrate your corporate security system and steal important files and databases. Because of this problem, it is very important that we understand all the details behind the different ways that browser/server communication works, and behind the way that different Web warehousing products are architected. Without this due diligence, we might design a Web warehousing solution that ultimately destroys our entire environment.

The Stateless Web

It is important for us to understand the exact nature of browser/server communications in order to stay sensitive to the security issues that working in a Web warehousing environment creates. It is equally important, however, for us to understand the nature of this traffic, to keep track of the integrity of individual transactions and the status of the databases and data warehouses from which we will be pulling information.

Since Web warehousing is fundamentally about accessing databases over the Web, it will be essential that we understand the basic "stateless" nature of the Web, and ways that we can work with it.

Statelessness

When we ask a server to execute a program from within the context of an HTML document, we create a situation that is operationally different than the one we created when we simply asked that a document be retrieved. In all our previous examples, we were dealing with a situation where a user looked at a document, clicked on a pointer to another document, and then waited around until the next document showed up.

Now, by all appearances, this series of events will seem like any other serially based computer operation. The user asks for something, the program takes control of the transaction, waits for a response, and then continues with the next operation. While the typical Web transaction may seem to work that way, it really does not. What actually happens in a typical Web transaction is that the browser sends off a request for something from the server and then makes itself available to do some other work.

There is no direct connection between client and server other than the actual passing of the request. After the request is sent, the transaction is over as far as the browser is concerned. In many situations, the server will immediately send back the page that was requested, and the browser will immediately display it, making it seem as if the two events were connected.

Consequences of Stateless Web Activities The fact that Web services are stateless has advantages and disadvantages. On the plus side, statelessness means that no matter how many Web servers go down, your browser will still be able to function. Statelessness provides an environment that is optimal for the sending and retrieving of a maximum number of read-only documents. In addition, statelessness is the natural condition of TCP/IP, and, since the Web is based on TCP/IP, it is the most natural way for the Web to have evolved.

Of course, when we decide that we would like the Web to do more than just display output, when we want it to keep track of database transactions or business transactions, for example, then it becomes critical that the Web somehow learn how to operate in a state-based mode. The maintenance of this physical, serial connection between browser and server, while only a minor issue where typical browser activity is concerned, can become a major issue when we start using the Web to execute programs.

Why? There are several reasons. First, when we ask a server to execute a program, the chances are very good that the server will take longer than just a few seconds to get back with a response. This may be a result of the workload on the server, the need to access a database, or any other of a number of reasons. When this happens, it will create a lull in response time that can cause the user to panic, worry, or get irritated. (Users may try issuing the command several more times because they think the computer didn't get the message the first time, or they may leave and do something else.)

Second, there will be situations where you may want to preserve some kind of integrity between one part of a session with a database and another part. For example, when scrolling through very large files it is common to set a placeholder in the database, return a small subset of data to the user, and then pick up the return of data where you left off when the user is ready to see more. This kind of operation will be impossible in a typical Web warehousing environment. The inability to ensure serial integrity means that you will be unable to truly "secure" transactions (unless you want users to input their password every time they see a new screen).

For all of these reasons, it is critical that we understand the stateless nature of the Web and the ways to get around it when necessary. Luckily for us, since Web warehousing usually involves a great deal of read-only activity, and only a very small amount of read/write activity, we will be able to skip a lot of this discussion. However, it is also important that we stay aware of this stateless nature of the Web, if we are going to understand how to make things work effectively.

Browser-Server Communication in Depth

Up until now we have been discussing different aspects of the nature of browser-server communication. At this point we are ready to summarize what we know, and show how it all fits together into a seamless Web transaction. We have talked about many of the different pieces of communication between the browser and server, but we haven't really talked about the complete communications package.

Complete Syntax of a Request

When a Web browser pulls a request off the input line and converts it into a command, it creates a message to be sent to the server. Included in this message are the following:

- A method, which describes the action that you want the server to perform
- The uniform resource locator (URL), which identifies the server, directory, and object being requested
- The protocol version (the HTTP version number)
- An optional set of fields that provides the server with additional information

Table 17-3 shows a collection of the current methods and the activities they call for. Included are the GET (return the named object), HEAD (return header information), and the POST, PUT, and DELETE commands (commands which ask the server to modify its own directories).

TABLE 17-3

HTTP Methods

Method Name	Method Activity
GET	Retrieve the object(s) I am asking for
HEAD	Return the header information about this object
*POST	Store the information being sent on the server
*PUT	Send a new copy of an existing object to the server
*DELETE	Delete this object from the server's directory
Other	New methods to be invented in the near future

*Many servers do not allow these commands to work (for obvious reasons).

In Table 17-4 we have assembled a collection of some of the standard "additional fields" that can also be sent to the server. These include the User-Agent (type of browser), If-Modified-Since (time sensitivity checking), Accept (MIME types accepted), and Authorization (security field).

If we wanted to send a request for the page `lazy_lion.htm`, from the `animal_server` site, the complete syntax for the command might look like this:

GET /cats/lions/lazy_lion.htm   *** Get command

HTTP/2.1   *** HTTP version

User Agent: Netscape Navigator 2.0   *** Browser type

Accept: text/plain   *** Accept commands to tell the server which types of response the browser can accept

Accept: text/html

Accept: image/gif

and so forth...

TABLE 17-4

Browser Communications Fields

Field Name	Information Sent
User-Agent	The type of browser
If-Modified-Since	Only return object if it is newer than the one currently held
Accept	MIME types the browser will accept
Authorization	Security field

TABLE 17-5

Server Response Fields

Field	Instructions
Server	The type of server
Date	The date and time of repsonse
Content-Length	How big the document is in bytes
Content-Type	The MIME type of the document
Content-Language	The national language of the document (English, Spanish, German, Chinese, etc.)
Content-Encoded	Compression or encoding scheme utilized
Last-Modified	Date and time the document was last modified

Complete Syntax of a Response

After receiving and processing the request, the server will need to send back not only what was asked for, but a lot of other status and content information as well. The different fields which can be sent from the server to the browser are shown in Table 17-5. Included as server response fields are the Server (type of Web server), Date (time stamp of the response), Content-Length (size of response in bytes), Content-Type (MIME type of the response), Content-Language (the national language of the response, e.g., German, English, Japanese), Content-Encoded (compression/encoding indicator), and Last-Modified (time stamp of last modification).

One of the most critical things that the server needs to send back to the browser is a status code. This code will tell the browser how its request is progressing. You can see a list of some status code values in Table 17-6.

TABLE 17-6

Server Status Codes

Code	Text	Explanation
200	Document follows	Request successful, document attached
301	Moved permanently	Document moved to new URL
404	Not found	No such document found
500	Server error	Server error experienced

Assuming that the `animal_server` in the previous example had the page requested and returned it, the response from the server could look like this:

```
HTTP/2.1
Status 200  Document follows
Server: Netscape Enterprise Server 4.x
Date: Mon., March 15, 1999 20:20:20 GMT
Content-type: text/HTML
Content-length: 9822
Last-modified : Wed. March 3, 1998 12:21:02 GMT
Contents of the lazy_lion.html document
```

Building on What Came Before As we continue to delve into the details of how the Web works, several things should become increasingly clear. First, the Web is not really any kind of invention in its own right. The Web is in fact a collection of approaches and technologies that have been under development for years, and which, when combined with other technologies, create a whole that is greater than the sum of its parts.

The Web builds on the power, flexibility, and standardization provided by the Internet and the TCP/IP protocol to define its technological infrastructure. It also builds on the power and flexibility of personal computers to provide browsers that are user-friendly and rich in features and functions. It then includes within its operational paradigm the power of hypertext and dynamic document navigation. And it makes use of the technology and approach to document search and retrieval pioneered through the development of WAIS services.

All in all, this combination provides a powerful but extremely complicated environment, which we, as Web warehousing practitioners, need to understand. In the next chapter, we will complete our investigation into the workings of the generic Web environment by examining, in detail, the workings of forms and CGI scripts.

CHAPTER 18

PPP and CGI

Database Access to the Web

- *What are the three major approaches used to deliver "traditional" data to users via the Web?*
- *What is the PPP approach to Web-based data access?*
- *In what ways can you collect input information from a Web user and pass it to the Web server?*
- *What are HTML forms, and how are they built?*
- *In what ways can you pass input data from the Web server to the programs accessing the databases?*
- *What is CGI, and how is it used to drive the management of programs and database access in the Web environment?*
- *What kinds of programs can be used to run Web database access?*
- *How do you gain access to the databases themselves?*

Up until now, we have continued to increase the depth and breadth of our understanding of the Web environment as a generic Web page search and retrieval environment. We started by developing an understanding of the simple Internet infrastructure and added to it an examination of HTML, HTTP, and browser-server communications. We also saw how this mechanism could be used to invoke programs. At this point, we are ready to see how we can harness this basic Web architecture to start delivering large amounts of business intelligence information (data warehousing data) through the same basic infrastructure.

Delivering Traditional Data over the Web

Although the Web infrastructure that we have described is certainly an ideal environment for the storage and retrieval of documents across a widely dispersed geography, it is hardly robust enough to support the needs of business people who want to gain access to traditional database resources. The new world of data processing being defined by Web warehousing will certainly include the retrieval of documents as one of its capabilities, but that capability, in and of itself, will still only define a small portion of the ultimate required functionality. Although traditional data retrieval may be less glamorous than surfing the Web, it is still critical to the running of a business.

Of course, we all know that the Web can and does support the distribution of this more traditional type of data on a regular basis. Our objective, for the rest of this chapter, will be to examine some of the different ways that this can be accomplished to see how we can use them to build the desired Web warehousing environment.

Methods for the Distribution of "Traditional" Data on the Web

Before we get into a lot of detail about how this data can be delivered via the Web, let's begin with a quick review of the three major categories of approaches. These include:

1. *PPP, or preprocess and publish, approach.* (This is not to be confused with the PPP protocol for Internet access.) Under this

Chapter 18: PPP and CGI

approach, data reports are published in HTML format and posted to the Web server just as any other HTML page would be.

2. *CGI, or common gateway interface.* Making use of CGI programs or scripts to drive the process is the de facto standard for database access through the Web. Under CGI you can write customized "database handler" programs which can work with a Web page and deliver data via the Web in a consistent, relatively efficient manner.

3. *Java.* Leveraging the power and flexibility of Java to create output is the latest, greatest option available, and it will soon overtake CGI as the Web developers' data delivery mechanism. Under Java, a developer can create true client/server type applications, built on top of the existing Internet infrastructure. (We will take a detailed look at Java and JDBC, the Java database connectivity protocol, in the next chapter.)

We will consider PPP and CGI in detail, and consider some of the strengths and weaknesses of each.

The PPP Approach

By far the easiest approach to the distribution of "traditional" data over a Web infrastructure is the PPP approach. To use this approach we do exactly what the name implies. We figure out in advance the kinds of information people will want and create the reports ahead of time (preprocessing), and then we convert them to an HTML format and publish them on a Web site (publish). It is then possible for users to gain access to the reports via the normal HTML channels.

While certainly the least glamorous of the approaches, the PPP approach is eminently practical, easily executable, and incredibly economical.

Architecture for the PPP Approach

The major components of the system using the PPP approach include the browser, the server, and an external database server which holds information of interest to some population of users.

To accomplish our objectives we simply run a report writing program on the database server, convert its output into HTML, and store it in the Web server. See Figure 18-1. Of course, to make this approach really

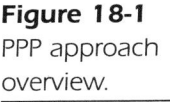
Figure 18-1
PPP approach overview.

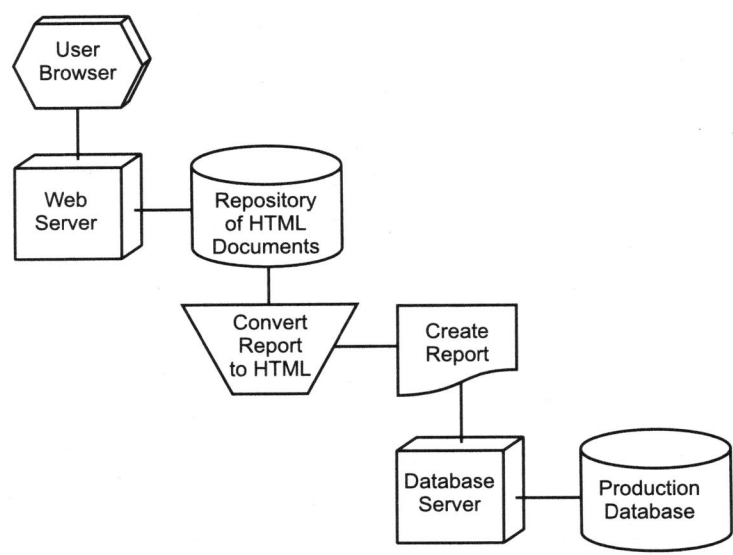

practical, the reports will need to be refreshed on an ongoing basis, something that is very easy to do.

Establishing Communication with the PPP Approach

Under the PPP approach, we make absolutely no changes to the way that the browser and server have been communicating all along. Users simply ask for the desired reports via the reports URL. The Web system takes care of the rest.

Special Issues Where PPP Is Concerned Although creating the PPP system is easy, the process of making it usable still requires that we do a few things. We can consider several options:

We can just tell the users which URLs to run for which reports and let them worry about it from there.

We can create menu HTML forms that will allow users to select the reports they want.

We can create sophisticated, dynamically generated menus that allow users to navigate through a large assortment of reports. (This option requires the use of CGI and will be considered under the next section.)

What are some of the issues regarding each of these approaches?

Giving the URLs to the Users The easiest way for the I/T department to get the HTML reports onto user screens is to simply give those users the URLs of the reports so that they can key them into their Web browser command lines. This is actually a lot more convenient for the user than it might sound. Consider this for a minute: If users are browser-literate at all, they will figure out how to save these URLs in their bookmarks file. This will allow the users to organize the access to the reports any way they want, and thus create an optimum environment.

Creating HTML Menus for the Reports An alternative approach is to create a Web page with menu selections and pointers to each of the reports. This is also relatively easy to do; however, maintenance of the screens and pointers can get to be challenging as the scope of the system increases. In fact, some product vendors have created automatic Web menu generation screens that take the detailed process of creating and maintaining these menus out of the hands of the developer altogether. Basically, every time reports are added to the environment, the menus are rebuilt simultaneously.

Simulated Navigation under PPP You can even get more sophisticated in your exploitation of this basic PPP approach. Several clever vendors of OLAP and query products have created systems that generate populations of interconnected reports. These reports are linked together at key points, in exactly the same way as HTML documents are linked together, via the hyperlinks mechanism.

When this linking of reports is done properly, it can seem to the user that the system is dynamically generating responses to questions, when in fact the reports were generated ahead of time.

The systems that create these environments generate a large population of different interrelated reports, and automatically post the hypertext linkage tags that tie them all together. Then the same system will generate menus that allow users to gain access to the system at strategic entry points.

In the last section of this book, we spend a considerable amount of time looking at some of the different ways that vendors provide Web access via their Web warehousing tools. You will be able to see several examples that help illustrate how this method is utilized.

In reality, the PPP approach is one of the best-kept secrets of the Web warehousing world. For some reason, people don't realize just how easy it really is to make the Web environment immediately useful. This is probably because the approach is so simple and straightforward that it just doesn't seem like it counts.

The CGI Approach

Where the PPP approach is simple and straightforward, the CGI approach, unfortunately, is quite the opposite. The PPP approach, in general, dictates that we change the way that *we do things* in order to get the job done. Under the CGI approach, in contrast, we try to get the Web to change the way that the *Web does things*, in order to get it to do *what we want* it to do.

CGI Background

Actually, the CGI approach was not engineered so much as it simply evolved over time. In the simplest terms, CGI figures out how to expand the capabilities of the Web architecture, making it possible for Web programmers to make the environment more responsive, without disrupting it too much. Because the requirement to make the Web an interactive, fully functional environment showed up long after the system was originally specified, you will find that, in many cases, the CGI approach seems to be extremely complicated and contrived. That is because, in many situations, it is.

The different performance, operational, and architectural limitations of the CGI approach are easy to find and frustrating to deal with. It is for this reason that Java is quickly replacing the CGI approach by many Web site developers. It is extremely important to understand the CGI approach, however, for several reasons:

- The vast majority of today's Web technology is crafted using this approach.
- A majority of Web warehousing tool vendors have leveraged the CGI capabilities heavily in the construction of their products.

- The CGI approach is an extremely useful tool to have in your toolkit when you need to figure out how to solve a specific Web warehousing problem.

What Is CGI?

CGI, the common gateway interface, is the standardized description of how standard (non-Java) programs are supposed to be run within the Web environment. CGI defines how Web servers and programs work together (just as HTTP defines how browsers and servers work together) to make it possible for the users of Web services to invoke programs from their browsers.

We introduced a little bit of the CGI approach in the last chapter, when we showed how you can issue an HTTP command to invoke a program on a Web server. (In the simplest situations, we can tell the Web server to execute a program by merely sending its URL to the server and waiting for that program's response to occur.)

Of course, if all we wanted to do were to blindly trigger off the execution of programs from the Web browser via HTML, then there would be no reason to invent a thing like CGI. But if we really intend to make our Web warehousing environment usable, we will have to do more than initiate simple programs.

What CGI defines for us is a way to turn the basic Web environment (a fundamentally one-way, read-only kind of system) into a dynamic setting where users can interact with the system to get more of the information that they need.

The Basic CGI-Based Architecture

As we consider briefly in the previous chapter, the CGI architecture involves the participation of the browser, Web server, and database server, just as the PPP model does. But in this case, the Web server plays a much larger role. In Figure 18-2 you can see how these elements relate. Our browser still sends messages to the Web server, but in this case, instead of requesting an HTML document, the browser requests that a CGI program, resident on the Web server's CGI directory, be run instead. When that program is run, it is able to execute the same traditional

Figure 18-2
The CGI approach.

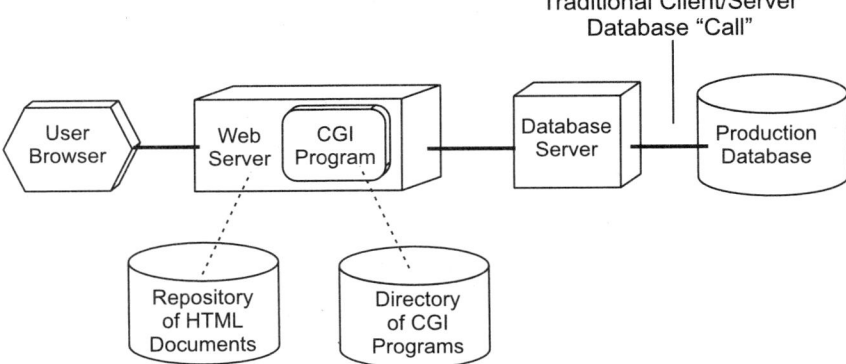

kinds of database queries that any other client/server program might. After retrieving the data requested, the CGI program can then format the response and send it back to the browser via the server.

A Model for Understanding CGI Components

To define a more robust and interactive Web environment, the developers of a CGI system need to include all of the traditional data processing components in their architectural mix. Fundamentally, we need to have components that support:

- *Input.* Providing users with a number of different ways to tell the system what kind of information they require.
- *Communication.* Standards for defining how to pass the information that the users input from the Web server to the program that needs it.
- *Processing.* The execution of computer instructions that do the work the user needs done.
- *Output.* The return of information to the user in a form that is useful.

We now take a few moments to consider each of these components in more detail.

INPUT with CGI

What kinds of information do we want the users to pass? There are many different kinds of data input needs that users of the Web may have in the "normal" business case, but in terms of Web warehousing, there are really only a few. These include:

- Search parameters
- Command line instructions
- SQL commands

So how can we use a simple command line interface (or alternatively, HTML forms) to pass parameters, commands, and even SQL commands? Well, believe or not, there is a way (although not a pretty one).

Using the Command Line

The first and most common way to communicate the user's wishes to the system is for the user to type instructions on the browser command line. As we have already seen, user command line input is the way every Web session starts. We have also seen that users, by typing in the URL of the page or program they would like to run, are able to retrieve or execute them in a relatively painless manner. What we have not seen, however, is any way that we could get this same command line input to allow the user to pass any additional information.

Parameter Passing from the Command Line Basically, the developers of the Web quickly found it necessary to develop a mechanism that allowed users and programs to pass things other than URLs via the HTTP interface. Specifically, all they did is develop a convention by which users can pass any additional information to the program that they would like by simply appending it to the end of the URL.

For example, suppose we have a program called `doggie_names`. Doggie_names goes out to the animal database, finds out the names of all of the dogs, and sends them back to us. Assume also that it is located at URL:

```
http://www.animal.com/animals/dog/doggie_names.exe
```

It is now possible for us to get a list of dog names from the database by simply typing this URL into the browser command line; however, the response we get could very well include the return of the names of hundreds of different dogs. There could be more dog names than we are really interested in. It would be nice if we could tell the `doggie_name` program to limit the names returned to any number we give it. For example, I might want to pass the number 10 to get 10 names back, or 20 to get 20 names back.

If the `doggie_names` program is set up properly, then we can accomplish this with the command line. All we need do is type the URL and then place a ? (the standard delimiter) after the program name and the number we want to pass to the program (in this case, the number 20). Specifically, our command line input would be:

```
http://www.animal.com/animals/dog/doggie_names.exe?20
```

The browser and server will both know how to handle the input.

Limitations with the Command Line Parameter Passing Option
While providing users with the ability to add parameters or commands to the end of a URL is certainly a big plus in terms of functionality, it still falls far short of being truly useful in many situations. The command line, after all, is only so big, and large command strings and SQL commands will be longer than it can handle. More important, by forcing users to use the manual command line option, you take away much of the user-friendliness of the system, and get back into the mode of trying to teach users how to be programmers (always a bad idea). What is needed is a way to allow users to input a lot of stuff, in a way that eases the amount of work that they have to do, and this is where HTML forms come in.

Using Forms to Make the Web Useful

HTML forms were created so that Web developers could create highly user-friendly environments that make it easy to collect user input. HTML forms are nothing more than HTML documents with special HTML data input tags included within them. Not too surprisingly, the syntax for an HTML form tag is very similar to that of any other HTML document tag. The two principal data input tags are called the FORM ACTION and INPUT TYPE tags.

The FORM ACTION Tag Obviously, if you are going to create a Web page that collects all kinds of input from the user, you will have to include within that form's description some mechanism which lets the browser know what should be done with the input when the user hits the

Chapter 18: PPP and CGI

submit button. That is the job of the FORM ACTION = tag. The syntax for this tag is:

```
<FORM ACTION = "insert the URL of the program that will process the form here">
```

For example, let's assume that we have created a form which makes it easy for users to request a list of all the different types of animals that live on a particular continent. They input the continent name and press the submit button, and then get back the list of animals. If the user inputs AFRICA the returned list will include lions, antelopes, elephants, and rhinos. If the user inputs ANTARTICA, the list could include penguins and seals.

If the program that conducts the search is located at www.animal.com, and the program is called continents, then the syntax for the FORM ACTION tag in this case would be:

```
<FORM ACTION = "http://www.animal.com/continents">
```

By placing the appropriate program URL in this space, you make it possible for the Web browser to know where to send the input received. See Figure 18-3 to see how the FORM ACTION tag is coded within an HTML document.

The INPUT TYPE Tag Now that the Web browser knows where to send the input it will receive, all we have to do is actually create the fields in which users can place the input. To perform this little trick, however, we will need a different tag. This one is called the INPUT

Figure 18-3
Coding for the continents program.

```
<FORM>
<FORM ACTION = "HTTP://www.animal.com/continents">
<B><FONT FACE = "Arial" SIZE = 6><P>The Animal Search Game</B></FONT> </P>
<B><FONT SIZE = 4><P>Fill in the name of a continent and see a list
                        of animals that live there !!!!!! </P>
.......  . .
........ . . (other coding here)
........ . .
</FORM>
</B>
</FONT>
</BODY>
</HTML>
```

TYPE tag. The INPUT TYPE tag allows the programmer to accomplish the following:

1. Pick the location on the Web page where the user input field(s) will be located.
2. Define the type of input that will be accepted (it can be a free-form-open text field, a checkbox, or any of a number of other types of input areas).
3. Give a unique name to the data that is being input and captured. (In other words, we assign a variable name to each data input field.)
4. Define a size and a default value for each field.

The syntax for the INPUT TYPE tag for a text entry field would be as follows:

```
<INPUT TYPE = "text" NAME = "Continent_Name" MAXLENGTH = 30> Input continent name here:
```

The message "Input continent name here:" will appear on the screen, with a 30-byte input box located right after it.

Submitting the Form Of course, we are still missing the one thing that we will need to make use of this form. We know where to collect the data, and we know where to send it when we collect it, but we haven't created a way to make it easy for the user to tell us that they are done filling in the form, and that it is ready to be sent. We accomplish this job through the use of the INPUT TYPE tag, and a special keyword, SUBMIT. An INPUT TYPE = SUBMIT command will place a button on the HTML screen with "Submit Query" written on it. When the user clicks on that button, the browser will know that it is time to send the form.

A Full Example of Form Building We have created a complete, ready-to-use form, so that you can become familiar with all of the aspects of HTML form programming. This example is a form called DOGLOVE.HTML. The DOGLOVE form collects survey information from dog lovers and offers to send them a prize if they fill it out.

In Figure 18-4 you can see the HTML coding for this form. Notice the FORM ACTION and INPUT TYPE tags. Notice also the three different kinds of INPUT TYPEs being used. We have an INPUT TYPE = TEXT, and INPUT TYPE = RADIO for radio buttons, and INPUT TYPE = SUBMIT for the submit button. In Figure 18-5 you can see how this form will look when activated by a Web browser.

Chapter 18: PPP and CGI

Figure 18-4
The dog lovers' survey—HTML code.

```
<HTML>
<BODY>
<FORM>
<P><B><FONT FACE = "Arial" SIZE = 6><P>Take our Dog Lovers
Survey</P></B></FONT>
    <P><B><FONT SIZE = 4><P>Fill in the information requested and win free
                dog food! </P></B></FONT>
<FORM ACTION = "HTTP://www.animal.com/doglove">
<P>What is your favorite name for a dog? <INPUT TYPE = "TEXT"
NAME = "DogName" WIDTH = "44"> </P>
<P> How many dogs do you own? </P>
<P> <INPUT TYPE = "RADIO" NAME = "One"> One Dog </P>
<P> <INPUT TYPE = "RADIO" NAME = "Two"> Two Dogs </P>
<P> <INPUT TYPE = "RADIO" NAME = "Lots"> More than 2 dogs</P>
<P> <INPUT TYPE = "SUBMIT"> </P>
</FORM>
</BODY>
</HTML>
```

Figure 18-5
The dog lovers' survey screen.

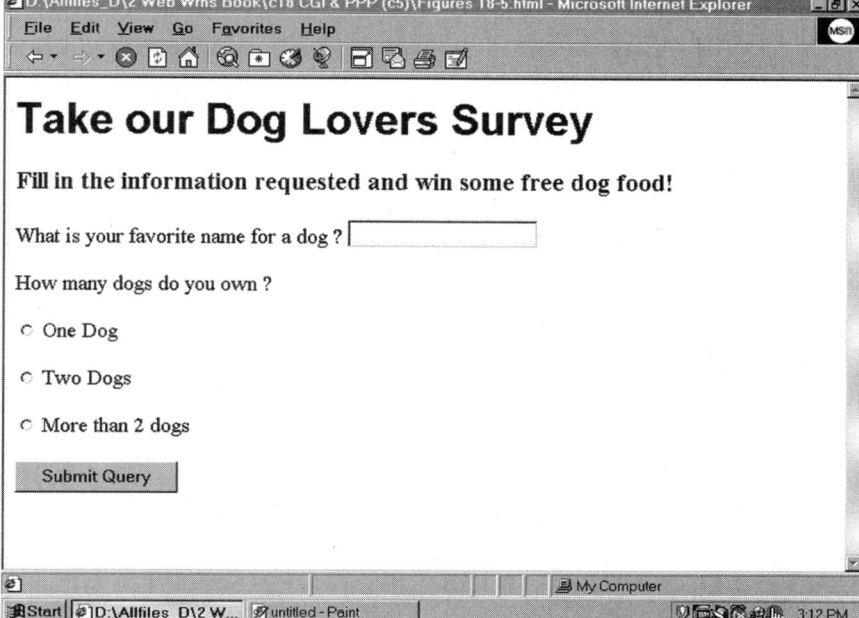

Communication within the CGI Environment

After the user's input has been collected, whether it be through a form or as a command line parameter, the system is now ready to package that input and send it off to the program for processing.

Passing User Input from the Browser to the Server

We already know the basic syntax for communications between the browser and the server, and luckily that syntax remains pretty much intact. (See Chapter 17 for a review of browser-server communications.) The only difference is that now when the URL is being passed, it is passed with all of the user input appended to it. (Obviously, the size of the URL field can get to be pretty large if the user has input a lot of information.) So, we now know that, when a browser sends a message to a server from a form, the message will include fields for a method (GET, POST, or another), a URL, a list of user input data, a protocol version, and the Accept list (which tells the server which MIME types will be accepted).

Naturally, the user input data is not mindlessly strung together and left for the program to figure out. What is actually sent is the name of the field that was filled by the user, followed by an equals sign, and then the actual value the user keyed in. So, for example, if a user input FIDO into our form and hit the submit button, the following message would be sent from the browser to the server:

```
GET HTTP://WWW.ANIMAL.COM/DOGLOVE?DogName = FIDO
HTTP/2.0
Accept text/html
Text/text
......
.......
```

Passing User Input from the Server to the Program

Adding the user's input to the end of the URL certainly makes for an easy and seamless way to deliver it to the server intact. But it tells us nothing about how the server will hand that same information to a program for processing.

Why is the interface between server and program so important? Why can't the server just pass the parameters on to the program the same way that they were received and let it go at that? It's simple. Remember our discussion of how the browser and server worlds are "stateless"? Well, this is where that information becomes critical. Since browsers and servers are stateless machines, when they hand-off work to some other program, they completely "forget" everything they ever knew about it.

That means that when the server tells a program to run and passes it some parameters, it will also have to tell that program everything about where the request came from, so that the program will know where to send the response back to. (Of course, the program will just do the work and then turn around and send all of this information back to the server, and ask the server to send the response back to the browser, but that is the nature of stateless processing!)

So what happens is that, when the Web server gets the command asking that a program be run, it will create and populate a large number of environmental variables, and then pass those variables off to the program when it starts. See Table 18-1 for a comprehensive list of these variables and their functions. Included in the list of environmental variables are many of the things that were passed from the browser to the server in the first place. In these situations, the server will parse the command string received, and populate all of the appropriate fields. Such variables include:

- HTTP_ACCEPT (which will hold a copy of the browser provider Accept list telling the program what kinds of MIME format material the browser will accept)
- USER_AGENT (which indicates the browser type)
- REQUEST_METHOD (which will tell the program which HTML method the browser originally requested—i.e., GET , POST, or some other HTML method.

Most important of all will be a variable called QUERY_STRING, which contains the already-formatted user input data. For example, our earlier example using the DOGLOVE program would leave us with a value of

QUERY_STRING = "DogName = FIDO")

TABLE 18-1

CGI Environmental Variables

Variable	Purpose
AUTH_TYPE	The security authentication method used
CONTENT_LENGTH	The length of the data sent by the browser
CONTENT_TYPE	MIME type of the data sent by the browser
GATEWAY_INTERFACE	Version of the CGI specification to which the server complies
HTTP_ACCEPT	A copy of the browser's Accept list
HTTP_USER_AGENT	The sending browser's type, name, and version number
QUERY_STRING	The information input by the user for processing by the program
REMOTE_ADDR	IP address of requesting browser
REMOTE_HOST	Full DNS hostname of requesting browser
REMOTE_USER	Authenticated user's name
REQUEST_METHOD	The HTML method requested by the browser (GET, POST, etc.)
SCRIPT_NAME	Path to the program being executed by the server
SERVER_NAME	The hostname, DNS, or IP address of the server
SERVER_PORT	The port number of the server
SERVER_PROTOCOL	HTTP version number used by server
SERVER_SOFTWARE	Name and version number of Web server

In addition to parsing, sorting, and passing on information that the browser sent, the server will include variables which tell the program about the server itself, including:

SERVER_NAME   The name or IP address of the server that is initiating the program

SERVER_SOFTWARE   The name and version number of the Web server

Finally, the Web server will figure out a lot of information that is not part of the message about where the request to run a program came from, information like:

REMOTE_ADDR   The IP address of the browser that sent the request

REMOTE_HOST   The host name of the machine where the browser resides

REMOTE_USER   The name of the user (for secure systems)

After preparing all of these variables and passing them on to the program, the Web server will stop running and wait for the next request.

Sending Information Back to the Browser

No small part of the work that a CGI program takes on is formatting a response to the browser that will be usable. As we have already considered, there are several ways that this can be done.

Passing Unformatted Text Data Back to the Browser In the simplest case, all the program needs to do to send information back to the browser is to prepare and send a simple text message. (Remember, almost every Web browser has the built-in ability to display unformatted text as a display option.)

Consider our continents program example from earlier in the chapter. A user inputs the name of a continent, and gets back a list of animal names. Although it would certainly be nice to create a pretty HTML screen with fancy formatting, we might not want to do all of the work necessary to make that happen. In that case, all we would need to do is have the program send the text back to the browser.

For example, assume that the user input the continent name of Africa, and that we want to send back a list that includes the names of lions, gazelles, and hyenas. In this case, the message we would want our program to send out to the browser would look something like the code you see in Figure 18-6.

There are several things to notice about the response displayed in Figure 18-6.

- The first three lines of the response—the status code "Document Follows" (200), date, and server type—are tagged onto the front of the message by the server.
- The program sends the content-type of text/text to the server. (This command tells the browser to use its own text formatting rules and *not* to expect HTML.)
- The rest of the response will be forwarded to the browser screen as is.

Figure 18-6
Continents program response sent back to the browser.

```
       HTTP/2.0 Document Follows
     Date: Mon, 04 June 1999 19:38:03 GMT
        Server: Netscape Navigator 2.2
          Content Type: text/text
          Animals from Africa
               Lions
               Gazelles
               Hyenas
```

Figure 18-7
Perl script creating the continents response.

```perl
        #!/usr/bin/perl
        ........
    ... other PERL commands
    print "Content-type: text/text\n\n";
    print "Animals from Africa\n";
        print "Lions \n";
        print "Gazelles \n";
        print "Hyenas \n";
        ........
    ... other PERL commands
        ........
```

The actual coding of this response will of course depend on the programming language, but the results should be the same. Figure 18-7 shows an example of how we could code the creation of this kind of output using a PERL script. In Figure 18-8 you can see how the browser will display what it receives. Notice the complete lack of formatting for the received text data.

Figure 18-8
The browser view of Continent = Africa.

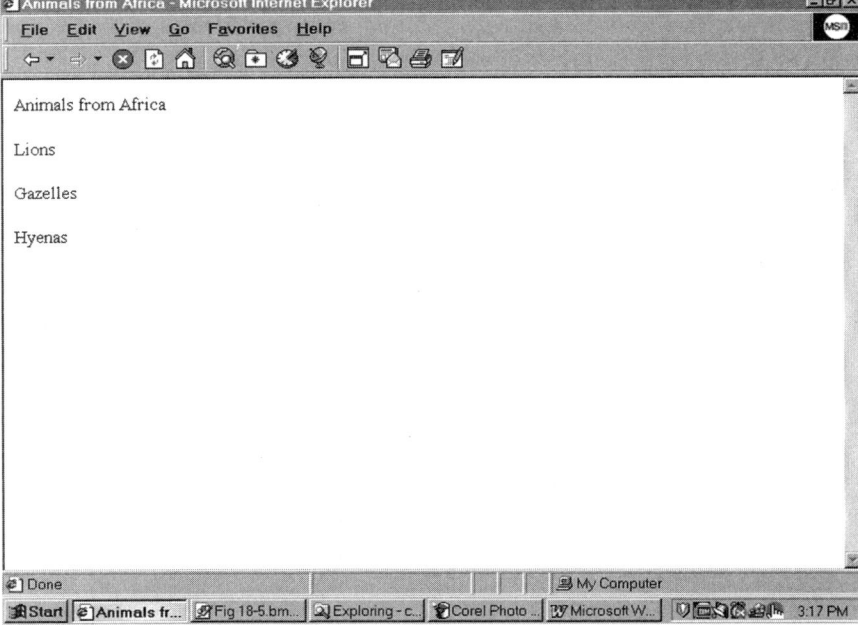

Dynamically Generating an HTML Document from within the Program By far, the most common approach that CGI programs use to get data back to the user's desktop is for the program to dynamically generate HTML. With this approach, the programmer has the ability to control all aspects of the response. (In a variation on this approach, some programs will actually dynamically create the HTML document and store it on the Web server's disk space, then issue a command to the server asking it to send the document to the user.)

The method for doing this is very similar to the technique we used in the previous example to generate a purely text response. The only difference is that we will write the program to output HTML format commands in addition to the actual data being returned.

Processing under CGI

Having defined the input and communications pieces of our robust Web programming model, we are ready to look at the actual programs that do the work.

Types of Programs in the World of the Web

In general, we can place these programs in one of three categories, according to the language they are written in:

- Scripts
- Standard Programming Languages
- Java

We will consider the first two categories of programs here, and save an examination of Java for the next chapter.

What Are Scripts? Scripts are programs written in a special-purpose programming language that has been developed to make it easy for programmers to do certain kinds of simple, repetitive programming tasks with a minimum of trouble. Scripting languages have existed almost as long as computers have, and it is common to find scripts in use on personal computers, on UNIX platforms, and on large mainframe systems.

Because of this, it is also common to find a fair share of scripts in the Web environment.

In the Web environment you will find scripts written in languages like Perl (the most popular of the UNIX Web scripting languages), UNIX shells (like the Korn or Bourne shell), the DOS command language (on the personal computer), REXX (IBM), or even Java-Script. While the syntaxes of these scripting languages may vary, they are basically the same, and they share many characteristics:

1. First, they are high-level languages. This means that they have a very limited number of commands within their syntax, but those commands are very powerful.
2. They are interpretive, or "real-time," languages. In other words, they are created, stored, and executed as simple, easily readable text files, and then interpreted by the operating system and turned into executable code "on-the-fly."
3. They are very easy to learn, write, and use.
4. They are very limited in the number of things they can do.

Scripts represent a large proportion of the total population of Web programming interfaces. This is because they are so easy to write. They are also often used as starting points from which "real" programs are run.

Unfortunately, there are several weaknesses that scripts exhibit which must be taken into account whenever you consider using them. These include the following:

- Scripts are not very secure (not compiled). Since script programs are written and stored in a plain text file format, and are not compiled the way other programming languages are, it is very easy for hackers to identify and modify scripts with no one even being aware of it.

- They are inefficient (unsophisticated and must be interpreted). Besides being easy to read and modify, scripts are also, in general, very inefficient in their execution. This is due in part to the fact that they must be interpreted (the system therefore suffers real-time compiler overhead every time the script is run). Additionally, it is a fact that, in general, scripting languages have a very limited set of sophisticated commands at their disposal, which means that when a script does some work, it will usually be done with a minimum of finesse.

- They are limited in what they can do. As we mentioned earlier, the scripting languages command set is limited. There are simply a lot of

Chapter 18: PPP and CGI

things that you cannot do with a script, but that can easily be done with a more sophisticated language.

What Are Standard Programs? Where scripts are small, high-level, general-purpose programs that are easy to write but limited in functionality, standard programs are exactly the opposite. While there are hundreds of programming languages available today, the most common types of programs that you will see in the Web world include C, C++, .exe, .dll, and the most popular of all, Java. These full languages:

Have extensive collections of commands and a sophisticated collection of rules and syntactical guidelines.

Are typically compiled. In other words they are written in English-like language and converted immediately into machine language by a compiler. This means that the program will run more efficiently, but it also means that the program is harder to change.

Are usually very difficult to learn, but are very powerful and flexible.

Between scripts and programs, the Web developer is provided with an extensive set of programming options to choose from. (From this point forward, we will pretty much use the terms *programs* and *scripts* interchangeably, which is also the way most people use the terms in the real world. When it is critical to make the distinction, we will make note of the fact.)

Where are CGI programs stored? Web servers today run a pretty good number of both scripts and standard programs to get their work done. These programs or scripts are usually referred to collectively as CGI-Scripts (even though they are not necessarily written in one of the scripting languages we mentioned earlier), and are often stored in a special directory called CGI-BIN (holding CGI binary programs). Of course, CGI rules will vary, depending on the platform the server is running on, the type of server it is, and the language the script is written in.

Alternatives to the CGI Standard It is also important to note that CGI is only one of several standards available today. Two of the other standards which are extremely popular are the Netscape Server Application Program Interface (NSAPI) to support Netscape servers and the standard DLL, OLE interfaces, and the ISAPI standard to support Microsoft server activities. In general, however, while the details behind these standards vary considerably, the basic working mechanisms and approaches are the same.

The CGI Runtime Environment

It is important that we, as Web warehousing designers and architects, understand not only how a program does the work it has been assigned to do, but also understand what the consequences of running that program will be for the performance of the system overall. It is not uncommon for the managers of Web sites to enjoy wonderful response times when they allow designers to implement purely HTML-based solutions. These managers find to their chagrin that, when they allow for CGI programming, they could be getting themselves involved in incredibly complex and difficult-to-resolve performance conflicts.

Remember, in most cases, when a Web server schedules a CGI-Script to run, that script will be running on the same machine as the Web server. This means that the more memory, CPU, and disk I/O capacity the CGI-Script takes, the less there will be available for the Web server to retrieve its next HTML page. This also means that the way a CGI-Script runs and the amount of resources it takes up are dependent upon the environment it is running in.

UNIX Task Management   In the UNIX environment, a CGI-Script will run as a distinct process. That means that each time the script is invoked, a new process, with a new pid (process identification), is spun off. This presents some advantages and some disadvantages.

Since each invocation of a script is spun off as a separate process, the system doesn't have to keep track of the status and the workings of each individual script. This means that the architecture for the UNIX-based environment is greatly simplified. Each process manages its own communication through its own stdin and stdout, and the Web server can pass the CGI environmental variables to the program through those mechanisms. In the same manner, the programs or scripts can pass their response back to the server via the same mechanism.

The down side of this arrangement however occurs whenever we get an environment where many people are executing the same CGI-Scripts over and over. In these cases, we will find that the system is using up a lot of system overhead that would be better managed through a multithreading capacity. This, alas, is beyond the ability of most CGI-Scripts (but not beyond the ability of Java).

Windows Task Management As in the UNIX environment, in the Windows NT world, a script is executed as a separate application, which is also invoked and run in its own space. Of course, the Windows NT operating system provides the architect with a lot more options for managing the priority and scheduling of these tasks. Ultimately, however, the need to multithread often-repeated scripts will still be in big demand.

Interestingly enough, since the standard Windows NT environment does not provide for the stdin/stdout capability, environmental variables are passed from the server to the CGI-Script through the use of temporary files. When the program finishes its work, and wants to send the response back to the Web server, then a temporary file is again used.

Provided with the CGI interface definitions, it becomes very easy for the managers of Web sites and the developers of Web-based applications to work together. To write a program to run on the Web, all they have to do is write a program or script that conforms with the CGI standard for the server and platform it is to run on, and they are ready to go!

Database Access under CGI

If you will recall, our CGI program usually resides on the same physical platform as the Web server machines that invoke it. This CGI program, however, although invoked by the Web server, is not actually part of the Web environment as such. It is actually another normal part of the corporate computer systems infrastructure. Thus, the way that these programs gain access to databases will totally depend on the way that the corporate infrastructure has been set up.

In general, however, there are several standard database access configurations that we will need to consider:

1. *Server native database.* In some situations, the database (or other data source) that a program needs to access will be a native system, resident on the same machine as the program (e.g., an Access database or an Excel spreadsheet). In these cases, programming database access will be identical to the way it would be done in any other situation. The only difference would be the coding which allows that program to accept the CGI environmental variables from the Web server and to pass the response back to the server for forwarding to the browser.

2. *ODBC database interface.* In cases when the database is not native, the second most common occurrence will be gaining access

through an ODBC interface. ODBC, the Open Database Connectivity standard, provides for a standardized data access mechanism to dozens of different database products across a wide range of platforms. Through ODBC, the programmer can gain access to any database almost anywhere within the corporate environment (as long as the ODBC interface has been installed on both ends).

3. *Native remote database interface.* Unfortunately, the ODBC interface, while convenient, is not especially the best way to gain access to remote databases. In those situations where performance and efficiency are critical, or where only one type of database is being accessed, it often makes sense to use the standard proprietary interface provided by the vendor. Most major vendors, including Oracle, Informix, Sybase, and DB2, furnish these interfaces. They provide the programmer with the means to gain access to these particular databases in a very efficient manner.

4. *Middleware-driven interface.* Some organizations are lucky enough to have installed any of a large number of sophisticated middleware products that ameliorate the need for direct vendor-provided interfaces, but which function better and more generically than ODBC.

What is particularly nice is that, for the most part, you will usually have many options to choose from when it is time to input the database information.

We now have a much better understanding of each of the parts of the CGI process. We have seen how CGI manages the passing of information and control back and forth from browser to network to Web server to CGI program to the database and back again. Given this information, we now are ready to take a look at some CGI programs to see how they are actually put together.

The Kinds of Work That CGI Programs Do

The way that a program is put together will depend, first and foremost, on the kind of work that you expect it to do. In general, when we talk about CGI programming and the world of Web warehousing, we will be putting together programs which:

Chapter 18: PPP and CGI

- *Run queries.* In many situations, we will be looking at applications that allow the user to input the SQL command themselves. In these cases, our program will need do nothing more than accept the query from the server, send it to the database, accept the answer set from the database, format it, and send it back to the browser again. In these cases, our programs are nothing more than database access managers and data formatters.
- *Build queries.* In other situations, the work of putting database queries together will be done by the program itself. In this case, the program will receive keywords, command words, and other key indicators that tell it the kind of work that will need to be done. Ultimately, the program either will place keywords into variables which are a part of prewritten SQL commands, or will dynamically create queries on the fly.
- *Perform more complicated work.* In some situations, the work to be done by the application will be more complicated than simply accessing data. CGI programs can be used to channel information from a variety of different sources (outside data feeds, public databases, internal document management systems, to name just a few). They can also be used to funnel things back to the browser that are not especially data (video, audio, images, stock tickers, etc.).

Standard CGI Database Program Flow

The writing of a fully functional CGI database accessing program is clearly a complicated exercise. To get a more complete picture of what all of the different components of a CGI program will be, look at Table 18-2. This table shows each of the steps in the process.

Conclusion

In this chapter, we complete our examination of the non-Java forms of database connectivity with a Web browser. In the next chapter we examine the Java programming options in detail, and show how Java solves the problem of getting database data out to a Web user. At that point we

TABLE 18-2

Process Flow for CGI Programming

Step	Name	Comments
1	Determine form method	Determine if the form initiated a GET or POST command
2a	Read QUERY_STRING	If the browser issued a GET, then read in the query string
2b	Read STDIN	If the browser issued a POST, then read in the stdin
3	Process user input	Perform whatever work is required to interpret and prepare the user input
4	Build a database query	Turn the user input into an SQL command
5	Logon to the database	Make the database connection with the database being targeted
6	Submit the query	Send the query to the database
7a	Initiate fetch loop	If the query will yield several response rows, then perform a fetch loop until all rows are retrieved
7b	Read the response	If the query will yield only one row returned, read in the record
8	End database connection	Disconnect from the database
9	Perform postprocessing	Do any additional work necessary to get the data into a usable format
10	Format as HTML and output	Print the response to the user, formatting the response as HTML

will be ready to investigate the issues revolving around Web warehouse design and performance tuning, and see how the different data access approaches provide for very different architectural profiles.

CHAPTER 19

Java

The Alternative Approach to Web Programming

- *What is Java, and where did it come from?*
- *How is it different from the other programming languages?*
- *What are applets, applications, and servlets?*
- *What are the major components of the Java language?*
- *What is the JDK (Java Development Kit)?*
- *What are the Java "packages," and why are they important?*

There isn't a person alive today who has anything to do with computers who hasn't heard of Java. Java is touted as the latest, greatest, and most powerful thing to happen in the computer world since the invention of programming itself.

It is certainly true that Java is a new, interesting, and powerful language. It is also true that there is a lot about the Java language and environment that we, as developers of Web warehousing environments, could care less about. It is also true, however, that there are certain things about Java that we need to know and understand in order to be effective warehouse developers. In this chapter, we will attempt to cut through the many volumes of information about Java and focus on the core collection of useful information.

An Introduction to Java

What is Java? Where did it come from? What makes it so different? And most important, why is it important to us? Let's start with a little history.

A Brief History

Java is an extremely young programming language. It was originally invented by a man named James Gosling who worked at Sun Microsystems. As most of us are aware, Sun is one of the biggest and most famous of the Silicon Valley computer manufacturers. Sun has been responsible for the development of a widely accepted line of UNIX-based computers for business, education, and the engineering community.

Because Sun is in an extremely competitive and volatile high-tech industry where fortunes are made or lost on a moment's notice, it is critical for it to seriously invest in the development of leading-edge technologies that can help it stay ahead of its competition. One of these research and development efforts eventually led to the invention of Java.

It seems that Sun had a systems development project code-named *Green*. It was the job of the developers on the Green team to figure out ways to computerize the new age of "smart" appliances. Although it was the intention of Gosling et al., to develop this capability using C++, they soon discovered that the language had several shortcomings. The result was the invention of a language then called *Oak*. Oak was object-oriented, easy to learn, platform-independent, and had many built-in safety features (a requirement for the programming of appliances that might hurt someone if handled improperly).

Unfortunately for Oak, the automated appliance industry idea fizzled, but Sun saw enough potential within it to resurrect it as the programming language for a new project, called *FirstPerson*. The FirstPerson team, organized in 1992, was supposed to figure out how Sun could help interactive cable television become a household medium.

By this time, the Oak language had started to exhibit many of the characteristics of the Java language as we know it today. Think about it. What was needed was a language which could be downloaded and run on remote devices (specifically the cable box in your front room), and do so in an efficient, secure, and timely manner. So the Oak language continued to grow in sophistication and capability and the real world continued to change.

Once again, fate had other ideas for this fledgling language. The FirstPerson project also stalled and Oak was without a home. But luckily for everyone involved, something else was going on in the computer industry, something much bigger than smart toasters or interactive cable boxes, something so big and so revolutionary that it would change the way people thought about computers, and change the way we use them—something that was so new and different and revolutionary that it would need its own special language to really get off the ground. We are referring, of course, to the creation of the World Wide Web.

While Sun and IBM and everyone else in the computer industry were off trying to figure out where the next great place to put computer technology would be, the Internet suddenly decided to take wings and soar. In 1993, the first Mosaic Web browser hit the Internet, and the World Wide Web phenomenon was well on its way. After the initial shock of the Web and its potential began to wear off, everybody started to scramble, trying to figure out how best to make it work. Although the Internet, CGI, and C++ were a good foundation, developers on the Web soon discovered that these tools were not quite right for the new environment. What was needed was something that could help developers put together systems based on the new distributed processing model that the Web defined, a language that could run anywhere, but would stay connected to other bits and pieces of itself spread willy-nilly around the globe. What was needed was a language that could function just like the Java language functions.

So, not being the types to walk away from a golden opportunity, the management team at Sun revamped the Oak language (a name which could not be used for copyright reasons), and gave it a new name, Java, and a new beginning.

Java Characteristics

Despite its rather humble beginnings and an apparent bit of bad luck, what we now know as the Java programming language has thrust itself into the limelight, and established itself as the COBOL of the twenty-first century. COBOL—which stands for COmmon Business prOgramming Language—was the well-established de facto programming standard for business data processing for several decades. However, since the inception of client/server technology, an environment that COBOL cannot support, the programming industry had been in chaos. Since there was no clear programming language standard that everyone could comply with, it was necessary to learn how to work with literally dozens of languages (a costly and wasteful process). Now all of that is changing. Java is here, and it looks like it's here to stay.

So what exactly is Java, and why is it unique? Let's look at a list of some of the major reasons. Java is powerful because:

1. It is an object-oriented (OO) programming language. People have been aware for some time now of the additional power and flexibility that the object-oriented approach to programming can provide, and Java is OO in spades.[1]

2. It is a safe language. This is critical for a language that has to be used and distributed across national, business, and hardware/ software boundaries. What do we mean by *safe*? We mean several things.

    a. Java has no pointers. One of the nicest little tricks that a programming language can use to increase efficiency are these little things known as *pointers*. A pointer is a programming technique that allows the program direct access to the memory of the computer it is working on, bypassing the programming language and the operating system in the process. While efficient, pointers also make it very easy for programs to do serious damage to the memory of a computer. Because of this potential, the developers of Java have made it impossible for a Java program to do anything like that.

---

[1]For more information about object-oriented technology see Rob Mattison, The Object Oriented Enterprise, published by McGraw-Hill, New York, 1994.

Chapter 19: Java: The Alternative Approach

  b. Java has a bytecode verifier. It has programs that can download themselves to a user's PC and execute themselves there. Although this is certainly a positive feature, in that it is no longer necessary to keep trying to load the latest versions of everything we run, it also means that we run a new kind of risk. What is to prevent someone from modifying the code that we are downloading, thereby turning an otherwise benign program into a destructive one? Java addresses this problem with bytecode verification. A bytecode verifier checks every program that is brought down to your computer before it is executed. This verifier ensures that the program is sound and safe to run. The chances of downloading a Java program and having it crash your system are rare because of this.

  c. Java applets cannot open, read, or write to native files. Another security measure has been built into the Java Web browser–programming world. When a Java program runs on a browser, it will never be allowed to read to, write from, or delete files on your own computer's file system. Thus, Java cannot house any of the nasty "hard drive eraser" programs that we hear so much about.

  d. Java windows are safe. Yet another safety feature built into Java has to do with the windows that pop up on the screen. In many situations in the past, unscrupulous programmers have been able to write "shadow programs"—programs that look just like the program you are supposed to be running, but that actually trick you into giving away your passwords, credit card numbers, and other important information. To prevent this kind of tampering, Java code is developed so that Java can place no window on the screen unless the Java logo is displayed. Therefore, the user can be assured that the program that is running has been through the bytecode verifier and is safe to run.

3. It is platform-independent. Because of Java's unique execution architecture, it can be run on almost any computer platform (and because of its history, you could probably run it on your toaster, dishwasher, and cable box as well).

4. It can run multithreaded. One of the biggest boons to computer systems development in recent years has been the creation of multiprocessors (computers with more than one CPU) and the leveraging of a capability known as *multithreading*. Multithreading

is the process of allowing a program to initiate and monitor several different "threads" of work at the same time. (For example, you could get the computer to check a database for a phone number, compute a paycheck amount, and write a payroll record to the payroll file, all at the same time.) While many operating systems are multithreaded, very few programming languages are. By allowing programmers to code multithreaded tasks, the Java language opens all kinds of new doors to the world of efficient and flexible programming.

5. It can be self-propagating. This nice feature of Java is a direct result of its legacy in the appliance and cable television days. A Java program can copy itself to a remote computer and execute itself without any intervention by the user. In fact, that program can then call down other programs that run themselves as well, ad infinitum. Thus, more and more work can be done for users in a way that is transparent to them but that can capitalize on their own hardware and software.

6. Java is an extremely powerful, flexible, and versatile language. You can use it not only to display data, but to manipulate sound, video, audio, and telephone messages.

7. It is industrial-strength. Unlike many of the earlier languages of this type, Java is built for production systems development. It does not exhibit a lot of the "flaky" and undependable behavior of other languages.

8. It is programmer-friendly. While certainly not the language for a novice computer user, as programming languages go, Java is relatively simple and straightforward, avoiding many of the complexities of earlier languages.

9. It runs on browsers, servers, and mainframes. You can write a Java program and run it on any or all of your systems. This provides for a consistency of approach and efficiency of effort unknown since the days of mainframes, VSAM, and COBOL.

10. With Java you can write the kind of Web application that you need—thin client, fat client, no client, all client, or client/server. As we saw in the previous chapter on the CGI approach, there were many limitations to what you could do, depending on the architecture. With Java, you can do it any way you want. You can write applications that function as CGI applications do, with "thin" clients handling display work and "fat" servers doing the bulk of the

processing. Then again, you might want to reverse it and write your applications so that all of the work is done on the client machine, and none is done on the server. Or you might put a system together that blends the two approaches. With Java, it is up to you.

11. Java puts states back on the Web. You may recall that the Internet, and therefore the Web, function in basically a stateless mode, with no dependent or logical connection between browser and server, and that statelessness can cause problems in certain situations. With Java, you can do something about that. With Java, you can write truly state-dependent programs that provide for full client/server transaction control for your Web applications. This is critical for many business applications and some Web warehousing needs.

The Java Runtime Environment

So, enough of all of the hype. Let's just see what the Java language is really all about. In this section we will look at some of the operational and architectural characteristics of Java, and actually examine some simple Java programs. In the next section, we will take a closer look at the components and toolkits that make up the Java programming environment. Then, in the last section we will take a very detailed look at the most important aspect of Java (for us, anyway): the way Java works with external files and databases.

Java the Language

At first glance, the Java language looks pretty much like any other compilable programming language. If you are familiar with the C or C++ programming language, then you will have very little trouble finding your way around a Java program.

Basic Organization of a Program A Java "program" (application or applet) is actually a collection of classes (miniprograms) that have been gathered together into one common file. These classes are just like programs (or free-standing subroutines) in that they each have sections for the declaration of variables, a declaration of subroutines (methods), and the organization of logical execution code (commands that move, copy, add, subtract, string, and unstring data as well as commands that test conditions, such as IF, THEN, ELSE, CASE, and DO UNTIL). These classes are organized into a logical flow that makes it possible for them to accomplish the work that the programmer wants them to do.

A typical application or applet starts out with the identification of any external libraries or files that the programmer wants included. Thus programmers can make the vast collections of prewritten commands and classes available for their programs to use. The simple IMPORT FILENAME command makes an external file or library available to the program for execution.

The different classes, or miniprogramming modules, that will make up the program are declared after the import commands. Each class definition includes:

- The declaration of variables
- The declaration of methods (subroutines)
- Procedural code (the work that the program does)

These different sections of the program are structured through the clever use of the {,}, (,) and (;) symbols. When all of this coding is complete, the programmer will be ready to compile the program and run it.

Java Is Both Compiled and Interpreted Every Time! It is at this point—the point at which we make our program ready for execution—that we see one of the big differences between Java and other programming languages.

In most computer programming languages the source code (the program that the programmer has written in English) is *compiled*—that is, converted from human language into computer language. The output of this process is a file called a *runtime module* or *object code*. It is the object code, written in the computer's language, that can then be placed on the computer and executed.

With Java, however, things are done differently. In the Java world, the source code, stored as a .java file, is compiled and turned into what is called a *bytecode file*. Bytecodes cannot be executed on a computer without help. But they also cannot be read and modified by humans. Our bytecode file is then taken to the computer that will run the program, and interpreted by another program, which finishes the process of converting it into computer language and executes it on the fly.

Although it may seem that this process adds some unnecessary complexity to our working environment, it is actually just the opposite. The process of creating bytecode files and exporting them to different platforms for final compilation and execution actually saves programmers all sorts of time and trouble.

Benefits of Bytecode Interpretation   Under the traditional mode of computer program preparation and execution, it is necessary for the programmer to know in advance which platform the program will run on. Then, when programming is complete, a special compiler for the system that the code will ultimately run on is used to create the object code specific to that platform.

While this approach works well in a world where a programmer need worry only about compiling programs for one or two platforms, imagine the nightmare this scenario creates for a programmer trying to develop code for the Web. In the Internet/Web environment, there are literally hundreds of different kinds of computers that a Web browser might be running on. To make a Web program usable, therefore, a programmer would need to have a compiler handy for each and every type of platform that might ask for its services and then compile the program hundreds of times, one time for each compiler, each time the code was changed.

Worse yet, the Web server would need to keep track of the different kinds of platforms that user requests come from. Then, when someone asks that some code be downloaded, the server would need to check for and send the right copy of the object code, the object code created by the compiler specific to that platform.

Java the Platform

So Java is a language that is compiled, turned into bytecode, and then interpreted and run on the targeted system. The process of turning Java code into bytecode is in fact called the compilation process, and the Java compiler (named javac in the Windows and UNIX environments) is used to get the job done.

The process of turning that bytecode into executable code, however, varies depending on where you want to run it. The environment that actually interprets and executes Java bytecode is referred to generically as the Java virtual machine, but you have different kinds of virtual machines for different kinds of environments. The general process of turning Java source code into a program that is actually run on a computer somewhere is therefore a many-step process. Figure 19-1 shows a diagram of these steps.

Figure 19-1

Preparing and running a Java program.

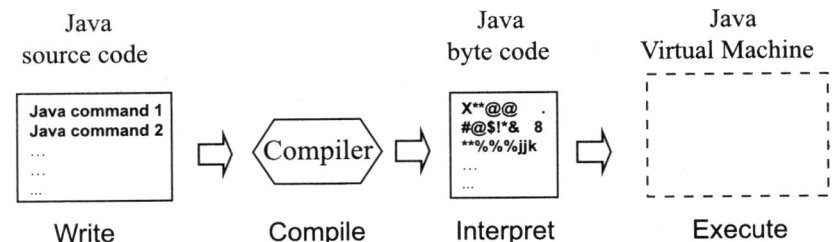

In general, there are two different kinds of environments that we may want to run a Java program in. Those are Web environments and non-Web environments.

Java on the Web Because so much of the work that people expect Java to perform has to do with Web processing, it should be no surprise that there are special rules and procedures for preparing and executing Java programs in this environment.

First, when you create Java programs for the Web, you don't call them programs or applications, you call them *applets*. An applet is a Java program that has been written with the idiosyncrasies of the Web in mind.

Second, when it comes time to prepare the applet to run on a Web page, you compile it, just like you would any other Java program, but you don't do anything else with it. In fact, you just send the applet, in its bytecode form, off to the Web browser, and let the Web browser worry about how to interpret and run it.

But how does the Web browser get the code interpreted and run? It is very simple; the Web browser must have a Java virtual machine built into it. (That is why you will see that there are some browsers that *can* run Java and some that cannot. If a Web browser is not Java-compliant it means that it has no Java virtual machine built into it, and therefore cannot interpret and run the bytecodes being sent to it.)

While making it a requirement that a Web browser have a Java virtual machine built into it before it can run Java code may seem limiting is in fact not that big of an issue. All the major Web browser manufacturers (specifically Netscape, Microsoft, and Sun) are already producing Java-compliant browsers and will continue to do so.

Writing and Running Java Applets

Let's take a few minutes to look at how this whole process will work in a Web environment. As we already stated, the Java applets will run over

Chapter 19:   Java: The Alternative Approach

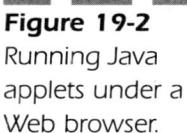
Figure 19-2
Running Java applets under a Web browser.

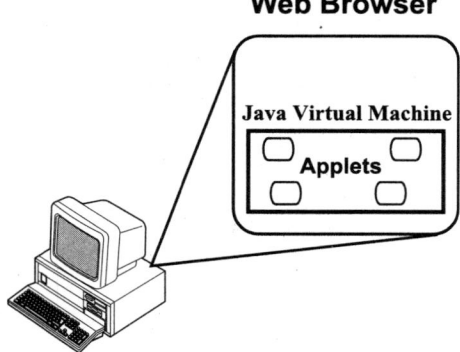

the Web only if the Web browser has a Java virtual machine built into it. See Figure 19-2. For a better look at how this works, let's write a simple program called Hi Mom! and see how we can get it to run.

Coding the Hi Mom! Applet   In Figure 19-3 you can see all of the code necessary to make our Hi Mom! applet work. Notice how this program works: there are 5 lines of code, which do the following:

1. Import the java.applet.Applet file (which makes it possible for this Java program to run under a browser)
2. Import the java.awt.Graphics file (which brings in the graphical display commands we want to exhibit)
3. Contain the definition for one class, the HiMom class
4. Contain one declaration (Graphics g), which tells the program to use the letter g to call the graphics display functions
5. Produce one line of code, which sends the words "Hi Mom!" and the size parameters 10 and 25 to the graphics program

So, what this program will do is display the words "Hi Mom!" wherever we place it on a Web page.

Figure 19-3
Coding the Hi Mom! applet.

```
import java.applet.Applet;
import java.awt.Graphics;
         public class HiMom extends Applet
              {public void paint(Graphics g)}
              {g.drawString("Hi Mom !!!",25,10);}
```

Placing the Applet on the Web Page Our next problem is trying to figure out how to get our applet to run in the right place on our Web page. This is done through the simple modification of the HTML language to include a tag pair for applets. The syntax for this tag is

```
<APPLET CODE = "insert applet name here," insert optional size/display parameters here>
```

Figure 19-4 shows an example of how we can place this applet onto a page called `himom.html`. As you can see from this example, our Web page will display the words: "This is just a chance to say:" and then execute the `Hi Mom!` applet.

The `Hi Mom!` Applet in Action Figure 19-5 shows the `himom.html` page displayed on a Netscape Navigator browser screen. Notice how the words "Hi Mom!" show up underneath the "This is just a chance to say:." That's because of the `<P> </P>` paragraph tag pairs, which put the applet on a separate line. Notice too how small the words "Hi Mom!" are on the screen. That's because this small print is the default for browser.

JAR (Java Archive) Files Of course, the real applets that you will write for a Web page will certainly be more complicated than this one. And usually these applications will include pictures, sounds, videos, and all sorts of other objects.

Unfortunately, when you start making applets that are very large and very complex, with lots of different files that need to get called in to make them work right, you get into a problem. As any Web HTML programmer will tell you, keeping track of all of the different pieces of a Web application and remembering to keep them all together so that when you move one, you move all the other parts as well, can get to be a serious problem.

Figure 19-4
Placing the Hi Mom! applet on your Web page.

```
<HTML>
<HEAD>
<TITLE> The Hi Mom Display Page </TITLE>
</HEAD>
This is just a chance to say :
<P>
<APPLET CODE = "HiMom.class">
</APPLET>
</P>
</BODY>
</HTML>
```

Chapter 19: Java: The Alternative Approach

Figure 19-5
The Hi Mom!
applet under
Netscape.

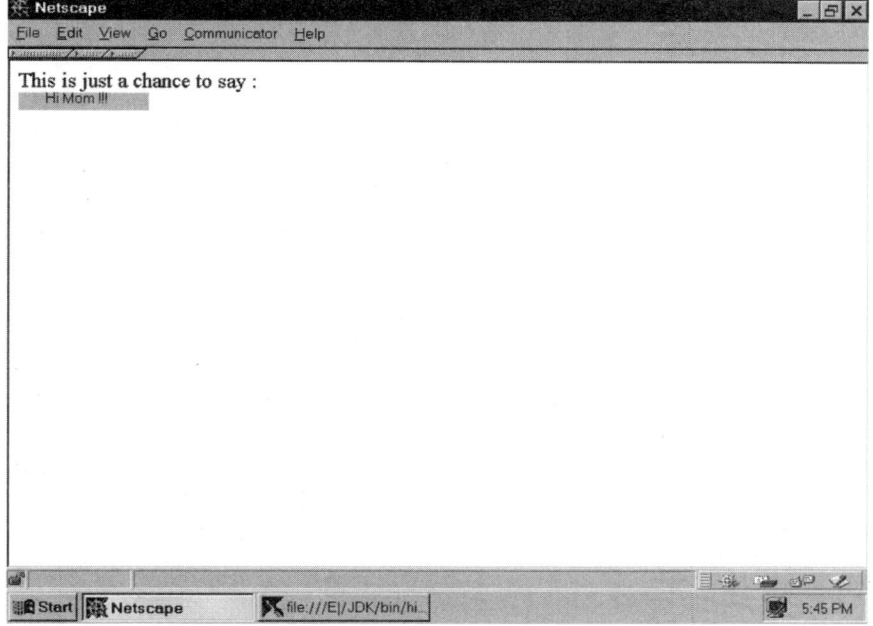

For example, let's say we make an applet called <Hi, my name is Rover!> This applet displays a message that says "Hello, my name is Rover!" In addition to this message, the applet shows a picture of Rover himself. So we write the applet, test it, place it on an HTML page, and run it and—blam!—your program doesn't work. What happened? Well, unless you were thinking ahead when you moved the HTML page to the Web server, you probably forgot to move the file with the picture of Rover when you moved the rest of the code. Therefore when the applet tried to pull in the picture and display it on the screen, nothing happened. This is a common problem, and one that causes untold hours of grief for Webmasters. As more and more objects get included in your applets, the problem gets worse.

To help programmers avoid these problems, the developers of Java created a special kind of file format called JAR. The JAR (Java ARchive) file format allows programmers to put all of the files called by an applet together into one special container. That way, when you move an applet, all you have to do is remember to move its JAR file and you no longer have to worry about keeping track of everything. Not only does the JAR file mechanism simplify the process of building and moving applets around, but also compresses these files, so it saves space at the same time.

When developing the JAR format, Java creators knew that it was important that it be:

Compact. It uses standard compression routines to save space.
Platform-independent. A JAR can go wherever an applet goes.
Unicode supportive. The textual information in headers is consistent.
Extensible. New features can be added.

JAR is a powerful and extremely useful feature within the applet development environment.

Writing and Running Non-Web-Based Java Applications

In the previous section we look at the coding and execution of Java applets in a Web environment. But what about running Java in a non-Web environment? What about running it just on any old computer to do "boring" non-Web work? The process is basically the same, but there are some differences that we need to be aware of.

First, a Java program that runs in a non-Web browser environment is referred to as a *Java application,* not an *applet.* This application is written, compiled, and turned into bytecode, just like any other Java program. However, when it comes time to run this program, we have several options to choose from. There are actually several non-browser-type Java virtual machines to choose from, depending on the work you want to do. For our purposes we will work with the generic Windows-based interpreter called Java. Figure 19-6 shows a diagram that recaps our under-

Figure 19-6
Running Java applications on a standard server.

Native Unix or DOS Environment

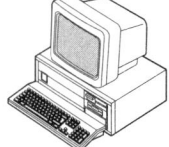

1. Compile Java Code with JAVAC
2. Run program with JAVA Interpreter

Chapter 19: Java: The Alternative Approach

standing of how to run a Java application in a non-Web browser environment.

Coding the Hi Mom! Application You can see in Figure 19-7 the code for our Hi Mom! application. The purpose of this application is the same as it was for the applet, to display the "Hi Mom!" message on the screen. (In this case, the screen will be the DOS window.)

Notice that this application only has three lines. That's because we don't have to do as much coding if we don't have to worry about graphical display. There are no import file lines because this program has no requirements for special libraries. The rest of the program is straightforward. The lines represent:

1. The class, which will be called himomapp
2. The main routine for the program
3. The System.out.println command, which routes our message to the stdout for the environment

Running the Hi Mom! Application Once the program is complete, we are ready to compile, interpret, and run it. In this case, we will want to run it on a plain old PC from the DOS prompt screen.

Figure 19-8 shows us the complete sequence that we go through to prepare this program. We review what is happening at each line:

1. We issue the <EDIT himomapp.java> command. This will take us into the MS-DOS editor program and allow us to write the program as you see it in Figure 19-7. After exiting that editor, our program file called himomapp.java will be saved in the directory and be ready to compile.
2. We execute the Java compiler (javac) and tell it to compile the himomap.java program. If there are no errors during the compile stage, then the program will return us to the DOS prompt.
3. We run the bytecode file called himomapp, using the DOS Java interpreter (called Java). By typing Java and the bytecode file name, we initiate the interpretation process.

Figure 19-7
Coding the Hi Mom! application.

```
class himomapp
   {public static void main(String[]args)
      {System.out.println("This is just a chance to say Hi
   Mom !!!");}
```

Figure 19-8
Output of the Hi Mom! application.

```
From the DOS prompt
C:\> edit himomapp.java
C:\> javac himomapp.java
C:\> java himomapp
This is just to say Hi Mom !!!
C:\>
```

4. We see the output of our program, the "This is just to say Hi Mom!" message.

Obviously, the size, complexity, and nature of real, production Java applications are much more extensive than these examples. They do, however, give you a good basic idea of how it all works.

Servers and Servlets There is another side to the world of Java, which we don't spend a lot of time with here: using Java to write servers. For example, the Java language was used to write the Sun Microsystems' server software. When Java is used to write servers (even servers like network servers, file servers, and security servers), then Java programs can also be written as special programs called *servlets*. The syntax for servlets is slightly different than it is for applets or applications, but the basic principles are the same.

Components of the Java Language

Given this solid basic overview of the Java programming environment, let's examine the many different facets of the language, and the way that they are organized. In this section we look at the Java development kit and the Java libraries and packages. In the next section, we explore a few of the libraries/packages of the most interest to us, namely Beans, the I/O package, and JDBC.

The Java Development Kit

When you create a new language in a new development environment, and you need to make it easy for programmers to learn to use it as quickly as possible, then you need a way to get as much useful documentation and sample code and as many useful utilities and toolkits into

Chapter 19: Java: The Alternative Approach

their hands as possible. That is exactly what the Java development kit (JDK) is. The kit, prepared and distributed by Sun, is free of charge to any programmer brave enough to take on the world of Java program development. If you would like to download a copy for yourself, you can find it at the Sun Microsystems' Java Web site at http://java.sun.com/.

For those who don't want to go through all of the trouble, here is what the kit includes:

- *The Java compiler.* A copy of the javac program, which turns Java source code into bytecode
- *Runtime interpreter.* A copy of the Java program, which provides for the real-time interpretation of Java bytecode
- *Applet viewer.* An application that will allow the programmer to see how applets will look before placing them on a Web page and displaying them via a browser
- *Debugger.* A copy of the `jdb` program, which will help the programmer debug applets and applications
- *Applet demos.* A vast assortment of fully functional applications and applets that will give any programmer a good starting point for learning the Java language
- *Other items.* Miscellaneous items such as a class file disassembler (which disassembles executable Java files), a header and stub file generator (which is used to generate those parts of a file necessary to run Java methods in C programs), and a documentation generator (which generates API documentation directly from Java source code)

Armed with all of this help, a programmer can get started on the road to Java programming with relative ease.

Core Java API Packages

Of course, the Java language does a lot more than the simple output of display lines that our earlier example showed. In reality, you can use Java to do almost anything you can do with a computer.

Unfortunately, when you have so many different options and capabilities that can all be made available through one programming language, it can get pretty difficult to organize and keep track of it all. To help ameliorate that problem, and to make it easy for people to find those parts of the language that they need, the Java language has been organized into packages. Each package includes all the different objects, classes, interfaces, exception definitions and error definitions that are a part of what is known collectively as the Java language. The packages are organized into logical groupings and are categorized as either standard packages (the major foundational packages that make up the language) or standard extension packages (several packages that define additional functionalities). In this section we review the standard package set (Language, Utilities, Networking, Windowing and AWT, and Standard I/O). In the next section, we review just a few of the extensions, including Beans and JDBC.

Language The language package, `java.lang`, provides all the classes that make up the core programming language itself. Included in `java.lang` are the object class (the superclass for all objects), data types (Boolean, character, double, float, integer, long), math (addition, multiplication, etc.), String (for the management of text strings), System (to access system resources from within the program), Runtime (to access runtime resources from within the program), and Thread (for the creation and coordination of thread activities). So, basically, the programming language core of Java is found in the language package.

Utilities The utilities package includes several miscellaneous utilitarian functions—things like Date (for the manipulation of current date, time, and date/time math), Data Structure (for the management of data within programs), Random (for the generation of random numbers), and others.

Networking This package provides network interface and communications support. It includes commands and classes such as

- *InetAddress classes,* which model an IP address and provide tools to help the programmer find out things about that address
- *URL classes* for the management and manipulation of URLs
- *Socket classes* for the creation and manipulation of networking sockets, the method used to establish direct connections between two programs over the network
- *ContentHandler,* a framework for handling the different Internet data types—i.e., for MIME types management

Windowing and AWT This package contains all the classes that make it possible for a programmer to use Java to manipulate a windowing environment. AWT, which stands for the Advanced Windowing Toolkit, includes the following classes: Graphical (drawing on the screen), Layout Management [controlling the physical layout of objects (borders, etc.)], Font (for the display of different printer fonts), Dimension (for the control of size, shape, and physical dimensions), and MediaTracker (for the tracking of media that have traveled over the network).

Standard I/O Of particular interest to us are the classes that make up the Standard I/O package. This package covers the commands that define the ways in which a standard Java program views external data sources and manages the reading and writing of those sources. We get an in-depth look at this package later in this chapter.

Java API Standard Extensions

In addition to the standard packages, there are several additional packages that greatly expand the breadth and depth of the Java language. There are many, many extensions to the Java language, most of which are not applicable to our discussion. However, there are a few standard extensions that are. These include the Enterprise extensions, (for database and remote access), Commerce (for Web business), Management (for integrated network management), Server (for server-side applications), Media [for 2-D, 3-D, video, audio, MIDI (Musical Instrument Digital Interface), telephony, etc.], Security (for security), and Java Beans (for componentized application development).

Enterprise Extensions—JDBC, RMI, and IDL Probably the most interesting set of extensions as far as we are concerned is the Enterprise extension set. The packages defined within these extensions provide the Java programmer with several capabilities that make it easy to manipulate information in a remote mode. These capabilities make it easy for the Java programmer to reach into the many different places where Web warehousing data may be stored, especially into legacy systems and legacy databases. Included within the Enterprise extensions definitions are:

JDBC (Java DataBase Connectivity). This package provides programmers with a standardized set of classes for the management of remote relational database objects. Included are commands for making connections to databases, submitting queries, defining cursors, and even executing stored procedures. These JDBC connections make it possible for Java programmers to work directly with Oracle, Informix, Sybase, DB2, and other relational databases in a relatively transparent manner. JDBC also provides for ODBC compatibility.

RMI (Remote Method Invocation). This capability makes it possible for Java programs to work interactively with programs running on other systems. Through RMI, the Java program can develop programs to trigger jobs on remote legacy systems and manage those programs' output in whatever way the Java program needs to.

IDL (Interface Definition Language). This set of APIs makes it possible to connect Java client programs to network servers running on other platforms. IDL provides an industry-standard way to transparently connect Java client programs to corporate legacy systems. Java IDL clients can be applications or applets.

Commerce The Commerce API contains a complete set of tools to develop applications for managing the processes of shopping, buying, selling, performing financial transactions, and conducting other forms of business via a Web/Java interface. Commerce API components include:

- *Infrastructure.* An architectural framework
- *Information database.* Repository for user transaction information
- *Payment cassettes.* Software modules that define a protocol for making electronic payments
- *Service cassettes.* Software modules that support value-added financial services (like financial analysis and tax preparation)
- *Administrative interfaces.* For the user, to help in the retrieval of administrative information

Management The Management API provides support for the management of integrated network systems. Included are modules for the support of:

- *Admin View Module (AVM).* An extension of the AWT, enhanced to provide support for graphs, charts, and other types of management reporting vehicles
- *Base object interfaces.* Core object types used to support distributed resources and services
- *Managed container interfaces.* Provides a method for the grouping together of similarly managed objects

Chapter 19: Java: The Alternative Approach

- *Managed notification interfaces.* Define a core of managed event notification interfaces
- *Managed data interfaces.* Provide a means of linking managed object attributes to relational databases under JDBC, and provide a transparent link between managed resources and external databases
- *Managed protocol interfaces.* Provide interfaces for the use of Java security APIs and Java RMI
- *Applet integration interfaces.* Allow applets to be integrated with the management core

Server API This API provides standards for the creation of Java programs for various kinds of shared-resource servers. For example, when you use Java to write a Web server (such as the Sun Microsystems' Hot Java server) or any other kind of server (such as a network server or commerce server), you would use the Server API set to do it. Included in the definition of the Server API are servlets (which are basically applets that work with a Java-based server).

Media API The media API set was established to greatly enhance the very limited alternative media capabilities of native Java [namely, GIF, JPEG (graphics), and AU (sounds)]. Included in the Media API are classes that model media types such as full-motion video, audio, 2-D and 3D graphics, and telephony. This API set includes:

- *Media Framework API.* Manages low-level timing of media applications
- *2-D Graphics API.* Includes extensions to AWT for the enhancement of print and other media
- *3-D Graphics API.* Supports high-performance VRML
- *Animation API.* For animation support
- *Video API.* For video images
- *Audio.* For sound
- *MIDI (Musical Instrument Digital Interface) API.* For musical pieces
- *Share API.* Support for synchronization and session management
- *Telephony API.* For telephone interface, teleconferencing, and caller ID

Java Beans Last but not least among the extensions to the standard Java package is Java Beans. The Beans extensions promise a long-awaited revolution in the way applications are programmed in the business world by bringing truly reusable software objects into the mainstream.

A Closer Look at Some Critical Extension APIs

While all the extensions that we have talked about have some bearing on our efforts to design, implement, tune, and troubleshoot Web warehousing systems, certain APIs deserve special attention because of their critical importance to the work we will be doing. We therefore take a closer look at a few of them.

A Closer Look at Java Beans

For over 30 years now, the developers of application programming languages have had a dream. The dream has gone under different names at different times, but basically, it went something like this: "If only there was a way to mass-produce programs the way we mass-produce other kinds of products. If only we could build programs out of interchangeable parts, instead of having to build each program from scratch every time." It is in response to this dream that the Java Beans environment was developed.

Java Beans (or simply Beans) are software components, built using the Java language, that are reusable. (In other words, if I write an applet, and build it in a way that is easy for someone else to pick it up and plug it into a program as a subroutine, then I have successfully built a Bean.)

The developers of Java realized that by simply imposing some additional structure and constraints around their environment and their language, they could produce the long-sought programming goal of reusable code and mass-producible applications. And so, the Java Beans API was born.

Of course, just because you are creating a lot of standardized code, according to a standard set of APIs, doesn't mean in and of itself that the much sought-after reusability will be achieved. No, we will need a little more help than that. Therefore, we also find that the Beans environment includes visually based programming tools (tools that allow programmers

Chapter 19: Java: The Alternative Approach   481

to point and click while looking for the code modules they need and then do simple cut and paste operations to make their programs a reality).

By combining the platform-independent and powerful nature of Java with the flexibility and ease of use of visually based, object-oriented programming techniques, the creators of Java and Java Beans are betting that they have finally created the ultimate programming environment.

Components of the Beans Environment   Included in the definition of the Beans API are:

- *GUI-merging APIs.*   Provide the mechanisms that allow programmers to merge graphical user interface (GUI) elements with a container document (Web page written in HTML). These APIs allow additional features to be added to the base Web page (container document) without having to rebuild it.

- *Persistence APIs.*   Provide for the storage and retrieval of objects within a container document (Web page). The Web page itself is stateless and, therefore, remembers nothing about the things the user selected on the screen a few minutes ago. The persistence APIs change that and make it possible for the page to remember a user's selections from one transaction to the next.

- *Event-handling APIs.*   Impose an additional layer of event-handling capabilities on top of the already robust AWT event-handling set.

- *Introspection APIs.*   Make it easy for development tools to "look at the insides" of a Bean without forcing the programmer to disassemble it.

- *Application-builder support API.*   Provides the overhead necessary for the editing and manipulating of components at run time.

Although still in its infancy, it is clear that the Web development world of the future and, consequently, the world of Web warehouse development and architecture, will not only be Java-based, but Java Bean-based as well.

The I/O Package up Close

No discussion of the warehousing of information in a Web environment would be complete without a review of the specifics of how the Java language manages standard I/O. While the JDBC package, which we will consider next, defines the way relational databases are handled by Java, it is clear that we will also need to understand how the base-level I/O will be handled if we are going to be able to handle any and all situations that may arise. As you may recall, the standard I/O handling package (named Java.IO) is part of the core Java standard API set.

The File Class The first thing we need to understand is how exactly Java views and manages files. Files themselves are defined to the Java program via the File class. This class includes methods such as:

getName()	Gets the name of a file and returns it as a string
.exists()	Tells whether a program exists or not
.canWrite(), .canRead()	Tell whether the file can be written to or read from
.mkdir()	Makes a directory
.delete()	Deletes a file
.renameTo()	Renames a file
.list()	Returns a list of filenames

By using the File class, programs can exert full control over their operating system–based file environment.

Reading Files with `FileInputStream` While the standard I/O package defines many classes, many of them are concerned with reading and writing data from keyboards, buffers, and other non-file-based sources. Our concern is only with file access, and here the class options are limited.

The `FileInputStream` class identifies a file that the program wants to read from. The syntax is simply:

```
FileInputStream("filename");
```

The in.read() method is then used to read the actual data out of the file. (Be forewarned, the reading of data from a file with Java is done in the same way as reading into a C or C++ program would be. That means you read data in as a stream, one byte at a time. The program logic is responsible for the building of records, fields, etc. This can result in some interesting I/O management routines.)

So, if we want to read a file called animals.txt into our program, we would code:

```
FileInputStream("animal.txt");
.in.Read(buf, 0,64)
```

where buf is the string that we defined to hold input records, and 0 and 64 provide additional starting and ending position and buffer utilization information.

Writing Files with `FileOutputStream` Writing files in the Java environment is handled much the same way. The class called `FileOutputStream` is used, and its syntax is:

```
FileOutputStream("filename");
```

Not too surprisingly, it uses the `out.write` method to output a record. Writing out to the `animals.txt` file might look like this:

```
FileOutputStream("animals.txt");

.out.write(buf);
```

where `buf` has once again been predefined as the string that will hold the record to be output.

Reading and Writing with `RandomAccessFile` Reading from and writing to files with the `FileInputStream` and `FileOutputStream` was improved significantly with the `RandomAccessFile` class. This class contains a long list of methods, which include most of the methods that you will find in both the `FileInputStream` and the `FileOutputStream` classes—for example, the read and write methods. This means that when you make use of the `RandomAccessFile` class you do not have to go through the trouble of calling in two classes to do all your I/O work.

In addition to this convenience, there is the powerful `getFilePointer()` method, which returns the current position of the file pointer in a file. This means that you can do simple random-access operations as you would with a simple database program. Accompanying `.getFilePointer` is `.seek()`, a method that allows you to skip ahead to the explicit place in the file you wish to move to.

While it is certainly more helpful and friendly than the other two classes, in general the standard I/O package leaves a lot to be desired. To say the least, programming standard I/O in the Java world looks pretty difficult and fairly complicated. Is it any wonder then that programmers love to work with relational databases?

Conclusion

At this point, we have covered just about all the basic information about Java that we need to know in order to get around in the environment. In the next chapter, we look specifically at how Java works with databases.

CHAPTER 20

JDBC

Accessing Databases with Java

- *What is JDBC?*
- *How do I get access to a database from within a Java program?*
- *What kinds of databases can I access with Java?*
- *What are the different database connectivity options?*
- *Can I use ODBC with Java?*
- *Are there any alternatives to JDBC and Java?*
- *What are DHTML and DXL, and how do they work?*

JDBC

Now, finally, we come to the crowning glory of the world of Java file and database manipulation, JDBC (Java Database Connectivity). The JDBC API defines the ways that a Java application or applet will work with "real" databases. (You may recall that JDBC is part of the Enterprise extensions to the standard Java API packages.)

As you might well imagine, Java started out without any kind of database interface at all. Originally, the only kind of file I/O that could be done with Java had to utilize the standard I/O package. By 1996, however, JavaSoft (the company that now manages Java development) realized that if Java was to become a true production language, then a database interface was required. Thus was born the idea for JDBC.

The current JDBC standard is based on the X/Open SQL CLI (call level interface). It is a low-level API supporting ANSI SQL-92 at the entry level.

Databases That You Can Access with JDBC

Since JDBC conforms to SQL-92, it is clear that there are many databases it can access. Included in this inventory are:

- *OODBMS*. Object-oriented database management systems
- *OORDBMS*. Object-oriented relational database management systems
- *RDBMS*. A plethora of relational database management systems, including:
  Oracle
  Sybase
  DB2
  Informix
- *ODBC*. Open database connectivity databases (which can include many nonrelational DBMSs and nondatabases as usable data sources). ODBC data sources can include:
  Spreadsheets
  Documents
  Notes databases
  Windows-based databases
  Legacy databases such as IMS, VSAM, and IDMS

The Database Access Process

Whether the language is Java, COBOL, or any other, the same basic, logical steps must be followed if a program is going to gain access to a database. Those steps include the following:

1. Include the JDBC classes and methods in the program. This will make it possible for JDBC to work.

2. Identify the database to the program. The first thing you have to do is tell the program how to find the database when it is needed. In the old days of data processing this was easy, since databases and programs ran on the same platforms. Nowadays, however, finding the database is not always that simple. Under Java, we use a special form of URL: the database URL.

3. Load the database drivers. Databases are software programs that have been built to meet the information management needs of a wide variety of individuals and systems. Because there are so many different kinds of databases, however, there is usually quite a bit of difference in the way a program can access and manipulate them. To make it easier for programs to hook up with different kinds of databases at different times, the developers of those databases have created customized interface programs called *drivers*. A database driver makes it possible for the developer of an application to simply "plug into" that database automatically. All you need to do is load the driver into your program and use it. Java programs are no exception to the rule. After figuring out where the database is, we then have the program load up the drivers that will allow it to work with that database. Drivers are loaded with the `forName` class.

4. Create a connection. Once all the identification and interface definition issues are resolved, our program will be ready to actually make a connection with the database and establish its own "thread," or working session. The Java program must issue a command that makes a connection with the database and opens up the lines of communication between them. This is accomplished with the `getConnection()` method.

5. Create and prepare an SQL statement. We accomplish this with the `createStatement()` method.

6. Submit the SQL statement for execution. Only after all the previously mentioned steps have been completed can the program actu-

ally submit the statement for execution. This is done in Java with the `executeQuery()` method.

7. Process the database results. As any programmer of database access knows, the reading of records out of a database can be a challenging task for a programming language. JDBC arranges for this operation with the ResultSet interface.

Table 20-1 provides a listing of each of these major steps in the database access process, and the corresponding Java JDBC method, interface, or class involved in its execution.

The `java.sql` Package

Before we dive into the details of the actual coding of JDBC database access, let's take a moment to review the different components of the `java.sql` (also known as the JDBC package). The JDBC package is composed of much the same kinds of components as the other packages. It includes objects, classes, methods, and interfaces. Some of the most critical of these are the `DriverManager` class (the only major instantiated class to be found in JDBC) and the major interfaces (Driver, Connection, Statement, and ResultSet).

TABLE 20-1

Program Flow for a Java Database Access Program

Step	JDBC Handling
Identify the JDBC classes and methods to the program	`import java.sql.*`
Identify the database to the program	Database URL
Load database drivers	`forName()`
Make connection to database / start thread	`getConnection()`
Create and prepare an SQL statement	`createStatement()`
Execute the query	`executeQuery()`
Read the results of the query	`ResultSet next()`
	`ResultSet getInt()`
	`ResultSet getString()`
Terminate the query and connection	`statement.close`
	`connection.close`

The `DriverManager` Class The `DriverManager` is really the core of JDBC functionality. It takes care of the management of different kinds of database drivers, and basically manages all the program interactions with that driver. (The preferred method for driver identification is to define the program's drivers in the `jdbc.drivers` property file. This should contain a list of classnames for driver classes that the program will need access to, and ameliorates the need for the explicit loading of the driver.)

There are a number of methods within the `DriverManager` class that provide many different ways in which drivers can be loaded and registered and database connections started. The methods include `getConnection` (which creates the connection between program and database), `registerDriver` (to make a new driver known to the `DriverManager`), `deregisterDriver` (to decommission a particular driver), and others. (Although it is not a part of the `DriverManager` class, the `Class.forName` method is the most commonly used command for the registration and initiation of drivers within a JDBC program. The decision to use `registerDriver` or `Class.forName` will depend on the way the `jdbc.drivers` and the entire database connectivity environment have been set up.)

The JDBC Interfaces Interfaces provide extensions to an object, but are not classes or objects themselves. They are collections of methods that supplement the functionality of a class. In this case, there are several interfaces that work with the `DriverManager` class which are very important to our understanding of how JDBC works. Table 20-2 contains a list of the major JDBC interfaces and their functions. These include:

- *Driver.* For the definition and management of different DBMS drivers. Each time the `DriverManager` loads a driver for a different database, it will create a new class for the management of interaction with that database. The Driver interface provides tools to help manage that process. Methods within the Driver interface include `acceptsURL` (which tells whether the driver can work with a specified database URL), `jdbcCompliant` (which indicates whether the database driver specified can actually work with JDBC or not), and others.

- *Connection.* For the establishment and management of connections to databases. Methods include `close` (to close the connection to the database), `commit` (to commit work), `createStatement` (to prepare a

TABLE 20-2

JDBC Interfaces and Their Functions

Interface	Function
`java.sql.Driver`	Manages the definition and utilization of database drivers
`java.sql.Connection`	Manages the creation of database connections and sessions
`java.sql.Statement`	Manages the creation and utilization of SQL statements
`java.sql.PrepareStatement`	Statement handling for precompiled queries
`java.sql.CallableStatement`	Statement handling for stored procedures
`java.sql.ResultSet`	Manages the handling of the data returned by a query
`java.sql.ResultSetMetaData`	Manages the retrieval of data about the data being retrieved (column names, data types, etc.)
`java.sql.DatabaseMetaData`	Manages the retrieval of data about the database being accessed (database name, version, etc.)

standard query for execution), `prepareCall` (to prepare for the execution of a stored procedure call), `prepareStatement` (to prepare for the precompilation of SQL commands) and others.

- *Statement.* For the construction and management of SQL statements. Methods include `executeQuery` (to execute a query), `executeUpdate` (to execute an update command), `setCursorName` (to establish a cursor name), and `setMaxRows` (to set the maximum number of rows to be retrieved), among others. Statement includes two subtypes:

    `PreparedStatement.` For the management of precompiled SQL (coupled with the `prepareStatement` method, which is part of the Connection interface).

    `CallableStatement.` For the management of stored procedures (coupled with the `prepareStatement` method, which is part of the Connection interface).

- `ResultSet.` For the management of the results of a query. A `ResultSet` provides access to a table of data generated by executing a Statement. The table rows are retrieved in sequence. Within a row, its column values can be accessed in any order. The `ResultSet` maintains an internal cursor and the `next` method is used to move that cursor. Column values are retrieved for each row, and individual columns can be referenced by column name or column number (from 1

Chapter 20: JDBC: Accessing Databases with Java

to *n* from left to right). When data is read in, it is automatically converted into Java data types. Actions within `ResultSet` include <Next> (to move the cursor), <Close> (to close the `ResultSet`), and a long list of `getxXX` commands, which are used to get different kinds of column values [e.g., `getInt` (get integer value), `getBignum` (to get a big number), `getAsciiStream` (to get an ASCII stream)]. (`ResultSet` also includes two subtypes:

`ResultSetMetaData`. For metadata about the result set (column name, type, etc.).

`DatabaseMetaData`. For metadata about the database itself (name, version, etc.).

Programming with JDBC

Armed with this background information, we are ready to begin the process of actually coding our JDBC program.

Import the JDBC Classes

To enable a Java program to execute JDBC we have to first make the JDBC classes and interfaces (and their methods) accessible to the program. This is done with the import command. In this case, the following commands will make this possible:

```
.import.java.sql.Connection
.import.java.sql.DriverManager
.import.java.sql.Statement
.import.java.sql.ResultSet
```

A shortcut version of the same command that will accomplish the same thing would be

```
import java.sql.*
```

Identifying the Database with the Database URL

As we noted earlier, the process of locating a database in today's highly distributed and volatile Internet/intranet world can be extremely challenging. The solution developed by JDBC is both eloquent and consistent with the underlying Internet technology it is based on. In the Java JDBC world, we identify databases by using a database URL.

The syntax for this URL varies depending on the type of Java program you are writing. For a Java application, the syntax will be:

```
.protocol-name:subprotocol-name: subname
```

where

```
protocol-name = jdbc
```

where `subprotocol-name` = a DBMS name or other identifier (e.g., Oracle, Sybase, DB2) and `subname` = any other DBMS-specific information as required by the database (e.g., the name of a particular logical database within the physical database environment).

So, if I had an Informix database named `animal_names` that I wanted to identify to a Java application, then it could be coded as:

```
."jdbc:informix:animal_names"
```

For a Java applet, we must include the remote server kinds of information, so the syntax will be:

```
.protocol-name:subprotocol-name: //server-name:port-number:database-name
```

where

- `protocol-name` = jdbc `subprotocol-name` = a DBMS name or other identifier (e.g., Oracle, Sybase, DB2)
- `server-name` = the name of the server running the database
- `port-number` = the physical port number for the database
- `database-name` = the name of the logical database being accessed

If I had a Sybase database running on the www.animals.com server at port number 298 and a database name of `animal_names` that I wanted to identify to a Java applet, then it could be coded as:

```
."jdbc:sybase://www.animals.com:298:animal_names"
```

We provide some other specific examples when we take a closer look at specific JDBC-database connections.

Chapter 20: JDBC: Accessing Databases with Java

Loading the Drivers with `forName()`

After telling the program where to find a database, the next thing we need to do is to have it load in the drivers that will allow the program to connect and work with the database. This is accomplished by using the `forName()` method. The syntax for this command is:

```
.internal-drivername = Class.forName(external-drivername)
```

Here

- `internal-drivername` = the name to be given to this particular driver when it is referred to by other commands within the program. (Remember that it will be possible to have accesses to more than one database from within the same program; therefore, we must create different driver names for each one.)
- `external-drivername` = the name of the driver as it is stored within the Java drivers directory.

If I wanted to initiate a driver for a Sybase database within my program, I could code:

```
.sybase-driver-1 = Class.forName("sybase.sql.SybaseDriver")
```

Besides making this explicit declaration of drivers, it is also necessary to define the external drivers to the Java environment via the <jdbc.drivers> system properties.

Creating a Connection with `getConnection()`

Having defined the location of the database to the program, and the driver that it should use, we are ready to actually initiate a transaction with that database and establish our logical unit of work, or transaction "thread." The establishment of this contact and the initiation of a work unit is called *making a database connection* in JDBC terminology. To create this connection, we need to create a new connection name and use the `getConnection` method (one of the methods belonging to the `DriverManager` class) to initiate it. The syntax for this operation is:

```
Internal-connection-name = DriverManager.getConnection(url, userid, password);
```

where

- `Internal-connection-name` is the name that we give to this particular connection so that it can be referenced by other parts of the program. (Remember, we can have more than one connection running at a time.)
- `url` is the database URL we mentioned earlier.
- `userid` is the login ID for gaining access to the database.
- `password` is the password for the specified `userid`.

Of course, the actual execution of this command can be handled by variables, or can be "hard-coded." In the case of hard coding, the command for creating a connection to our Sybase database would look like this:

```
Sybase_Connection_1 = DriverManager.getConnection("jdbc:sybase://
192.192.192.1:finance_db","IAMBOB","BOBPW")
```

where `IAMBOB` is the `userid` and `BOBPW` is the `IAMBOB` password.

If we had wanted to, we could have created variables to hold `url`, `userid`, and `password` and inserted them into the command instead. If we had used the variables called `dburl`, `dbuserid`, and `dbpw` and primed them with the appropriate values, we could have accomplished the same thing by coding:

```
Sybase_Connection_1 = DriverManager.getConnection(dburl,dbuserid,dbpw);
```

Creating and Preparing a Statement with `createStatement()`

Before we can execute this query, we have to prepare it. Preparing the query in the JDBC environment is a two-step process.

In the first part of the process, the program builds the query itself. This can be done by simply hard coding an SQL command right into the program (and enclosing it in quotes). Alternatively, the program can construct the query on the basis of information that it pulled in and put that query into variables, which are then used to populate the command. (You may recall that JDBC supports normal queries, inserts, updates, deletes, stored procedures, and precompiled programs as well as just queries. The example we are giving here is the bare-bones "query" version. The syntax for these other operations is basically the same, but involves different commands for obvious reasons.)

After the query has been built, we are ready to "prepare it" via the `createStatement()` method, which is part of the Connection interface. The syntax for the `createStatement()` method is:

```
.statement-name = connection-name.createStatement()
```

where `statement-name` = a unique name we give this statement so that it can be referred to from other parts of the program and `connection-name` = the name of the connection that we used to uniquely identify the database session started with the `getConnection()` command. For example, building on our previous examples, we could code:

```
Sybase-statement-1 = Sybase-connection-1.createStatement()
```

On successful execution of this method, we are ready to run our query.

Executing a Statement with `executeQuery()`

The `executeQuery()` method (part of the Statement interface) is used to submit the query to the database for execution. It can be invoked only if all of the previously mentioned methods have been invoked successfully. We must also have our query built and ready to submit if it is going to work. The syntax for the command is:

```
.statement-name.executeQuery(sql-call)
```

where `statement-name` = the name given to the statement in the previous step and `sql-call` = the fully expressed SQL command, either in hard-coded form or with variables (where all variables have been resolved). The syntax for an invocation of this command using our earlier examples would be:

```
Sybase-statement-1.executeQuery("Select Name, Breed, Color from Animal_DB");
```

Processing Results with `ResultSet` Interface Methods

After the query has been executed, all that is left to do is read in the results. This is done by several methods. Remember that the executed query will return an internal table to the Java program, which must be read through one record at a time. The methods that we use to do this are `next()`, which gets the next record, and the `getXXX` commands (`getInt`, `getASCII`, etc.).

The procedure for this operation is as follows:

1. We declare a variable that will represent the `ResultSet`. The syntax

```
ResultSet result-set-name
```

will accomplish this.

2. We set the `ResultSet` name equal to the `executeQuery` statement:

```
Result-set-name = statement-name.executeQuery(sql-call)
```

This will leave us with the named `ResultSet`, which we can manipulate. We can then work with this `ResultSet`.

3. We read the next record with the command:

```
Result-set-name.next()
```

4. We read different columns out of the retrieved row with:

```
Result-set-name.getString();
```

and so on.

Closing with `close()`

After we have finished with the database, we want to close the various connections, statements, etc. We do this with the `close()` method. The syntax is simply:

```
Statement-name.close
```

or

```
Connection-name.close
```

A Review of JDBC Programming

Now that we have successfully walked through the entire life cycle of a JDBC database call, let's review the entire process.

Chapter 20: JDBC: Accessing Databases with Java

JDBC Methods Summary As we have seen, JDBC makes it possible to gain access to remote databases from within your Java program through a series of classes, methods, and interfaces. These function as follows.

- `DriverManager`. Each program has only one `DriverManager`. The `DriverManager` keeps track of and manages all connections to all databases.
- `Drivers`. Each database that you want to access from within the program must have a unique driver associated with it; that driver makes the connection to the database possible.
- `Connections`. Each unique connection to a database is managed by a different connection. Connections are given unique names within the program.
- `Statements`. For each connection, any number of unique statements can be run. These statements cannot be run simultaneously; however, they can be serially executed within the same program.
- `Query`. When a statement is sent to the database for execution, it becomes a query. Each statement has a query associated with it.
- `ResultSet`. The `ResultSet` is a collection of data, stored as a table (array) within the program, and read into the program with the `next()` method.
- `Close`. Each statement and connection should be closed when completed.

Figure 20-1 shows a diagram of the relationships between these elements. In this figure we can see three connections (one each for Sybase,

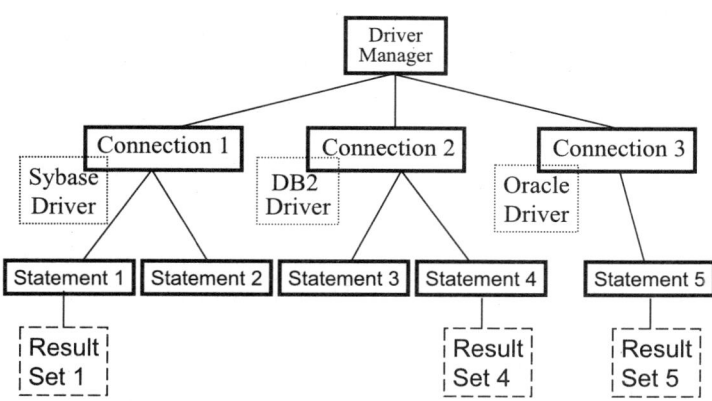

Figure 20-1
JDBC methods interaction for a JDBC program.

DB2, and Oracle), with the appropriate drivers loaded, some statements associated with each connection, and result sets associated with some of the statements (remember insert, update, and delete commands have *no* result sets).

Example Program To help you to put all of these pieces together, Figure 20-2 provides a copy of a simple sample program that illustrates the use of the methods we have been talking about.

Additional JDBC Capabilities

As we have already seen, JDBC offers the programmer more options than just the simple query processing we have been talking about. There are also capabilities for the support of:

Stored procedures. Make it possible to leverage queries built and stored within the database

Precompiled queries. Make it possible to precompile programs and simply execute them from the program

Cursor-managed queries. Provide the programmer with explicit cursor control

Transaction management. Give the program explicit control over logical units of work and the commit process

Multiple ResultSets. When a stored procedure returns more than one `ResultSet`, the `Statement.getMoreResults()` method will handle their processing

Query metadata access. Allows programs to query about the names, sizes, and types for the columns of a return set

Database metadata access. Allow programs to query about the nature, version, and status of the database being polled

JDBC Working with Specific Databases

In addition to the standard JDBC approaches discussed, several other models can be used. As we continue to explore the world of Java and database connectivity, it will be important for us to remember several things:

Chapter 20: JDBC: Accessing Databases with Java

Figure 20-2
Programming example for database access.

```java
//* The animal listing program lists all animals in the database and their ages

import java.sql.*;

public class Samplet extends java.applet.Applet{
  public void paint (Graphics g) {
    //* declare string variables to hold values
      String driver = "oracle.sql.OracleDriver"
      String url    = "jdbc:oracle:thin:bob@animaldb"
      String user   = "bob"
      String pass   = "bobpw"
      String query1 = "Select name, age from animal"

      try {
      //* Load the driver
        Class.forName(driver);
      //* Make the connection
        Connection c;
        c = DriverManager.getConnection(url,user,pass);
      //* Create the statement
        Statement stmt;
        stmt = c.createStatement();
      //* Execute the Query and load into the ResultSet called rs
        ResultSet rs = stmt.executeQuery(query1);
      //* Create loop for the processing of results
      //* the value of next will be incremented(the next row will be read) until
      //* there are none left. Then rs.next() will be false and the while loop will end
        while (rs.next()) {
            //* get the two columns from the next row
            //* the first column, name, is a String, so use getString
            //* the second column, age, is an Integer, so use getInt
            //* print them out
            String c1 = rs.getString(1);
            Integer c2 = rs.getInt(2);
            g.drawstring(c1,20,y);
            g.drawstring(c2,100,y);
            y = y + 10 ;
            }
      //* Close the statement and the connection
        stmt.close();
        c.close();
      }
```

1. JDBC is an "open standard." That means that it has been put together in such a way that it is easy for vendors and independent developers to generate creative variations on the theme. This openness is not only allowed, it is encouraged. Therefore the number of variations on the standard JDBC operational model will

continue to rise, making the environment more complicated, but more versatile at the same time.
2. Each vendor of a database product to which JDBC connects will probably create interfaces unique to its product set.
3. The supporters of previously established database connectivity standards (such as ODBC, OLE, and CORBA) will continue to promote their standards, and develop interfaces and bridges that will tie JDBC to their initiatives.
4. The manufacturers of database connectivity middleware such as Intersolv, XDB, and Simba will continue to create viable third-party alternatives and enhancements to JDBC.

We will continue by looking at some of these variations.

JDBC and ODBC

Up until now, no database connectivity standard has done more to promote the use of databases than ODBC. ODBC, the Open DataBase Connectivity standard, initiated by Microsoft, has made it possible for millions of users to access hundreds of thousands of databases from hundreds of different software packages, without ever having to worry about the connectivity issues involved. Because of this, it should come as no surprise that the developers of Java and JDBC wanted to figure out a way for Java-JDBC applications to gain access to these databases as quickly and seamlessly as possible.

To encourage this process, there is a copy of the JDBC-ODBC bridge shipped with every copy of the Java development kit (JDK). This bridge makes it possible for Java programs to access ODBC registered data sources with native Java-JDBC code. This means that all of the spreadsheets, documents, tables, PC databases (e.g., Access and dBaseIV), Lotus Notes databases, flat files, legacy databases (e.g., IMS and IDMS) can be accessed by using SQL commands issued via the standard JDBC interface.

To make an ODBC database usable to your program, you need to do several things:

1. Create an ODBC database connection using the ODBC control panel. You can find the control panel under the Start...Settings... Control Panel option under Windows 95. Be sure to use the 32-bit ODBC and not the older 16-bit version!

Chapter 20: JDBC: Accessing Databases with Java

2. Use the ODBC control panel to select the ODBC data source you want to work with and give it a name. (Make note of this name; you will need to refer to it from within the Java program later.)
3. Code the Java program, using all the guidelines we have established for any JDBC program with the following exceptions:
4. Use the name of the Java developers kit (JDK) -provided JDBC-ODBC driver, in place of a database driver name. In this case, the name is `sun.jdbc.odbc.JdbcOdbcDriver`. Use that as the parameter for the `Class.forName()` method.
5. Use the special JDBC-ODBC URL convention. Specifically, `jdbc.odbc:odbc-name`. The `odbc-name` is the name you gave the ODBC data source from the ODBC control panel (see steps 1 and 2).
6. Aside from these few variations, you can proceed to access your ODBC just as if it were any other relational database.

For an overview of the JDBC-ODBC bridge process, see Figure 20-3.

JDBC and ORACLE

Without a doubt, the most popular database in the world today is Oracle. And Oracle has done a good job of making it easy for Java programmers to access their databases.

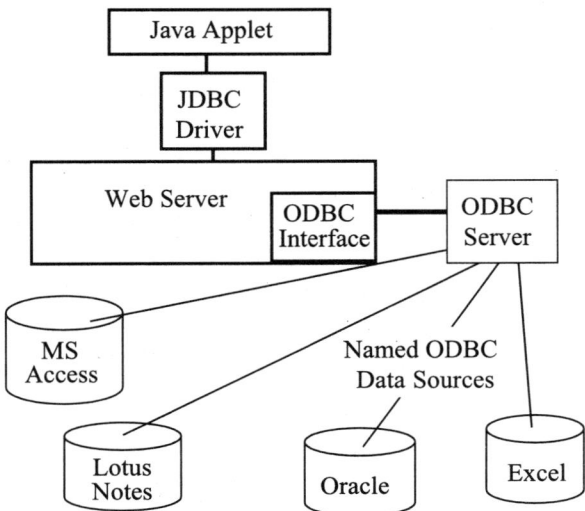

Figure 20-3
JDBC-ODBC overview.

Oracle programming with JDBC is done much the same way as any other JDBC programming. The program must still declare the `java.sql.*` files for input, the Oracle drivers must still be loaded and the connections, statements, and queries are still handled in exactly the same way. There are, however, a few small variations of which developers should be aware, and one very large one.

Oracle Connection Types Oracle actually supports two different kinds of database connections, each with its own sets of drivers, URLs, and other syntax. These two types are the "thin" connection type for applet programming and the OCI, or Oracle call interface connection type for applications.

Coding the Oracle Thin Connection Type The Oracle thin connection type for applets is a Type 4 driver that uses Java sockets to connect the applet directly to the Oracle database. This means that a JDBC thin implementation is platform-independent and does *not* make use of any existing SQL*NET capabilities. The Oracle JDBC thin driver is written in Java and can therefore be downloaded to any browser and run dynamically. To code an applet for Oracle thin use, you must load the Oracle thin driver and code the URL. In this case, the URL syntax is

`jdbc:oracle:thin:user/password@database`

where `thin>` is the connection type name and `user/password@database` is the standard Oracle `username/password@database` name syntax.

Coding the Oracle OCI Connection Type The Oracle OCI connection type for applications is a Type 2 driver that uses Java native methods to call C language entry points to the OCI (Oracle call interface) library. OCI is the native Oracle call level interface mechanism. Oracle JDBC-OCI drivers require the installation of SQL*NET version 2.3 or higher on the client, and are totally platform-dependent, but support all standard OCI connection types including IPC, named pipes, and DEC-NET. The procedure for the connection of Oracle OCI is (1) load the Oracle OCI driver and (2) code the URL—in this case:

`jdbc:oracle:oci:user/password@database`

where `oci` is the connection type name and `user/password@database` is the standard Oracle database naming convention.

General Oracle JDBC Information In addition to these differences, some other, smaller idiosyncrasies to be aware of include:

Streaming. Oracle JDBC drivers support the streaming of data in either direction between client and server. They support all stream conversions including binary, ASCII, and Unicode. (This means that it is possible to create very fast and efficient Oracle database operations where a lot of data needs to be moved and streaming can save a lot of overhead.)

Stored procedures. The Oracle JDBC drivers support execution of PL/SQL procedures and anonymous blocks.

Database metadata. You can gain access to the database metadata through standard database calls to the Oracle system tables.

JDBC and Other Databases

Of course, JDBC functionality is not limited to ORACLE and ODBC databases. Some of the others include DB2, Sybase, and Informix. The treatment of the JDBC interfaces is fairly consistent for all of them.

JDBC and DB2 For example, the IBM DB2 Universal Database, version 5, provides full support for the JDBC interface including the provision for "thin" applet programming and "not-thin" application programming using a CLI (call level interface) and the IBM CAE (call application enabler). This capability is very similar to the Oracle OCI capability.

Third-Party JDBC Connectivity Middleware In addition to the different ways that the vendors of databases are making it possible to directly work with Java, there is also a large group of middleware software vendors who would like to make accessing these databases even easier still. (Middleware vendors create third-party database-neutral connectivity packages that enable effortless attachment to many different databases for many different products.)

Why would anyone need to buy a middleware product to connect programs and databases, when JDBC already provides so many different options? There are two good reasons.

1. *Simplification of multidatabase access.* Probably the biggest single reason that people use middleware is to help them to simplify their programming and support environment. In many cases, pro-

grammers may be forced to provide support for two, three, and up to seven different databases, all at the same time (and maybe even from within the same program). When this happens, the process of trying to manage so many different databases, drivers, and their many different versions and nuances can get to be a big problem. In these cases, a middleware product provides a vendor-neutral environment that ameliorates all these problems and provides programmers with one centralized facility to work with.

2. *Performance optimization.* The other reason that people like middleware is for the performance improvements they can sometimes gain. Third-party vendors can sometimes figure out ways to optimize query processing better than the database vendor can.

In the next two subsections, we will provide some information about a couple of these middleware products—XDB Expresslane and SimbaExpress—so that the reader can develop an appreciation for what middleware does and how it works.

The XDB ExpressLane Product The XDB company's product ExpressLane is a good example of a middleware product that helps make the world of JDBC programming easier. ExpressLane focuses primarily on making it easy for Java programs to gain access to mainframe-based legacy systems (primarily those written in IMS or VSAM on an MVS390 operating system).

While it is possible to gain access to these types of database files using a standard ODBC interface, there are many reasons that this kind of connection may not be desirable. Unfortunately, the immense size, complexity, and idiosyncratic nature of mainframe legacy systems often leave the ODBC interface with extremely poor performance and complex connectivity problems.

With the ExpressLane product, all of that is taken care of. XDB Company has been in the business of making mainframe legacy data available to other environments for years, and it was an easy matter for them to broaden the scope of their products to include JDBC connectivity. In the standard JDBC configuration, ExpressLane makes use of a gateway machine, which serves as an intermediary between the mainframe and browser. This gateway supports both applet and application programming, and is implemented through the inclusion of the ExpressLane driver and URL in the Java program.

SimbaExpress and JDBC While ExpressLane focuses on simplifying and speeding up access to mainframe data sources, Simba and its

SimbaExpress product are in the business of speeding up the process of dealing with multiple UNIX and Windows databases such as Oracle, Sybase, Informix, and MS-SQL. The Simba solution comes with two components:

- The SIMBA JDBC client, which is a 100 percent Java driver that can be incorporated into an applet or application.
- The SimbaExpress server, which receives and processes all JDBC-based data requests from the Web environment. This server manages all incoming JDBC-based database traffic, converts it from JDBC to ODBC, and then submits the queries to the data sources in the ODBC format.

This product has proved to several customers that it can simplify database traffic (by eliminating the need to manage multiple database drivers across multiple Web browsers) and speed up database query processing (faster than standard CGI-type interfaces).

The Next Generation of Web Technology

Although it is clear that the combination of Java and JDBC brings a whole new, bigger, better, and richer programming environment to the world of the Web, many individuals feel that the Java approach:

- Brings a lot more complexity to the Web environment than is necessary
- Could be improved upon even more, if enhancements were made to the core Internet/Web/HTML architecture, making them more robust and functional

And, of course, in a world where things are changing faster than you can keep track of them, these complaints have been heard. There are several initiatives currently underway to make improvements to the Web environment on several levels. These include:

1. The release of a new version of IP, one which will ameliorate some of the bothersome "statelessness" problems, as well as make improvements to packet delivery speeds.
2. The development of a replacement for HTML called Dynamic HTML, or DHTML
3. The development of a superform of HTML called XML.

We briefly review each of these ongoing improvement efforts. Alas, these changes and improvements come at such a rapid pace that by the time you are reading this, things will have most certainly moved forward significantly. However, these three initiatives do seem to be good, strong indicators of the general direction that the technology is moving in.

The Next Generation of Internet Protocol: IPv6

Although the current Internet and Web environments have been working quite well for some time now, it is clear to most people that the current levels of system usage and the current state of networking technology call out for the implementation of a new underlying network protocol infrastructure.

Of course, changing network infrastructure protocols is not quite as simple as one might expect. The whole value and attractiveness of the Internet is the fact that it is based on the leveraging of a good, simple least-common-denominator approach to network management. Any changes to the core IP infrastructure of this environment, therefore, must be approached with a great deal of caution.

But changes will take place nevertheless. The current generation of IP used on the Web today, IP version 4 (IPv4), has been in service for over 20 years, and it has been decided that it is time for a change. Among the weaknesses of IPv4 that are being addressed with this new release are:

Security features. It is very difficult to "secure" IP traffic.

Configuration management. It is very difficult to reconfigure the environment (right now, every address on the system must be hard-coded, making it very difficult to change configurations around in order to meet the needs of new traffic demands).

Addressing issues. The current IP addressing scheme was not configured with the current Internet world in mind. There are more nodes on the Internet today than people ever thought imaginable, and continued growth and expansion means that there is a serious IP address shortage problem.

Version 6 of the IP protocol addresses these issues. Under IPv6, addresses are bigger (128 bits versus the IPv4 32-bit size). This greater capacity allows for more flexibility in addressing and address management and will enable the Internet to manage automatic readdressing.

Along with this new addressing scheme is a built-in dynamic routing, rerouting, and configuration management scheme, which will make it easier for the managers of the IP environment to adjust to the ever-increasing demands of the marketplace. This same functionality will make it possible to maintain better and more stringent security over the entire environment. All told, the new version of IP will allow the existing Internet infrastructure to support today's Internet traffic load, and a lot more to come.

Dynamic HTML

Many nice things can be said about HTML and the Web environment of today. It is clear, however, that HTML has some deficiencies that make it difficult to work with. If the Web environment of the future is to meet the demands that business and consumers are placing on it, then some changes have to be made. While it is true that the use of Java and JDBC do a lot to help move the environment forward, there are those who would like to see the fundamental nature of HTML itself shift, in order to make it more usable as a programming environment in the future.

What is Dynamic HTML (DHTML)? Simply put, it is an HTML page that can change its content after it has been invoked. With DHTML, Web programmers can put up a page and allow the objects on that page (the pictures, the words, etc.) to continuously change without requiring the browser to go back to the server for more input.

There are actually several different initiatives underway, sponsored by various organizations that would like to see a new, improved HTML replace the existing language. Two of the biggest are efforts sponsored by Sun and by Microsoft. These initiatives are designed to help HTML programmers to create much more interactive, complicated, and state-sensitive types of applications using basic HTML-like commands and tags.

DHTML Core Characteristics The new DHTML approaches attempt to address the many shortcomings of standard HTML with the following three functional enhancement areas.

1. *Client-side scripting.* With client-side scripting, the Web programmer writes a script that is run on the browser and interacts with the HTML document that is currently being displayed. Client-side scripting can be done with the Visual Basic scripting language (VBScript) or the Java scripting language (JavaScript).

In either case, additional functionality and control are the results, along with a reduced network and server load.

2. *Cascading style sheets (CSS).* CSSs provide Web programmers with fuller control over the Web pages they design. In today's HTML/Web environment, the Web page designer can place formatting tags on a page, but the Web browser decides how to interpret them. With a style sheet, programmers can develop ways to override local browser decisions about formatting, and impose the designer's specific wishes. These same style sheets can be used to establish a display style for a complete population of Web pages, and allow the designer to make changes to the style which are then reflected across all the pages in the group.

3. *The document object model (DOM).* The DOM is a platform- and language-neutral interface that allows scripts (and programs) to dynamically access and update the content, structure, and style of an HTML document. This means that scripts can modify tags on the fly, thereby dramatically altering the appearance of a page interactively.

In these three areas, DHTML will provide Web programmers with a much wider variety of techniques and approaches that will enhance the quality and usability of Web pages in the future.

XML—The New Meta-HTML Approach

XML (Extended Markup Language) is quickly shaping up as the replacement for the HTML approach to Web design. While HTML (HyperText Markup Language) was originally developed to deliver document management and hypertext to the world, its functionality represents only a small portion of what a fully enabled hypertext environment would be like.

The great-grandfather of all hypertext languages and all document definition languages is a language called SGML (Standard Generalized Markup Language). SGML specifies the grammar for a wide range of document markup languages. This grammar is dictated by the definition of its document type (DTD or document-type definition). HTML is one of the types of documents that SGML can define, and it was based on SGML standards.

Now, however, as people seek ways to get even more leverage out of the Web environment, they are turning to SGML for further inspiration.

Chapter 20: JDBC: Accessing Databases with Java

Unfortunately, SGML is still too large, cumbersome, and generalized to meet the needs of an environment as big and diverse as the World Wide Web. There is another subset of SGML, however—a subset bigger than HTML and yet smaller than the complete SGML set. That subset, XML, is quickly establishing itself as the new standard language for the Web.

What Is XML? Extensible Markup Language provides the Web designer with a radically new and different way to define Web pages. Although HTML allows designers to define how a page looks, XML is used to define what a page contains.

In general, XML is content-aware (responding to the nature of the information being managed) and format-ignorant, while HTML is content-ignorant (it does not react to the nature of the information it displays), but totally format-aware. A comparison should help us understand the differences.

Programming HTML Style An HTML programmer trying to write an order entry form for an on-line book company needs to create a page by defining the individual headings, separator lines, input fields, field descriptors, and a host of other details. In other words, HTML provides the programmer with the means to define the presentation of collection of meaningless objects. The programmer can place tags such as <H1>, <p>, and <color = xxxxx> around words like "Customer Name" and "Customer Address" to define the layout, and then assign variables such as cust-name-field and cust-address-field, to specify how the page will look and act. It is the way in which the programmer arranges these objects that gives them meaning. After all these elements have been arranged in the right way, an HTML browser document will read them in and display them on the screen the way you want.

Programming with XML The HTML approach to page display and design involves the use of only one document, the HTML document itself, and the services of an HTML browser to display it. To create that same page display with XML, two documents are blended together through the services of an XML browser.

The two parts that make up a fully displayed XML session are the XML page definition itself (which defines what information the page will manage) and a DTD (which defines how what was specified in the XML will be managed and displayed). (DTDs, or document-type definitions, are templated document definitions that are created and managed for a wide range of industry- and function-specific applications. For example, you could have a retail order entry DTD that defines all the fields needed to create a retail order entry system. Then a Web designer could develop a custom application of that type by simply locating the correct DTD and defining the application according to the specific data values that are required.)

An XML programmer defines a page on the basis of the information that the page holds, not on how individual elements will look or behave. To define the order entry page referred to in our previous example using XML, a programmer would define the page by inputting tags with names like <Customer Name> and <Customer Address> (names that describe the kind of information that is being managed). At the same time, the DTD will be partnered with the XML definition. The DTD holds all the rules for how to format, display, and manage those things called <Customer Name> and <Customer Address>.

Benefits of the XML Approach In addition to relieving the programmer of the burden of defining all the individual elements of a screen, XML provides many other benefits as well:

- *Content-rich tags.* Because XML and DTD documents are content-specific, it will be possible for Web sites to manage information that is more accurate and accessible to individuals. For example, a browser search for the word *chip* today on the Web will yield information about potato chips, people named Chip, and microchips. In a content-rich-tag world, the industry specification for the document content will allow the search engines to zero in on the specific kind of chips being looked for.

- *XLL.* Another feature of XML is XLL (Extensible Link Language). This language eliminates the hard-coded, one-way links of HTML and replaces them with dynamic, self adjusting "soft" links, which can be redirected as the object being pointed to changes.

- *Industry-standard treatments.* As the population of DTD documents grows, industry-standard treatments for fields will make programming easier and easier with each generation.

- *Publishing across media types.* XML and XML browsers are publishing-neutral. The same XML document can be used to produce Web page, printed, and CD-ROM-based output, all with a consistent look and feel, and a minimum of rework.

The Future of XML XML is quickly moving into the forefront of Web technology. The Web standards bodies have approved a very liberal XML standard, XML browsers are starting to hit the market, and XML capabilities are being built into existing browsers. We will surely be seeing a lot more of XML as the technology progresses.

Conclusion

In this chapter, we cover a significant amount of territory. We see the different components that make up the JDBC interface, how they are coded, and how they look in a program. With the closing of this chapter, we finish our review of the basic Web environment from a technological perspective. Armed with this information, we are in a position to truly understand and evaluate different Web warehousing architectural and performance tuning alternatives.

CHAPTER 21

Architecture, Performance, and Management

- *What are the typical configurations of a Web warehouse?*
- *How do you measure the performance of a Web warehousing environment?*
- *What are the key tactics utilized to monitor and control Web warehouse performance?*
- *How do you troubleshoot performance problems in a Web warehousing environment?*

To complete our picture of the Web warehouse, we briefly review its overall architecture. After that we tackle one more important issue, the system's performance, how to monitor and improve it.

Web Warehousing Topology

The architecture for a typical corporate data warehouse is complicated because corporate information systems are complicated. Despite the designer's best intentions, one must ultimately compromise when one starts to deal with dozens of legacy systems and hundreds or even thousands of users. Our Web warehousing architecture will end up being equally complex for the same reasons.

Typical Configurations

Let's look at a couple of "typical" configurations.

An Intranet Configuration   One of the most frequently developed Web warehousing configurations is the secure intranet layout. See Figure 21-1. Under this model, the organization chooses to leave out any connection to the outside world of the Web, but does leverage the power and flexibility of Web technology by assembling an architecture that includes:

1. Installation of Web browsers on all end-user terminals.
2. Connection of all browsers to a Web server via the internal LAN using the TCP/IP protocol.
3. Connection of that Web server to an application server that manages CGI, Java, and other application service functions.
4. Connection of that application server to a data warehouse server where all data of interest to the users is stored.

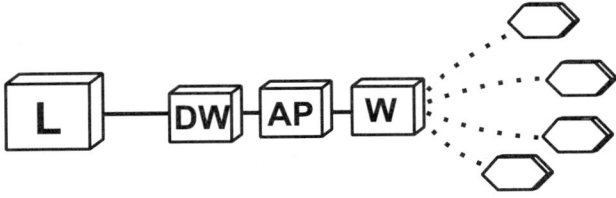

Figure 21-1
A typical intranet-based Web warehouse configuration.

Chapter 21:   Architecture, Performance, and Management

5. Connection of the data warehouse server to the legacy systems (in this case, the mainframes that house the corporation's key operational systems).

Looking at this architecture in terms of the functionalities of a data warehousing environment that we have already discussed, we can see that under this configuration:

- The acquisition functions are managed by a combination of legacy system and data warehouse server machine physical components. In this case, the acquisition components make no use of Web technology at all.
- The data warehouse server manages the storage functions.
- The access functions are managed by a combination of application server, Web server, and users with their Web browsers. See Figure 21-2.

Leveraged Inbound Configuration   Putting a Web warehousing environment together so that the organization can take advantage of Web technology, without actually hooking up to the Web, is one option. Another option that many organizations choose is the leveraged inbound configuration. See Figure 21-3. Under this configuration, the organization leverages the power, flexibility, availability, and low cost of Web connectivity to deploy applications around the world, without the need for expensive dedicated internally managed networks.

End users gain access to the Web via a local access provider and to the corporate applications via a publicly recognized Web server, which is in turn hooked up to an application server that is safely situated *behind* a corporate firewall. This firewall guarantees that only authorized corpo-

Figure 21-2
Allocation of Web warehouse functionality.

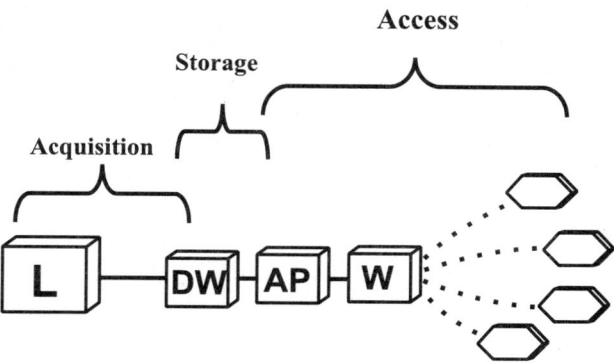

Figure 21-3
The leveraged inbound configuration.

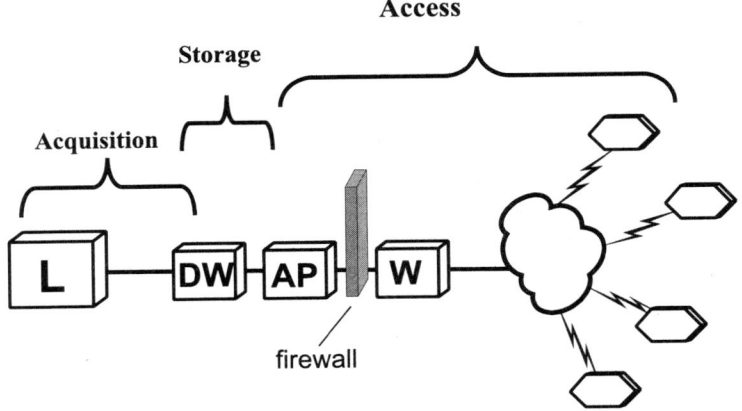

rate users are allowed access to the internal systems. The application server is then hooked up to the data warehouse server, which again is fed by data from the legacy systems.

Just as in the previous example, we can see that the acquisition and storage components of the Web warehouse exist without any reference to or awareness of the Web or Web technology. In this case, however, the access component not only makes use of Web technology, but also actually includes the World Wide Web itself as part of the overall architecture.

Leveraged Outbound Configuration Just to show you how complicated and topsy-turvy this can get, let's consider another kind of configuration. See Figure 21-4. In this situation, we have an almost complete reversal of roles:

Figure 21-4
The leveraged outbound configuration.

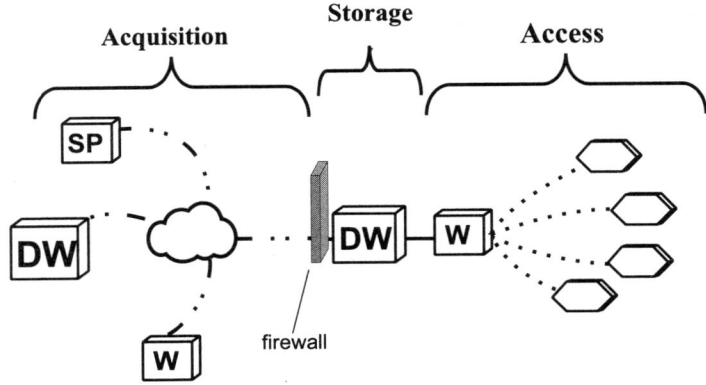

Chapter 21: Architecture, Performance, and Management

Acquisition. The acquisition component of this system consists almost completely of World Wide Web–based servers. Here, our warehouse receives input from a public Web page server (W), a specialty image server (SP), and a corporate data warehouse (DW) that has been made available via a Web gateway.

Storage. The required data, images, and text from these three sources are identified, prepared, and stored on a locally controlled data warehouse, located internally.

Access. The information is then accessed via Web browsers hooked up to an internally managed LAN.

A Dual-Leveraged Configuration And of course it is very possible for an organization to put a system into place that gains some of its input from the Web and some from internal legacy systems, while supporting user access via both World Wide Web and internal communications channels. See Figure 21-5. In this situation, we have all the options:

Acquisition. The acquisition component of this system consists of both World Wide Web–based servers and internal legacy systems.

Storage. The required data, images, and text from these sources are identified, prepared, and stored on a locally controlled data warehouse located internally.

Access. The information is then accessed via Web browsers hooked up to an internally managed LAN and remotely via the World Wide Web.

Figure 21-5
A dual-leveraged configuration.

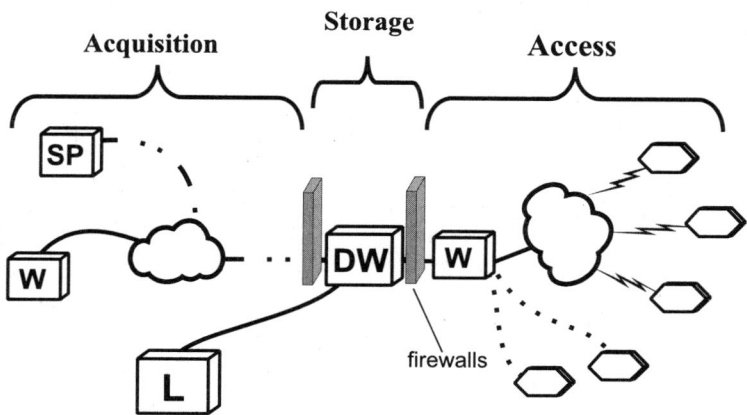

Capacity Planning, Performance Tuning, and Troubleshooting

With so many different configurations to choose from, managing the speed, responsiveness, and capacity of these kinds of environments presents some special challenges, and requires some special skills. Luckily, over the past several years, a relatively large body of knowledge about the management and support of client/server and other kinds of network- and computer-based systems has been accumulated. This has led to the development of a large number of techniques that can be of value in these situations. To start with, let's consider some of the fundamental concepts necessary to attack these issues.

Nodes, Links, and Capacity

The first thing that we have to realize when we look at performance and capacity issues in an environment like this is that the system is a very large and complicated one. Since it is so large and complicated, there is *no way* that we can make evaluations without understanding all the pieces that make it up.

The performance of any system like this depends both on the performance of each component and on the way all of the them work together. Figuring out capacity, therefore, requires that we calculate the workload that each component will place on the system, and then look at how well the other components are able to deal with it.

Capacity itself is measured and calculated by three kinds of metrics, all of them revolving around the concept of a transaction. We attempt to evaluate the system's ability by measuring items such as:

- *Rates.* How often or at what rate transactions are generated or responded to
- *Volumes.* How much data or information gets moved or handled for each transaction
- *Quantities.* How many transactions are generated or handled within a given time frame

In general, these rates, volumes, and quantities are combined to give us our two principal measures: transactions per hour (TPH; how many activities are initiated in a given time frame), and megabytes per hour (MPH; how much information is moved in a given time frame). The

Chapter 21: Architecture, Performance, and Management

transactions per hour measurement will help us understand how much workload a component of the system generates and how well other components will be able to deal with that workload. The megabytes per hour measurement will help us determine how well the network linkages are able to handle the throughput demands of the system.

While there are many different kinds of platforms, servers, and network connections that we need to deal with when putting a system like this together, as far as capacity planning goes there are only two types: nodes and links.

Measuring Node Capacity and Stating Node Workload Generation A node is a component of the Web warehouse environment that does some kind of work for the user. End-user workstations, Web servers, data warehouse servers, legacy systems, specialty servers, and application servers are all nodes. Nodes will therefore have a given capacity and a queue that allows requests to stack up and wait for service as they come in. Nodes can both generate demand (that is, they can create work to be passed to another node) and satisfy demand (that is, perform work for another node). The basic terminology is as follows:

Nodes generate *workloads*.

Workloads are interpreted by the other components of the system as *requirements*.

The ability of a node to satisfy a requirement is called its *capacity*.

To figure out how many transactions, and ultimately how much work is created by a node that generates workload for the system, we again deal with metrics to obtain meaningful estimates. The most common metrics include:

- Average and maximum number of generating agents (i.e., number of users) stated in terms of maximum and concurrent number of agents [i.e. concurrent users (CU), maximum number of users (MU)]
- Average and maximum transactions generated per agent per time frame (second, minute, hour, etc.) stated in terms of transactions per time frame (i.e., TPS, TPM, TPH, etc.)

Given these metrics, we will be able to figure out:

How much load a population of users will place on the system

How much load a processing node will create for another node (i.e., how much work a Web server will place on an application server or how much work an application server will place on a data warehouse server)

How much capacity the links of the system will have to support

After calculating how much workload a node will create, we need to figure out how well another node will be able to satisfy that workload. Workload satisfaction is typically measured in terms of:

- *Average response time (ART).* A measure, in real (wall time) seconds, of how long it takes the server to answer the request. Measured in transactions per second, minute, or hour (TPS, TPM, TPH).
- *Concurrency.* A measure that indicates the number of concurrent transactions that a server can manage before queuing or rejecting any more transactions. Stated in terms of a simple count [i.e., concurrent transactions (CT)]. Concurrent handling numbers are important only when the workload is so high that concurrent processing will be required. For simplicity's sake, we limit our examples to situations where this is not required.

Given these metrics, we can figure out:

How much work a node will be able to support

What kinds of response times users can expect

When we need to consider enhancement of node capacities or alteration of an architecture

Although we will need to use several different kinds of metrics to put the capacity picture together, ultimately node workload, requirements, and capacity are stated in terms of transactions per time frame (TPS, TPM, or TPH).

Measuring Link Capacity A link is a component of the Web warehouse environment that connects two nodes together. Internet, LAN, TCP/IP, and internal high-speed connections are all examples of links within our system. Links also have a capacity and a queue, but it is of a different nature. A link's only job is to move things from one node to another.

The capacity of links is usually defined in terms of their bandwidth and stated in baud or megabits per second. Typical link speeds include numbers like 14.4, 28.8, 56 kbps (modem speeds), or T1, T2, T3, etc. (for very high end capacities). The measures of significance to us, however, appear only when we translate these abstract engineering terms into operational capacity terms. We therefore examine capacity—using metrics such as:

1. *Average and maximum packet size (APS, MPS).* The volume of data or information being forwarded from one node to the next
2. *Average and maximum packets per transaction (APPT, MPPT).* The average number of packets created by each transaction.
3. *Packets per time frame (second, minute, hour, etc., or PPS, PPM, PPH, etc.).* The average number of packets that will traverse the link in one time frame.

By combining the system generation metrics, network capacity metrics, and service satisfaction metrics we are able to get a good picture of the capacities of both individual components and the overall system. To help us understand how these metrics and configuration modeling techniques can be utilized to solve real problems, we look at how they can be used to evaluate the performance of a simple Web warehousing system.

Step-by-Step Guide to Capacity Planning

Our first example will show how these basic tools can be used to help address capacity planning situations. In a capacity planning scenario, the Web warehouse architect is provided with only the sketchiest amount of information about the kinds of workloads the end users will be placing on the system and the kinds of work the system will be expected to do. And yet, the architect is expected to make decisions about whether the network, hardware, and software components selected will be big enough to meet the demands of the system.

In this case, the best one can do is develop a capacity planning model that uses best-guess estimates to get some kind of approximation of workload and capacity. However, by applying this discipline and these metrics, we can determine whether our proposed or existing architecture will be able to handle the workload we expect. These insights will help us figure out things like:

- How big different nodes need to be (how large the Web server, application server, and data warehouse server need to be)
- How much network (link) capacity is required to provide the desired level of service

- How the architectural components can best be arranged to maximize performance at the lowest possible cost

To put together a capacity plan for a given architecture, we need to go through the following steps:

1. Develop a capacity map for the system.
2. Create a capacity inventory report for each node and link on the map (and calculate the corresponding workloads, requirements, and capacities).
3. Identify capacity shortfall situations.
4. Reconfigure the architecture (upgrade appropriate components) and recalculate.

By calculating these values, an analyst will be able to quickly determine where potential bottlenecks and performance trouble areas will be. In the following section, we develop some detailed information about how this discipline can be applied in using a simplified example.

Developing a Capacity Map

To prepare for our performance evaluation, we need to capture on paper exactly what our configuration looks like. As we stated earlier, it is absolutely critical that we be aware of all of the components of our architecture and how they fit together if we are to have a real chance of addressing performance and capacity issues.

Too often, people called on to do capacity planning or performance tuning will automatically zero in on one or two aspects of the system (e.g., network bandwidth, database capacity, Web server capacity) without taking all of the components into account. While this ad hoc approach to performance can sometimes be effective, more often than not it leads to more problems and confusion.

The method of putting this configuration model together is simple and straightforward. All you need to do is:

1. Determine what the different nodes in the environment are. We need to include both those nodes that we are in control of (e.g., a data warehouse server) and those which we are not (e.g., a remote Web server).
2. Determine the nature of each of the links between those nodes, again including both those you can control (internal LAN/WAN)

Chapter 21: Architecture, Performance, and Management

and those you cannot (the World Wide Web itself and independent Internet service provider facilities).

3. Diagrammatically represent this model (see Figure 21-6). In this simple example, we illustrate a capacity map for a simple Web warehouse environment. This system involves only three nodes (user workstations, a Web server, and a data warehouse server) and two network links (a LAN connection between the users and the Web server and a high-speed link between the Web server and the data warehouse).

Creating the Capacity Worksheets

Once we have identified what each of the nodes and links in the system are, our next step is to figure out and document the workload each will be able to generate and/or support. We do this by creating a series of worksheets. The purpose of these worksheets is to provide us with the means to analyze and understand how each component (platform and link) will contribute to the creation and satisfaction of system demand. Each worksheet describes a different component of the system, and that component's participation in the system's workload, as either a generator of workload or a satisfier of workload. In the following examples, we will show several worksheet reports so that you can get a general idea about how this process works. We will show reports for a few of the platforms and links within the system, to illustrate how these calculations are developed.

In a real-world situation, the job of putting an evaluation like this together would require that we develop at least two worksheets for every system component. The first set of worksheets would be used to show us what kind of workload the components will generate, and the demand that will place on the rest of the system. The second set would be used to help

Figure 21-6
Capacity map example.

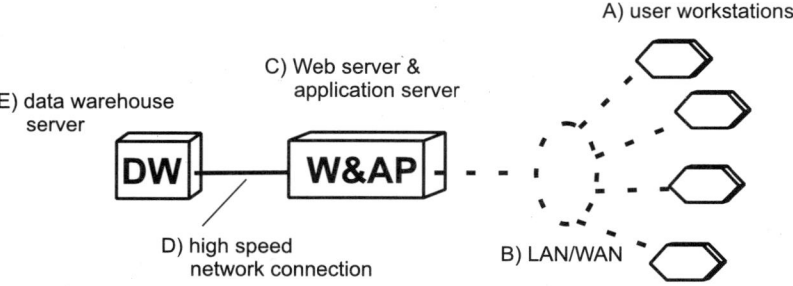

evaluate how well the system will be able to handle the information and workload passed back to the end user from the servers originally invoked.

For example, if you look at the example capacity map in Figure 21-6, you can see that we have five components: user workstations (A), LAN/WAN (B), Web and application server (C), high-speed network connection (D), and data warehouse server (E). To develop a comprehensive collection of worksheets we would require the worksheets in the following order:

1. User workload generation (A). How much workload will the users create?
2. LAN/WAN user workload handling (B). How well will the LAN/WAN be able to handle the demand generated by the users?
3. Web and application server workload handling from end user (C). How well and how quickly will the Web and application server handle the demands placed on it by the users?
4. Web and application server workload generation to data warehouse (C). How much work will the Web and application server pass on to the data warehouse for execution?
5. High-speed-link workload handling from Web and application server (D). How well will the high-speed link handle the workload being transported from the Web and application server to the data warehouse?
6. Data warehouse workload handling from Web and application server (E). How well will the data warehouse handle the workload sent to it?
7. Data warehouse workload generation to Web and application server (E). After the data warehouse gets its instructions (in this case, a database request) it will hopefully retrieve a lot of data and pass it back to the Web and application server. This response set of information represents a second set of workloads, which must be passed back upstream to the user.
8. High-speed-link workload handling to Web and application server (D). In this case we need to see what effect the data being returned to the program and ultimately the user will have on the network link. We must be sure to analyze both inbound and outbound network traffic when considering the system's capacity.
9. Web and application server workload handling from data warehouse (C). The workload placed on the Web and application server when the requested data is returned.

Chapter 21: Architecture, Performance, and Management   **525**

10. Web and application server workload generation to end user (C). The volume of information that will be sent back to the end user.
11. LAN/WAN workload handling from Web and application server (B). The ability of the LAN/WAN to handle the data being passed back to the end user, including the inbound traffic as well.
12. End-user workstation workload handling from Web and application server (A). The user workstation's ability to handle the demand placed on it by its response from the system.

Accuracy versus Cost Issues   Obviously, as with all steps in this process, the person performing the analysis will need to make some decisions about the quality and accuracy of the estimates being worked with. The world of system performance evaluation is a tricky one under the best of conditions, and hardly anyone ever has the time to get all of the conditions right.

There are basic facts that you always have to deal with when it comes time to do performance evaluation: Performance evaluations are estimates and they cost money to run. It is a simple law of statistics, that the more time, energy, and money you spend on making your estimates accurate, the more precise they will be. Unfortunately, the only way to get a *completely* accurate estimate is to actually build the system and see what happens.

In general, the techniques that we are talking about here are *very high level*, and yield *very rough estimates*. These approaches are most effective when used as very quick, very inexpensive "sanity checks," just to make sure that nothing obvious has been overlooked. Much more sophisticated and advanced tools and techniques can be applied should these suggestions fail to yield good results.

Worksheet Development and Analysis (Some Examples)

Given this basic high-level understanding of the process, we will proceed to demonstrate how this approach can be used in a more detailed situation. The examples here will provide the reader with a general idea of how the worksheet development and analysis process works.

End-User Workstation (Initial Workload Generation)   Before we can calculate capacity we have to determine how much workload the users will be creating. To do this, we usually make some educated assumptions about what we expect the user's behavior to be, and act accordingly.

Our first example, Figure 21-7, shows a typical capacity worksheet, developed for our system's end-user workstation environment. This report tells us that we have approximately 200 users, all with PCs housing Intel type-586 chips, 10 gigabytes of disk, and Windows 95 with Netscape browser software. It also tells us that we can expect:

1. An average of 20 users to be on at any one time.
2. These users will generate approximately 12 transactions per hour (average user transaction rate or AUTR), or one every 5 minutes.
3. Each of these transactions will generate approximately three packets of outbound network traffic (APPT).

Figure 21-7
Initial end-user workload (user to Web server).

Web Warehouse Capacity Planning	End-User Workstation	Initial Generation Workload
Description		
Population		Corporate assigned PC, 200 users across 3 office locations
Hardware		586 PC with 10 gigabyte hard Ethernet drive and network card
Software		Windows 95, Netscape
Network hookup		Corporate LAN/WAN
Capacity		
Total users	TU	200
Concurrent users	CU	20
Average user transaction rate	AUTR	12 TPH (transactions per hour)
Average packet size	APS	50 kilobytes
Average packets per transaction	APPT	3 PPT
Average system packet rate ASPR = ASTR × APT	ASPR	720 PPH (packets per hour)
Average system capacity requirement ASCR = ASPR × APS	ASCR	36,000 KPH (kilobytes per hour)
Requirements (load placed on the environment)		
Network requirement (36,000 KPH = 36 MPS)		36 MPH (megabytes per hour)
Transaction processing requirement (12 TPH × 20 ACU)		240 TPH

Chapter 21: Architecture, Performance, and Management

4. The average packet will be approximately 50 kilobytes in size (APS).
5. This will result in a workload of approximately 720 packets per hour (PPH) (12 transactions per hour times 20 users times 3 packets per transaction).
6. The ultimate outbound network load will be 36,000 kilobytes per hour, or 600 kilobytes per minute (36,000/60) or 10 kilobytes per second (600/60).

LAN/WAN Capacity—User to Web Server Our second example, Figure 21-8, shows us the inventory data for the LAN/WAN connection between the workstations and the Web server. In this case, we already know what the load on the network link will be (from the value computed on the workstation worksheet), and we know what the capacity of the network should be. Therefore, all we need to do is report these facts and be sure that the demand is not greater than the capacity.

Figure 21-8
LAN/WAN capacity (user to Web server).

Environment Description Capacity Planning	LAN/WAN	Calculating the Ability of the LAN to Carry the Initial User Traffic
Environment Description		
Population		500 corp. users supported (200 involved in the Web warehouse)
Hardware		Fiber-optic backbone with Ethernet BNC local connections
Software		TCP/IP
Capacity		
Capacity/second		1 MPS (megabytes per second)
Capacity/hour		3600 MPH (megabytes per hour)
Workstation Load Requirements		
Average system capacity requirement	ASCR	36 MPH (megabytes per hour)
Computations		
Capacity		3600 MPH (megabytes per hour)
Requirement (36 MPH)	(see Figure 21-7)	36 MPH (megabytes per hour)
Difference (available capacity)		3564 MPH (megabytes per hour)

Figure 21-8 shows how one typically figures out whether the network link connection can handle the capacity or not. The first section of the worksheet gives us a brief narrative description of the physical and operational network environment and its inherent capacity. In this case, the LAN/WAN in question:

1. Supports 500 users (including our 200 Web warehouse users)
2. Consists of a fiber-optic backbone, with Ethernet physical connections back to the users' PCs
3. Supports a transmission rate of 1 megabyte per second (MPS) or 3600 megabytes per hour (MPH), computed by multiplying 1 MPS times 3600 seconds/hour = 3600 MPH

The second section contains information that we carried forward from the end-user workstation worksheet. This information is used to figure out what the capacity requirements for the outbound LAN/WAN traffic will be. In this case, the number we are looking for is the ASCR (average system capacity requirement), which is 36,000 kilobytes per hour (KPH). This number is equivalent to 36 megabytes per hour (MPH).

The last section summarizes both the capacity of the link and the requirements that will be placed on it, allowing us to see whether we have a surplus or a deficit of capacity. In this case, we have a surplus capacity of 3564 MPH. In other words, we have plenty of network capacity available for this workload.

Web and Application Server Capacity Once we have determined what the workload on the Web server will be, and proved that the network will get all of the work delivered to it on time, we are ready to evaluate how well it will be able to get the job done. See Figure 21-9. This worksheet tells us that:

1. Our combination Web and application server is a Windows NT–based PC, running the MS Web server.
2. The system has a measured average response time (ART) for this type of workload of 960 transactions per hour (approximately 16 transactions per minute, or 1 every 3.8125 seconds).
3. The system can also handle as many as five user requests at the same time, with a concurrent transaction capacity (CTC) of 5 concurrent transactions.

We already know, from the first worksheet in Figure 21-7, end-user workload generation, that the server will need to be able to handle at least 240 transactions per hour (TPH). The last section of the sheet sum-

Chapter 21: Architecture, Performance, and Management

Figure 21-9
Web server capacity (user to Web server).

Web Warehouse Capacity Planning	Web Server	Handling Initial User Workload
Environment Description		
Description		Local Web server supporting Web HTML request and CGI programs
Hardware		486 PC, 10 gigabytes hard disk
Software		Windows NT, MS Server
Capacity		
Average response time	ART	960 TPH (transactions per hour)
Concurrent transaction capacity	CTC	5 CT (concurrent transactions)
Requirements (from user workstations)		
Transaction processing requirement	(see Fig. 21-7)	240 TPH
Computations		
Capacity		960 TPH
Requirement		240 TPH
Surplus capacity		720 TPH

marizes our findings: with a capacity of 960 TPH and a workload of 240 TPH, we will in fact have a surplus of 720 TPH on this server.

Web Server Workload Generation Of course, just because the Web server can handle this workload does not mean that the entire system can. The next thing we have to do is figure out how much workload the Web and application server will create for the data warehouse that it is connected to. Our next worksheet, in Figure 21-10, shows us these calculations.

This worksheet summarizes what we know about the kind of work that the user transactions typically ask the Web server to perform. It tells us that we can expect an average of two database calls to be a part of every user transaction (database calls per transaction or DBT). We also know that when a call is made to the data warehouse, the database SQL command will be sent in a packet that is an average of 100 kilobytes in size (APS). The worksheet also tells us that, in general, each database call will be contained within one packet [yielding an average packets per transaction (APPT) measure of 1 PPT].

It is important that the reader not get confused by the APS and APPT measures used on this worksheet, and the ones from previous worksheets. Remember, the user generated a series of transactions and sent

Figure 21-10
Web server workload (Web server to data warehouse).

Web Warehouse Capacity Planning	Web Server	Data Warehouse Workload Generation
Environment Description		
Description		Local Web server supporting Web HTML request and CGI programs
Hardware		486 PC, 10 gigabytes hard disk
Software		Windows NT, MS Server
Capacity/Metrics		
Database calls per transaction	DBT	2 DBT
Average packet size (query)	APS	100 K
Average packets per transaction	APPT	1 PPT
Average Web server transaction rate	AWTR	480 TPH
Average system packet rate ASPR = AWTR × APPT	ASPR	480 PPH (packets per hour)
Average system capacity requirement	ASCR	48 KPH (kilobytes per hour)

them to the server. When the server gets those transactions, however, it processes them, and creates its own transactions. (In this case the Web and application Server will create two database transactions for every user transaction it receives.) Along this same line, while a user transaction may consist of 3 packets of an average size of 50 kilobytes, our application server will end up sending different-sized packets downstream to the data warehouse for processing.

Finally, our worksheet tells us that the system will generate an average of 480 transactions per hour (an average Web server transaction rate or AWTR of 480 TPH). (Remember, this represents 480 database requests.) And the network workload that will be generated between the Web and application server and the data warehouse will amount to little more than 48 KPH (an ASCR of 48 KPH), since the system generates 480 TPH, each transaction consists of only one packet, and each packet is 100 kilobytes in size (480 × 1 × 100 = 48,000 or 48 kilobytes).

Etc., etc., etc. While a fully illustrated example would require carrying calculations like this all the way through the system, the brief examples shown here provide the reader with a pretty good idea about what is involved. As stated earlier, the critical thing about using this process is to be sure of your objectives before you start. The process just outlined is helpful only in situations where you want to make sure that there is no obvious capacity problem that has been overlooked and you need a quick way to isolate a potential problem area and find where it might be. In different situations, other approaches will be more useful.

A Step-by-Step Guide to Performance Troubleshooting

In the previous example, we demonstrated a technique that can help you get some best-guess estimates about performance and the capacity of individual components and the system overall before the system has been built. That method, however, though useful in some situations, will be of little value when you are faced with a real-world troubleshooting situation.

While the chance to proactively plan for the capacity of a Web warehouse will happen once in a while, an even more common situation is to find that an existing Web warehousing system is suffering from extremely poor performance. In such situations, you will need to make use of a slightly different kind of approach.

When a production Web warehousing system is having serious performance problems, there is usually little time for any kind of thorough, sophisticated analytical approach. Usually, end users will be clamoring for reports, management will be fuming, and the warehouse support staff will be in a panic. For these situations, an even less scientific method of diagnosis will have to suffice.

What you need in a situation like this is a technique that will help you figure out, in the shortest amount of time possible, exactly where the problem area is within a distressed system. First you need to figure out whether the problem is caused by the users, the network, the Web server, the database, or whatever other component your particular system might happen to involve. Then you can call on the right specialist who can quickly diagnose the source of the problem and figure out how to fix it.

While there are many approaches to addressing such problems, the simplest and most commonly used technique is the "divide and conquer" approach.

The Divide and Conquer Approach

There seems to be some kind of weird law of the universe that convinces people that if their system is large and complex (like a Web warehouse) then there is no way that it can be analyzed by anyone but an "expert." In reality, we have found that if you simply attack the problem of large systems performance in a simple and straightforward manner, you can pinpoint the problem area with a minimum of expert intervention.

It is hardly ever the case that a large complex Web warehouse system is so badly engineered that the entire system is performing poorly. What usually happens is that one piece of the system becomes overloaded with work, and that component's failure to perform slows down the rest of the system.

The principles underlying the divide and conquer approach are simple. The basic steps of the process are:

1. Develop an inventory of components (nodes and links)
2. Select a set of transactions and test their overall performance
3. Disassemble the transactions into their component parts
4. Test the performance of each part
5. Analyze the results and pinpoint the problem component

This process allows us to isolate the problem component within the Web warehousing environment in a minimum amount of time. The following sections provide a more detailed breakdown of the process.

Step 1—Develop an Inventory of Components (Nodes and Links)

The first thing we do in an analysis of this kind is figure out exactly what all the different pieces of the system are and how they fit together. To accomplish this we will go through the same process we did in the previous case.

- We develop a capacity map. This map shows us the different components that make up the system and how they are related and connected to each other. (See Figure 21-6 for an example of a capacity map.)

- We create systems inventory worksheets. These inventory worksheets will list each component and its characteristics. (Again, we proceed exactly as we did in the previous section.) The inventory we put together should consist of just some basic capacity and configuration information for each component. We do not need to include all the detailed transaction and capacity metrics. (See Figures 21-7 through 21-10 for examples of some component inventory worksheets.)

Once we have assembled this prerequisite configuration and architecture information, we are ready to start the next phase of the process.

Chapter 21: Architecture, Performance, and Management

Step 2—Test Transactions Once we understand how the system is put together, the next thing we do is select a sample population of transactions to use as our test bed. In general, we will accomplish this as follows:

1. We select a small representative sample of transactions to test. (It usually helps to pick one or two of the transactions that perform the worst and combine them with a few chosen at random.)
2. Each transaction in the sample is tested and stopwatched a certain number of times. (*Stopwatching* is the process of running a transaction from a user terminal, waiting to see how long it takes to run, and then logging the amount of time that it took.) You use a stopwatch in this situation, just as you would use one to measure how long it takes a runner to finish a race course.
3. The results for each transaction are then added up and averaged out. We will then have an average wall time (AWT) for each transaction.
4. For those transactions whose average wall times are unacceptable, we begin the disassembly process.

Figure 21-11 shows a spreadsheet that tracks the stopwatched times for five representative transactions:

- *Display main menu.* The first screen displayed when you enter the system
- *Display query screen.* A screen that allows you to select the types of queries you want to run
- *Execute simple query.* The transaction that runs after you have input your simple query instructions
- *Execute complex query.* The transaction that runs after you have input your complex query instructions

Figure 21-11
Transaction stopwatch times, in seconds.

	Display Main Menu	Display Query Screen	Execute Simple Query	Execute Complex Query	Multiple Query Search
1	1	2	25	56	25
2	2	3	13	111	16
3	3	4	15	33	39
4	5	3	22	15	55
5	7	5	5	100	120
Average	**3.6**	**3.4**	**16**	**63**	**51**

- *Multiple query search.* A transaction that involves the scanning of several database tables with complex calculations between them

As we can see, there is a significant difference between the execution times. The worst performers are the execute complex query and the multiple query search transactions.

Step 3—Transaction Disassembly Once we have run the full system tests, we are ready to begin the process of disassembly. Basically, disassembly is the process of separating out that piece of a complete end-to-end transaction that occurs within each component of the overall architecture, and testing to see exactly how long it takes just that piece to execute. We start the disassembly process by listing each of the components of our architecture. In this case, our list consists of:

End-user workstation (A)

LAN/WAN connection (B)

Web and application server (C)

High-speed connection between Web and application server and the data warehouse (D)

Data warehouse (E)

We then take each of the transactions that we want to disassemble (in this case, the bad performers, execute complex query and multiple query search) and determine what actions they perform and what loads they place on each component.

Figure 21-12 shows an example of this breakdown for these two transactions. As we can see, each of these transactions:

1. Sends an HTML screen to the Web and application server
2. Puts a small data transport load on the LAN
3. Triggers the execution of a CGI program which then calls the data warehouse
4. Puts another very light data transport load onto the high-speed connection
5. Puts a significant load on the data warehouse (invoking several queries)

Each query in item 5 results in the sending of a significant amount of data back to the Web and application server. This causes the Web and application server to finish the processing and send a small answer

Chapter 21: Architecture, Performance, and Management

Figure 21-12
Disassembly of the poor performance transactions.

	Execute Complex Query	Multiple Query Search
User Workstation	Sends one HTML screen to the Web server	Sends 1 HTML screen to the Web server
LAN/WAN	Transports 2552 bytes to the server (size of HTML page)	Transports 12,354 bytes to the server (size of the HTML page)
Web & Application Server	Receipt of page triggers a CGI program that generates 5 SQL queries, forwarded to the data warehouse	Receipt of page triggers a CGI program which generates 15 SQL queries, forwarded to the data warehouse
High-Speed Connection	Transports 5000 bytes (5 × 1000 bytes) of SQL commands to the data warehouse	Transports 15,000 bytes (15 × 1000) of SQL commands to the data warehouse
Data Warehouse	Executes 5 queries and returns 50,000 bytes of data	Executes 15 queries and returns 150,000 bytes of data
High-Speed Connection	Transports 50,000 bytes back to the Web and application server	Transports 150,000 bytes back to the Web and application server
Web & Application Server	Receives data, processes it, returns 2500 bytes to end user	Receives data, processes it, returns 2500 bytes to end user
LAN/WAN	Transports 2500 bytes to end user	Transports 2500 bytes to end user
User Workstation	Receives answer and displays	Receives answer and displays

screen to the end user. This places a very light burden on the LAN/WAN and finally results in the answer being displayed on the user's screen.

Step 4—Testing Each Part of the Transaction After we have finished disassembling the transaction, we are in a position to start testing different components. Our objective is to end up with estimates that give us a good indication of how long each component takes to do its job. To accomplish this, we perform tests on those components that allow us direct access, and we find ways to derive the performance of those components that we cannot directly measure.

For example, in a typical Web warehousing environment, it is fairly easy to test end-user, Web server, application server, and data warehouse commands via direct manual input. Since these server devices usually have direct input capabilities built in, we can break down our testing process into smaller pieces.

In the worst-case scenario, we would usually try to test each leg of the journey of our transaction from one end of the system to the other, to see how much each contributes to the overall performance problem. The following procedure illustrates one way that this might be accomplished.

1. *Initial LAN/WAN transmit times.* First we want to see how long it takes the system to send a simple HTML screen to the server. This time is relatively easy to measure. We simply invoke any plain HTML transaction and see how long it takes. For example, the average execution time for the display main menu, or the display query screen transaction shown in Figure 21-11, provides good estimates for the first part of our transaction's journey. We will therefore assume that the typical LAN/WAN transmit time is approximately 3.6 seconds (a value that we derived using the transaction test times in Figure 21-11 as a guide).

2. *Web and application server time.* The next thing we need to estimate is exactly how long it takes the system to run the specified CGI program and get its response. The trick, of course, is to get that execution time without the burden of the LAN/WAN and end-user workstation as a part of it. The quickest way to get this number is to run the CGI program itself, directly on the Web and application server, and then measure the response time from that location. This kind of server-side execution of a program is usually easy to set up and do and should be a part of your Web warehousing environment set up. After running the server-side CGI program test, we have a number that represents the time it takes the rest of the system to satisfy the workload. We still do not know, however, how much of that measured response time is created by the Web and application server, how much is created by the network, and how much is caused by the data warehouse.

3. *Data warehouse time.* Next we test the data warehouse itself. To test this part we need to get copies of the queries that the CGI programs are executing over the network, and input them manually, keeping track of how long it takes them to run. Luckily, every major data warehousing product (database software) has a built-in direct query input capability (like the Oracle or DB2 ISQL facility). Manually running these queries will let us know exactly how long it takes the system to do the database portion of the process.

Chapter 21: Architecture, Performance, and Management

Step 5—Analyze the Results After we have tested the back-end database portion by itself, we will be ready to put together a very accurate picture of how much workload each component of the system is contributing to this transaction.

Figure 21-13 shows a summarization of our findings for the execute complex query example. The figure lists each component in the Web warehouse environment and the source of the measurement number we will be using. The overall system response, from end-user workstation to the data warehouse and back again, is an average of 63 seconds (as reported in Figure 21-11). We then see that the manual execution of this CGI program at the Web server yields a response time of 56 seconds. Given this information, we can calculate that the LAN/WAN portion of the transaction time must take approximately 7 seconds (63 − 56 = 7). We then input the SQL commands into the data warehouse and find that it is able to answer all queries in 5 seconds. This leaves us with a total of 51 seconds of response time unaccounted for (7 seconds for the LAN/WAN traffic, 5 seconds for the data warehouse adds up to 12 seconds: 63 − 12 = 51).

We know, by a process of elimination, therefore, that either the application server or the high-speed connection between the Web and application server and the data warehouse is slowing the system down. If we do some simple math, taking the network bandwidth and amount of data being transported into account, we find that the high-speed network component should add no more than 5 seconds to the transaction time. This leaves us with the conclusion that 46 seconds of the entire transaction response time is application server-based.

Figure 21-13
Disassembly of the poor performance transactions.

	Measurement Source	Measure Results	Derived Values
User Workstation	Overall average response time (see Fig. 21-11)	63 seconds	0 seconds
LAN/WAN	Derived from other samples		7 seconds
Web and Application Server	Manual execution of the CGI program	56 seconds	46 seconds
High-Speed Connection	Computed based upon bandwidth and data volumes		5 seconds
Data Warehouse	Direct data warehouse input of queries	5 seconds	5 seconds

Given that information, it is obvious that, to improve the system's performance, we have to either (1) upgrade the hardware supporting the Web and application server or (2) rewrite the CGI programs to run more efficiently.

Other Aids to the Troubleshooting Process

Of course, the painstaking manual process that we described here is only one approach that you can take. This divide and conquer approach, however, works amazingly well in many situations. The process of manually inputting and measuring response times is not always possible, however. When that is true, some other tools may be helpful.

Log Files The old tried-and-true method of system performance management has always been the trusty system log file. System log files are created by the server to help the administrator keep a record of everything that happened on the system. Whether the node in question is a Web server, an application server, a data warehouse, or any other kind of hardware, the chances are good that the product has a log file and a log file analyzer software package associated with it.

Web server log files typically keep track of every transaction run by a user, and Web browser log files sometimes keep track of every single keystroke and mouse movement. Application servers typically keep track of all users and of all transactions run on the system. Data warehouse servers almost without fail have log files that document every database I/O, the person requesting it, the transaction that asked for it, and the response time that the system was able to deliver. Log files can add a significant amount of extra input into the performance evaluation process.

Transaction Simulators In those situations where the organization has an extremely large, complex, and mission-critical system to worry about, it is quite common to enhance the existing performance monitoring toolkit with a special kind of program called a *transaction simulator*.

Transaction simulators can be written by a member of the computer systems staff in their simpler forms, or can be purchased as sophisticated, complete transaction measurement software packages. In either case, the architect gains a tool that allows preloading a large population of transactions into the system, then runs the transactions and measures the response times electronically.

Transaction simulators help the managers of very large systems estimate workloads and simulate overloaded system situations. Simulators provide managers with the information necessary to anticipate system outages and performance bottlenecks, and address them before they become a problem.

Conclusion

In this chapter we consider some of the different interpretations of the term *Web warehouse* and develop our own comprehensive description. We review some of the major issues involved in the management and control of these Web warehousing environments. We then review some of the many different ways that the Web warehouse architect can analyze an architecture and troubleshoot performance problem areas.

APPENDIX

TOPOLOGY DOCUMENTATION CONVENTIONS

As an aid to comprehending the process of designing, developing, and managing Web warehouse architectures, this appendix presents a diagramming technique that allows you to quickly understand exactly what kind of environment you are dealing with.

Platform Symbols

Figure A-1 shows our convention for the identification of servers or platforms, a cube. We consider a server/platform to be any hardware component whose principle purpose is to serve the requests of multiple users. We include as platforms Web servers, application servers, database servers, and legacy system platforms (mainframe, UNIX, and any other).

When the designation of the type of platform is important, we include the initials of the type of server inside of the cube, such as:

Figure A-1
Web warehouse platform symbols.

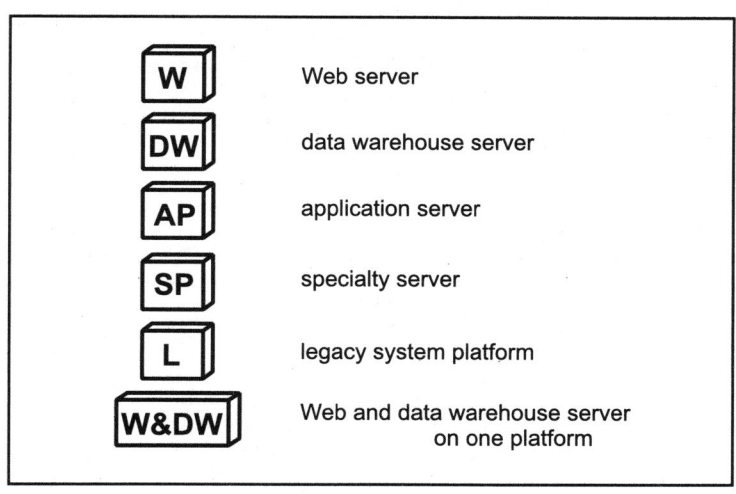

1. W for Web server, a machine that:
   a. Has its own TCP/IP address and InterNIC-registered domain name.
   b. Manages a population of Web (HTML) pages.
   c. Manages the scheduling of CGI (and possibly Java) programs. A Web server may or may not be the actual site where CGI and Java programs are executed. It may simply schedule the programs to run on application servers.
2. AP for application server, a machine that:
   a. Does not have an InterNIC-registered domain name.
   b. Does not manage Web pages or database activity.
   c. Hosts the execution of application programs that are usually triggered for execution by a Web server.
   d. Often gains access to data warehouse servers to process data.
3. DW for data warehouse server, a machine that:
   a. May or may not have InterNIC-registered domain name (depending on the database connectivity requirements).
   b. Does not execute application programs (though it does manage and execute stored procedures).
   c. Usually includes acquisition and storage components, but uses the Web as its primary access delivery vehicle.
   d. Is responsible for the storage, management, and retrieval of large volumes of data.
4. SP for specialty server, a machine dedicated to the management and retrieval of special-purpose objects like:
   a. Images
   b. Graphics
   c. Video
   d. Audio
   e. 3-D/4-D
   f. Stock price monitoring
   g. Usenets
   h. News services
   i. Clipping services
5. L for legacy system machine, any platform that houses an organization's operational computer system. Legacy systems can be found on

Appendix

mainframes, UNIX platforms, personal computers, and any other kind of platform.

When the platform in question has more than one function, we include the initials for all of its roles (e.g., W & AP for a machine that serves as both a Web server and an application server).

Workstation Symbols

We use similar convention to signify the different kinds of end-user workstations. The basic symbol is a hexagon. When it is important to know what type of workstation we are dealing with, we include the following initials within the figure to identify them. (Also see Figure A-2.)

1. WB for a PC running with a Web browser
2. WB-J for a PC/Web browser running a Java applet
3. WB-C for a PC/Web browser running a CGI application
4. NB-J for a PC running Java without a Web browser
5. TCP for a PC running a native (non-Web) application, but using the TCP/IP connection to establish a client/server relationship with a database somewhere on the Internet/intranet
6. UNIX for a UNIX workstation

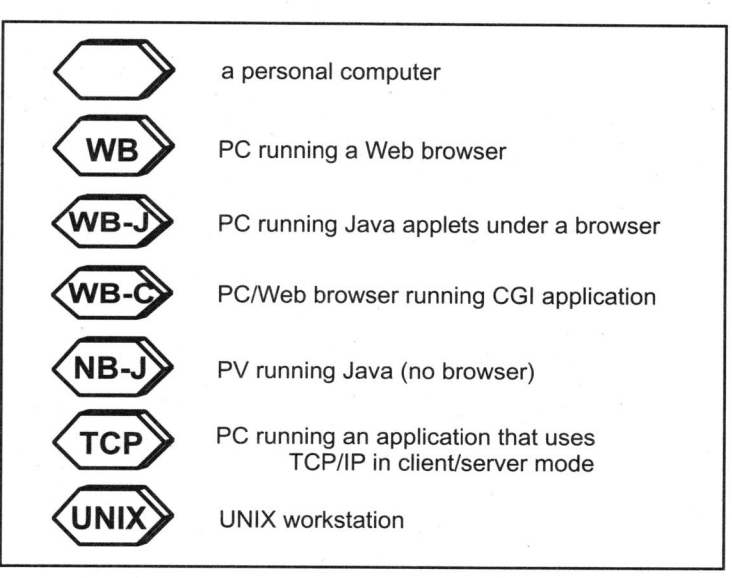

Figure A-2
Workstation symbols.

Figure A-3
Network symbols.

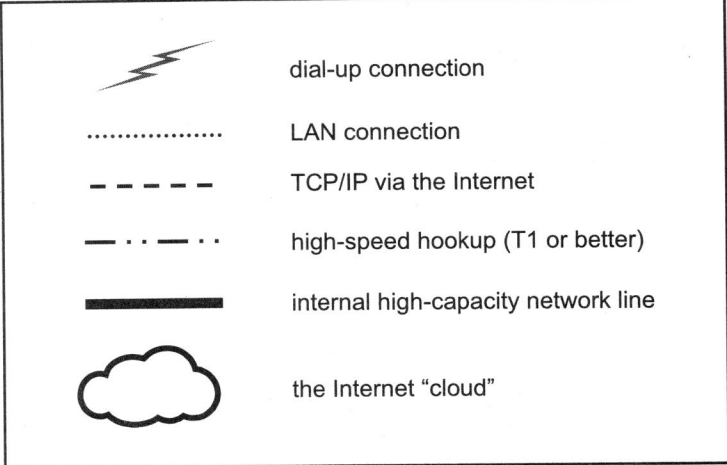

Network Symbols

Finally, we also need a convention for showing the different kinds of network connectivity that the Web warehouse architecture might include. See Figure A-3. We show the different kinds of network connections through the following symbols:

1. Cloud for the Internet itself
2. Solid black line for a high-capacity network connection
3. Dotted line for a LAN connection
4. Combination dot-dash line for a high-speed (T1 or better) connection
5. Dashed line for a normal TCP/IP Internet connection
6. Thunderbolt for a dial-in connection

When the specific speed of a line is pertinent, we include the speed (e.g., 28.8 kbps for a modem), along the length of the line.

GLOSSARY

A HREF = Tag that creates a hypertext pointer within a Web page. This tag underlines the text it refers to and specifies the URL to which it points.

Abstract representation The application of graphical software to display extremely complex, multidimensional conditions in a way that helps users better understand the complex relationships between the different variables.

Abstract windowing toolkit (AWT) Alternative name for the (package) library of windowing components from the Java API.

Accept-type Browser request field that tells the server what MIME types the browser can accept.

Access That component of a data warehouse environment concerned with the delivery of information to end users in a usable, manageable, and manipulable form. Access includes query, OLAP, statistical analysis, data discovery, and graphical information management tools.

Acquisition That component of the data warehouse environment concerned with the identification, extraction, cleansing, and preparation of data for loading into the warehouse. Acquisition technology includes data extraction, data repository, and metadata management software.

Agent A specialized type of software that can act on the instructions it has been given by the user, without that user's direct and immediate intervention.

Agent-based model Approach to text information delivery that allows a user to make use of software agents, which can then do work without requiring the user's immediate participation or presence.

ANOVA (analysis of variance) Approach used to measure the adjusted rate of variance across a population. It measures how much "real" variance there is in a population compared to a random variance.

Applets Java programs written to be executed from within Web browsers.

Application programming interface (API) A standard definition of how certain kinds of work are to be done in a programming language.

Application server A platform dedicated to the execution of application programs (CGI, Java, and others) that is generally invoked by a Web server and usually gains access to data via a data warehouse server.

Application value proposition A statement that describes the potential value that the application will deliver to the business and a description of how the business organization that will implement that benefit will make it work.

Architectural principles The collection of core, high-level descriptions of how a new technology solution can be organized.

Average response time (ART) A measure, in real (wall-time) seconds, of how long it will take the server to answer a request.

Average wall time (AWT) The average amount of time it takes a transaction to run, measured in elapsed time.

Beans Colloquial name for Java Beans.

Broadcast model Approach to text information management delivery wherein the information being sent is broadcast to the complete set of receivers all at the same time with no discrimination for individuals.

Business knowledge The collection of information, assembled and applied to the solution of a specific business problem is what we define as business knowledge (data + context + application to a specific business problem = business knowledge).

Capacity map A diagrammatic representation of a Web warehousing environment's physical configuration, showing the nodes (server platforms) and links (network components) and their capacities and capabilities.

Capacity planning The process of figuring out what the overall capacity of a system will be (measured in terms of number of users, number of concurrent users, number of transactions).

Cascading style sheets (CSS) A mechanism that allows the creator of a Web page to attach styles (fonts, sizes, colors, etc.) to the HTML document. With style sheets, page authors can create a consistent style for pages, or Web users can superimpose their own style.

Categorization The process of analyzing documents and, depending on content, placing them into predefined categories.

CGI-BIN Special UNIX directory used to hold programs that are to be executed by the Web server on the behalf of a user.

Glossary

CGI-SCRIPTS Generic name for all programs that have been written for, and been made available to, a Web server for execution. CGI-SCRIPTS include both script and standard programming language programs.

CHAID (chi-square automatic interaction detection) Data discovery technique that searches for interdependencies between variables in a population on the basis of chi-square analysis.

Class.forName() Method used to load database drivers into a Java program.

Client application enabler (CAE) Component that allows JDBC calls to access DB2 applications. Similar to the Oracle OCI.

Cluster analysis Statistical analysis approach used to analyze large populations of data. Cluster analysis looks for the most common "clustering" of variables within subsets of the population.

Clustering The process of grouping like documents according to the occurrence of similar words, expressions, phrases, or other characteristics.

Codification The process of interpreting text and converting it into meaningful codes for analysis.

Collaborative work environment System environment that allows individuals to collectively participate in the completion of tasks through their shared participation in the development of textual materials.

Common gateway interface (CGI) A standard for establishing communication between Web servers and Web browsers. The CGI standard defines the way in which commands and data are passed between browsers and servers in a vendor- and language-neutral format.

Compile The process whereby an English-language-like programming language module is turned into a machine-readable executable module.

Computer-aided design (CAD) The utilization of computer software to assist engineers and designers in the creation and manipulation of graphical engineering and construction drawings.

Computer-aided manufacturing (CAM) The utilization of computer software to assist organizations in the manufacture of products by feeding computer-generated specifications into manufacturing processes.

Concurrent transaction capacity (CTC) The number of concurrent transactions the server can manage before queuing or rejecting any more transactions.

Connection One of the four interface definitions that make up the JDBC set. Connection is concerned with the creation of connections to databases.

Conscription service Service that forces users to receive the latest information available for a given subject area as specified by someone else.

Content-type Server response field that tells the browser the MIME type of the document being sent.

Context-limiting search parameters Capabilities that allow the user to limit the population of files that the search engine will access, to save time and effort.

Corporate digital library Corporate-sponsored collection of digitally stored documents (and often other media as well), which are made available to corporate users through the mechanism of a search engine and/or enabling tools.

Correlation matrices Statistical analysis approach that identifies natural groupings of variables within the same population. Correlation analysis attempts to discover the strength of the relationships between bivariate (two) variables.

.createStatement() Method that prepares an SQL statement for execution.

Cultural hierarchy The collection of different cultural identity groups an individual belongs to.

Customer value proposition The offer a company makes to the consumer, stating which wants and needs the company is willing to satisfy.

Data analysis The process of investigating the relationships between variables in a population of data to discover meaningful patterns or dependencies.

Data discovery The form of data analysis that makes use of the newer, nontraditional, non-mathematically based methods to analyze populations of data. Examples of data discovery approaches are neural networks, CART, CHAID, and decision trees.

Data mart A generalized term used to describe data warehouse environments that are somehow smaller than others. A relative and sub-

Glossary

jective term often used to describe small, single-purpose minidata warehouses.

Data mining The application of statistical or data discovery techniques to an unknown population of data to try to discover meaningful characteristics or trends.

Data mining The process of identifying a large population of relatively unprocessed data, which is analyzed by statistical analysis or data discovery tools to attempt to discover new insights or patterns of value to the business.

Data warehouse applications The contiguous assembly of acquisition, storage, and access components, organized to deliver a value proposition from within the data warehouse environment.

Data warehouse server A platform dedicated to the acquisition and storage of data and other objects of interest to end users, with provision made for access via Web or client/server technology.

Data warehouse Any of a very large group of data management applications which involve the extraction, preparation, storage, and accessing of corporate legacy information systems data, for the purpose of achieving newer or better business benefits through the manipulation of that data. From a business perspective, a data warehouse is an environment, dedicated to the extraction of information out of legacy systems, and the conversion of that data into meaningful business information.

Data warehousing An approach to the building of computer systems whose primary functions are the storage, cataloging, retrieval, and analysis of information (in the form of data), through the use of client/server technology.

Data The raw material (numbers and words) that databases and documents are composed of.

Database object High-level abstraction of the different components of a data sourcing environment. A database object provides the user with a business view of the data source (as opposed to a technical or administrative view).

Database URL Special format for the identification and location of databases within the JDBC specification. The format for the Database URL is `jdbc:<subprotocol name>:<subname>`.

Descriptive statistics Statistical approaches that help describe a population (for example, the mean, mode, and average).

Desktop publishing The process of creating, storing, and producing publications by specialized personal computer based software that allows the user to set type, spacing, and all of the other features required for published documents.

Document object model (DOM) A platform- and language-neutral interface that allows scripts (and programs) to dynamically access and update the content, structure, and style of an HTML document.

Document-type definition (DTD) Document metafile that holds the standardized description for the formatting of information specified in an XML document.

Domain name service (DNS) Facility that keeps track of the alternative names given to servers on a network. The DNS server translates an IP address to a server name.

DriverManager One of the four interface definitions that make up the JDBC set. DriverManager is concerned with the overall management of the relationship between program and database and includes DriverManager, the foundational class of the JDBC package.

Dynamic HTML (DHTML) An HTML page that can change itself *after* it has been invoked.

Dynamically generated HTML screen An HTML screen that a program writes dynamically and sends directly to the browser, on the basis of the input that the program received.

.executeQuery() Method used to send an SQL command to a JDBC-connected database.

Exploratory/explanatory statistics Approaches that explain why things happen or provide insight into how they happen.

Extended Markup Language (XML) Advanced generation of markup language that brings content-based programming to Web development.

Extranet An Internet-like service that incorporates the Internet with a company's internal computer network and systems environment.

Factor analysis Approach used to determine how many and which factors actually contribute to an outcome. Factor analysis is used to help define market segments.

Feature extraction The process of identifying and analyzing those features which help determine what a document means, what it refers to, what its principle context is, and any other aspects that help determine how it applies to user-defined important criteria.

Glossary

Feature extractor Software component that analyzes image input and translates the definition of one particular feature of that image into a codified "description."

File transfer protocol (FTP) Internet service that allows people to copy files from anywhere to anywhere (assuming FTP clients and servers are in place).

FileInputStream Part of the standard I/O package which describes how standard file input is read into a Java application or applet.

FileOutputStream Part of the standard I/O package which describes how standard file output is managed by a Java application or applet.

FileRandomAccess Part of the standard I/O package which describes how random access to a data file can be managed from within a Java application or applet.

Financial model Model of how the application of a new technology will be financially measured, controlled, and accounted for.

FORM ACTION Special HTML tag that allows the programmer to specify which program on the server should be used to process the form input.

FORM A specialized type of HTML document that allows the user to input items for processing by programs or scripts on the Web server.

Functional model Model of how a new technology will function to meet the needs of users and consumers.

Gains chart Graphical display that shows the user how much better or worse a selected population will respond to a campaign, charted against a statistically random sampling.

Generalization Creating the definition of a product, system, or capability in such generalized terms that, while the definition is certainly true, it actually fails to provide people with the detailed information that would help them make a truly informed decision.

Geographic information system (GIS) Category of graphical information systems that specialize in the display and manipulation of geographical representations, combined with traditional tabular data.

.getConnection() Method that creates a connection between a Java program and a database.

Gopher Internet service that allows people to look for cataloged documents using structured directories and menus. A precursor of the Web paradigm.

Graphical information system Any of the category of information systems that collect traditional tabular type data and display it graphically.

Graphing software Software that converts tabular data into graphical displays (pie charts, bar charts, etc.).

Hypertext Approach to managing the process of navigating between documents; allows readers to select keywords or icons and immediately branch to a new document.

HyperText Markup Language (HTML) The language used to build Web pages and manage Web network traffic.

HyperText Transfer Protocol (HTTP) The language/protocol used to send messages over the Web.

Imaging The process of capturing the textual images on a document in electronic form.

IMG SRC = Tag that identifies an image to be displayed on a Web page.

Inbound Web configuration A Web architecture that allows users outside of the corporate infrastructure to gain access to systems via the World Wide Web.

Index builder That aspect of a search engine concerned with the collection of information and its placement within the product's indexing scheme.

Index searching mechanism (query builder) That aspect of a search engine application which is concerned with the conversion of the search parameters provided by the user into a meaningful query that can be run against the indexes to determine which entries best meet the user's request.

Information The combination of data and contextual information which gives that data a specific meaning.

In-line display objects Images that are displayed automatically and simultaneously with text within a Web page.

INPUT TYPE Special HTML tag line that allows the programmer to define input fields for the user.

Interface Definition Language (IDL) Provides a way to connect Java client programs to network servers running on other platforms. Allows you to transparently connect Java client applications or applets to legacy systems.

Glossary

Internet relay chat (IRC) Internet service that allows users to converse electronically within chat rooms.

Internet service provider (ISP) A business or organization that provides dial-up access to the Internet to consumers or employees.

Internet A worldwide network of machines, all communicating via a common infrastructure, protocol, and rules of operation. The Internet uses a variety of services including the Web, FTP, gopher, and many others.

InterNIC Cooperative agency that manages many aspects of the Web environment.

Interpret The process that a computer goes through when it reads a script file and turns it into an executable program.

Intranet An Internet-like network infrastructure managed and controlled by a company for its own internal utilization. An intranet can run Internet browsers and servers, but does not access the World Wide Web.

Invention Process of creating something that never existed before.

IP address A unique network address assigned to each machine connected to the Internet. IP addresses are assigned by InterNIC.

Java Programming language and execution environment created by Sun Microsystems and utilized extensively for Web development.

Java API extensions Collection of nonstandard API packages which support video, 3-D, telephony, and other nontraditional interfaces to Java.

Java archive (JAR) files Standard format for the compression and storage of all of the components of an applet.

Java Beans Java classes (subroutines or programs) which can be managed and manipulated via visually based development tools.

Java bytecodes The output generated by a Java compiler.

Java core API Collection of standard packages supporting Java development (includes language, utilities, networking, windowing, and standard I/O capabilities).

Java database connectivity The Java language package that addresses database connectivity issues.

Java development kit (JDK) Collection of tools, utilities, documentation, and sample code used to help support programmers in the development of Java applications and applets.

Java virtual machine Another of a number of software defined "platforms" that will interpret and run Java bytecode programs. Java-compliant Web browsers contain built-in Java virtual machines.

`java.sql` The name of the file holding the JDBC class and interface definitions.

Killer application A computer system implementation that radically changes the way an industry is run, and consequently the positions and strengths of competitors within that industry.

Knowledge base manager The component of the IQ/Objects product family that provides users with the ability to manage metadata about data sources.

Knowledge economics The study of those issues pertaining to the production, distribution, and use of knowledge within the organization.

Knowledge exchange The economic system through which people place value on the creation, storage, manipulation, distribution, and application of knowledge and define the terms under which they will participate in the knowledge economy.

Knowledge management theory An approach to the study of business that attempts to describe the effectiveness of organizations as a function of the efficiency with which they create, store, and apply knowledge to the creation of goods and services.

Knowledge neighborhood A group of individuals who share a common vocabulary, a common set of perspectives and objectives, and a common responsibility for the efficient management of one of the links of the corporation's value chain.

Knowledge network A group of individuals who share a common interest in the same collection of information and knowledge about a particular subject area.

Knowledge worker Term coined by Peter Drucker to describe the type of worker who makes no direct contribution to the creation of goods and services, but who applies knowledge to the more efficient deployment of goods and services by others.

Legacy platform Any platform whose primary purpose is to house a corporation's core operational systems.

Leveraged architecture The configuration of a Web warehouse environment in such a way that some aspect of the World Wide Web is leveraged to the advantage of the organization.

Glossary

Lift Measure of the improvement in response that one statistical model will yield compared to another.

Manually loaded indexes An approach to building indexes in which humans read, interpret, and catalog all the documents in the search universe, and manually load those categorizations into the search index.

Mechanical principles The core, detailed description of how a new technology actually works.

Media-based search scheme Approach to the storage and retrieval of multimedia information that makes use of multimedia objects themselves to describe, index, and retrieve them.

Middleware Any of a class of software products that helps programs connect to different kinds of databases.

MIME types Designations of the various types of objects managed over the Internet. MIME types include text/ASCII, text/HTML, IMG/GIF, and others.

Misdirection Defining a product, system, or capability in such a way that the purchaser is led to draw false conclusions about what the system can do or deliver.

Modeling The process of figuring out how a new technology will fit into the day-to-day world of the business.

Multimedia information management systems (MIMS) A category of software products that allow users to store and retrieve non-data and non-textually based objects, in order to address specific business objectives.

Multipurpose Internet mail extensions (MIME) International standard established to standardize the transport and handling of multimedia objects in an Internet and, consequently, the Web environment.

Obfuscation The process of intentionally making things seem more complicated and confusing than they really are in order to make a sale.

Object database connectivity (ODBC) Microsoft-established standard for connecting databases from multiple sources to multiple database types. ODBC makes it possible for almost any program to access almost any database using a standard set of commands and protocols, as long as they both conform to the ODBC standards.

Object types Definitions of types of files based on the naming convention. These conventions include, for example, .doc (MS Word), .html (HTML document), .xls (Excel), .wk4 (Lotus), and .wav (sound).

OCI connection type One of two types of Oracle JDBC connections. The OCI, or Oracle Call Interface, is utilized for Java applications only and makes use of Oracle's native OCI libraries to enable database connections.

Operating principles The core fundamentals that describe how a new technology works. These include mechanical and architectural principles.

Operational infrastructure The policies, procedures, roles, responsibilities, and system software, which define how the data warehouse environment is used, managed, tuned, and configured.

Operational model A model that describes how the presence of a new technology can change the way a company operates.

Operational model Model of how the use of a new technology will fit into the way people currently do things.

Optical character recognition (OCR) A computer system that can scan handwritten or printed documents (images) and convert those images into textual characters.

Organizational model A model of the new roles and responsibilities required by the use of a new technology, and the way the business organization is going to change to capitalize on the technology.

Organizational model Model of the way that people will change their organizational structure, and the definition of new roles and responsibilities necessary to support the implementation of a new technology.

Outbound Web configuration A Web architecture that allows users within the corporate infrastructure to gain access to external data sources accessible via the World Wide Web.

Overlay A layer of a geographical display that lays a new set of images on top of the already existing image (for example, a street map overlay over a map of zip code boundaries).

PERL High-level scripting language popular for the programming of UNIX-based Web sites.

Physical infrastructure Those aspects of the data warehousing environment having to do with the physical support of the environment including hardware, network, operating system, and other core physical components.

Glossary

Predictive model An analytically based view of the world that attempts to effectively identify those characteristics of a population that can best predict that population's behavior. You can create a model to try to predict the behavior of populations of humans (e.g., customers' buying patterns), machines (e.g., machine failure rates), or systems (e.g., companies' responses to changing conditions).

Predictive statistics Statistical methods that allow practitioners to predict the future behavior of a population.

Program-loaded indexes Approach to index loading that involves the explicit scheduling and running of document interpretation and categorization programs which create the index load data automatically. Also called job-loaded indexes.

Promotion The process of attempting to create interest in and acceptance of new technological solutions through the use of proactive advertising and evangelizing techniques.

Pull model Approach to text information management delivery that requires the user to specifically ask for and "pull" the information from a centralized storage source.

Push model Approach to text information management delivery that requires the system to be aware of the kinds of information that a user is supposed to get and send it to the user whether or not it has been asked for specifically.

Reality representation The process of making use of virtual reality software to provide users with a graphical representation of a real-world situation to help them understand and/or diagnose its condition or situation.

Regression analysis Statistical analysis approach used to identify underlying multivariable patterns within a population.

Remote method invocation (RMI) Allows a program on one machine to communicate with a program on another machine via simple Java methods.

`ResultSet` One of the four interface definitions that make up the JDBC set. `ResultSet` is concerned with the processing of the results of an SQL query.

Script language A programming language consisting of a limited number of high-level commands. Examples are PERL, shell script, and JAVA-SCRIPT. Script programs are usually not compiled and run dynamically. They are also known as interpretive languages.

Scripts Typically small, single-threaded programs written in a high-level command language to drive server programs and processing.

Search enabler software Software product that allows users to ask the system to retrieve text information related to the topics, concepts, and documents They have supplied it.

Search engine Software product that allows users to ask the system to retrieve text information related to the keywords they have supplied it.

Search pipeline The series of processing steps that a user query will go through when being prepared for execution by the Excalibur RetrievalWare product.

Search template Those characteristics of a document that a search engine will accept from a user as input into its searching mechanism.

Search universe The full population of documents from which the search engine can select.

Security and personal identity information systems Information systems that attempt to establish the identity of a person through physical characteristics such as fingerprints, retina, or hand-span.

Servlets Mini-Java applications that support and enhance the capability of Java-based server applications. Servlets are to servers what applets are to browsers.

Software developers kit A collection of program logic, tools, and components that allows a programmer to develop a particular type of application. A toolkit of programming parts and tools.

Software development kit (SDK) A collection of software development components and modules that can be assembled by the developer to deliver a specific application functionality. An SDK is a toolkit of programming components that programmers use to build specific applications.

Specialty server A platform dedicated to the management of special types of objects (images, pictures, graphics, video, audio, 3-D, 4-D, etc.).

Spider Specialized software agent that can (1) identify documents of interest to the user, (2) travel to the location where they are stored, (3) read them, (4) analyze their contents, and (5) report on those contents through the creation or population of indexes.

Spider-loaded indexes Approach to index loading that involves the use of spider programs, programs that proactively search the Web or search universe for documents of interest.

Glossary

Standard generalized markup language (SGML) Core language used to define markup languages (including HTML and XML).

Standard programming language A programming language that consists of a large number of commands, and which is usually compiled. Examples are Java, BASIC, C++.

Stateless That characteristic of the Internet and the Web that dictates the nature of the relationship between browser and server. In a stateless environment, browsers and servers operate without keeping track of what the other is doing, and without maintaining an awareness of the state of transactions they are working on.

Statement One of the four interface definitions that make up the JDBC set. Statement is concerned with the creation and running of SQL statements,

Static display objects Objects made available to users via an icon placed on the Web page. A static object is a sound clip, graphic, video, or document that is invoked only when the user clicks on its icon.

Statistical analysis The form of data analysis that makes use of the traditional, mathematically based, statistical disciplines. Examples of statistical analysis approaches include regression analysis, factor analysis, correlation studies, and ANOVA.

Stopwatching The process of running transactions from a user terminal, and measuring how long it takes them to run (often done with a stopwatch).

Storage That component of the data warehouse environment concerned with the storage of usable data in a database, directory, or some other form of manageable data storage structure. Storage technology includes any form of database management system, including relational, star schema, object/oriented, and many others.

Subscription service Service that provides users with the latest information available for a given subject area in response to users' requests.

Targeted model Approach to text information management delivery wherein the individual user receives the specific information required on a personalized basis.

Telnet Internet service that allows users to log onto and issue commands on a remote server.

Text analysis The process of analyzing the content of textual documents through the use of software that applies quantitative and statistical disciplines to help develop a better understanding of their content.

Text-based search scheme Approach to the storage and retrieval of multimedia information that makes use of words and sentences to describe, index, and retrieve different multimedia objects.

Textual information management system (TIMS) An information system used to identify, categorize, and organize textual information and make that information available to users according to their unique search and retrieval requirements (also referred to as text information system).

Thin connection type One of two types of database connection. The thin connection is developed for the support of applet programming and is provided by ORACLE, IBM, and other database vendors.

Topology The arrangement of physical, logical, and/or functional components within an architecture.

Transactions per hour (TPH) The number of transactions a node can process (or generate) in an hour, on average.

Transactions per minute (TPM) The number of transactions a node can process (or generate) in a minute, on average.

Transactions per second (TPS) The number of transactions a node can process (or generate) in a second, on average.

Uniform resource locator (URL) A Web addressing method. A URL identifies a resource on the Web.

User request facility Those parts of a search engine application concerned with the collection of search information parameters from the user.

User response facility Those aspects of a search engine application concerned with the reporting of information back to the user.

User-based model Approach to text information delivery that requires the user to interact with the system in order to get the information requested.

Value chain The set of activities an organization performs to create and distribute its goods and services.

Value chain component A specific activity that provides one part of the overall value chain.

Value proposition A statement that defines the value a company proposes to provide to a customer.

Glossary

Virtual reality software Software that converts tabular data into graphical representations of a real-world object or event.

Visioning The process of helping people figure out how the implementation of new technology models will affect them, and how they can adjust to using them.

Visual data mining The process of providing users with a graphical display of complex data and information interrelationships, which can then be visually and interactively explored, reviewed, imploded, exploded, and manipulated by using graphical manipulation options.

Web server A platform dedicated to the management of Web pages (HTML) and the scheduling of CGI applications.

Web warehouse A corporate information system dedicated to the identification, classification, and management of any and all information resources available to the business user, which can help contribute to the attainment of higher profits and/or lower expenses through that information's extraction, preparation, storage and dissemination.

Web warehousing An approach to the building of computer systems whose primary functions are the identification, cataloging, retrieval (possibly storage), and analysis of information (in the form of data, text, graphics, images, sounds, videos, and other multimedia objects) through the use of Web technology, in order to help people find the information they are looking for and analyze it effectively.

Web Colloquial name for that assortment of Internet services having to do with the management of HTML via HTTP commands, browsers, and servers.

Wide-area information service (WAIS) Internet service that gathers collections of index information about a population of documents and allows people to search for documents of interest using these indexes.

Word processing The process of creating, storing, and printing documents using specialized hardware and/or software. Word processing packages include products like MS Word, WordPerfect, and Lotus Word Pro.

INDEX

A

Abstract analysis, 297
Acceptance of new technologies, 53
Access (data warehousing), 159–162
   and data discovery tools, 161
   graphical/geographic information systems, 161
   hardware architecture for, 161–162
   network architecture for, 162
   OLAP tools, 160
   query/reporting tools, 160
   and statistical analysis, 160–161
Acquisition (data warehousing), 153–156
   components of, 153–154
   hardware architecture for, 154–155
   support software for, 155–156
   and Web warehousing, 156
Actionability, 89–90
ActiveX, 171, 195
Adaptive Pattern Recognition Processing (APRP), 330
Addressing (on Internet), 378–380
Administration Edition (IQ/Objects), 180
Advanced Windowing Toolkit (AWT), 477
Agent-based model (text delivery systems), 305
Air transportation, 47–48
Alignment, 71–72, 82–84
AltaVista, 312–313
American Hospital Supply, 80
Analytical toolkits area, 222
Analytical tools, 222
   business value from, 223–228
   categories of, 223–224
   determining, 227–228
   examples of, 224–227
   data discovery tools, 229–230
   applications, 230–232
   architectural approaches, 234–235
   statistical analysis vs., 232–234

Analytical tools (*Cont.*):
   IM for RM, 235–244
   architecture, 244
   Business Insights area, 243–244
   Customer Focus section, 242–243
   Data Preparation functions, 237–239
   Model Build area, 239–243
   multimedia analysis, 358
   statistical analysis, 227
   applications, 227–228
   architectural approaches, 234–235
   data discovery vs., 232–234
Aperio (Influence Software), 212–219
   Aperio Administrator, 213
   application development with, 215–219
   architecture, product, 213–215
   product offerings, 213
Aperio Knowledge Agent, 213
Aperio Knowledge Gallery, 213
Aperio OLAP, 213, 215–219
Applets, 468–472
Application value propositions, 92
Applications layer, 164–165
APRP (Adaptive Pattern Recognition Processing), 330
Archie, 410
Architectural principles, 43–44
Area objects (IQ/Objects), 185
Armstrong, Edwin, 42, 43, 46
Arpanet, 375
AT&T, 382
Audion, 41–42
AutoCAD, 258
Autodesk Inc., 258–259
Autodesk MapGuide, 258–265
   architecture of, 260–261
   operation of, 261
   sample implementations using, 259
   starting/manipulating displays with, 262–265

AWT (Advanced Windowing Toolkit), 477

B

Base reports (OLAP), 199–200
Bell, Alexander Graham, 43
Berners-Lee, Tim, 42
Biomedical research, 342
Boolean operators, 328
BPR (*see* Business process reengineering)
Broadcast model (text delivery systems), 304
Brokered information, 305
Browser-server communication, 429–431
   requests, 429–431
   responses, 431–432
Budgeting, knowledge management-based, 56
Bush, Vannevar, 416
Business applications of Web warehousing, 12–15
   closed-feedback-loop systems, 14–15
   collaborative work groups, 13
   data warehousing on Web, 12
   document-based knowledge, delivery of, 12
   learning, corporate, 14
   multimedia, 12–13
   paperless bureaucracy, 14
   raw information, analysis of, 14
Business behavior, 11
Business Insights area (IM for RM), 243–244
Business knowledge, 30–31
Business process reengineering (BPR), 63–64
Business value, 152
   from analytical tools, 223–228
   categories of value, 223–224
   determining value, 227–228
   examples, 224–227
   categories of, 223–224
   descriptive information, 223
   exploratory/explanatory discovery, 224
   predictive information, 223
   specialized insights, 224
   from graphical information systems, 248–249
   of OLAP, 203–205
   from traditional charting/graphing software, 250–252
Business(es), 67–72

Business(es) (*Cont.*):
   alignment in, 71–72
   and customer needs, 68–69
   definition of, 67
   key to survival of, 67
   and knowledge exchange, 120–121
   organizational structures in, 69–71
   and right to knowledge, 121–122, 126–127
Buying behavior, predicting, 225–226
Bytecode files (Java), 466

C

Capacity, 518–531
   measuring, 518–521
   link capacity, 520–521
   node capacity, 519–520
   planning, 521–531
   map, capacity, 522–523
   worksheets, capacity, 523–531
Cascading style sheets (CSS), 507
Categorization tool (Intelligent Miner for Text), 351–353
Cell phone locations, analyzing, 258
CERN, 42
CGI (*see* Common Gateway Interface)
CHAID (*see* Chi-square automatic interaction detection)
Charting software, traditional, 249–252
Chi-square automatic interaction detection (CHAID), 231–232
Class A addresses, 379
Class B addresses, 379
Class C addresses, 379
Client/server technology, 137–138, 273
Clipping services, on-line, 300–301
`close()` method (JDBC), 496
Closed-feedback-loop business systems, 14–15
Cluster analysis, 339, 349–351
Coarse-grain ranking, 329
COBOL, 136, 462
Collaborative problem solving, 299–300
Collaborative work environments, 13, 291, 298–300
Column objects (IQ/Objects), 184
Command line FTP, 395, 397
Commerce API (Java), 478

Index

Common Gateway Interface (CGI), 168, 171, 191, 326, 438–458
  as approach to data delivery, 438–439
  architecture of, 439–440
  communication within, 446–451
    from browser to server, 446
    returning information back to browser, 449–451
    from server to program, 446–448
  database access under, 455–456
  input with, 440–445
    command line, using, 441–442
    forms, using, 442–444
  processing under, 451–458
    and database access, 455–456
    database program flow, standard, 457, 458
    and runtime environment, 454–455
    with scripts, 451–453
    with standard programs, 453
    and type of work, 456–457
Competitiveness, 270–271
Component objects (IQ/Objects), 185
Composite objects (IQ/Objects), 185
Computer systems, 70, 81–83
  components of, 290
  first-generation, 135, 279–280
  and knowledge management, 27–31
  second-generation, 135–137
Conscription services, 291, 300–302
Consultants, 104, 124
Consumer applications:
  of knowledge management, 26
  of Web warehousing, 15–16
Consumer behavior, 11
Consumer Internet hookups, 384–386
Consumer needs, meeting, 68–69
Content search, 339
Content summarization, 339
ContentHandler, 476
Context evaluation, 297
Convenience, 91
Corporate conscription services, 302
Corporate digital libraries, 293
Corporate identity, 116
Corporate Internet hookups, 386–387
Corporate learning, 14
Corporate property, 305–306

Corporate strategic initiatives, 62–66
  business process reengineering, 63–64
  convergence of, 66
  customer-centric approach, 65–66
  efficient customer response, 64–65
Corporation(s):
  knowledge management view of, 20–21
  traditional, 19–20
Correlation analysis, 227–228
`createStatement()` method (JDBC), 494–495
CRM (*see* Customer relationship management)
CSS (cascading style sheets), 507
Cubes, 209, 215
Cultural hierarchy, 116–117, 121–122
Cultural memberships, 115–116
Cultural shift, 113–117
Customer Focus section (IM for RM), 242–243
Customer Relationship Intelligence, 342–347
  analysis with, 345–346
  architecture, 347
  input identification/collection with, 345
  input standardization with, 345
  report generation with, 346–347
Customer relationship management (CRM), 33, 65–66
Customer service, text management systems in, 277
Customer-centric approach, 65–66

D

DASD (direct-access storage devices), 135
Data:
  dimensional, 201
  factual, 201
Data discovery, 161, 222
Data discovery tools, 229–230
  applications of, 230–232
  CHAID, 231–232
  neural networks, 230–231
  architectural approaches to, 234–235
  statistical analysis vs., 232–234
Data mart:
  architectural deployment models, 149–150
  data warehouse vs., 148–149
Data mining, 222, 229
  text mining vs., 340–341

Data mining (*Cont.*):
  visual, 254–256
  See also Text mining
Data Preparation area (IM for RM), 237–239
Data processing, 28
Data warehousing, 4–7, 134–165
  access component of, 159–162
    data discovery tools, 161
    graphical/geographic information systems, 161
    hardware architecture, 161–162
    network architecture, 162
    OLAP tools, 160
    query/reporting tools, 160
    statistical analysis, 160–161
  acquisition component of, 153–156
    hardware architecture, 154–155
    support software, 155–156
    and Web warehousing, 156
  architectural deployment models, 149–150
  barriers to successful, 140–146
    political issues, 145–146
    sourcing, 141–143
    system specifications, 143–145
  and business value, 152
  data mart vs., 147–149
  definition of, 139
  economic justification for, 139–140
  as environment, 152–153
  failed approaches to, 146–148
  information systems architecture before, 134–138
    client/server technology, 137–138
    first-generation systems, 135
    relational databases, 136–137
    second-generation systems, 135–136
  layers in, 162–165
    applications layer, 164–165
    operational infrastructure, 163
    physical infrastructure, 163
    query tools, 160
  "real" warehouse as model for, 150–152
  reporting tools, 160
  storage component of, 156–159
    hardware architecture, 158
    network architecture, 158–159
    support software, 159
  successful approaches to, 148–153
  See also Web warehousing

Databases:
  CGI, access under, 455–456
  relational, 29, 136–137
DB2, 503
De Forest, Lee, 41–42, 46
Decision support systems (DSS), 5
Dependence on technology, 54
Descriptive information, 223
Design, knowledge management-based, 55
Desktop publishing, 282
DHTML (*see* Dynamic HTML)
Dictionaries, 330
Dictionary lookup, 327–328
Digital libraries, corporate, 293
Digital word, 287
Dimensional data, 201
Direct-access storage devices (DASD), 135
Disk drives, 135
DNS (*see* Domain name services)
Doctors, 123–124
Document categorization, 339
Document-based knowledge, delivery of, 12
Domain name services (DNS), 380–382
Drucker, Peter, 18
Drug development, 255–256, 342
DSS (decision support systems), 5
Dual-leveraged configuration, 517
Due diligence, 172–173
Dumb terminals, 162
Dynamic HTML (DHTML), 507–508
Dynamic IP address allocation, 380

E

E-commerce, 16
Economics, knowledge (*see* Knowledge economics)
ECR (*see* Efficient customer response)
Edison, Thomas, 43, 44, 51
Efficient customer response (ECR), 33, 64–65
Electric utility companies, 343
Electricity:
  functional vision for, 46–47
  invention of, 42
Email, 282–283, 304, 404–405
Engelbart, Douglas, 416
Enterprise resource planning (ERP), 35

Index

Excalibur Internet Spider, 324
Excalibur RetrievalWare, 323–335
   accuracy of, 334–335
   HTML interface architecture, 325–326
   index building with, 330–331
   query building approach in, 327–330
   scalability of, 335
   screen examples, 332–334
   search templates in, 326
   synchronization with, 331–332
   user interface, 325
Excalibur RetrievalWare FileRoom, 324
Excalibur Screening Room, 324
Excalibur Technologies Corporation, 323
Excalibur Visual RetrievalWare, 324, 363–369
   feature extractor in, 364–365
   practice applications, 366–368
   vector indexes in, 365–366
Exchange, knowledge (*see* Knowledge exchange)
Excite, 314
executeQuery() method (JDBC), 495
ExpressLane, 504
Extended Markup Language (XML), 508–511
Extranets, 388–389

F

Factor analysis, 228
Faraday, Michael, 42, 43
Feature extractors (Excalibur Visual RetrievalWare), 364–365
File transfer protocol (FTP), 394–397, 410
   architecture of, 394–395
   command line FTP, 395, 397
   power/flexibility of, 397
FileInputStream, 482
FileOutputStream, 483
Financial models, 49–50
Fine-grain ranking, 329
Fingerprint identification systems, 359
First-generation computer systems, 135, 279–280
Forecasting, 173
Forms (in CGI), 442–444
forName() method (JDBC), 493
FTP (*see* File transfer protocol)
Functional models, 45–47

Functional vision, 104–105
Fuzzy spelling, 328

G

Gains charts, 240
Games, interactive, 105
General Atomics, 382
Generalization, 88
Geographic information systems (GIS), 161, 256–265
   Autodesk MapGuide, 258–265
   architecture of, 260–261
   displays, starting/manipulating, 262–265
   operation of, 261
   sample implementations, 259
   examples of, 257–258
   functionality of, 257
getConnection() method (JDBC), 493–494
GIS (*see* Geographic information systems)
Global positioning systems (GPS), 254
Global Sports (case example), 174–188
   creation of database objects, 180–182
   data sources, identification of, 180
   problem summary, 175
   reports, 183–188
   distribution of, 186–188
   formatting of, 184–186
   validation of, 183
   software, choice of, 175, 177
Gopher, 397–399, 410
Gosling, James, 460
GPS (global positioning systems), 254
Grammatical analysis, 339
Graphical display products, 161
Graphical information systems, 248–256
   business value provided by, 248–249
   definition of, 248
   traditional charting/graphing software, 249–252
   virtual-reality products, 252–254
   layering applications, 253
   medical systems, 254
   oil well drilling services, 254
   power plant example, 252–253
   traffic/transportation management, 254
   visual data mining applications, 254–256

Graphing software, traditional, 249–252
Groupware, 298

H

Hand pattern recognition, 359
Handwriting, 287–288
Hosting, 157–158
HOSTS file, 381–382
Hot objects (IQ/Objects), 185
HotBot, 313–314
HTML (*see* Hypertext markup language)
Hybrid search systems, 357
Hypertext functionality, 415
Hypertext markup language (HTML), 190–194, 280, 392, 393
   Dynamic HTML, 507–508
   and Excalibur RetrievalWare, 325–326
   and hypertext paradigm, 415–417
   managing program execution with, 424–427
   and MIME, 421–424
   object management with, 417–421
   browser settings, 421
   nontext objects, placement of, 419–420
   types of objects, 420–421
   and OLAP, 209, 211, 215, 217
   as universal document display language, 411–415

I

IDL (Interface Definition Language), 478
IDMS (Information Data Management System), 135
IM for RM (*see* Intelligent Miner for Relationship Marketing)
Imaging systems, 283–284
Implied models, 99–100
IMS (Information Management System), 135
Index builders, 310
Index building, 311, 330–331
Indexes, 310, 316–323, 330–331
   loading, 318–323
   manually loaded indexes, 319–320
   program-built (job-based) indexes, 320–321
   spider-based approach to, 321–323

Indexes (*Cont.*):
   multimedia, 360–363
   organization of, 317–318
   query building/execution techniques with, 318
Industry value proposition, 73
Information:
   brokered, 305
   businessperson's need for, 270–271
   descriptive, 223
   predictive, 223
   public domain, 305
Information Data Management System (IDMS), 135
Information management, 28–29
Information Management System (IMS), 135
Infoseek, 314–315
Infrastructure, 69–71
In-line display objects, 419
Insurance industry, text management systems in, 278–279, 299
Intelligent Miner for Relationship Marketing (IM for RM), 235–244
   architecture of, 244
   Business Insights area of, 243–244
   Customer Focus section of, 242–243
   Data Preparation area of, 237–239
   Model Build area of, 239–243
Intelligent Miner for Text, 341–342, 347–353
   categorization tool, 351–353
   clustering tool, 349–351, 353
   feature extraction tool, 348
Intelligent Query, 178
Intelligent software agents, 305
Interactive games, 105
Interface Definition Language (IDL), 478
Internal email, 304
Internet, 116–117, 119–120, 375–406
   addressing on, 378–380
   architecture of, 376–380
   and domain name services, 380–382
   and extranets, 388–389
   FTP services, 394–397
   Gopher, 397–399
   hooking up to, 384–389
   consumer hookup, 384–386
   corporate hookup, 386–387
   and InterNIC, 382–383
   and intranets, 388–389

Index

Internet (*Cont.*):
  IRC, 404
  mail via, 404–405
  and TCP/IP protocol, 376–378
  Telnet, 403
  topology of, 376
  URLs, 383–384
  WAIS, 399–403
  See also World Wide Web
Internet relay chat (IRC), 404
Internet service providers (ISPs), 385–388
InterNIC, 382–383
Interviews, 105
Intranets, 388–389, 514–515
Inuit, 114
Invention of new technologies, 41–42
Inventory control, 74
IP addresses, 379–380, 382–383, 506
IP protocol, 377
  version 4 of, 506
  version 6 of, 506–507
IQ Software, 175, 177–179
  product family, 177–178
  strategy of, 178–179
IQ/LiveWeb, 178
IQ/Objects, 179–185
  architecture, 189
  data sources, identification of, 180
  database objects, creation of, 180–182
  editions of, 179–180
  queries, developing, 182–183
  reporting with, 183–185
IQ/SmartServer, 178, 186–188
  architecture for, 189–191
  publishing reports with, 191–192
  real-time report generation with, 192–195
IQ/Vision, 178
IRC (Internet relay chat), 404
ISPs (*see* Internet service providers)
I/T departments, knowledge management for, 55–57

J

Java, 171, 211, 326, 460–483
  API packages, core, 475–477
  API standard extensions, 477–483

Java (*Cont.*):
  Commerce API, 478
  enterprise extensions, 477–478
  I/O package, 481–483
  Java Beans, 479–481
  Management API, 478–479
  Media API, 479
  Server API, 479
  characteristics of, 462–465
  COBOL vs., 462
  history of, 460–462
  as language, 465–466
  as platform, 467–468
  runtime environment of, 465–474
  applets, writing/running, 468–472
  compiling/interpreting, continuous, 466–467
  non-Web-based applications, 472–474
  program organization, 465–466
  on Web, 468
  on Web, 468
Java Beans, 479–481
Java DataBase Connectivity (JDBC), 168, 171, 477–478, 481–482, 486–511
  accessible databases, 486
  and java.sql package, 488–491
  and next generation of Web technology, 505–511
  process of accessing databases with, 487–488
  programming with, 491–498
    additional capabilities, 498
    closing, 496
    connection, creating, 493–494
    drivers, loading, 493
    importing classes, 491
    locating/identifying databases, 491–492
    processing results, 495–496
    query statement, 494–495
  with specific databases, 498–505
    DB2, 503
    ExpressLane, 504
    middleware products, 503–504
    and ODBC standard, 500–501
    Oracle, 501–503
    SimbaExpress, 504–505
Java Development Kit (JDK), 474–475, 500
Java Report Requestor (IQ Software), 196
JavaSoft, 486
java.sql package, 488–491

JDBC (*see* Java DataBase Connectivity)
JDK (*see* Java Development Kit)
Job-based approach (to index building), 320–321

K

Keyboard analysis, 297
Killer applications, 79–80, 271
Knowledge:
   business, 30–31
   delivery of document-based, 12
   right to, 121–122, 126–127
   storage of, 268
Knowledge bases, 32
Knowledge community, 110
Knowledge economics, 25, 111
   broadcast radio and movies, role of, 118–119
   definition of, 112
   examples of, 122–124
   Internet and Web, role of, 119–120
   in primitive societies, 117
   printing press, role of, 117–118
   television, role of, 119
   and Web warehousing, 125
Knowledge exchange, 112, 130
   business applications of, 120–124
   conflict over, 125–127
   definition of, 112–113
   ownership issues, 125–126
   security issues, 125
Knowledge factories, 18–20
Knowledge management, 17–36
   and breakdown of traditional corporate model, 18–20
   and computer systems, 27–31
   business knowledge, role of, 30–31
   data processing, 28
   information management, 28–29
   consumer applications, 26
   for corporate I/T departments, 55–57
   corporation from perspective of, 20–21
   definitions of, 21–22, 26–27
   future applications of, 54–55
   organizational structures based on, 58–59
   principles of, 23–26
   scope of, 22
   and system architecture, 57

Knowledge management (*Cont.*):
   and systems development life cycle, 127–130
   theory, knowledge management, 23
   and value chains, 57–58, 80–82
Knowledge management systems, 31–36
   automatic systems, 34–35
   classification of, 34
   definitions of, 31–32, 35–36
Knowledge management theory, 23
Knowledge neighborhoods, 25, 33, 110–111, 130
Knowledge networks, 25, 108–110
Knowledge workers, 18
KnowledgeBase, 32
Knowledge-is-power paradigm, 271

L

LANs (*see* Local-area networks)
Layering applications, virtual-reality, 253
Learning, corporate, 14
Legacy systems, 142–143
Legal profession, text management systems in, 278
Leveraged inbound configuration, 515–516
Leveraged outbound configuration, 516–517
Lexical analysis, 339
Life cycle, knowledge management-based systems, 56, 127–130, 142
Lift (random response rate), 241–242
Linguistic analysis, 339
Link capacity, measuring, 520–521
Local-area networks (LANs), 5, 273, 387, 522–528, 534–537
Lotus Notes, 33
Lycos, 315, 316

M

Mail, Internet (*see* Email)
Management API (Java), 478–479
Management information systems (MIS), 5, 29
Manufacturing, text management systems in, 275
Map Visualizer, 255

Index

Marconi, 43, 46
Marketing, 55, 74
Marketing conscription services, 301
Marketing databases, 98–99
Marketing knowledge neighborhood, 111
Marketing materials, 305
Matrix management, 19
MDBS (Multidimensional Database Management Systems), 208
Mechanical principles, 43
Media, 9–11
Media API (Java), 479
Medical systems, virtual-reality, 254
Memex, 416
Merchandising, 74
Microkeypads, 11
Microsoft Excel, 256
Microsoft Windows 95, 51, 161, 381
Microsoft Windows NT, 455
Middle management, 19
Middleware, 503–504
MIME (*see* Multipurpose Internet mail extensions)
MIS (*see* Management information systems)
Misalignment, 82–83
Model Build area (IM for RM), 239–243
Modeling, 129
    completion of, 102
    of new technologies, 44–50
    process of, 24–25
Models, 96–102
    definition of, 99
    development of, 100–102
    by consultants, 101
    functional/financial models, 97–98
    with help from outside parties, 101–102
    by internal research and development departments, 100
    by special study teams, 101
    implied, 99–100
    operational/organizational, 98–99
    See also Visioning
Mosaic, 461
Movies, 118–119
Multidimensional Database Management Systems (MDBS), 208
Multihosting, 158
Multimedia, business utilization of, 12–13

Multimedia management information systems, 356–369
    categories of, 357–359
    indexing in, 362–363
    textual search systems vs., 359–362
    Visual RetrievalWare, 363–369
    feature extractor in, 364–365
    practice applications, 366–368
    vector indexes in, 365–366
Multipurpose Internet mail extensions (MIME), 421–424
Multithreading, 463–464

N

Name extraction, 348
National Science Foundation, 382
Nationalism, 119
NBC, 46
Network protocols, 377–378
Network service providers (NSPs), 410–411
Network Solutions, Inc., 382
Networks, knowledge (*see* Knowledge networks)
Neural networks, 230–231
News services, 300
Newspapers, on-line, 343
Node capacity, measuring, 519–520
NSAPI, 214
NSPs (*see* Network service providers)

O

Oak language, 460–462
OCR (optical character recognition), 284
ODBC (*see* Open Database Connectivity)
Oil well drilling services, virtual-reality, 254
OLAP (*see* On-line analytical processing)
OLAP reporting, 198
OLE objects (IQ/Objects), 185
OLTP (*see* On-line transaction processing)
On-line analytical processing (OLAP), 5, 48, 144, 160, 198–219
    with Aperio, 212–219
    business value of, 203–205
    cubes, 209

On-line analytical processing (*Cont.*):
   data management approaches with, 208–209
   design challenges with, 205–207
   features of, 198
   relational, 208
   reporting with, 199–202
   base reports, 199–200
   navigation, 200–202
   Web approaches with, 209–212
   client/server-based front end, 210–211
   hybrid approaches, 211–212
   publishing as Web pages, 209–210
On-line clipping services, 300–301
On-line newspapers, 343
On-line transaction processing (OLTP), 5, 17, 76–77, 89, 96
Open Database Connectivity (ODBC), 456, 500–501
Operating principles, 42–44
Operational enhancement, 169, 173
Operational infrastructure, 163
Operational models, 47–48
Operations, 74
Optical character recognition (OCR), 284
Oracle, 501–503
Organizational models, 48–49
Organizational structures, 58–59, 69–71, 277–278
OS/2, 161

P

Panning, 263
Paperless bureaucracy, 14
Parsers, 400–401
Parsing, 328
"Partial paint" phenomenon, 409
Pattern searches, 330
Personal computers, 280–281
Personal Edition (IQ/Objects), 179
Personal identification management systems, 358–359
Phrase counts, 297
Physical facilities, 70
Physical infrastructure, 163
Physical intranets/extranets, 388–389
Planning, knowledge management-based, 56
Policies, 70–71

Political issues, 145–146
Porter, Michael, 73
Power plant virtual-reality application, 252–253
PPP (*see* Pre Process and Publish)
Pre Process and Publish (PPP), 168, 170, 191, 435–438
   architecture for, 435–436
   establishing communication with, 436–438
Predictive information, 223
Primitive societies, 114, 117
Printed information, 286–287
Printing press, 117–118
Problem solving, collaborative, 299–300
Procedures, 70–71
Processes, 70–71
Production problems, discovering cause of, 226–227
Promotion of new technologies, 51–53
Prompt objects (IQ/Objects), 184
Propaganda, 118–119
Protestant Reformation, 118
Protographic identification system, 359
Public domain search engines, 292
Public domain text information, 305
Publishing software, 282
Pull model, 303
Purchasing, 74
Push model, 303–304

Q

Query building/execution, 310, 318, 327–330
Query Edition (IQ/Objects), 179
Query tools, 160
Querying:
   delivery capabilities, 170–171
   developing queries, 182–183
   with IQ/Objects, 179
   tools for, 168–170

R

Radio, 41–43, 46, 118–119
Random response rate, 240–241
`RandomAccessFile`, 483
Ranking, coarse- vs. fine-grain ranking, 329

Index

Raw information, analysis of, 14
RCA, 46
Real estate industry, text management systems in, 277
Reality representation services, 252
Regression analysis, 228
Relational databases, 29, 136–137
Relational OLAP, 208
Remote Method Invocation (RMI), 478
Renaissance, 118
Report Edition (IQ/Objects), 179–180
Reporting:
   ActiveX, 195
   delivery capabilities, 171
   with IQ/Objects, 179–180
   Java-based, 196
   tools for, 160, 168–170
Reports:
   with Customer Relationship Intelligence, 346–347
   distributing
     for viewing, 186–187
     for viewing via Web, 187–188
   formatting, 184–186
   real-time generation of, 192–195
   validating, 183–185
Research and development, 100, 275–276
Retail industry, value chains in, 73–75, 78–79
Retinal scans, 359
RMI (Remote Method Invocation), 478
ROLAP, 215
Role playing, 105

S

Sabre reservation system, 80
Sales, 74
Sales cycle management, 299
Sales people, 123
Sarnoff, David, 46
Scripts, 451–453, 507–508
SDK (*see* Software Developer's Kit)
Search enablement products, 296
Search enablers, 291
Search engines, 291–296, 308–323
   architecture of, 309–311
   corporate digital libraries, 293
   critical role of Web, 308–309

Search engines (Cont.):
   functionality of, 293–296
   keyword searches, 293
   targeting of search population, 293, 295
   future role of, 309
   indexes in, 316–323, 330–331
   loading, 318–323
   organization, 317–318
   query building/execution, 318
   multimedia-based, 357–358
   principal components of, 310–311
   subscription search services, 292–293
   with text analysis, 2987
   variations in, 311–323
   indexing schemes, 316–323
   templates, search, 312–316
   user interfaces, 311–312
   Web-based public domain search engines, 292
   See also Excalibur RetrievalWare
Search pipeline, 327
Search templates, 310, 312–316, 326
Search universe, 310
Second-generation computer systems, 135–137
Security, 125, 358–359
Semantic analysis, 339
Semantic expansion, 328
Semantic networks, 329–330
Server API (Java), 479
Shared reference libraries, 299
Silicon Graphics Inc., 255
SimbaExpress, 504–505
Soft dollars, 273
Software Developer's Kit (SDK), 324, 364
Software development, 55
Software procurement, 56–57
Sourcing, data, 141–143
Special-interest groups, 301
Spiders, 305, 321–323, 330
Splat and Scatter Visualizer, 255
Spotfire Inc., 255–256
Spreadsheets, 224–225
SQL, 136
Standard programs, 453
Stat Visualizer, 255
Statelessness (of World Wide Web), 427–429
Static display objects, 419
Statistical analysis, 160–161, 222, 227, 297
   applications of, 227–228
   correlation analysis, 227–228

Statistical analysis (*Cont.*):
  factor analysis, 228
  regression analysis, 228
  architectural approaches to, 234–235
  data discovery vs., 232–234
Status, 91
Stock quotes, 300
Stop words, 331
Stopwatching, 533
Storage (data warehousing), 156–159
  hardware architecture for, 158
  network architecture for, 158–159
  support software for, 159
Store layout design, 74
Store location planning, 74, 257–258
Strategic initiatives (*see* Corporate strategic initiatives)
Study teams, special, 101
Subscription search services, 292–293, 300–301
Subscription services, 291
Sun Microsystems, 460–462
Superheterodyne, 42
Surveys, 104
Synchronization, 331–332
System objects (IQ/Objects), 184

T

Targeted model (text delivery systems), 304
TCP/IP protocol, 376–378, 380–383, 385, 386
Technology Watch, 342
Technology(-ies), new:
  assimilation process for, 40–54
  acceptance, 53
  and cultural shift, 113–117
  as cycle, 128–129
  dependence, 54
  invention, 41–42
  modeling/visioning, 44–50
  operating principles, development of, 42–44
  promotion, 51–53
  and cultural shift, 113–117
  deployment of, 87–91
  and actionability, 89–90
  cost factors, 90
  functions, 87–89
  noneconomic aspects of, 90–91
  and redefining roles, 272–274

Technology(-ies) (*Cont.*):
  value chain-based view of, 81–82
  Web warehousing as, 38–40, 50
Telecommunications industry:
  knowledge neighborhoods in, 110
  value chains in, 75
Television, 119
Telia, 259
Telnet, 403
Term extraction, 348
Text analysis, 291, 296–298
Text information management systems (TIMS), 290–306
  and businessperson's need for information, 270–271
  challenges with, 285–288
  contextual differences, 286
  language differences, 285
  storage media, 286–288
  stylistic differences, 285–286
  in collaborative work environments, 298–300
  current state of, 281–285
  delivery/execution models, 303–305
  functional components of, 302–306
  history of, 279–283
  imaging systems, 283–284
  and new technologies, 272–274
  objectives of, 291
  optical character recognition, 284
  potential of, 268–269
  search engines/enablers, 292–296
  corporate digital libraries, 293
  functionality of, 293–296
  subscription search services, 292–293
  Web-based public domain search engines, 292
  shortcomings in current Web-based, 269
  sources, information, 305–306
  subscription/conscription services, 300–302
  successful applications of, 274–279
  customer service, 277
  insurance, 278–279
  legal profession, 278
  manufacturing, 275
  organizational structure, 277–278
  real estate, 277
  research and development, 275–276
  travel/transportation, 276–277
  as systems, 290–291
  text analysis with, 296–298

Index

Text information management systems (*Cont.*):
  Text Knowledge Miner, 341–342
  Text mining, 338–353
    business applications using, 342–343
    with Customer Relationship Intelligence, 343–347
    data mining vs., 340–341
    with Intelligent Miner for Text, 341–342, 347–353
    categorization tool, 351–352
    clustering tool, 349–351, 353
    clustering versus categorization, 353
    feature extraction tool, 348
    process of, 339–340
    as separate discipline, 338–339
    tools for, 339
    special language classification, 352
    summarization, 353
  Text mining solutions, 338
  Text objects (IQ/Objects), 184
  Text search, multimedia search vs., 359–362
  Think tank applications, 299–300
  Think tank databases, 283
  Time constraints, 86
  TIMS (*see* Text information management systems)
  Token typing, 328
  Tokenization, 327
  Traffic/transportation management systems, virtual-reality, 254
  Transaction simulators, 538–539
  Travel industry, text management systems in, 276–277
  Tree Visualizer, 255
  Trend analysis, 339
  Triode, 41
  Troubleshooting, 531–539
    component inventory, development of, 532
    and disassembly of transactions, 534–535
    divide and conquer approach to, 531–532
    log files, use of, 538
    and testing transactions, 533–538
    with transaction simulators, 538–539

U

Universal resource locators (URLs), 383–384, 437

UNIX, 157, 162, 381, 454
URLs (*see* Universal resource locators)
U.S. Department of Defense, 375
User request facility, 310
User response facility, 310
User-based model (text delivery systems), 304

V

Value:
  business (*see* Business value)
  delivery of, 95–96
Value chains, 24, 33, 57–58, 72–84, 128
  and alignment, 82–84
  definition of, 73
  implementation of, 77–78
  and killer applications, 79–80
  and knowledge management, 80–82
  and legacy/OLTP systems, 76–77
  in retail industry, 73–75, 78–79
  in telecommunications industry, 75
  uses of, 72–73
  and value propositions, 92
  and Web warehousing, 77
Value propositions, 24, 91–95, 128, 164, 173
  application, 92
  definition of, 93
  identifying, 95
  uses of, 92–94
  and value chains, 92
Vector indexes (Excalibur Visual RetrievalWare), 365–366
Veronica, 410
Virtual intranets/extranets, 389
Virtual-reality graphical information systems, 252–254
  layering applications, 253
  medical systems, 254
  oil well drilling services, 254
  power plant example, 252–253
  traffic/transportation management, 254
Visioning, 44–50, 102–105, 129
  objectives of, 103
  as process, 25, 104–105
  See also Models
Visual data mining applications, 254–256
Visual displays, 11

Index

Visual RetrievalWare (*see* Excalibur RetrievalWare)
Voice matching systems, 359
Voice response systems, 11

W

WAIS (*see* Wide-area information service)
WalMart, 80
Wang, 280
WANs (*see* Wide-area networks)
Warehousing (*see* Data warehousing; Web warehousing)
"Waterfall" data warehouse model, 149–150
Web OLAP (*see* On-line analytical processing)
Web technology, 6–7
Web Viewer (IQ Software), 195
Web warehousing, 4–17
    benefits of, 174
    business applications of, 12–15
    closed-feedback-loop systems, 14–15
    collaborative work groups, 13
    data warehousing on Web, 12
    document-based knowledge, delivery of, 12
    learning, corporate, 14
    multimedia, 12–13
    paperless bureaucracy, 14
    raw information, analysis of, 14
    and business value, 152
    consumer applications, 15–16
    definition of, 8
    deployment of, 86–87
    functional model for, 47
    future of, 10–11
    and knowledge economics, 125
    media delivered by, 9
    as new technology, 38–40, 50
    potential of, 9–10
    purpose of, 8–9
    successful implementation of, 58
    topology of, 514–517
        dual-leveraged configuration, 517
        intranet configuration, 514–515
        leveraged inbound configuration, 515–516
        leveraged outbound configuration, 516–517
    and value chains, 57–58, 77

Web-based public domain search engines, 292
Wide-area information service (WAIS), 399–403, 410, 522, 524–528, 535–537
    indexer, WAIS, 400–401
    search and retrieve functions, 401–403
Wide-area networks (WANs), 387
Word combination counts, 297
Word counts, 297
Word processing, 281–282
Word reduction, 328
Work areas, 162
Work flow management systems, 299
Work groups, collaborative, 13
World War II, 119
World Wide Web (WWW), 6, 42, 282–283, 374–375, 390–393
    architecture of, 392–393, 408–409
    browser-server communication on, 429–432
        requests, 429–431
        responses, 431–432
    CGI approach to data delivery on. (*see* Common Gateway Interface)
    Java on, 468
    PPP approach to data delivery on, 435–438
    server-based services on, 391–392
    stateless nature of, 427–429
    traditional data delivery over, 434–435
    unique features of, 409–411
    See also Hypertext markup language; Internet
Writing, 268, 286–288
WWW (*see* World Wide Web)

X

XDB company, 504
Xerox Corporation, 280
XML (*see* Extended Markup Language)

Z

Zooming, 263–264
Zzm:
    ck. courier font (underline)
    ck. MGH style
    ck. sort

ABOUT THE AUTHOR

Rob Mattison is a world-renowned author and recognized thought leader in the development of Web warehousing and knowledge management solutions. As a Silicon Valley–based consultant, he works with hardware, software, and consulting organizations to develop easy-to-use and highly effective business solutions that increase operational efficiency and profitability through the deployment of these technologies. Rob welcomes your questions, comments, and suggestions. He can be reached via email at RMATTISON@compuserve.com.

Knowledge Management and Web Warehousing Experience Rob Mattison has more than 20 years' experience in the development of knowledge management–based solutions to business problems that have included projects involving:

Value Chain Analysis. Development of "killer applications" that redefine an organization's value chain and the competitive aspects of the business.

Value Proposition Development. Identification, cataloging, prioritization, and utilization of value propositions to help drive the system development and design process and guarantee good return on investment for project development.

Knowledge Engineering and Knowledge Economics. Mapping of a company's organizational and procedural aspects into the corresponding knowledge economies. Diagnosis of those economies to create a more efficient knowledge network.

Knowledge Management System Design and Implementation. Identification of knowledge-based needs and development of systems to meet those needs.

Knowledge Management Interests Rob is available and interested in opportunities to teach, write, and speak about knowledge management concepts and their application to business problems and solutions.

He can also participate in the development of product offerings with hardware, software, and consulting companies that synergize the capabilities these technologies offer into new, efficient knowledge management systems.

Rob is also interested in opportunities to directly assist organizations with harnessing the vast power that improvements in different knowledge management capabilities represent and making them tangible and viable additions to the corporation's inventory of revenue-producing/enhancing systems.